Bieber's Dictionary of Legal Abbreviations Reversed

A DICTIONARY OF TERMS AND TITLES WITH THEIR ABBREVIATIONS

by
IGOR I. KAVASS, Editor

with
Lois A. O'Brien and Duane A. Strojny
Contributing Editors

William S. Hein & Co., Inc.
Buffalo, New York
1994

Library of Congress Cataloging-in-Publication Data

Kavass, Igor I.
    Bieber's dictionary of legal abbreviations reversed : terms
and titles to abbreviations / by Igor I. Kavass, editor, with Lois A.
O'Brien and Duane A. Strojny, contributing editors.
          p.   cm.
    ISBN 0-89941-874-0
    1. Law--Abbreviations. 2. Citation of legal authorities. I.
O'Brien, Lois A. II. Strojny, Duane A. III. Title.
K89.K37 1994
340'.0148--dc20   94-32503
                                          CIP

Printed in the United States of America.

This volume is printed on acid-free paper by
William S. Hein & Co., Inc.

Table of Contents

Introduction

In the course of writing articles, briefs, opinions, treatises and other types of professional publications, the legal profession has always been in the habit of using abbreviations wherever this is convenient or possible. Much of legal writing is repetitive and technical. References to other publications are frequent, and on occasion they are more abundant than the writer's own narrative text. Use of abbreviations is both necessary and inevitable in such circumstances. Titles of law journals, law reports, legislative compilations, and other serial law publications are especially suited to be abbreviated; and so are many legal terms, as well as the names of government agencies and other public or private organizations. Many abbreviations are eventually turned into acronyms. The desire to shorten references and citations is ever present in legal writing.

In general, writers and editors are free to devise whatever abbreviations or acronyms they prefer to construct within the limits of their imaginative skills. In other words, there are no uniform national or international rules for abbreviations and acronyms. There are a few prerequisites, but they are very limited in scope, as well as in the manner of their use. They consist of prescriptions established by some courts or government agencies, which may require that in writings addressed to them (or produced by them) certain publications are abbreviated in a prescribed manner. Of course, elsewhere or for other purposes, such abbreviation forms do not need to be used, and largely they are not. Writers and editors are free to devise their own abbreviations, and frequently readers are put in a position of using wit and imagination to decipher the intentions of the former. There have been attempts by various editorial groups to adopt agreed sets of abbreviations or, at least, to formulate common abbreviation rules (the most successful of such attempts have resulted in the production of such guides as the Harvard "Bluebook" or the University of Chicago "Maroon Book"). However, none of these efforts have achieved meaningful uniformity. For most titles, names, and terms there are many different abbreviations or acronyms in use. They are particularly abundant for the earlier English, Scottish, and American law reports.

The situation is not improving today. Abbreviations and acronyms for the same items continue to proliferate, and whilst there is some discussion on an international level of establishing uniform abbreviation rules, prescribed "official" abbreviations are not likely to emerge in the foreseeable future.

Fortunately, there is now a work which helps readers unravel the meanings of the multitude of abbreviations and acronyms used in different legal publications. This work is *Bieber's Dictionary of Legal Abbreviations* (hereinafter referred to as *Bieber's Dictionary*). Published by William S. Hein & Co., Inc., its current editions are compiled and edited by Mary Miles Prince.

Bieber's Dictionary has so far identified about 30,000 abbreviations and acronyms, and with every new edition this number becomes more extensive, not only because there are more abbreviations, but also because there are many new publications which tend to have their titles abbreviated in legal writings.

Bieber's Dictionary lists the identified abbreviations and acronyms in alphabetical order. Alongside each entry it includes the full meaning of the respective abbreviation or acronym (in the case of a publication its full title).

The present work is a companion volume to *Bieber's Dictionary*. It is compiled at the request and recommendation of many users of *Bieber's Dictionary* who would like to have the facility of searching for abbreviations or acronyms from titles, terms and names, as well as for the latter from abbreviations and acronyms. This work accomplishes that requirement. It offers, so to speak, the **"reverse"** of the information contained in *Bieber's Dictionary*.

In an alphabetical order it lists titles, names and terms which appear in the current edition of *Bieber's Dictionary*. Each title, name, or term entry includes all of the abbreviations or acronyms identified in *Bieber's Dictionary* as being or having been used in legal publications. The abbreviations and acronyms are listed in alphabetical order. No preferences in their use are indiated or suggested. Through an effective use of data processing it is hoped that it might be possible in later editions of this work to indicate the abbreviation forms recommended, for example, by the Harvard "Bluebook" or used in such important bibliographic reference tools as the *Index to Legal Periodicals*. No such information is available herein.

The entries in this work are arranged in a strict alphabetical order. Nevertheless, for easier searching, many publications are listed several times under a variety of alternative title formats. This is particularly done for publications with complex or composite titles. Further references and cross references are listed alphabetically in the Addendum which supplements the dictionary.

The work is expected to be regularly updated in coordination with the forthcoming edition of *Bieber's Dictionary*. In such updates, the information is expected to be further improved and expanded, and thereby become more easily retrievable.

The Editor.
August 1994

Bieber's Dictionary of Legal Abbreviations Reversed

A DICTIONARY OF TERMS AND TITLES WITH THEIR ABBREVIATIONS

A

A/E Legal Newsletter
A/E Legal Newsl.
Ab Initio (from the beginning) (Lat.)
Ab init.
Abandoned Property
Aband.Prop.
Abandoned, Lost, and Unclaimed Property
Aband.Prop.
Abatement, Survival, and Revival
Abat. & R.
Abbot (Lord Tenterden) on Shipping
Abb. Sh., Abb. Ship.
Abbot on Criminal Trial Practice
Abbott, Crim. Tr. Pr.
Abbott
A, Ab, Abb
Abbott's, Admiralty Reports
Abb., Abb. Ad., Abb. Ad.R. Adm., Ad., Adm. Ad.R., Abbot's Adm., Abbott's Adm., Abbott's Ad.Rep.
Abbott's Appeals Decisions
Abb. App.Dec.
Abbott's Circuit Court Reports
Abb. U.S., Abb.C.Court
Abbott's Civil Jury Trials
Abbott, Civ. Jury Trials
Abbott's Clerks and Conveyancers' Assistant
Abb. Cl. Ass.
Abbott's Court of Appeals Decisions
Abb. Ct. App., Abb. Ct. of App.Dec., Abb. Ap.Dec., Abb. N.Y. App.
Abbott's Decisions
Abb. Dec.

Abbott's Dictionary
Abb. Dict., Abbott
Abbott's Digest of the Law of Corporations
Abb. Dig. Corp
Abbott's Forms of Pleading
Abb. F.
Abbott's Forms of Pleading, Supplement
Abb. F. Sup.
Abbott's Indiana Digest
Abb. Ind. Dig.
Abbott's Introduction to Practice under the Codes
Abb. Int.
Abbott's Law Dictionary
Abb. L. Dic., Abb. Law Dict.
Abbott's Legal Remembrancer
Abb. Leg. Rem.
Abbott's Merchant Ships and Seaman
Abbott
Abbott's Merchant Ships and Seamen by Story
Story, Merchants
Abbott's Monthly Index
Abb. Mo. Ind.
Abbott's National Digest
Abb. Nat. Dig.
Abbott's New Cases, New York
A.N., A.N.C., Abb. N.Cas., Abb. New Cas., Abbott's N.C., Abb. N.C.
Abbott's New York Digest
Abb. Dig., Abb. N.Y. Dig.
Abbott's New York Digest, Second Series
Abb. N.Y. Dig.2d

Abbott's Pleadings under the Code
Abb. Pl.
Abbott's Practice in the United States Courts
Abb. U.S. Pr.
Abbott's Practice Reports, New York
Abb. Pr., Abb. P.R., Abb. Pr. Rep., Abb. Prac., Abbot's Prac. Rep., Abbott P.R., Abbott Pr. Rep., Abbott Pract. Cas., Abbott's Pr.Rep.
Abbott's Practice Reports, New Series, New York
Abb. N.S., Abb. Pr. N.S., Abb. Prac. N.S.
Abbott's Real Property Statutes
Abb. R.P.S.
Abbott's Reports of the Beecher Trial
Abb. Beech. Tr.
Abbott's Reports, United States Circuit and District Courts
Abb., Abbott U.S. Rep., Abb. U.S.C.C., Abbott U.S.R.
Abbott's Trial Evidence
Abb. Tr. Ev.
Abbott's Year Book of Jurisprudence
Abb. Y.Bk.
Abbreviation[s]
Abbr.
Abduction
Abduct.
Abduction and Kidnapping
Abduct.
Abdy and Walker's Gaius & Ulpian
A. & W. Gai.
Abdy and Walker's Justinian
A. & W. Just., Abdy & W. Just.

Abdy's Civil Procedure among the Romans
Ab. Rom. Proc.
Abdy's Roman Civil Procedure
Abdy R. Pr.
A'Beckett 's Reserved Judgments, Equity, New South Wales, Australia
A'B.R.J.N.S.W., A'Beck. R.J.N.S.W., Eq. Judg., Res. & Eq.J., Res. & Eq. Judg.
A'Beckett's Reserved Judgments, Port Philip, New South Wales, Australia
A'B.R.J.P.P., A.'Beck. R.J.P.P.
A'Beckett's Reserved Judgments, Victoria, Australia
A'Beck. Judg.Vict., Res. & Eq. J., Res. & Eq. Judg., A'Beck. Res. Judgm.
A'Beckett's Comic Blackstone
Com. Black.
ABF Research Newsletter (American Bar Foundation)
ABF Res. Newsl.
Able and Available
AA
Able Seaman
A.B.
Abortion
Abort.
Abortion Law Reform Association
A.L.R.A.
Abortion Law Reform Association News Letter
A.L.R.A.N.L.
Abortion Law Reporter
Abortion L. Rep.
Above
Abv.
Abraham Rees' English Cyclopaedia
Rees' Cyclopaedia

Abridge[d]
Abr.
Abridgement
Ab., Abr.
Abridgement of Cases in Equity.
Abr. Ca. Eq., Eq.Ab., Eq. Ca.
Abr., Eq. Ab., Eq. Ca. Abr.
Absent
Abs.
Absent without leave (military term)
A.W.O.L.
Absentees
Absent.
Absolute
Abs.
Abstain
Abs.
Abstract
Ab., Abstr.
Abstracted Reappraisement Decisions
R.
Abstracted Valuation Decisions
V.
Abstracts of Star Chamber Proceedings
Mundy
Abstracts of Title
Abstr.T.
Abstracts of Treasury Decisions
Ab., Abs.
Abstracts on Criminology and Penology
Abs. Crim. Pen., Abstr.Crim. & Pen.
Abstracts, Treasury Decisions, New Series
Abs, Abs(NS), Abs., Ab.N.
Abuse of Process
Abuse P.
Academic
Acad., ACAD

Academy
Acad.
Academy Law Review, Kerala, India
Acad. L. Rev.
. **Academy of Human Rights**
A.H.R.
Academy of Political Science Proceedings
Acad. Pol. Sci. Proc.
Accelerated Cost Recovery System
ACRS
Accession
Access.
Accession Treaty and Decision Concerning the European Coal and Steel Community
A.T.D.
Accident Compensation Journal, Madhva Pradesh, India
A.C.J. (Mad.Pr.)
Accident Investigation Branch
A.I.B.
Accident Offices' Association
A. O. A.
Accident/Injury/ Damages
AID, A.I.D.
Accord
Acc.
Account
A/C, Acct., acct.
Account Sales
AS or A/S or A/s.
Accountancy
A., acct.
Accountancy Board
Accy
Accountancy Law Reporter, Commerce Clearing House
Accountany L. Rep (CCH)

Accountancy Law Reports, Commerce Clearing House
Accountany L. Rep (CCH)

Accountant Law Reports
Acct. L. Rep.

Accountant[s]
Acct., acct., Acctants.

Accounting
Acct., acct., Acctg., acctg.

Accounting for Law Firms
Acct. for L. Firms

Accounting Principles Board Opinions
A. P. B. Op.

Accounting Research Board Opinion
A. R. B.

Accounts and Collection Unit Circulars
A. & C. Cir.

Acknowledgement[s]
Acknowl.

Acquiescence
A

Acquiescence by Commissioner in Tax Court of Board of Tax Appeals Decisions
Acq.

Acquired Immune Deficiency Syndrome
AIDS

Acquittal
acq.

Acquitted
acq.

Acquitted In Result
acq. in result

Acret on Architects and Engineers
AE

Acret's California Construction Law Manual
CCLM

Acret's Construction Arbitration Handbook
CAH

Acret's Construction Arbitration Handbook, Supplement
CAH(s)

Acret's Construction Law Digests
CLD

Acret's Construction Litigation Handbook
CLH

Acret's Construction Litigation Handbook, Supplement
CLH(s)

Act of Sederunt,Scotland
Act of Sed., Act. Sed., A.S.

Acta Academiae Universalis Jurisprudentiae Comparativae, Berlin, Germany
Acta

Acta Cancellariae by Monroe
Act. Can., Monro., Monro. A.C.

Acta Criminologica
Acta Crim.

Acta Curiae Admiralatus Scotiae by Wade
Act. Cur. Ad. Sc.

Acta Juridica
Acta Jur.

Acta Juridica Academiae Scientiarum Hungaricae
Acta Juridica, Acta Jur.
Acad.Sci. Hung., Acta Juridica
Acad. Sci. Hungaricae

Acta Juridica, Cape Town, South Africa
Acta Jur. (Cape Town), Acta Juridica

Acta Oeconomica Academiae Scientiarum Hungaricae
Acta Oeconomica

Acta Regia, an Abstract of Rymer's Foedera
Act. Reg.
Action on Decision
AOD
Active Corps of Executives
ACE
Act[s]
Act., St., L., Law
Acton
Act.
Acton's Prize Cases, Privy Council
Act., Acton, Act. Pr. C.
Acts and Ordinances of South Australia
S. Austl. Acts & Ord.
Acts and Joint Resolutions of South Carolina
S.C. Acts
Acts and Joint Resolutions of the State of Iowa
Iowa Acts
Acts and Ordinances of the Interregnum
Acts & Ords. Interregnum.
Acts and Resolves of Massachusetts
Mass. Acts
Acts of Alabama
Ala. Acts.
Acts of Lawting Court, Scotland
Act. Lawt. Ct.
Acts of Lords Auditors of Causes, Scotland
Act. Ld. Aud. C.
Acts of Lords of Council in Civil Causes, Scotland
Act. Ld. Co. C.C.
Acts of Privy Council, ed. Dasent
Dasent, Act. P.C.
Acts of the Privy Council, New Series
Act. P.C.N.S.

Acts of South Australia
Acts S. Austl.
Acts of Tasmania
Acts Tasm.
Acts of the Australian Parliament
Acts, Austl. Acts P., Austr. Acts, Acts Austl. P., Austr. Acts P. (See also Acts of the Parliament of the Commonwealth of Australia)
Acts of the General Assembly of the Commonwealth of Virginia
Va. Acts
Acts of the General Assembly, Church of Scotland
Act. Ass.
Acts of the Legislature of West Virginia
W.Va. Acts
Acts of the Lords of Council in Public Affairs, Scotland
Act. Ld. Co. Pub. Aff.
Acts of the Parliament of Victoria
Acts. Vict.
Acts of the Parliament of Scotland (1124-1707) (1814-1875)
A.P.S., Scot. Parl. Acts
Acts of the Parliament of the Commonwealth of Australia
Austl. Acts, Acts Austr.P., Austr. Acts P. (See also Acts of the Australian Parliament)
Acts of the Privy Council
P.C.A.
Acts of the Privy Council, Colonial Series
P.C.C., Act. Pr. C. Col.S.
Acts of Van Diemen's Land, Australia
Acts Van Diem. L., Van Diem. L. Acts

Acts, Resolves and Constitutional Resolutions of the State of Maine
Me. Acts

Ad Finem (near the end) (Lat.)
Ad.fin.

Ad Hunc Locum (at this place) (Lat.)
a.h.l.

Ad Hunc Vocem (at this word) (Lat.)
a.h.v.

Ad Initium (at, or to, the beginning) (Lat.)
ad init.

Ad Interim (in the meantime) (Lat.)
ad int.

Ad Locum (at the place) (Lat.)
ad loc.

Ad Sectum (at suit of) (Lat.)
Ads.

Ad Usum (according to custom) (Lat.)
ad us.

Ad Valorem (in proportion to the value of; according to the value for goods) (Lat.)
ad val.

Adair on Law of Libels
Adair Lib., Ad. Lib.

Adam on the Law of Slavery in British India
Adam Sl.

Adam on Trial by Jury
Adam Jur. Tr.

Adams and Durham on Real Property
Ad. & Dur. R.P.

Adams County Legal Journal
Adams, Adams L.J.

Adams Legal Journal
Adams Leg. J. (Pa)

Adams on Ejectment
Ad. Ej.

Adams on the Education Act
Ad. Ed. Act

Adams on Trade Marks
Ad. Tr.M.

Adam's Equity
Ad. Eq., Adam's Eq.

Adam's Justiciary Reports
Ad. Jus.

Adams' Essay on Anglo-Saxon Law
Ad. Ang. Sax. L.

Adams' Reports (1 New Hampshire)
Adams

Adams' Reports (41-42 Maine)
Adams

Adam's Roman Antiquities
Ad. Rom. Ant., Adams, Rom. Ant.

Adby and Walker's Gaius & Ulpian
Abdy & W. Gai., Add Ecc., Add. Eccl., Addams, Ad., Add., Add. Eccl. Rep., Add. E.R., Addams Ecc.(Eng.)

Added Value Tax
A.V.T.

Addenda and Corrigenda
A. & C.

Addendum
Ad.

Addington's Abridgment of Penal Statutes
Add. Abr.

Addison on Charges
Add. Ch.

Addison on Contracts
Add. C., Add. Con., Add. Cont.

Addison on the Agricultural Holdings Act
Add. Agr. Act

Addison on Torts
Ad. Torts, Add. T., Add. Tor., Add. Torts.

Addison's Pennsylvania Reports
Add. Penn., Add.

Addison's County Court Reports, Pennsylvania
Add.Pa., Add. Rep., Addis, Addison (Pa.)

Additional
Add., addit.

Additional Personal Allowance
A. P. A.

Additional Requirements
AR

Adelaide
Adel.

Adelaide Law Review
Adel. L. Rev., Adel. L.R., Adelaide L. Rev., A.L.R.

Adelphia Law Journal
Adelphia L.J.

Adjoining Landowners
Adj.L.

Adjourned Session
Adj. Sess.

Adjudg[ed, ing, ment]
Adj.

Adjust
Adj.

Adjusted Current Earnings
ACE

Adjusted Gross Income
AGI

Adjustment
Adj.

Adjutant General's Office, U.S.
AGO

Adkinson on Township and Town Law in Indiana
Adk. Town

Administration[ive]
Ad., Admin., administrn.

Administration of Aging
AOA

Administrative Code
Admin. Cd.

Administrative Committee on Co-ordination
ACC

Administrative Court Digest
Ad. Ct. Dig.

Administrative Decisions
Admin. Dec.

Administrative Decisions Under Immigration and Nationality Laws of the United States
B.I.A.

Administrative Interpretations
Adm. Interp.

Administrative Law
Ad. L., Admin. L.

Administrative Law Bulletin
Ad. L. Bull., Ad. L.B.

Administrative Law Decisions
A.L.D.

Administrative Law Journal
Admin. L.J.

Administrative Law Journal of the American University
Admin. L.J. Am. U.

Administrative Law Judge
A.L.J.

Administrative Law News
Ad. L. News

Administrative Law Newsletter
Ad. L. Newsl.

Administrative Law Reporter, Pike and Fischer
Ad. L. Rep. (P & F), Admin. L. (P & F)

Administrative Law Reporter Second, Pike and Fischer
Ad. L. Rep.(P & F), Admin. L. (P&F)

Administrative Law Review
Ad. L. Rev., Adm. L. Rev.,
Admin. L. Rev., Admin. L.R.
Administrative Office of the Courts Newsletter
A. O. C. Newsl.
Administrative Order
A. O.
Administrative Orders or Directives
A. O.
Administrative Procedure Act
APA
Administrative Rules and Regulations of the Government of Guam
Guam Admin R.
Administrative Rules of Montana
Mont. Admin. R.
Administrative Rules of South Dakota
S.D. Admin. R.
Administrative Rules of the State of Utah
Utah Admin. R.
Administratix
Admx.
Administrator
Ad., Adm., Admin., adminstr.,
Admr.
Administrator of Civil Aeronautics
ACA
Admiralty
Adm., Admir., Admty.
Admiralty and Ecclesiastical
A. & E.
Admiralty Decisions of Hopkinson in Gilpin's
Hopk. Adm. Dec.
Admiralty Decisions tempore Hay & Marriott
Dec. t. H. & M.

Admiralty Division
Admir.
Admiralty Fleet Order
A.F.O.
Admiralty Instruction
A .I.
Admission
Admis.
Admitted
Adm.
Adolphus and Ellis' English King's Bench Reports
Ad. & El., Adolph & E., Ad. &
E., Ad. & El.(Eng)
Adolphus and Ellis's English Queen's Bench Reports
Ad. & El., A. & E.
Adolphus and Ellis's English Queen's Bench Reports, New Series
Ad. & El. N.S., Ad. & El. N.S.,
A. & E., Ad. & El. N.S., Adol.
& El.N.S., A. & E.N.S., Ad &
El (NS), Adol. & El., A. &
E.(n.s.)
Adoption
Adopt.
Adult and Vocational Education
A/V
Adultery
Adult.
Advance California Appellate Reports
ACA, A.C.A.
Advance California Reports
A.C.
Advance Opinions
Adv. Ops.
Advance Opinions in Lawyers' Edition of United States Reports
Adv.O.

Advance Sheet
Adv. Sh., Ad. Sh.
Advanced Legal Education, Hamline University School of Law
ALEHU
Advanced Management Research
AMR
Advanced Professional Programs, University of Southern California Law Center
USCAPP
Advanced Record System
A.R.S.
Advanced Student in Law
A.S.L.
Advanced Wastewater Treatment
AWT
Advancement[s]
Advancem.
Adverse Possession
Adv. Poss.
Advertising
Adv, Advert., Advertis., Advt.
Advisory
Adv.
Advisory Committee on Administrative and Budgetary Questions
ACABQ
Advisory Committee on Drug Dependence
A.C.D.D.
Advisory Council on the Penal System
A.C.P.S.
Advisory Tax Board Recommendation United States Internal Revenue Bureau
T.B.R.
Advoca[te, cy]
Advoc., adv., Advoc.

Advocate, Students' Law Society, University of Toronto
Advocate (Toronto)
Advocate, Vancouver Bar Association
Advocate ·
Advocates' Chronicle, India
Adv. Chron.
Advocates' Quarterly.
Advocates' Q., Advoc. Q.
Adye on Courts-Martial
Adye C.M.
AELE Legal Liability Reporter
AELE Legal Liab. Rep.
Affair[s]
Aff.
Affidavit[s]
Aff., afft., Affi.
Affirmative Action Compliance Manual for Federal Contractors, Bureau of National Affairs
Aff. Action Compl. Man. (BNA)
Affirmed
A, Aff'd
Affirmed in
Aff.
Affirmed on rehearing, or affirming on rehearing
aff reh
Affirming
Aff'g
Affirming in
App.
Afghan
Af
Afghanistan
Afgh., Afg.
Aforesaid
afsd.
Africa
Afr.

Africa Law Reports, Commercial Series
  A.L.R.Comm.
African
  Afr.
African Affairs
  Afr. Aff.
African and Malagasy Associated States
  AMAS
African Journal of International Law
  Afr. J. Int'l L.
African Law Digest
  Afr. L. Dig., Afr. L. Digest, A.L.D.
African Law Reports
  Afr. L.R.
African Law Reports, Commercial Law Series
  A.L.R.Com.,A.L.R. Comm., African L.R. Comm.
African Law Reports, Malawi Series
  A.L.R. (Malawi ser.), Afr. L.R., Mal.Ser., African L.R. Mal., A.L.R.Mal., African L.R. S.L., A.L.R. S.L.
African Law Reports, Sierre Leone Series
  A.L.R. (Sierra L. ser.), African L.R. S.L., A.L.R. S.L., Afr. L.R., Sierra L.Ser., Afr. L.R., Sierre L.Ser.
African Law Studies
  Af. L. Studies, Afr. L. Stud., African L.S.
African Peanut (Groundnut) Council
  APC
African States associated with the European Economic Community
  EAMA

African, Caribbean, and Pacific States
  ACP
Afrikaans
  Afr.
Afro-Asian People's Solidarity Organization
  AAPSO
After Sight
  AS or A/S or A/s.
Against
  Ag.
Age Discrimination Act of 1975
  ADA
Age, Newspaper in Melbourne, Australia (Law Reports)
  (The) Age
Agency
  Ag., Agcy., agy.
Agency for International Development
  AID
Agency for International Development Procurement Regulations
  AIDPR
Agency for Toxic Substances and Disease Registry
  ATSDR
Agent
  Agt.
Agnew on Patents
  Agn. Pat.
Agnew on the Statute of Frauds
  Agn. Fr.
Agra High Court Reports, India
  Agra H.C.
Agreed Case
  Agr. C.
Agreement[s]
  Ag., Agr., Ag.
Agree[s]
  Ag., Agr.

Agricultur[al, e]
Agric., Agr., Agri., Agric.
Agricultural Adjustment Act
AAA
Agricultural Code
Agric. C.
Agricultural Conservation and Adjustment
Agric. Conserv. & Adj.
Agricultural Conservation and Adjustment Administration
ACAA
Agricultural Credit Corporation
ACC
Agricultural Law Journal
Agr. L.J.
Agricultural Marketing Service, P. & S. Docket
A. M. S. , P. & S.
Agricultural Marketing Services
AMS
Agricultural Research Administration
ARA
Agricultural Research Service
A.R.S.
Agricultural Stabilization and Conservation Service
ASCS
Agriculture and Markets
Agric. & Mkts.
Agriculture Conservation Program
A.C.P.
Agriculture Decisions
A.D., Ag Dec, Agri. Dec.
Agriculture, Nutrition, and Forestry
ANF
Aid to Families with Dependent Children
AFDC, A.F.D.C.

Aid to the Aged, Blind, or Disabled
A.A.B.D.
Aid to the Blind
A.B.
Aid to the Permanently and Totally Disabled
A. P. T. D.
AIDS Law and Litigation Reporter
AIDS L. & Litig. Rep.
AIDS Law Reporter
AIDS L. Rep.
AIDS Litigation Reporter
AIDS Litigation Rep.
Aiken's Digest of Alabama Statutes
Aik. Dig., Aik. Stat.
Aikens' Vermont Report
Aik., Aik. Rep., Aikens (Vt.), Aikens's Rep., Aik.(Vt.)Rep., Aik.
Ainsworth's Latin-English Dictionary
Ainsworth, Lex.
Ainsworth's Lexicon
Ainsw.
AIPLA Quarterly Journal
AIPLA Q.J.
Air
Air
Air and Space Lawyer
Air & Space Law.
Air Force
A.F.
Air Force Base
AFB
Air Force JAG Law Review
A.F. JAG L. Rev.
Air Force Law Review
A.F. L. Rev., A.F.L.R., Air Force L.R.

Air Force Procurement Instruments
AFPI
Air Law
Air L.
Air Law Review
Air L. Rev., Air L.R.
Air Registration Board
A. R. B.
Air Safety Board
ASB
Air University Review
Air U. Rev.
Aird's Civil Laws of France
Aird Civ. Law.
Aiyar's Company Cases
Aiyar, Aiyar C.C.
Aiyar's Leading Privy Council Cases
Aiyar L.P.C.
Aiyar's Unreported Decisions
Aiyar Unrep. D.
Ajmer-Merwara Law Journal, India
A. M. L. J., Ajmer-Merwara L.J.
Aker, Beam and Walsh on Mental Capacity
MNC
Akron Law Review
Akron L. Rev.
Akron Tax Journal
Akron Tax J.
Alabama
Al., Ala.
Alabama Acts
Ala. Acts
Alabama Appellate Court
Ala.A.
Alabama Appellate Court Reports
Ala. App.
Alabama Bar Bulletin
Ala. Bar Bull.

Alabama Civil Appeals
Ala. Civ. App.
Alabama Code
Ala. Code
Alabama Constitution
Ala. Const.
Alabama Court of Appeals
Ala. App., Ala. Cr. App.
Alabama Institute for Continuing Legal Education
AICLE
Alabama Law Journal
Ala. L.J.
Alabama Law Review
Alabama L. Rev., Ala. L. Rev., L.R.
Alabama Lawyer
Ala. Law., Ala. Law, Law.
Alabama Public Service Commission
Ala. P.S.C.
Alabama Public Service Commission Decisions
A. P. S. C.
Alabama Railroad Commission
Ala. R.C.
Alabama Reports
A., Ala., Ala. Rep.:, Ala. Reps.:, Alab. Rep., Alabama Rep., Ala.R., Al.Rep.
Alabama Reports, New Series
Ala. N.S., Ala. R. N.S.:, Alab.(N.S.)
Alabama Select Cases, Supreme Court, by Shepherd (vols. 37, 38 & 39)
Ala. Sel. Cas.
Alabama State Bar Association
Ala. S.B.A., Ala. St. B.A., Ala. St. Bar Assn.
Alabama State Bar Foundation Bulletin
Ala. St. B. Found. Bull.

Alabama Supreme Court
Ala.
Alabama Supreme Court Reports
Ala.
Alaska
Ak, Alas., Alk
Alaska Administrative Code
Alaska Admin. Code
Alaska Bar Brief
Alaska B. Brief, Alaska B.B.
Alaska Bar Journal
Alaska B.J.
Alaska Codes
Alaska Co.
Alaska Constitution
Alaska Const.
Alaska Federal Reports
A.F.Rep., Alas F, Alaska Fed.,
Alaska Fed. Rep.
Alaska Law Journal
Alaska L.J.
Alaska Law Review
Alaska L. Rev.
Alaska Native Claims Appeals Board
A. N. C. A. B.
Alaska Reporter
Alaska
Alaska Reports
Alaska, Alk
Alaska Session Laws
Alaska Sess. Laws
Alaska Statutes
Alaska Stat.
Albania, Albanian
Alb., Al.
Albany
Alb.
Albany Law Journal
Alb. Law J., Alb. L.J., A.L.J.
Albany Law Journal of Science and Technology
Alb. L.J. Sci. & Tech.

Albany Law Review
Alb. L. Rev., Albany L. Rev.
Albany Law School Journal
Alb. L.S. Jour.
Albert on Arbitration (Lord Cairns' Decisions)
Alb. Arb., Cairns Dec.
Alberta
A, AB, Alta.
Alberta Gazette
Alta. Gaz.
Alberta Law
Alta. L.
Alberta Law Quarterly
Alb. L.Q., Alberta L.Q., Alta.
L.Q.
Alberta Law Reports
Alb. L.R., Alberta L.(Can),
Alta., Alta. L.R., A.L.R.
Alberta Law Reports, Second Series
Alta. L.R.(2d)
Alberta Law Review
Alberta L. Rev., Alta. L. Rev.
Alberta Reports
A. R.
Alberta Revised Statutes
Alta. Rev. Stat.
Alberta Statutes
Alta. Stat.
Albuquerque Bar Journal
Albuquerque B.J.
Alcock and Napier's Irish King's Bench Reports
Al. & N., Alcock & N, Alc. &
N., Ale. & N., Al. & Nap., Alc.
& Nap., A. & N.
Alcock on Personal Property
Alc. Per. Prop.
Alcock's Irish Registry Cases
Alc. Reg. Cas., Alc., Alc. Reg.
C., Alc. Reg. Cas.

Alcohol and Tobacco Taxation Division, United States Internal Revenue Bureau
A.T.
Alcohol Tax Unit, Internal RevenueBulletin
A.T.
Alcohol Tobacco and Firearms Cumulative Bulletin
A.T.F.C.B.
Alcohol, Drug Abuse, and Mental Health Administration
ADAMHA
Alcoholic Beverage
Alco. Bev.
Alcoholic Beverage Control
Alco. Bev. Cont.
Alcoholism Treatment Quarterly
Alcohol Treat. Q.
Alden and Van Hoesen's Digest of Mississippi Laws
Ald. & V.H.
Alden Law Reports
A.L.R.
Alden's Abridgment of Law
Ald. Abr.
Alden's Condensed Reports
Ald.
Alden's Index of United States Reports
Ald. Ind.
Aldred's Questions on the Law of Property
Ald. Ques.
Aldrich's Edition of Anson on Contracts
Ald. Ans. Cont.
Aldridge's History of the Courts of Law
Ald. Hist.
Alexander on Life Insurance in New York
Alex. Ins.

Alexander's British Statutes in Force in Maryland
Alex. Br.S tat.
Alexander's Chancery Practice in Maryland
Alex. Ch. Pr.
Alexander's Practice of the Commissary Courts, Scotland
Alex. Com. Pr.
Alexander's Reports, (66-72 Mississippi)
Alexander.
Alexander's Texas Digest
Alex. Dig.
Alexandra Case Report by Dudley
Alex. Cas.
Aleyn's English King's Bench Reports
Al., Aleyn (Eng.), Allen, Aleyn
Alfred's Laws
LL. Alfred's, Leg. Alfred
Algemene Mededelingen, Netherlands
Alg. Med.
Algeria, Algerian
Alg.
Alger's Law in Relation to Promoters and Promotion of Corporations
Alger's Law Promoters & Prom. Corp.
ALI-ABA CLE Review
ALI-ABA CLE Rev.
ALI-ABA Course Materials Journal
ALI-ABA Course Mat. J., ALI-ABA Course Materials J.
ALI Federal Income Tax Project
ALI Fed. Income Tax Project
Alien Property Custodian
APC
Alien Property Division
A. P. D.

Alison on Scottish Criminal Law
    Al. Sc. Cr. L.
Alison's Practice, Scotland
    Alison Pr.
Alison's Principles of the Criminal Law of Scotland
    Alis. Princ. Scotch Law.
All Courts
    All.
All England Law Reports
    A.E.L.R., A.E.R., All Eng, All.E.R.
All England Law Reports Reprint
    All E.R. Repr., A.E.R. Rep., All E.R. Rep.
All England Law Reports Reprint Extension Volumes, Australia
    A.E.R. Rep. Ext., All E.R. Rep. Ext.
All India Criminal Decisions
    A.I.Cr.D., All India Crim. Dec.
All India Criminal Times
    All Ind. Cr. T.
All India Law Reporter
    A.I.R.
All India Reporter
    All Ind. Rep., All India Rptr.
All India Reporter, Allahabad Series
    All., All.Ser.
All India Reporter, Andhra Pradesh Series
    Andh. Pra.
All India Reporter, Andhra Series
    Andh., And.
All India Reporter, Assam Series.
    Asm., Assam
All India Reporter, Bhopal Series
    Bhop.
All India Reporter, Bilaspur Series
    Bilas.

All India Reporter, Bombay Series
    B
All India Reporter, Calcutta Series
    C, Cal.
All India Reporter, Dacca Series
    Dacca
All India Reporter, East Punjab Series
    East Punjab
All India Reporter, Federal Court Series
    F.C.
All India Reporter, Himachal Pradesh Series
    H.P., Him. Pra.
All India Reporter, Hyderabad Series
    Hy., Hyd.
All India Reporter, Indian Digest
    Ind. Dig.
All India Reporter, Jammu and Kashmir Series
    J.& K.
All India Reporter, Kerala Series
    Kerala
All India Reporter, Kutch Series
    Kutch
All India Reporter, Madhya Bharat Series
    M.B.
All India Reporter, Madhya Pradesh Series
    Madh. Pra., M.P.
All India Reporter, Madras Series
    Mad.
All India Reporter, Manipur Series
    Manip.
All India Reporter, Mysore Series
    Mys.

All India Reporter, Nagpur Series
Nag., All India Rep.
All India Reporter, New Series
All Ind. Rep. N.S.
All India Reporter, Orissa Series
Oris., Orissa
All India Reporter, Patiala and East Punjab States Union Series
Pepsu.
All India Reporter, Patna Series
P.
All India Reporter, Peshawar Series
Peshawar
All India Reporter, Privy Council Series
P.C.
All India Reporter, Punjab Series
Pun.
All India Reporter, Rajasthan Series
R., Raj.
All India Reporter, Saurashtra Series
Sau.
All India Reporter, Simia Series
Simia
All India Reporter, Sind Series
Sind
All India Reporter, Supreme Court Reports
S.C.
All India Reporter, Travancore-Cochin Series
T.C.
All India Reporter, Tripura Series
Trip.
All India Reporter, Vindhya Pradesh Series
V.P.
All India Reports
All.I.R.

All India Reports Manual: Unrepealed Central Acts
India A.I.R. Manual
All Indian Criminal Reports
All I.C.R., All Ind. Cr. R.
All Nigeria Law Reports
All Nig. L.R., All N.L.R.
All Pakistan Legal Decisions
All Pak. Leg. Dec., All Pak. Legal. Dec.
All South Africa Law Reports
A.S.A.R.
All-State Sales Tax Reporter, Commerce Clearing House
All-St. Sales Tax Rep. (CCH)
All States Tax Guide, Prentice-Hall
All States Tax Guide (P-H)
Allahabad Criminal Cases
All. Cr. Cas., A. Cr. C., A.C.C.
Allahabad Criminal Reports
A.Cr.R.
Allahabad Law Journal and Reports
All.L.J. & Rep.
Allahabad Law Journal
A.L.J., Alla. L.J.
Allahabad Law Review
All.L.R.
Allahabad Law Times
All.L.T.
Allahabad Weekly Notes (and Supplement)
A.W.N., All.W.N.
Allahabad Weekly Reporter
All.W.R., A.W.R.
Allen
Al.
Allemanian Laws
L.All.
Allen & Morris' Trial
All. & Mor. Tr.

Allen's (Charles) Reports (1-14 Massachusetts)
Allen's Rep.

Allen on Sheriffs
All.Sher.

Allen's Telegraph Cases
All.Tel.Cas., Al.Tel.Ca., Al. Tel. Ca.

Allen's Massachusetts Reports
All., Allen

Allen's New Brunswick Reports
N.B.R. All., All., All.N.B.

Allen's Washington Territory Reports
Allen

Allen's Washington Territory Reports, New Series
Wash. Ter. N.S.

Alleyne's Legal Decrees of Marriage
All.L.D. of Mar.

Alliance for Labor Action
ALA

Allinson's Pennsylvania Superior and District Court Reports
Allinson, Allin.

Allison's American Dictionary
Allison's Am. Dict.

Allnat on Law of Partition
Alln. Part.

Allnutt on Wills
Alln. Wills

Allowing Appeal
Allowing app.

Allowing Rehearing
allowing reh.

Allwood's Appeal Cases under the Weights & Measures Act
Allwood

Alsager's Dictionary of Business Terms
Alsager.

Also Known As
a.k.a.

Alteration of Instruments
Alt. Inst.

Alternative
Alt.

Alternative County Government
Alt. County Gov't.

Alternative Dispute Resolution
Alt. Disp. Res.

Alternative Minimum Tax
AMT

Alternative Minimum Taxable Income
AMTI

Ambassadors
Ambass.

Ambler's Reports, Chancery
Amb., Ambl.

Amend[ed, ing, ment, ments]
A., Am., Amd., Amend., Amend'g., Amends.

Amendment to Constitution
Const. Amend.

Amendment to the Constitution of the United States
Const. U.S. Amend., A.C.U.S.

Amendments and Additions
A. & A.

America Law Journal (Hall's)
Am. L. J. (O. S.)

America; American
A, Am., Amer.

American and English Annotated Cases
A. & E. Ann Cas., A. & E. Anno., A. & E. Cas., Am. & Eng. Ann. Cas., Ann. Cas.

American and English Corporation Cases
A. & E. Corp. Cas., Am. & E. Corp. Cas., Am. & Eng.Corp.Cas., Cor. Cas.

American and English Corporation Cases, New Series
Am. & E. Corp. Cas. N.S., Am.
& Eng.Corp.Cas.N.S.

American and English Decisions in Equity
Am. & E. Eq. D., Am. & Eng.
Eq. D.

American and English Encyclopedia of Law
A. & E. Enc. L., A. & E. Ency.,
Amer. & Eng. Enc. Law

American and English Encyclopedia of Law & Practice
A. & E. Enc. L. & Pr., Am. &
Eng. Enc. Law & Pr., Ency. L.
& P., A. & E. Enc., A. & E.
Ency. Law

American and English Patent Cases
A. & E.Pat.Cas., Am. & Eng.
Pat. Cas.

American and English Pleading and Practice
A. & E.P. & P., A. & E.P. & Pr.

American and English Railroad Cases
A. & E.R.Cas., A. & E.R.R.C.,
A. & E.R.R.Cas., Am. & E.R.
Cas.

American and English Railroad Cases, New Series
Am. & E.R. Cas. N.S., A. &
E.R.Cas., N.S., A. &
E.R.R.Cas.(N.S.), Am. &
Eng.Ry.Cas.N.S.

American and English Railway Cases
A. & E.R.C., Am. & Engl. R.C.,
Am. & Eng. Ry Cas.

American Academy of Judicial Education
AAJE

American Academy of Matrimonial Lawyers Journal
Am. Acad. Matri. Law. J.

American Academy of Political and Social Science
Am. Acad. Pol. & Soc. Sci.

American Academy of Psychiatry and the Law Bulletin
Am. A. Psych. L. Bull.

American Annotated Cases
Ann. Cas., Anno. Cases, Am.
Ann. Cas.

American Anthropologist
Amer. Anthrop.

American Arbitration Association
AAA

American Association of Law Libraries
AALL

American Association of University Professors
A.A.U.P.

American Association of University Professors Bulletin
Am. Assoc. Univ. Prof. Bull.

American Bankers' Association
A.B.A.

American Bankruptcy
Am. Bankr.

American Bankruptcy Journal
Am. Bankr. J.

American Bankruptcy Law Journal
Am. Bankr. L.J.

American Bankruptcy, New Series
Am. Bankr. N.S., Am. B. (N.S.)

American Bankruptcy Register
Am. Bankr. Reg.

American Bankruptcy Reports
A.B. Rep., A.B.R., Am. Bank.
R., Am. Bankr. Rep., Am.
Bankruptcy Reps., Am. B'Kc'y.
Rep., Am. B.R.

American Bankruptcy Reports, New Series
   A.B.R.N.S., Am. Bankr. Rep. N.S., Am. Bankr. R.(N.S.), Am. B.R.(N.S.)

American Bankruptcy Review
   A.B. Rev., Am. Bank. Rev., Am. Bankr. Rev.

American Bar Association
   ABA, A.B.A., Am. B.A.

American Bar Association Antitrust Law Journal
   ABA Antitrust L.J.

American Bar Association Center for Professional Discipline
   ABACPD

American Bar Association Comparative Law Bulletin
   A.B.A. Comp. L. Bull

American Bar Association Comparative Law Bureau. Bulletin
   Bull. Comp. L.

American Bar Association Journal
   A.B.A. J., A.B.A. Jo., Am. Bar. Ass. J., A.B.A. Jour., Am. Bar Asso. Jour.

American Bar Association Model Business Corporation Act Annotated
   Model Business Corp. Act

American Bar Association Model Business Corporation Act Annotated, Second Series
   Model Bus. Corp. Act. Anno.2d.

American Bar Association Model Code of Professional Responsibility
   Model Code of Professional Responsibility

American Bar Association Reporter
   ABA Rep, A.B.A. Rep., Am Bar Asso Rep

American Bar Association Section of Insurance, Negligence and Compensation Law
   ABA Sect. Ins. N & CL

American Bar Association Section of Labor Relations Law
   ABA Sec. Lab. Rel. L.

American Bar Association International and Comparative Law Section Reports
   A.B.A. Rep. Int'l. & Comp. L. Sec.

American Bar Foundation
   ABF, A.B.F.

American Bar Foundation Annotated Code of Professional Responsibility.
   Annot. Code of Professional Responsibility

American Bar Foundation Research Journal
   A.B.F. Research J., A.B.F. Research Reptr. J., A.B.F.Res. J., Am. B. Found. Res. J., Am. Bar Found. Res. Y.

American Bar Foundation Research Reporter
   A.B.F. Research Reptr.

American Bar News
   Am. B. News

American Business Law Association
   A.B.L.A.

American Business Law Journal
   Am. Bus. L.J.

American Chancery Digest
   Am. Ch. Dig.

American Civil Law Journal
   Am. Civ. L.J., A.C.L.J., Am. C. L.J.

American Civil Liberties Union
   A.C.L.U., ACLU

American Civil Liberties Union Foundation
ACLUF

American Civil Liberties Union Legislative Action Bulletin
A.C.L.U. Leg. Action Bull.

American Consular Bulletin
Am. Consul. Bul.

American Corporation Cases
Amer. Corp. Cas., Am. Corp. Cas., A.C.C.

American Criminal Justice Association
A.C.J.A., ACJA

American Criminal Law Quarterly
Am. Crim. L.Q.

American Criminal Law Review
Am. Crim. L. Rev.

American Criminal Reports
Am. Cr., Am. Cr. R. (Hawley), Am. Cr. R., A.C.R.

American Criminal Trials, Chandler's
Am. Cr. Tr.

American Decisions
A.D., Am.D., Amer. Dec., Am. Dec., Am. Dec's.

American Digest
Am. Dig.

American Digest Century Edition
Am Cent Dig, Am. Dig. Cent. Ed.

American Digest Decennial Edition
Am. Dig. Dec. Ed. (or Dec. Dig., Decen. Dig. [Am. Dig. Second Dec.Ed. or Am. Dig. Secd. Dec. Ed., Am Dig. Third Dec.Ed., Am. Dig. Fourth Dec.Ed., etc.] Decen.Ed.)

American Digest Key Number Series
Am. Dig. Key No. Ser.

American District Telegraph Company
ADTC

American Economic Review
Am. Econ. Rev., Amer. Econ. Rev.

American Edition
Am. Ed.

American Electrical Cases
A.E.C., Am. Elect. Cas., Am. Electr. Cas., Amer. Elec. Ca.

American Encyclopedic Dictionary
Am. Enc. Dict.

American Enterprise
Am. Ent.

American Federal Tax Reports, Prentice Hall
AFTR, Am. Fed. Tax R., Am. Fed. Tax Rep., P.-H. Cas.

American Federal Tax Reports Second Series, Prentice Hall
AFTR2d, A.F.T.R.2d (P-H), Am. Fed. Tax R. 2d

American Federation of Labor
A.F.L.

American Federation of Labor and Congress of Industrial Organizations
A.F.L.-C.I.O.

American Foreign Insurance Association
AFIA

American Foreign Law Association Newsletter
Am. For. L. Ass'n Newsl.

American Historical Review
Am. Hist. Rev.

American Hospital Association
AHA

American Independent Party
AIP
American Indian Journal
Am. Ind. J., Am. Indian J.
American Indian Law Newsletter
Am. Ind. L. Newsl.
American Indian Law Review
Am. Ind. L. Rev., Am. Ind. L.R.,
Am. Indian L. Rev.
American Indian Movement
AIM
American Insolvency Reports
A. Ins. R., Am. Ins. Rep., Am.
Insolv. Rep.
**American Institute for Certified
Public Accountants Profes-
sional Standards, Commerce
Clearing House**
AICPA-Prof. Stand. (CCH)
American Institute of Banking
AIB
**American Institute of Manage-
ment**
AIM
**American Intellectual Property
Law Association**
AIPLA
**American International Law
Cases**
A.I.L.C.
**American Journal of Trial Advo-
cacy**
Am. J. Trial Advoc.
American Journal Law Review
Am. J. L.Rev.
**American Journal of Compara-
tive Law**
A.J.C.L., Am. J. Comp. L., Am.
J. Comp. Law, Amer. J. Comp.
L.
**American Journal of Criminal
Law**
Am. J. Crim. L.

**American Journal of Economics
and Sociology**
Amer. J. Econ. & Soc.
American Journal of Family Law
Am. J. Fam. L.
**American Journal of Forensic
Psychiatry**
Am. J. For. Psych.
**American Journal of Interna-
tional Arbitration**
Am. J. Int'l Arb.
**American Journal of Interna-
tional Law**
A.J.I.L., Am. J. Int. L., Am J
Intl L, Am. J. Int'l. L., Amer.
J. Int'l. L.
**American Journal of Interna-
tional Law, Proceedings**
Am. J. Int. Law Proc.
**American Journal of Jurispru-
dence**
Am. J. Juris., Am. J. Jurispr.,
Am. J. Jurisprud.
**American Journal of Law and
Medicine**
Am. J. L. & Med., Am. J. Law
& Med., Am. J. of Law & Med.
**American Journal of Legal His-
tory**
Am. J. Leg. Hist., Am. J. Legal
Hist.
American Journal of Philology
Am. J. Philol.
**American Journal of Police Sci-
ence**
Am. J. Police Sci.
**American Journal of Political Sci-
ence**
Am. J. Pol. Sc.
American Journal of Politics
Am. Jour. Pol.

American Journal of Social Sciences
Am. J. Soc. Sci.

American Journal of Sociology
Am. Jour. Soc.

American Journal of Tax Policy
Am. J. Tax Pol'y

American Journal of Trial Advocacy
Am. J. Trial Advoc.

American Judicature Society Bulletin
AJS, Am. Jud. Soc., Am. Jud. Soc. Bull.

American Judicature Society Journal
AJS, Am. Jud. Soc., Am. Jud. Soc. J.

American Jurisprudence
Am. Jur.

American Jurisprudence Legal Forms
Am. Jur. Legal Forms, Am. J. Leg. Forms Anno., Am. Jur. Leg. Forms Anno.

American Jurisprudence Legal Forms, Second Series
Am. Jur. Legal Forms 2d.

American Jurisprudence Pleading and Practice Forms Annotated
Am. J. Pl. & Pr. Forms Anno., Am. Jur. Pl. & Pr. Forms

American Jurisprudence Pleading and Practice Forms, Revised Editions
Am. Jur. Pl. & Pr. Forms (Rev. ed.)

American Jurisprudence Proof of Facts
Am. J. Proof of Facts, Am. Jur. Proof of Facts

American Jurisprudence Proof of Facts Annotated
Am. Jur. Proof of Facts Anno.

American Jurisprudence Proof of Facts, Second Series
Am. Jur. POF2d

American Jurisprudence, Second Series
Am. Jur. 2d, Am.J.2d

American Jurisprudence Trials
Am. J. Trials, Am. Jur. Trials

American Jurist
A.J., Am. Jur., Am. Jurist, Amer. Jur.

American Labor Arbitration Awards, Prentice Hall
A.L.A.A., Am. Lab. Arb. Awards (P-H), P-H Am. Lab. Arb. Awards, Am. Lab. Arb. Cas.

American Labor Arbitration Services
Am.Lab. Arb.Serv.

American Labor Cases, Prentice Hall
A.L.R.., Am. Lab. Cas., Am. Lab. Cas. (P-H), P-H Am. Lab. Cas.

American Labor Legislation Review
Am. Lab. Leg. Rev., Am. Labor Legis. Rev.

American Law Institute
A.L.I., Am. L. Ins.

American Law Institute-American Bar Association Committee on Continuing Professional Education
ALIABA

American Law Institute-American Bar Association Course Materials Journal
ALI-ABA Course M. J.

American Law Institute Model Land Development Code
Model Land Dev.Code

American Law Institute Model Penal Code
Model Penal Code

American Law Institute Proceedings
A.L.I. Proc.

American Law Institute, Restatement of the Law
Am. L. Ins., Am. L. Inst., Am. Law Inst.

American Law Journal
Am. Law J., A.L.J., Am. L. J.

American Law Journal, Ohio
Am. L. J., Am. L. J. (O)

American Law Journal, New Series
Am. L. J. N. S., Am. Law J. N.S.

American Law Magazine
Am. Law Mag., Am. L. Mag., A.L.M., Am. L. M.

American Law of Elections, by McCrary
Am. L. Elec.

American Law of Property
Am. Property

American Law of Veterans
Am. Vets., A.L. Rec.

American Law Record
Rec., Am. Law Rec., Am. Law Record

American Law Record, Ohio
Am. L. Rec.(Ohio)

American Law Register,Cincinnati
Am. Law Reg., A.L.R., Am. Law Reg. (old ser.), Am. Law Register

American Law Register
A.L.R.

American Law Register and Review
Am. L. Reg. & Rev.

American Law Register, New Series
A.L.Reg.(N.S.), Am. L. Reg. (N. S.), Am. Law Reg. N. S., Amer. Law Reg. (N. S.)

American Law Register, Old Series
A.L.Reg.(O.S.), Am. L. Reg., (O. S.), Am. Law Reg. O. S., Amer. Law Reg. (O. S.)

American Law Register, Philadelphia
A.L.Reg., Am. L. Reg., Law Reg., Am. L. Rep.

American Law Reporter, Davenport, Iowa
A.L.Rep.

American Law Reports
A.L.R.

American Law Reports, Annotated
A.L.R.

American Law Reports Annotated, Federal
A.L.R. Fed.

American Law Reports Annotated, Fifth Series
A.L.R.5th, AL5

American Law Reports Annotated, Fourth Series
A.L.R.4th, AL4

American Law Reports Annotated, Second Series
A.L.R.2d, AL2

American Law Reports Annotated, Third Series
A.L.R.3d, AL3

American Law Reports Later Case Service
A.L.R.L.C.S.

American Law Reports, Federal
A.L.R. Fed.

American Law Review
Am. L. Rev., Am. Law Rev.,
Amer. Law Rev., A.L.Rev.

American Law School Review
Am. L. S. Rev., Am. L. Sch.
Rev., Am. Law S. Rev., Am.L.
School Rev.

American Law Times
A.L.T.

**American Law Times Bank-
ruptcy Report**
A.L.T. Bankr., Bank. Rep., Am.
L. T. Bankr., Am. L. T. Bankr.
Rep., Bank. Ct. Rep.

American Law Times Reports
A.L.T.R., Am. L. T. R., Am. L.
T. Rep., Am. Law T. Rep.

**American Law Times Reports,
New Series**
A.L.T.R.N.S., Am. L. T. R. N. S.

American Lawyer
Am. Law., Am. Lawy., Amer.
Lawy., Amer. Law.

American Leading Cases
A.L.C., Am. L. Cas., Am. Lead.
Ca. (ed. of 1871), Am. Lead.
Cases, Am. Leading Cas., Am.
Leading Cases, notes by Hare
and Wallace, Amer. Lea. Cas.,
Am. Lead. Cas. (H & W), Am.
Lead. Cas., Am. L. C., Hare &
Wallace Amer. Leading Cases,
Lead. Cas. Am., Hare & Wal.
L.C., Hare & Wallace Lead.
Cases (Am.)

American Legal News
Am. Leg. N.

American Legislator
Am. Leg.

American Library Association
ALA

**American Management Associa-
tion**
AMA

American Maritime Cases
Am. Mar. Cas., Am Marit
Cases, A.M.C., M.C.

American Medical Association
A.M.A.

American Monthly Review
Am.Mo.Rev.

**American National Standards In-
stitute**
ANSI

American Negligence Cases
Am. Neg. Ca., Am. Neg. Cas.,
Am. Neg. Cases, Am. Negl.
Cas., A.N.C.

American Negligence Digest
Am. Neg. Dig.

American Negligence Reports
Am. Neg. Rep., Am. Negl. R.,
Am. Negl. Rep.

**American Negligence Reports,
Current Series**
A. N. R.

American Notary
Am. Notary

**American Oriental Society Jour-
nal**
Am. Oriental Soc'y

American Patent Law Association
APLA

**American Patent Law Associa-
tion Bulletin**
Am. Pat. L. A. Bull., Am. Pat.
L. Assoc. Bull., APLA Bull.

**American Patent Law Associa-
tion Quarterly**
APLA Q.

**American Patent Law Associa-
tion Quarterly Journal**
APLA Q. J.

American Patent Law Quarterly Journal
Am. Pat. L. Q. J.

American Philosophical Quarterly
Am. Phil. Q.

American Pleader's Assistant
Am. Pl. Ass.

American Political Science Journal
Am. Pol. Sci. J.

American Political Science Review
A. P. S. R., Am. Pol. Sc. Rev., Am. Pol. Sci. Rev., Am. Pol. Science Rev.

American Politics Quarterly
Am. Pol. Q.

American Practice
Am. Pr.

American Practice Reports
Am. Pr. Rep.

American Practice Reports, New Series
Am. Pr. Rep. NS

American Probate, New Series
Am. Prob. N. S.

American Probate Reports
Am. Pro. Rep., Am. Prob., Am. Prob. Rep.

American Quarterly Register
Am. Q. Reg.

American Quarterly Review
Am. Q. Rev.

American Railroad and Corporation Reports (or Reporter)
Am. R. R. & C. Rep., Am. R. & C. Rep.

American Railroad Corporation
Am. R. & Corp.

American Railway Association
A. R. A.

American Railway Cases
A. R. C., Am. R. Ca., Am. R. R. Ca., Am. Rail. Cas., Am. Ry. Ca., Am. Ry. Cases, Am. R. R. Cas., Am. Railw. Cas.

American Railway Reports
Am. R. Rep., Am. Rail. R., Am. Ry. Rep., Amer. R'y. Rep., A.R.R., A.R.R.R., Am. R. R. Rep.

American Red Cross
A. R. C.

American Reports
A. R., A. Rep., Am. R., Am. Rep., Am. Reports, Amer. Rep., Amer. Reports, Amer. Reps., American Repts.

American Review of East-West Trade
Amer. Rev. E. -W. Tr.

American Review of History and Politics
Am. Rev. of Hist. & Politics

American Review of International Arbitration
Am. Rev. Int'l Arb.

American Review of Soviet and Eastern European Foreign Trade
Sov. & E. Eur. For. Tr.

American Review on the Soviet Union
Am. Rev. on the Soviet Union

American Revolution Bicentennial Administration
ARBA

American Ruling Cases
A. R. C.

American Samoa
Am. Sam., Am. Samoa, A.S.

American Samoa Administrative Code
ASAC

American Samoa Code
 A. S. Code
American Samoa Code Annotated
 Am. Samoa Code Ann.
American Slavic and East European Review
 Am. Slav. & East Europ. Rev.
American Society for Legal History
 ASLH
American Society of Hospital Attorneys
 ASHA
American Society of International Law
 Am. Soc. Int. L., ASIL
American Society of International Law Proceedings
 Am. Soc. Int. L. Proc., Am. Soc. Int'l. L. Proc., Am. Soc'y Int'l L. Proc., ASIL Proc. Amer. Soc. of Internat. L.
American Sociological Review
 Am. Soc. Rev., Am. Sociolog. Rev.
American Standards Association
 ASA
American State Papers
 Am. St. P., Am. St. Papers, Am. State Papers
American State Reports
 Am. S. R., Am. St. Rep., Am. St. Reports, Am. Sta. Rep., Am. State Rep., Amer. St. Rep., Amer. State Reps., American State Rep., A.S.R, Am. St. R.
American Stock Exchange Guide, Commerce Clearing House
 Am. Stock Ex. Guide
American Street Railway Decisions
 Am. St. R. D., Am. St. Ry. Dec.

American Street Railway Reports
 Am. St. Ry. Rep.
American Taxpayer's Quarterly
 Am. Tax Q., Am. Taxp. Q.
American Telephone and Telegraph Co.
 AT & T
American Telephone and Telegraph Co. Commission Leaflets
 A.T. & T. Co. Com. L.
American Telephone and Telegraph Co. Commission Telephone Cases
 A.T. & T. Co. T.C.
American Themis
 Am. Them., Them.
American Trade Mark Cases
 Am. Trade Mark Cas., Am. T.-M. Cas.
American Trial Lawyers Association Journal
 A.T.L.A.J., A.T.L.J.
American Trial Lawyers Journal
 Am. Trial Law. J.
American Trial Lawyers Law Journal
 Am. Trial Law. L. J.
American University Intramural Law Review
 Am. U. Intra. L. Rev., Am. U. Int. L. Rev.
American University Journal of International Law & Policy
 Am. U. J. Int'l L. & Pol'y
American University Law Review
 Am. U.L., Am. U. L. Rev., Am. Univ. L. Rev., Amer. Univ. L. Rev., A.U.L.R., AULR
American[s]
 Am.
Americans for Constitutional Action
 ACA

Americans for Democratic Action
ADA
Americans With Disability Act
Amer. with Disab. Act
Amerman's Reports (111-115 Pennsylvania Reports)
Amer.
Ames Foundation Yearbook
Y.B.Ames
Ames' Cases on Bills and Notes
Ames Cas. B. & N.
Ames' Cases on Partnership
Ames Cas. Par.
Ames' Cases on Pleading
Ames Cas. Pl.
Ames' Cases on Suretyship
Ames Cas. Sur.
Ames' Cases on Trusts
Ames Cas. Trusts.
Ames' Reports (1 Minnesota)
Ames
Ames' Reports (4-7 Rhode Island)
Ames
Ames, Knowles and Bradley's Reports (8 Rhode Island)
Ames, K. & B.
Amharic
Am.
Amicus Curiae (friend of the court) (Lat.)
am.cur.
Amicus, South Bend, Indiana
Amicus
Amicus, Thousand Oaks, California
Amicus
Amnesty International
A .I.
Amos and Ferard on Fixtures
A. & F.Fix., Am. & Fer., Ferard, Fixt., Amos & F. Fixt., Amos & F.

Amos' Fifty Years of the English Constitution
Amos Fifty Years
Amos on an English Code
Amos Eng. Code
Amos on International Law
Amos Int. Law
Amos on Laws for Regulation of Vice
Amos Reg. Vice
Amos' Primer of the English Constitution
Amos Engl. Const.
Amos' Science of Jurisprudence
Amos Jur.
Amusements and Exhibitions
Amuse.
Analysis
Anal.
Analysis and Digest of the Decisions of Sir George Jessel by A.P. Peter
Peter
Analysis and Digest of the Decisions of Sir George Jessel
Jes.
Analytical Review: A Guide to Analytical Procedures
ARAP
Ancient
Anc., anc.
Ancient Charters, 1692
Anc. Charters
Ancient Dialogue upon the Exchequer
Anc. Dial. Exch.
And Husband
et vir.
Anderson on Church Wardens
And. Ch. W.
Anderson, Chapter 11 Reorganizations
CER

**Anderson and Morris, Chapter 12
Farm Reorganizations**
　FaR
Anderson's Agricultural Decisions
　And. Agr. Dec.
Anderson's Agriculture Cases
　And.
**Anderson's English Common
Pleas Reports**
　And.
Anderson's Examination Questions and Answers
　And. Q. & A.
Anderson's History of Commerce
　And. Com.
Anderson's Law Dictionary
　And. Law Dict.
**Anderson's Reports, English
Court of Common Pleas**
　Ander. (Eng.), Anders., Anderson
**Anderson's Uniform Commercial
Code**
　Anderson UCC
Andhra Weekly Reporter, India
　Andhra W. R., An. W. R., And.
　W. R., Andh. W. R.
Andhra, India
　And. Ind.
**Andrew's English King's Bench
Reports**
　And.
**Andrews and Stoney's Supreme
Court of Judicature Acts**
　And. & Ston. J. A.
Andrews' Criminal Law
　And. Cr. Law.
**Andrews' Digest of the Opinions
of the Attorneys-General**
　And. Dig.

**Andrews' English King's Bench
Reports**
　Andr., Andrews (Eng.)
**Andrews' Manual of the United
States Constitution**
　And. Man. Const.
Andrews' Precedents of Leases
　And. Pr. Lea.
Andrews' Precedents of Mortgages
　And. Pr. Mort.
Andrews' Reports (63-73 Connecticut)
　And.
Andrews' Revenue Law
　And. Rev. Law
**Andrews' United States Laws and
Courts**
　And. L. & Cts.
**Androphy, White Collar Crime
Cases**
　WCC
Angell and Ames on Corporations
　A. & A. Corp., Ang. & A. Corp.,
　Ang. Corp.
Angell and Durfee on Highways
　Ang. Highw., A. & D. High.,
　Ang. High., Ang. & D. High
**Angell and Durfee Reports (1
Rhode Island)**
　Ang., Ang. & Dur.
Angell on Adverse Enjoyment
　Ang. Adv. Enj.
Angell on Assignment
　Ang. Ass.
Angell on Bank Tax
　Ang. B.T.
Angell on Carriers
　Ang. Car.
Angell on Insurance
　Ang. Ins.
Angell on Limitation of Actions
　Ang. Lim.

Angell on Tide Waters
Ang. Tide Water, Ang. T.W.

Angell on Water Courses
Ang. Water Courses, Ang. Wat.

Angell's Rhode Island Reports
Ang.

Anglo American Law Review
A.A.L.R., Anglo-Am. L. Rev., Anglo-Am. L.R., Ang. & A. L. Rev.

Anglo Saxon
A.S.

Anglo-Soviet Journal
Anglo-Soviet J.

**Animal and Plant Health Inspec-
tion Service**
APHIS

Animal Rights Law Reporter
Animal Rights L.Rep.

Animal[s]
Ani.

Annals
Annals

Annals of Air and Space Law
Annals Air & Space, Annals Air
& Space L., Annals of Air L. &
Space

Annals of Congress
Ann. Cong., Ann.C.

**Annals of the American Academy
of Political and Social Science**
Ann. Am. Acad., Annals, Annals Am. Acad. Pol. & Soc. Sci.

**Annals of the Chinese Society of
International Law. Taipei, Tai-
wan**
Chinese Soc'y. Int'l. L. Annals

**Annals of the Hitotsubashi Acad-
emy, Japan**
Ann. Hitotsubashi Acad.

**Annaly's English King's Bench
Reports, Tempore Hardwicke,
7-10 Geo. II**
Ann.

Annesley on Insurance
Ann.Ins.

**Anno Ante Christum Natum (the
year before the birth of Christ)
(Lat.)**
A.A.C.N.

**Anno Ante Christum (the year
before Christ) (Lat.)**
A.A.C.

**Anno Christi (in the year of
Christ) (Lat.)**
A.C.

**Anno Domini (in the year of Our
Lord) (Lat.)**
A.D.

Anno Futuro (next year) (Lat.)
a.f.

**Anno Post Christum Natum (the
year after the birth of Christ)
(Lat.)**
A. P. C. N.

**Anno Post Roman Conditam
(year after the foundation of
Rome) (Lat.)**
A. P. R. C.

**Anno Regni (in the year of the
reign) (Lat.)**
A. R.

**Anno Regni Regis/ Reginae (in
the year of the King's/Queen's
reign) (Lat.)**
A.R.S.

**Anno Regni Victoriae Regina (in
the year of Queen Victoria's
Reign) (Lat.)**
A.R.V.R. (and the year)

**Anno Reparatae Salutis (in the
year of redemption) (Lat.)**
A.R.S.

Annotated
Ann., Anno.

Annotated Cases
  A.C.
Annotated Code
  Ann. Code
Annotated Code of Maryland.
  Md. Ann. Code, Md. Code Ann.
Annotated Law Reporter
  Ann. L. Rep.
Annotated Laws of Massachusetts
  Mass. Ann. Laws
Annotated Legal Forms Magazine
  Ann. Leg. Forms Mag.
Annotated Statutes
  Ann. St.
Annotated Statutes of Indian Ter-
  ritory
  Ann. St. Ind. T.
Annotated Tax Cases
  A.T.C., Ann. Tax Cas.
Annotations to Official Florida
  Statutes
  Fla. Stat. Anno.
Announcements by the Internal
  Revenue Service
  Ann.
Annual
  A, Ann.
Annual Conference on Intellec-
  tual Property
  Ann. Conf. on Intell. Prop.
Annual Digest and Reports of In-
  ternational Law Cases
  A.D., Ann. Dig.
Annual Digest and Reports of
  Public International Law Cases
  A.D.I.L.R., Ann. Dig. I. L. C.
Annual Digest of International
  Law
  A.D.I.L.
Annual Law Register of the
  United States
  Ann. Law Reg., Ann.L.Reg.U.S.

Annual Legal Bibliography
  Ann. Leg. Bibliog.
Annual Notre Dame Estate Plan-
  ning Institute
  Ann. Notre Dame Est. Plan.
  Inst.
Annual of Industrial Property
  Law
  Ann. Ind. Prop. L., Ann. Indus.
  Prop. L.
Annual Practice
  Ann. Pr., A. P.
Annual Proceedings of the Na-
  tional Association of Railway
  Commissions
  Ann. Proc. Nat. Asso. R. Coms.
Annual Register
  A. R., Ann. Reg.
Annual Register, New Series
  Ann. Reg. N. S.
Annual Report
  Ann. Rep.
Annual Report and Official Opin-
  ions of the Attorney General of
  Indiana
  Ann. Rep. & Op. Ind. Att'y. Gen.
Annual Report and Official Opin-
  ions of the Attorney General of
  Maryland
  Ann. Rep. & Op. Md. Att'y. Gen.
Annual Report of the Attorney
  General for the State of South
  Carolina to the General Assem-
  bly
  Ann. Rep. S. C. Att'y. Gen.
Annual Report of the Attorney
  General, State of Florida
  Ann. Rep. Fla. Att'y. Gen.
Annual Report of the Inter-Ameri-
  can Commission on Human
  Rights
  Inter-Am. C.H.R.

Annual Return
A. R.
Annual Review of Banking Law
Ann. Rev. Banking L., Ann.
Rev. Banking Law
Annual Review of International Affairs
Ann.Rev. Int'l Aff.
Annual Survey of African Law
Ann. Surv. Afr. L., Annu. Surv.
of Afr. L., A.S.A.L.
Annual Survey of American Law
Ann. Surv. Am., Ann. Surv.
Am. L., Ann. Survey Am. L.,
Annu. Surv. of Amer. L., ASAL
Annual Survey of Australian Law
Ann. Surv. Austl. L.
Annual Survey of Banking Law
Ann. Surv. Banking L.
Annual Survey of Colorado Law
Ann. Surv. Colo. L.
Annual Survey of Commonwealth Law
Ann. Surv. Comm. L., Ann.
Surv. Commonw. L., A.S.C.L.,
Ann. Surv. Commonw. L.
Annual Survey of English Law
A.S.E.L.
Annual Survey of Indian Law
Ann. Surv. Ind. L., ASIL,
Annu. Surv. of Indian L.
Annual Survey of Massachusetts Law
Ann. Surv. Mass. L., Ann. Survey
Annual Survey of South African Law
Ann. Surv. S. A. L., Ann. Surv.
S. Afr. L., A.S.S.A.L., Annu.
Surv. of South Afr. L.
Annuities
Annui.

Annulment of Marriage
Annul.
Anonymous
A, anon.
Anonymous Reports at End of Benloe or Bendloe, England
A.B., An. B., An.
Another
Anr.
Anson on Contracts
Ans. Con., Anson, Cont.
Anstey's Guide to the English Law and Constitution
Anst. Eng. Law.
Anstey's Pleader's Guide
Anst. Pl. Gui.
Anstruther's English Exchequer Reports
Anst., Anstr., Anstr. (Eng)
Ante Christum (before Christ) (Lat.)
A.C.
Ante Christum Natum (before the birth of Christ) (Lat.)
A.C.N.
Anthon's Abridgment of Blackstone
Anth. Black.
Anthon's Law Student
Anth. L.S.
Anthon's New Precedents of Declarations
Anth. Prec.
Anthon's New York Nisi Prius Reports
Anth., Anthon NP (N. Y.)
Anthon's Nisi Prius Reports
Anth. N.P., Anthon's N. P., Anthon's Rep., Anth. N. P. R., Anthon Rep., Anthon's N. P.
Anthon's Study of Law
Anth. St.

Anthony on Consolidation of Railroad Companies
Anth. R.R. Cons.

Anthony's Edition of Shephard's Touchstone
Anth. Shep.

Anti-Ballistic Missiles
ABM

Anti-Discrimination Board Newsletter
ADB-INK Newsletter

Antigua and Barbuda
Ant. & Barb.

Antitrust
Antitrust

Antitrust and Trade Regulation Report, Bureau of National Affairs
Antitrust & Trade Reg. Rep. (BNA)

Antitrust and Trade Regulation Reporter, Bureau of National Affairs
A.T.R.R.

Antitrust Adviser
AA

Antitrust Bulletin
Antitrust Bull.

Antitrust Law and Economics Review
Antitrust L. & Econ. Rev.

Antitrust Law Journal
Antitrust L. J.

Antitrust Law Symposium
Antitrust L. Sym.

Antitrust Newsletter
Antitrust Newsl.

Apartment
Apart

Aphorisms of Bacon (Sir Francis)
Bac. Aphorisms

APLA Quarterly Journal, American Patent Law Association
APLA Q. J.

Appeal Allowed
App. allowed

Appeal and Error
A. & E.

Appeal Cases
A.C., App.

Appeal Cases in Canada
A.C.

Appeal Cases in Ceylon
A.C.

Appeal Cases in the United States
App. Cas.

Appeal Cases of the different states of the United States
App. Cas.

Appeal Cases, District of Columbia
App. Cas. (D. C.), App. D.C.

Appeal Cases, English Law Reports
App. Cas.

Appeal Court Reports, Ceylon
A.C.R.

Appeal Court Reports, New Zealand
App. Ct. Rep.

Appeal Denied
App. den.

Appeal Dismissed
App. dism.

Appeal Reports, New Zealand
App. N.Z.

Appeal Reports, New Zealand, Second Series
App. N.Z.2d

Appeal Reports, Upper Canada (1846-66)
A. R.

Appeal Tribunal
App. Trib., AT

Appeals and Review Memorandum Committee, Internal Revenue Bulletin
A. R. M.

Appeals and Review Recommendation
A.R.R.

Appeal[s] Examiner
App. Exam.

Appeals from Fisheries Commission
App. Fish. Com.

Appeals Notes
A. N.

Appeal[s] Referee
App. Ref.

Appeals Relating to Tax on Servants, 1781
App. Tax Serv.

Appearance
Appear.

Appellant
App.

Appellate Court
A.C., App Ct

Appellate Court Administration Review
App. Court Ad. Rev., App. Ct. Admin. Rev.

Appellate Decisions, New York
AD

Appellate Decisions 2d Series, New York
AD2d

Appellate Department
App. Dep't.

Appellate Division
App. Div.

Appellate Division Reports
A.D.R.

Appellate Jurisdiction Act, 1876
App. Jur. Act 1876

Appendices of Proceedings of the Scottish Land Court
S.L. Co., S.L. Co. R.

Appendices to Scottish Land Court Reports
Sc. La. Rep. App.

Appendix[es]
App.(s), Append., Appx.

Appendix to 11 Peters, U.S. Reports
Bald. App.

Appendix to Breese's Reports, Illinois
Ap. Bre., Appx. Bre.

Appendix to Tidd's Practice
Tidd App.

Appendix to Volume 10 of Hare's Vice-Chancellor's Reports
Ha. App.

Appleton's Reports
App., Appleton.

Appleton's Rules of Evidence
App.Ev.

Applicable
Appl.

Application for Certiorari Denied
C.D.

Application for Mandamus Granted in Part
M.G.P.

Application for Review Decisions
ARD

Application for Writ of Error Dismissed by Agreement of Parties
DAP

Application for Writ of Error Dismissed for Want of Jurisdiction
D.

Application for Writ of Error Dismissed, Judgment Correct
DJC

Application for Writ of Error Granted
    G.

Application for Writ of Mandamus Dismissed for Want of Jurisdiction
    M.D.

Application for Writ of Mandamus Refused
    M.R.

Application for Writ of Mandamus Refused in Part
    M.R.P.

Applied
    Appl.

Appointed
    Apptd.

Appropriation[s]
    Approp.

Approved
    Appd.

Approved in
    Appr.

Approving
    Appr.

April
    Apr.

Apud (in the works of an author) (Lat.)
    Ap.

Apud Justinianum (or Justinian's Institutes)
    Ap. Just., Ap. Justin.

Arab Common Market
    ACM

Arabian American Oil Company
    A. R. A. M. C. O.

Arabic
    A

Arbitration
    Arb., Arbitr.

Arbitration and Award
    Arb. & A.

Arbitration in the Schools
    Arb. Schools

Arbitration Journal
    Ar. J., Arb. J., Arbitration J.

Arbitration Journal of the Institute of Arbitrators
    Arb. J. of the Inst. of Arbitrators

Arbitration Journal, New Series
    Arb. J. (N. S.)

Arbitration Journal, Old Series
    Arb. J. (O. S.)

Arbitration Law; A Digest of Court Decisions
    Arb. L. Dig.

Arbitration Materials
    Arb. Mat'l, Arb. Nat'l

Arbitrator[s]
    Arb.

Arbuthnot's Select Criminal Cases
    Arbuth.

Archbold on Baines' Acts on Criminal Justice
    Arch. Baines' Acts

Archbold on Bankruptcy
    Arch. Bank.

Archbold's Abridgment of Poor Law Cases
    Arch. Pl. Cas., Arch. P. L. Cas.

Archbold's Bankruptcy Law
    Arch B.L.

Archbold's Civil Pleading and Evidence
    Archb. Civil Pl., Arch. Civ. Pl.

Archbold's Common Law Practice
    Arch. C. L. Pr.

Archbold's Criminal Law
    Arch. Cr. L.

Archbold's Criminal Pleading
    Arch. Cr. Pl., Arch. Cr. Pl. (or Archb. Crim. Pl.), Archb. Crim. Pl.

Archbold's Criminal Practice
Arch. Cr. Prac.
Archbold's Criminal Procedure
Arch. Cr. Proc.
Archbold's Edition of Blackstone's Commentaries.
Arch. Black.
Archbold's Forms in King's Bench and Common Pleas
Arch. K. B. Forms
Archbold's Forms of Indictment
Arch. Forms Ind.
Archbold's Indictments, with Forms
Arch. Forms
Archbold's King's Bench Practice
Arch. K. B. Pr.
Archbold's Justice of the Peace
Arch. J. P.
Archbold's Law of La
Archbold's Law of Arbitration and Award
Arch. Arb.
Archbold's Law of Landlord and Tenant
Arch. L. & T., Archb. Landl. & Ten.
Archbold's Law of Nisi Prius
Arch. N. P.
Archbold's Law of Partnership
Arch. Part.
Archbold's Lunacy Laws
Arch. Lun.
Archbold's Municipal Corporations Act
Arch. Mun. Corp.
Archbold's New Practice
Archb. N. Prac., Archb. New Pr.
Archbold's New Practice in Poor Law Removals and Appeals
Arch.P.L.
Archbold's Nisi Prius Law
Archb. N. P.

Archbold's Pleading and Evidence in Criminal Cases
Archb. Cr. Law, Archb. Cr. Prac. & Pl., Arch. Cr.
Archbold's Pleas of the Crown
Arch. P. C.
Archbold's Poor Law
Arch. P. L.
Archbold's Poor Law Cases
A. P. L. Cas., Arch. P.L.C.
Archbold's Practice
Archb. Pr.
Archbold's Practice by Chitty
Arch. P. Ch., Arch. Pr. Ch.
Archbold's Practice in Judges Chambers
Arch. J. C. Pr., Arch. Pr. J.C.
Archbold's Practice in Quarter Sessions
Arch. Pr. Q. S.
Archbold's Practice in the Common Pleas
Arch. C. P., Arch. Pr. C.P., Arch. P.C.P.
Archbold's Practice in the King's Bench
Arch. P. K. B., Arch. Pr. K.B.
Archbold's Practice in the Queen's Bench
Arch. Q.B.
Archbold's Summary of Laws of England
Arch. Sum.
Archer and Hogue's Reports (2 Florida)
Archer & H., Archer & Hogue
Archer's Reports (2 Florida)
Archer
Archibald's, Country Solicitor's Practice in the Queen's Bench
Arch. C. S. Pr.
Architects
Arch.

Architects Law Reports
  Arch. L. R.
Architects' Law Reports
  Architects' L. R.
**Area Redevelopment Administra-
tion**
  ARA
Argentina
  Arg., Argen.
**Argles' French Law of Bills of Ex-
change**
  Arg. Bilis Ex.
**Argles' Treatise Upon French
Mercantile Law**
  Arg. Fr. Merc. Law.
Arguendo (in arguing) (Lat.)
  Arg.
Argus Law Reports, Australia
  Argus L. Rep., Argus L.R.,
  Arg. L. R.
**Argus Law Reports Current
Notes, Australia**
  A.L.R.(C.N.)
Argus Reports, Australia
  A. R., Am.Rep., Arg. Rep.
**Argus Reports, Newspaper, Aus-
tralia**
  Argus (Newspr)(Vic.)
Aristotle
  Arist.
Aristotle, Nicomachean Ethics
  Eth. Nic.
Arizona
  Ariz., Az.
Arizona Administrative Digest
  Ariz. Admin. Dig.
Arizona Appeals Reports
  Ariz. App.
Arizona Attorney
  Ariz. Att'y
Arizona Bar Journal
  Ariz. B. J.

Arizona Constitution
  Ariz. Const.
Arizona Corporation Commission
  Ariz. C. C.
Arizona Court of Appeals Reports
  Az. A.
**Arizona Journal of International
and Comparative Law**
  Ariz. J. Int'l & Comp. L., Ari-
  zona J. Int'l & Comp. L.
Arizona Law Review
  Ariz. L. Rev., Arizona L. Rev.,
  Az. L., Az. L.R.
Arizona Lawyer
  Ariz. Law
Arizona Legislative Service
  Ariz. Legis. Serv.
**Arizona Official Compilation of
Administrative Rules and
Regulations**
  Ariz. Admin. Comp., Ariz.
  Admin. Comp. R.
Arizona Railway Commission
  Ariz. R. C.
Arizona Reports
  Ariz., Az.
Arizona Revised Statutes
  Ariz. Rev. Stat., Ariz. Rev.
  State, A.R.S.
**Arizona Revised Statutes Anno-
tated**
  Ariz. Rev. Stat. Ann.
Arizona Session Laws
  Ariz. Sess. Laws
Arizona State Law Forum
  Ariz. St. L. F.
Arizona State Law Journal
  Ariz. St. L. J., Ariz. State L.J.,
  Arizona State L. J.
Arizona Supreme Court Reports
  Ariz.
Arkansas
  A, Ark.

Arkansas Appeals Reports
Ark. App.
Arkansas Appellate Reports
Ark. App. Rep.
Arkansas Bar Association
ARBA, Ark. B. A.
Arkansas Bar Association, Proceedings
Ark. B. A.
Arkansas Constitution
Ark. Const.
Arkansas Corporation Commission Reports
Ark. C. C.
Arkansas Department of Public Utilities Reports
Ark. P. U.
Arkansas General Acts
Ark.Acts
Arkansas Institute for Continuing Legal Education
ARKCLE
Arkansas Law Journal
Ark. L.J.
Arkansas Law Notes
Ark. L. Notes
Arkansas Law Review
Ark. L. Rev., Arkansas L. Rev.
Arkansas Lawyer
Ark. Law.
Arkansas Lawyer Quarterly
Ark. Law. Q.
Arkansas Railroad Commission
Ark. R. C.
Arkansas Register
Ark. Admin. Reg., Ark. Reg.
Arkansas Reports
Ak, Ark., Ark. R., Ark. Rep.,
Ark's
Arkansas Statutes
Ark. Stats.
Arkansas Statutes Annotated
Ark. Stat. Ann.

Arkansas Supreme Court Reports
Ark.
Arkley's Justiciary Reports
Ark., Ark. Just., Arkley, Arkl.
Armed Services
A.S.
Armed Services Procurement Regulation
ASPR
Armed Services Renegotiation Board
ASRB
Arms Control and Disarmament Agency
ACDA
Armstrong, Macartney and Ogle's Irish Nisi Prius Reports
Arms. M. & O., A.M. & O.,
Arm. & O., Arm. Mac. & Og.,
Arm. M. & O., Arms. Mac. &
Og., Armstrong M & O (Ir)
Armstrong's Breach of Privilege Cases, New York
Arms. Br. P. Cas.
Armstrong's Cases of Contested Elections, New York
Arms. Elect. Cas.
Armstrong's Contested Election Cases
Arms. Con. El., See also New
York Election Cases
Armstrong's Limerick Trials
Arms. Tr.
Armstrong's New York Contested Elections
Arms. Con. Elec.
Army Lawyer
Army Law., Army Lawy.
Army Order
A. O.
Army Procurement Procedures
APP

Army Regulations
    A. R.

Army Routine Order
    A.R.O.

Arnold and Hodges' English Bail Court Reports
    Arn. & H. B. C., Arn. & Hod. B. C.

Arnold and Hodges' Practice Cases
    Arn. & Hod. P. C., Arn. & Hod. Pr. Cas.

Arnold and Hodges' Queen's Bench Reports
    Arn. & H., A. & H., Arnold & H, Arn. & Hod.

Arnold on Marine Insurance
    Am. Ins.

Arnold on the Law of Public Meetings
    Arn. Pub. Meet., Arn. Pub. M.

Arnold's Common Pleas Reports
    Arnold

Arnold's Election Cases
    Arn. El. Cas.

Arnold's English Common Pleas Reports
    Arn.

Arnold's Municipal Corporations
    Arn. Mun. Cor.

Arnolds, Carroll, Lewis and Seng. Eyewitness Testimony, Strategies and Tactics
    ET

Arnot's Criminal Cases
    Arnot Cr. C.

Arnot's Criminal Trials
    Arn.

Arnould on Marine Insurance
    Arn., Arn. ins.

Aron and Rosner. How to Prepare Witnesses for Trial
    HPWT

Aron, Duffy and Rosner. Cross Examination of Witnesses
    CEW

Aron, Duffy and Rosner. Impeachment of Witnesses Cross-Examiner's Art
    IW

Arrangement
    Arrang.

Arrets et Avis du Conseil d'Etat (Judgments and opinions of the Council of State), Belgium
    A.A.C.E.

Arrête
    Ar.

Ars Aequi, Juridisch Studentenblad, Netherlands
    AA

Art
    Art

Art and the Law
    Art & L., Art & Law

Article[s]
    Art., (arts.)

Articled Clerk[s]
    Artic. Cl.

Articled Clerk and Debater
    Artic. Cl. Deb.

Articled Clerks' Journal and Examiner
    Artic. Cl. J. Exam.

Articles of War
    A.W.

Articuli Cleri (articles of the clergy) (Lat.)
    Artic. Cleri

Articuli Super Chartas (articles upon the charters) (Lat.)
    Artic. sup. Chart.

Artificial Insemination
    A .I.

Artificial Insemination by Donor
    A.I.D.

Arts
Arts
Arundell on the Law of Mines
Arun. Mines
Asbestos Hazard Emergency Response Act of 1986
AHERA
Ashburner's Principles of Equity
Ashb.
Ashe's Tables to the Year Books, Coke's Reports, and Dyer's Reports
Ashe
Ashmead's Pennsylvania Reports
Ashm., Ash., Ashm. (Pa.), See also Ashmead's Reports
Ashmead's Reports
Ashmead, Ashmead (Pa.), Ashmead's Penn. Rep.
Ashton's Reports (9-12 Opinions of the United States Attorneys General)
Ashton., Ashurst
Ashurst's Manuscript Reports, printed in vol. 2, Chitty
Ashurst MS.
Ashurst's Paper Books, in Lincoln's Inn Library
A. P. B., Ashurst, Ashurst MS.
Asia Quarterly
Asia Q.
Asian-African Legal Consultative Committee
AALCC
Asian and African Studies
Asian & Afr. Stud.
Asian and Pacific Council
ASPAC
Asian Comparative Law Review
Asian Comp. L. Rev.
Asian Pacific Commercial Lawyer
Asian Pac. Comm. Law.

Asian Survey
Asian Surv.
Asiatic Society of Japan, Transactions, Tokyo
Asiatic Soc. of Japan
Association of Student International Law Societies International Law Journal
ASILS Intl. L.J., ASILS Int'l L.J.
Aspect[s]
Asp.
Aspinall's Maritime Cases (or Reports)
Mar.L. Cas. (N.S.), Mr. L.C. N.S.,
Aspinall's Maritime Cases (or Reports), New Series
Asp. M.C.L., Mar.L. Cas. (N.S.), Mar. L.C. N.S., Asp. Rep., Asp., Asp. Cas., Asp. M.C., Aspin., Asp. Mar. L. Cas.(Eng.), Asp. Mar. Law Cas.
Assault and Battery
Asslt. & B.
Assembly (state Legislature in the United States)
Assem.
Assembly Bill (in the United States state legislatures)
A.B.
Assessed Tax Case
A.T.C.
Assessed Taxes, Decisions of Judges
Ass. Tax.
Asset Depreciation Range
AOR
Asset Depreciation Range System
ADR
Asset Depreciation System
AOS

Assia Regis David, Scotland
Ass. Reg. Da.
Assigned
Assd.
Assignments
Assign.
Assignments for Benefits of Creditors
Assign. for Crs.
Assistance Payments Administration
APA
Assistance, Writ of
Assist.
Assistant[s]
Asst., asst.
Assistant Judge Advocate General for Procurement (Army); Contract Division Office of Judge Advocate General of Army
CSJAGE
Assistant Vice-Chancellor
A.V.Ch.
Assizes of Jerusalem
Ass. Jerus.
Asso and Manuel's Institutes of Spanish Civil Law
Asso & Man.
Associate
Assoc.
Associate Judge
A.J.
Associate of the Institute of Arbitrators
A.I. Arb.
Associated African States and Madagascar
AASM
Associated Scottish Life Offices
A.S.L.O.
Association[s]
Ass'n., Assn., Asso., assoc.

Association for the Study of Abortion Newsletter, Australia
A.S.A. Newsl.
Association Francaise de Droit Aerien
AFDA
Association of American Law Schools
AALS
Association of American Law Schools Proceedings
AALS Proc.
Association of Attenders and Alumni of the Hague Academy of International Law.
AAA
Association of British Chambers of Commerce
A.B.C.C.
Association of Chief Police Officers
A.C.P.O.
Association of Data Process Service Organizations
ADPSO
Association of Fire Loss Adjusters
A.F.L.A.
Association of Iron Ore Exporting Countries
AIOEC
Association of Natural Rubber Producing Countries
ANRPC
Association of Professional, Executive, Clerical and Computer Staff
APEX
Association of Scientific, Technical and Managerial Staffs
A.S.T.M.S.

Association of Southeast Asian Nations
ASEAN
Association of Special Libraries and Information Bureaux
A.S.L.I.B.
Association of Student International Law Societies
ASILS
Association of the Bar of the City of New York
A.B.C.N.Y.
Association of the Bar, City of New York, Committee on Amendment of the Law, Bulletin
C.A.L. Bull.
Association of Trial Lawyers of America
ATLA
Association of Trial Lawyers of America Law Journal
A. Trial Law. Am. L.J.
Association of Trial Lawyers of America Newsletter
Ass'n Trial Law. Am. Newsl.
Associations and Clubs
Asso., assoc.
Aston's Entries, 1673
Ast. Ent.
At Sight Of
Ats., ASOL, A/S or A/s.,
Atcheson's Election Cases
Atch. E.C.
Atchison's English Navigation and Trade Reports
Atch.
Ateneo Law Journal
Ateneo L.J.
Athelston's Laws
LL. Athelst.
Atherley on Marriage Settlements
Ath. Mar. Set.

Atkinson on Conveyancing
Atk. Con.
Atkinson on Marketable Titles
Atk. Titles
Atkinson on Sheriffs
Atk Sher.
Atkinson's Chancery Practice
Atk. Ch. Pr.
Atkinson's Law of Solicitors' Liens
Atkinson
Atkinson's Quarter Sessions Records, Yorkshire
Atk.
Atkyns' English Chancery Reports
Atk.
Atkyn's Parliamentary Tracts
Atk. P.T.
Atlantic
Atl.
Atlantic Community Quarterly
Atl. Comm. Q.
Atlantic Monthly
Atl. Mo., Atlan.
Atlantic Province Reports
Atl.P.R., A. P. R., Atl.Prov., A. P. R.
Atlantic Reporter
A., A, A. R., At., Atl., Atl. R., Atl. Rep., Atl. Repr., At.Rep., A. Rep.
Atlantic Reporter, Second Series
A.2d, Atl.2d
Atomic
Atom.
Atomic Energy
A.E., Atomic E.
Atomic Energy Agency
AEA
Atomic Energy Commission
A.E.C.

Atomic Energy Commission Procurement Regulations
AECPR

Atomic Energy Commission Reports
A.E.C., AEC

Atomic Energy Law Journal
A.E.L.J., Atom Ener L J, Atom. Energy L.J., Atomic Energy L.J., Atomic Eng. L.J.

Atomic Energy Law Reporter, Commerce Clearing House
Atom. En. L. Rep. CCH., CCH Atom. En. L. Rep.

Attachment
Attach.

Attorney[s]
Att., Atty. (Attys), Att'y(s)

Attorney-General
A.G., Att. Gen., A.G., Atty. Gen., Att'y Gen.

Attorney General's Annual Report
Att'y Gen. Ann. Rep.

Attorney General's Decisions
A.G. Dec.

Attorney General's Information Service
A.G.I.S.

Attorney General's Law Journal
Att'y Gen. L.J.

Attorney General's Opinions
AG, Atty. Gen. Op.

Attorney-General's Opinions, New York
Atty. Gen. Op. N.Y.

Attorney General's Reports
Rep. Atty. Gen.

Attorney Sanctions Newsletters
AtSN

Atwater's Reports (1 Minnesota)
Atw., Atwater.

Atwood and Brewster. Antitrust and American Business Abroad
AABA

Auckbourn's Jurisdiction of the Supreme Court of Judicature
Ayck. Jur.

Auckland University Law Review
Auck. U. L. Rev., Auckland U. L. Rev., Auckland Univ. L. Rev.

Auction[s]
Auct.

Auction Register and Law Chronicle
Auct. Reg. & L. Chron.

Audit
Aud.

Audita Querela
Aud. Q.

Auditor
Aud.

Auditor-General
Aud.-Gen.

August
Au., Ag., Aug.

Auli Gellii Noctes Atticae
Aul. Gell. Noct. Att.

Auoniam Attachiamenta
Quon. Attach.

Austin's Ceylon Reports
Austin (Ceylon).

Austin's English County Court Cases
Aust., Austin C.C.

Austin's Jurisprudence
Aust. Jur.

Austin's Kandran Appeals
Aust. K.A.

Austin's Lectures on Jurisprudence
Aust. Jr., Aust. Jur.

Austin's Lectures on Jurisprudence, Abridged
Aust. Jur. Abr.

Australia[n]
Aust., Austral.

Australia, Acts of the Parliament
Acts, Austl. Acts P., Austr. Acts, Acts Austl. P., Austr. Acts P. (See also Acts of the Australian Parliament and Acts of the Parliament of the Commonwealth of Australia)

Australia, Commonwealth, Acts of Parliament
Austl. Acts, Acts Austl. P., Austl. Acts P.

Australia, Commonwealth Law Reports
Austr. C.L.R. (see also Commonwealth Law Reports)

Australia Legal Monthly Digest
A.L.M.D., Austl. L.M.D. (see also Legal Monthly Digest)

Australian and New Zealand Conveyancing Report
A.C.V.

Australian Accountant
Aust Accountant, Aust Acc, Aust Acctnt

Australian Accounts Preparation Manual
ACTP

Australian and New Zealand Environmental Report
A. N. V.

Australian and New Zealand Income Tax Reports
A.N.Z.I.T.R.

Australian and New Zealand Journal of Criminology
Austl. & N.Z. J. Crim., Austl. & N.Z. J. Criminology, Aust. & N.Z. J. Crim.

Australian Annual Digest
Austl. A.D.

Australia-New Zealand-United States Security Treaty 1851
ANZUS

Australian Argus Law Reports
Aust. Argus L. Rep., Austl. Argus L.R. (see also Argus Law Reports)

Australian Army Legal Department
A.A.L.D.

Australian Banker
Aust Banker

Australian Bankruptcy Cases
A.B.C., Aust. Bankr. Cas., Austl. Bankr. Cas., Austr. B.C.

Australian Bar Gazette
Aust. Bar Gaz.

Australian Bar Review
Austl. B. Rev.

Australian Business Law Review
A.B.L.R., Austl. Bus. L. Rev., A. Bus. L. Rev., Aust. Bus. L. Rev.

Australian Capital Territory
A.C.T.

Australian Capital Territory Law Reform Commission
ACTLRC

Australian Capital Territory Subsidiary Legislation
Austl. Cap. Terr. Subsdy., Subs. Leg. Austl. Cap. Terr.

Australian Capital Territory Reports
A.C.T.R.

Australian Capital Territory Supreme Court
SC (ACT)

Australian Commercial Journal
Austl. Com. J.

Australian Company Law Cases
A.C.L.C.

Australian Company Law Reports
A.C.L.R.

Australian Conveyancer and Solicitors Journal
Austl. Convey. & Sol. J., Aust. Conv. Sol. J.

Australian Corporate Affairs Reporter
A.C.A.

Australian Criminal Reports
A. Crim. R.

Australian Current Law
A.C.L.

Australian Current Law Digest
A.C.L.D.

Australian Current Law Review
A.C.L.R., Aust. C. L. Rev., Aust. Curr. L. Rev., Austl. Current L. Rev., A.C. L. Rev.

Australian Digest
A.D., Austl. D., Aust. Digest, Austl. D.2d

Australian Digest, Second Edition
Austl. D.2d

Australian Director, Institute of Directors in Australia
Aust Director

Australian Estate and Gift Duty Cases
A.E.G.R.

Australian Estate and Gift Duty Reporter
A.E.G.

Australian Family Law and Practice
A.F.L.

Australian Family Law Cases
F.L.C.

Australian Federal Tax Reporter
A.F.T.

Australian High Court and Federal Court Practice
A.H.F.

Australian Income Tax Decisions by Ratcliffe and M'Grath
R. & McG.

Australian Income Tax Guide
A.T.G.

Australian Income Tax Reports
I.T.R.

Australian Industrial Law Review
Aust. Ind. L.R.

Australian Industrial Review
A.I.L., A.I.L.R.

Australian Institute of Criminology
A.I.C.

Australian Institute of International Affairs
A.I.I.A.

Australian Journal of Corporate Law
Austl. J. Comp. L.

Australian Journal of Family Law
Austl. J. Fam. L.

Australian Journal of Forensic Sciences
Austl. J. For. Sci.

Australian Journal of Labour Law
Austl. J. Lab. L.

Australian Journal of Law and Society
Austl. J. L. Soc'y

Australian Journal of Public Administration
Aust. J. Pub. Admin.

Australian Jurist
Aust. Jr., Aust. Jur., Austl. Jr., Austr. Jur.

Australian Jurist Reports
A. Jur. Rep., A.J.R., Austl. Jur. R., Aust. Jr. R., Aust. Jur. Rep.

Australian Jurist Reports, Notes of Cases
    A.J.R.(N.C.)
Australian Law Journal
    A.L.J., Aust. L.J., Austl. L.J., Austr. L.J.
Australian Law Journal Reports
    Aust. L.J. Rep., Austl. L.J. Rep., A.L.J.R., Austl. L.J.
Australian Law News
    Aust. Law News, Aust. L.N.
Australian Law Reform Agencies Conference
    A.L.R.A.C.
Australian Law Reform Commission
    A.L.R.C.
Australian Law Reports
    A.L.R., Aust. L. Rep., Austl. L.R.
Australian Law Times
    A.L.T., Austl. L. Times, Austr. L.T., Aust. L.T.
Australian Lawyer
    Austl. Law., Aust.Law., Aust. Lawyer
Australian Leave and Holidays Practice Manual
    Alive
Australian Mining and Petroleum Law Journal
    A. M. P. L. J.
Australian National Bibliography
    ANB
Australian Personnel Management
    APM
Australian Public Affairs Information Service
    APAIS
Australian Quarterly
    Aus. Quart., Aust. Quart., AQ

Australian Sales Tax Guide
    A.T.X.
Australian Securities Law Cases
    A.S.L.C.
Australian Securities Law Reporter
    A.S.R.
Australian Statutory Rules, Consolidation
    Austl. Stat. R. Consol.
Australian Superannuation Practice
    A.S.P.
Australian Tax Cases
    A.T.C.
Australian Tax Decisions
    A.T.D., Austl. Tax, Austr. Tax
Australian Tax Planning Report
    A. P. X.
Australian Tax Reports
    A.T.R.
Australian Tax Review
    Aust. Tax Rev., Austl. Tax Rev., A.T. Rev.
Australian Trade Practices Reports
    A.T.P.R.
Australian Yearbook of International Law
    Aust. Y. Int.L., Aust. Yearbook Int.L., Aust. Yr. Bk. I.L., Austl.Y.B. Intl L., Austl. Y.B. Int'l L., Aust. Yb. Int'l L., A.Y.B.I.L.
Austria[n]
    Aus., Aust.
Authentica (Lat.)
    Auth.
Authorised
    Auth.
Authority[ies]
    Auth.

Automated Data and Telecommu-
nications Service
 ADTS
Automatic Data Processing
 ADP
Automobile Cases
 Auto. C., Auto. Cas.
Automobile Cases, Second Series
 Auto. Cas.2d
Automobile Insurance
 Auto. Ins.
Automobile Insurance Cases
 Auto. Ins. Cas.
Automobile Insurance Reporter,
Commerce Clearing House
 Auto. Ins. Rep.(CCH)
Automobile Law Reporter, Com-
merce Clearing House
 Auto. L. Rep. (CCH)
Automobile Law Reports, Com-
merce Clearing House
 Auto. L. Rep. (CCH)
Automobiles and Highway Traffic
 Auto
Avenue
 Ave.
Average
 Av.
Averbach on Handling Accident
Cases
 Averbach Acci.Cas.
Avery and Hobb's Bankrupt Law
 Av. & H.B.L., A. & H. Bank.
Aviation
 Av., Avi.

Aviation Cases
 Av. Cas.
Aviation Law Reporter, Com-
merce Clearing House
 Av. L. Rep. (CCH)
Aviation Law Reports, Com-
merce Clearing House
 Av. L. Rep. (CCH)
Aviation Reports
 U.S. Aviation
Ayckbourn's Chancery Forms
 Ayck. Ch. F.
Ayckbourn's Chancery Practice
 Ayck. Ch. Pr.
Ayliffe's Calendar of Ancient
Charters
 Ayi. Char.
Ayliffe's Introduction to the Cal-
endar of Ancient Charters
 Ayl.Int.
Ayliffe's Pandects of the Roman
Civil Law
 Ayl. Pan., Ayl. Pand., Ayliffe
Ayliffe's Parergon Juris Canonici
Anglicani
 Ayliffe, Ayl. Par.
Ayr and Wigton's Registration
Cases
 Ayr & Wig.
Ayr's Registration Cases
 Ayr
Ayrton's Land Transfer Act
 Ayr. Land Tr.
Azuni on Maritime Law
 Azuni Mar.Law, Az. Mar. Law.

B

Babington's Law of Auctions
Bab. Auc.
Babington's Law of Set-off
Bab. Set-off.
Baccalaureus Juris
B.Jur.
Baccalaureus Procurationis
B.Proc.
Bachelor of Arts
B.A.
Bachelor of Cannon Law
B.C.L.
Bachelor of Civil Law
B.C.L.
Bachelor of General Laws
B.G.L.
**Bachelor of Juridical and Social
Sciences**
B.Jur. & Soc.S.
Bachelor of Law[s]
B.L., LL. B, B.L.L.
Bachelor of Letters
B.L.
**Bache's Pennsylvania Justice's
Manual**
Bache Pa. Just.
**Bach's Reports (19-21 Montana
Reports)**
Bach.
Backus on Sheriffs
Back. Sher.
**Bacon on Benefit Societies and
Life Insurance**
Bac. Ben. Soc., Bac. Ins.
Bacon on Government
Bac. Gov., Bacon

**Bacon on Leases and Terms of
Years**
Bac. Lease., Bacon
Bacon on Uses
Bacon, Bac. Uses.
Bacon's Abridgment
Bacon, Bac. Ab., Bac. Abr.
Bacon's Aphorisms
Bacon, Bac. Aph., Bac. Apho-
risms
Bacon's Arguments in Law
Bacon
Bacon's Case of Treason
Bac. Ca.
Bacon's Chancery Cases
Bac. Chanc.
Bacon's Complete Arbitrator
Bacon, Bac. Comp. Arb.
Bacon's Decisions
Bac. Rep., Bac. Dec.
**Bacon's Elements of the Common
Law**
Bac. El., Bacon
Bacon's Georgia Digest
Bac. Dig.
Bacon's Law Tracts
Bac. Law Tr., Bac. Law Tracts,
Bacon, Bac. Tr.
Bacon's Liber Regis
Bacon
**Bacon's Liber Regis, vel Thesau-
rus Rerum Ecclesiasticarum**
Bac. Lib. Reg. (or T.E.)
Bacon's Maxims of the Law
Bacon, Bac. Max., Bacon Max.
Reg.

Bacon's Reading Upon the Statute of Uses
Bac. Read. Uses., Bac. St. Uses.
Bacon's Works
Bac. Works.
Bagehot's English Constitution
Bag. Eng. Const., Bag. Engl. Const.
Baggett's Texas Foreclosure-Law and Practice
TF
Bagley and Harman's Reports (17-19 California)
Bag. & Har., Bagl. & H., Bagl. & Har., Bagl. & Har. (Cal.)
Bagley's Practice (1834)
Bag. Ch. Pr.
Bagley's Reports (16-19 California)
Bagl., Bagl. (Cal.)
Bahamas
Bah.
Bahamas Law Reports
B.L.R., Bah. L.R.
Bahrain
Bahr.
Bail and Recognizance
Bail & R.
Bail Bond
B.B.
Bail Court
Bail Ct., B.C.
Bail Court Cases, Lowndes and Maxwell
B.C.C., B.C.R., B.C. Rep.
Bail Court Reports, Saunders and Cole
B.C.R., B.C. Rep., B.C.C., Bail Ct. R.
Baildon's Select Cases in Chancery (Selden Society Publication, 10)
Baild.

Bailey on Bills
B.B.
Bailey's Chancery Reports, South Carolina
Bailey, Ch.
Bailey's English Dictionary
Bailey. Dict.
Bailey's Equity or Law Reports, South Carolina
Bailey
Bailey's Equity Reports, South Carolina
Bail. Eq., Bai. Eq., Bail. Eq. (S.C.), Bailey Eq.
Bailey's Law of Master's Liability for Injuries to Servant
Bailey, Mast. Liab.
Bailey's Law Reports, South Carolina
Bai., Bail. L., Bail. L.(S.C.), Bail.
Bailey's North Carolina Digest
Bail. Dig.
Baillie's Digest of Mohammedan Law
Baill. Dig.
Baillie's Mohammedan Law of Inheritance
Baill. Inher.
Bailment
Bailm.
Bainbridge on the Law of Mines and Minerals
Bainb. Mines, Bainb. M. & M.
Baker on the Law Relating to Burials
Bak. Bur.
Baker/Seck. Determining Economic Loss
DEL
Baker's Health Laws
Bak. Health L.

Baker's Law of Highways
Bak. Highw.

Baker's Law of Quarantine
Bak. Quar., Baker, Quar.

Baker's New York Corporation Laws
Bak. Corp.

Balance
Bal.

Balance of Payments Report[s]
Balance of Payments
Rep.(CCH), Bal. Pay't Rep.

Balance Sheet
b.s.

Balasingham's Notes of Cases, Ceylon
Balas. N.C.

Balasingham's Reports, Ceylon
Bal.

Balasingham's Reports of Cases, Ceylon
Balas. R.C.

Balasingham's Supreme Court Reports, Ceylon
Balas.

Baldasseroni on Maritime Law
Bald., Bald. C.C.

Baldeva Ram Dave, Privy Council Judgments, India
Bal. R.D., Baldev. P.C.

Baldus and Cole, Statistical Proof of Discrimination
SPD

Baldus, Commentaries on the Justinian Code
Bald., Bald. C.C.,

Baldwin
Baldw.

Baldwin, Appendix to 11 Peters
Bald. App. 11 Pet.

Baldwin on Bankruptcy
Baldwin, Bald. Bank

Baldwin's Connecticut Digest
Bald. Conn. Dig., Baldw. Dig.

Baldwin's Kentucky Revised Statutes Annotated
Ky. Rev. Stat. Ann.

Baldwin's Patent, Copyright, Trademark Cases
Bald. Pat. Etc. Cas., Bald. Pat. Cas.

Baldwin's United States Circuit Court Reports
Bald., Bald. C.C., Baldw.,
Bald. Cir. C., Bald. Rep., Baldwin's C.C. U.S.Rep., Baldwin's Rep.

Baldwin's View of the United States Constitution with Opinions
Bald. Const. (or Op.)

Balfour's Practice, Laws of Scotland
Balf. Pr., Balf.

Ball and Beatty's Irish Chancery Reports
B. & B., Ba. & Be., Ball & B. (Ir.), Ball & B., Ball & Beatty

Ball on National Banks
Ball Banks, B.B.

Ballantine on Limitations
Bal. Lim., Ball. Lim., Ball. Lim.

Ballard's Somerton Court Rolls (Oxford Arch. Soc. No. 50)
Ball.

Ballentine's Law Dictionary
Ballentine, Balletine's Law Dict.

Ballentine's Self Pronouncing Law Dictionary
Ballentine's Law Dict.

Ballinger's Annotated Codes and Statutes,Washington
Bal. Ann. Codes, Ballinger's Ann. Codes & St.

Ball's Digest of the Common Law
Ball Dig.
Ball's Index to Irish Statutes
Ball. Ind.
Ball's Popular Conveyancer
Ball Conv.
Ball's Student Guide to the Bar
Ball St. Guide
Balsam and Zabin's Disability Handbook
DH
Baltimore City Reports
Balt. C. Rep., B.R.
Baltimore Law Transcript
Balt. L. Tr., Balt. L.T., B.L.T.
Bamberg's Reports of Cases decided by the Railway and Canal Commission
Bamber.
Banaras Law Journal
Banaras L.J., Ban. L.J.
Banbury's English Exchequer Reports (145 ER)
Banbury (Eng.)
Bancus Reginae (Queen's Bench)
B.R.
Bancus Regis (King's Bench)
B.R.
Bancus Superior (Upper Bench)
B.S.
Bangala Law Reporter, India
Bang.L.R.
Bangladesh
Bangl.
Bank
Bk
Bank and Trust
B. & T.
Bank for International Settlements
BIS

Bank of England Quarterly Bulletin
Bank Eng. Q.B., B.E.Q.B.
Banker's Law Journal
Banker's L.J.
Banker's Magazine
Bank. Mag.
Banking Cases
Bank. Cas.
Banking Code
Bank. C.
Banking Law Journal
Bank. L.J., Banking L.J., Bk. L.J.
Banking Law Review
Banking L. Rev.
Banking, Finance and Urban Affairs
B.F.U.A.
Banking, Housing and Urban Affairs
BHUA
Bankrupt Court Reporter
Bank. Ct. Rep.
Bankrupt Register
B. Reg.
Bankruptcy
Bank., Bankr., Bcy., Bky.
Bankruptcy Act
Bankr. Act.
Bankruptcy and Insolvency Cases
B. & I., Bank. Insol. Rep., Bank. & Ins., Bank. & Ins. R., Bank. & Insol. Rep., Banks. & Ins.
Bankruptcy Annulment Order
B.A.O.
Bankruptcy Bar Bulletin
Bankr. B. Bull.
Bankruptcy Cases
B.C.

Bankruptcy Court
  Bank.
Bankruptcy Court Decisions
  Bankr. Ct. Dec. (CRR), B.C.D.
Bankruptcy Developments Journal
  Bankr. Dev. J.
Bankruptcy Fee
  B.f.
Bankruptcy Forms
  Bankr. Form
Bankruptcy Gazette
  Bank. Gaz.
Bankruptcy Law Reporter, Commerce Clearing House
  Bankr. L. Rptr., Bankr. L. Rep. (CCH)
Bankruptcy Law Reports, Commerce Clearing House
  Bankr. L. Rep. (CCH)
Bankruptcy Register
  Bank. Reg., B.R.
Bankruptcy Reporter
  BRW
Bankruptcy Reports
  B.R.
Bankruptcy Rules
  Bankr. Rule
Bankruptcy and Insolvency Reports
  Bankr. Ins. R.
Banks' Reports (1-5 Kansas)
  Banks.
Bankter's Institutes of Scottish Law
  Bank. I., Bank. Inst.
Bankton's Institutes of the Laws of Scotland
  Bankt. I.
Banning and Arden, Patent Cases
  Bann. & Ard., Bann. & A., Bann. & A. Pat. Cas., Ban. & A., B. & A.

Banning's Limitations of Actions
  Bann. Lim.
Bannister's Edition of O. Bridgman's English Common Pleas Reports
  Bann. Br.
Bannister's English Common Pleas Reports
  Bann.
Bar
  B
Bar and Legal World
  Bar & Leg. W.
Bar Association Bulletin, Los Angeles
  B.A. Bull. L.A.
Bar Association of Metropolitan St. Louis Bankruptcy Reporter
  BAMSL
Bar Association of San Francisco
  BASF
Bar Association of the District of Columbia
  DCBA
Bar Bulletin
  B. Bull.
Bar Bulletin, New York County Lawyers'
  Bar Bull. (N.Y. County L.A.)
Bar Examination Annual
  Bar. Ex. Ann.
Bar Examination Guide
  Bar Ex. Guide
Bar Examination Journal
  B.Exam.J., Bar Ex. J., Bar Ex. Jour.
Bar Examiner
  Bar Exam., B.Exam.
Bar Gazette
  Bar Gaz.
Bar Leader
  B. Leader, Bar Lead.

Bar Reports
Bar Re., Bar.
Bar Reports (1-12 Law Times Reports)
Bar Rep.
Barbados
Barb.
Barbados Law Reports
Barb. L.R., B.L.R.
Barber
Barber
Barber on Insurance
Barb. Ins.
Barber's Digest
Barb. App. Dig.
Barber's Digest of Kentucky
Barb. Dig.
Barber's Gold Law
Barber, B, Barb.
Barber's Reports (14-24 Arkansas)
Barb. Ark., Bar., Barb., Barber, Barbe.
Barbeyrac's Edition of Grotius on War and Peace
Barb. Gro.
Barbeyrac's Edition of Puffendorf's Law of Nature and Nations
Barb. Puf.
Barbour and Carroll's Kentucky Statutes
Barb. & C. Ky. St.
Barbour on Parties in Law and Equity
Barb. Par.
Barbour on the Law of Set-Off
Barb. Set-Off
Barbour's Abstracts of Chancellor's Decisions
Barb. Abs.

Barbour's Chancery Practice
Barb. Ch. Pr., Barb. Ch., Barb. Ch. Rep., Barb. Chancery Rep., Barb. Ch.(N.Y.), Barbour's Ch.Pr., Barbour's Ch.R., B.Ch.
Barbour's Criminal Law
Barb. Cr. L., Barb. Cr. Law
Barbour's Criminal Pleadings
Barb. Cr. P.
Barbour's Criminal Practice
Barb. Cr. P.
Barbour's New York Reports
B
Barbour's Supreme Court Reports
Barbour's Sup. Court Rep., Bar. S.C. Rep., Barb., Barb. (N.Y.)S.C.R., Barb. R., Barb. S.C., Barb. S.C.R., Barb. Sup. Ct., Barb. Sup. Ct. Reports, Barbour, Barbour (N.Y.)
Barclay's Digest of the Law of Scotland
Bar. Dig., Barc. Dig. Law Sc.
Barclay's Digest, or Legislative Manual of Congress
Barc. Dig. (or Leg.Man.)
Barclay's Law of Highways
Barc. High.
Barclay's Missouri Digest
Barc. Dig., Barc. Mo.Dig.
Barham's Student's Guide to the Preliminary Examinations
Barh. Pre. Ex.
Barlow's Justice of Peace
Barl. Just.
Barnardiston's English Chancery Reports Temp. Hardwicke
Barnard.

Barnardiston's English Chancery Reports
Bar., Barnardiston C.C., Bar. Ch., Bar. Chy., Barn. Ch., Barnard. Ch., Barnard.Ch. (Eng.)

Barnardiston's English King's Bench Reports
Barnard., Barn. K.B., Bar., Barn., Barnard. K.B.

Barnes' English Common Pleas Reports
Barn.

Barnes' Equity Practice
Barn. Eq. Pr.

Barnes, Exposition of the Law Respecting Sheriff
Barn. Sh.

Barnes' Notes of Cases of Practice in Common Pleas (94 ER)
Barn. No., Barnes, Barnes Notes, Barnes Notes (Eng.), Barnes, N.C., Bar. N.

Barnes's Federal Code
Barnes's Fed. Code

Barnet's English Central Criminal Courts Reports
Barnet.

Barnewall and Adolphus' English King's Bench Reports
B. & A., B. & Ad., Barn. & Adol., Barn. & A., Bar. & Ad., Barn. & Ad., Barn & Ad. (Eng.)

Barnewall and Alderson's English King's Bench Reports
Barn. & A., Barn. & Ald., Barn. & Ald.(Eng.), B. & Ald., Bar. & Al.

Barnewall and Alderson's English King's Bench Reports, 1st Part
Selw. & Barn.

Barnewall and Cresswell,'s English King's Bench Reports
Bar. & Cr., B. & C., Barn. & C., Barn. & C.(Eng.), Barn. & Cr., Barn. & Cress.

Barnfield and Stiness' Reports (20 Rhode Island)
Barnf. & S.

Barnfield's Reports (19-20 Rhode Island)
Barn.

Barnstaple's Printed Minutes and Proceedings
Barn. Pr.M.

Barnwall's Digest of the Year Books
Barnw. Dig.

Baroda Law Reports, India
Baroda L.R.

Baron
Bn.

Baron (judge), Court of Exchequer, England and Wales
B

Baron of the Court of Exchequer
B.E.

Baron on Chattel Mortgages
Baron Ch. Mort.

Barony of Urie Court Records
Baron., Barron

Barradall's Manuscript Reports, Virginia
Barr.MSS., Barr.M.

Barrington's Magna Charta
Bar. Mag.

Barrington's Observations Upon the Statutes
Bar. Anc. Stat.

Barrington's Observations Upon the Statutes from Magna Charta to 21 James I
Bar. Ob. Stat., Barr Ob. (or Stat.), Barr. Obs. St., Bar. Obs. St., Barr. St., Barring. Obs. St., Barring. St.

Barrister
Bar.

Barrister [The]
Barr.

Barrister-at-Law
B.L.

Barrister, Chicago
Barrister

Barrister, Coral Gables, Fla.
Barrister

Barrister, Davis, Cal.
Barrister

Barrister, Fort Lauderdale, Fla.
Barrister

Barrister, Toronto
Barrister

Barroll's Chancery Practice
Barr. Ch. Pr.

Barron and Arnold's English Election Cases
Bar. & Arn., Barr. & Arn., B. & A., B. & Arn.

Barron and Austin's English Election Cases
B. & Aust. Cases (Eng.), Barr. & Aus., B. & A., B. & Aust., Bar. & Au., Bar. & Aust.

Barron and Holtzoff's Federal Practice and Procedure
Barron & H. Fed. Pr. & Proc.

Barron's Mirror of Parliament
Barron Mir.

Barrow's Reports (18 Rhode Island)
Bar., Barrows (R.I.), Barr., Barrows

Barr's Reports (1-10 Pennsylvania)
Barr., Barr. (Pa.)

Barry on Building Societies
Barry Build. Soc.

Barry on Forms and Precedents in Conveyancing
Barry Forms Conv.

Barry on Tenures
Barr. Ten., Barry Ten.

Barry's Chancery Jurisdiction
Barry Ch. Jur.

Barry's Practice of Conveyancing
Barry Conv.

Barry's Statutory Jurisdiction of Chancery
Barry Ch. Pr.

Bartholoman's Reports, Yorkshire Lent Assize, March 9, 1911
Bartholoman

Bartlett's Congressional Election Cases
Bart. El. Cas., Bart. Elec. Cas., Bart.Cong. Election Cases

Bartlett's Index of the Laws of Rhode Island
Bart. Ind.

Bartlett's Law of Mining
Bart. Mines

Barton's Florida Taxation
FLT

Barton's Modern Precedents in Conveyancing
Bart. Prec. Conv.

Barton's Science of Conveyancing
Bart. Conv.

Barton's Law Practice
Bart. L. Pr.

Barton's Maxims in Conveyancing
Bart. Max.

Barton's Precedents in Convey-
ancing
    Bar. Prec. Conv.
Barton's Suit in Equity
    Bar. Eq., Bart. Eq.
Bass' Products Liability: Design
and Manufacturing Defects
    PLDM
Bassett's Illinois Criminal Plead-
ing and Practice
    Bass. Crim. Pl.
Bastard[s]
    Bast.
Batchelder's Law of Massachu-
setts Manufacturing Corpora-
tions
    Batch. Mfg. Cor.
Bateman on Agency
    Bate. Ag.
Bateman's Commercial Law
    Bate. Com. L.
Bateman's General Laws of Ex-
cise
    Bate. Exc.
Bateman's Law of Auctions
    Bate. Auct.
Bateman's United States Consti-
tutional Law
    Bate. Const.
Bates' Annotated Revised Stat-
utes, Ohio
    Bates' Ann. St.
Bates' Delaware Chancery Re-
ports
    Bates Ch. Bates
Bates' Digest, Ohio
    Bates' Dig.
Bates' Law of Partnership
    Bates, Part.
Bateson's Leicester Records
    Bateson

Batten on Specific Performance
in Contracts
    Bat. Sp. Perf.
Batten on the Stannaries Act
    Bat. Stan.
Battle's Digest, North Carolina
    Bat. Dig.
Battle's Revisal of the Public Stat-
utes of North Carolina
    Bat. Rev. St., Battle's Revisal
Battle's Revised Statutes of
North Carolina
    Bat. Stat.
Batts' Annotated Revised Civil
Statutes, Texas
    Batts' Ann. St., Batts' Rev. St.
Batty's Irish King's Bench Re-
ports
    Batty (Ir.), Batt.
Bauernfeind's Income Taxation:
Accounting Methods and Peri-
ods
    AMP
Bavarian Laws
    L. Bai.
Baxter on Judicature Acts and
Rules
    Bax. Jud. Acts
Baxter's Reports (60-68 Tennes-
see)
    Baxt., Bax., Baxt. (Tenn.),
    Baxter
Bayard on Evidence
    Bay. Ev.
Bayard on the Constitution of the
United States
    Bay. Cons.
Bayley on Bills and Notes
    Bay. Bills, Bayl. B., Bayley, Bills
Bayley on Fines and Recoveries
    Bayl. F. & R.
Bayley's Chancery Practice
    Bayl. Ch. Pr.

Bayley's Commentaries on the Laws of England
Bayl. Com.

Bayley's Questions and Answers for Students
Bayl. Q. & A.

Baylies' Digested Index of English and American Reports
Bay. Dig. Ind.

Baylies on Domestic Servants
Bay. Dom. Serv.

Baylles on Sureties and Guarantors
Baylles, Sur.

Baylor Law Review
Baylor L. Rev., B.L.R., By. L.R.

Bay's Reports (1-3, 5-8 Missouri)
Bay

Bay's South Carolina Reports
Bay

Beach on Contributory Negligence
Beach, Contrib. Neg.

Beach on Injunctions
Beach, Inj.

Beach on Private Corporations
Beach, Priv. Corp.

Beach on Public Corporations
Beach, Pub. Corp.

Beach on the Law of Receivers
Beach, Rec.

Beach's Commentaries on Modern Equity Jurisprudence
Beach, Mod. Eq. Jur.

Beach's Modern Practice in Equity
Beach, Eq. Prac.

Beame's Commitments in Bankruptcy
Bea. Bank.

Beames' Costs in Equity
Bea C.E., Bea. Costs (or C.E.)

Beames' Equity Pleading
Bea. Eq. Pl.

Beames' Glanville
Beames, Glanv.

Beames on the Writ of Ne Exeat Regno
Bea. Ne Ex.

Beames' Orders in Chancery
Bea. Ord.

Beames' Pleas in Equity
Bea. Pl. Eq.

Bearblock's Treatise upon Tithes
Bear. Tithes

Beasley's New Jersey Chancery Reports
Beas.

Beasley's New Jersey Equity Reports
Beas., Beasl.

Beatty's Irish Chancery Reports
Beat., Beatt., Beatty, Beatty Ir. Ch.

Beaumont's Bills of Sale
Beau. Bills

Beaumont's Life and Fire Insurance
Beau. Ins.

Beavan
Bea.

Beavan and Walford's English Railway and Canal Cases
Beav. & W. Ry. Cas., Beav. & Wal. Ry. Cas., Beav. R. & C. Cas.

Beavan and Walford's English Railway and Canal Parliamentary Cases. 1846
Beav. & Wal.

Beavan and Walford's English Railway Cases
Beav. & W.

Beavan's English Railway and Canal Cases
Beav. R. & C.

Beavan's English Rolls Court Reports
 B, Beavan, Ch., Beav., Beav. (Eng.)
Beavan's Ordines Cancellariae
 Beav. O.C.
Beaver County Legal Journal
 B. Co. Leg. J'nal., Beaver, Beaver County L.J., Beaver Co. L.J. (Pa.)
Beawes' Lex Mercatoria
 Beaw., Beaw. Lex Mer.
Beawes' Lex Mercatoria Rediviva
 Lex. Mere. Red.
Beccaria on Crimes and Punishments
 Bec. Cr.
Beck's Colorado Reports (12-16 Colorado, and 1 Colorado Court of Appeals)
 Beck, Beck (Colo.)
Beck's Medical Jurisprudence
 Beck, Med. Jur.
Bedell's Reports (163-191 N. Y.)
 Bedell
Beebee's Analysis of Common Law Practice
 Bee. Anal.
Beebe's Ohio Citations
 Beebe Cit.
Beeler's Reports, Tennessee
 Beeler
Bee's Admiralty. An Appendix to Bee's District Court Reports, United States
 Bee Adm.
Bee's EnglishCrown Cases Reserved
 Bee C.C.R.
Bee's United States District Court Reports
 Bee

Before
 Bef.
Before Christ
 B.C.
Begg's Conveyancing Code
 Begg Code
Begg's Law Agents
 Begg L. Ag.
Behavior
 Behav.
Behavior Sciences and the Law
 Behav. Sci. & L.
Belasis' Bombay Reports
 Bel.
Belgian
 Belg.
Belgian Review of International Law
 Belg. Rev. Int'l L.
Belgium
 Belg.
Belgium-Luxembourg Economic Union
 BLEU
Belgium, Netherlands, Luxembourg Economic Union
 BENELUX
Beling and Vanderstraaten's Ceylon Reports
 Beling & Van., B. & V.
Beling's Ceylon Reports
 Bel., Beling
Belknap's Probate Law of California
 Bel. Prob.
Bellasis' Bombay Reports
 Bell.
Bellasis' Civil Cases for Bombay
 Bell C. C.(Eng.), Bell C.C., Bellas.

Bellasis' Criminal Cases for Bombay
Bell C.C. (Eng.), Bell C.C., Bellas.

Beller's Criminal Cases for Bombay
Bell Cr. C., Bell Cr. Ca., Bell Cr. Cas.

Beller's Delineation of Universal Law
Bell. U.L., Bell. Del.

Bellewe's Cases Tempore Henry VIII, Brooke's New Cases
Pet. Br., Bel. Ca.t.H.VIII

Bellewe's English King's Bench Reports
Bellewe, Bellewe (Eng.), Bel., Bell. Cas.t.Rich.II, Bell. Cas.t.R.II, Bellewe's Ca. Temp.R.II

Bellinger and Cotton's Annotated Codes and Statutes, Oregon
B. & C. Comp., Ann. Codes & St.

Bellinger's Reports (4-8 Oregon)
Bell., Bell. (Or.), Bel., Bellinger.

Belli's Modern Trials
Belli's Mod. Trials

Bell on Completing Titles
B.C.T.

Bell on Excise
Bell Ex.

Bell on Expert Testimony
Bell Exp. Test.

Bell on Landlord and Tenant
Bell L. & T.

Bell on Leases
B.L., Bell Leas.

Bell on Sales
Bell S.

Bell's Appeals to House of Lords from Scotland
Bell Sc. App.

Bell's Calcutta Reports
Bell.

Bell's Cases in Parliament: Scotch Appeals
Bell P.C.

Bell's Commentaries on the Laws of Scotland
B.C., Bell's Comm., Bell Comm.

Bell's Completing Titles
Bell C.T.

Bell's Dictionary and Digest of the Laws of Scotland
Bell Dict.

Bell's Dictionary of Decisions, Court of Session
Bell Dict. Dec., Bell's Dict.

Bell's Election Law of Scotland
Bell Elec.

Bell's English Crown Cases Reserved
Bell., Bell C. C.(Eng.), Bell C.C., Bell Cr. C., Bell Cr. Ca., Bell Ca. Cas.

Bell's Folio Reports, Scotch Court of Session
Bell fol.

Bell's House of Lords Appeal Cases
Bell App., Bell's App., Bell App. Cas., S. Bell., Bell H.L., Bell H.L. Sc.

Bell's Illustrations of Principles
Bell Illust.

Bell's Law of Arbitration in Scotland
Bell Arb.

Bell's Law of Awards
Bell Aw.

Bell's Lecture on Conveyancing
Bell Convev.

Bell's Medico Legal Journal
Bell Med. L.J.

Bell's Octavo Reports, Scotch Court of Sessions (1790-92)
Bell Oct.

Bell's on the Testing of Deeds
B.T.D.

Bell's Principles of the Law of Scotland
Bell Prin.

Bell's Property as Arising from the Relation of Husband and Wife
Bell H.W.

Bell's Putative Marriage Case
Bell Put. Mar.

Bell's Reports, Calcutta High Court
Bell C.H.C., Bell (In.), Bell H.C.

Bell's Reports, Court of Session, Scotland
Bell, C.

Bell's Reports, India
Bell (In.)

Bell's Sale of Food and Drugs
Bell Sale

Bell's Scotch Appeal Cases
Bell Sc. App.Cas. (Scotland), Bell.

Bell's Scotch Appeals
Bell Ap.Ca.

Bell's Scotch Court of Sessions Cases
Bell Sc. Cas., Bell Ct. of Sess., Bell Ct. of Sess.Pol., Bell Poli., Bell Ses. Cas., Bell Cas.

Bell's Scotch Session Cases
Bell., Bell. C.

Bell's Scottish Digest
Bell Sc.Dig., Bell Scot. Dig.

Bell's Supplemented Notes to Hume on Crimes
Bell No.

Bell's System of Forms of Deeds
Bell Deeds, Bell Sty.

Bell's System of the Forms of Deeds (Styles) of Scotland
Bell Sty. (or Syst.)

Bell's Testing of Deeds
Bell T.D.

Belt's Edition of Brown's English Chancery Reports
Belt Bro.

Belt's Edition of Vesey Senior's English Chancery Reports
Belt Ves. Sen.

Belt's Supplement to Vesey Senior's English Chancery Reports
Belt. Sup., Belt. Sup.Ves., Belt's Supp. (Eng.), Belt Supp.

Ben Monroe's Kentucky Reports (40-57) (Ben Monroe's Kentucky Supreme Court Reports)
Ben. Monroe, B.Mon., B.M., B.Monr., B.Mon. (Ky.)

Benchmark
Bench.

Bendloe's English Common Pleas
Bendl., Bendloe

Benecke on Marine Insurance
Ben. Ins.

Benedict on Admiralty
Benedict, Admiralty

Benedict's Admiralty Practice
Ben. Adm. Prac., Ben. Adm.

Benedict's New York Civil and Criminal Justice
Ben.Just. (or J.P.), Benedict, Bt., Ben., Bened., Bene.

Benedict's United States District Court Reports
Ben.Just. (or J.P.), Benedict, Bt., Ben., Bened., Bene.

Beneene on Average
Ben.Av.

Beneficiary
Benef.
Benefit and Donation Claims, Se-
lected Decisions of Umpire
O.U.U.I.S.D.
Benefit Decisions of the British
Empire
O.U.U.I.B.D.
Benefit Principles
BP
Benefit Series Service, Unemploy-
ment Insurance, United States
Department of Labor
BSSUI
Benefits Law Journal
Benefits L.J., Benefits L.J.
Benefits Review Board Service,
Matthew Bender
Ben. Rev. Bd. Serv.(MB),
B.R.B.S.
Benelux Economic Union
B.E.U.
Benet on Military Law and
Courts-Martial
Benet Ct.-M
Benevolent Order[s]
Ben. Ord.
Bengal
Beng.
Bengal Full Bench Rulings,
North-Western Provinces
Full B.R.
Bengal Law Reports
Ben., Beng., Beng. L.R.
Bengal Law Reports, Appeal Cases
B.L.R.A.C., Beng. L.R. App.
Cas.
Bengal Law Reports, High Courts
B.L.R.
Bengal Law Reports, Privy Council
Beng. L.R.P.C.

Bengal Law Reports, Supplemen-
tal Volume, Full Bench Rulings
Beng. L.R. Supp., B.L.R. Suppl.
Vol.
Bengal Sadr Diwani Adalat
Cases, India
Beng. S.D.A.
Bengal Sadr Diwani Adalat Deci-
sions, India
Dec. S. D. A.
Benjamin's and Slidell's Louisi-
ana Digest
Ben. & S.Dig.
Benjamin's. New York Annotated
Cases
Benj.
Benjamin on Sales
Benj. Sa., Benj. Sales, Benj.
Benjamin's Chalmer's Bills and
Notes
Benj. Chalm. Bills & N.
Benlie at the End of Ashe's Tables
Benl. in Ashe., Benl. & D., B.
& D., Benl.
Benloe and Dalison's English
Common Pleas Reports
Benl. Old., B. & D., Ben. & Dal.,
Bend., Ben. & D., Dal., Old
Ben., Old Benloe., Bend. & D.
(Eng.)
Benloe or Bendloe in Keilway's
Reports
Benl. in Keil.
Benloe's English Reports, King's
Bench and Common Pleas
Ben.
Benloe's King's Bench Reports
Benl. K.B., Ben. in Keil., Benl.,
Benl. (Eng.), Benloe
Bennet and Heard's Criminal
Cases
B. & H. Crim. Cas.

Bennett and Heard's Leading Criminal Cases
B. & H. Cr. Cas., B. & H. Lead. Cas., Ben. & H.L.C., Benn. & H. Cr. Cas., B. & H. Lead. Ca.

Bennett and Heard's Massachusetts Digest
B. & H. Dig., Benn. & H. Dig.

Bennett on Receivers
Benn. Rec.

Bennett's Dakota Cases
Benn.(Dak.)

Bennett's Dissertation on Practice of Masters in Chancery
Benn. Pr. M.C.

Bennett's Fire Insurance Cases
Ben. F.I. Cas., Benn. F.I. Cas.

Bennett's Insurance Cases
Ben. Ins. Cas.

Bennett's Missouri Cases
Benn. (Mo.)

Bennett's Reports (1 California)
Bennett, Benn., Benn. Cal.

Bennett's Reports, (1 Dakota)
Bennett, Benn.

Bennett's Reports (16-21 Missouri)
Bennett, Benn.

Bennett's Rights and Liabilities of Farmers
Benn. Farm.

Benson's Remarkable Trials and Notorious Characters
Rem. Tr. No. Ch.

Bentham's Act of Packing as Applied to Special Juries
Bent. Pack. Jur.

Bentham's Codification
Bent. Cod.

Bentham's Constitutional Code for all Nations
Bent. Const. Code

Bentham's Judicial Evidence
Bent. Ev.(or Jud.Ev.), Benth. Jud. Ev.

Bentham's Principles of Morals and Legislation
Bent. Mor. & Leg., Bent. Mor. Leg.

Bentham's Rationale of Judicial Evidence
Benth. Ev., Benth. Jud. Ev.

Bentham's Rationale of Punishment
Bent. Pun.

Bentham's Theory of Legislation
Bent. The. Leg.

Bentley's Reports, Irish Chancery
Bent.

Bentley's Reports (13-19 Attorneys-General's Opinions)
Bentl. Atty.-Gen.

Benton's Abridgment of the Debates of Congress
Bent. Abr.

Beor's Queensland Law Reports
Q.L. Beor.

Bequeath[ed]
Beqd.

Bequest[s]
Beqt.

Berar Law Journal, India
Berar

Berkeley Women's Law Journal
Berkeley Women's L.J.

Berk's County Law Journal
Berk Co. L.J., Berks, Berks Co LJ (Pa), Berks Co.:

Bermuda
Berm.

Bermuda Law Reports
B.L.R.

Bernard's Church Cases, Ireland
Bern. Ch. Cas., Bern.

Berry's Reports (1-28 Missouri Appeals)
Berry

Berton's New Brunswick Reports (2 New Brunswick Reports)
Ber., N.B.R. Ber., Bert.

Besson's New Jersey Precedents
Bess. Prec.

Best and Smith's English Queen's Bench Reports
B. & S., Best & Sm., Best & S., Best & S. (Eng.)

Best on Evidence
Best Ev.

Best on Presumptions of Law and Fact
Best, Pres., Best, Presumptions

Best on the Right to Begin and Reply
Best Beg. & Rep.

Best on Trial by Jury
Best Jur. Tr.

Best's Law Dictionary
Best Law Dic.

Betts' Admiralty Practice
Betts' Adm. Pr.

Beven and Siebel's Reports, Ceylon
Bev. & Sieb., B. & S.

Beven on Negligence in Law
Beven

Beven's Ceylon Reports
Be. (Ceylon), Beven

Beverage[s]
Bev

Beverly Hills Bar Association Journal
Bev. Hills B.A.J., Beverly Hills B. Ass'n J.

Bevil on Homicide
Bev. Hom.

Bevill's English Patent Cases
Bev. Pat.

Bevin and Mill's Reports, Ceylon
Bev. & M.

Bevin on Employer's Liability for Negligence of Servants
Bev. Emp. L.

Bewley and Naish on Common Law Procedure
Bew. & N. Pr.

Bi-Monthly Law Review, University of Detroit
Bi-Mo. L. Rev.

Bibb's Kentucky Reports (4-7 Kentucky)
Bibb., Bibb. (Ky.)

Bicknell and Hawley's Reports (10-20 Nevada)
Bick., Bick. & H., Bick. & Hawl.

Bicknell's Indiana Civil Practice
Bick. Civ. Pr.

Bicknell's Indiana Criminal Practice
Bick. Cr. Pr.

Bicknell's Reports, India
Bick. (In.)

Bidder's Court of Referees Reports, England
Bid.

Bidder's Locus Standi Reports, England
Bid., Bidd.

Biddle on Insurance
Bid. Ins.

Biddle on Retrospective Legislation
Bid. Retr. Leg.

Biddle on Warranties in Sale of Chattels
Bid. War. Sale Chat.

Biddle's Table of Statutes
Bid. Tab. Stat.

Biennial Report and Official Opinions of the Attorney General of the State of West Virginia
Biennial Rep. & Op. W.Va. Atty's Gen.

Biennial Report of the Attorney General of the State of Michigan
Mich. Att'y Gen. Biennial Rep.

Biennial Report of the Attorney General of the State of South Dakota
Biennial Rep. S.D. Att'y Gen.

Biennial Report of the Attorney General of the State of Vermont
Biennial Rep.Vt. Att'y Gen.

Biennial Report of the Attorney General, State of Iowa
Biennial Rep. Iowa Att'y Gen.

Bigelow's Life and Accident Insurance Reports
Life & Acc. Ins. R., Big. L. & A. Ins. Rep.

Bigelow on Equity
Big. Eq.

Bigelow on Estoppel
Big. Est., Bigelow, Estop.

Bigelow on Frauds
Big. Fr.

Bigelow on Torts
Big. Torts

Bigelow's Bench and Bar of New York
Big. B. & B.

Bigelow's Cases on Bills and Notes
Big. B. & N., Big. Cas. B. & N.

Bigelow's Cases, William I. to Richard I.
Big. Cas., Cas. Wm. I.

Bigelow's Edition of Jarman on Wills
Big. Jarm. Wills

Bigelow's English Procedure
Big. Eng. Proc., Big. Proc.

Bigelow's Leading Cases on Bills and Notes, Torts, or Wills
Bigelow, Lead. Cas., Big. Lead. Cas.

Bigelow's Leading Cases in Torts
Big. Cas. Torts

Bigelow's Life and Accident Insurance Cases
Big. L. & A. Ins. Cas., Big. L.I. Cas., Bigg. L.I.Cas.

Bigelow's Life and Accident Insurance Reports
Life and Acc. Ins. R.

Bigelow's Overruled Cases
Big. Ov. Cas.

Bigelow's Placita Anglo-Normanica
Plac. Ang. Nor., Big. Plac.

Bigg on Acts Relating to Railways
Bigg R.R. Acts

Bigg's Criminal Law
Bigg Cr. L.

Bignell's Reports, India
Big., Bign.

Bihar and Otissa Selected Decisions of the Board of Revenue, India
B. & O. Bd. of Rev.

Bihar Law Journal Reports, India
B.L.J., Bih. L.J. Rep.

Bihar Reports, India
Bih. Rep., Bih. Rep.

Bill of Exchange
B.e.

Bill[s] of Lading
B/L, B/l, B.l., B.L. [Bs/L, Bs.L., Bs./l., Bs.l.]

Bill of Rights Journal
Bill of Rights J., Bill Rights J., Bill Rts. J., B.R.J.

Bill of Rights of Virginia
  B.R.V.
Bill of Rights Review
  Bill Rights Rev.
Bill of Sale
  B/S
Billing
  Bill.
Billing and Prince's Law and Practice of Patents
  Bil & Pr. Pat.
Billing's Law of Awards and Arbitration
  Bil. Aw.
Billing's Law Relating to Pews
  Bil. Pews
Bills and Notes
  B. & N.
Bills Receivable
  b.r., b.rec.
Binder's Hearsay Handbook (and Second or Third Editions)
  HHb, [HHb(2), HHb(3)]
Bingham and Colvin on Rents
  Bing & Colv. Rents
Bingham on Actions and Defences in Real Property
  Bing. Act. & Def.
Bingham on Infancy and Coveture
  Bing. Inf.
Bingham on Judgments and Executions
  Bing. Ex., Bing. Judg.
Bingham on Landlord and Tenant
  Bing. L. & T.
Bingham on the Law of Real Property
  Bing. R.P.
Bingham on the Laws of Descent
  Bing. Des.

Bingham's English Common Pleas Reports
  Bing., Bing. (Eng.)
Bingham's Executory Contracts
  Bing. Ex. Cont.
Bingham's New Cases, English Common Pleas
  Bing. N. Cas., New. Cas., N.C., Bing. N.C., Bing. N.C. (Eng.), B.N.C.
Binmore's Digest, Michigan
  Bin. Dig.
Binmore's Index-Digest of Michigan Reports
  Binm. Ind.
Binney's Pennsylvania Reports
  Binn. (Pa.)
Binney's Pennsylvania Supreme Court Reports
  Binn.
Binney's Reports, Pennsylvania
  Bin.
Binns' Justice, Pennsylvania
  Binns' Just., Binn. Jus.
Binn's Pennsylvania Justice
  Binn Jus., Binns' Just.
Biographical
  Biog.
Biography
  Biog.
Bioren and Duane's United States Laws
  Bior. & D. Laws
Bird's Laws Respecting Landlords, Tenants and Lodgers
  Bird L. & T.
Bird's New Pocket Conveyancer
  Bird Conv.
Bird's Solution of Precedents of Settlements
  Bird Sol. Pr.

Bird's Supplement to Barton's Conveyancing
Bird. Supp.

Birdseye's Statutes (Birdseye's New York Statutes)
Birds. St.

Birdwood's Printed Judgments
Birdw.

Birkenhead's Judgments, House of Lords
Birk. J.

Birth Control
Birth Con.

Bishop on Contracts
Bish. Con., Bish. Cont.

Bishop on Criminal Law
Bish. Cr. Law, Bish. Cr.L.

Bishop on Criminal Procedure
Bich. Crim. Proc., Bish. Cr. Proc.

Bishop on Insolvent Debtors
Bish. Ins.

Bishop on Marriage and Divorce
Bish. Mar. & Div.

Bishop on Marriage, Divorce, and Separation
Bish. Mar., Div. & Sep.

Bishop on Married Women
Bish. Mar. Wom.

Bishop on Non-Contract Law, Rights and Torts
Bish. Non-Cont. Law

Bishop on Statutory Crimes
Bish. St. Crimes, Bish. Stat. Cr.

Bishop on Written Law
Bish. Wr. L.

Bishop's Digest, Montana
Bishop Dig.

Bishop's Edition of Burrill on Assignments
Bish. Burr.

Bishop's First Book of the Law
Bish. First Bk.

Bishop's Law of Nolle Prosequi
Bish. Noll. Pros.

Bishop's New Criminal Law
Bish. New Cr. Law

Bishop's New Criminal Procedure
Bish. New Cr. Proc.

Bishop's Trials
B.Tr.

Bispham's Principles of Equity
Bisp. Eq., Bisph. Eq.

Bissell's Minnesota Statutes
Biss. Stat.

Bissell's United States Circuit Court Reports
Bis., Biss., Biss. (U.S.), Bissell

Bisset's Estates for Life
Biss. Est.

Bisset's Partnership and Joint Stock Companies
Biss. Part.

Bissett and Smith's Digest
Biss. & Sm.

Bissett on Estates for Life
Bissett, Est.

Bittleston and Wise's English New Magistrate Cases
Bit. & Wise

Bittleston, Wise, and Parnell's English New Magistrates Cases
Mag. Cas., N.Mag. Cas., New Mag. C.

Bittleston, Wise and Parnell's English New Practice Cases
Bitt. W. & P.

Bittleston's English Chamber Cases
Rep.in Cha., Bitt. Cha. Cas.

Bittleston's English Practice Cases under Judicature Act
Bitt. Pr. Case, Bitt. P.C., Bitt. Pr. Cas., Bit. Prac. Cas.

Bittleston's Reports in Chambers, English Queen's Bench Division
Bitt. Ch. Cas., Bitt., Bitt. Ch., Bitt. Chamb. Rep., Bitt. Rep. in Ch.

Bituminous Coal Labor Board
BCLB

Black Book of the Exchequer
Lib. Nig. Seace, L.N., Lib.N.g.

Black Law Journal
Black L.J., Bl.L.J.

Black Legal Workers' Association
B.L.W.A.

Black Letter
B.L.

Black on Constitutional Law
Black, Const. Law

Black on Construction and Interpretation of Laws
Black St. Const., Black, Interp. Laws

Black on Employer's Liability
Black Emp. Li., Bl.Emp.L.

Black on Judgments
Bl. Judgm., Black, Judg., Black, Judgm.

Black on Tax Titles
Black Tax Titles

Black on the Laws Regulating the Manufacture and Sale of Intoxicating Liquors
Black, Intox. Liq.

Black's United States Supreme Court Reports
Black Rep., Bk.

Blackburn on Sales
Blackb. Sales, Blackb., Black. Sal.

Blackerby's Justice of the Peace
Black. Just.

Blackerby's Justices' Cases, England
Black. Jus.

Blackerby's Magistrates Reports, England
Black

Blackford's Indiana Reports
Bl., Black., Blackl., Blackl.(Ind.), Blackford's Ia. R., Black.R., Blackf., Blackf.(Ind.)

Blackham, Dundas and Osborne's Irish Nisi Prius Reports
Bl.D. & O., Bl.D. & Osb., Black. D. & O., B.D. & O.

Black's Constitutional Prohibitions
Black, Const. Prohib.

Black's Decisions in Shipping Cases
Black Ship. Ca.

Black's Law Dictionary
Bl. Dict., Black. Dict., Black L.D., Black, Law Dict., Black's Law Dict., Bl.L.D.

Black's Reports (30-53 Indiana)
Black

Black's Supreme Court Reports (66-67 of United States Reports)
Black, Bl., Black R.

Blackstone on Magna Charta
Black. Mag. Ch., Bl.W., Bla.

Blackstone's Analysis of the Laws of England
Black. Anal.

Blackstone's Commentaries, Abridged
Black. Abr.

Blackstone's Commentaries by Kinne, edited by Devereux
Dev. Kin. Bl.

Blackstone's Commentaries by Reed, Pennsylvania
Reed Pa. Black.

Blackstone's Commentaries on the Law of England
Bl., Bl. Com., Bla. Com., Black. Com., Com., Comm., Bl. Comm., Blackstone's Commen.

Blackstone's (H.) English Common Pleas Reports
H.Bl., H. Black, H.B., Black, Hem. Bl, Hy. Bl. Be., Blg. H., Hen. Bl., Bl. H.

Blackstone's Law Tracts
Bl. Law Tracts, Black L.Tr., Bl.L.T.

Blackstone's Reports in King's Bench. Temp.George II & III; and Common Pleas,George III (1746-80)
Blackst., Bl. W., Bla., Black.R., Black.

Blackstone's (William) English King's Bench Reports
Bl., Black. W., Wm. Bl., Blackst. R.

Blackwell's Condensed Illinois Reports
Black. Cond., Black. Cond. Rep., Blackw. Cond.

Blackwell's Scotch Acts
Blackw. Sc. Acts, Blackw. Sc. Act.

Blackwell's Tax Titles
Black. Tax Tit., Bl. T.T., Blackw. T.T., Blackw. Tax Titles

Blair County Law Reports
Blair Co., Blair Co. L.R., Blair Co. L.R.(Pa.)

Blair's Manual for Scotch Justices of the Peace
Blair

Blake and Hedges' Reports (2-3 Montana)
Bl. & H., Blake & H.

Blake's Chancery Practice
Bl. Chy. Pr., Blake Ch. Pr.

Blake's Reports (1-3 Montana)
Blake

Blanchard and Weeks' Leading Cases on Mines
Bl. & W. Mines, Blanc. & W.L.C., Blan. & W. Lead. Cas., Bl. Chr. R., Bland.Ch.R., Bland's Ch., Bland's Ch. R., Bland's Chy. Rep., Bla. Ch., Bland Ch.(Md.), Bland, Bland's Ch.

Blanshard on Statute of Limitations
Blan. Lim., Blansh. Lim.

Blashfield's Instructions to Juries
Blash. Juries.

Blasphemy
Blas.

Blasphemy and Profanity
Blas.

Blatchford and Howard's Dist.Ct.Rep.(34 and 35 Georgia Reports)
Blatch. & H.

Blatchford and Howland's United States District Court Reports
B. & H., Betts' Dec., Bl. & H., Bl. & How., Blatchf. & H., Blatchford & H.

Blatchford's Prize Cases, United States
Bl. Pr. Cas., Blatch.Pr.Cas., Bl. Prize, Blatchf. Pr. Cas., Blatchf.Prize Cas.

Blatchford's United States Circuit Court Reports
Bl., Blatchf., Blatchf. C.C., Bl.C.C., Blat. C.C.R., Blatch., Blatch. (U.S.Cir.Ct.), Blatchf. C.C. Rep., Blatchf. (U.S.Circ.Ct.), Bl.C.C.R.

Blaxland's Codex Legum Angelicanum
Blax. Eng. Co.

Blayney on Life Annuities
Blay. Ann.

Blayney on Life Assurance
Bla. Life Ass., Blay. Life Ins.

Bleckley's Reports (34 and 35 Georgia Reports)
Bleck., Bleckley

Blickenaderfer's Law Student's Review
Blick. Rev.

Bligh's English House of Lords Reports
Bli.

Bligh's English House of Lords Reports, New Series
Bli.N.S., Bl. N.S., Bligh N.S. (Eng.)

Bligh's English House of Lords Reports, Old Series
Bli. (O.S.)

Bliss' Annotated New York Code
Bliss N.Y. Code

Bliss on Code Pleading
Bliss Co. Pl.

Bliss on Life Insurance
Bliss Ins.

Bliss's New York Code
Bliss N.Y. Co.

Block on Tithes
Bl.Ti.

Bloomfield' Manumission (or Negro) Cases, New Jersey
Bloom. Man., Manum. Cas., Manum. Cases, Negro. Cas., Neg. Cas., Bloom. Man. Neg. Cas.

Bloomfield's Negro Cases, New Jersey
Blm. Neg.

Blount on Tenures
Blount Ten.

Blount's Fragmenta Antiquitatis
Blount Frag.Ant.

Blount's Impeachment Trial
Blount Tr.

Blount's Law Dictionary
Bl., Bl.L.D., Blount, Blount L.D.

Blue Sky Law Reporter, Commerce Clearing House
Blue Sky L. Rep. (CCH)

Blue Sky Law Reports, Commerce Clearing House
Blue Sky L. Rep. (CCH)

Bluett's Advocate's Note Book, Isle of Man
Blu.

Bluett's Isle of Man Cases
Bluett

Blumenstiel on Bankruptcy
Blum. B'k'cy.

Blydenburgh on Law of Usury
Bly.Us.

BNA Banking Reports, Bureau of National Affairs
BNA Banking Rep.

Board
Bd., Brd.

Board of Contract Appeals
BCA

Board of Contract Appeals Decisions, Commerce Clearing House
CCH BCA Dec., B.C.A. (CCH), Bd. Cont. App. Dec.

Board of Control
B.C.

Board of Directors
Bd of Dirs

Board of Economic Welfare
BEW

Board of Examiners in Watchmaking
Watch.

Board of Immigration Appeals
B.I.A.

Board of Inland Revenue
B.I.R.

Board of International Broadcasting
BIB

Board of Review
Bd. of Rev., BR

Board of Review and Judicial Council of the Army
B.R. & J.C.(Army), B.R.-J.C. (Army), B.R. (Army)

Board of Review, U.S. Army
B.R.

Board of Tax Appeals
T.A.

Board of Tax Appeals Decisions, Commerce Clearing House
B.T.A.C.C.H.

Board of Tax Appeals Decisions, Prentice-Hall
B.T.A.P.H.

Board of Tax Appeals Memorandum, Prentice-Hall
B.T.A.M. (P-H)

Board of Trade
B.o.T.

Board of Trade Journal
B.O.T.Jo.

Boddam and Greenwood's Notanda Digest
Not. Dig.

Bogert on Trusts and Trustees
Bogert, Trusts

Bohun's Cursus Cancellariae
Boh. Curs. Can., Bohun. Curs. Canc.

Bohun's Declarations and Pleadings
Boh. Dec.

Bohun's Ecclesiastical Jurisdiction
Boh. Eccl. Jur.

Bohun's Election Cases, England
Bohun

Bohun's English Lawyer
Boh. Eng. L.

Bohun's Practising Attorney
Boh. Att.

Bohun's Titles
Boh Ti.

Bolivia
Bol.

Bombay High Court Printed Judgments
B.H.C.P.J., P.J.

Bombay High Court Reports
Bomb. H.Ct., B.H.C.R., Bom. H.C.R., B.H.C., Bom., Bomb. Hg.Ct.

Bombay High Court Criminal Rulings
Bomb. Cr. Rul.

Bombay Law Journal
Bombay L.J., Bom. L.J.

Bombay Law Reporter
Bomb. L.R., B.L.R., Bom. L.R., Bom. L.R.J.

Bombay Law Reports
Bom. L. Rep.

Bombay Reports, Appellate Juris-diction
Bom. A.C.
Bombay Reports, Civil Jurisdiction
Bom. O.C.
Bombay Reports, Crown Cases
Bomb. Cr. Cas.
Bombay Reports, Oudh Cases
Bom. O.C.
Bombay Select Cases, Sadr Di-wani Adalat
Bomb. Sel. Cas.
Bombay Sudder Dewanny Adawlut Reports
Bellasis
Bombay Unreported Criminal Cases
Bom. Unrep. Cr. C., Unrep. Cr. C.
Bona Fide Occupational Qualifi-cation
BFOQ
Bona Fide Purchaser
B.f.p.
Bond Law Review
Bond L. Rev.
Bonded Goods
B/g
Bond's Maryland Court of Ap-peals Proceedings (in Ameri-can Legal Records, Vol. 1)
Boul Md. App.
Bond's United States Circuit Re-ports
Bond
Bone's Precedents in Conveyanc-ing
Bone Prec.
Bonnetti's Italian Dictionary
Bonnetti, Ital. Dict.
Bonney on Insurance
Bonn. Ins., Bon. Ins.
Bonney on Railway Carriers
Bonn.Car., Bon. LR.R. Cas.

Bonum Factum (a good or proper act, deed, or decree) (Lat.)
B.F.
Book[s]
Bk., (Bks.)
Book of Feuds [The]
Feud. Lib.
Book of Judgments
Jud., Bk. Judg., Book of Judg.
Book of Ramsey
Lib. Rames.
Book Value
B/V
Books of Regiam Majestatem
Reg. Maj.
Books of Sederunt
Books S., Books Sed.
Boone on Corporations
Boone Corp.
Booraem's Reports (6-8 California)
Boor., Booraem
Boote's Action at Law
Boote Act.
Boote's Chancery Practice
Boote Ch. Pr.
Boote's Suit at Law
Boote, Boote S.L., Boote, Suit at Law
Booth on Real Action
Booth, Real Act., Booth R. Act., B.R.Act., Boo. R. Act.
Booth on Indictable Offenses
Booth Ind. Of.,Booth In. Of.
Booth on Law of Wills
Booth Wills
Borough Court
Bor. Ct.
Borradaile's Civil Cases, Bombay
Borr.
Borthwick's Modes of Prosecut-ing for Libel
Borth.

Bosanquet and Darby's Limitations
Bos. & D. Lim.

Bosanquet and Puller's English Common Pleas, Exchequer and House of Lords Reports
B. & P., Bos. & P. (Eng.), Bos. & Pul., Bos. & Pul., Bos. & P., Bos. & Pu.

Bosanquet and Puller's New Reports, English Common Pleas
B. & P.N.R., N.R., New Rep., Bos. & Pul. N.R., Box. & Pul. N.R., Bos. & P.N.R., Bos. & P.N.R. (Eng.), B.P.N.R.

Bosanquet's Rules of Pleading
Bos. Pl.

Boscawen on Convictions
Bosc. Con.

Boston
B

Boston Bar Journal
B.B.J., Boston B.J.

Boston College Environmental Affairs Law Review
B.C. Envtl. Aff. L. Rev.

Boston College Industrial and Commercial Law Review
B.C. Ind. & Com. L.R., B.C. Ind. & Com. L. Rev., B.C. Ind. Com'l. L. Rev., B.C. Indus. & Com. L. Rev., Bost. Coll. Ind. L. Rev., Boston Col. Ind. Com. L. Rev., B.C. Int'l. & Comp. L.J., Boston Col. Int'l. & Comp. L.J., B.C. Int'l. & Comp. L. Rev., Boston Col. Int.Comp. L. Rev.

Boston College Law Review
B.C. L. Rev., Boston College L. Rev.

Boston College Third World Law Journal
B.C. Third World L.J., Bos. C. Third World L. J.

Boston Law Reporter
Bost. Law Rep., Bost. L.R.

Boston Police Court Reports
Bost. Pol. Rep.

Boston Police Reports
Bos. Pol. Rep.

Boston University International Law Journal
Bos. U. Int. L.J., B.U.Int'l L.J.

Boston University Journal of Tax Law
B. U. J. Tax L., B.U.J. Tax Law

Boston University Law Review
Boston U. L. Rev., Bost.U. L.Rev., B.U.L., B.U.L.Rev.; BU L Rev

Boston University Public Interest Law Journal
B. U. Pub. Int. L.J.

Boston University School of Law
BUSL

Bostworth's Superior Court Reports
Bos.

Boswell's Reports, Scotch Court of Sessions
Bosw.

Bosworth's New York Superior Court Reports (14-23)
Bosw.

Botswana
Bots.

Botswana Law Reform Committee
Botswana L.R.C.

Bott's Poor Law Cases, England
B.P.L. Cases, Bott's P.L., B.P.L. Cas., Bott P.L. Cas., B.P.L.

Bott's Poor Law Settlement
Cases, England
　　Bott., Bott Set. Cas., Bott Poor
　　Law Cas.
Bott's Poor Laws by Court, Eng-
land
　　Court
Bott's Poor Laws by Constant,
England
　　Const.
Bott's Poor Laws, England
　　Bott P.L.
Bouldin's Reports (119 Alabama)
　　Bould.
Boulnois' Reports, Bengal, India
　　Bouln., Boulnois
Boundary[ies]
　　Bound.
Bounty[ies]
　　Bount.
Bourdin on Land Tax
　　Bourd. L.T.
Bourke on the Indian Law of
Limitations
　　Bourke Lim.
Bourke's Lefevre's Parliamen-
tary Decisions
　　Lef. Dec.
Bourke's Parliamentary Prece-
dents
　　Bourke P.P.
Bourke's Reports, Calcutta High
Court
　　Bourke
Boutwell's Manual of the United
States Tax System
　　Bout. Man.
Bouvier's Institutes of American
Law
　　Bou. Inst., Bouv. Inst.
Bouvier's Law Dictionary
　　Bouv. L. Dict., Bouv. Law Dict.,
　　Bouvier, Bouv., Bou. Dic.

Bovill's Patent Cases
　　Bov. Pat. Cas.
Bowen's Political Economy
　　Bowen, Pol. Econ.
Bowler and Bowers (2-3 U.S.
Comptroller's Decisions))
　　Bow., B. & B.
Bowler's London Session Re-
cords
　　Bow.
Bowles on Libel
　　Bowl. Lib.
Bowstead on Agency
　　Bowstead
Bowyer's Commentaries on the
Constitutional Law of England
　　Bow. Cons. Law
Bowyer's Commentaries on Uni-
versal Public Law
　　Bow. Com., Bow. Pub. Law
Bowyer's Introduction to the
Study and Use of the Civil Law
　　Bow. Int.
Bowyer's Modern Civil Law
　　Bow. Civ. Law, Bowyer,
　　Mod.Civil Law
Boyce's Delaware Supreme Court
Reports
　　Boyce
Boyce's Practice in the United
States Courts
　　Boyce U.S. Pr.
Boyd's Admiralty Law, Ireland
　　Boyd. Adm.
Boyd's Justice of the Peace
　　Boyd Jus.
Boyd's Merchant Shipping Laws
　　Boyd Sh.
Boyle's Law of Charities
　　Boy. Char., Boyle Char.
Boyle's Precis of an Action at
Common Law
　　Boyle Act.

Boys on Coroners
  Boys Cor.
Brabrook's Industrial and Provident Societies
  Bra. Ind. Soc.
Brabrook's Law of Trade Unions
  Bra. Tr. Un.
Brackenridge on the Law of Trusts
  Brack. Tr.
Brackenridge's Miscellanies
  Brack. Misc.
Bracton
  Br.
Bracton de Legibus et Consuetudinibus Angliae
  Bra., Brac., Bract., Bracton
Bracton's (James S.) Digest of Maxims
  Bract.
Bracton Law Journal
  Brac. L.J., Bracton L.J.
Bracton's Note Book, English King's Bench, Temp. Henry III
  B.N.B., Brac., Br. N.B.
Bradbury's Pleading and Practice Reports, New York
  Bradb.
Bradby on Distresses
  Brad. Dis.
Bradford
  Br.
Bradford's Iowa Supreme Court Reports
  Bradford
Bradford's Kentucky Statutes
  Brad.
Bradford's New York Surrogate Court Reports
  Bradf. Sur., Bradf. Surr., Brad., Bradf., Brad. R., Brad. Sur., Bradf. Rep., Bradf. Sur. R., Bradford's R., Bradford's Sur. R.

Bradford's Proceedings in the Court of Star Chamber (Somerset Record Society Publications, 27)
  Bradf., Brad.
Bradford's Reports, Iowa
  Bradf., Brad.
Bradley's Point Book
  Bradl. P.B.
Bradley's Rhode Island Reports
  Bradl., Bradl.(R.I.)
Bradwell
  Br.
Bradwell's Illinois Appeal Court Reports
  App. Ct. Rep.
Bradwell's Reports (1-20 Illinois Appellate Court Reports)
  Brad., Bralw.
Brady's English History
  Bra.
Brady's Historical Treatise on Cities
  Bra. Cit.
Brady's History of the Succession of the Crown of England
  Brad.
Brady's Index, Arkansas Reports
  Brady Ind.
Brady's Treatise upon Cities and Boroughs
  Brady's Tr.
Brainard's Legal Precedents in Land and Mining Cases
  Brain. L.P., B.L.P.L. & M.Cas.
Braithwaite's Oaths in Chancery
  Braith. Oaths
Braithwaite's Oaths in the Supreme Court
  Braith. Oaths

Braithwaite's Record and Writ Practice of the Court of Chancery
Braith. Pr.

Braithwaite's Register
Br. Reg.

Braithwaite's Times of Procedure in Chancery
Braith. Chy.

Brame's Reports (vols. 66-72 Mississippi)
Brame.

Branch's Maxims
Branch, Max.

Branch's Principia Legis et Equitatis
Branch, Princ., Branch Pr.

Branch's Reports (1 Florida)
Branch.

Brandenburg's Bankruptcy
Brandenburg Bankr.

Brandenburg's Bankruptcy Digest
Brandenburg Dig.

Brandenburg's Reports (21 Opinions of Attorneys-General)
Brand.

Brande's Dictionary of Science
Brande.

Brandon on Foreign Attachment
Brand. For. Att., Brand.F. Attachm. (Or Brand.For. Attachm.)

Brandon's Practice of the Mayor's Court
Brand. May. Ct.

Brandt on Suretyship and Guaranty
Brandt, Sur.

Branson's Digest, Bombay
Brans. Dig.

Brantly's Reports (80-90 Maryland)
Brantly, Brant.

Brayton
Br.

Brayton Vermont Reports
Brayt., Brayton (Vt.), Bray. R., Brayt. Rep., Brayton's Rep., Bray.

Brazil
Braz.

Breach of Peace and Disorderly Conduct
Breach P.

Breach of Promise
Breach Prom.

Breese
Br.

Breese's Reports (1 Illinois)
Breese

Brett's Cases in Modern Equity
Brett Ca. Eq.

Brevard
Br.

Brevard's Digest of the Public Statute Law, South Carolina
Brev. Dig.

Brevard's South Carolina Reports
Brev.

Brevia Judicialia (Judicial Writs)
Brev. Ju.

Brevia Selecta (Choice Writs)
Brev. Sel.

Brewer's Reports (19-26 Maryland)
Brewer, Brew., Brew. (Md.)

Brewing Trade Review Licensing Law Reports
B.T.R. L.R., B.T.R.

Brewster
Br.

Brewster's Pennsylvania Digest
Brewst. Pa. Dig.

Brewster's Pennsylvania Reports
Brewst., Brews., Brews. (Pa.), Brewster

Brewster's Reports, Pennsylvania
Brews., Brewst., Brews. (Pa.), Brewster
Bribery
Brib.
Brice's Law Relating to Public Worship
Bri. Pub. Wor.
Brice's Ultra Vires
Bri. Ult. V., Brice Ult.V.
Brickell's Alabama Digest
Brick. Ala. Dig., Brick. Dig.
Bridgeport Law Review
Bridgeport L. Rev.
Bridgman
Br.
Bridgman on Conveyancing
Bridg. Conv.
Bridgman's Digested Index
Bridg. Dig. Ind.
Bridgman's English Common Pleas Reports
Bridg., Carter (Eng.), Rep.t.O.Br., Cart., Carter
Bridgman's Index to Equity Cases
Bridg. Eq. Ind.
Bridgman's Legal Bibliography
Bridg. Leg. Bib.
Bridgeman's (Orlando) English Common Pleas Reports
O.B., O. Bridgm., O. Bridg., O. Bridg. (Eng.), Orl. Bridg., Orl. Bridgman
Bridgman's Reflections on the Study of the Law
Bridg. Ref.
Bridgman's Thesaurus Juridicus
Bridg. Thes.
Brief
Br.

Brief Case, National Legal Aid Association
Brief Case
Brief of the Phi Delta Phi
Brief
Briefcase
Briefcase
Briggs' General Railway Acts
Briggs Ry. Acts
Brigham Young University Journal of Public Law
B.Y.U. J. Pub. L.
Brigham Young University Law Review
Brig. Yo. U. L.R., Brigham Young U. L. Rev., Brigham Young Univ. L. Rev., Brigham Y.U.L.R., B.Y.U. L. Rev., B.Y.U. L.R.
Bright on Husband and Wife
Bright H. & W.
Bright on Pennsylvania Taxation
PaT
Brightly
Br.
Brightly on the Law of Costs in Pennsylvania
Bright. Costs
Brightly's Analytical Digest of the Laws of the United States
Bright. Dig., Brightly Dig.
Brightly's Annotated Bankrupt Law
Bright. Bank. Law
Brightly's Digest (of New York Laws)
Bright. Dig., Brightly Dig.
Brightly's Digest of United States Laws
Bright. U.S. Dig.
Brightly's Digest (of Pennsylvania Law)
Bright. Dig., Brightly Dig.

Brightly's Edition of Purdon's Digest of Pennsylvania Laws
Bright. Pur. Dig., Bright. Purd.

Brightly's Edition of Troubat and Haly's Practice
Bright. Tr. & H. Pr.

Brightly's Election Cases, Pennsylvania
Brightly El. Cas., Brightly's Elec. Cas.

Brightly's Equitable Jurisdiction
Bright. Eq. Jur.

Brightly's Federal Digest
Br. Fed. Dig., Bright. Fed. Dig.

Brightly's Leading Cases on Elections, Pennsylvania
Brightly's Elec. Cas, Brightly El. Cas., Brightly El., Bright. E.C., Brightly Elect. Cas., Brightly Election Cas.(Pa.), Brightly El. Cas., Brightly El., Bright. E.C., Bright. Elec. Cas.

Brightly's New York Digest
Bright. N.Y. Dig.

Brightly's Pennsylvania Digest
Bright. Pa. Dig.

Brightly's Pennsylvania Nisi Prius Reports
Bright. (Pa.), Brightly's Rep., Brightl, N.P., Pa. N.P., Bright. N.P., Bright., Brightly

Brisbin
Brisb.

Brisbin's Reports (1 Minnesota)
Brisb. Minn., Brisbin

Britain
Brit.

Britannia
Brit.

Britannica
Brit.

British
Br., Brit.

British and Colonial Prize Cases
Br. & Col., Brit. & Col. Pr. Cas., Trehern, P.C., B. & C. Pr. Cas., Br. & Col. Pr. Cas.

British and Foreign State Papers
B.F.S.P.

British and Irish Association of Law Librarians
B.I.A.L.L.

British Association of Social Workers
B.A.S.W.

British Burma
Br. Bur., Brit. Burm.

British Columbia
B.C., Br. Col., Brit. Col.

British Columbia Annual Law Lectures
B.C.L. Lectures

British Columbia Branch Lectures
B.C. Branch Lectures

British Columbia Gazette
B.C. Gaz.

British Columbia Law Notes
B.C.L. Notes

British Columbia Law Reform Commission
B.C.L.R.C.

British Columbia Law Reports
B.C., B.C. Rep., B.C.C., B.C.L.R., B.C.R.

British Columbia Revised Statutes
B.C. Rev. Stat.

British Columbia Statutes
B.C. Stat.

British Columbia Tax Reporter, Commerce Clearing House
B.C. Tax Rep. (CCH)

British Crown Cases
Br. Cr. Cas., Brit. Cr. Cas.

British Crown Cases (American Reprint)
Br. Cr. Ca., Br.C.C.
British East Africa
B.E.A.
British European Airways
B.E.A.
British Guiana
Brit. Gui.
British Guiana Full Court Reports (Official Gazette)
F.C.
British Guiana Law Reports (Old and New Series)
B.G., B.G.L.R.
British Guiana Limited Jurisdiction (Official Gazette)
L.J.
British Guiana Official Gazette Reports
O.G.B.G.
British Guiana Reports of Opinions
R.B.G.
British Guiana Supreme Court, Appellate Jurisdiction
A.J.
British Honduras
Brit. Hond.
British Institute of Human Rights
B.I.H.R., B.I.H.R.
British Institute of International and Comparative Law
B.I.I.C.L.
British Institute of International and Comparative Law Newsletter
B.I.I.C.L. Newsl.
British Insurance Association
B.I.A.
British Insurance Brokers' Association
B.I.B.A.

British Insurance Law Association
B.I.L.A.
British Insurance Law Association Bulletin
B.I.L.A. Bull.
British International Law Cases
B.I.L.C.
British International Law Society
B.I.L.S.
British Journal of Administrative Law
B.J.A.L., Brit. J. Ad. L., Brit. J. Adm. L., Brit. J. Admin. Law
British Journal of Criminology
B.J. Crim., Brit. J. Criminol., Brit. J. Criminology, Brit. J. of Crimin.
British Journal of Delinquency
B.J. Delinq., Brit. J. Delinq., Brit. J. of Delinquency
British Journal of Industrial Relations
B.J. Ind. Rel., B.J.I.R., Brit. J. Ind. Rel.
British Journal of International Law
Brit. J. Int'l. L.
British Journal of Law and Society
B.J.L.S., Brit. J. Law & Soc., Brit. J.L. & Soc'y.
British Legal Association
B.L.A.
British Legal Services Agency
B.L.S.A.
British Library
B.L.
British Maritime Law Association
B.M.L.A.
British Museum
B.M.
British North America Act
B.N.A. Act.

British Practice in International Law
Brit. Prac. Int'l L.

British Quarterly Review
Brit. Quar. Rev.

British Ruling Cases
Br. Rul. Cas., B.R.C., Brit. Rul. Cas.

British Section of the International Commission of Jurists
Justice

British Shipping Laws, A Series Published by Stevens
Brit. Ship. L.

British Standard
B.S.

British Standards Institute
BSI

British Tax Review
Brit. Tax Rev., B.T.R., Brit. Tax Rev.

British Treaty Series
Brit. T.S.

British West Indies
B.W.I.

British Yearbook of International Law
Brit. Y.B. Int'l., Brit. Y.B. Int'l.L., B.Y.I.L.

Britton
Br.

Britton's Ancient Pleas of the Crown
Brit., Britt.

Britton's Shepard's California Legal Filing Directory
SCLF

Brockenbrough
Br.

Brockenbrough and Holmes's Virginia Cases
Brock. & Hol. Cas., Brock. & H., Brock. & Hol., Brock. & Ho.

Brockenbrough's Marshall's Decisions, United States Circuit Court
Brock., Brock. C.C., Brock. Marsh.

Broderick and Freemantle's Ecclesiastical Cases, England
Brod. & F. (Eng.), Brod. & Fr., Bro. & F., Bro. & Fr., Brod. & F. Ecc. Cas., Brod. & Fr. Ecc. Cas., Br. & F. Ecc., Br. & Fr., Brod., B. & F., Brod. & Frem.

Broderip and Bingham's English Common Pleas Reports
Br. & B., B. & B., Brod. & B., Brod. & Bing.

Brodie's Notes and Supplement to Stair's Institutions
Bro. St., Bro. Stair, Brod. Stair.

Brodix's American and English Patent Cases
Brodix Am. & El. Pat. Cas., Brodix Am. & E. Pat. Cas., Brodix Am. & Eng. Pat. Cas.

Bromberg and Lowenfels' Securities Fraud and Commodities Fraud
SFCF

Brooke
Br.

Brooke on the Office and Practice of a Notary in England
Brooke Not., Bro. Not.

Brooke's Abridgment
Bro. Ab., Bro. Abr., Brooke, Abr., Br. Abr.

Brooke's Bibliotheca Legum Angliae
Brooke Bib. Leg.

Brooke's Churchwarden's Guide
Brooke Ch. W.

Brooke's Ecclesiastical Judgments (or Cases), England
Brooke, Brooke Eccl. Judg.

Brooke's New Cases (collected by Bellewe), England
Bell. Cas.t.Hen.VIII, Bellewe's Ca. temp.Hen.VIII, Bell. Cas.t.H.VIII, Bellewe t.H.VIII

Brooke's New Cases, English King's Bench
Bro. N.C., B.N.C., Brooke N.C., Brooke (Petit), Br. N.Cas., Brook N. Cas. Petit Br.

Brooke's New Cases (Petit Brooke), England
Little Brooke, Pet. Br., Br. N.C., Lit. Brooke, Brooke

Brooke's New Cases, Translation by March, England
March N.C.

Brooke's Reading on the Statute of Limitations
Bro. Read., Brooke Lim.

Brooke's Six Ecclesiastical Judgments (or Cases), England
Brooke Eccl., Brooke Six Judg., Bro. Ecc.

Brooklyn Bar Association
Brookl. Bar.

Brooklyn Barrister
Brooklyn Bar.

Brooklyn Daily Record
Brooklyn Daily Rec., Brookl. Rec.

Brooklyn Journal of International Law
Brook. J. Int'l L., Brookl. J. Int. L., Brooklyn J. Int. L., Brooklyn J. Int'l. L.

Brooklyn Law Review
B.R., Br. L.R., Brook L. Rev., Brookl. L. Rev., Brooklyn L. Rev.

Brook's Abridgments
Brook Abr.

Brooks' Reports (106-119 Michigan)
Brooks.

Broom
Br.

Broom and Hadley's Blackstone's Commentaries on the Law of England
Broom & H. Comm., Broom & H. Com., B. & H. Black.

Broom and Hadley's Commentaries on the Laws of England
Br. & Had.

Broom on Parties to Actions
Broom Part.

Broom's Commentaries on the Common Law
Br. Com., Bro. Com., Broom C.L., Broom, Com. Law.

Broom's Constitutional Law
Broom Const. L., Br. Cns. Law

Broom's Legal Maxims
Br. Leg. Max., Bro. Leg. Max., Bro. Max., Broom, Leg. Max. (or Broom, Max.), Br. Max.

Broom's Philosophy of the Law
Broom Ph. Law, Br. Phil. Law.

Broom's Selection of Legal Maxims
Broom

Brother[s]
Bro., (Bros.)

Brotherhood
Bhd.

Brough's Law of Elections
Brough Elec.

Brought forward
B.f.

Broughton's Indian Civil Procedure
Bro. Civ. Proc., Brough. Civ. Pro.

Broun's Reports, Scotch Justiciary Court
Broun., Bro. Just., Broun. Just.

Brown
Br.

Brown and McCall's Yorkshire Star Chamber (Yorkshire Arch. Society Record, Series 44, 45, 51, 70)
Bro. & M.

Brown and Rader's Reports (vol. 137 Missouri)
Brown & R., Br. & R.

Brown on Agency and Trust
Bro. Ag.

Brown on Fixtures
Bro. Fix.

Brown on Forestalling, Regrating and Monopolizing, with Cases
Bro. For.

Brown on Limitations as to Real Property
Bro. R.P.L.

Browne
Br.

Browne and Gray's Reports (110-114 Massachusetts)
Browne & Gray, Browne & G.

Browne and Hemingway's Reports (53-59 Mississippi)
Bro. & H., Browne & H., Browne & H., Browne & Hemingway.

Browne and Macnamara's Railway Cases, England
B. & M., B. & Macn., Bro. & M., Brown & MacN., Bro. & Mac., B. & Mac., B. & M., Browne & Macn.

Browne and Theobald on Railways
Browne & Th. Railw.

Browne on Civil and Admiralty Law
Browne Civ. L.

Browne on Statute of Frauds
Browne, St. Frauds

Browne on the Companies' Acts
Bro. Co. Act.

Browne on the Statute of Frauds
Bro. Fr.

Browne on Usages and Customs
Browne Us.

Browne's Actions at Law
Bro. Ac., Bro. Act.

Browne's Admiralty and Civil Law
Bro. A. & C.L., Bro. Adm. & C.L., Browne Adm. & C.L., Bro. C. & A.L., Bro. Civ. Law, Browne, Civ. Law

Browne's Civil Procedure Reports
Browne

Browne's Digest of Decisions on Divorce and Alimony
Bro. Dig. Div.

Browne's Divorce Court Practice
Bro. Div. Pr., Browne, Div.

Browne's Georgia Pleading and Practice and Legal Forms Annotated
Brown, Ga.Pl. & Pr.Anno.

Browne's Humorous Phrases of the Law
Bro. Humor.

Browne's Judicial Interpretation of Common Words and Phrases
Browne, Jud. Interp.

Browne's Law of Carriers
Bro. Car., Browne Car.

Browne's Law of Rating of Hereditaments
Bro. Hered.

Browne's Law of Usages and Customs
Bro. Us. & Cus.

Browne's Medical Jurisprudence of Insanity
Bro. Ins.

Browne's National Bank Cases
Browne Bank. Cas., Browne N.B.C., Bro. N.B. Cas.

Browne's New Abridgment of Cases in Equity
Bro. Abr. In Eq.

Browne's Parliamentary and Municipal Registration Act
Bro. Reg. Act

Browne's Patent Office Practice
Bro. Pat. Pr.

Browne's Practice in Divorce and Matrimonial Causes
Browne Div. Pr.

Browne's Practice of the High Court of Chancery
Bro. Ch. Pr,

Browne's Probate Practice
Bro. Prob. Pr., Browne, Prob. Pr.

Browne's Reports, Ceylon
Bro., Br. R., Brown

Browne's Reports (97-109 Massachusetts)
Browne

Browne's Pennsylvania Reports
Browne Pa. R., Browne's Rep., Brown's (Penn.), Brown's Penn. Rep., P.A. Browne (Pa.), P.A. Browne R., Bro., Browne

Browne's Treatise on the Law of Trademarks
Bro. Tr. M., Browne Tr. M.

Browning and Lushington on Marriage and Divorce
Bro. & Lush. M. & D., Brown & Lush. M. & D.

Browning and Lushington's English Admiralty Reports
Br. & L., Br. & Lush, B. & L., Brown. & L., Brown. & L. (Eng.), Brown. & Lush., Bro. & L., Bro. & Lush.

Browning on Marriage and Divorce
Bro. M. & D., Brown. M. & D.

Browning's Divorce Court Practice
Brown. Div. Pr.

Brownlow
Br.

Brownlow and Goldesborough's English Common Please Reports Tempore Eliz. & Jac
Brown. & Gold., Brownl., Brownl. & G., Brown. & G. (Eng.), Brownl. & Gold., Br. & Gold., Bro. & G., Brown, Brn., B. & G., Br. & G.

Brownlow's Brevia Judicialia
Brow. Brev., Brownl. Brev., Br. Brev. Jud., Br. Brev. Jud. & Ent.

Brownlow's Entries
Brown. Ent., Brownl. Ent., Br. Ent.

Brownlow's Latine Redivivus, or Entries
Brownl. Redv., Bro. Ent.

Brown's (David Paul) Speeches
Bro. Sp.

Brown's English Chancery Cases or Reports
B.C.R., B.C. Rep., B.C.C., Br. P.C., Brown Ch., Brown Ch. C., Br.C.C., Brown, C.C., Brown C., Bro.C.C. (or C.R.), Bro. C.C., Bro., Brown, Bro. Ch., Bro. Ch. Cas., Bro. Ch. R.,

Brown's Civil and Admiralty Law
Brown, Civ. & Adm. Law.
Brown's Ecclesiastical Cases, England
Brown Ecc., Br. Eccl., Bro. Eccl.
Brown's English Parliamentary Cases or Reports
Brown, Bro. Parl. Cas., B.P.C., Bro. P.C., Bro., Brown, Parl. Cas. B.P.C., Bro. Parl. Cas., B.P.R.
Brown's Entries
Bro. Ent.
Brown's Divorce Tax Planning Strategies
DTPS
Brown's Epitome and Analysis of Savigny's Treatise on Obligations in Roman Law
Brown's Roman Law
Brown's Formulae Bene Placitandi
Bro. Form., For. Pla.
Brown's House of Lords Cases
Brown Parl., Brown Parl.Cas., Brown P.C.
Brown's Law Dictionary
Brown, Brown Dict., Brown, Bro. Law Dic.
Brown's Michigan Nisi Prius Reports
Bro., Bro. NP., Brown, Brown N.P., Mich. Nisi Prius, Bro. NP., Brown N.P.Cas., Brown N.P. (Mich)
Brown's Modus Intrandi
Mod.Int.
Brown's or Howell's Michigan Nisi Prius Reports or Cases
Mich. N.P.
Brown's Parties to Actions
Br. Par.

Brown's Practice (Praxis), or Precedents in Chancery
Bro. Prac., Bro. Prac. (or Prax.), Prax.
Brown's Reports (53-65 and 80-136 Missouri)
Bro.
Brown's Reports (4-25 Nebraska)
Brown
Brown's Reports (53-65 Mississippi)
Brown
Brown's Reports (vols. 80-137 Missouri)
Brown
Brown's Scotch Reports
Brown
Brown's Supplement to Morrison's Dictionary of Decisions, Court of Sessions, Scotland
Bro. Sup. to Mor., Brown Sup. or Brown Sup. Dec., Br. Sup., B.S., Bro. Supp.
Brown's Synopsis of Decisions of the Scotch Court of Session
Brown Syn., Bro. Syn., Bro. Synop., Br. Syn.
Brown's Tax Strategies for Separation and Divorce
TSSD
Brown's The Forum
Bro. For.
Brown's Treatise on Law of Sale
Bro. Sal.
Brown's United States Admiralty Reports
Bro. Adm., Brown, Brown Adm.
Brown's United States Admiralty Reports (Appendix)
Brown's Adm. App.
Brown's United States District Court Reports
Brown

Brown's United States District Court Reports (Admiralty and Revenue Cases)
Brown A. & R., Bro. A. & R.

Brown's Vade Mecum
Bro. V.M.

Bruce and Williams' Admiralty Jurisdiction
Bru. & Wil. Adm.

Bruce's Principia Juris Feudalis
Bru. Princip.

Bruce's Military Law, Scotland
Bru. M.L.

Bruce's Scotch Court of Session Reports
Bru., Br., Bruce

Brunker's Irish Common Law Digest
Brunk. Ir. Dig.

Brunner's Collected Cases, United States
Brun. Col. Cas., Brunn Col. Cas. (F), Brunn. Coll. Cas., Brunner, Col. Cas.

Brunner's Selected Cases, United States Circuit Courts
Brun. Sel. Cas., Brunn. Sel. Cas., Brunner Sel. Cas.

Brunskill's Land Cases, Ireland
Brunskill, Bruns. L.C.

Brushwood's Medical Malpractice: Pharmacy Law
MMPL

Bruxelles (Brussels)
Brux.

Bruzard's Mauritius Reports
Bruzard

Bryant and Stratton's Commercial Law
Bry. & Str.Com.L.

Bryce's Registration of Trade Marks
Bryce Tr. M.

Bryce's Study of the Civil Law
Bryce Civ. L.

Bryne on Bills of Sale
Byrne B.S.

Buchanan, Cape Colony Court of Appeal Reports
A.C., App. Ca., Buch., B.A.C., Buch. Rep., Buch. App. Cas., Buch. Ct. App. Cape G.H., Buch. A.C.

Buchanan, Cape Colony Supreme Court Reports
Buch., Buch. S.C. Rep., B., Buch.J. Cape G.H.

Buchanan (Eben J. or James) Reports, Cape of Good Hope
Buch., A.C., App. Ca., B.A.C., Buch. App. Cas., Buch. A.C., Buch. Rep., Buch. Ct. App. Cape G.H.

Buchanan's Appeal Court Reports for the Cape Colony
B.A.C., A.C., Buch., App. Cas., Buch. App. Cas., Buch. Rep., Buch. A.C., Buch. E. Cape G.H., Buch. App. Cas., Buch. Ct. Ap. Cape G.H.

Buchanan's Court of Session Cases, Scotland
Buch., Buchanan

Buchanan's Eastern District Reports, Cape of Good Hope
Buch. E.D. Cape G.H.

Buchanan's New Jersey Equity Reports (71-85)
Buch. Eq. (N.J.), Buch.

Buchanan's Precedents of Pleading
Buch. Pr. Pl.

Buchanan's Remarkable Criminal Cases
Buch. Cas. (or Tr.)

Buchan's California Lien Laws
Buch. Lien Law

Buck's Alternative Energy
  AEn
**Buck's English Cases in Bank-
ruptcy**
  Buck, Buck. Cas., Buck Bankr.
  (Eng.)
Buckley on the Companies Acts
  Buckl.
**Buckley's Law and Practice Un-
der the Companies' Act**
  Buck. Comp. Act
**Buckner's Decisions (in Free-
man's Mississippi Chancery Re-
ports 1839-43)**
  Buck. Dec.
Bucknill on Care of the Insane
  Buck. Ins.
Bucknill on Lunacy
  Buck Lun.
**Bucknill's Cooke's Cases of Prac-
tice Common Pleas, England**
  Buck., Buck. Cooke
**Buck's Bankruptcy Cases, Eng-
land**
  Buck Cas., Buck, Buck Bankr.
  (Eng.)
**Bucks County Law Reporter,
Pennsylvania**
  Bucks Co. L. Rep., Bucks Co.
  L.R. (Pa), Bucks
**Buck's Massachusetts Ecclesiasti-
cal Law**
  Buck. Eccl. Law
Buck's Reports (vols. 7-8 Montana)
  Buck
Budget
  B
Buffalo Law Review
  Bu. L.R., Buff. L. Rev., Buffalo
  L. Rev.
**Buffalo Law Review Weekly Law
Bulletin**
  Buffalo L. Rev. Bull.

Building[s]
  Bldg.
**Building and Construction Con-
tracts**
  Bldg. Contr., Bldg. Contr.
Building and Construction Law
  Bldg. & Constr. C. L.
Building and Loan Associations
  B. & L. Assoc.
Bulgaria[n]
  Bulg., B.
**Bullard and Curry's Louisiana Di-
gest**
  Bull. & C. Dig., Bull. & Cur.
  Dig.
**Bullen and Leake's Pleadings on
Actions in King's Bench Deci-
sions**
  Bull. & L.
**Bullen and Leake's Precedents of
Pleading**
  B. & L. Pr., Bull. & L. Pr.
**Buller and Bund's Manual of
Bankruptcy**
  Bull & B. Bank.
Buller's Law of Distress for Rent
  Bull. Dis.
Buller's Law of Nisi Prius
  Bull. N.P., Bull. NP (Eng.),
  B.N.P., Buller N.P.
**Buller's Paper Book, Lincoln's
Inn Library**
  B.P.B., Buller
Bulletin
  Bul., Bull.
**Bulletin, Committee on Criminal
Courts' Law and Procedure, As-
sociation of the Bar, New York
City**
  C.C.C.Bull.
**Bulletin, Comparative Law Bu-
reau**
  Bulletin Comp. L.

Bulletin for International Fiscal Documentation
B.I.F.D., Bull. Int. Fisc. Doc., Bull. for Internat. Fiscal Docum., Bull. for Int'l. Fisc. Doc.

Bulletin of Canadian Welfare Law
Bull. Can. Welfare Law, Bull. Can.Welfare L.

Bulletin of Comparative Labour Relations
Bull. Comp. Lab. Rel.

Bulletin of Czechoslovak Law
Bull. Czech. L.

Bulletin of International Association of Law Libraries
I.A.L.L.Bull.

Bulletin of Judge Advocate General of Army
Bull. JAG

Bulletin of Law, Science and Technology
Bull. L.Sci. & Tech., Bull. L. Science & Tech

Bulletin of Legal Developments
Bull. Leg. Dev., Bull. Legal Devel.

Bulletin of Medieval Canon Law
Bull. Mediev. Canon L.

Bulletin of the American Academy of Psychiatry and the Law
Bull. Am. Acad. Psych. & L.

Bulletin of the American Patent Law Association
APLA Bull.

Bulletin of the Anglo-Soviet Law Association
Bull. Anglo-Sov.L.A.

Bulletin of the Association of the Bar of New York City
N.Y.C.B.A. Bull., New York City B.A. Bul.

Bulletin of the Copyright Society of the U.S.A.
Bull. Cop. Soc., Bull. Copyright Soc'y., Bull. Cr. Soc., Bull. C'right Soc'y. Copy. Soc. Bull.

Bulletin of the European Communities
Bull. Eur. Communities

Bulletin of the Industrial Law Society
Indust. L. Soc. Bull.

Bulletin of the International Bar Association
Bull. I.B.A.

Bulletin of the International Civil Aviation Organization
ICAO Bull.

Bulletin of the International Commission of Jurists
Bull. I.C.J.

Bulletin of the International Law Association
Int'l. L. Ass'n. Bull.

Bulletin of the National Tax Association
Bull. N.T.A., Bull. Nat. Tax Assoc.

Bulletin of the Quebec Society of Criminology
Bull. Que. Soc. Crim.

Bulletin of United States Trademark Association
Trademark Bull.

Bulletin Weekly Law Bulletin
Bull.

Bulletin, Waseda University Institute of Comparative Law
Bull. Waseda U. Inst. Comp. L.

Bullingbroke's Ecclesiastical Law
Bull. Eccl.

Bulstrode's English King's Bench Reports
  Bulstr., Buls, Bulst.
Bump on Bankruptcy
  Bump B'k'cy
Bump on Composition in Bankruptcy
  Bump Comp.
Bump on Federal Procedure
  Bump Fed. Pr.
Bump on Fraudulent Conveyances
  Bump Fr. Conv., Bump. Fraud. Conv.
Bump's Internal Revenue Laws
  Bump Int. Rev., Bump's Int. Rev. Law
Bump's Law of Patents, Trade-Marks, & c.
  Bump Pat.
Bump's Notes on Constitutional Decisions
  Bump N.C., Bump Const. Dec.
Bump's United States Stamp Laws
  Bump St. L.
Bunbury's English Exchequer Reports
  Bunb.
Bunyon on Domestic Law
  Buny. Dom. L.
Bunyon on Life Assurance
  Buny. Life Ass.
Bunyon on Life Insurance
  Buny. Life Ins.
Bunyon's Fire Insurance
  Buny. Fire Ins.
Burdick's Law of Crime
  Burdick, Crime
Burdick's Principles of Roman Law
  Burdick, Roman Law

Bureau
  Bur.
Bureau of Agricultural Economics
  BAE
Bureau of Animal Industry Docket
  B.A.I.
Bureau of Domestic Commerce
  BDC
Bureau of East-West Trade
  BEWT
Bureau of Employees' Compensation
  BEC
Bureau of Employment Security
  BES
Bureau of Indian Affairs
  BIA
Bureau of Internal Revenue
  BIR
Bureau of International Commerce
  BIC
Bureau of International Economic Policy and Research
  BIEPR
Bureau of Labor-Management Reports
  BLMR
Bureau of Labor Statistics
  BLS
Bureau of Land Management
  BLM
Bureau of Mines
  BOM
Bureau of Narcotics and Dangerous Drugs
  BNDD
Bureau of National Affairs
  BNA, B.N.A.
Bureau of Product Safety
  BPS

Bureau of Resources and Trade Assistance
BRTA
Bureau of the Budget
BOB
Bureau of the Census
Census
Bureau of Unemployment Compensation
UCB
Burford's Reports (6-18 Oklahoma)
Burf.
Burge on Appellate Jurisdiction
Burge App.
Burge on Colonial and Foreign Law
Burg, Col. & For. Law, Burge Col. Law
Burge on Conflict of Laws
Burge, Confl. Law.
Burge on Maritime International Law
Burge Mar. Int. L.
Burge on Suretyship
Burge, Sur.
Burgerlijk Wetboek Civil Code, Netherlands
B
Burgess' Reports (16-49 Ohio)
Burgess
Burglary
Burgl.
Burgundian Laws
L.L. Burgund.
Burgwyn's Maryland Digest
Burg. Dig., Burgw. Md. Dig.
Burke on Copyright
Burke Cop.
Burke on Criminal Law
Burke Cr. L.
Burke on International Copyright
Burke Int. Cop.

Burke on the Law of Public Schools
Burke Pub. Sch.
Burke's Celebrated Trials
Burke Cel. Tr., Burke Tr., Cel.Tr.
Burkina Faso
Burk, Faso
Burks' Reports (91-98 Virginia)
Burks
Burlamaqui's Principles of Natural and Politic Law
Burl. Natural & Pol. Law, Burlamaqui., Burl. Nat.
Burma Law Institute Journal
B.L.I.J., Burma L. Inst. J.
Burma Law Journal
Burma Law Inst. J., Burma L. Inst. J., B.L.J., Bur. L.J., Burm. L.J.
Burma Law Reports
Burma L.R., Bur. L.R., Burm. L.R.
Burma Law Times
B.L.T., Bur. L.T., Burm. L.T.
Burn on Stock Jobbing
Burn St. Job.
Burnet's Criminal Law of Scotland
Burn. Cr. L.
Burnet's Manuscript Decisions, Scotch Court of Session
Burnet
Burnett and Kafka's Litigation of Federal Tax Controversies
LFTC
Burnett's Reports (20-22 Oregon)
Burnett
Burnett's Wisconsin Reports
Burn., Burnett, Burnett (Wis.), Burnett's Rep., Bur.
Burns' Annotated Statutes, Indiana
Burns' Ann. St., Burns' Rev. St.

Burn's Attorney's Practice
Burn Att. Pr.
Burn's Conveyancing Practice
Burns Pract.
Burn's Ecclesiastical Law
B. Ecc. L., Burn Eccl., Burn,
Ecc. Law, Burns' Ecc. Law
Burn's Indiana Administrative Rules and Regulations
IND. Admin. R.
Burn's Indiana Statutes Annotated Code Edition
Ind. Code Ann.
Burn's Justice of the Peace
Burn's JP (Eng.), B.Just.,
Burn J.P. (or Jus.), Burn, J.P.
Burn's Law Dictionary
Burn Law Dict., Burn, Dict.
Burn's Marine Insurance
Burn Mar. Ins.
Burrell's Admiralty Cases
Burr. Adm.
Burrell's Reports, Admiralty, ed. by Marsden, England
Burrell, Burrell (Eng.)
Burrill on Assignments
Burr. Ass., Burrill, Assignm.
Burrill on Circumstantial Evidence
Bur. Circ. Ev., Burr. Circ. Ev.,
Burrill, Circ. Ev.
Burrill on Voluntary Assignment
Bur. Ass., Burrill Ass.
Burrill's Forms
Bur. Forms, Burr. Forms
Burrill's Law Dictionary
Bur. Law Dic., Burr. Dict.,
Burr. Law Dict., Burrill
Burrill's New York Practice
Bur. Pr., Burr. Pr.
Burrill's Practice
Burrill, Pr.

Burrnett's Oregon Reports (20-22 Oregon)
Burrnett.
Burroughs and Gresson's Irish Equity Pleader
Burr. & Gr. Eq. Pl., Bur. &
Gres. Eq. Pl.
Burrough's History of the Chancery
Bur. Chy., Burr. Ch.
Burroughs on Public Securities
Burr. Pub. Sec.
Burroughs on Taxation
Bur. Tax., Burr. Tax.
Burrow's English King's Bench Reports Tempore Lord Mansfield
Bur., Burr., Burr. (Eng.)
Burrow's English Settlement Cases
Burrow, Sett. Cas., Burr. S.C.,
Burr. S.Cas., Burr. Sett. Cas.,
Burr. Sett. Cas. (Eng.), Bur.
S.C., Burr. S. Cases, Sett. Cas.
Burr's Trial, Reported by Robertson
Burr. Tr., Burr. Tr. Rob.
Burton's Cases and Opinions
Cas. Op., Burt. Cas.
Burton on Bankruptcy
Burt. Bank.
Burton on Real Property
Burt. Real Prop., Burt. R.P.
Burton's Collection of Cases and Opinions
Burt.Cas., Cas. Op.
Burton's Manual of the Laws of Scotland
Burt. Man.
Burton's Parliamentary Diary
Burt. Parl.
Burton's Scotch Trials
Burt. Sc. Tr.

Busbee Law
Busb. L.
Busbee's Criminal Digest, North Carolina
Busb. Cr. Dig.
Busbee's Equity Reports (44 North Carolina)
Busb. Eq., Busbee Eq. (N.C.)
Busbee's North Carolina Law Reports (44-45 North Carolina)
B.N.C., Busb.
Bushby, Parliamentary Elections
Bush. Elec.
Bush's Digest of Florida Laws
Bush Dig.
Bush's Kentucky Report, (64-77 Kentucky)
Bush (Ky.), Bush
Business
Bus.
Business America
Bus. Am.
Business and Commerce
Bus. & Com.
Business and Defense Services Administration
BDSA
Business and Law
Bus. & L.
Business and Professions
Bus. & Prof.
Business and Professions Code
Bus. & Prof. C.
Business and Society Review
Bus. & Soc'y. Rev.
Business Corporation
Bus. Corp.
Business Franchise Guide, Commerce Clearing House
Bus. Franchise Guide (CCH)
Business Insurance Trust
BIT

Business Law Cases for Australia
A.B.L.
Business Law Journal
Bus. L.J., Business L.J.
Business Law Reports
Bus. L. Rep., B.L.R.
Business Law Review
B.L.R., Bus. L. Rev., Bus. L.R., Bus. L.R., Business L.R., Bus. L.R., Bus. L. Rev. (Butterworths)
Business Lawyer
BL, Bus. L., Bus. Law., Bus. Lawyer
Business Lawyer, Special Issue
BLS
Business Quarterly
Business Q.
Business Regulation
Bus. Reg.
Business Regulation Law Report
Bus. Reg. L. Rep.
Business Trust
Bus. Trust
Business Unreported Profits
BURPs
Business Week
Bus. Wk.
Buskirk's Indiana Practice
Busk. Pr.
Buswell and Wolcott's Massachusetts Practice
Busw. & Wol. Pr.
Butler County Legal Journal
Butler
Butler's Horae Juridicae Subsecivae
Butler, Hor. Jur., Butl. Hor. Jur.
Butler's Lawyer and Client
But. Law. & Cl.

Butler's Notes to Coke on Little-ton
  Butl. Co. Litt., Butler, Co. Litt.
Butterworth's Current Law
  B. Current L.
Butterworth's Rating Appeals.
  Butt. R.A., B.R.A., Butt. Rat. App.
Butterworth's South African Law Review
  Butt. S.A. Law Rev., Butterworth's S.A. Law Review, Butterworth's South Afr. L. Rev.
Butterworth's Workmen's Compensation Cases, England
  Butt. W.C.C., Butt. Work. Comp. Cas., B.W.C.C. (Eng.), B.W.C.C.
Butts' Edition of Shower's English King's Bench Reports
  Butts Sh.
Buxton's Reports (123-129 North Carolina)
  Buxton, Buxton (N.C.)

Byles on Law of Exchange
  Byl. Exch.
Byles on Bills of Exchange
  Byl. Bills., Byles, Byles Bills
Byles on Usury Laws
  Byl. Us. L.
Bynkershoek's Law of War
  Byn. War
Bynkershoeks Observationum Juris Roman Libri
  Bynks. Obs. Jur. Rom.
Bynkershoek's Quaestionum Juris Publici
  Bynk.
Byrne on Patents
  Byrne Pat.
Bythewood and Jarman's Precedents
  Jar. Prec.
Bythewood's Precedents in Conveyancing
  Byth. Conv., Byth. Prec.

C

Cababe and Ellis' English Queen's Bench Reports
Cab. & Ell., Cab. & E., Cab. & El., Cab. & El. (Eng.)

Cababe on Interpleader and Attachment of Debts
Cab. Int.

Cabinet Lawyer by John Wade
Cab. Lawy.

Cadwalader on Ground Rents
Cadw. Gr. R.

Cadwalader's Cases, U.S. District Court, Eastern District of Pennsylvania
Cadwalader.

Cadwalader's Digest of Attorney-General's Opinions
Cadw. Dig.

Cahiers de Droit Fiscal International (International Fiscal Association)
C. de D., C. D. Fisc. Int'l

Cahill's Illinois Statutes
Cahill's Ill. St.

Caii (or Gaii) Institutiones
Caii

Caines and Leigh's Crown Cases, England
C. & L. C.C.

Caines' Cases in Error, New York
C.C.E., Cai. Cas., Cai. Ca., Cain. Cas. in Error, Cain. C.E., Cain. E., Caines Ca. in E., Caines' Ca. in Er., Caines' Cas. in Er., Cains. C., N.Y. Cas. in Error, Cai. Cas., Cai. Cas. Err., Cai. R., Cai.Cas. (or Cas.Err.), Cain, Caines, Caines Cas.,

Caines (N.Y.), N.Y. Cas. Err., Cai.

Caines' Lex Mercatoria Americana
Cai. Lex Mer.

Caines' Practical (New York) Forms
Cai. Forms

Caines' Practice
Cai. Pr.

Caines' Reports, New York Supreme Court
Cai. (N.Y.), Caine. R., Caines' R., Caines Rep., Cain's. R., Cai., Cai. R., Cain, Caines, Caines Cas., Caines (N.Y.), Cai. Cas.

Caines' Term Reports, New York Supreme Court
T.R. (N.Y.), T.R., Cai., Cai. Cas., Cai. R., Cai. T.R., Cain, Caines, Caines Cas., Caines (N.Y.), Caines Term. Rep. (N.Y.), N.Y.T. Rep.

Cairns' Decisions in the Albert Arbitration (Reilly)
Cairns Dec.

Calcutta
C, Cal.

Calcutta Law Journal
Calcutta L.J., C.L.J., Calc. L.J.

Calcutta Law Journal Reports
Cal. L.J.

Calcutta Law Reporter
C.L.R., Cal. L.R.

Calcutta Legal Adviser
Cal. Leg. Adv.

Calcutta Legal Observer
Cal. Leg. Obs.

Calcutta Reports of Cases in Appeal
Sevestre
Calcutta Sadr Diwani Adalat Reports
Cal. S.D.A., Cal. Ser., Calc. Ser.
Calcutta Weekly Notes
Calcutta W.N., W.N., W.N. (Calc.), Cal. W.N., C.W.N., Calc. W.N.
Calcutta Weekly Reporter
Cal. W.R.
Caldecott's Magistrates' and Settlement Cases, England
Cal., Cald., Cald. (Eng.), Cald. J.P., Cald. Mag. Cas., Cald. S.C., Cald. Set. Cas., Cald. M. Cas., Cald. S.C., Cald. Sett. Cas.
Caldwell on Arbitration
Cald. Arb.
Caldwell's Reports (25-36 West Virginia)
Cald.
Calendae
Cal.
Calendar
Cal.
Calendar of Coroners Rolls of the City of London
Sharpe
Calendar of Proceedings in Chancery Tempore Elizabeth
Ch. Cal., Cal. Ch., Cal. P. Ch.
Calendarium Rotulorum Patentium
C.R.P.
Calendars of the Proceedings in Chancery, Record Commission
Cal.
California
C, Cal.

California Administrative Code
Cal. Adm. Code., Cal. Admin. Code
California Administrative Register
Cal. Admin. Reg.
California Advance Appellate Reports
ACA, A.C.A.
California Advance Legislative Service
Cal. Adv. Legis. Serv.
California Advance Reports
A.C.
California Agriculture Code
Cal. Agric. Code
California Appellate Decisions
Cal. App. Dec.
California Appellate Department of the Superior Court
C.A.
California Appellate Reports
C.A., Ca. A., Cal. App.
California Appellate Reports Supplement
C.A. Supp., Cal. App. Supp.
California Appellate Reports, Second Series
C.A. 2d, Ca. A. 2d, Cal. App. 2d
California Appellate Reports, Second Series Supplement
C.A. 2d Supp., Cal. App. 2d Supp.
California Appellate Reports, Third Series
C.A. 3d, Ca. A. 3d, Cal. App. 3d
California Appellate Reports, Third Series Supplement
C.A. 3S., Cal. App. 3d Supp.
California Bankruptcy Journal
Cal. Bankr. J.
California Board of Railroad Commissioners
Cal. Bd. R. Co.

California Code Statutes and Amendments
Cal. Stat.
California Compensation Cases
Cal. Comp. Cases, C.C.
California Constitution
Cal. Const.
California Continuing Education of the Bar
CEB
California Decisions
Cal. Dec.
California General Corporation Law
Ca. G.C.L.
California Industrial Accident Commission, Compensation Cases
Cal. I.A.C. C.C.
California Industrial Accident Decisions
Cal. I.A.C. Dec., Cal. Ind. Acct. Dec., Cal. Ind. Acci. Dec.
California International Practioner
Cal. Int'l Prac.
California Jurisprudence
Cal. Jur.
California Jurisprudence, Second Edition
Cal. Jur. 2d
California Jury Instructions, Civil
CAJI
California Jury Instructions, Criminal
CAJC, Cal. J.I.C.
California Law Journal
Cal. L.J., C.L.J.
California Law Journal and Literary Review
C.L.J. & Lit. Rev.

California Law Review
C. L. Rev., Ca. L.R., Cal. L. Rev., Cal LR, Calif. L. Rev.
California Law Revision Commission
Calif. L.R.C.
California Lawyer
Cal. Law.
California Legal Filing Directory (Britton)
SCLF
California Legal Record
C. Leg. Rec., Cal. Leg. Rec.
California Legislative Service, West Publishing Co.
Cal. Legis. Serv.
California Management Review
Calif. Management Rev.
California Penal Code
Cal. Penal Code
California Practice
Cal. Prac.
California Public Defenders Association
CAPDA
California Railroad Commission Decisions
Cal. R.C. Dec., C.R.C.
California Railroad Commission Digest of Decisions
Cal. R.C. Dec. Dig.
California Railroad Commission Opinions and Orders
Cal. R. Com.
California Real Property Journal
Cal. Real Prop. J.
California Regulatory Law Reporter
Cal. Reg. L. Rep.
California Reporter
CaR, Ca.R., Cal. Rptr.

California Reporter, Second Series
CaR 2d

California Reports
C, Cal., Cal. Rep., Calif.

California Reports, Second Series
Cal. 2d

California Reports, Third Series
Cal. 3d

California State Bar Journal
Cal. S.B.J., Cal. St. B.J., Calif. S.B.J.

California State University, Los Angeles
CSULA

California Superior Court, Reports of Cases in Appellate Departments
Cal. Sup., Cal. Sup. (Cal.), Cal. Supp.

California Supplement
Cal. Sup.

California Supreme Court Reports
C., Cal

California Supreme Court Reports, Second Series
C. 2d

California Supreme Court Reports, Third Series
C. 3d

California Trial Lawyers Journal
C.T. L.J.

California Unreported Cases
Ca. U., C.U., Cal. Unrep., Cal. Unrep. Cas.

California Western International Law Journal
Ca. W. I. L.J., Cal. W. Int'l. L.J., Calif. W. Int. L.J., Calif. W. Int'l. L.J., Calif. West. Int'l. L.J., Calif. Western Int. L.J.

California Western Law Review
Ca. W. L.R., Cal. W. L. Rev., Calif. W. L. Rev., Calif. West. L. Rev., Calif. Western L. Rev., California West. L. Rev., C.W. L.R.

Call's Virginia Reports (vols. 5-10 Virginia)
Call. (Va.), Call.

Callaghan and Co.
Callaghan

Callan's Military Laws of the United States
Cal. Mil. Laws, Call. Mil. L.

Callis on Sewers
Callis, Sew., Call.Sew., Cal. Sew.

Callis' (Robert) Reading on the Statute of Sewers, 23 Hen.8.85.
Callis

Callman on Unfair Competition and Trade Marks
Callman, Unfair Comp.

Calthorpe on Copyholds
Calth. Copyh.

Calthrop's City of London Cases, King's Bench, England
Calth., Calth. (Eng.), Calthr.

Calthrop's English King's Bench Reports
Calth., Cal., Cal. Rep., Calth. (Eng.), Calthr.

Calvert's Parties to Suits in Equity
Calv. Par., Calv. Parties

Calvininus Lexicon Juridicum
Calv. Lex., Calvin Lex., Calvin., Calvin. Lex. Jurid.

Cambria County Legal Journal
Cambria, Cambria Co. L.J., Cambria Co. (Pa.)

Cambria County Reports
Camb. Co. L.J.

Cambrian Law Review
Cambrian L. Rev., Cambrian L.R., Camb. L.J.
Cambridge Law Journal
Cambridge L.J., C.L.J.
Cambridge Philological Society, Proceedings of
Proceed. of the Cambridge Philol. Soc.
Cambridge University Library
C.U.L.
Camden Society
Camd. Soc., C.S.
Camden's Britannia
Cam. Brit., Camd. Brit., Camden
Camera Ducata (Executive Chamber) (Lat.)
Cam. Duc.
Camera Scaccaria (Exchequer Chamber) (Lat.)
Cam.Scac., Cam. Scacc.
Camera Stellate (Star Chamber) (Lat.)
Cam. Stell.
Cameron and Norwood's North Carolina Conference Reports
C. & N., Cam. & N., C.N. Conf., Cam. & Nor.
Cameron on Intestate Succession in Scotland
Cam. Int. Suc.
Cameron on Joint Stock Companies
Cam. J.S. Comp.
Cameron's Legal Opinions, Toronto
Cam. Op.
Cameron's Practice, Canada
Cameron Pr., Cameron Pr. (Can.)
Cameron's Privy Council Decisions
CAM

Cameron's Reports, Upper Canada, Queen's Bench
Cam.
Cameron's Supreme Court Cases, Canada
Cameron, Cameron S.C., CAM, Cam. S.C., Cameron (Can.), Cameron Cas. (Can.), S.C.C., Cam. Cas.
Cameron's Supreme Court Practice, Canada
Cam. Prac.
Campaign for Justice in Divorce
C.J.D.
Campaign Law Reporter
Campaign L. Rep.
Campbell Law Review
Camp L Rev, Campbell L. Rev.
Campbell on Citation and Diligence
Camp. Cit.
Campbell on Executors and Administrators in Pennsylvania
Camp. Ex.
Campbell on Negligence
Camp. Neg.
Campbell, on Sale of Goods and Commercial Agency
Camp. Sale, Com. Ag.
Campbell's Compendium of Roman Law
Camp., Camp. Rom. L., Camp. Rom. L. Comp., Camp. Rom. L. (or Comp.), Campb., Campbell
Campbell's English Nisi Prius Reports
C.N.P.C., Camp., Campb., Campbell, Campb. (Eng.), Camp. N.P.
Campbell's Legal Gazette
Campb. L.G.

Campbell's Legal Gazette Reports
Camp., Campb. (Pa.), Campbell, Campb., Leg. Gaz. R., Leg. Gaz. Rep.

Campbell's Lives of the Chief Justice
Campbell, Camp. Ch. Jus.

Campbell's Lives of the Lord Chancellors
Camp. Ld. Ch., Camp. Lives Ld.Ch., Campbell

Campbell's Mercantile Law
Camp. Merc. L.

Campbell's Reports (27-58 Nebraska)
Camp., Campb., Campbell

Campbell's Reports of Taney's Decisions, U.S. Circuit Court
Camp. Dec., Campb. Dec., Camp., Campb., Campbell

Campbell's Ruling Cases
Rul. Cas.

Camp's Reports (1 North Dakota)
Camp.

Canada
Can.

Canada Criminal Acts, Taschereau's Edition
Can. Cr. Acts., Tasch. Cr. Acts

Canada Criminal Cases Annotated
Can. C.C.

Canada Exchequer Court Reports
Can. Exch., Ex. C.R., Can. Ex. C.R., E.C.R.

Canada Fortnightly Law Journal
F.L.J.

Canada Gazette
C. Gaz., Can. Gaz.

Canada in World Affairs
Can. in Wld. Aff.

Canada Law Journal
C.L.J., Can. L.J., Can. L.J.

Canada Law Journal, New Series
C. L.J. N.S., Can. L.J. N.S.

Canada Law Journal, Old Series
C. L.J. O.S., U.C.L.J. O.S.

Canada Law Reform Commission
C.L.R.C.

Canada Law Reports
C.L.R., Can. L.R.

Canada Law Reports, Exchequer Court
Ex. C.R., Can. Exch., Can. L.R., Exch. C., Exch. Ct. (Can.)

Canada Law Reports, Federal Court
F.C.

Canada Law Reports, Supreme Court
Can. S.Ct.

Canada Legal News
Can. Leg. N.

Canada Railway Cases
Can. Ry. Cas.

Canada Railway Commission
Can. R.C.

Canada Recent Laws
Rec. Laws

Canada Supreme Court
Can. S.C., S.C.C., C.S.C.

Canada Supreme Court Reports
Can. S.C., S.C.R., Can. S.C. Rep., Can. S.Ct., Can. Sup.Ct., Can. S.C. R., S.C.R.

Canada Tax Appeal Board Cases
Can. Tax App. Bd., Tax A.B.C.

Canada Tax Cases
Can. Tax Cas., C.T.C.

Canada Tax Cases Annotated
Can. Tax Cas. Ann., Cas. Tax

Canada Treaty Series
Can. T.S.

Canada Uniform Law Conference Proceedings
   Unif. L. Conf.
Canada-United States Law Journal
   Can. U.S. L.J.
Canada-U.S. Business Law Review
   Can.-U.S. Bus. L. Rev.
Canadian Abridgment
   Can. Abr.
Canadian Abridgment, Second Edition
   Can.Abr. (2d)
Canadian-American Law Journal
   Can.-Am. L.J.
Canadian Annual Digest
   C.A.D.
Canadian Appeal Cases
   Can. App. Cas., C.R. [date] A.C.
Canadian Appeal Reports of Upper Canada (1846-66)
   A.R.
Canadian Banker
   Can. Bank.
Canadian Bankruptcy Reports
   Can. Bank. R., Can. Bankr.,
   Can. Bankr. Rep., C.B.R.
Canadian Bankruptcy Reports Annotated
   Can. Bankr. Ann.
Canadian Bankruptcy Reports Annotated, New Series
   C.B.R. (N.S.), Can. Bankr. Ann. (N.S.)
Canadian Bar Association, British Columbia Branch Meeting Program Reports
   B.C. Branch Lec.
Canadian Bar Association Journal
   Can. B.A. J., Can. Bar. A.J.,
   Can. B.A.J.

Canadian Bar Association, Proceedings
   Can. B.A.
Canadian Bar Association Year Book
   Can. B. Year Book., Can. B.
   Ass'n Y.B., Can. Bar Year Book
Canadian Bar Journal
   Can. Bar J., Can. B.J.
Canadian Bar Journal, New Series
   Can. Bar J. (N.S.)
Canadian Bar Review
   Can. B. Rev., Can. Bar. Rev.,
   Can. B.R.
Canadian Business Law Journal
   Can. Bus. L.J.
Canadian Cases on the Law of Torts
   Can. Cases L. Torts, C.C.L.T.
Canadian Chartered Accountant
   Can. Chart. Acc.
Canadian Commercial Law Guide, Commerce Clearing House
   Can. Com. L. Guide (CCH)
Canadian Commercial Law Reports
   Can. Com. Cas., Can. Com.
   L.R., Can. Com. R.
Canadian Communications Law Review
   Can. Com. L. Rev.
Canadian Community Law Journal
   Can. Com. L.J., Can. Community L.J.
Canadian Court Martial Appeal Reports
   C.M.A.R.
Canadian Criminal Cases
   Can. Cr. Cas., C.C.C.

Canadian Criminal Cases Annotated
Can. Crim. Cas., Can. Crim. Cas. Ann.

Canadian Criminal Cases, New Series
Can. Crim. Cas. (N.S.)

Canadian Criminal Reports
Can. Cr. R.

Canadian Department of Industry, Trade and Commerce
Canada Commerce.

Canadian Encyclopedic Digest
C.E.D.

Canadian Environmental Law Association Newsletter
C.E.L.A. Newsletter

Canadian Environmental Law News
C. Environ. L. N., Can. Env. L. News, Can. Environ. L. N.

Canadian Environmental Law Reports
C.E.L.R.

Canadian Exchequer Reports
Can. Ex. R.

Canadian Green Bag
Can. Green Bag

Canadian Human Rights Advocate
Can. Hum. Rts. Advocate

Canadian Human Rights Reporter
Can. Human Rights Rep.

Canadian Journal of Administrative Law and Practice
Can. J. Admin. L. & Prac.

Canadian Journal of Correction
Can. J. Correction

Canadian Journal of Criminology
Can. J. Criminol., Can. J. Criminology

Canadian Journal of Criminology and Corrections
Can. J. Crim. & Corr., Can. J. Corr., Can. J. Crim. & Correct., Can. J. Criminology & Corr.

Canadian Journal of Family Law
Can. J. Fam. L.

Canadian Journal of Law and Jurisprudence
Can. J.L. & Juris.

Canadian Journal of Political Science
Can. J. Pol. Sc.

Canadian Journal of Women and the Law
Can. J. Women & L.

Canadian Labour
Can. Lab.

Canadian Labour Law Cases
C.L.L.C.

Canadian Labour Relations Board Reports, 1974-
Can. L.R.B.R.

Canadian Law Review
Can. L. Rev.

Canadian Law Review and Corporation Legal Journal
C.L.R.

Canadian Law Times
Can. L. Times, Can. L.T., Canada L.T., C.L.T.

Canadian Law Times Occasional Notes
Can. L.T. Occ. Notes, C.L.T. Occ. N., Can. L.T. Occ. N.

Canadian Lawyer
Can. Law., Can. Lawyer

Canadian Legal Aid Bulletin
Can. Legal Aid Bul.

Canadian Legal Studies
Can. Leg. Stud., Can. Leg. Studies, Can. Legal Stud.

Canadian Municipal Journal
Can. Mun. J., C.M. J.
Canadian National Railways
C.N.R.
Canadian Native Law Reporter
Can. Native L. Rep.
Canadian Oil and Gas
Can. Oil & Gas
Canadian Pacific Railway Company
C.P.R.
Canadian Patent Office Record
Can. Pat. Off. Rec.
Canadian Patent Reports
Can. Pat. Rep., Can. P.R., C.P.R.
Canadian Patent Reports, Second Series
C.P.R. (2d)
Canadian Perspectives on International Law and Organization
Can. Persp.
Canadian Public Administration
Can. Pub. Ad., Can. Pub. Admin.
Canadian Railway and Transport Cases
C.R.T.C., Can. Ry. & T. Cas.
Canadian Railway Cases
Can. R. Cas., C.R.C.
Canadian Reports, Appeal Cases
Can. R. A.C., Can. R. App. Cas., C.R., A.C., C.R.A.C.
Canadian Reports, Appellate Cases
Can. App.
Canadian Sales Tax Reporter, Commerce Clearing House
Can. Sales Tax Rep. (CCH)
Canadian Tax Cases
C. Tax C.
Canadian Tax Foundation, Conference Report
Can. Tax Found.

Canadian Tax Foundation Report of Proceedings of the Tax Conference
Can. Tax Found. Rep. Proc. Tax Conf.
Canadian Tax Journal
Can. Tax J.
Canadian Tax Law Journal
Can. Tax L.J.
Canadian Tax News
Can. Tax News
Canadian Tax Reporter, Commerce Clearing House
Can. Tax Rep. (CHH)
Canadian Tax Reports, Commerce Clearing House
Can. Tax Rep. (CHH)
Canadian Transport Commission
CTC
Canadian Welfare
Can. Wel.
Canadian Yearbook of International Law
Can. Y.B. I.L., Can. Y.B. Int. Law, Can. Y.B. Int'l. L., Can. Yearbook Int. L., Can. Yb. of Internat.
Canal Zone
Canal Z., C.Z., C.Z. Code, C.Z.C.
Canal Zone Laws
L.C.Z.
Canal Zone Order
CZO
Canal Zone Reports, Supreme and District Courts
C.Z. Rep.
Canal Zone Supreme Court
Canal Zone
Canal Zone Supreme Court Reports
Canal Zone Sup. Ct.

Cancelariae, English Chancery Reports
Acta
Cancellation of Instruments
Canc. Instr.
Candy and Birdwood's Printed Judgments of Sind, India
Candy.
Candy on Mayor's Court Practice
Candy M.C.
Cane and Leigh's Crown Cases Reserved, England
Cane & L.
Cannon House Office Building
CHOB
Cannons Enacted under King Edgar
Edg. C.
Canon[s]
Can.(s)
Canons of Aelfric
AelLC.
Canterbury Law Review
Canterbury L. Rev.
Canterbury's Texas Construction Law Manual
TCLM
Cantor's Traumatic Medicine and Surgery for the Attorney
Cantor, Med. & Surg.
Cantwell's Cases on Tolls and Customers, Ireland
Cantwell
Cape and Orange Free State Native Appeal and Divorce Court, Selected Decisions
N.A.C. & O., N.A. & D., C & O.
Cape Colony Supreme Court Reports
S.C.R., Cape S.C.R.
Cape Law Journal
C.L.J., Cape Law J., Cape L.J.

Cape Law Reports
C.L.R.
Cape of Good Hope
C.G.H.
Cape of Good Hope Cases in the Supreme Court
Cas. S.C. (Cape G.H.)
Cape of Good Hope Reports
S.C.
Cape Province
C.P.
Cape Provincial Division Report
C.P.D., C, Cape P. Div., Cape T. Div.
Cape Times
C.T.
Cape Times Common Law Reports
C.T.C.L.R.
Cape Times Law Reports, edited by Sheil
Sheil.
Cape Times Supreme Court Reports, Cape of Good Hope
C.T.R., Cape T.R.
Capias ad Respondendum (a judicial writ) (Lat.)
Ca. resp.
Capias ad Satisfaciendum (writ of execution) (Lat.)
Ca. sa.
Capital
Cap.
Capital Defense Digest
Cap. Def. Dig.
Capital Gains Tax
C.G.T.
Capital Stock Tax Ruling, Internal Revenue Bureau
C.S.T.
Capital Transfer Tax
C.T.T.

Capital University Law Review
Cap. U. L. Rev., Capital U. L.
Rev., Capital U. L.R., Capital
Univ. L. Rev.

Capitulo
Cap.

**Cardozo Arts and Entertainment
Law Journal**
Cardozo Arts & Ent. L. J., Car-
dozo Arts & Entertainment L.J.

Cardozo Law Review
Cardozo L. Rev.

**Cardozo Studies in Law and Lit-
erature**
Cardozo Stud. L. & Lit.

Care Of
c/o

Caribbean Common Market
CARICOM

**Caribbean Free Trade Associa-
tion**
CARIFTA

Caribbean Law Journal
Carib. L.J., Caribbean L.J.

Caribbean Law Liberation
Caribbean L. Libr.

**Carleton's New Brunswick Re-
ports**
Carl., N.R.B. Carl.

**Carmody-Witt's Cyclopedia of
New York Practice**
Carmody-Wait, N.Y. Prac.

Carolina
Car.

Carolina Law Journal
Car. L.J., Carolina L.J.

**Carolina Law Repository
(4 North Carolina Reports)**
Law Repos., Car. L. Repos., Car.
L. Rep., Car. Law Repos., Car.
L.R., Carolina L.Repos., L. Rep.,
Law Repository, N. Car. Law
Rep.

Carolina Regina (Queen Caroline)
C.R. (Charles)

Carolus (as 4 Car. II)
Car.

Carolus Rex (King Charles)
C.R.

**Carpenter's Reports (52-53 Cali-
fornia)**
Carp., Carpenter

**Carpmael's Patent Cases, Eng-
land**
Carp., Carp. Pat. Cas., Carp.
P.C.

Carran's Summary Cases, India
Carr. Cas., Carran.

Carried Over
c/o

Carrier[s]
Carr.

Carrier's Tax
C.T.

**Carriers Taxing Ruling, Internal
Revenue Bulletin**
C.T. Rul.

**Carrington and Kirwan's English
Nisi Prius Reports**
C.T., Car. & K., Car. &
K.(Eng.), Car. & Kir, C. & K.

**Carrington and Marshman's Eng-
lish Nisi Prius Reports**
C. & Marsh., C. & M., Car. &
M., Car. & M. (Eng.), Car. &
Mar., Carr. & M., C. & Mar.

**Carrington and Payne's English
Nisi Prius Reports**
C. & P., Car. & P., Car. & P.
(Eng.)

Carrington's Criminal Law
Car. Cr. L.

**Carrow and Oliver's English Rail-
way & Canal Cases**
C. & O. R. Cas., Car. & Ol., Car.
& O.

Carrow, Hamerton and Allen's New Sessions Cases, England
Car. H. & A., Carr., Ham. & Al., C.H. & A., New Sess. Cas.

Carshaltown's Court Rolls
Carsh.

Carswell's Practice Cases
Carswell's Prac., C.P.C.

Cartel, Review of Monopoly, Developments and Consumer Protection, London, England
Cartel

Carter's English Common Pleas Reports Tempore O. Bridgman (same as Orlando Bridgman)
Bridg., Carter (Eng.), Rep.t.O.Br., Cart., Carter

Carter's Reports (1-2 Indiana)
Cart., Carter

Carthew's English King's Bench Reports (1686-1701)
Carth., Carth. (Eng.), Cart.

Cartmell's Trade Mark Cases
Cartm.

Cartwright's Cases, Canada
Cart. Cas. (Can.), Cartwr. Cas.

Cartwright's Cases on British North America Act
Cart.

Cartwright's Constitutional Cases, Canada
Cart. B.N.A., Cartw. C.C.

Caruther's History of a Lawsuit: Cases in Chancery
Car. Laws.

Carver on the Law Relating to the Carriage of Goods by Sea
Carv. Carr., Carver.

Cary on Juries
Cary Jur.

Cary on Partnership
Cary Part.

Cary's Commentary on Littleton's Tenures
Cary Lit.

Cary's English Chancery Reports
Cary., Cary (Eng.)

Case and Comment
C. & C., Case & Com., Case & Comm

Case of the City of Chester, on Quo Warranto
Chest. Ca.

Case on Appeal
A.C.

Case or Placitum
Ca.

Case Western Reserve Journal of International Law
Case W. Res. J. Int.L., Case W. Res. J. Intl L., Case West. Res. J. Int'l L.

Case Western Reserve Law Review
Case W. Res. L. Rev., Case West. Res. L. Rev., Case West.Reserve L. Rev., C.W.L.

Case[s]
c., C.

Cases and Opinions in Law, Equity and Conveyancing
Ca., cas., Cas.Eq.

Cases Argued and Decreed in Chancery
Cas. Arg. & Dec.

Cases at Nisi Prius
C.N.P.

Cases at the end of Popham's Reports
Poph.(2).

Cases Banco Regis Tempore William III (12 Modern Reports), England
Cas. B.R.

Cases in Chancery
Cas. Ch.

Cases in Chancery Tempore Car. II, England
Chan. Cas., Ch. Ca., Ch. Cas., Ch. Cas. (Eng.), Cas. Ch., Cas. in C., C.C., Cas. Ch. 1, 2, 3

Cases in Chancery Tempore George II, England
Temp. Geo. II., Ca. temp. King, Ca. temp. K.

Cases in Chancery Tempore Plunkett, England
Ca. t. Plunk.

Cases in Chancery Tempore Talbot
Ca. temp. Talb.

Cases in Crown Law, England
Cas. C.L.

Cases in Equity Abridged
Cas. Eq. Abr.

Cases in Equity, Gilbert's Reports, England
Cas.Eq.

Cases in Gold Coast Law
Danquah

Cases in King's Bench (8 Modern Reports), England
Cas. K.B.

Cases in King's Bench Tempore Hardwicke, England
B.R.H.

Cases in King's Bench Tempore 7-10 Geo. II, England
Ann.

Cases in King's Colorado Civil Practice
King Cas.

Cases in Law and Equity (10 Modern Reports), England
Cas. L. Eq., Cas. L. & Eq., Ca. t. Mac.

Cases in Parliament
Cas. P., Cas. Parl., Ca.P., Ca. Parl.

Cases in the Eastern District's Local Division of the Supreme Court of South Africa
E.

Cases in the Griqualand West Local Division of the Supreme Court of South Africa
G.L.D., G.W.

Cases in the House of Lords
Cas. H.L.

Cases in the Supreme Court, Cape of Good Hope
Cas. S.C. (Cape G.H.)

Cases of Appeal to the House of Lords
Cas. App.

Cases of Contested Elections
C.C.E., C. of C.E.

Cases of Practice, in Common Pleas, England
Cas. Pra. C.P., Cas. Prac. C.P., Cas. Pr. C.P., Cas. Pr.

Cases of Practice in King's Bench, England
Cas. Prac. K.B., Cas. Pr., Cas. Pra. K.B., Cas. Pr. K.B.

Cases of Settlement and Removals
Cas. Sett., Ca. Sett.

Cases of Settlement, King's Bench, England
Cas. S.M.

Cases on the Six Circuits, England
Six Circ., Cas. Six Cir.

Cases Taken and Adjudged (Report in Chancery), England
Cas. Tak. & Adj.

Cases Tempore Charles II, England
Ca. t. Ch.2

Cases Tempore Charles II (3 Reports in Chancery), England
Cas.t.ch.II.

Cases Tempore Finch in Chancery, England
Ca. temp. F., Rept. I. Fich., Cas. temp.F., Cas. t. Finch (Eng.), Cas. t.F.

Cases Tempore George I, Chancery (8-9 Modern Reports), England
Cas. t. Geo.I.

Cases Tempore Hardwicke, England
Cas. temp. Hardw., Ca. temp. H., Cas. t. Hardw., Cas. t. H.

Cases Tempore Hardwicke by Lee, England
Hardw., Hardw. (Eng.), Cas. t. Hard. (byLee), Cas. t. Hardw., Cas. T. H.

Cases Tempore Hardwicke by Lee and Hardwicke, England
Cas. t. Hard., Hardw. Cas. Temp., Cas. t. Hardw., Cas. t. H.

Cases Tempore Hardwicke, by Ridgeway, England
Hardw., Hardw. (Eng.), Cas. t. Hardw., Cas. t. H.

Cases Tempore Hardwicke, King's Bench, by Annaly, England
Anny. Ca. temp. Hard., Ca. t. H., Ca. t. Hard., Cas. temp.H., Cas. t. Hardw., Cas. t. H.

Cases Tempore Hardwicke (W. Kelynge, English King's Bench Reports)
Cas. K.B.t.H., Cas. K.B.t.Hard.

Cases Tempore Holt (11 Modern Reports), England
Ca. t. H., Rept. t. Holt, Ca. t. Holt., Ca. t. Q.A.

Cases Tempore Holt, King's Bench (Holt's Reports), England
Cas. t. H., Cas. t. Holt., Ca. temp. Holt

Cases Tempore King (Macnaghten's Select English Chancery Cases)
C. t. K.

Cases Tempore King, Chancery, England
Ca. t. K., Ca. t. King

Cases Tempore Lee, England
Ca. t. Lee, Cas. temp. Lee.

Cases Tempore Maccelesfield (10 Modern Reports), England
Cas. t. Maccl., Cas. t. Mac.

Cases Tempore Northington (Eden's English Chancery Reports)
C. t. N., Cas. t. Northington

Cases Tempore Queen Anne (11 Modern Reports), England
Cas. t. Q. Anne, Cas. t. Q.A.

Cases Tempore Sugden, Irish Chancery
Cas. t. Sugd.

Cases Tempore Talbot, England
Cas. temp. Talb., Ca. temp. Talbot, Cas. t. Talb., Ca. t. Talb., C.t.T., Tal., Talb., Cas. t. Tal.

Cases Tempore Talbot, by Forrester, English Chancery
Cas. F.T.

Cases Tempore William III (12 Modern Reports), England
Ca. t. Wm.3, Cas. t. Wm. III., Cas. C.R.

Cases under Sugden's Act
Cooke
Cases with Opinions, by Eminent Counsel, England
Cas. w. Op., Cas. & Op.
Casey's Reports (25-36 Pennsylvania)
Casey., Cas. R., Cas.
Cash on Delivery
C.O.D.
Cash or Deferred Arrangements
CODAs
Casper's Forensic Medicine
Casp. For. Med.
Cassel's Digest
Cass. Dig.
Cassels' Practice Cases
Cass. Prac., Cass. Prac. Cas.
Cassell's Procedure in the Courts of Canada
Cas. Proc., Cass. Proc.
Cassels' Supreme Court Decisions
Cass. S.C.
Cassell's Supreme Court Digest
S.C. Dig.
Cassel's Supreme Court Practice
Cass. Sup. C. Prac.
Cassiodori Variarum
Cassiod. Var.
Casson's Local Government Board Decisions
Cass. L.G.B.
Castle on Rating
Cast. Rat.
Castle's Law of Commerce in Time of War
Cast. Com.
Casualty
Cas.
Caswall on Copyholds
Casw. Cop.
Catalogue[s]
Cat.

Cataloguer[s]
Cat., cat.
Cataloguing
cat.
Cates' Reports (109-127 Tennessee Reports)
Cates
Catholic
C, Cath.
Catholic Lawyer
Cath. Law., Cath. Lawyer, Catholic Law.
Catholic University Law Review
Cath. U. L. Rev., Cath. U. L.R., Catholic U. L.R., Catholic U. L.Rev., Catholic Univ. L. Rev., C.U. L.R.
Catholic University of America Law Review
Cath. U. A. L.R., Cath. U. L. Rev., Catholic U. A. L.R., C.U.A. L.R.
Catholic University of America Law School
CUALS
Causa Mortis (by reason of death) (Lat.)
C.m.
Causes Celebres (famous trials) (French)
C.C.
Causes Celebres, Quebec Provincial Reports
Ca. Celeb.
Causes of Action
COA
Cavanagh's Law of Money Securities
Cav. Mon. Sec.
Caveat Emptor (let the buyer beware) (Lat.)
C.e.

Cavender's Debates on Canada
Cav. Deb. Can.

**Cavendish's Debates, House of
Commons**
Cav. Deb.

Cawley's Laws Concerning Jesuits, etc.
Cawl.

**Cay's Abridgment of the English
Statutes**
Cay Abr.

Ceiling Price Regulation
C.P.R.

Cemetery[ies]
Cem.

Center[s]
Ctr.

Center for Advanced Legal Training
CALT

Center for Computer Assisted Legal Instruction
CCALI

Center for Continuing Education
CCE

Centers for Disease Control
CDC

**Center for International Legal
Studies**
CILS

**Center for Latin American Studies, University of Wisconsin-
Milwaukee**
UWCLA

Center for Transnational Corporations
CTC

Central
Cent.

Central Acts, India
India Cen. Acts

Central African Republic
Cent. Afr. Rep.

Central American Common Market
CACM

**Central Criminal Court Cases,
England**
C.C. Ct. Cas., Cent. Crim. C.
Cas.

**Central Criminal Court (Old
Bailey), England**
C.C.C.

**Central Criminal Court Reports,
England**
Cent. Crim. C.R.

**Central Criminal Court Session
Papers**
C.C.C. Sess. Pap., C.C.C. Cas.,
Cent. Crim. C. Cas., Sess. Pap.
C.C.C., Centr. Cr. Ct. R.

Central District
CD

Central Intelligence Agency
CIA

Central Law Journal
Centr. L.J., C.L.J., Central L.J.,
Cent. Law J., Cent. L.J.

Central Law Monthly
Cent. L.Mo.

Central Office of Information
C.O.I.

Central Provinces
C.P.

Central Provinces, India
C.P. Ind.

**Central Provinces, India, Select
Cases**
Sel. Cas.

Central Provinces Law Reports
Cent. Prov. L.R., C.P.L.R.

Central Reporter
Cent. Rep., C.R., Cent., Cent.
R.(Pa.)

Central Statistical Office
C.S.O.

Central Treaty Organization
    CENTO
Centre County Legal Journal
    C.C.L.J.
Centre International D'Etudes Criminologiques (International Centre of Criminological Studies) (French)
    C.I.E.C.
Centum
    C.
Century
    C
Century Dictionary
    Cent. Dict.
Century Dictionary and Cyclopedia
    Cent. Dict. and Cyc., Cent. Dict. & Ency.
Century Digest (American Digest System)
    C.D., Cent. Dig.
Cepi Corpus
    C.C., Ce.C.
Cepi Corpus and Bail Bond
    C.C. & B.B.
Cepi Corpus and Committitur
    C.C. & C.
Certificate[s]
    Ctf., cert.
Certificate of Competency
    COC
Certificate of Deposit
    C/D
Certified From
    Cert.
Certified Public Accountant
    C.P.A.
Certified To
    Cert.
Certify
    Cert.

Certiorari
    Cert.
Certiorari Denied
    cert. den., Cert. denied
Certiorari Denied by U.S. Supreme Court
    U.S. cert. den.
Certiorari Dismissed
    Cert. dis., Cert. dismissed
Certiorari Dismissed by U.S. Supreme Court
    U.S. cert. dis.
Certiorari Granted
    Cert. Gr.
Ceylon Appeal Cases
    A.C.
Ceylon Appeal Court Reports
    A.C.R.
Ceylon Criminal Appeal Reports
    Ceyl. Cr. App. R.
Ceylon Labour Law Journal
    Ceyl. Lab. L.J.
Ceylon Law Journal
    Ceyl. L.J., C.L.J.
Ceylon Law Recorder
    Ceyl. L. Rec., Ceyl. L.R., Ceylon Law Rec., Law Rec., Rec.
Ceylon Law Reports
    C.L.R.
Ceylon Law Review
    Ceyl. L. Rev., Ceylon L. Rev.
Ceylon Law Review and Reports
    Ceylon L.R.
Ceylon Law Society Journal
    Ceylon L. Soc. J.
Ceylon Law Weekly
    Ceyl. L.W.
Ceylon Legal Miscellany
    Ceyl. Leg. Misc.
Chaffe and Nathanson's Administrative Law, Cases and Materials
    Chaffee & Admin. Law

Chairman
Chmn.
Challis on Real Property
Challis
Chalmers' Colonial Opinions
Ch., Ch. (Eng.), Ch. Col. Op.
Chalmers on Bills of Exchange
Chalmers
Chalmers' Opinions, Constitutional Law
Chal. Op.
Chamber of Commerce
C.C.
Chamberlin's American Commercial Law
Cham. Com. Law.
Chambers and Parsons' Railroad Laws
Cham. & P.R.R.
Chambers and Pretty's Cases on Finance Act
Ch. & P.
Chambers' Chancery Jurisdiction as to Infants
Cham. Chy. Jur.
Chambers' Common Law
C.L. Chambers, C.L. Chamb.
Chambers' Digest of Public Health Cases
Chamb. Dig. P.H.C.
Chambers on Commons and Open Spaces
Cham. Com.
Chambers on Estates and Tenures
Cham. Est.
Chambers on Landlord and Tenant
Cham. L & T., Cha. L. & T.
Chambers on Leases
Cham. Leas.
Chambers on Rates and Rating
Cham. Rat.

Chambers Practice
Cham. Pr.
Chambers' Upper Canada Reports
Cham., Chamb., Cham. Rep., Chr. Rep., Chamber.
Champerty and Maintenance
Champ.
Champion's Cases, Wine and Beer-Houses Act
Champ.
Chance on Powers
Chance Pow., Chanc. Pow.
Chancellor
C, Chan., Chanc.
Chancellor of the Exchequer
Chanc. Ex.
Chancellor's Court
Ch.
Chancery
C, Chan., Chanc.
Chancery Appeal Cases, England
L.R. Ch. App., Cha. App., Ch.App.Cas.
Chancery Appeals
C.A.
Chancery Cases
C.C.
Chancery Cases Chronicle, Ontario
C.C. Chr., C.C. Chron.
Chancery Cases Tempore Talbot
Forester
Chancery Cases (2 Kenyon's Notes of King's Bench Cases), England
Keny. Ch.
Chancery Chambers' Reports, Ontario
Chamb. Rep.

Chancery Chambers Reports, Upper Canada
Chan. Chamb., Ch. Chamb., Ch. Chamb. (Can.)

Chancery Court
Ch. ct., Chan. Ct.

Chancery Court or Division
Ch.

Chancery Division
C.D.

Chancery Divisional Court
Ch. Div'l.Ct.

Chancery Practice
Ch. Pr.

Chancery Reports Tempore Car. I to Queen Anne
C.R.

Chancery Reports (2 Kenyon's King's Bench Reports), England
Keny. Chy. (2 Keny.)

Chancery Sentinel, New York
N.Y. Ch., Chan. Sentinel, Ch. Sent., Ch. Sent. (NY)

Chandler's American Criminal Trials
Chand. Cr. T., Chand. Cr. Tr., Chand. Crim. Tr.

Chandler's Reports (20, 38-44 New Hampshire)
Chand., Chand. (NH), Chandl.

Chandler's Wisconsin Reports
Chand., Chand. (Wis.), Chandl., Chand. R., Chandler, Chandler Wis.

Chaney's Michigan Digest
Ch. Dig., Cha. Dig.

Chaney's Reports (37-58 Michigan)
Chan., Chaney, Chaney (Mich.)

Channel Islands
C.I.

Chaplain
Chap.

Chapman's Addenda
Cha. Add.

Chapman's Practice of the Court of King's Bench
Cha. Pr.

Chappell and Shoard on Copyright
Chap. & Sh.

Chapter[s]
C, c., Cap., Ch., Chap., Chs.

Charging Party
CP

Charity[ies]
Char.

Charles
Cha., Chas.

Charley's Chamber Cases, England
Char.Cham.Cas., Charl. Cha. Cas., Charl. Chas.Ca., Charley Ch. Cas.

Charley's Pleading under the Judicature Acts
Charl. Pl.

Charley's Practice Cases, England
Char. Pr. Cas., Charl. Pr. Cas., Charley Pr. Cas.

Charley's Real Property Statutes
Charl. R.P. Stat.

Charlton's Georgia Reports
T.U.P.C., Charlt. T.U.P., Ch. R.M., Charl. R., Charlton's R., Charlton's (Rob't M.) Rep., R.M.C., Charl. R.M., Charl. (Ga.), Charlt., Charlt. R.M., R.M. Charlt. (Ga.), T.U.P. Chrlt., R.M.A., Ch. T.U.P., Charl. T.U.P., Charlt.

Charta Mercatoria
Char. Merc.

Chartae Antiquae
Chart. Antiq.

Charter K, United States Home Loan Bank Board
Ch. K.

Charter of the United Nations
U.N. Charter

Charter Party
C.P.

Chartered
Chtd

Chartered Accountant
C.A.

Chartered Institute of Patent Agents
C.I.P.A.

Chartered Insurance Institute
C.I.I.

Chartered Life Underwriter[s]
C. L. U.

Chartered Life Underwriter Journal
CLU J.

Chartered Property and Casualty Underwriter
C.P.C.U.

Chartered Surveyors Voluntary Service
C.S.V.S.

Chase on Stephens' Digest of Evidence
Chase, Steph. Dig. Ev.

Chase, Shields, Lambert, Baker and Shillito's Small Business Financing
SBF

Chase's Blackstone
Ch. Black., Chase's Bl.

Chase's United States Circuit Court Decisions
Chase Dec.

Chase's United States Circuit Court Decisions, edited by Johnson
John., John[s].

Chase's Statutes at Large, Ohio
Chase's St.

Chase's Trial (Impeachment) by the United States Senate
Chase Tr.

Chase's United States Circuit Court Decisions
Chase.

Chattel Mortgage
C/M

Cheever's Medical Jurisprudence for India
Cheev. Med. Jur.

Chemical
Chem.

Chemical Regulation Reporter, Bureau of National Affairs
Chem. Reg. Rep. (BNA)

Cherokee Case
Cher. Ca.

Chesapeake Case Report
Ches. Ca.

Chester County Reports
Chest., Ches. Co., Ches. Co Rep., Chest. Co., Chest. Co. Rep., Chester, Chester Co. (Pa.), Chester Co. Rep., Chest. Co. (Pa.)

Chester Palatine Courts
Booth

Cheves' South Carolina Equity Reports
Cheves Eq. (SC), Chev. Ch., Chev. Eq., Cheves L. (SC), Chev., Cheves.

Chicago
Chi.

Chicago Bar Association Record
Chi. B.A. Rec.

Chicago Bar Record
Chi. B. Rec., Chi. B. Record, Chicago B. Rec., Chicago Bar Rec.

Chicago Board Options Exchange Guide, Commerce Clearing House
  Chicago Bd. Options Ex. Guide (CCH)
Chicago-Kent University Law School
  Chi.-Kent
Chicago-Kent Law Review
  Chi-Kent L. Rev., Chi-Kent Rev., Chicago-Kent L. Rev., C.K. L.R., C.K.
Chicago Law Bulletin
  Chi. L.B., Chic. L.B., Chicago L.B.
Chicago Law Journal
  Chi. L.J., Chic. L.J., Chicago L.J., C.L.J.
Chicago Law Record
  Chi. L.R., Chicago L. Rec., Chicago L. Record (Ill.), Chic.L.R.
Chicago Law Times
  Chi. L.T., Chic. L.T., Chicago L.T.
Chicago Legal News
  Chicago Leg. News (Ill.), C.L.N., Chi. Leg. N., Chic. Leg. N.
Chicago Tribune
  Chi. Trib.
Chicano-Latino Law Review
  Chicano-Latino L. Rev.
Chicano Law Review
  Chicano L. Rev.
Chief Accountant
  C.A.
Chief Baron
  C.B.
Chief Baron of the Exchequer
  Ch. B. Ex., CB
Chief Court of Cochin, Select Decisions, India
  Coch. Ch. Ct.

Chief Executive Officer
  CEO
Chief Judge
  Ch. J.
Chief Judge in Bankruptcy
  C.J.B.
Chief Justice
  Ch. J., C.J.
Chief Justice of Nigeria
  C.J.N.
Chief Justice of the Common Pleas, Canada
  C.J.C.P.
Chief Justice of the Common (Upper) Bench, Canada
  C.J.U.B.
Chief Justice of the Court of Common Pleas
  Ch. C.P.
Chief Justice of the Federation, Nigeria
  C.J.F.
Chief Justice of the King's Bench
  C.J.K.B.
Chief Justice of the Queen's Bench
  C.J.Q.B., Ch. Q.B.
Chief Justices Law Reform Committee, Victoria, Australia
  V.C.J.C.
Chief of Naval Operations
  CNO
Chief Registrar's Reports
  C.R.R.
Child Poverty Action Group
  CPAG
Children's Court
  Child. Ct.
Children's Legal Rights Journal
  Child. Legal Rights J., Child. Legal Rts. J.
Children's Rights Reports
  Chil. Rts. Reports

China
Ch.
China Law Reporter
China L. Rep.
China Law Review
China L. Rev., China Law Rev.
China, People's Republic of
P.R.C.
Chinese
C
Chinese Law and Government
Chin. L. and Gov., Chin. Law &
Gov., Chinese L. & Govt.
Chinese Law Journal
Chinese L. J.
Chipman on the Law of Contracts
Chip. Cont.
**Chipman's Manuscript Reports,
New Brunswick**
Chip. Ms.
Chipman's New Brunswick Reports
Chip. W., Chip., N.B.R. Chip.
Chipman's Principles of Government
Chip. Gov.
Chipman's Vermont Reports
Chip., N. Chip., N. Chip. (Vt.),
N. Chipm., Chipm. V., Chip
(Vt.), Chip. D., D. Chip (Vt.), D.
Chipm., D. Chip.
Chitty and Hulme on Bills of Exchange
Chit. & H. Bills.
**Chitty and Patell's Supreme
Court Appeals**
Chitt. & Pat.
Chitty and Temple on Carriers
Chit. & T. Car.
Chitty (Junior) on Bills
Chit. Jun. B.
Chitty Law Journal
Chitty L.J.

Chitty on Bills
Ch. Bills., Chit. Bills, Chit. Bills
(or B. & N.)
Chitty.
Chitty on Carriers
Chit. Car.
Chitty on Commercial Law
Chit. Com. Law., Chitty, Com.
Law.
Chitty on Constables
Chit. Const.
Chitty on Contracts
Chit. Con., Chit. Cont., Chitty,
Contracts
Chitty on Medical Jurisprudence
Chit. Med. Jur.
Chitty on Pleading
Ch. Pl., Chit. Pl.
Chitty on the Game Laws
Chit. G.L.
Chitty on the Law of Descents
Chit. Des., Chit. Nat., Chitty
B.C.
Chitty's Bail Court Reports, England
Chitty BC (Eng.)
**Chitty's Commercial and General
Lawyer**
Chit. Lawy.
Chitty's Criminal Law
Ch. Cr. L., Chit. Cr. L., Chit. Cr.
Law, Chit. Crim. Law
**Chitty's Edition of Archbold's
Practice**
Chit. Arch. Pr., Chit. Archb. Pr.
**Chitty's Edition of Blackstone's
Commentaries**
Chit. Bl. , Ch. Black., Chi. Black
(See also Chitty's Blackstone),
Chit. Bl. Comm., Chitty, Bl.
Comm.

Chitty's Edition of Burn's Justice
  Chit. Burn's J., Ch. Burn's J.
  (See also Chitty's Burn's Justice)
Chitty's English Bail Court Reports
  Chit., Chit. R., Chitt., Chit. B.C.
Chitty's English King's Bench Reports
  Ch. R.
Chitty's English King's Bench Practice Reports
  Chit.
Chitty's Equity Digest
  Chit. Eq. Dig.
Chitty's Equity Index
  Chit. Eq. Ind., Chitty Eq. Ind.
Chitty's General Practice
  Chit. Gen. Pr., Chit. Pr.
Chitty's King's Bench Forms
  Chit. F.
Chitty's Law Journal
  Chitt. L.J., Chitty's L.J.
Chitty's Law of Apprentices
  Chit. Ap.
Chitty's Law of Nations
  Chit. L.of N., Chit. Nat.
Chitty's Mew's Supplement to Fisher's English Digest
  Chit. & M. Dig.
Chitty's Precedents in Pleading.
  Chit. Prec.
Chitty's Prerogatives of the Crown
  Chit. Prer.
Chitty's Stamp Act
  Chit. St. A.
Chitty's Statutes of Practical Utility
  Chit. St., Chit. Stat.
Chitty's Summary of the Practice of the Superior Courts
  Chit. Sum. P.

Choyce's Cases in Chancery, England
  C.C.C., Ch. Cas. Ch., Ch. Ca.
  Ch., Ch. Cas. in Ch., Cho. Ca.
  Ch., Cho. Ca. Ch., Choyce Cas.
  Ch., Choyce Cas. (Eng.)
Christian's Bankrupt Law
  Chris. B.L.
Christian's Charges to Grand Juries
  Chr. Ch.
Christie's Precedents of Wills
  Chr. Pr. W.
Chronica Juridicalia
  Chron. Jur.
Chronicle
  Chron.
Chronicles of the Divorce Courts
  Chron. Div. Cts.
Chronological
  Chron.
Chrostwaite's Pennsylvania Municipal Law Reporter
  Mun. L. Rep.
Church
  Ch.
Church Assembly Measure
  CAM
Church of England
  C. of E.
Church of Scotland, Acts of the General Assembly
  Act. Ass.
Churchill and Bruce on Office and Duties of Sheriff
  Church. & Br. Sh.
Chute's Equity under the Judicature Act
  Chute, Eq.
Cicero's De Oratore
  De Orat.
Cincinnati
  Cin., Cinc.

Cincinnati Bar Association Journal
Cin. B. Ass'n J., Cin. B.A. J.
Cincinnati Law Bulletin
Cin. L. Bull., Cin. Law Bul.,
Cinc. L. Bul.
Cincinnati Law Review
Ci. L.R.
Cincinnati Municipal Decisions
Cin. Mun. Dec.
Cincinnati Superior Court Decisions
Hosea's Rep.
Cincinnati Superior Court Reporter
Cinc. Sup. Ct. Rep., C.S.C.R.,
Cinc. Super., Cin. Sup. Ct. R.,
Cin. Super. Ct., Cin. R., Cin.
Rep., Cin. S.C. R., Cin. S.C.
Rep., Cin. Sup. Ct. Rep., Cin.
Super. Ct. Rep'r., Cin. Super.
(Ohio), Cinc. (Ohio), Cin. Sup.
Ct.
Cincinnati Weekly Law Bulletin
Weekly Cin. Law Bull.
Circa (about) (Lat.)
C.
Circuit
C, Cir., Circ.
Circuit Court
C.C., Cir.
Circuit Court Decisions
Cir. Ct. Dec.
Circuit Court Decisions, Ohio
Cir.Ct.Dec. (Ohio)
Circuit Court of Appeals, United States
Cir., C.C.A. (U.S.)
Circuit Court of Appeal[s] states of the United States
Cir. Ct. App.
Circuit Court of the United States
C.C. U.S.

Circuit Court Reports
C.C.R., Cir. Ct. R.
Circuit Court Reports, the United States
Hughes'
Circuit Court Rule
Cir. Ct. Rule
Circuit Courts of Appeals (prior to Sept. 1, 1948)
C.C.A.
Circuit Court[s], states of the United States
Cir. Ct.
Circuit Decision[s]
C.D.
Circuit Judge[s]
C.J.
Circular Orders, Northwestern Provinces, India
Cir. Ord. N.W.P.
Citation[s]
Cit.
Citation in Examiner's Decision
Ex.
Citator
Cit.
Citator and Indian Law Journal
Cit.
Cited
C.
Cited as Controlling
F (used in Shepard's Citations)
Cited in
Cit.
Citing
Cit.
City Court
C.C., City Ct.
City Court Reports
City Ct. R., City Ct. Rep.

City Court Reports, Supplement
C.C. Supp., City Ct. Rep. Supp., City Ct. Supp. (NY), City Ct. R. Supp.

City Hall Recorder (Ropers), New York City
C.H. Rec., City Hall Rec. (NY)

City Hall Reporter (Lomas), New York City
C.H. Rep., City H. Rep., City Hall Rep., City Hall Rep. (NY)

City of London Law Review
London L. Rev.

Civil
Civ., C.

Civil Aeronautics Administration
C.A.A.

Civil Aeronautics Authority
C.A.A.

Civil Aeronautics Authority Opinions
C.A.A. Op.

Civil Aeronautics Authority Reports
C.A.A.

Civil Aeronautics Board
C.A.B.

Civil Aeronautics Board Reports
C.A.B.

Civil Aeronautics Journal
C.A.J.

Civil Aeronautics Manual
CAM

Civil Air Patrol
CAP

Civil Air Regulations
C.A.R.

Civil and Commercial Code
CCom.C, CComm.C

Civil and Criminal Law Series, India
Civ. & Cr. L.S.

Civil and Military Law Journal, India
Civ. & Military L.J., Civ. and Mil. L.J.

Civil Appeals
Civ.

Civil Appeals, Texas
CATx.

Civil Aviation Licensing Act
C.A.L.A.

Civil Code
C.C., Civ. Code

Civil Code of Louisiana
Code La.

Civil Code of Practice
Civ. Code Prac., Civ. Code Practice

Civil Court
C.C., Civ. Ct.

Civil Court of Record
Civ. Ct. Rec.

Civil Defense Committee
CDC

Civil District Court
CDC, Civ. D. Ct.

Civil Justice Quarterly
Civ. Just. Q.

Civil Law
C.L.

Civil Liberties Docket
Civ. Lib. Dock., Civil Lib.Dock.

Civil Liberties Reporter
Civ. Lib. Rptr.

Civil Liberties Review
Civ. Lib. Rev., Civil Liberties Rev.

Civil Liberty
Civ. Lib.

Civil Litigation Reporter
Civ. Litigation Rep.

Civil Power
C.P.

Civil Practice Act
Civ. Prac. Act, C.P.A.
Civil Practice Law and Rules
Civ. Prac., C.P.L.R.
Civil Procedure
Civ. Proc., C.P.
Civil Procedure Reports, New York
Civ. Pr., Civ. Pr. Rep., Civ. Pro., Civ. Pro. R., Civ. Proc. R., Civ. Proc. Rep., C.P., Civ. Pro. Reports, Civil Pro. R., N.Y. Civ. Proc. Rep., N.Y.C.P.
Civil Procedure Reports, New Series, New York
Civ. Pro. R. (N.S.), Civ. Proc. Rep. N.S., Civ. Proc.R. (N.S.), Civ. Proc. (N.S.), C.P.R. (N.S.), C.P.R.C. (N.S.)
Civil Rights
Civ. R., Civ. Rights
Civil Rights-Civil Liberties
C.R.-C.L.
Civil Rights Digest
Civ.Rts.Dig.
Civil Servant[s]
C.S.
Civil Service
Civ. S., Civ. Serv., C.S.
Civil Service Arbitration Awards
C.S.A.A., C.S.A.B.
Civil Service Commission
C.S.C.
Civil Service Department
C.S.D.
Civil Service Pay Research Unit
C.S.P.R.U.
Civilian
Civ.
Civilian Conservation Corps
C.C.C.

Civilian Health and Medical Program of Uniformed Services
CHAMPUS
Claim[s]
Clm[s.], Cl[s.]
Claims Court
Cl Ct
Claims Court Reporter
ClC
Clancy's Treatise of the Rights, Duties and Liabilities of Husband and Wife
Clancy Rights, Clancy, Husb. & W.
Clarendon's Parliamentary Chronicle
Clar. Parl. Chr.
Clark
Cl.
Clark and Finnelly's House of Lords Cases (or Reports)
Cl. & F., C. & F., Cl. & Fin., Clark & Fin., Clark & F., Clark & F. (Eng.)
Clark and Finnelly's House of Lords Reports (New Series)
Clark & F. (N.S.), CC. & Fin. (N.S.), Clark & Fin. (N.S.), Clark. & F. (N.S.)
Clark, Cobb and Irwin's Georgia Code
Irwin's Code
Clark on Receivers
Clark, Receivers
Clarke and Hall's Cases of Contested Elections in Congress
C. & H. Elec. Cas., Clarke & H. Elec. Cas.
Clarke and Hall's Contested Elections in Congress
Cl. & H.

Clarke and Scully's Drainage Cases
Cl. & Sc. Dr. Cas., Clarke & S. Dr. Cas., C. & S.
Clarke on Bills and Notes
Cl. Bills, Clarke B.
Clarke on Extradition
Cl. Extr., Clarke Extr.
Clarke's Admiralty Practice
Clarke Adm. Pr.
Clarke's Bibliotheca Legum
Clarke Bib. Leg.
Clarke's Canada Insolvent Acts
Cl. Can. Ins.
Clarke's Chancery Reports, New York
Clarke's Chy. (N.Y.)
Clarke's Constable's Manual
Clarke Const.
Clarke's Criminal Law
Clarke Cr. L.
Clarke's Early Roman Law
Cl. R. L., Clarke Rom. L.
Clark's House of Lords Cases
H.L. Cas., H.L. Cas. (Eng.), H.L.
Clarke's Insolvent Acts
Clarke Insol.
Clarke's Insurance Law
Clarke Insur.
Clark's Jamaica Supreme Court Judgments
Clark
Clarke's New York Chancery Reports
Clarke Ch., Clarke Ch. (NY), Cl.R., Cl. Ch., Clarke
Clarke's Notes of Cases
Clarke
Clarke's Notes of Cases, in his "Rules and Orders," Bengal
Clarke Not., Clarke R. & O.

Clarke's (or Clerke's) Praxis Admiralitatis
Clarke Pr.
Clarke's Pennsylvania Reports
Clarke, Clarke (Pa.)
Clarke's Reports (1-8 Iowa)
Clarke, Clarke (Ia.)
Clarke's Reports (19-22 Michigan)
Clarke, Clarke (Mich.)
Clark's Appeal Cases, House of Lords
Cl. App., Clark App.
Clark's Colonial Laws
Cl. Col., Clark Col. Law
Clark's Digest, House of Lords Reports
Clark Dig., Clark's House of Lords Cases , Ho. Lords C., Ho. L. Cas., Ho. Lords Cas., H.L.C.
Clark's North Carolina Annotated Code of Civil Procedure
Clark's Code.
Clark's Pennsylvania Law Journal Reports
Clark (Pa.), Pa. L.J.R.
Clark's Reports (58 Alabama)
Clark, Clark (Ala).
Clark's Summary of American Law
Clark's Summary
Clark's Treatise on Elections
Cl. Elec.
Class Action Reports
Class Act. Rep.
Clause[s]
Cl[s.]
Claydon on Landlord and Tenant
Clay. L. & T.
Clay's Digest of Laws of Alabama
Clay's Dig.
Clayton on Conveyancing
Clay. Conv.

Clayton's English Reports, York Assizes
Clayt., Clayton, Clayton (Eng.)

Clayton's Pleas of Assize at York
Rep. York Ass.

Clayton's Reports and Pleas of Assizes at York
Clay.

Clayton's Reports of Assizes at Yorke
Rep. Ass. Y., York Ass., Yorke Ass.

CLE Journal and Register
CLE J. & Reg., (see Continuing Legal Education for CLE)

Clean Air Act
CAA

Clean Water Act
CWA

Clearinghouse Review
Clearinghouse Rev.

Cleary's Registration Cases, England
Cleary R.C., Cleary Reg. Cas.

Cleaveland on the Banking System
Cleve. Bank.

Cleaveland's Banking Laws of New York
Cleav.Bank. L.

Clemens on Corporate Securities
Clem. Corp. Sec.

Clemens' Reports (57-59 Kansas)
Clem.

Clerk
Clk.

Clerk of Session
C.S.

Clerk of the Peace
C.P.

Clerk of the Privy Council
C.P.C.

Clerk to the House of Commons
C.H.C.

Clerk to the Signet
C.S.

Clerke and Brett on Conveyancing
Clerke & Br. Conv.

Clerke's American Law and Practice
Clerke Am. L.

Clerke's Digest, New York
Clerke Dig.

Clerke's (or Clarke's) Praxis Admiralitatis
Clerke Pr., Clerke Prax.

Clerke's Rudiments of American Law and Practice
Clerke Rud.

Clerk's Assistant
Cl. Ass.

Clerk's Magazine
Clk's. Mag., Clk's. Mag., Clk's. Mag., Clk. Mag., Clk. Mag.

Clerks of Court
Clk. Ct.

Cleveland
Clev.

Cleveland Bar Association Journal
Clev. B. Assn. J., Clev. B.A. J., Clev. Bar Ass'n. J.

Cleveland Law Record
C. L. Rec., C.L.R., Clev. L. Rec., Cleve. L. Rec. (Ohio), Cleve. Law Rec.

Cleveland Law Register
C. L. Reg., Clev. L. Reg., Cleve. L. Reg., Cleve. L. Reg. (Ohio), Cleve. Law Reg.

Cleveland Law Reporter
C. L. Rep., Clev. L. Rep., Cleve.
L. Rep., Cleve. Law R., Cleve.
Law Rep., Cleve. L.R. (Ohio),
Clev. Law Rep., Clev. R., Cleve.
Rep.

Cleveland-Marshall Law School
Clev.-Mar.

Cleveland Marshall Law Review
Clev.-Mar. L. Rev., Cleve. Mar.
L. Rev., C.M. L.R., C.M.

Cleveland State Law Journal
Cleveland S. L.J.

Cleveland State Law Review
Clev. St. L. Rev., Clev. St. L.
Rev., Clev. St. L.R., C.M.,
C.S.L.R.

**Clevenger's Medical Jurispru-
dence of Insanity**
Clev. Insan.

**Clifford and Richard's English
Locus Standi Reports**
Clif & R., Clif & Rick., Clif. &
Rich., Cliff. & Rich., Cliff. &
Rick.

**Clifford and Stephen's English
Locus Standi Reports**
C. & S., Clif. & St., Clif. &
Steph., Cliff. & Steph.

**Clifford's United States Circuit
Court Reports**
Clif., Cliff., Cliff. (c.c.),

**Clifford's English Southwick
Election Cases**
Cliff., Clif. El., Clif. El. Cas.,
Clif. South. El., Clif. South. El.
Cas.,

Clifford's Probate Guide
Clif. Prob.

Clift's Entries, England
Clift

Clinical
Clin.

Clinton's Digest, New York
Clin. Dig.

Clode's Martial Law
Clode M.L.

Clow's Leading Cases on Torts
Clow L.C. on Torts.

**CLU Journal (Chartered Life Un-
derwriters)**
CLU J.

Cluskey's Political Text Book
Clusk. Pol. T.B.

Co-operative
Co-op.

**Co-operative Digest, United
States Reports**
Co-op. Dig.

Co-transfer Agent
Co-T/Agt.

Co-trustee
Co-Tr.

Coast Guard
CG

**Coast Guard Court Martial Man-
ual**
CGCMM

**Coast Guard Court of Military Re-
view**
CGCMR

Coast Guard Law Bulletin
C.G. L. Bull.

**Coast Guard Marine Safety Man-
ual**
M.S.M.

**Coast Guard Procurement Regu-
lations**
CGPR

Coast Guard Regulations
CGR

**Coast Guard Supplement to Man-
ual for Courts-Martial**
CGSMCM

Cobb on Slavery
Cobb. Slav.

Cobbett on Pawns and Pledges
Cobb. P. & Pl.

Cobbett's (afterwards Howell's) State Trials
Cobb.St.Tr., Cob. St. Tr.

Cobbett's Parliamentary History
Cobb. Parl. Hist.

Cobbett's Political Register
Cobb. Pol. Reg.

Cobbey's Nebraska Annotated Statutes
Cobbey's Ann. St.

Cobbey's Practical Treatise on the Law of Replevin
Cobbey, Repl.

Cobb's Georgia Digest of Statute Laws
Cobb, Dig.

Cobb's New Digest, Laws of Georgia
Cobb.

Cobb's Reports (121 Alabama)
Cobb.

Cobb's Reports (4-20 Georgia)
Cobb.

Cochin Law Journal
Cochin L.J., Co. L.J.

Cochin Law Reports
Cochin, Cochin L.R.

Cochrane's Hindu Law
Cochr. Hind. L.

Cochran's Nova Scotia Reports
Cochr., Coch., Coch. N.Sc., N.S.R. Coch.

Cochran's Reports (3-10 North Dakota)
Cochr., Cochran.

Cockburn and Rowe's English Election Cases
Cockb. & Rowe, Cockb. & R., Cock. & Rowe, C. & R., Cock. & R.

Cockburn on Nationality
Cock. Nat.

Cockburn's Charge in the Tichborne Case
Cock. Tich. Ca.

Cocke's Reports (14-15 Florida)
Cocke

Cocke's Reports (16-18 Alabama)
Cocke

Cocke's Common and Civil Law Practice of the U.S. Courts
Cocke U.S. Pr.

Cocke's Constitutional History of the United States
Cocke Const. Hist.

Coddington's Digest of the Law of Trade Marks
Codd. Tr. M.

Code
C.

Code Amendments
Code Am.

Code Civil France
C.C.

Code de Procedure Civile
Code P.C.

Code Municipal Quebec
Code M.

Code Napoleon
C.C., C.N., Code N., Code Nap.

Code of Alabama
Ala. Code

Code of Civil and Commercial Procedure
CC Com. Proc.

Code of Civil Procedure
C.C.P., CCProc., Code Civ. P., Code Civ. Pro., Code Civ. Proc., Code of Civ. Proc.

Code of Civil Procedure for Quebec
C.P.Q.

Code of Colorado Regulations
Colo. Admin. Code.

Code of Criminal Procedure
C. Cr. Pr., C. Crim. Proc., Code
Cr. Pro., Code Cr. Proc., Code
Crim. P., Code Crim. Proc.

Code of Federal Regulations
C.F.R.

Code of Georgia
Ga. Code

Code of Georgia Annotated
Ga. Code Ann.

Code of Iowa
Iowa Code

Code of Judicial Procedure
C. Jud. Proc.

Code of Justinian
Jus. Code, Code.

Code of Laws of South Carolina
S.C. Code

Code of Laws of South Carolina Annotated
S.C. Code Ann.

Code of Maryland Regulations
Md. Admin. Code

Code of Massachusetts Regulations
Mass. Admin. Code

Code of Practice
Code Prac., C.P.

Code of Procedure
C. Pr., Code Pro., Code Proc.,
C.P.

Code of Public General Laws
Code Pub. Gen. Laws

Code of Public Local Laws
Code Pub. Loc. Laws

Code of Theodosius
Code Theod.

Code of Virginia
Va. Code

Code Penal
Code P.

Code Reporter
C.R.

Code Reporter, New York
Co. R. (N.Y.), Co. Rep., Co.R.,
Code N.Y. Rep., Code R., Code
Rep.

Code Reporter, New Series, New York
Co. R.N.S., Code R.N.S., Code
R.N.S. (NY), C.R.N.S.

Code Reports, New York
Code R. (NY)

Codex
C.

Codex Juris Civilis
Cod. Jur. Civ.

Codex Justinian
Code., Cod.

Codex Theodosius
Cod. Theodos., C.Theod., Code
Theodos.

Codified Statutes
Cod. St.

Codifying Act of Sederunt
C.A.S.

Coe, Practice of the Judges' Chambers
Coe Ch. Pr.

Cofer's Kentucky Digest
C of. Dig.

Coffey's California Probate Decisions
Coffey's Prob. Dec., Cof., Cof.
Prob. Dec. (Cal.), Coff. Prob.,
Cof. Pro., Cof. Prob., Coffey, Coffey Probate Dec., Coffey
Prob.Dec., Coffey's Prob. Dec.

Coghlan's Epitome of Hindu Law Cases
Cogh. Epit.

Cohanand and Hemmerling on Inter Vivos Trusts
IVT

Cohen and Gobert on The Law of Probation and Parole
LLP
Cohen and Lee's Maryland Digest
C. & L. Dig.
Cohen's Admiralty Jurisdiction, Law, and Practice
Cohen, Adm. Law
Cohen's Criminal Appeals Reports
Crim. App. Rep.
Cohen's Nova Scotia Reports
N.S.R. Coh.
Coke on Littleton
Coke Lit., Litt., Co. Lit., Co. Litt., Co. Litt. (Eng.)
Coke's 4th Institute
Co. on Courts
Coke's Bankrupt Law
Co. B.L.
Coke's Compleat Copyholder
Co. Cop.
Coke's Courts (4th Institute)
Co. Cts.
Coke's English King's Bench Reports
Rep., Co., Coke, Coke (Eng.), Co. Rep., R., The Rep., Reports
Coke's Entries
Ent., Coke Ent., Co. Ent., Ent.
Coke's Institutes
Co., Coke Inst., Co. Inst., Co. inst. (Eng.), Inst.
Coke's Institutes, Epilogue to
Inst. Epil.
Coke's Pleadings
Co. Pl.
Coke's Pleas of the Crown (3d Institute)
Co. P.C.
Coke's 2d Institute (Magna Charta)
Co. M.C.

Coke's 3d Institute (Pleas of the Crown)
Co.P.C.
Colby on Mortgage Foreclosures
Col. Mort.
Colby's Criminal Law and Practice, New York
Col. Crim. Law
Colby's Massachusetts Practice
Col. Mass. Pr.
Colby's Practice
Colb. Pr.
Coldstream's Scotch Court of Session Procedure
Colds. Pr.
Coldwell's Reports (41-47 Tennessee)
Cold. (Tenn.), Coldwell, Col., Coldw., Coldw. (Tenn.)
Coldwell's Tennessee Supreme Court Reports
Cold.
Cole's Criminal Informations
Cole Cr. Inf.
Cole's Ejectment
Cole Ejec.
Cole's Particulars and Conditions of Sale
Cole Cond.
Colebrooke's Digest of Hindu Law
Cole. Dig.
Coleccion de los Decretos
Dec. Col.
Coleman and Caines' Cases (Common Law), New York
C. & C., Col. & Cai. Cas., Col. & Caines Cas. (N.Y.), Cole. & Cai. Cas., Col. & C. Cas., Colem. & C. Cas., Col. & Cai.,

Coleman's New York Cases
Col. Cas. (NY), Col. Cas.,
Colem. Cas., C. & C., Colem.,
Coleman, Cole. Cas. Pr., Cole.
Cas., Cole. Cases, C.C.

Coleman's Reports (99, 101-106, 110-129 Alabama)
Cole., Col.

Coler's Law of Municipal Bonds
Col. Mun. B.

Cole's Edition of Iowa Reports
Cole.

Cole's Law and Practice of Ejectment
Cole Eject.

Colin on French Interstate Successions
Col. Fr. Suc.

Collateral Trust
Coll. Tr.

Collect on Delivery
C.O.D.

Collectanea Juridica
Co. Jurid., Coll. Jurid.

Collection and Credit Agency
Coll. & Cr. A.

Collection des Causes Celebres, Paris, France
Coll.Caus.Cel.

Collection of Abstracts of Acts of Parliament
Smee.

Collections of Decisions of the European Commission of Human Rights
Eur. Comm'n H.R. Dec. & Rep.

Collective Bargaining Agreement
CBA

Collective Bargaining Negotiations and Contracts, Bureau of National Affairs
Collective Bargaining Negot. & Cont. (BNA)

Collective Measures Commission
CMC

Collector[s]
Coll.

College[s]
C

College Law Bulletin
Coll. L. Bull.

College Law Digest
Coll. L. Dig., College L. Dig.

College of Law, University of Utah
CLUU

Colleges and Universities
Coll. & U.

Colles' English Parliamentary (House of Lords) Cases
Colles, Colles (Eng.), Coll. P.C.,
Coll., Colles, P.C.

Collet on Torts and Measure of Damages
Coll. Tor.

Collier and Eaton's American Bankruptcy Reports
Coll. & E. Bank., Collier & E.
Am. Bank.

Collier and Miller on Bills of Sale
C. & M. Bills, Coll. & Mil.B.S.

Collier on Law of Contribution
Coll.Contr.

Collier's Bankruptcy Cases
Collier Bankr. Cas.Collier
Bank. C.B.C.

Collier's Bankruptcy Cases, Second Series
Collier Bankr. Cas. 2d

Collier's Law of Bankruptcy
Coll.Bank., Collier, Bankr.

Collier's Law of Mines
Col. Mines, Coll. Min.

Colliers on Patents
Coll. Pat.

Collins and Postlewaite, on International Individual Taxation
IIT

Collins, Lombard, Moses and Spitler's Drafting the Durable Power of Attorney
DDPA

Collinson on the Law of Idiots and Lunatics
Coll. Id. (or Lun.), Collin. Ind. (or Lun.)

Collinson on the Stamp Laws
Coll. St. L.

Collyer on Partnership
Colly. Part., Collyl. Partn., Coll. Part., Col. Part.

Collyer's Chancery Cases, England
Colly Ch. Cas. (Eng.), Coll., Coll. C.C.

Collyer's English Chancery Cases Tempore Bruce, V.-C.
Coll.N.C.

Collyer's English Chancery Reports
Coll.C.R.

Collyer's English Vice Chancellors' Reports
Colly.

Colombo Law Journal
Colombo L.J.

Colombo Law Review
Colombo L. Rev.

Colombo Plan
CENTO

Colonial
Col.

Colonial Law Journal, New Zealand
Col. L.J. N.Z., Col. L.J.

Colonial Law Journal Reports, New Zealand
C.L.J.

Colonial Lawyer
Colonial Law.

Colonial Office
C.O.

Colorado
C, Co., Colo.

Colorado Appeals Reports
Col. App.

Colorado Bar Association
Colo. B.A.

Colorado Constitution
Colo. Const.

Colorado Court of Appeals Reports
Colo. App., Co. A.

Colorado Decisions
Colo. Dec.

Colorado Decisions Supplement
Colo. Dec. Supp.

Colorado Decisions, Federal
Colo. Dec. Fed.

Colorado Industrial Commission Report
Colo. I.C.

Colorado Journal of International Environmental Law and Policy
Colo. J. Int'l Envtr. L. & Pol'y

Colorado Law Reporter
Col. L. Rep., Col. Law Rep., Colo. L.R., Colo. L. Rep., Colo. Law Rep.

Colorado Lawyer
Colo. Law.

Colorado Nisi Prius Decisions
Col. N.P., Colo N.P. Dec.

Colorado Public Utilities Commission Decisions
Colo. P.U.C.

Colorado Public Utilities Commission Report
Colo. P.U.C. Rep.

Colorado Register
Colo. Admin. Reg

Colorado Reports
Co., Col., Colo., Col.Rep.

Colorado Revised Statutes
Col. Rev. Stat.

Colorado Session Laws
Colo. Sess. Laws

Colorado State Bar Association. Report
Colo. St. B.A.

Colorado State Railroad Commission
Colo. S.R.C.

Colquhoun on Roman Civil Law
Colq. Civ. Law., Colq. C.L., Colq. Rom. Civ. Law, Colq. Rom. Law

Colquhoun on the Judicature Acts
Colq. Jud. A.

Colquit
Colq.

Colquit's Reports (1 Modern Reports)
Colq., Colquit.

Coltman's Registration Appeal Cases
Colt. Reg. Cas., Coltm., Colt. (Reg.Ca.)

Columbia
Col., Colom., Colum.

Columbia Business Law Review
Colum. Bus. L. Rev.

Columbia Human Rights Law Review
Col. Hum. R. L. Rev., Colum. Hum. Rts. L. Rev., Colum. Human Rights L. Rev.

Columbia Journal of Environment Law
Colum. J.Environ. L., Col. J. Environ. L., Colum. J. Env. L., Colum. J.Envt'l L.

Columbia Journal of Gender and Law
Colum. J. Gender & L.

Columbia Journal of International Affairs
Colum. J.Int'l Aff.

Columbia Journal of Law and Social Problems
Colum. J.L. & Soc.Prob., CJL, Col. J. L. & Soc. Probl., Colum. J.L. & Soc.Probs., Colum. J.Law & Soc.Prob., Columbia J. of L. and Soc.Probl.

Columbia Journal of Law and the Arts
Colum J L & Arts

Columbia Journal of Transnational Law
Col. J. Transnat'l L., Colum. J. Transnat. L., Colum. J.Transnat'l. Law, Columbia J. of Transnat. L.

Columbia Journal of World Business
Col. J. World Bus., Colum. J.World Bus.

Columbia Jurist
Colum. Jur., Colum. Jr.

Columbia Law Review
Cb.L.R., C.L.R., Col. L. Rev., Col. Law Review, Colum. L. Rev., C.R.

Columbia Law Times
Colum. L.T.

Columbia Society of International Law Bulletin
Colum. Soc. Int. L. Bull., Colum. Soc'y. Int'l. L. Bull.

Columbia Survey of Human Rights Law
Colum. Surv. Hum. Rts. L., Colum. Survey Human Rights L.

Columbia - VLA Journal of Law & the Arts
Colum. - VLA J. L. & Arts

Column[s]
Col., Cols.

Colvil's Manuscript Decisions, Scottish Court of Session
Colvil.

Colyar on Guarantees
Coly.Guar.

Comberbach's English King's Bench Reports
Comb., Com.

Comer's Forms of Writs
Com. Forms

Combined Transport Bill of Lading
FBL

Command Papers
Cd., Cmd., Cmnd.

Commanded
comd.

Comment[s]
Com.

Commentary[ies]
Comm.

Commerce
Comm., Com.

Commerce Clearing House, Inc.
CCH

Commerce Court
Comm. Ct.

Commerce, Science, and Transportation
C.S.T.

Commercial
Cml., com., com'l., Comm., comml.

Commercial and Legal Reporter
Com. & Leg. Rep.

Commercial and Municipal Law Reporter
Com. & Mun. L. Rep.

Commercial Agent
C.A.

Commercial and Industrial Bulletin
C.I.B.

Commercial Arbitration Yearbook
Y.B. Com. Arb.

Commercial Cases
Com. Cas.

Commercial Cases, Small Cause Court, Bengal
Rep. Com. Cas., Com. Cas. S.C.C.

Commercial Code
Com. C., Comm. C., Comm. Code

Commercial Law
Com. Law, Com. L.

Commercial Law Annual
Com. L.A., Com. Law Ann.

Commercial Law Association Bulletin
C.L.A. Bulletin

Commercial Law Journal
Com. L.J.

Commercial Law League Journal
Com. L. League J.

Commercial Law League of America
Com. L. L. A.

Commercial Law Reports
Comm. L.R.

Commercial Laws of the World
C.L.W.

Commission
Com.,Comm., Commiss., Commn.

Commission Decision
CD

Commission for Racial Equality
    C.R.E.
Commission Leaflets, American Telephone and Telegraph Cases
    C.L.
Commission of Human Rights
    H.R. Comm.
Commission on International Commodity Trade
    CICT
Commission on the Isle of Man Constitution. Report
    MacDermott Commission
Commission Telephone Cases Leaflets
    Comm. Tel. Cas.
Commissioned
    commd.
Commissioner[s]
    Commr., Comm., Com., Com'r., Commrs.
Commissioner Delegation Order
    CDO
Commissioner of Appeals
    Com. App.
Commissioner of Banking and Insurance
    Comr. of Bkg. and Ins.
Commissioner of Internal Revenue
    C.I.R.
Commissioner of Patents
    Com. Pat.
Commissioner of Patents and Trademarks
    Com'r Pat.
Commissioner of the Public Debt
    C.P.D.
Commissioners' Decisions (Patent)
    Com. Dec.

Commissioner's Decisions, U.S. Patent Office
    C.D.
Commissioner's Delegation Order
    Comm. Del. Order
Commissioners of the Great Seal
    Com. G.S.
Committee[s]
    Com., Comm.
Committee for Industrial Organization
    CIO
Committee for Privileges
    C. Priv.
Committee for Programme and Co-ordination
    CPC
Committee of Inspection
    C.I.
Committee of Senior Officials
    CSO
Committee of the Whole House
    C.W.H.
Committee on Political Education
    COPE
Committee on Professional Education of The Philadelphia Bar Association
    CPEPBA
Commodity Credit Corporation
    C.C.C.
Commodity Exchange Authority
    CEA
Commodity Futures Law Reporter, Commerce Clearing House
    Comm. Fut. L. Rep. (CCH), Commodity Futures L. Rep.
Commodity Futures Law Reports, Commerce Clearing House
    Comm. Fut. L. Rep. (CCH)

Commodity Futures Trading Commission
CFTC
Commodity Stabilization Service
CSS
Common
Com.
Common Bench
B, C.B., CB
Common Cause
Comm. Cause
Common Customs Tariff
C.C.T.
Common External Tariff
CET
Common Law
C.L., Com. Law
Common Law Chamber Reports
C.L. Ch., C.L. Chamb., C.L. Chamb. Rep.
Common Law Lawyer
Comm. L. Law.
Common Law Procedure
C.L.P.
Common Law Procedure Acts
C.L.P.A.
Common Law Reports
C.L.R., Com. L.Rep., C.L.(See also Dasent's Common Law Reports, England)
Common Law Reports, Canada
C.L.R. (Can.)
Common Law Reports, published by Spottiswoode
See also Spottiswoode's Common Law Reports
Common Market
Comm. Mkt.
Common Market Law Reports
Comm. Mkt. L. Rep., Comm. Mkt. L.R., C.M. L.R.

Common Market Law Review
C.M. L. Rev., C.M. L.R., Comm. Mkt. L. Rev., Common Mkt. L. Rev., Comm. Market L. Rev.
Common Market Reporter, Commerce Clearing House
CCH Comm. Mkt. Rep., C.M.R., Comm. Mkt. Rep.
Common Market Reports, Commerce Clearing House
Common Mkt. Rep. (CCH)
Common Orders
C.O.
Common Pleas
C.P.
Common Pleas Division, English Law Reports
Com. P.Div., Com. Pl. Div., C.P. Div., C.P. (Eng.), C.P.Div. (Eng.), Com. Pl.
Common Pleas Practice Cases, England
Cas. Pra. C.P., Cas. Prac. C.P., Cas. Pr. C.P., Cas. Pr.
Common Pleas Reporter
Com. P. Reptr., C.P. Rept., Com. Pl. R. (Pa.), Com. Pl. Reptr., C.P. Rep.
Common Pleas Reports, Upper Canada
C.P.U.C., Com. Pl.
Common Professional Examination
C.P.E.
Common Scold
Com.S.
Common Serjeant
C.S.
Commonwealth
Com., Commonw., Commw., Com'w'th.
Commonwealth Act
Com. Act, Commonw. Act

Commonwealth Acts of Australia
Austl. C. Acts (See also Acts of
the Australian Parliament and
Acts of the Parliament of the
Commonwealth of Australia)
Commonwealth Arbitration Reports, Australia
Comm. A.R., Commw. Arb.,
Commw. Art., C.A.R.
Commonwealth Court
Commw. Ct.
**Commonwealth International
Law Cases**
C.I.L.C.
Commonwealth Judicial Journal
Comm. Jud. J., Commw. Jud. J.
Commonwealth Law Bulletin
C.L.B., Comm. L.B., Commw.
L.B.
Commonwealth Law Reports
Commonw. L. Rep., C.L.R.,
C.L.R. Aust., Comm. L.R.,
Commw. L.R.
Commonwealth Law Review
Commonw. L. Rev.
**Commonwealth of Australia Acts
of Parliament**
Austl. Acts., Acts Austl. P.,
Austl. Acts P. (See also Acts of
the Australian Parliament and
Acts of the Parliament of the
Commonwealth of Australia)
**Commonwealth of Puerto Rico
Rules and Regulations**
P.R.R. & Regs.
**Commonwealth Public Service
Arbitration Reports**
C.P.S.A.R.
Commonwealth Record
Cwlth. Record
Commonwealth Secretariat
Comm. Sec., Commw. Sec.

Communication[s]
Com., Comm.
Communications and the Law
Com. & L., Com. & Law.,
Comm. & L., Commun. & Law
Communications Satellite Corporation
C.O.M.S.A.T.
**Communications Workers of
America**
CWA
Community Affairs
Com. Affrs.
Community Enterprise Programme
C.E.P.
Community Property
Community Prop.
Community Property Journal
Comm. Prop. J., Community
Prop. J.
Community Relations Service
C.R.S.
Community Services Administration
CSA
Company
Co.
**Company and Securities Law
Journal**
Company & Sec. L.J.
Company Cases
Com. Cas., Comp. Cas.
Company Law Journal
Comp. L.J.
Company Lawyer
Comp. Lawy., Company Law
Comparative
Comp.
Comparative Administrative Science Quarterly
Comp. Admin. Sci. Q.

Comparative and International Law Journal of South Africa
Comp. & Int. L.J. S. Afr., Comp. & Int. L.J. South Africa, Comp. & Int. L.J. South Africa, Comp. & Int'l. L.J. S.Afr., C.I. L.J. S.A.

Comparative Juridical Review
Comp. Jur. Rev., Comp. Jurid. Rev.

Comparative Labor Law
Comp. Lab. L., Comp Labor L, Comp. Lab. L.J.

Comparative Law Review. The Japan Institute of Comparative Law, Tokyo, Japan
Comp. L. Rev. (Japan Inst.), Comp. L. Rev.

Comparative Law Series, U.S. Bureau of Foreign and Domestic Commerce General Legal Bulletin
Comp. L.S., Comp. L. Ser.

Comparative Law Yearbook
Comp. L. Yb.

Compare
Comp., Cp.

Comparisons in Law and Monetary Comments
Comparisons in L. & Monet. Com.

Compendium of Laws of Armed Forces
Comp. Armed Forces

Compensation
Comp.

Compensation Review
Comp. Rev.

Compilation
Comp.

Compile
Comp.

Compiled
Comp.

Compiled Laws
C.L., Comp. Laws

Compiled Statutes
Comp. St., Comp. Stat., C.S.

Compiler
Comp.

Complaint Docket
C.D.

Compleat Lawyer
Compleat Law.

Complete Attorney
C. Atty., Com. Att.

Complete Solicitor
C. Sol, Comp. Sol.

Compliant
Compl.

Composer
Comp.

Composition with Creditors
Comp. Cred.

Compounding Crimes
Comp. Crimes

Comprehensive Employment and Training Act
CETA

Compton, Meeson, and Roscoe's English Exchequer Reports
C.M. & R.

Comptroller General
Comp. Gen.

Comptroller General's Opinion
Comp. Gen. Op., C.G.O.

Comptroller Treasury Decisions
Comptr. Treas. Dec.

Computer[s]
Computer

Computer-Assisted Legal Research
CALR

Computer Law and Practice
Computer L. & Prac.

Computer Law and Tax Report
Computer L. & T. Rep., Computer L. & Tax
Computer Law Association
CLA
Computer Law Journal
Computer/L. J.
Computer Law Service Reporter
C.L.S.R., Computer L. Serv. Rep. (Callaghan)
Computer Lawyer
Computer Law.
Computers and Law
Comp. & Law, Comput. & Law, Computers & L.
Comstock on Executors
Comp. Ex.
Comstock on Guardian and Ward
Com. G. & W.
Comstock's Digest of the Law of Dower
Com. Dow.
Comstock's Reports (1-4 New York Court of Appeals)
Coms., Comst.
Comyn on Landlord and Tenant
Com. L. & T.
Comyn on Law of Usury
Com. Us., Comyn, Usury
Comyn's Digest, by Day
D.C.D.
Comyn's Digest of the Laws of England
Com. Dig., Comyns' Dig.
Comyns' English King's Bench Reports
Comyns., Com., Comyn., Com. Rep.
Comyn's Law of Contracts
Com. on Con., Com. Con., Com.
Concentrated Employment Program
CEP

Conclusion
concl.
Condemnation
c., Condem.
Condensed Ecclesiastical Reports
Cond. Ecc. R., Cond. Eccl.
Condensed English Chancery Reports
Cond. Eng. Ch., Cond. Ch. R.
Condensed English Exchequer Reports
Cond. Ex. R., Cond. Exch. R.
Conders' Highway Cases
Cond H.C.
Conditional Sale Chattel Mortgage Reporter
Condit. Sale
Condominiums and Cooperative Apartments
Condomin.
Conductor Generalis
Cond. Gen.
Condy's Edition of Marshall on Insurance
Cond. Marsh.
Conference
Conf.
Conference of American Legal Executives
CALE
Conference of Commissioners on Uniformity of Legislation in Canada
Conf. Comm. Uniformity Legis.
Conference of Teachers of International Law
Conf. Teach. Int'l L.
Conference on Charitable Foundations Proceedings, New York University
N.Y.U. Conf. on Char. Found. Proc., Conf. on Char. Found. N.Y.U. Proc.

Conference on Personal Finance Law, Quarterly Report
Conf. Pers. Fin. L.Q.R.

Conference on Security and Co-operation in Europe (Helsinki Accords)
CSCE

Conference Proceedings, Inter-American Bar Association
Conf. Proc. Inter-Amer. Bar Assoc.

Conference Report
Conf. Rept.

Conference Reports by Cameron and Norwood, North Carolina
Conf., Conference (NC), Conf. R.

Conferre (compare)
cf.

Confirmatio Chartarum
Conf. Chart.

Confirmation
Conf.

Confirming
Conf.

Conflict of Laws
Conf. L.

Conflict Prevention Center
CPC

Congdon's Digest
Cong. Dig.

Congdon's Mining Laws of California
Cong. Min. L.

Congregational
Congl.

Congress
C, Cong.

Congress of Industrial Organizations
CIO

Congress of World Unity
CWU

Congressional
Cong., Congl.

Congressional Budget Office
CBO

Congressional Committee Prints
Comm. Print

Congressional Debates
Cong. Deb.

Congressional Digest
Cong. Dig.

Congressional Election Cases
Cong. El. Cas.

Congressional Globe
Cong. Gl., Cong. Globe

Congressional Index
Cong. Index

Congressional Quarterly Weekly Reports
Cong. Q. W. Repts.

Congressional Record
Cong. Rec.

Congressional Research Service
C.R.S.

Conkling's Admiralty
Conk. Adm.

Conkling's Executive Powers
Conk. Ex. Pow.

Conkling's Iowa Justice of the Peace
Conk. J.P.

Conkling's Treatise on Jurisdiction and Practice of the United States Courts
Conk. Treat. (or U.S.Pr.)

Connected Case
cc (used in Shepard's Citations)

Connecticut
C, Conn., Ct.

Connecticut Bar Association
CBA

Connecticut Bar Association Record
CBA Rec.

Connecticut Bar Journal
    C. B.J., Con. B.J., Conn. Bar J.,
    Conn. B.J.
Connecticut Circuit Court Reports
    Cir., Conn. Cir. Ct., Conn.Cir.
Connecticut Compensation Commissioners, Compendium of Awards
    Conn. Comp. Com.
Connecticut Constitution
    Conn. Const.
Connecticut Decisions
    Conn. Dec.
Connecticut General Statutes
    Conn. Gen. Stat.
Connecticut General Statutes Annotated
    C.G.S.A., Conn. Gen. Stat. Ann.
Connecticut Journal of International Law
    Conn. J. Int'l L.
Connecticut Law Journal
    Conn. L.J., Conn. Sup.
Connecticut Law Review
    Con. L. Rev., Con. L.R., Conn.
    L. Rev., Connecticut L. Rev.
Connecticut Legislative Service
    Conn. Legis. Serv.
Connecticut Probate Law Journal
    Conn. Prob. L. J.
Connecticut Public Acts
    Conn. Pub. Acts
Connecticut Public and Special Acts
    Conn. Acts
Connecticut Public Utilities Commission
    Conn. P.U.C.
Connecticut Railroad Commissioners
    Conn. R.C.

Connecticut Reports
    Conn., Conn. Reports, Ct.,
    Conn. R., Conn. Rep., Connecticut R., Connecticut Rep., Connect.Rep.
Connecticut Reports, by Day
    Day (Conn.)
Connecticut Special Acts
    Conn. Spec. Acts, Conn. Spec.
    Acts
Connecticut State Agencies Regulations
    Conn. Agencies Reg.
Connecticut State Board of Labor Relations
    SBLR
Connecticut Supplement
    Conn. S., Conn. Sup., Conn.
    Supp., C.S.
Connecticut Workmen's Compensation Decisions
    Conn. Comp. Dec.
Connell on Parishes
    Con. Par.
Connoly's New York Reports
    Con.
Connoly's New York Surrogate Reports
    Conn. Surr., Connoly., Conn.,
    Conn. Surr. Rep., Connoly Sur.
    Rep., Connoly Surr. Rep.,
    Con.Sur., Cy.
Connor and Lawson's Irish Chancery Reports
    Con. & L., C. & L., Connor & L.,
    Con. & Law.
Connor and Simonton's South Carolina Digest
    C. & S. Dig.
Connor and Simonton's South Carolina Equity Digest
    Con. & Sim.

Connor's Irish Digest
  Con. Dig.
Conover's Digested Index
  Con. Dig. Ind.
Conover's Reports (16-153 Wisconsin Reports)
  Conover, Conov., Con.
Conroy's Custodian Reports
  Conr., Con. Cus.
Conservative Party
  C
Conservator
  Cons.
Conservatorship
  Consv.
Consistorial Decisions, Scotland, by George Ferguson, Lord Hermand
  Ferg.
Consolato del Mare
  Cons. del M.
Consolidated
  Cons., Consol.
Consolidated General Orders in Chancery
  Cons. Ord. in Ch., Consolid. Ord.
Consolidated Omnibus Budget Reconciliation Act
  COBRA
Consolidated Statutes
  Con. St., Con. Stat., C.S.
Consolidated Statutes of British Columbia
  C.S.B.C.
Consolidated Statutes of Canada
  C.S.C.
Consolidated Statutes of Lower Canada
  C.S.L.C.
Consolidated Statutes of Manitoba
  C.S.M.

Consolidated Statutes of New Brunswick
  C.S.N.B.
Consolidated Statutes of Upper Canada
  C.S.U.C.
Consolidated Treaty Series
  C.T.S.
Consortium Newsletter
  Consort. Newsl.
Conspiracy
  Consp.
Constable
  Cons.
Constitution
  Cons., Const., constn.
Constitution of the United States
  Const. U.S.
Constitution of Virginia
  C.V.
Constitutional
  Cons., Const., constl.
Constitutional and Parliamentary Information
  Const. & Parliam. Inf.
Constitutional Commentary
  Const. Commentary, Const Comm.
Constitutional Instrument
  C.I.
Constitutional Law
  Const. L.
Constitutional Law Journal
  Const. L.J.
Constitutional Reports
  Const. Rep.
Constitutional Reports, South Carolina, printed by Treadway
  Const. S.C., Const.

Constitutional Reports, South Carolina New Series, Printed by Mills
Const. S.C.N.S., Const. N.S., Cont.

Constitutional Reports, South Carolina, Vol. 1, by Harper
Const.

Constitutional Review
Const. Rev.

Constitutiones Othoni (found at the end of Lyndewood's Provinciale)
Const. Oth.

Constitutiones Tiberii
C.T.

Constitutions and Laws of the American Indian Tribes
C.L.A.I.T.

Constitutions of African States
Const. Afr. States

Constitutions of Dependencies and Special Sovereignties
Const. Dep. & Sp. Sov.

Constitutions of Nations
Const. Nations

Constitutions of the Countries of the World
Const. World

Construction
Const., Constr.

Construction Lawyer
Construction Law

Construction Litigation Reporter
Co LR

Const's Edition of Bott's Poor Law Cases
Bott P.L. Const., Const Bott, Const.

Consuetudines Feudorum; or, the Book of Feuds
F, Consuet. Feud.

Consul
Cons., Cos.

Consules
Coss.

Consult[ant, ing]
Cons.

Consumer
Consumer

Consumer and Borrower Protection
Cons. & Bor. Pro.

Consumer and Commercial Credit, Prentice-Hall
Cons. & Com. Cred. (P-H)

Consumer Credit Guide, Commerce Clearing House
Cons. Cred. Guide., Consumer Cred. Guide (CCH)

Consumer Federation of America
CFA

Consumer Finance Law Quarterly Report
Consumer Fin. L.Q. Rep.

Consumer Law Today
Cons. L. Today

Consumer Price Index
CPI

Consumer Product Safety Act
CPS Act

Consumer Product Safety Commission
CPS Commission, CPSC

Consumer Product Safety Guide, Commerce Clearing House
Consumer Prod. Safety Guide (CCH), Consumer Prod. Saf'y Guide

Consumer Product Warranty Acts
Cons. Prod. Warr.

Consumer Protection Advisory Committee
C.P.A.C.

Consumerism
Consumerism
Consumers' Association
C.A.
Containing
Cont.
Contemporary
Contemp.
Contemporary Drug Problems
Contemp. Drug Prob.
Contemporary Law Review
Cont. L. Rev.
Content[s]
Cont.
Contested Election Cases
Cont. Elect. Case.
Continent
Cont.
Continental
Cont.
Continental United States
CONUS
Continuance
Contin.
Continuation of Rolle's Reports (2 Rolle), England
Con.
Continue
Cont.
Continued
Cont.
Continuing Legal Education
CLE
Continuing Legal Education for Wisconsin
CLEW
Continuing Legal Education in Colorado, Inc.
CCLE
Continuing Legal Education of New Mexico, Inc.
NMCLE

Continuing Legal Education of the Bar, University of California Extension
CCEB
Continuing Legal Education, University of Kentucky College of Law
KCLE
Continuing Legal Education, University of Montana
CLEM
Continuing Legal Education, University of Oklahoma Law Center
OCLE
Contra (against) (Lat.)
Cont.
Contract Adjustment Board
CAB
Contract Appeals Decisions, Commerce Clearing House
Cont. App.Dec. (CCH)
Contract Cases Federal
C.C.F., Cont. Cas. Fed.
Contract Settlement Appeal Board
C.S.A.B.
Contractors' Bond
Cont. Bond
Contracts
Cont.
Contre (against, versus) (Fr.)
c.
Contribution
Contrib.
Control of Banking, Prentice-Hall
Cont. of Banking (P-H)
Controlled Materials Plan Regulation
CMP Reg.
Control[s]
Cont.

Controverted Elections Judges
Cont. El.
Convention[s]
conv.
Convention of the Estates of Scotland
Conv. Est.
Convention on the Contract for the International Carriage of Goods by Road (Geneva, 19 May 1956)
CMR
Coventry's Mortgage Precedents
Cov. Mort.
Conversion
conv.
Convertible
conv.
Conveyancer
Conv., Convey
Conveyancer and Property Lawyer
Conv. & Prop. Law.
Conveyancer and Property Lawyer, New Series
conv. & prop law (N.S), Conv. & Prop. Law (N.S.), C.P.L., Conv. (N.S.)
Conveyancer's Assistant
Conv. Asst.
Conveyancers' Year Book
Conv. Y.B.
Conveyancing
Conv.
Conveyancing Review
C.R., Conv. Rev.
Convicted Poacher
C.P.
Coode on the Written Law
Coode Wr.L.
Coode's Legislative Expression
Coode Leg. Exp.

Cook on Corporations
Cook, Corp.
Cook on Stock, Stockholders, and General Corporation Law
Cook, Stock, Stockh. & Corp.Law.
Cooke and Alcock's Irish Kings Bench Reports
C. & A., Cooke & Al.(Ir.), Coo. & Al.
Cooke and Alcocke's Irish Reports
Co. & Al., Cooke & A., Cooke & Al., Cooke & Alc.
Cooke and Harwood on Charitable Trusts
C. & H. Char. Tr.
Cooke and Harwood's Charitable Trust Acts
Cooke & H.Ch.Tr., Coo. & H.Tr.
Cooke on Agricultural Tenancies
Cooke Agr. T.
Cooke on Life Insurance
Cooke, Ins.
Cooke on Rights of Common
Cooke Com.
Cooke on the Agricultural Holdings Act
Cooke Agr. Hold.
Cooke on the Law of Defamation
Cooke Def.
Cooke's Act Book of the Ecclesiastical Court of Whalley
Cooke
Cooke's Admiralty Cases, Quebec
Cook Adm.
Cooke's Agricultural Tenancies
Coo. Agr.T.
Cooke's Bankrupt Laws
Cooke B.L., Coo. Bankr.
Cooke's Enfranchisement of Copyholds
Coo. Cop.

Cooke's English Common Pleas Reports
Cooke C.P.

Cooke's Inclosure Act
Cooke I.A., Coo. I.A., Cooke. Incl. Acts

Cooke's Law of Copyhold Enfranchisement
Cooke Cop.

Cooke's Law of Defamation
Coo. Def.

Cooke's New York Highway Laws
Cooke High.

Cooke's Practical Register of the Common Pleas
Cooke Pr. Reg.

Cooke's Practice Cases, English Common Pleas
Rep. Cas. Pr., Cooke (Eng.), Cooke Pr. Cas., Cooke

Cooke's Reports (3, Tennessee)
Cooke, Cooke's Rep., Cooke (Tenn.)

Cook's Lower Canada Admiralty Court Cases
Co. A.

Cook's Penal Code, New York
Cook's Pen. Code.

Cook's Vice Admiralty Reports
Cook Adm., Cook V. Adm., Cook Vice-Adm.

Cooley Law Review
Cooley L. Rev.

Cooley on Constitutional Limitations
Cooley, Const.Lim., Cooley, Const.Limit., Cool. Con. Lim.

Cooley on Taxation
Cool. Tax., Cooley, Tax, Cooley, Tax'n.

Cooley on Torts
Cool. Torts, Cooley, Torts.

Cooley's Constitutional Law
Cool. Con. Law, Cooley, Const.Law.

Cooley's Edition of Blackstone's Commentaries
Cool. Black., Cooley, Bl. Comm.

Cooley's Michigan Digest
Cool. Mich. Dig.

Cooley's Reports (5-12 Michigan)
Cooley.

Coopers' Effect of a Sentence of a Foreign Court of Admiralty
Coop. For. Ct.

Cooper's English Cases (or Reports) Tempore Cottenham
Coop.t.Cott. (Eng.), Cooper t. Cott., Cooper, Coop. & Cott., Coop. C. Cas., Coop.C.C., & Cooper, G. Coop., G. Cooper (Eng.), Coop. Temp.Cottenham, Coop.

Cooper's (C.P.) English Chancery Practice Cases
C.P. Cooper, Coop., Cooper, Coop. Cr. Pr., C.P.C., Coop. Ch. (Eng.), Coop. P.C., Coop. Pr. C., Cooper Pr. Cas., Cooper Pr. Cas. (Eng.)

Cooper's English Chancery Reports Tempore Brougham
Coop., Coop.t. Brougham (Eng.), Coop. Temp. Brougham, Coop. Temp. Brough., Coop. & Br., Coop. & Brougham, Cooper.

Cooper's English Chancery Reports (or Cases) Tempore Eldon
Coop., Coop. temp. Eldon, Cooper, Coop. & Eld., Coop. & Eldon, Cooper t. Eldon, C.P. Cooper, Coop., Cooper, Coop. Cr. Pr., C.P.C., Coop. Ch. (Eng.), Coop. P.C., Coop. Pr. C., Cooper Pr. Cas., Cooper Pr. Cas. (Eng.), Coop. & Eld. (Eng.)

Cooperative
   Coop.
Cooperative Association
   Coop. Asso.
Cooperative Corporations
   Coop. Corp.
Cooperative State Research Service
   CSRS
Cooper's Equity Digest
   Coop. Eq. Dig.
Cooper's Equity Pleading
   Coop. Eq. Pl.
Cooper's Florida Reports (21-24 Florida)
   Cooper
Cooper's Institutes of Justinian
   Coop. Inst., Coop. Inst. Just.,
   Cooper, Just. Inst.
Coopers' International Union of North America
   CIA
Cooper's Judgment
   Coop. Judg.
Cooper's Law of Libel
   Coop. Lib.
Cooper's Medical Jurisprudence
   Coop. Med. Jur.
Cooper's Public Records of Great Britain
   Coop. Rec.
Cooper's Select Cases Tempore Brougham
   Sel. Cas.t.Br.
Cooper's Select Cases Tempore Eldon
   Coop. Sel. Ca.
Cooper's Select Early Cases
   Coop. Sel. E.C.
Cooper's Tennessee Chancery Reports
   Coop. Ten.Chy., Coop. Tenn.
   Ch., Coop. Chy., Cooper Tenn.

Ch., Cooper, Tenn. Ch., Coop.
   Ch., Coop., Cooper Ch.
Coordinator
   Coord.
Coote on Mortgages
   Coo. Mort., Coote, Coote Mor.
Coote's Admiralty Practice
   Coote Adm.
Coote's Ecclesiastical Court Practice
   Coote Ecc. Pr.
Coote's Law of Landlord and Tenant
   Coote L. & T.
Coote's Practice of the Court of Probate
   Coote Pro. Pr.
Coote's Probate Court Practice, Edited by Tristram
   Coote & Tr. Pr. Pr.
Cope's Reports (63-72 California)
   Cope.
Copinger on Title Deeds
   Cop. Tit. D.
Copinger's Copyright
   Cop. Cop.
Copinger's Index to Precedents
   Cop. Ind. Pr.
Coppe's Manual for Courts-Martial
   Copp. Ct. Mar.
Copp's Land Office Decisions
   Copp Land.
Copp's United States Mining Decision
   Copp. Min. Dec.
Copp's United States Public Land Laws
   Copp. Pub. Land Laws, Copp.
   Pub. L.L., Copps. L.L.
Copyright
   Copy.

Copyright and Literary Property
Copy. & Lit. P.

Copyright Bulletin
Copy. Bull

Copyright Decisions
Copy. Dec.

Copyright Law Decisions, Commerce Clearing House
Copyright L. Dec. (CCH)

Copyright Law Reporter, Commerce Clearing House
Copyright L. Rep. (CCH)

Copyright Law Symposium (American Society of Composers, Authors and Publishers)
Ascap Sympos., Copyright L. Symp. (ASCAP), A.S.C.A.P. Cop.L.Symp., A.S.C.A.P. Copyright L.Symp., Copyright L.Sym. (ASCAP)

Copyright Society of U.S.A. Bulletin
Bull. Cop. Soc., Bull. Copyright Soc'y., Bull. Cr. Soc., Bull. C'right Soc'y., Copy. Soc. Bull.

Copyright World
Copyright World

Copyright; Monthly Review of the International Bureau for the Protection of Intellectual Property (BIRPI), Geneva, Switzerland
Copyright

Coran Nobis and Allied Statutory Remedies
Coran N.

Corbett and Daniell's Election Cases, England
Corb. & D, Corb. & Dan., C. & D.

Cord on Legal and Equitable Rights of Married Women
Cord Mar. Wom.

Cordery on Solicitors
Cord. Sol.

Cornell International Law Forum
Cornell Int'l L.Forum, Cornell Internat. L.J.

Cornell International Law Journal
Cornell Int'l. L.J.

Cornell Law Forum
Cornell L.F.

Cornell Law Journal
Cornell L.J.

Cornell Law Quarterly
Cor. L.Q., Corn L Q, Cornell L.Q., C.L.Q.

Cornell Law Review
Cor., Cornell L. Rev.

Cornell Law School
CLS

Corner's Forms of Writs on the Crown Side
Corn. Wr.

Corner's Queen's Bench Practice
Corn. Pr.

Cornish on Purchase Deeds
Corn. Deeds., Corn. Pur. D., Cornish, Purch. Deeds

Cornish on Remainders
Corn. Rem.

Cornish on Uses
Corn. Us.

Cornwall's Table of Precedents
Cornw. Tab.

Cornwell's Digest
Corn. Dig.

Coroners
Coron.

Coroner's Society Cases
Cor. Soc. Cas.

Corporate
Corp.

Corporate and Business Law Journal
Corp. & Bus. L.J.
Corporate Counsel Reporter
Corp. Couns. Rep.
Corporate Counsel Review
Corp. Counsel Rev.
Corporate Counsel Review Journal of the Corporate Counsel Section, State Bar of Texas
Corp. Counsel Rev. J. Corp. Counsel Section, St. B. Tex.
Corporate Counsel Weekly, Bureau of National Affairs
Corp. Couns. Wkly. (BNA)
Corporate Depositary
Corp. Dep.
Corporate Management Tax Conference
Corp. Mgt. Tax Conf.
Corporate Practice Commentator
Corp. Prac. Com., Corp. Prac. Comm., Corp. Prac. Comment., Corp. Pract. Comment.
Corporate Practice Review
Corp. Prac. Rev., Corp. Pract. Rev.
Corporate Practice Series, Bureau of National Affairs
Corp. Prac. Ser. (BNA)
Corporate Reorganization and American Bankruptcy Review
Corp. Reorg. & Am. Bank. Rev.
Corporate Reorganization Reporter
CRR
Corporate Reorganization[s]
Corp. Reorg.
Corporate Trust[s]
C.Tr.
Corporate Trustee[s]
Corp. Tr.

Corporation[s]
Corp.
Corporation Forms, Prentice-Hall
Corp. Forms (P-H)
Corporation Guide, Prentice-Hall
Corp. Guide (P-H)
Corporation Journal
Corp. J.
Corporation Law Guide
Corp. L. Guide
Corporation Law Review
Corp. L. Rev.
Corporation-Management Edition, Prentice-Hall
Corp. Mgmt.Ed. (P-H)
Corporation, Prentice-Hall
P-H Corp.
Corporation Tax
C.T.
Corporations and Associations
Corp. & Ass'ns.
Corporations Code
Corp. C
Corpus (body) (Lat.)
C., cor.
Corpus Juris
C.J., Corp. Jur.
Corpus Juris Annotations
C.J. Ann.
Corpus Juris Canonici
C.J. Can., Corp. Jur. Can.
Corpus Juris Canonique
Corp. Jus. Canon.
Corpus Juris Civilis
C.J. Civ., C.J.C., Corp. Jur. Civ.
Corpus Juris Germanie
Corp. Jur. Germ.
Corpus Juris Secundum
C.J.S.
Correction
Cor., Correc.
Corrective
Cor.

Correspond
  Corr.
Correspondances Judiciaires (French)
  Cor. Jud.
Correspondence
  Corr.
Correspondent
  Corr.
Corresponding
  Corr.
Corvinus' Elementa Juris Civilis
  Corvin. El., Corvin. Et.
Corvinus' Jus Feodale
  Corv. Jus.
Cory on Accounts
  Cory Acc.
Coryton on Copyrights
  Cory. Cop.
Coryton on Patents
  Cor. Pat., Cory. Pat.
Coryton on Stage Rights
  Cory. St. R.
Coryton's Reports
  Cory., Coryton
Cosmetic[s]
  Cosm.
Cost Accounting Standards Guide, Commerce Clearing House
  Cost Accounting Stand. Guide (CCH), Cost Acc'g. Stand. Guide
Cost and Freight
  C.A.F., C. & F.
Cost-Plus-a-Percentage-of-Cost
  CPPC
Cost-Plus-Fixed-Fee
  CPFF
Cost-Plus-Incentive-Fee
  CPIF
Cost, Freight and Insurance
  C.F. & I., C.I.F.

Cost, Insurance, Freight and Commission
  C.I.F. & C.
Cost, Insurance, Freight and Exchange
  C.I.F.E.
Cost, Insurance, Freight and Interest
  C.I.F.I.
Cost, Insurance, Freight, Commission and Interest
  C.I.F.C.I.
Costa Rica
  Costa R.
Cotenancy and Joint Ownership
  Coten. & Jt. O.
Cothran's Annotated Statutes of Illinois
  Coth. Stat.
Cottenham English Chancery Reports
  Cott.
Cottonian Manuscripts (British Museum)
  Bibl. Cott., Cott. Mss.
Cotton's Abridgment of the Records
  Cot. Abr.
Coulston and Forbes on Waters
  Coul. & F. Wat.
Council
  Coun.
Council for Economic Mutual Assistance
  CEMA
Council of Economic Advisers
  CEA
Council of Europe
  C. of E., CE, CENTO
Council of Europe, Debates of the Consultative Assembly
  Eur. Conslt. Ass. Deb.

Council of Europe, Debates of the Consultative Assembly
Eur.Consult. Ass. Deb.
Council of Legal Education
C.L.E.
Council of Ministers
COM
Council of Ministers, European Community, European Union
COM
Council on Environmental Quality
CEQ
Council on International Economic Policy
CIEP
Council on Legal Education for Professional Responsibility. Newsletter
Council Legal Educ. Prof. Resp. Newsl.
Council on Tribunals
C.O.T., C.T.
Counsel
Couns.
Counsellor, New York City
Counsellor.
Counsellors' Magazine
Couns. Mag.
Counterclaim
Countcl.
Counterfeiting
Counterf.
Counties
Cty.
Counties Palatine
Co. Pal.
County
Co., Cty.
County Council
C.C.
County Council Cases
County Co. Cas.

County Court
C.C., Co. Ct., County Ct., Cty. Ct.
County Court Appeals
C.C.A.
County Court Cases
Co. Ct. Cas.
County Court Chronicle
Co.Ct.Ch.
County Court Judge
C.C.J.
County Court Reports, Pennsylvania
Co. Ct. Rep. (Pa.)
County Court Rules Committee
CCRC
County Courts and Bankruptcy Cases
County Cts. & Bankr. Cas.
County Courts Chronicle
C. Cts. Chr., County Cts. Chron., Cty. Ct. Chron., Count. Cts. Ch., Count. Cts. Chron., C.C. Chron., Co. Ct. Chr.
County Courts Reporter (in Law Journal), England
C.C. Rep.
County Courts Reports
C.C.R., County Cts. Rep., Co. Ct. R., Cty. Ct. R., Co. Ct. Rep.
County Judge's Court
County J.Ct.
County Reports
County R.
Couper's Judiciary Cases
C.J.C.
Couper's Justiciary Reports
Coup., Cou., Coup. Just. Couper
Cour d'Appel (French)
App.
Cour de Cassation (French)
Cass.

Court[s]
  C, Cot., Ct.(s)

Court Decisions Relating to the National Labor Relations Act
  Ct. Dec. N.L.R.A., Ct. D.

Court Journal and District Court Record
  Court J. & Dist. Ct. Rec.

Court Management Journal
  Court Mgt. J., Ct. Mgmt. J.

Court-Martial Report, Army Cases
  C.M.

Court-Martial Reports of the Judge Advocate General of the Air Force
  C.M.R. (Air Force), CMR JAG AF., CMR (AF)

Court Martial Reports of the Judge Advocate General of the Armed Forces and the Court of Military Appeals
  CMR JAG & US Ct. of Mil. App.

Court-Martial Reports, Air Force Cases
  A.C.M.

Court Martial Reports, Citators and Indexes
  CMR, Cit. & Ind.

Court Martial Reports, Coast Guard Cases
  CGCM

Court-Martial Reports, Judge Advocates General of the Armed Forces and the Court of Military Appeals
  C.M.R.

Court-Martial Reports, Navy Cases
  N.C.M.

Court-Martial, European Theater of Operations
  C.-M.E.T.O.

Court of Appeal
  C.A., Cs. App.

Court of Appeal for East Africa Digest of Decisions of the Court
  E. Afr. Ct. App. Dig.

Court of Appeal in Chancery
  Ch.App.Cas.

Court of Appeal Reports
  Rep. in C.A.

Court of Appeals
  C.A., Ct. of App., Ct. App.

Court of Appeals, Parish of Orleans, Louisiana
  La. App. (Orleans)

Court of Appeals Reports, New Zealand
  C.A., Ct. App. N.Z., Ct. Rep. N.Z.

Court of Arches
  C.A., Arch.

Court of Chancery
  Ch.

Court of Civil Appeals
  Civ. App.

Court of Claims Act
  Ct. Cl. Act.

Court of Claims Reports
  Ct. Cl. N.Y., C.Cl.

Court of Claims Rules
  Ct. Cl. R.

Court of Claims Trial Division
  Ct Cl Tr Div

Court of Common Pleas
  C.C.P., C.P., Ct. Com. Pl., Ct. Com. Pleas, Ct. of Com. Pleas

Court of Criminal Appeal[s]
  C.C.A., Ct. Crim. App., Crim. App.

Court of Crown Cases Reserved
  C.C.R.

Court of Customs and Patent Appeals
Ct. Cust. & Pat. App.
Court of Customs and Patent Appeals Reports
C.C.P.A., C.A.
Court of Customs Appeals
Ct. Cust. App.
Court of Customs Appeals Reports
C.A., Ct. Cust. App.
Court of Delegates
Deleg.
Court of Divorce and Matrimonial Causes
D.
Court of Error
Ct. Err.
Court of Errors and Appeals
Ct. Err. & App., Ct. Errors and App., Ct. of Er. and Appeals
Court of Exchequer
Ex., C.E.S., Exch.
Court of General Sessions
Ct. Gen. Ses., Ct. Gen. Sess.
Court of Human Rights
H.R. Court
Court of International Trade
Ct. Int'l Trade
Court of International Trade Reports
C.I.T.
Court of International Trade Rules
C.I.T.R.
Court of Justice of the European Communities
C.J.E.C., E.C.J.
Court of Justiciary
Ct. Just.
Court of Justiciary Cases
S.C.,J.

Court of Military Appeals
C.M.A.
Court of Military Appeals Reports
C.M.A.
Court of Military Review
C.M.R.
Court of Probate
C.P., P.
Court of Review Decisions, Ratcliffe and M'Grath, New South Wales
R. & McG. Ct. of Rev.
Court of Scotland, Act of the General Assembly
Act. Ass.
Court of Session, Scotland
Ct. of Sess., C. Sess., C.S., Ct. Sess.
Court of Session Cases, Scotland
C. of S. Ca., Court Sess. Ca., C.S.C., Ct. Sess. Cas., S.C.
Court of Session Cases, Fifth Series, Scotland
C. of S. Ca. 5th Series.
Court of Session Cases, First Series, Scotland
C. of S. Ca. 1st Series
Court of Session Cases, Fourth Series, Scotland
C. of S. Ca. 4th Series
Court of Session Cases, House of Lords, Scotland
S.C.H.L., H.H.L
Court of Session Cases, Second Series, Scotland
C. of S. Ca. 2d Series.
Court of Session Cases, Third Series, Scotland
C. of S. Ca. 3rd Series.
Court of Special Appeals
Ct. of Sp.App.
Court of Special Sessions
Ct. Spec. Sess.

Court of [General, Special] Sessions
Ct. [Gen., Spec.] Sess.
Court Order
Ct/O.
Court Practice Institute
CPI
Court Review
Court R., Ct. Rev.
Court Rolls of Ramsey Abbey
Ault.
Court Trust
C.T.
Courtenay and Maclean's Scotch Appeals
Cour. & Macl., Court. & Macl.
Courts and Judicial Proceedings
Cts. & Jud. Proc.
Court's Bott's Poor Laws, England
Court
Courts-Martial Appeal Court
C.-M.A.C.
Courts-Martial Manual
M.C.M.
Coutlee's Digest, Canada Supreme Court
Cout. Dig.
Coutlee's Supreme Court Cases, Canada
Coutlee
Coutlee's Unreported Cases, Canada
Coutlee Unrep. (Can.), Coutlee, Cout.
Coutumes de Normandy
Cout. de N.
Coutumes de Paris
Cout. de P.
Covenant[s]
Coven.

Coventry's and Hughes' Digest of the Common Law Reports
C. & H. Dig., Cov. & H. Dig.
Coventry's Common Recoveries
Cov. Rec.
Coventry's Conveyancers' Evidence
Cov. Conv. Ev.
Cowan on Warrants of Attachment
Cow. Att.
Cowan's Land Rights in Scotland
Cow. L.R.
Cowdery's Law Encyclopaedia
Cowd. L. Enc.
Cowell's East India Digest
Cow. Dig.
Cowell's Institutiones Juris Anglicani
Cow. Inst.
Cowell's Interpreter
Cow. Int., Cowell.
Cowell's Law Dictionary
Cow. Dic., Cowell.
Cowen's Criminal Digest
Cow. Cr. Dig.
Cowen's Criminal Reports
Cow. Crim. (NY), Cow. Cr.,
Cow. Cr. R., Cow. Cr. Rep.
Cowen's New York Criminal Law
Cow. Cr. L.
Cowen's New York Justice of the Peace
Cow. Just., Cow. J.P., Cow. Tr.
Cowen's New York Reports
Cow., Cow. N.Y.
Cowen's Reports
Cow. R.
Cowper's Cases, England
Cowp. Cas.
Cowper's English King's Bench Reports
Cow., Cowp., Cowp. (Eng.)

Cowperthwaite on Insanity in its Medico-Legal Relations
Cowp. Ins.
Cox and Atkinson's Registration Appeal Cases
Cox & Atk.
Cox and Saunders on Criminal Law Consolidation Acts
Cox & S.Cr. L.
Cox on Joint Stock Companies
Cox J.S. Comp.
Cox on the Law and Science of Ancient Lights
Cox Anc. L.
Cox's Advocate
Cox Adv.
Cox's Common Law Practice
Cox C.L. Pr.
Cox, Macrae and Hertslet's English County Court Reports
Mac. & H., Cox & M'C., C.M. & H., Cox, M. & H., Cox, McC. & H., Cox, Mc. & H.
Cox's Principles of Punishment
Cox Pun.
Cox's Registration and Elections
Cox Elect.
Coxe's Reports (1 New Jersey)
Coxe
Coxe's Translation of Guterbach's Bracton
Coxe Bract.
Cox's American Trade Mark Cases
Am. Tr. M. Cas., Cox Am. T.M. Cas., Cox Tr. M. Ca., Cox Tr. M. Cas., Cox Am. T. Cas.
Cox's English County Court Cases
Cox C.C., Cox Cty. Ct. Cas., Cox Cty. Ct. Ca.
Cox's Criminal Law Digest, England
Cox Cr. Dig.

Cox's Crown Cases, England
Cox C.C.
Cox's ed. of Peere Williams' Reports, England
Cox P.W.
Cox's English Chancery Cases
Cox Ch., Cox Ch. Cas. (Eng.), Cox
Cox's English Chancery Reports
Cox, Cox Ch., Cox Ch. Cas. (Eng.), Ch. Pr.
Cox's English Criminal Cases
Cox, Cox Cr. Cas., Cox C.C., Cox Crim. Cas., C.C.C., Cox Cr. Ca.
Cox's English Equity Cases
Cox Eq., Cox Eq. Cas.
Cox's Institutions of the English Government
Cox Gov., Cox Inst.
Cox's Joint Stock Cases, England
Cox J.S. Cas., Cox Jt. Stk.
Cox's Magistrate Cases, England
Cox Mag. Ca., Cox M.C.
Cox's Manual of Trade-Mark Cases
Cox Man. Tr. M., Cox Tr. M.
Cox's Practice of Registration and Elections
Cox Reg.
Cox's Questions for the Use of Students
Cox. Ques.
Cox's Reports (25-27 Arkansas)
Cox
Crabb on Real Property
Crabb R.P.
Crabb on the Common Law
Crabb C.L., Crabb, Com. Law
Crabb on the Law of Real Property
Crabb, Real Prop.

Crabbe's United States District Court Reports
Crab., Crabbe, Crabbe

Crabb's Digest of Statutes
Crabb Dig. Stat.

Crabb's English Synonyms
Crabb, Eng.

Crabb's History of the English Law
Crabb Eng. L., Crabb, Hist. Eng. Law

Crabb's Precedents in Conveyancing
Crabb Prec.

Crabb's Technological Dictionary
Crabb, Technol. Dict., Techn. Dict.

Crabb's Treatise on Conveyancing
Crabb Conv.

Craig and Phillips' English Chancery, Reports
Craig & Ph., C. & P., Cr. & Ph., Craig & Ph. (Eng.), Craig & P.

Craig on Trees and Woods
Craig Tr. & W.

Craig (Sir T.), Jus Feudale
Cr., Craig Jus. Feud., Craigius, Jus Feud.

Craigie, Stewart and Paton's Scottish Appeal Cases
Craig. & St., Craig. St. & Pat., Craig. S. & P., C.S. & P., Cr.S. & P., Cr. & St., Paton., Craig. St. & Pat.

Craigie, Stewart and Paton's House of Lords Appeals from Scotland
Pat. App.

Craig's Etymological, Technological, and Pronouncing Dictionary
Craig, Dict.

Craig's Practice
Craig Pr.

Craik's English Causes Celebres
Craik C.C.

Cranch (William) United States Circuit Court Reports
Cr. C.C. Rep., Cran.C.C.R., Cranch C.C.Rep., Cr. C.C., Cr., Cra., Cra.C.C., Cranch (C.Ct.), Cranch C.C., Cranch R.

Cranch's District of Columbia Reports (1-5 District of Colombia)
Cranch, Cranch D.C.

Cranch's Patent Decisions
Cranch Pat. Dec., Cr. Pat. Dec.

Cranch's (William) United States Supreme Court Reports (vols. 5-13 United States Reports)
Cran., Cr., Cranch, Cran. Rep., Cranch Rep.

Cranenburgh's Criminal Cases
Crane. C.C.

Crane's Reports (22-29 Montana)
Crane

Crary's New York Practice, Special Pleading
Crar. Pr., Cra. N.Y. Pr.

Crawford and Dix's Abridged Cases, Ireland
Ab.Ca., Craw. & D. Ab. Cas., Craw. & D., Abr. Cas., Craw. & D. Abr. Cas., Cr. & Dix Ab. Ca., C & D. A. C., Crawf. & D. Abr. Cas., Ir. Cir. Crt., Cr. & Dix Ab. Cas.

Crawford and Dix's Circuit Cases, Ireland
Craw. & Dix, Crawd. & Dix, Craw. & D., Craw. & D.C.C., Crawf. & D., C. & D., C. & D.C.C., Cr. & Dix., Ir. Cir. Cas., Cr. & Dix C.C.

Crawford and Dix's Criminal Cases, Ireland
Crawf. & Dix
Crawford County Legal Journal
Craw Co.Leg.J. (Pa.), Crawford Co. Leg. Jour.
Crawford's Reports (53-69, 72-101 Arkansas Reports)
Craw., Craw (Ark)
Creasy on International Law
Creas. Int. L.
Creasy's Ceylon Reports
Creasy.
Creasy's Colonial Constitutions
Creas. Col. Const.
Creasy's Rise and Progress of the English Constitution
Creas. Eng. Cons.
Credit
Cr.
Credit Card
Letter Cred., Cred. C., Cred. Card
Creditor
Cr.
Creditors' Bill
Cred. B.
Creighton Law Review
Creighton L. Rev.
Cresswell's English Insolvency Cases
Cress. Ins. Ca., Cress., Cress. Ins. Cas., Cress. Insolv. Cas.
Crime
Crime
Crime and Delinquency
Crime & Delin., Crime & Delin'cy, Crim. & Delin., Crime & Del., Crime & Delinq.
Crime and Delinquency Abstracts
Crime & Delin'cy Abst.

Crime and Delinquency Literature
Crime & Delin'cy Lit.
Crime and Justice
Crime & Just.
Crime and Social Justice
Crim. & Soc. Just., Crime & Soc. Just.
Criminal
Cr., Crim.
Criminal Act
Cr. Act.
Criminal Appeal Reports, England
Cr. App. R., Cr. App. Rep., Crim. App. R., C. App. R., C.A.R., Crim. App., Crim. App. (Eng.)
Criminal Appeals
Cr. App.
Criminal Case and Comment
Crim. Case & Com.
Criminal Code
Cr. Code., Crim. Code
Criminal Code and Code of Criminal Procedure, Kansas
Kan. Crim. Code & Code of Crim. Proc.
Criminal Code of Practice
Cr. Code Prac.
Criminal Conspiracy
Crim. con.
Criminal Conversation
Crim. con.
Criminal Conversion
Crim. con.
Criminal Defense
Crim. Def.
Criminal Injuries Compensation Board
Crim. Inj. Comp. Bd.

Criminal Investigation Department
 C.I.D.
Criminal Justice
 Cr. Just., Crim. Just.
Criminal Justice and Behavior
 Crim. Just. & Behavior
Criminal Justice Ethics
 Crim. Just. Ethics
Criminal Justice Journal
 Crim. J.J., Crim. Just. J.
Criminal Justice Newsletter
 Crim. Just. Newsl.
Criminal Justice Quarterly
 Crim. Just. Q.
Criminal Justice Review
 Crim. Just. Rev.
Criminal Law
 Crim. Law
Criminal Law Audio Series
 C.L.A.S.
Criminal Law Bulletin
 Crim. L. Bull.
Criminal Law Forum
 Crim. L.F.
Criminal Law Journal
 Crim. L.J., C.L.J., C.L.J., Cr.
 L.J.
Criminal Law Journal of India
 Crim. L.J. I., Crim. L.J. Ind.
Criminal Law Journal Reports
 India Crim. L.J.R.
Criminal Law Magazine
 Cr. L. Mag., Crim. L. Mag., Cr.
 Law Mag.
Criminal Law Magazine and Reporter
 Crim. L. Mag. & Rep., Criminal
 L. Mag. & Rep.
Criminal Law Quarterly
 Crim. L.Q., Criminal L.Q.
Criminal Law Recorder
 Cr. Law Rec., Crim. L. Rec.

Criminal Law Reporter
 Cr. Law Rep., Crim. L. Rptr.,
 Crim. L. Rptr., Crim. L. Rep.,
 Crim. L. Rep., Cr.L.R.
Criminal Law Reports by Green
 Crim. Law Reps. (Green), Green
 Cr. Rep., Green Cr. L. Rep.,
 Green. Cr. Law R., Green Crim.
 Reports
Criminal Law Review
 Crim. L. Rev., Crim. L.R.,
 Crim.L.Rev. (England)
Criminal Law Revision Committee
 C.L.R.C., Crim. Law Rev.Cttee.,
 Crim. L.R.C.
Criminal Lawyer, India
 Cr.L.
Criminal Office
 C.O.
Criminal Practice
 Cr. Prac.
Criminal Practice Act
 Cr. Prac. Act.
Criminal Practice Law Review
 Crim. Prac. L. Rev.
Criminal Procedure
 Cr. Proc., Crim. Pro., Crim.
 Proc., Cr.P.
Criminal Procedure Act
 Cr. Proc. Act.
Criminal Recorder
 Crim. Rec., Crim. Rec., Crim.
 Rec.
Criminal Reports, Canada
 Crim. R., Crim. Rep., Cr. Rep.,
 Can. Crim., C.R.
Criminal Reports, New Series, Canada
 C.R.N.S., Crim. Rep. (N.S.)
Criminal Reports, Third Series, Canada
 C.R. (3d)

Criminal Rulings, Bombay
Cr. Rg.
Criminal Statute[s]
Cr. St.
Criminologist
Criminol.
Criminology
Criminol., Criminology
Cripps' Church and Clergy Cases
Cripps, Ch. & Cl. Cas., Cripp
Ch. Cas., Cripps Cas., Cripp's
Ch. Cas., Cripps Church Cas.
Cripps' Church Law
Cripp Ch.L. (or Ecc.L.)
**Cripps' Compulsory Acquisition
of Land**
Cripp Comp.
**Cripps' Law Relating to Church
and Clergy**
Cripp Ch.L. (or Ecc.L.)
Critchfield's Reports (5-21 Ohio)
Critch., Critch (Ohio St.)
Critical Path Method
CPM
**Criticised (soundness of decision
or reasoning in cited case criti-
cised for reasons given)**
c., (Used in Shephard's Cita-
tions)
Criticized in
Crit.
Criticizing
Crit.
**Crockford and Cox's English
Maritime Law**
Mar. Cas.
**Crockford's English Maritime
Law Reports (or Cases)**
Crockford, Mar. L.C., Mar. L.R.
**Crocker on Sheriffs and Consta-
bles**
Crock. Sh.

**Crocker on the Duties of Coro-
ners in New York**
Crock. Cor.
**Crocker's Notes on Common
Forms**
Crock. Forms
**Crocker's Notes on the Public
Statutes of Massachusetts**
Crock. Notes
**Croke's English King's Bench Re-
ports**
Cro., Croke
**Croke's English King's Bench Re-
ports Tempore Elizabeth**
Cro. Eliz. (Eng.), Cro. Cas., R.1
Cro.
**Croke's English King's Bench Re-
ports Tempore Charles I**
R.3 Cro., Cro. Cas., Chs. Cas.
(Eng.), Cro. Cas.
**Croke's English King's Bench Re-
ports Tempore James I**
R.2 Cro., Cro. Jac., Cro. Jac.
(Eng.), Cro. Cas.
**Crompton and Jervis's English
Exchequer Reports**
Cr. & J., Cromp. & J., Cromp. &
J. (Eng.), C. & J., Cromp. &
Jerv., Cromp. & Jer.
**Crompton and Meeson's English
Exchequer Reports**
Cromp. & M., Cromp. & M.
(Eng.), C. & M., Cr. & M.,
Cromp. & Mees.
**Crompton. Meeson and Roscoe's
English Exchequer Reports**
Cr. M. & R., Cromp. M. & R.,
Cromp. M. & R. (Eng.)
**Crompton's English Exchequer
Reports**
Cromp. Exch. R., Cromp. Ex. R.

Crompton's Jurisdiction of Courts
Cromp. Cts., Cromp. J.C.,
Cromp. Jur.

Crompton's Office of a Justice of the Peace
Crom., Cromp. Just.

Crompton's Rules and Cases of Practice
Cromp. R. & C.Pr.

Crompton's Star Chamber Cases
Cromp., Crompt.

Crosley on Wills
Cros. Wills

Cross-claim
Cross-cl.

Cross on Lien and Stoppage in Transitu
Cross Lien

Croswell's Collection of Patent Cases, United States
Crosw. Pat. Ca., Crosw. Pat. Cas.

Crounse's Reports (3 Nebraska)
Crounse.

Crown
Cr.

Crown Agent
C.A.

Crown Cases
C.C.

Crown Cases Reserved
Cr. Cas. Res., C.C.R.

Crown Circuit Assistant
Cr. C.A.

Crown Circuit Companion
Crown C.C., Cr. Cir. Comp.

Crown Land Cases
Crown L.C.

Crown Land Reports
C.L.Q.

Crown Lands Law Reports, Queensland
Queensl. Cr. Lands L.R.,
C.L.L.R., Q.C.L.L.R., C.L.R.

Crown Office
C.O.

Crown Office Rules
C.O.R.

Crown Pleas
C.P.

Crowther's Ceylon Reports
Crowth., Crowther., Crow.

Cruise on Dignities
Cru. Dign.

Cruise on Titles of Honor
Cru. Titl.

Cruise on Uses
Cru. Us.

Cruise's Digest of the Law of Real Property
Cru. Dig., Cru., Cruise Dig.,
Cruise's Dig.

Cruise's Fines and Recoveries
Cru.Fin.

Crump on Marine Insurance
Crump Ins., Crump Mar. Ins.

Crump on Sale and Pledge.
Crump S. & Pl.

Crump's Practice Under the Judicature Acts
Crump Jud. Pr.

Crumrine's Reports (116-146 Pennsylvania)
Crumrine

Cucin,'s Medical Malpractice: Handling Plastic Surgery Cases
MMPSC

Cudden on the Copyhold Acts
Cudd. Copyh.

Cujacius' Opera, quae de Jure fecit, etc.
Cujacius

Cullen's Bankrupt Law
    Cull. B.L.
Culpabilis (guilty) (Lat.)
    Cul.
Cum Testamento Annexo (with will annexed) (Lat.)
    C.T.A.
Cumberland
    Cum.
Cumberland Law Journal
    Cumberland L.J. (Pa.), Cumb., Cumb. Law Jrnl.
Cumberland Law Review
    Cum. L. Rev., Cumb. L. Rev., Cumberland L. Rev.
Cumberland-Samford Law Review
    Cum.-Sam., Cum. Sam. L. Rev., Cumb.-Sam. L. Rev., Cumberland-Samford, Cumberland-Samford L.Rev.
Cumberland's Law of Nature
    Cumb. Nat.
Cummins and Dunphy's Remarkable Trials
    Cum. & Dun. Rem. Tr., Rem. Tr.
Cummins' Reports
    Cummins
Cummuns' Manual of Civil Law
    Cum. Civ. L.
Cumulative
    Cum.
Cumulative Bulletin, Internal Revenue Bureau, Treasury
    C.B., Cum. Bull.
Cumulative Index
    C.I.
Cumulative Pocket Parts
    Cum. P.P.
Cumulative Supplement
    Cum. Supp.
Cunningham on Hindu Law
    Cun. Hind. L.

Cunningham on Simony
    Cun. Sim.
Cunningham's Dictionary
    Cun. Dict.
Cunningham's English King's Bench Reports, Tempore George II
    Cun., Cunn., Cunningham, Cunningham (Eng.), Ann.
Cunningham's Law Dictionary
    Cun. L.D.
Cunningham's Law of Notes and Bills of Exchange
    Cun. Bill. Exch., Cun. Bills
Cunningham's Maxims and Rules of Pleading
    Cun. Pl.
Curia Advisare Vult (court will be advised)
    Cur. adv. vult, C.A.V.
Curia (court) (Lat.)
    CUR, Cur.
Curia Phillippica
    Cur. Phil.
Curia Regis (King's Court) (Lat.)
    C.R.
Curia Regis Rolls
    Cr.R., Cur. Reg. R.
Current Cases
    C.C.
Current Comment and Legal Miscellany
    Cur. Com., Current Com. & Leg. Mis.
Current Court Decisions
    Current Ct. Dec.
Current Indian Cases
    Cur. I.C., Cur. Ind. Cas., C.I.C.
Current Indian Statutes
    Curr. Indian. Stat.
Current Law
    Current L.

Current Law and Social Problems
Current L. & Soc. Prob.
Current Law Consolidation
C.L.C.
Current Law Monthly
C.L.M.
Current Law Reports
Cur. L.R., C.L.R.
Current Law Statutes Annotated
C.L. Stats.
Current Law Year Book
Curr. L. Y.B., C.L. Y.B., Current L. Y.B., Current L.Y.
Current Legal Bibliography
Cur. Leg. Bibliog., Current Leg. Bibliog.
Current Legal Forms with Tax Analysis
C.L.F.
Current Legal Problems
C.L.P., Cur. Leg. Prob., Curr. Legal Prob., Current Leg. Prob., Current Legal Probs., Curr. Leg. Probl.
Current Legal Thought
Cur. Leg. Thought
Current Medicine for Attorneys
Current Med., Current Med. for Att'ys
Current Municipal Problems
Cur. Mun. Prob.
Current Property Law
Cur. Prop. L., Current Prop. L., C.P.L.
Curry's Abridgment of Blackstone
Cur. Bl.
Curry's Reports (6-19 Louisiana)
Curry.
Cursus Cancellariae
Curs. Can.
Cursus Scaccarii
Cur. Scacc.

Curteis' English Ecclesiastical Reports
Curt., Curt. Ecc., Curt. Eccl., Curt. Eccl. (Eng.)
Curtis' Admiralty Digest
Curt. Adm. Dig.
Curtis' American Conveyancer
Curt. Conv.
Curtis' Commentaries on the United States Courts
Curt. U.S. Courts
Curtis' (Condensed) Decisions, United States Supreme Court
Curt. Cond.
Curtis' Digest, United States
Curt. Dig.
Curtis' Edition, U.S. Supreme Court Reports
Curt., Curt. Cond., Curtis
Curtis' Equity Precedents
Curt. Eq. Pr.
Curtis' History of the Constitution of the United States Courts
Curt. U.S. Const.
Curtis on Patents
Curt. Pat.
Curtis on the Jurisdiction of United States Courts
Curt. Jur.
Curtis' Rights and Duties of Merchant Seaman
Curt. Mer. Sea.
Curtis' United States Circuit Court Decisions
Curt. C.C., Curt. Dec.
Curtis' United States Circuit Court Reports
Cur., Curt., Clurtis, Curtis C.C.
Curtis on Copyright
Curt. Cop.

**Curtis's Decisions of the U.S. Su-
preme Court**
  Curt. Cond. Rep., Curtis S.C.
  Reports, Curtis' U.S. Sup. Ct. R.
Curwen on Abstracts of Title
  Curw. Abs. Tit., Cur. Ab. Tit.
Curwen's Laws of Ohio
  Curw. L.O
Curwen's Overruled Ohio Cases
  Curw., Cur. Ov. Ca., Curw. Ov.
  Cas.
**Curwen's Revised Statutes of
Ohio**
  Curw. R.S.
Curwen's Statutes of Ohio
  Curw., Cur. Stat.
Cushing on Trustee Process
  Cush. Trust. Pr.
**Cushing, Storey and Joselyn's
Election Cases, Massachusetts**
  C.S. & J.
**Cushing's Election Cases in Mas-
sachusetts**
  Cush. Elec. Cas.
**Cushing's Law and Practice of
Legislative Assemblies**
  Cush. Law & Prac. Leg. Assem.,
  Cush. Leg. Ass., Cush. Parl.
  Law.
**Cushing's Manual of Parliamen-
tary Law**
  Cush. Man.
**Cushing's Massachusetts Su-
preme Judicial Court Reports
(55-66 Massachusetts)**
  Cush., Cushing., Cush. (Mass.)
**Cushing's Study of the Roman
Law**
  Cush. Rom. Law
**Cushman's Mississippi Reports
(23-29 Mississippi)**
  Cush., Cushman, Cushm.

Custer's Ecclesiastical Reports
  Cust. Rep.
Custody
  Cust.
Custom Court Reports
  Cust. Ct.
**Customs and Patent Appeals Re-
ports (Customs)**
  Cust. & Pat. App. (Cust.)(F)
**Customs and Patent Appeals Re-
ports (Patents)**
  Cust. & Pat. App. (Pat.XF)
Customs and Usages
  Cus. & Us.
Customs Appeals Decisions
  C.A.D.
Customs Bulletin
  C.B., Cust. Bull.
Customs Bulletin and Decisions
  Cust. B. & Dec.
Customs Cooperation Council
  CCC
Customs Court Decisions
  C.D.
Customs Court Reports
  Cu.Ct.
**Customs Court Rules (Rules of the
United States Customs Court)**
  Cust. Ct. R.
**Customs Decisions, U.S. Treasury
Department**
  C.D.
**Customs Duties and Import Regu-
lations**
  Cust. D.
Customs Penalty Decisions
  Cust. Per. Dec.
Customs Rules Decisions
  CRD
**Custos Rotulorum (Keeper of the
Rolls)**
  C.R.

Custos Sigilli (Keeper of the Seal)
    C.S.
Cutler on Naturalization Laws
    Cut. Nat.
Cutler on Settlements
    Cut. Sett.
**Cutler's Insolvent Laws of Massa-
chusetts**
    Cut. Ins. L.
**Cutler's Legal System of the Eng-
lish, the Hindoos, etc., India**
    Cut. Leg. Sys.
Cutler's Reports of Patent Cases
    Cutler's
**Cutler's Trademark and Patent
Cases**
    Cut. Pat. Cas.

Cuttack Law Times, India
    Cutt. L.T., Cut. L.T.
Cyclopedia Law Dictionary
    Cyc. Dict.
**Cyclopedia of Law and Proce-
dure Annotations**
    Cyc. Ann., Cyc. Law & Proc.,
    Cyc., C.Y.C.
Cyprus Law Reports
    Cyprus L.R., C.L.R.
**Czechoslovak Journal of Interna-
tional Law**
    Czech. J. Int'l L., Czech. Y.B.
    Int'l L.
Czechoslovakia
    Czech.

D

Dacca Reports, India
DR

Dadyburjar's Small Court Appeals, India
Dady.

Dagge's Criminal Law
Dag. Cr. L.

D'Aguilar on Courts-Martial
Dag. Ct. M.

Dahlgren's Maritime International Law
Dahl. Mar. Int. L.

Daily Law and Bank Bulletin
L. & B. Bull.

Daily Legal News
D. L. N., Daily Leg. News (Pa.), Daily L.N.

Daily Legal Record
Daily L.R., Daily Leg. (Pa.)

Daily Register, New York City
Reg.

Daily Telegraph Reports (Newspaper)
D. T. (Newspr)

Dakota
Da., Dak.

Dakota Law Review
Dak. L. Rev., Dak. Law Rev.

Dakota Reports
Dakota

Dakota Territory Reports
Da., Dak.

Dale's Clergyman's Legal Handbook
Dale Cl. H.B.

Dale's Ecclesiastical Reports, England
Dale Ecc., Dale Eccl.

Dale's Judgments
Dale

Dale's Law of the Parish Church
Dale Par. Ch.

Dale's Legal Ritual (Ecclesiastical Reports)
Dale Leg.Rit.

Dale's Reports (2-4 Oklahoma)
Dale

Dalhousie Law Journal
Dalhousie L.J.

Dalison's English Common Pleas Reports
Dal. C.P., Dal., Dalison, Dalison (Eng.)

Dalison's Reports in Keilway, England
Dal. in Keil.

Dallam's Texas Decisions, From Dallam's Digest
Dall. Dec.

Dallam's Texas Digest and Opinions
Dallam Dig. (Tex.), Dall. Dig.

Dallam's Texas Supreme Court Decisions
Dall., Dall. (Tex.)

Dallas Bar Association
DALBA

Dallas' Laws of Pennsylvania
Dall. L., Dall., Dall. Laws

Dallas' Pennsylvania and United States Reports
D., Dallas, Dall., Dal.

Dallas' Report of Cooper's Opinion on the Sentence of a Foreign Court of Admiralty
Dal. Coop., Dall. Coop.

Dallas' Styles of Writs, Scotland
Dall., Dall. Sty.
Dallas' United States Supreme Court Reports (1-4 United States Reports)
Dal., Dall. S.C., D.
Dallison's Reports in Keilway's King's Bench Report, England
Dall. in Keil
Dalloz-Sirey
D. S.
Dalrymple on Feudal Property
Dalr. Feud. Prop.
Dalrymple on Stair's Decisions, Court of Session
Dalr.
Dalrymple on Tenures
Dalr. Ten.
Dalrymple on the Polity of Entails
Dalr. Ent.
Dalrymple's Decisions, Court of Sessions
Dalr. Dec., Dalr., Dal.
Dalrymple's Feudal Property in Great Britain
Dalr. Feu. Pr.
Dalrymple's (Lord Hailes) Decisions of the Court of Session
Hailes
Dalton on Sheriffs
D. S., Dalt. Sh., Dal. Sh.
Dalton's County Justice
Dalt. Just.
Dalton's Justices of the Peace
Dalt.
Daly's Hand-Book on Practice in the Lord Mayor's Court
Daly May. Ct.
Daly's Nature and Cases of Surrogate's Courts, New York
Daly Sur.

Daly's New York Common Pleas Reports
Daly, Daly (NY), Daly's R., Dal.
Damages
Damg.
Dampier and Maxwell's British Guiana Reports
Alves
Dampier's Paper Book, Lincoln's Inn Library
D. P. B., Dampier MSS.
Dana's Edition of Wheaton's International Law
Dana Wh.
Dana's Kentucky Supreme Court Reports (31-39 Kentucky)
Dana, Dana (Ky.), Dan
Dane's Abridgement of American Law
Dan. Abr., Dane Abr., Dane's Abr.
Dangerous Drugs Act
D. D. A.
Daniel on Trademarks
Dan. T. M., D. C. P.
Daniell's Chancery Pleading and Practice
Daniell, Ch. Pl & Prac., Daniell, Ch. Pr., Daniell, Ch. Prac.
Daniell's Chancery Practice
Dan. Ch., Dan. Ch. Pr., D.C.P.
Daniell's Exchequer in Equity Reports, England
Dan. Exch. (Eng.), Dan
Daniell's Forms and Precedents in Chancery
Dan. Forms
Daniels' Compendium Compensation Cases
Dan
Daniel's Law of Attachment
Dan. Att.

Daniel's Negotiable Instruments
Dan. Neg. Ins., Daniel, Neg.
Inst.
Danish
Da., Dan
Danish Ordinances
Dan. Ord.
Danner's Reports (42 Alabama)
Dann., Dan, Dann, Danner
Dann's Reports (1 Arizona)
Dann
Dann's Reports (22 California)
Dann
Danquah, Akan Laws and Customs of Ghana
D.A.L.C.
Danquah, Cases in Akan Law of Ghana
D. C. A. L.
Danson and Lloyd's English Mercantile Cases
Dan. & Lld., Dans. & L., Dans.
& LL., Dans. & Lld., Dan. & L.,
Dan. & Ll.
D'Anvers' Abridgment of Common Law
D.Abr., D'An., Danv. Abr.,
Danv., D'Anv. Abr., D.Abr.
Dar es Salaam Law Journal
D. es S. L.J.
Dar es Salaam University Law Journal
D. es S. U. L. J.
Darby and Bosanquet's Statutes of Limitations
Darb. & B. Lim., Da. & Bos.
Darling's Practice of the Court of Session
Darl. Pr. Ct. Sess., D.Pr.
Dart on Vendors and Purchasers
Dart, Vend., Dart
Dartmouth College Case
Dart. Col. Ca.

Darwin's Criminal Law
Darw. Cr. L.
Dasent's Bankruptcy and Insolvency Reports, England
Dasent, Das.
Dasent's Common Law Reports, England
Das.
Dassler's Edition, Kansas Reports
Dass. Ed., Dass. Ed. (Kan.)
Dassler's Kansas Digest
Dass. Dig.
Dassler's Kansas Statutes
Dass. Stat.
Data Processing
D. P.
Date of Birth
DOB
Dauphin County, Pennsylvania
Dauph. Co., Dauph. Co. (Pa.)
Dauphin County Reports, Pennsylvania
Dauph., Dauph. Co. Rep., Dau.
Co. Rep., Dauphin, Dauphin Co.
Reps.
Daveis' District Court Reports (2 of Ware)
Daveis, See also Davies' District
Court Reports
David on Building Societies
Dav. Bdg. Soc.
Davidge and Kimball's Compendium of Internal Revenue
D & K Int. Rev.
Davidge and Kimball's Internal Revenue Laws
Dav. & Kim. I.R.L.
Davidson and Dicey's Concise Precedents in Conveyancing
Dav. & Dic. Pr.
Davidson on Agricultural Law
AgL

159

Davidson on Banks and Banking
    Dav. B. & B.
Davidson's Conveyancing
    Dav. Conv.
**Davidson's Precedents in Convey-
ancing**
    Dav. Prec. Conv.
**Davidson's Reports (92-111 North
Carolina)**
    Davidson
**Davies' District Court Reports (2
of Ware)**
    Dav. (U. S.), Davies
Davies' English Patent Cases
    Dav., Davies (Eng.), Dav. P. C.,
    Dav. Pat. Cas.
**Davies' Irish King's Bench and
Exchequer Reports**
    Davy, Dav., Davies, Davis, Dav.
    Rep., Dav. Ir., Dav. Ir. K.B.,
    Davies (Ir.)
Davies on Annuities
    Dav.Ann.
Davies on French Mercantile Law
    Dav. Fr. Merc. Law
Davis
    D.
**Davis' Abridgment of Coke's Re-
ports**
    Dav. Coke.
**Davis' Administrative Law Trea-
tise**
    Davis, Admin. Law
Davis' Criminal Law
    Dav. Cr. Law, Davis Cr. Law
**Davis' Criminal Law Consolida-
tion Acts**
    Dav. Cr. Cons.
Davis' English Church Canons
    Dav. Eng. Ch. Can., Dav. Can.
**Davis' Hawaiian Reports (2 Ha-
waii**
    Davis, Davis Rep., Dav.

Davis' Indiana Digest
    Dav. Dig., Dav. Ind. Dig.
Davis' Justice of the Peace
    Dav. Jus.
Davis' Land Court Decisions
    Dav. Land. Ct. Cas., Davis L.
    Ct. Cas.
Davis' Law of Building Societies
    Davis Bdg., Davis, Bldg. Soc.
Davis' Law of Master and Servant
    Dav. M. & S.
**Davis' Law of Registration and
Election**
    Dav. Elec.
**Davis' Massachusetts Convey-
ancer's Handbook**
    Davis, Mass. Convey. Hdbk.
**Davis on Friendly Societies and
Trade Unions**
    Dav. Fr. Soc.
**Davis on Industrial and Provi-
dent Societies**
    Dav. Ind. Soc.
Davis on the Labor Laws
    Dav. Lab. L.
Davis' Precedents of Indictment
    Dav. Prec. Ind., Dav.
Davis' Trade Unions
    Dav. Tr. Un.
**Davis' United States Supreme
Court Reports**
    Dav., Davis (J. C. B.), Davis
**Davison and Merivale's English
Queen's Bench Reports**
    Dav. & Mer., Dav. & M., Dav. &
    M. (Eng.), D. & M., D. M., D. &
    Mer.
**Davison on Registration and Elec-
tions**
    Dav. Reg.
**Davys' English King's Bench Re-
ports**
    Davys, Davys (Eng.)

Dawe on Arrest in Civil Cases
Daw. Ar.
**Dawe on Crimes and Punish-
ments**
Daw. Cr. & Pun.
**Dawe's Epitome of the Law of
Landed Property**
Daw. Land. Pr.
Dawe's Real Estate Law
Daw. Real Pr.
Dawson's Attorney's
Daw. Att.
**Dawson's Colorado Code of Civil
Procedure**
Dawson's Code
Dawson's Origo Legum
Daw. Or. Leg.
Dax's Exchequer Precedents
Dax Exch.Pr.
**Dax's Practice in the Offices of
the Masters**
Dax Mast.Pr.
Day Book
D. B.
Days After Acceptance
D/a
**Days After Date (in bills of ex-
change)**
D. d.
Day's Connecticut Reports
Day, Day's Ca., Day's Ca. Er.,
Day's Cases, Day's Conn. Rep.
Day's English Election Cases
Day Elect. Cas.
Dayton's Law of Surrogates
Day. (or Dayt.) Sur.
Dayton's Ohio Reports
Dayton, Dayton (Ohio), Dayton
Rep., Dayton
Dayton's Term Reports, England
Dayt. Term Rep.

**De Bene Esse, (conditionally)
(Lat.)**
D. B. E.
**De Bonis Asportatis (trespass to
person) (Lat.)**
d. b. a.
**De Bonis Non (of the goods not
administered) (Lat.)**
D. B. N.
**De Burgh's Maritime Interna-
tional Laws**
DeB. Mar. Int. L.
**De Colyar's English County
Court Cases**
De Coly., De Col.
De Colyar's Law of Guaranty
De Col. Guar.
**De Ea Re Ita Censuere (concern-
ing that matter have so de-
creed) (Lat.)**
D. E. R. I. C.
De Fooz on Mines
DeF. Min.
**De Gex and Jones' English Bank-
ruptcy Reports (1857-59)**
D. & J.B., De G. & J.B., D. G. &
J. B., D.G. & J., DeG. & J. By.
**De Gex and Jones' English Chan-
cery Reports**
D & J.
**De Gex and Smale's English
Chancery Reports**
D. & S., De G. & S., De G. & Sm.
**De Gex and Smale's Tempore
Knight-Bruce and Parker Re-
ports, Vice-Chancellor's Court**
D. & Sm.
**De Gex's English Bankruptcy Re-
ports**
De G. Bankr. (Eng.), D. G., De-
Gex, DeG., DeG. Bankr.

De Gex, Fisher, and Jones' English Bankruptcy Reports
D. F. & J. B., De G. J. & J. By.,
D. G. F. & J. B., F. & J. Bank

De Gex, Fisher, and Jones' English Chancery Reports
D. G. F. & J., De Gex, F. & J.,
D. F. & J., De G. F. & J.

De Gex, Jones, and Smith's English Chancery Reports
D. G. J. & S., De Gex, J. & S.,
De G. J. & Sm., D. J. & S., De
G. J. & S., De G. J. & S. (Eng.),
De G. J. & S. By., D. G. J. & S.
B., D. J. & S. B.

De Gex, Macnaghten and Gordon's English Bankruptcy Reports
De Gex, M. & G., D. G. M. & G.
B., D. M. & G. B., D. M. & G.,
De G. M. & G. By., D. G. M. &
G., De G. M. & G., D. M. & G.,
De Gex, M. & G.

De Hart's Military Law and Courts-Martial
De H.M.L.

De Lolme on the English Constitution
De L. Const., De Lolme, Eng.
Const.

De Mello's Extradition Cases
De M.

De Paul Law Review
D. P. L.R.

De-Rating and Rating Appeals, England and Scotland
DR, D. R. A.

De Verborum Obligationibus
V.O.

De Witt and Weeresinghe's Appeal Court Reports, Ceylon
W. & W.

Deacon and Chitty's English Bankruptcy Reports
Dea. & Chit., Deacon & C.
Bankr. Cas. (Eng.), Deacon &
C., Dea. & Ch., Deacon & C.
Bankr. Cas., Deac. & Ch., D. &
C., Deac. & C., D. & Ch., D. &
Chit., Deac. & Chit.

Deacon on Bankruptcy Law and Practice
Deacon Bankr. (Eng.), Deacon,
Bankr. Cas, Deac. Bank. Pr.

Deacon on Criminal Law of England
Deac. Cr. Law

Deacon's Digest of the Criminal Law
Deac. Dig.

Deacon's English Bankruptcy Reports
Deac.

Dead Bodies
Dead B.

Dead Freight
D. f.

Dead on Arrival at Hospital
DOA

Deady and Lane's Oregon General Laws
Dead. Or. Laws

Deady's Circuit and District Court Reports
Dea., Deady

Deane and Swabey's English Ecclesiastical Reports
D. & Sw., Deane & S. Eccl.
(Eng.), D. & S., Dea. & Sw.,
Deane, Deane Ecc., Deane & S.
Eccl., Deane & S. Eccl. Rep.,
Deane & Sw., Deane Ecc. Rep.,
Deane Ecc. Rep. B.

**Deane and Swabey's English Pro-
bate and Divorce Reports**
Deane

**Deane on the Effect of War as to
Neutrals**
Deane Neut.

Deane's Blockade Cases
Deane

Deane's Law of Blockade
Deane Bl.

Dean's Medical Jurisprudence
Dean Med. Jur.

Deane's Reports (24-26 Vermont)
Deane

**Dearsley and Bell's English
Crown Cases**
D. & B. C.C., Dears. & B.,
Dears. & B. C. C., Dears. & B.
Crown Cas.

Dearsly on Criminal Process
Dearsl. Cr. Pr., Dears. Cr. Pr.

**Dearsley's English Crown Cases
Reserved**
Dears, Dears. C.C.

**Deas and Anderson's Court of
Session Decisions**
Deas & A., Deas & And., D. & A.

**Deas on the Law of Railways in
Scotland**
Deas Ry.

Death Certificate
D. C.

Death Penalty Reporter
Death Pen. Rep.

Debate[s]
Deb.

Debates on the Judiciary
Deb. Jud.

Debenture
Deb.

Debit
Deb.

**Debitum Sine Brevi (debt with-
out writ) (Lat.)**
D. S. B.

Debtor[s]
Dr.

Debtor and Creditor
Debt. & Cred.

Decalogue Journal
Decalogue, Decalogue J.

Deceased
D, Dec., Dec'd.

December
Dec., De., Dc.

**Decessit Sine Prole (died without
issue) (Lat.)**
D. s. p.

**Decessit Sine Prole Legitima
(died without legitimate issue)
(Lat.)**
D. s. p. l.

**Decessit Sine Prole Mascula
(died without male issue) (Lat.)**
D. s. p. m.

**Decessit Sine Prole Mascula Su-
perstite (died without surviving male issue) (Lat.)**
D. s. p. m. s.

**Decessit Sine Prole Superstite
(died without surviving issue)
(Lat.)**
D. s. p. s.

**Decessit Sine Prole Virile (died
without male issue) (Lat.)**
D. s. p. v.

**Decessit Vita Patris (died during
his father's life) (Lat.)**
D. v. p.

Decimal
Dec.

Decimal Currency Board
D. C. B.

Decision[s]
Dec.(s)

Decision of Sergeant Arabin
Arabin.
Decisions From the Chair (Parliamentary)
Dec. Ch.
Decisions Given by the Office of the Umpire (Unemployment Insurance) Respecting Claims to Out-of-work Donation
O.U.U.I.
Decisions of General Appraisers
GA
Decisions of Joint Commission
Dec. Jt. Com.
Decisions of the California Public Utilities Commission
Cal. P.U.C.
Decisions of the Commissioner of Patents
Dec. Com. Pat., Pat. Dec.
Decisions of the Commissioners Under the National Insurance (Industrial Injuries) Acts Relating to Wales
C.W.I.
Decisions of the Commissioners Under the National Insurance (Industrial Injuries) Acts Relating to Scotland
C.S.I.
Decisions of the Comptroller General of the United States
Comp. Gen., Dec. U. S. Comp. Gen., Dec. U.S. Compt. Gen.
Decisions of the Comptroller of the Treasury
Comp. Dec.
Decisions of the Department of the Interior
Interior Dec.

Decisions of the Department of the Interior, Pension and Retirement Claims
P. and R.D.
Decisions of the Employee's Compensation Appeals Board
ECAB, Empl. Comp. App. Bd.
Decisions of the Equal Employment Opportunity Commission, Commerce Clearing House
CCH EEOC Dec., EEOC Dec. (CCH)
Decisions of the Federal Maritime Commission
Dec. Fed. Mar. Comm'n., F.M.C.
Decisions of the First Comptroller of the United States Treasury
Bowler's First Comp. Dec.
Decisions of the Income Tax Board of Review
Board of Review Decisions
Decisions of the Industrial Accident Commission of California
Cal. I.A.C., Cal. Ind. Acc. Com., Cal. Ind. Acc. Com. Dec., Cal. Ind. Com., Calif. Ind. Accdt. Com. Dec., Dec. of Ind. Acc. Com., I.A.C. Dec., I.A.C. of Cal., Ind. Acc. Com., Industrial Acc. Com.
Decisions of the Judicial Committee of the Privy Council re the British North American Act, 1867, and the Canadian Constitution, Canada
Olms.
Decisions of the Lands Tribunal (Rating)
LVC
Decisions of the Sudder Court in India
S.D.

Decisions of the United States
Maritime Commission
  Dec. U. S. Mar. Comm'n.
Decisions of the United States
Merit System Protection Board
  M.S.P.B.
Decisions of the United States
Railroad Labor Board
  U.S. R.R. Lab. Bd. Dec.
Decisions of the Water Court in
South Africa
  Hall., Krummeck
Decisions of the Zillah Courts,
Lower Provinces, India
  Beng. Zillah
Declaration[s]
  Dec., Decl.
Declaratory Judgement[s]
  Decl. J.
Declination
  Dec.
Decoration[s]
  Dec.
Decree[s]
  D., D
Decreta Childeberti ad Legem
Salicam
  Decret. Childeb. ad L. Salic.
Decretalia of the Canon Law
  Decretal.
Dedicated
  Ded.
Dedication
  Ded., Dedic.
Deering's California General
Laws Annotated
  Cal. Gen. Laws Ann., Deering's
  Cal. Gen. Laws. Ann.
Deering's Annotated California
Code
  Cal. Code, Cal. [subject] Code
  (Deering), Deering's Cal. Code
  Ann.

Deering's California Advance
Legislative Service
  Deering's Cal. Adv. Legis. Serv.
Dees on the Law of Insolvent
Debtors
  Dees Ins.
Defence Act
  D.A.
Defendant[s]
  dft., Defs.['], Def.[s]
Defense[s]
  Def.[s]
Defense Acquisition Circular
  D.A.C.
Defense Acquisition Regulation
  D.A.R.
Defense Advanced Research Pro-
jects Agency
  DARPA
Defense Air Transportation Ad-
ministration
  DATA
Defense Civil Preparedness
Agency
  DCPA
Defense Contract Audit Agency
  DCAA
Defense Contract Finance Regu-
lations
  DCFR
Defense Counsel Journal
  Def. Couns. J.
Defense Electric Power Admini-
stration
  DEPA
Defense Fisheries Administra-
tion
  DFA
Defense Food Order (Production
and Marketing Administra-
tion)
  DFO

Defense Food Order, Sub-Order
DFO, SO
Defense Intelligence Agency
DIA
Defense Investigative Service
DIS
Defense Law Journal
Def. L.J., Defense L.J.
Defense Manpower Administration
DMA
Defense Materials Exploration Agency
DMEA
Defense Materials Procurement Agency
DMP
Defense Materials System
DMS
Defense Mobilization Board
DMB, DMO
Defense Nuclear Agency
DNA
Defense of the Realm Act
D. O. R. A.
Defense Production Administration
DPA
Defense Relocation Corporation
DRC
Defense Research Institute
DRI
Defense Security Assistance Agency
DSAA
Defense Solid Fuels Administration
DSFA
Defense Solid Fuels Order
SFO
Defense Supply Agency
DSA

Defense Supply Procurement Regulations
DSPR
Defense Systems Acquisition Review Council
DSARC
Defense Transport Administration
DTA
Defined
Def.
Definition[s]
Def.[s]
Defunctus (deceased) (Lat.)
Def.[s]
Degge's Parson's Counsellor and Law of Tithes
Deg., Degge
Degree
D, Deg.
DeHart on Military Law
DeHart, Mil. Law
De Hovenden's Chronicle
Rog. Hov.
DeKretser's Matara Appeals for Ceylon
De Krets.
Delafield on Post Mortem Examinations
Del. P.M. Ex.
Delafon on Naval Courts Martial
Del. Ct. M.
Delane's English Election Revision Cases
Del. El. Cas., Del., Delane
Delaware
De., Del.
Delaware Cases
Del. Cas.
Delaware Chancery Reports
D. Ch., De. CH., Del. Ch., Del. Civ. Dec.

Delaware Chancery Reports, Supplement
Del. Ch. Supp.
Delaware Code
Del. Code
Delaware Code Annotated
De. C. Ann., Del. Code Ann.
Delaware Constitution
Del. Const.
Delaware County
Del. Co.
Delaware County Law Journal
Del. Co. L.J. (Pa.)
Delaware County Reports
Del. County, Del. Co. (Pa.), Del.
Co. R., Del. Co. Reps., Del.
County Rep., Delaware Co.
Reps., Bliss, Del.
Delaware Court of Chancery
DCh
Delaware Criminal Cases
Del. Cr. Cas., Houst. Cr. Rep.,
Houst. Crim. Cas., Houst. Crim.
Cases, Houst. Crim. Rep.
Delaware General Corporation Law
Del. G. C. L.
Delaware Journal of Corporate Law
Del. J. Corp. L.
Delaware Laws
Del. Laws
Delaware Lawyer
Del. Law.
Delaware Register of Regulations
Del. Reg. of Regs.
Delaware Reports
D., Del.
Delaware Supreme Court Decisions
Del. Sup.
Delaware Supreme Court Reports
Del. County Rep.

Delaware Term Reports
Del. Term R.
Deleatur (omit) (Lat.)
dele.
Delegate
Del. County Rep.
Delegation Order
Del. Order, DO
Delete
D
Delhi
Del.
Delhi Civil Decisions
Del. Civ. Dec.
Delhi Law Review
Del. L.R., Delhi L.R., Delhi L.
Rev.
Delhi Law Times
Delhi L. Times
Delinquent, Delinquency
Delinq., delinq.
Delivered
delv.
Delivered Alongside Ship
d.a.s.
Delivered At Dock
d. d.
Dellam's Texas Opinions
Dell.
Demangeat's Condition Civile, Etrangers en France
Dem. Cond. Etran.
Demarest's New York Surrogate's Court Reports
Demarest, Dem. Sur., Dem.
Surr., Dem., Dem. (NY)
Democrat
D.
Democrat-Farmer-Labor Party
DFL
Democratic People's Republic of Korea
Korea (DPR)

Demolombe's Code Napoleon
Demol., Demol. C. N.
Demurrer
Dem.
Denied
D., Den.
Denio's New York Reports or New York Supreme Court Reports
D., Den., Denio, Denio (N. S.), Denio R.
Denis' Reports (32-46 Louisiana)
Den., Denis
Denison and Pearce's English Crown Cases
Den. & P., Den. & P. C. C., D. & P., Den.
Denison and Scott's House of Lords Appeal Practice
Den. & Sc. Pr.
Denison's English Crown Cases
D., Den. C.C., Denison, Cr. Cas.
Denmark
Den.
Denning Law Journal
Denning L.J.
Denning Law Review
Denning L Rev
Denomination
Denom.
Denslow's Notes (1-3 Michigan)
Dens.
Denver
Den.
Denver Bar Association Record
Den. B. A. Rec.
Denver Journal of International Law
Denver J. Int'l. L.

Denver Journal of International Law and Policy
Denv. J. I. L. P., Denv. J. Int'l. L. & Pol'y., Denver J. Int. L. & Policy
Denver Law Center Journal
Den. L. C. J.
Denver Law Journal
Den. L.J., Denver L. J., Dn. L.J., D. J.
Denver Legal News
Den. L. N., Denver L. N.
Denver University Law Review
Den. U. L. Rev., Denv. U. L. Rev.
Deny[ing]
Den.
Denying
den'g
Denying Appeal
den. app.
Denying Reargument
den. rearg.
Denying Rehearing
den. reh.
Denying Writ of Error
den. writ of error
Department
Dep., Dept.
Department of Agriculture (for a state)
Ag.
Department of Agriculture Procurement Regulations
AGPR
Department of Commerce
DOC
Department of Commerce Procurement Regulations
COMPR
Department of Defense
DOD
Department of Defense (forms)
DD

Department of Defense Index of Specifications and Standards
    DODISS

Department of Economic Security
    DES

Department of Employment
    D. E.

Department of Employment and Productivity
    D. E. P.

Department of Employment Security
    DES

Department of Energy
    DOE

Department of Health and Social Security
    D. H. S. S.

Department of Health, Education and Welfare
    HEW

Department of Health, Education and Welfare Procurement Regulations
    HEWPR

Department of Housing and Development
    HUD

Department of Industrial Relations
    DIR

Department of Interior
    DOI

Department of Interior, Office of Coal Research
    O.C.R.

Department of Justice
    DOJ

Department of Labor
    DOL

Department of Labor and Industry
    DLI

Department of Public Instruction
    PI

Department of Public Welfare (for a state)
    P.W.

Department of State
    DOS, DS

Department of State Bulletin, United States
    Dept. State Bull., Dep't. St. Bull.

Department of State Procurement Regulations
    DOSPR

Department of Taxation
    Tax

Department of the Interior
    DOI

Department of the Interior, Decisions Relating to Public Lands
    Pub. Lands Dec.

Department of the Interior Procurement Regulations
    DIPR

Department of State Bulletin
    Dept. St. Bull.

Department of Trade and Industry
    D. T. I.

Department of Transportation
    DOT

Department Reports, New York State Department
    Dept. R.

Departmental Decisions
    Dept. Dec.

DePaul Business Law Journal
    DePaul Bus. L.J.

DePaul Law Review
    DePaul L. Rev., DeP.

Dependent Relative Allowance
    DRA

Deposit
    Dep.

Depositary
Dep.
Deposition
Dep.
Deposition and Discovery
Depos. & D.
Deposit in Court
Dep. in Ct.
Department of Health and Human Services
HHS
Deputy
Dep.
Deputy Advocate
D.A.
Deputy Assistant Director
D.A.D.
Deputy Assistant Judge Advocate General
D.A. J.A.G.
Deputy Assistant Provost Marshall
D. A. P. M.
Deputy Chief
D. C.
Deputy Clerk of Session
D. C. S.
Deputy Commissioner
D. C.
Deputy Counsel
D. C.
Deputy Director-General
D. D. G.
Deputy Judge Advocate General
D. J. A. G.
Deputy Keeper of the Signet
D. K. S.
Deputy Remembrancer
D. R.
Deputy Sheriff
DS
Der Betrieb
DB

Desaussure's South Carolina Equity Reports
Desaus, Desaus. Eq., Des., See also Dessaussure's South Carolina Equity Reports
Descent and Distribution
Desc. & D.
Description
Descr.
Descriptive Word Index
D. W. I.
Desertion and Nonsupport
Desert. & N.
Desiderio and Taylor's Planning Tax-Exempt Organizations
PTO
Designation of Scarce Materials
DSM
Dessaussure's South Carolina Equity Report
Dess., Dessaus., See also Desaussure's South Carolina Equity Reports
Desty on Commerce and Navigation
Dest. Com. & Nav.
Desty on Federal Constitution
Dest. Fed. Cons.
Desty on Shipping and Admiralty
Dest. Sh. & Adm.
Desty on Taxation
Desty, Tax'n.
Desty's California Citations
Dest. Cal. Cit.
Desty's California Digest
Dest. Cal. Dig.
Desty's Criminal Law
Dest. Cr. L.
Desty's Federal Citations
Dest. Fed. Cit.
Desty's Federal Procedure
Dest. Fed. Proc.

Detachable
Det.
Detached
Det.
Detective
Det.
Detroit
Det.
Detroit Bar Journal
Det. B.J.
Detroit Bar Quarterly
Detroit B.Q.
Detroit College Law Review
Det. C.L. Rev., Det. Coll. L.
Rev., Det. C. L.R., Det. Coll. L.R.
Detroit College of Law
Detroit Coll. L.
Detroit Law Journal
Det. L. J., Detroit L.J.
Detroit Law Review
Det. L. Rev., Detroit L. Rev.
Detroit Lawyer
Detroit L., Det. Law
Detroit Legal News
Det. Leg. N., Detroit Leg. N.
Development
Dev., Devel
Development Assistance Committee, Organization of Economic Cooperation and Development
DAC
Devereux and Battle's North Carlina Equity Reports
Dev. & B. Eq., Dev. & Bat. Eq.
Devereux and Battle's North Carolina Law and Equity Reports
D. & B., D. & B., Dev. & B.,
Dev. & Bat., Dev. & BL. (NC),
Dev. & B.
Devereux's Kinne's Blackstone
Dev. Kin. Bl.

Devereux's Kinne's Kent
Dev. Kin. Kent
Devereux's North Carolina Equity Report
Dev. Eq.
Devereux's North Carolina Law Reports
Dev. L., Dev. L. or Dev.N.B.,
Dev.
Devereux's Reports, United States Court of Claims
Dev., Dev. C. C., Dev. Ct. Cl.
Deviation Clause
D. C., D/C
Devisavit Vel Non (issue of fact as to whether a will in question was made by the testator) (Lat.)
d. v. n.
Devlin on Deeds and Real Estate
Devl. Deeds, Dev. Deeds.
D'Ewes' Journal and Parliamentary Collection
D'Ewes J.
Dewey Decimal Classification
D. D. C.
Dewey on Divorce Law
Dew. Div.
Dewey's Compiled Statutes of Michigan
Dew. St.
Dewey's Kansas Court of Appeals Reports (60-70 Kansas)
Dew.
DeWitt's Reports (24-42 Ohio)
DeWitt
Dialogus de Scaccario
Dial. de Scacc.
Dibb's Forms of Memorials
Dibb F.
Dice's Reports (79-91 Indiana)
Dice

Dicey and Morris on Conflict of Laws
Dicey & Morris
Dicey on Conflict of Laws
Dicey, Confl. Laws
Dicey on Law of Domicil
Dic. Dom., Dicey, Dom., Dicey, Domicil
Dicey on Parties to Actions
Dic. Par.
Dicey's Lectures Introductory to the Study of the Law of the English Constitution
Dicey, Const.
Dickenson's Reports (46-58 New Jersey Equity)
Dick.
Dickinson International Law Annual
Dick. Int'l L. Ann.
Dickinson Journal of International Law
Dick. J. Int'l L.
Dickinson Law Review
Dick. L. Rev., Dick. L.R., Dickinson. L. Rev., Dk. L.R., D. L. R.
Dickens' English Chancery Reports
Dick. Ch., Dick. Ch. (Eng.), Wy. Dick., Dickens, Dick.
Dickinson's Equity Precedents for New Jersey
Dick. Eq. Pr.
Dickinson's Justice
Dick. Just.
Dickson's Law of Evidence in Scotland
Dick. Ev.
Dickinson's Lawyers
Dick. Law.
Dickinson's New Jersey Equity
Dick. (NJ)

Dickinson's Practical Guide to the Quarter Sessions
Dick. Quar. Ses.
Dickson's Analysis of Blackstone's Commentaries
Dick. Black.
Dickson's Analysis of Kent's Commentaries
Dick. Kent.
Dicta
D., Dic.
Dicta of Denver Bar Association
Dicta
Dictionary
Dict., D.
Dictum
D.
Died Without Issue
D. W. I.
Diedrich & Gaus' Defense of Equal Employment Claims
DEEC
Dieser's Year Books, England
Y.B., Year b.
Digby's History of the Law of Real Property
Digby, R. P., Dig. R. Pr.
Digby's Sales and Transfer of Shares
Dig. Shares
Digest
Dig., D., Dig.
Digest of Decisions of the Workmen's Compensation Board, Pennsylvania
Pa. W.C. Bd. Dec. Dig.
Digest of International Law by Hackworth
D.I.L. (Hack.)
Digest of International Law by Moore
D.I.L. (Moore)

Digest of International Law by Whiteman
D.I.L. (White.)

Digest of Justinian
Dig., Just. Dig., Dig. Proem., Digest, D.

Digest of Manx Cases
Farrant

Digest of Maxims by James S. Bracton
Bract.

Digest of Ontario Case Law
Ont. Dig.

Digest of Opinions of Judge Advocate General, United States
Dig. Ops. J. A. G.

Digest of Opinions of the Attorney General of Texas
Tex. Dig. Op. Att'y Gen.

Digest of Reports of the Average Adjusters Association
Av. Adj. Assoc. Dig.

Digest of the Commercial Laws of the World
Dig. C.L.W.

Digest of the Law of Libel
Dig. L.L.

Digest of Writs
Dig.

Digest to Cowen's New York Reports
Cow. Dig.

Digesta of Justinian
Dig.

Digestum
Dig.

Dignum Deo Donum Dedit
D.D.D.D.

Dillon on Municipal Bonds
Dill. Mun. Bonds

Dillon on Municipal Corporation
Dillon, Mun. Corp., Dill. Mun. Cor., Dill. Mun. Corp.

Dillon on the Irish Judicature Act
Dill. Ir. Jud. A.

Dillon on the Removal of Causes
Dill. Rem. Caus.

Dillon's Laws and Jurisprudence of England and America
Dill. Laws Eng. & Am.

Dillon's United States Circuit Court Reports
Dil. Cir. Court Rep., Dill. Rep., Dillon C. C., Dillon Cir. Court Rep., Dil., Dill., Dillon

Diocesan Consistory Court
D. C. C.

Diplomacy
Dipl.

Diplomatic Corps
D. C.

Diplomatic Correspondence of the United States, Edited by Sparks
Dip. Cor.

Diprose and Gammon's Reports of Law Affecting Friendly Societies
D. & G.

Director[s]
Dir.(s)

Director of Public Prosecutions
D. P. P.

Dirksen Senate Office Building
DSOB

Dirleton's Decisions, Court of Sessions
Dirl., Dirl. Dec.

Dirleton's Doubts and Questions in the Law
Dirl. D.

Disapproved In
Disappr.

Disapproving
Disappr.

Disarmament Commission,
United Nations
 D. C.
Disaster Loan Corporation
 DLC
Disciplinary Law and Procedure
 Advance Sheets
 Disc. L. & Proc. Adv. Sheets
Discount
 Disc.
Discovered
 Disc.
Discovery
 Disc.
Discussion Paper
 D. P.
Dismissed
 Dism'd., D.
Dismissed for Want of Bond
 DWB
Dismissed for Want of Prosecu-
 tion
 DWP, D.
Dismissing
 Dism'g.
Dismissing Appeal
 dism. app.
Disney on Gaming
 Disn. Gam.
Disney's Ohio Superior Court Re-
 ports
 Dis. R., Disney (Ohio), D., Dis.,
 Disn. (Ohio), Disn.
Disorderly Houses
 Disord. H.
Dispute
 Disp.
Dispute Resolution Notes
 Dispute Res. N.
Dissenting Opinion
 Dis. op., j (used in Shepard's Ci-
 tations)

Dissertation
 diss.
Distinguish[ed, ing]
 Dist.; d (used in Shepard's Cita-
 tions)
Distribute or Distributing
 Distrib.
Distribution
 Distr.
Distribution Regulation, Office of
 Price Stabilization United
 States
 DR
Distributive
 Distr.
Distributor
 Distrib.
District
 Dist.
District and County Reports for
 Pennsylvania
 D. & C.
District and County Reports, Sec-
 ond Series, for Pennsylvania
 D. & C.2d
District Attorney
 D.A.
District Commissioner
 D. C.
District Court
 D. C., Dist. C., Dist. Ct., D. Ct.,
 D.
District Court Law Reports
 District Court L.R.
District Court of Appeal
 Dist. Ct. App.
District Court Reports
 D. C. R.
District Court (usually U. S.)
 D. Ct.
District Court, District of Colum-
 bia
 D. D. C.

District Judge
D. J.
District Lawyer
District Law, District Law.
(D.C.)
District of Columbia
D. C., Dist. Col.
District of Columbia Appeal Cases
App. Cas. (D.C.), App. D.C.
District of Columbia Appeals Cases (1-5 United States Reports)
Cranch C.C.
District of Columbia Appeals Reports
D.C. App.
District of Columbia Bar Association
DCBA
District of Columbia Bar Association Journal
Distr. Col. B. A. J.
District of Columbia Bar Journal
D.C. B. J.
District of Colombia Circuit Court Rules
D.C. Cir. R.
District of Columbia Code
D.C. Code
District of Columbia Code Annotated
D.C. Code Ann.
District of Columbia Code Encyclopedia
D.C. C. E.
District of Columbia Code Legislative and Administrative Service
D.C. Code Legis & Admin. Serv.
District of Columbia Compensation Act
DCCA

District of Columbia Court of Appeals
DC Ct App, Dist. Col. App.,
C.A.D.C.
District of Columbia Court of Appeals Cases
D.C. Cir.
District of Columbia Manpower Administration
DCMA
District of Columbia Public Utilities Commission
Dist. Col. P. U.
District of Columbia Reports
D. C.
District of Columbia Rules and Regulations
D.C.R. & Regs.
District of Columbia Supreme Court Reports (1-5 United States Reports)
Cranch C.C.
District of Columbia Supreme Court Reports
S.C.D.C.
District of Columbia Supreme Court Reports, New Series
S.C.D.C.N.S.
District Registry
D. R.
District Reports
Dist. Rep.
Disturbing Meetings
Disturb. M.
Divide
Div.
Dividend
Div.
Dividend Disbursing Agent
DDA
Divinity
Div.

Division
Div.
Division Court
Div. C.
Division of Employment
D. E.
Division of Employment Security
DES
Division of Placement and Unemployment Compensation
D. P. U. C.
Division of Placement and Unemployment Insurance
UID, D.P.U.I.
Division of Unemployment Compensation
DUC
Divisional and Full Court Judgments of Ghana
D. & F.
Divisional Court
D. C.
Divisional Court Selected Judgments, Divisional Courts of the Gold Coast Colony
Div. Ct.
Divorce and Matrimonial Causes Court
Div. & Mat. Ct.
Divorce and Separation
Div. & S.
Divorce Proceedings
Div.
Dixbury
D.
Dixon on General Average
Dix. Av.
Dixon on Title Deeds
Dix. Tit. D.
Dixon on Law of the Farm
Dix. Farm
Dixon on Partnership
Dix. Part.

Dixon on Probate and Administration Law and Practice
Dix. Pr.
Dixon's Abridgment of the Maritime Law
Dix. Mar. Law
Dixon's Law of Shipping
Dix. Ship.
Dixon's Law of Subrogation
Dix. Subr.
Dixon's Marine Insurance and Average
Dix. Mar. Ins.
Dix's School Decisions, New York
Dix. Dec. (NY), Dix. Dec.
Djibouti
Djib
Dock Brief
D. B.
Dock Dues and Shipping
D. D. & Shpg.
Docket
Dkt., Docket
Dockett, Tennessee Bar Association Newsletter
Docket
Doctor
D., Doc., Dr.
Doctor and Student
Doct. & St., D. & S., D. S., Doct. & Stud., Doct. and Stud.
Doctor of Canon Law
D. Cn. L.
Doctor of Civil Law
D. C. L.
Doctor of Commerical Law
D. Com. L.
Doctor of Comparative Law
D. C. L.
Doctor of Divinity
D.D.
Doctor of Juridical Science
J.S.D.

Doctor of Jurisprudence
JD, J.D.
Doctor of Juristic Science
J.S.D., S.J.D.
Doctor of Law
D. L., Ju.D., LL. D.
Doctor of Medicine
M.D.
Doctor of the Science of Law
S.J.D.
Doctrina Placitandi
Doct. Pl., Doct. Plac.
Doctrine of Demurrers
Doct.Dem.
Document
dct., Doc.
Documents Against Acceptance
D/A, d/a
Documents Against Payment
D. a. p., d. a. p.
Dodd and Brook's Probate Court Practice
Dodd & Br. Pr. Pr., D. & B. Pr. Pr.
Dodd on Burial and Other Church Fees
Dodd Bur. Fees
Doderidge on the Antiquity and Power of Parliaments
Dod. Ant. Parl.
Doderidge's English Lawyer
Dod. Eng. Law
Doderidge's Nobility
Dod. Nobility
Doderidge's The Lawyer's Light
Dod. Law L.
Dod's Parliamentary Companion
Dod.
Dodson's English Admiralty Reports
Dod., Dod., Dods., Dodson Adm. (Eng.), Dod. Adm.

Doing Business As
d/b/a
Domat's Droit Civil (Domat's Civil Lw)
Dom. Civ. Law, Domat, Civ. Law, Domat
Domat's Droit Publique (Domat's Public Law)
Domat, Dr. Pub., Domat, Liv. Prel.
Domesday Book
D. B., Dom. Boc., Dom. Book, Domes., Domesday
Domestic
Dom.
Domestic and International Business Administration
DIBA
Domestic International Sales Corporation
DISC, DISC
Domestic Relations
Dom. Rel.
Domestic Relations Court
Dom. Rel. Ct.
Dominican Republic
Dom. Rep.
Dominion
Dom.
Dominion Companies Law Reports
D. C. L. R. (Can.)
Dominion Law Reporter
D. L. R.
Dominion Law Reports
D. L. R., Dom. L.R.
Dominion Law Reports, 2d Series
D. L. R. 2d.
Dominion Law Reports, 3d Series
D. L. R. 3d.
Dominion of Canada Labour Service
D. C. Lab. S.

Dominion of Canada Statutes in the Reign of Victoria
C.Vict.

Dominion Report Service
D. R. S.

Dominion Tax Cases, Commerce Clearing House
D. T. C., Dominion Tax Cas. (CCH), D. Tax

Dominus
Dom.

Domus Procerum
D. P., Dom. Proc.

Donaker's Reports (165 Indiana)
Donaker

Donation Land Claim
DLC

Donnell's Irish Land Cases
Donn., Dona., Donn. Ir. Land Cas.

Donnelly's English Chancery Reports
Dona., Donn. Eq., Donnelly, Donnelly (Eng.)

Dono Dedit (given as a gift) (Lat.)
D.D., d. d.

Donovan's Modern Jury Trials
Don. Tr.

Doria's Law and Practice in Bankruptcy
Dor. Bank

Dorion's Quebec Queen's Bench Reports
Dor. Q. B., Dorion, Dorion (Can.), Dorion Q. B., D. C. A., Dor.

Dorsay's Law of Insolvency
Dor. Ins.

Dorsey's Maryland Laws
Dor. Md. Laws

Dos Passos on Stock-Brokers and Stock Exchanges
Dos Passos, Stock-Brok.

Doshisha Law Journal
Doshisha L.J.

Doshisha Law Review
Doshisha L. Rev.

Douglas' English Election Cases
Doug. El. Cas., Doug. El. Ca., Doug., Dougl. El. Cas.

Douglas' English King's Bench Reports
Doug., Doug. K. B., Dougl. K.B., Dougl. K.B. (Eng.)

Douglas' Michigan Supreme Court Reports
Doug., Doug. (Mich.), Dougl. (Mich.)

Dow and Clark's English House of Lords Cases
D. & C., Dow N. S., Dow & C., Dow & C. (Eng.), Dow & Cl., D. & Cl.

Dow's English House of Lords Cases, New Series
D. N. S.

Dowdeswell on Life and Fire Insurance
Dowd. Ins.

Dowell's Income Tax Acts
Dow. Inc.

Dowell's Stamp Duties
Dow. St.

Dowling and Lowndes' English Bail Court Reports
Dowl. & L., Dowl. & Lownd., Dow. & L., D. & L.

Dowling and Lowndes' English Practice Cases
Dow. & Lownd.

Dowling and Ryland's English King's Bench Reports
Dow. & Ry. K. B., D. & R., Dow. & Ry., New Term Rep., Dowl. & R., Dowl. & R. (Eng.), Dowl. & Ryl.

Dowling and Ryland's English Magistrate Cases
D. & R. M.C., Dow. & Ry. M. C., Dowl. & Ryl. M. C., Dowl. & R. Mag. Cas., D. & R. Mag. Cas.

Dowling and Ryland's English Nisi Prius Cases
D. & R. N. P. C., Dow. & Ry., Dow. & Ry. K. B., Dow. & Ry. N. P., Dowl. & Ryl. N. P., D. & R. N.P., New Term Rep., D. & R. Mag. Cas., Dowl. & R. Mag. Cas. (Eng.), Dowl. & R. NP (Eng.), Dowl. & R. N. P.

Dowling and Ryland's English Queen's Bench and Magistrates' Cases
Dowl. & R.

Dowling English Practice Reports
Dowl. P. R.

Dowling's Common Law Practice
Dowl. Pr.

Dowling's English Bail Court (Practice) Cases
Dowl. (Eng.), Dowl. P. C., Dowl. PC (Eng.), Dowl.

Dowling's English Bail Court Reports, New Series
Dowl. N. S., Dowl. NS (Eng.), Dow. N.J., D.N.S.

Dowling's English Practice Cases
Dow, Dow. PC (Eng.), Dow P. C., Dow N. S., Dow. P. R., Dowl. Pr. Cas., D.P.C.

Dowling's English Practice Cases, New Series
Dowl. P. C. N. S., D. N. S., Dowl. Pr. C. N. S.

Downton and Luder's English Election Cases
Down. & Lud.

Dow's House of Lords (Parliamentary) Cases
Dow, Dow P. C., Dow. PC (Eng.)

Draft
dft.

Drake and Homer's Bankruptcy Practice
BP

Drake and Morris, Chapter 13 Practice and Procedure
PP

Drake and Mullins' Bankruptcy Practice
BP

Drake Law Review
Dr. L.R., Drake L. Rev., DR

Drake on Attachment
Dr. Att., Drake Att., Drake Attachm.

Draper on Dower
Dra. Dow.

Draper's Upper Canada King's Bench Reports
Dra., Draper (Can.), Draper (Ont.), Draper

Drawer
Dr.

Dresse on Internal Revenue Laws
Dres. Int. Rev.

Drewry and Smale's English Vice Chancellor's Reports
D. & Sm., Drew. & S., D. & S., Drew. & S. (Eng.), Drew. (Eng.), Drew. & Sm., Dr. & Sm., Dr., Drew.

Drewry's Chancery Forms
Drew. Ch. F.

Drewry's Injunctions
Drew. Inj.

Drewry's Patent Law Amendment Act
Drew. Pat.

Drewry's Trademarks
Drew. Tr. M.
Drewry's Equity Pleading
Drew. Eq. Pl.
Drew's Reports (13 Florida)
Drew.
Drinkwater's English Common Pleas Reports
Drinkw. (Eng.), Drinkw., Drinkwater, Drink.
Driving While Intoxicated
D. W. I.
Drone on Copyrights
Drone Cop.
Drug Abuse Law Review
Drug Abuse L. Rev., Drug Abuse L.R.
Drug Enforcement
Drug Enforce.
Drug Enforcement Administration
DEA
Drug Law Journal
Drug L.J.
Drug Supervisory Body, United Nations
DSB
Drunk and Disorderly
D. & D.
Drury and Walsh's Irish Chancery Reports
Dr. & Wal., D. & Wal., Drury & Wal. (Ir.), D. & W., Dru. & Wal., Drury & Wal.
Drury and Warren's Irish Chancery Reports
Drury & War. (Ir.), D. & W., D. & War., Dr. & War., Dru. & War., Drury & War.
Drury's Irish Chancery Reports
Drury, Drury (Ir.)

Drury's Irish Chancery Reports Tempore Napier
Dr. t. Nap., Ca. & Nap., Dr. R. t. Nap., Dru. t. Nap., Cas. t. Nap., Dr., Dr. & Nap., Dru. & Nap., Drury t. Nap.
Drury's Irish Chancery Reports Tempore Sugden
Dr. R. t. Sug., Ca. & Sugd., Dru., Drury t. Sug., Dr., Dr. & Sug., Dr. t. Sug., Dru. & Sug., Dru. t. Sugden, Dru. t. Sug.
Du Cange's Glossarium
Du Cange.
Duane on the Law of Nations
Duane Nat.
Duane's Road Laws of Pennsylvania
Duane Road L.
Dubitante
Dub.
Dubitatur
Dub.
Dublin University Law Journal
Dublin U. L.J., D.U.L.J. (N.S.)
Dublin University Law Review
D. U. L.R., Dublin U. L. Rev.
Ducange's Glossarium
Duc.Gl.
Duchy of Cornwall Office
D. C. O.
Dudley's "Alexandra" Case Report
Alex. Cas.
Dudley's Georgia Reports
Dud., Dud. (Geo.), Dud. (Ga.), Dudl., Dudley (Ga.), Dud. R., Ga. Dec. (Dudley), G.M. Dud., G.M. Dudl.

Dudley's South Carolina Equity Reports
Dudl., Dud. Eq. (S. C.), C.W. Dud. Eq., C.W. Dudl. Eq., C.W.Dud., Dud. Ch., Dud. Eq., Dud., Dud. L., Dud. L. S. C., Dud. Law., Dud. S. C., Dudl.

Duer on Insurance
Duer, Ins.

Duer on Marine Insurance
Duer Mar. Ins.

Duer on Representation
Duer Rep.

Duer's Constitutional Jurisprudence
Duer Const. Jur.

Duer's New York Superior Court Reports
Duer., Duer (NY)

Duff on Conveyancing
Duff Conv.

Duff on Feudal Conveyancing
Duff.

Dufresne's Glossary
Dufresne

Dugdale on Summons
Dug. Sum.

Dugdale's Monasticon
Dug. Mon.

Duke
D.

Duke Bar Association Journal
Duke B. A. J., Duke B. Ass'n J.

Duke Bar Journal
D. B. J., Duke Bar J.

Duke Journal of Comparative and International Law
Duke J. Comp. & Int'l L.

Duke Law Journal
Du. L.J., Duke L.J.

Duke on Charitable Uses
Duke Ch. Us.

Duke University Bar Association Journal
Duke B. A. Jo., Duke B.J.

Duke's Law of Charitable Uses
Duke

Dulcken's Eastern District Reports, Cape Colony
Dulck.

Duncan
Dun.

Duncan's Manual of Summary Procedure
Dunc. Man.

Duncan's Mercantile Cases
Dunc. Mer. Cas., Dunc. Merc. Cas.

Duncan's Scotch Entail Cases
Dunc. Ent. Cas.

Duncan's Scotch Parochial Ecclesiastical Law
Dunc. Eccl. L.

Duncombe on the Law of Evidence
Dunc. Ev.

Duncombe's Nisi Prius
Dunc. N. P.

Dundee Law Chronicle
Dund. L. C.

Dunglison's Dictionary of Medical Science and Literature
Dungl. Med. Dict.

Dunkle's Guide to Pension and Profit Sharing Plans
GPPS

Dunlap's Abridgment of Coke's Reports
Dunl. Abr.

Dunlap's Admiralty Practice
Dunl. Pr.

Dunlap's Forms
Dunl. F.

Dunlap's Paley on Agency
Dunl. Paley Ag.

Dunlop on Parochial Law, Scotland
Dunl. Par., D.P.L.

Dunlop, Bell and Murray's Court of Session Cases
D. B. & M.

Dunlop, Bell and Murray's Reports, Court of Session Cases, Second Series
Dunl. B & M., Dunl., Dunlop, Second D.

Dunlop's Admiralty Practice
Dunl. Adm. Pr.

Dunlop's Laws of Pennsylvania
Dunl. L. Pa.

Dunlop's Laws of the United States
Dunl. L. U.S.

Dunning's English King's Bench Reports
Dunn., Dunning

Dunphy's and Cummins' Remarkable Trials
Dun. & Cum.

Dun's Landlord and Tenant in Ireland
Dun L. & T.

Duponceau on Jurisdiction of United States Courts
Duponceau, U.S. Cts., Dup. Jur.

Duponceau on the Constitution
Dup. Const.

Duquesne Law Review
Duq. L. Rev., Duq.

Duquesne University Law Review
D. U. L.R., Duq.U. L. Rev., Duquesne L. Rev., Duquesne U. L. Rev.

Durandi Speculum Juris
Durand. Spec. Jur.

Durfee's Reports (2 Rhode Island)
Durf, Durfee

Durie's Court of Session Decisions
Durie

Durnford and East's (Term) Reports, King's Bench, England
D. & E., Durn. & E.

Dutch
D.

Dutcher's Reports (25-29 New Jersey)
Dutch.

Dutton and Cowdrey's Revision of Swift's Digest of Connecticut Laws
Dut. & Cowd. Rev.

Duvall's Reports (62-63 Kentucky)
Duv.

Duvall's Reports, Canada Supreme Court
Duv. (Can.), Duvall, Duvall, Duv.

Duxbury's Reports of the High Court of the South African Republic
Dux., D.

Dwarris on Statutes
Dw. Stat., Dwar. St., Dwar.

Dwight's Charity Cases
Dwight

Dwyer on the Militia Laws
Dw. Mil.

Dyche and Pardon's Dictionary
Dyche & P. Dict.

Dyer's English King's Bench Reports
D., Dy., Dyer, Dyer (Eng.), Di.

Dyett's Summary Proceedings
Dy. Sum. Proc.

Dymond on Death Duties
Dym. Death Dut.

E

Eagle and Younge's English Tithe Cases
    Eag. & Y., E. & Y., Eag. & Yo.
Eagle on the Law of Tithes
    E.L.T., Eag. T.
Eagle's Magistrate's Pocket Companion
    Eag. Mag. Com.
Earl
    E.
Early English Text Society
    E.E.T.S.
Earnshaw's Gold Coast Judgments
    Earn., Earnshaw
Earth Law Journal
    Earth L.J., Earth Law J.
Earth Resources Observation Systems
    EROS
Earwalker's Manchester Court Leet Records
    Earw.
Easements and Licenses
    Ease.
East
    E.
East Africa Court of Appeals Reports
    East Af
East Africa Law Reports
    E. Afr. L. Rep., E. Afr. L.R., E.A.L.R., East Afr. L. Rep.
East Africa Protectorate Law Reports
    E.A. Prot. L.R., E.A.P.L.R.
East African Community
    EAC

East African High Commission
    E.A.H.C.
East African Journal of Criminology
    E.A.J. Criminol., East Afr. J. Criminol.
East African Law Journal
    E. Afr. L.J., E.A.L.J., East Afr. L.J., E. African L.J.
East Asian Executive Reports
    E. Asian Executive Rep.
East European Constitutional Review
    E.E. Const. Rev., E.E. Con. Rev.
East India
    E.I.
East India Company
    E. India Co., E.I.C.
East Indian
    E.I.
East Indies
    E.I.
East Pakistan
    East Pak.
Easter
    E.
Easter (Paschal) Term
    P.
Easter Term
    E., E.T., East. T.
Eastern
    E.
Eastern Africa Law Reports
    E.A., East Afr. L. Rep.
Eastern Africa Law Review
    E. Afr. L. Rev., E.A.L. Rev., East. Afr. L.R., East. Afr. L. Rev.

Eastern District Court Reports, Cape of Good Hope
E.D., E.D.C., East. D.C., Gane

Eastern Districts, Local Division, South African Law Reports
East. D.L.

Eastern Journal of International Law, Madras, India
Eastern J. Int'l. L., East. J. Int. L., Eastern J. of Internat. L.

Eastern Law Reporter
East. L.R., East. L.R. (Can.), E.L.R., East., East. Rep.

Eastern Mineral Law Institute
E. Min. L. Inst.

Eastern Nigeria Law Reports
E.N.L.R.

Eastern Nigeria Legal Notice
E.N.L.N.

Eastern Region
E.R.

Eastern Region of Nigeria Law Reports
E.N.L.R., E.R.L.R., E.R.N.L.R.

Eastern Region of Nigeria Public Notice
E.R.P.N.

Eastern Reporter
East. Rep.

Eastern School Law Review
E. School L. Rev.

Eastern United States Business Law Review
East. U.S. Bus.L.Rev.

Eastern War Time
E.W.T.

East's English King's Bench Reports
Ea., East, East (Eng.), E.R.

East's Notes of Cases in Morley's East Indian Digest
Ea., East, East N. of C.

East's Pleas of the Crown
East PC (Eng.), East Pl. Cr., East P.C., E.P.C.

Eaton's Supplement to Chipman on Contracts
Eat. Cont.

Eavesdropping
Eaves.

Ebersole's Reports (59-80 Iowa)
Ebersole, Ebersole (Ia.)

Ebsworth on the Law of Infants
Ebs. Inf.

Ecclesiastical
E., Ec., Ecc., Eccl.

Ecclesiastical and Admiralty
Eccl. and Ad.

Ecclesiastical and Admiralty Reports
E. and A.

Ecclesiastical Commissioner
E.C.

Ecclesiastical Compensations
E.B.

Ecclesiastical Court
Eccl. Ct.

Ecclesiastical Institute[s]
E.I.

Ecclesiastical Law Journal
Ecc. L.J.

Ecclesiastical Reports
Eccl. Rep.

Ecclesiastical Statutes
Eccl. Stat.

Eck on Asset Valuation
ASV

Ecology Law Quarterly
Ecol L Q, Ecol. L. Quart., Ecology L.Q.

Economic and Monetary Union
EMU

Economic and Social Commission for Asia and the Pacific, United Nations
ESCAP

Economic and Social Committee, United Nations
ESC, ECOSOC

Economic and Social Council
ESCOR

Economic Bulletin for Europe
Econ. Bull. Eur., Econ. Bull. for Europe

Economic Commission for Africa, United Nations
ECA

Economic Commission for Asia and the Far East, United Nations, United Nations
ECAFE

Economic Commission for Europe, United Nations
ECE

Economic Commission for Latin America, United Nations
ECLA

Economic Commission for Western Asia, United Nations
ECWA

Economic Community of West African States
ECOWAS

Economic Controls, Commerce Clearing House
Econ. Contr., Econ. Contr. (CCH)

Economic Corporation Administration
ECA

Economic Development Administration
EDA

Economic Recovery Tax Act of 1981
ERTA

Economic Regulations
E.R.

Economic Research Service
ERS

Economic Stabilization Agency
ESA

Economic Standards, Commerce Clearing House
Econ. Stand. (CCH)

Economic[s]; Economy
Econ.

Economist
Economist

Eddis on Administration of Assets
Ed. Ass.

Eddis on Bills of Exchange
Ed. Bills

Eden's Bankrupt Law
Eden. Bankr., Ed. B.L.

Eden's Edition of English Chancery Reports Tempore Northington
Ca. t. N., Ca. t. North., Cas. t. North., Ed. Bro., Ed.

Eden's Injunctions
Ed. Inj.

Eden's Principles of Penal Law
Ed. P.L., Eden, Pen. Law, Eden's Prin. P.L., Prin. P.L.

Edgar's Reports, Court of Session, Scotland
Edgar, Ed., Edg.

Edges' Forms of Leases
Edg. Leas.

Edicts of Justinian
Edict, Edicta

Edinburgh
Ed.

Edinburgh Law Journal
Edinb. L.J., Ed. L.J.

Edited
  Edit.
Edition[s]
  ED, ed., Eds., Edit., Edited
Editor[s]
  ed., Eds., Edit., Edited
Editorial Comment
  Ed. Comment
Edmands' Address to His Law Students
  Edm. Addr.
Edmonds' Edition of the New York Statutes
  Edm. Stat.
Edmonds' New York Select Cases
  Edm. Sel. Ca., Edm. Sel. Cas., Edm. Sel. Cas. (NY)
Edmonds' New York Statutes at Large
  Edmonds' St. at Large
Edmund's English Law Reports, Appeal Cases
  App. Cas.
Edmund's Exchequer Practice
  Edm. Exch. Pr.
Edmund's Laws
  Leg. Edm.
Education; Educational
  Educ.
Education and Labor
  E.L.
Education Department Reports
  Ed. Dept. Rep.
Education for the Handicapped Law Report
  Ed. H.L.R, EHLR
Education Law Reporter
  Educ. L. Rep. (West)
Education Order
  Ed. O.
Edward
  Edw.

Edward I Yearbooks
  Y.B.Ed.I., Yearb.Ed.I
Edward The Confessor
  Edw. Conf.
Edward The Confessor's Laws
  L.L.Edw.Conf.
Edwards' Abridgement of Prerogative Court Cases
  Edw. Pr. Ct. Cas., Edw.Abr.
Edward's Abridgment Privy Council Cases
  Edw. Abr.
Edwards' Admiralty Jurisdiction.
  Edw. Adm. Jur.
Edwards' Chancery Reports, New York
  Ed. Ch (N. Y.), Ed. Ch. R., Ed. Cr., Edw. Chan., Edw. (N. Y.), Edwards' Chr. R., Edwards' Rep., Edw.Ch. (NY), Ed.Ch., Ed.C.R., Edw., Edw.Ch., Edw.Rep.
Edwards' Chester Palatine Courts
  Edw.
Edwards' English Admiralty Reports
  Edw., Edw. (Tho.), Edw.Adm., Edw.Adm. (Eng.), Edw.Lead.Dec.
Edwards' Factors and Brokers
  Edw. Fac.
Edwards' Juryman's Guide
  Edw. Jur.
Edwards' Justices' Treatise
  Edw. Treat.
Edwards' Law of Gaming
  Edw. Gam.
Edwards on Bills and Notes
  Edw. Bills, Edw. Bills and N.

Edwards on Ecclesiastical Jurisdiction
Edw. Eccl. Jur.

Edwards on Factors and Brokers
Edw. Brok. and F.

Edwards on Parties in Chancery
Edw. Part.

Edwards on Receivers in Equity
Edw. Rec.

Edwards on the Law of Bailments
Edw. Bail., Edw. Bailm.

Edwards on the Law of Referees
Edw. Ref.

Edwards on the Stamp Act
Edw. St. Act

Edwards' Pleasantries of the Courts of New York
Edw. Pleas.

Edwards' Prize Cases (English Admiralty Reports)
Edw. P.C., Edw. Pr. Cas.

Edward's Reports (2-3 Missouri)
Edw. Mo., Edw.

Edwardus Rex (King Edward)
E.R.

Equal Employment Opportunity Commission (EEOC) Compliance Manual, Bureau of National Affairs
EEOC Comp. Man.

Equal Employment Opportunity Commission (EEOC) Compliance Manual, Commerce Clearing House
EEOC Comp. Man.

Effective
Eff.

Efird's Reports (45-56 South Carolina)
Efird

Egan on Bills of Sale
Egan Bills

Egan on Extradition
Eg. Ext.

Eggleston on Damages
Egg.Dam.

Eglit on Age Discrimination
AgD

Egremont on the Law of Highways
Egr. High.

Eiffe on the Irish Judicature Act
Eif. Jud. Act

Eighteen-Nation Disarmament Committee
ENDC

Eiloart on Laws relating to Women
Eil. Wom.

Ejectment
Eject.

El Paso Trial Lawyers Reviews
El Paso Trial Law. Rev.

El Salvador
El. Sal.

Elchies' Court of Session Cases, Scotland
Elchies, El., Elch.

Elchies' Dictionary of Decisions, Court of Session, Scotland
El. Dict., Elchies' Dict.

Elder
Eld.

Eldest
Eld.

Eldest Son
E. s.

Election
Elec.

Election Cases
E.C., Elect. Cas., El. Cas.

Election Law Reports, England
Elec. L.R., E.L.R.

Election of Remedies
Elect. Rem.

Election Reports
Elect. Rep., E.R.

Elections Code
Elec. C.

Electrical
Elec.

Electricity
Elec.

Electronic
Elec.

Electronic Data Processing
EDP

Electronic Fund Transfers
EFT

Elevator[s]
Elev.

Elizabeth Regina (Queen Elizabeth)
E.R.

Eller's Minnesota Digest
El. Dig.

Ellesmere's Post Nati
Ellesm. Post N., Ellesm. Postn.

Ellet on the Laws of Trade
Ell. Trade

Elliot's American Diplomatic Code
Ell. Dip. Code

Elliot's Debates on the Federal Constitution
Ell. Deb., Elliot, Deb. Fed. Const.

Elliott on Roads and Streets
Elliott, Roads and S.

Elliott's Appellate Procedure
Elliott, App. Proc.

Elliott's Supplement to the Indiana Revised Statutes
Elliott, Supp.

Ellis and Blackburn's English Queen's Bench Reports
Ell. & Bl., El. & B., El. & Bl., El. & Bl. (Eng.), E. & B, Ellis & Bl.

Ellis and Ellis' English Queen's Bench Reports
Ell. & Ell., El. & El., El. & El. (Eng.), E. & E.

Ellis on Fire and Life Insurance and Annuities
Ell. Ins.

Ellis on Insurance
Ellis

Ellis on the Law of Debtor and Creditor
Ellis Dr. & Cr.

Ellis, Best and Smith's English Queen's Bench Reports
El. B. & S., E.B.& S., Ell. B. & S., El. B. & S. (Eng.)

Ellis, Blackburn and Ellis' English Queen's Bench Reports
El. B. & El., E.B. & E., El. B. & E., Ell. Bl. & Ell., El. Bl. & El. (Eng.), El., Bl. & El.

Ellis' Debtor and Creditor
Ell. D. & Cr.

Ellison's Law of Annuities
Ell. Ann.

Ellsworth's Copyright Manual
Ells. Cop. Man.

Elmer's Digest of New Jersey Laws
Elm. Dig.

Elmer's New Jersey Laws
Elm. N.J. Laws

Elmer's Practice in Lunacy
Elm. Lun., Elmer, Lun.

Elmes' Executive Departments of the United States
Elm. Exec. Dep.

Elmes on Architectural Jurisprudence
Elm. Arch. Jur.

Elmes on Ecclesiastical Civil Dilapidation
Elm. Dilap.

Elphinstone, Norton and Clark on Interpretation of Deeds
Elph.

Elphinstone's Introduction to Conveyancing
Elph. Conv.

Elphinstone's Rules for Interpretation of Deeds
Elph. Interp. Deeds

Elsley's Edition of William Blackstone's English King's Bench Reports
Els. W. Bl.

Elsynge on Parliaments
Elsyn. Parl.

Elton on Commons and Waste Lands
Elt. Com., Elton, Com.

Elton on Copyholds
Elt. Copyh., Elton, Copyh.

Elton's Tenures of Kent
Elt. Ten. of Kent

Elwell on Malpractice and Medical Jurisprudence
Elw. Mal., Elw. Med. Jur.

Emalfarb's Illinois Construction Law: Manual and Forms
ICLM

Embezzlement
Embez.

Embracery
Embrac.

Emergency Court of Appeals
Em. App., Em. Ct. App., Emer. Ct. App.

Emergency Petroleum and Gas Administration
EPGA

Emergency Powers Act
E.P.A.

Emergency Powers (Defence) Act
E.P.D.A.

Emerigon on Insurance
Emer. Ins., Emerig. Ins.

Emerigon on Maritime Loans
Emer. Mar. Lo., Emerig. Mar. Loans

Emerson and Haber's Political and Civil Rights in the United States
Emerson & Haber, Pol. & Civ. Rits.

Eminence
E.

Eminent Domain
Em. Dom.

Emory International Law Review
Emory Int'l L. Rev.

Emory Journal of International Dispute Resolution
Em. J. Int. Disp. Resol.

Emory Law Journal
Em. L.J., Emory L.J.

Emperor
Emp.

Empire
Emp.

Employee Benefits Cases, Bureau of National Affairs
EBC, Employee Benefits Cas. (BNA)

Employee Relations Law Journal
Empl. Rel. L.J., Employee Rel. L.J.

Employee Stock Ownership Plan
ESOP

Employers' Liability
Empl'rs. Liab.

Employment Agency
Employ. Ag.
Employment and Training Administration
ETA
Employment and Training Reporter, Bureau of National Affairs
Empl. & Training Rep. (BNA)
Employment Appeals Tribunal
E.A.T.
Employment-At-Will Reporter
E.A.W.R.
Employment Commission
E.C., Empl. Com.
Employment Coordinator, Research Institute of America
Empl. Coordinator (R.I.A.)
Employment Practice Decisions, Commerce Clearing House
E.P.D., Empl. Prac. Dec. (CCH),
Employment Practices Guide, Commerce Clearing House
Empl. Prac. Guide (CCH)
Employment Protection (Consolidation) Act
EP(C)A
Employment Relations Board
ERB
Employment Relations Income Security Act
ERISA
Employment Safety and Health Guide, Commerce Clearing House
Empl. Saf'y & Health Guide (CCH), Empl. Safety & Health Guide (CCH)
Employment Security Agency
ESA
Employment Security Board
ESB

Employment Security Commission
ESC
Employment Security Department
ESD
Employment Security Division
ESD
Employment Service Automated Reporting System
ESARS
Employment Service Division
ESD
Employment Services Bureau
ESB
Employment Stabilization Commission
ESC
Employment Standards Administration
ESA
Employment Tax Ruling
Em. T.
Employment Taxes, Social Security Act Rulings, United States Internal Revenue Service
Em. T.
Empress
Emp.
Encyclopedia Americana
Enc. Amer.
Encyclopedia Britannica
Enc. Brit.
Encyclopedia Dictionary, edited by Robert Hunter
Enc. Dict.
Encyclopedia of European Community Law
E.E.C.L.
Encyclopedia of Evidence
Ency. of Ev.
Encyclopedia of Forms
Enc. Forms

Encyclopedia of Forms and Precedents
Ency. of Forms
Encyclopedia of Georgia Law
E.G.L.
Encyclopedia of Law and Practice
Ency. of L. & Pr.
Encyclopedia of Pennsylvania Law
P.L.E.
Encyclopedia of Pleading and Practice
Ency. P. & P., Enc. Pl. & Pr., Enc. Pl. & Prac., Ency. of Pl. & Pr.
Encyclopedia of Pleading and Practice Supplement
Ency. U.S. Sup. Ct. Rep.
Encyclopedia of the Laws of England
Encyc.
Encyclopedia of United States Reports
U.S.E.
Encyclopedia of United States Supreme Court Reports
Enc. U.S. Sup. Ct. Rep., Ency. U.S. Sup. Ct.
Endlich on Building Associations
End. Bdg. Ass., Endl. Bidg. Ass'ns.
Endlich's Commentaries on the Interpretation of Statutes
End. Interp. St.
Energy
Energy
Energy and Natural Resources
ENR
Energy Conservation and Production Act
ECPA
Energy Controls, Prentice-Hall
Energy Cont. (P-H)

Energy Information Administration
EIA
Energy Information Council
EIC
Energy Law Journal
Energy L.J.
Energy Law Service, Callaghan
Energy L. Serv. (Callaghan)
Energy Management, Commerce Clearing House
Energy Mgmt. (CCH)
Energy Policy and Conservation Act
E.P.C.A.
Energy Research and Development Administration
ERDA
Energy Resources Council
ERC
Energy Users Report, Bureau of National Affairs
Energy Users Rep. (BNA)
Energy Users Report, Commerce Clearing House
En. Users Rep.
Enforc[ed, ment, ing]
Enfd., Enf., Enf'g.
Enforcement Denied
Enf'. den.
Engineer Contract Instructions
ECI
Engineer
Eng'r.
Engineering
Eng'g.
England
E., Eng., Engl.
England and Wales
E. and W.
England and Wales, High Court of Justice
High Court

English
Eng., E.

English and Scotch Ecclesiastical Reports
Eng. Sc. Ecc.

English Admiralty
Eng. Ad., Eng. Adm.

English Admiralty Reports
Eng. Ad., Eng. Adm. R.

English and Empire Digest
E. & E. Dig., E. & E.D.

English and Irish Appeals, House of Lords
E. & I.

English Chancery
E.C., Eng. Ch.

English Chancery Appeals
Equity Rep.

English Chancery Records
Acta Cancelariae

English Chancery Reports (American Reprint)
E.C., Eng. Ch.

English Chancery Reports Tempore Finch
Finch., Finch (Eng.)

English Common Law Procedure Act
C.L.P.Act.

English Common Law Reports
Com. Law Rep., Eng. Com. L.R., Com. Law R., Com. L.R.

English Common Law Reports (American Reprint)
Eng. C.L., C.L., E.C.L. (Eng.)

English Common Law Reports, (American Reprint edited by Sergeant and Lowber)
Serg. & Lowb.Rep.

English Consistorial Reports by Haggard
Consist. Rep., Consist. See also Haggard's English Consistory Reports

English Crown Cases (American Reprint)
Eng. C.C., Eng. Cr. Cas.

English Ecclesiastical Reports
Eccl. R., Eng. Ecc. R., Eng. Eccl.

English Ecclesiastical Reports (American Reprint)
E.E.R.

English Exchequer Reports
Eng. Exch., Exch., Ex.

English Exchequer Reports (American Reprint)
Exch. Rep., E.E.

English Historical Review
Eng. Hist. Rev.

English Law and Equity Reports
L. & E.

English Law and Equity Reports (American Reprint)
Eng. L. & Eq., Eng. L. & Eq. R., Eng. Law & Eq., E.L. & Eq.

English Law Reports, Chancery Appeals
Ch., Ch. (Eng.)

English Law Reports, Admiralty and Ecclesiastical
Adm. & Ecc., Adm. & Eccl., L.R.A. & E.

English Law Reports, Appeal Cases
L.R.A.C., L.R. App., L.R. App. Cas., L.R. App. Cas. (Eng.)

English Law Reports, Chancery Division
Ch., Ch. Div., Ch. Div. (Eng.), Ch. (Eng.), Ch.D., L.R.Ch. D.

English Law Reports, Chancery Division, Second Series
Ch.D. 2d

English Law Reports, Common Pleas Division
L.R.C.P. Div. (Eng.), L.R.C.P.D.

English Law Reports, Crown Cases Reserved
L.R.C.C. (Eng.), L.R.C.C.

English Law Reports, Equity
L.R. Eq., L.R. Eq. (Eng.)

English Law Reports, Exchequer
Exch., L.R. Ex., L.R. Ex. Cas., L.R. Exch., L.R. Exch. (Eng.)

English Law Reports, Exchequer Division
L.R. Ex. Div., L.R. Exch. D., L.R. Exch. Div. (Eng.), Exch.D., E.D.

English Law Reports, House of Lords, Scotch and Divorce Appeal Cases
H.L.Sc. App.Cas., L.R.H.L. Sc., L.R.H.L. Sc. App. Cas. (Eng.)

English Law Reports, Indian Appeals
L.R. Indian App., L.R. Indian App. (Eng.), L.R.I.A., L.R. Ind. App.

English Law Reports, Indian Appeals Supplement
L.R. Ind. App. Supp., I. A.Sup.Vol.

English Law Reports, King's Bench
K.B., K.B. (Eng.)

English Law Reports, King's Bench Division
L.R.K.B.

English Law Reports, Privy Council Appeal Cases
L.R.P.C., L.R.P.C. (Eng.)

English Law Reports, Probate
Prob.

English Law Reports, Probate Division
L.R.P.

English Law Reports, Probate, Divorce and Admiralty Division
L.R. Prob. & Div., L.R. Prob. & M. (Eng.), L.R. Prob. Div., L.R. Prob. Div. (Eng.), L.R.P. Div.

English Law Reports, Queen's Bench
Q.B., L.R.Q.B. (Eng.), L.R.Q.B

English Law Reports, Queen's Bench Division
L.R.Q.B. Div., L.R.Q.B. Div. (Eng.), Q.B.D., L.R.Q.B.D.

English Law Reports, Scotch and Divorce Cases before the House of Lords
L.R. Sc. & D.

English Law Reports, Sessions Cases
L.R. Sess. Cas.

English Law Reports, Statutes
L.R. Stat.

English Maritime Law Reports, by Crockford
Crockford.

English on Church Pews
Eng. Pews

English Pleader
Eng. Pl.

English Privy Council Reports
P.C. Rep.

English Railway and Canal Cases
Eng. R. & C. Cas., Eng. Ry. & C. Cas., Ra. Ca., Rail. & Can. Cas., Eng.R.R.Ca.

English Railway and Canal Cases, by Beavan and others
Beav. R. & C. Cas.

English Railway and Canal Cases, by Nichale, etc.
Nichale
English Reports Annotated
Eng. Rep. Anno., E.R.A.
English Reports, Full Reprint
Eng. Re., Eng. Rep. R., Eng. Rep. Re., Reprint, Eng. Rep., E.R.
English Reports (Moak's American Reprint)
Eng. Rep. See also Moak's English Reports
English Reprint
Eng. Reprint
English Ruling Cases
Eng. Ru. Ca., Eng. Ru.Cas., Eng. Rul. Cas., E.R.C., E.R.C. (Eng.)
English's Digest of the Arkansas Statutes
Dig. St.
English's Reports (6-13 Arkansas)
Eng., Eng. Rep., English
Enjoin[ed, ing]
Enjoin
Enter[ed, ing]
Enter
Enterprise
Enter.
Entertainment
Ent.
Entertainment and Media Law
Entertainment & Med. L.
Entertainment and Sports Lawyer
Ent. & Sports Law.
Entertainment Duty
E.D.
Entertainment Law Journal
Entertainment L.J.
Entertainment Law Reporter
Entertainment L.R.

Entertainment Tax
E.T.
Entry Clearance Officer (Immigration)
E.C.O.
Environment
Env't
Environment and Public Works
EPW
Environment Law Review
Environ. L. Rev.
Environment Regulation Handbook
Env't Reg. Handbook (Env't Information Center)
Environment Reporter, Bureau of National Affairs
Envir. Rep., Env't. Rep. (BNA)
Environment Reporter Cases, Bureau of National Affairs
Env't Rep. Cas. (BNA)
Environmental
Envtl.
Environmental Affairs
Env. Aff., Envtl. Affairs
Environmental and Planning Law Journal
Envtl. and Plan. L.J.
Environmental Claims Journal
Envtl. Claims J.
Environmental Conservation
Envir. Conserv.
Environmental Forum
Envtl.F.
Environmental Health Services
EHS
Environmental Impact Statement
E.I.S.
Environmental Law
Env. L., Environ. L., Environm. L., Environmental Law, Envtl. L., Envtl.L.

Environmental Law Institute
ELI
Environmental Law Journal
Envtl. L.J.
Environmental Law Quarterly
Newsletter
Envt'l. L.Q. Newsl.
Environmental Law Reporter
Env. L. Rptr., Envir. L. Rep.,
Envt'l. L. Rep. (Envtl. L. Inst.),
Envtl. L. Rptr.
Environmental Law Review
Env. L. Rev., Envtl. L. Rev.
Environmental Policy and Law
Environm. Policy & L., Envtl.
Pol'y & L.
Environmental Protection
Agency
E.P.A.
Environmental Reporter Cases,
Bureau of National Affairs
E.R.C.
Envoy Extraordinary
Env. Extr.
Envoy Extraordinary and Minis-
ter Plenipotentiary
E.E. & M.P.
Eodem (in the same place or un-
der the same title) (Lat.)
E., Eod.
Equal Access to Justice Act
EAJA
Equal Employment Compliance
Manual
Eq. Empl. Compl. Man.
Equal Employment Opportunity
EEO
Equal Employment Opportunity
Commission
EEOC

Equal Employment Opportunity
Commission Compliance Man-
ual, Commerce Clearing House
EEOC, E.E.O.C. Compliance
Manual
Equal Opportunities Commission
E.O.C.
Equal Pay Act of 1963
EPA
Equatorial Guinea
Eq. Guinea
Equipment
Equip.
Equitable
Eq.
Equitable Conversion
Eq. Conv.
Equitable Distribution Reporter
Equi. Dist. Rep.
Equity
E., Eq.
Equity Cases Abridged
Ab. Eq. Cas., Abr.Eq.Cas., Abr.
Cas. Eq., Eq. Cas. Abr., Eq. Cas.
Abr. (Eng.)
Equity Cases, Modern Reports
Eq. Cas. Mod., Eq. Cas.
Equity Court or Division
Eq.
Equity Exchequer
E.E.
Equity Reports
Eq. R. (Eng.), Eq., Eq. Rep., Eq-
uity Rep., Eq. Rep.
Erck's Ecclesiastical Register
Erck
Ergänzung (Amendment, Supple-
ment) (German)
Erg.
Erie County Law Journal
Erie Co. L.J. (Pa.), Erie Co. Leg.
J., Erie, Erie L.J.

Erle on the Law of Trade-Unions
Erle Tr. Un.
Erroneous[ly]
Erron.
Error and Appeal
E. & A.
Errors and Omissions Excepted
E. & O.E., E. & O.E.
Errors Excepted
E.E.
Erskine's Institutes of the Law of Scotland
Ersk., Ersk. Inst., Erskine I., Erskine, Inst.
Erskine's Principles of the Law of Scotland
Ersk., Ersk. Prin.
Erskine's Speeches
Ersk. Speech, Ersk. Speeches
Erskine's United States Circuit Court, etc. , Decisions (vol. 35 Georgia)
Ersk. Dec.
Escriche's Dictionary of Jurisprudence
Escriche, Dict.
Escrow
Esc.
Espinasse on Penal Evidence
Esp. Pen. Ev.
Espinasse on Penal Statutes
Esp.P. St.
Espinasse on Evidence
Esp. Ev.
Espinasse on Law of Bankrupts
Esp. Bank
Espinasse's Actions on Statutes
Esp. Act.
Espinasse's Digest of the Law of Actions and Trials
Esp. Dig.

Espinasse's English Nisi Prius Reports
Esp., Esp. N.P.
Esquire
Esq.
Esquirol on Insanity
Esq. Ins.
Essays on Anglo-Saxon Law
Ess. Ang. Sax. Law
Established
Est.
Established Church
E.C.
Establishment
Estab.
Estate and Gift Tax Ruling
E.T.
Estate Duties Investment Trust
E.D.I.T.
Estate Dut[y, ies]
E.D.
Estate Gazette
E.G.
Estate Planning
E.P., Est. Plan.
Estate Planning Institute
Est. Plan. Inst.
Estate Planning, Prentice-Hall
P-H Est. Plan.
Estate Planning Review
Est. Plan. Rev.
Estate Tax Division, United States Internal Revenue Service
E.T.
Estate Tax Ruling
E.T.
Estate[s]
Est.
Estates and Trusts Journal
Est. & Tr. J.
Estates and Trusts
Est. & Trusts

Estates and Trusts Quarterly
Estates Q., Est. and Tr. Q.
Estates and Trusts Reports
Est. & Tr. Rep., E.T.R.
Estates Gazette
Est. Gaz., Estates Gaz.
Estates Gazette Digest of Cases
E.G.D., E.G.D.C.
Estates Gazette Digest of Land and Property Cases
Est. Gaz. Dig.
Estates, Gifts and Trusts Journal
Est. Gifts & Tr. J.
Estates, Powers and Trusts
Est. Powers & Trusts
Estee (Morris M.), United States District Court Reports for Hawaii
U.S. Dist. Ct. Haw. (Estee), Estee, Estee (Hawaii)
Estee's Code Pleading Practice and Forms
Est. Prac. Pl., Est. Prac.
Estimated
Estm.
Estoppel and Waiver
Estop. and W.
Et Alia (and other things) (Lat.)
Et al.
Et Alibi (and elsewhere) (Lat.)
Et al.
Et Alii (and others) (Lat.)
Et al.
Et Cetera (and the others, and so forth) (Lat.)
Etc.
Et Sequens (and the following) (Lat.)
et seq.
Et Sequitur (and as follows) (Lat.)
et seq.
Et Uxor (and wife) (Lat.)
et ux.

Ethelred's Laws
Leg. Ethel.
Ethics
Ethics
Ethiopia
Eth.
Etting's American Admiralty Jurisdiction
Ett. Ad.
Euer's Doctrina Placitandi
Euer
Eurolaw Commercial Intelligence
Eurolaw Com. Intel.
Europe
Eur.
Europe Archiv
E.A.
European
Eur.
European Agreement concerning the International Carriage of Dangerous Goods by Road
ADR
European Agricultural Guidance and Guarantee Fund
EAGGF
European Arbitration
Eur. Arb.
European Assurance Arbitration
Eur. Ass. Arb.
European Atomic Energy Community
EURATOM, Euratom
European Bank for Reconstruction and Development
EBRD
European Coal and Steel Community
ECSC
European Commission of Human Rights
EC Human Rights, Eur. Comm. on Human Rights

European Committee on Crime Problems
  E.C.C.P.
European Common Market
  E.C.M.
European Communities
  E.C.
European Communities Bulletin
  Bull. Eur. Communities
European Communities Committee of Permanent Representatives
  COREPER
European Communities Court of Justice
  E.C.C.J.
European Community Cases
  CEC
European Community Convention on the Jurisdiction of the Courts and Enforcement of Judgments in Civil and Commercial Matters, 27 Sept Sept. 1968
  Conv. F.J.
European Company Statute
  ECS
European Competition Law Review
  E.C.L.R.
European Conference of Ministers of Transport
  ECMT
European Convention on Human Rights Yearbook
  Y.B.Eur.Conv. on Human Rights, Y.B.Eur.Conv. on H.R., Yb. of Eur.Conv. on Human Rights, Y.B. Europ. Conv. H.R.
European Court of Human Rights
  Eur. Ct. H.R.
European Court of Justice
  Eur. C.J.

European Court Reports
  E.C.R.
European Currency Unit
  ECU
European Defence Community
  E.D.C., EDE
European Development Fund
  EDF
European Documentation Centre
  E.D.C.
European Economic Area
  EEA
European Economic Community
  EEC
European Economic Review
  E.E.R.
European Free Trade Association
  EFTA
European Human Rights Reports
  E.H.R.R.
European Industrial Relations Review
  E.I.R.R.
European Inland Transport Organization
  ECITO
European Intellectual Property Review
  Eur. Intell. Prop. Rev., Europ. Intell. Prop. Rev.
European Investment Bank
  EIB
European Law Digest
  Eur. L. Dig.
European Law Newsletter
  Eur. L. Newsl.
European Law Review
  E.L. Rev., E.L.R., Eur. L. Rev., European L. Rev.
European Monetary Agreement
  EMA

European Monetary and Coopera-
tion Fund
   EMCF
European Nuclear Energy Agency
   E.N.E.A.
European Parliament Working
Documents
   Eur. Parl. Doc., Eur. Parl. Docs.
European Parliamentary Assem-
bly Debates
   Eur. Parl. Deb.
European Payments Union
   EPU
European Recovery Program
   ERP
European Regional Organisation
of the International Confedera-
tion of Free Trade Unions
   E.R.O.
European Space Agency
   ESA
European Space Research Or-
ganization
   ESRO
European Space Vehicle Launch-
er Development Organization
   ELDO
European Taxation
   Eur. Tax., Eur. Taxation
European Transport Law, Jour-
nal of Law and Economics
   Eur. Trans. L., Eur. T.L., Eur.
   Transp. L.
European Treaty Series, Agree-
ments and Conventions of the
Council of Europe
   Europ. T.S., E.T.S.
European Union
   EU
European Works Council
   E.W.C.
European Yearbook
   Eur. Y.B., Europ. Y.B.

Europen Human Rights Reports
   Eur. H.R. Rep.
Evaluation Quarterly
   Eval. Q.
Evaluation Review
   Eval. Rev.
Evans' Collection of Statutes
   Ev. Stat.
Evans' Edition of Harris' Modern
Entries
   Ev. Harr.
Evans' Great War Prize Cases
   Pr.Ca.
Evans' English King's Bench Re-
ports
   Evans
Evan's Lord Mansfield's Deci-
sions, England
   Evans
Evans' Maryland Practice
   Ev. Md. Pr.
Evans on Agency
   Ev. Ag.
Evans on Pleading
   Ev. Pl.
Evans on the Law of Principal
and Agent
   Ev. Pr. and Ag.
Evans' Practice of the Supreme
Court of Judicature
   Ev. Jud. Pr.
Evans' Reports, Washington Ter-
ritory (announced, but never
published)
   Evans
Evans' Road Laws of South Caro-
lina
   Ev. R.L.
Evans' Translation of Pothier on
Obligations
   Ev. Poth.
Evans' Trial
   Ev. Tr.

Everybody's Law Magazine
Everybody's L.M.
Evidence
Ev., Evid.
Ewell on the Law of Fixtures
Ewell Fix.
Ewell's Edition of Blackstone
Ewell Bl.
Ewell's Edition of Evans on Agency
Ewell Evans Ag.
Ewell's Essentials of the Law
Ewell Ess.
Ewell's Leading Cases on Infancy, etc.
Ewell Cas. Inf. (or L. C.), Ewell L.C.
Ewing's Justice
Ewing Just.
Ex Parte (on behalf of one party only) (Lat.)
Exp.
Ex Relatione (on the relation of) (Lat.)
Ex rel.
Ex warrants
X.W.
Examiner
Exam.
Examiner's Decision
Ex.
Example
Ex.
Exceptional Circumstances Allowance
ECA
Exceptional Needs Payment
ENP
Excess Profit Duty
E.P.D.
Excess Profits Tax
E.P.T.

Excess Profits Tax Council Ruling or Memorandum, United States Internal Revenue Bureau
E.P.C.
Exchange
Ex., Exch.
Exchange of Property
Exch. P.
Exchequer
Ex., Exch.
Exchequer Cases, England
Exch. Cas.
Exchequer Chamber
Exch. Cham.
Exchequer Court, Canada
Can. Ex.
Exchequer Court Reports, Canada
Exch. C.R.
Exchequer Division
Exch.
Exchequer Reports, Canada
Exch. Can.
Execution
Exec.
Executive
Ex., Exec.
Executive Agreement Series, United States Treaties and Agreements
EAS, E.A.S.
Executive Disclosure Guide, Commerce Clearing House
Exec. Disclosure Guide (CCH)
Executive Document
Exec. Doc.
Executive Enterprises, Inc.
EEI
Executive Instruments
E.I.
Executive Orders
Ex. Or.

Executor[s]
Ex., Exec., Ex'r., Exor., Exr.,
Exor[s]
Executor[s] and Administrator[s]
Ex. and Ad.
Executrix
Execx., Exx., Ex'x.
**Exempt Organizations Guide,
Commerce Clearing House**
Exempt. Org. Rep. (CCH)
Exemption[s]
Exemp.
Expense[s]
Exp.
Experimental Safety Vehicle
ESV
Expert Evidence Reporter
ExER
Expired
Exp.
Expiring Law Continuance Acts
E.L.C. Acts
Explained
E., Exp., Expld.
Explosions and Explosives
Explos.
Export Administration Bulletin
E.A.B.
Export Credit Guarantees
ECG
Export Credits Guarantee Department
E.C.G.D.
Export-Import Bank
Eximbank, EXIMBANK

Export Marketing Service
EMS
Expression
Exp.
Expropriation[s]
Exp.
Extended
Extd., Ext.
Extension[s]
Extn., Ext.
External
Ext., Extl.
Exton's Maritime Dicaeologie
Exton Mar. Dic.
Extortion
Extort.
Extortion, Blackmail and Threats
Extort.
Extra Session
Ex. Sess.
Extract[s]
Ex.
Extradition
Extrad.
Extraordinary Session
Extra. Sess.
Extravagantes Communes
Ex. Com.
**Eyre's Manuscript Notes of
King's Bench Cases, England**
Eyre, MS
Eyre's King's Bench Reports Tempore William III, England
Eyre

F

Facsimile
Facs.
Factories Journal Reports
F.J.R.
Faculty
Fac.
Faculty Collection of Decisions, Court of Sessions, Scotland
FC (Scott), Fac. Coll., Fac. Dec., F.C., F
Faculty of Advocates Collection of Decisions, Court of Session, Scotland
Fac., Fac. Coll. N.S.
Faculty of Law Review, University of Toronto
Fac. of L. Rev. (Toronto), Fac. L. Rev., Fac. of L.R., U.T. Faculty L.R.
Fair Access to Insurance Requirements
FAIR
Fair Employment Board
FEB
Fair Employment Practice Cases, Bureau of National Affairs
F.E.P. Cas., FEP, Fair Empl. Prac. Cas. (BNA)
Fair Employment Practices Commission
FEPC
Fair Labor Standards Act
FLSA
Fair Trade Laws
Fair Tr.
Fairbanks' Marriage and Divorce Laws of Massachusetts
Fair. M. & D.

Fairfield's Reports (10-12 Maine)
Fairf., Fairf. (Me.), Fairfield
Falconer and Fitzherbert's English Election Cases
Falc. & Fitz., Falc. & F., F. & Fitz.
Falconer's English County Court Cases
Falc. Co. Cts.
Falconer's Marine Dictionary
Falc. Marine Dict.
Falconer's Scotch Court of Session Cases
Falc., Pres. Fal., Pr. Falc., Pres. Falc.
Falkland Islands
Falk. Is.
Fallen Building Clause
F.b.c.
Fallen Building Clause Waiver
F.b.c.w.
False Imprisonment
False Imp.
False Personation
False Pers.
False Pretenses
False Pret.
Family
Fam.
Family Advocate
Fam. Adv., Fam. Advocate, Family Adv.
Family Court
Fam. Ct.
Family Court Act
Fam. Ct. Act.
Family Division
Fam. Div., F.D., Fam.

Family Divisional Court
   Fam. Div'l Ct.
Family Income Supplement
   FIS
Family Law
   Fam. Law
Family Law Commentator
   Fam. L. Commtr.
Family Law Newsletter
   Fam. L. Newsl.
Family Law Notes
   Fam. L.N.
Family Law Quarterly
   Fam. L.Q., Family L.Q.
Family Law Reporter, Bureau of National Affairs
   Fam. L. Rep. (BNA), F.L.R.
Family Law Reports
   Fam. L.R.
Family Law Review
   Fam L. Rev.
Family Law Tax Guide, Commerce Clearing House
   Fam. L. Tax Guide (CCH)
Family Rights Group
   FRG
Famous Cases of Circumstantial Evidence, by Phillips
   Fam. Cas. Cir. Ev.
Fanton's Tables of Roman Law
   Fan. Rom. Law
Far Eastern Commission
   FEC
Far Eastern Economic Review
   Far Eastern Econ. Rev.
Far Eastern Law Review
   Far East. L. Rev., Far East L.R., F.E.L.R., F.E.U.L. Rev.
Farm Credit Administration
   FCA
Farm Security Administration
   FSA

Farmer Cooperative Service
   FCS
Farmers Home Administration
   Fm. H.A.
Farquharson's Court of Chancery
   Farq. Chy.
Farrar's Manual of the United States Constitution
   Farr. Const.
Farren on Life Assurance
   Farr. Life Ass.
Farren's Bill in Chancery
   Farr. Bill
Farren's Masters in Chancery
   Farr. Mas.
Farresley's Cases in Holt's King's Bench Reports
   Far.
Farresley's Reports (7 Modern Reports)
   Farr., Mod. Cas. Per. Far., Mod. Cas. T. Holt, Mod. Cas. per Far. (T. Holt), Farresley, Far.
Farr's Medical Jurisprudence
   Farr Med. Jur.
Farwell on Powers
   Farw. Pow., Farwell
Fascicule (installment) (Lat.)
   fasc.
Faust's Compiled South Carolina Laws
   Faust
Fawcett on Landlord and Tenant
   Fawc. L & T., Fawc.
Fawcett's Court of Referees
   Fawc. Ref.
Fayette Law Journal
   Fayette Leg. J. (Pa.), Fay. L.J.
FBI Law Enforcement Bulletin, Federal Bureau of Investigation
   FBILEB

FDA Consumer, Food and Drug Administration
F.D.A. Cons.
Fearne on Contingent Remainders
F.C.R., Fear. Rem.
Fearne's Posthumous Works
Fea. Posth.
February
Fe., Fb., Feb.
Federal
Fed.
Federal Acquisition Regulation
F.A.R.
Federal Alcohol Administration
Fed. Alc. Adm.
Federal Anti-Trust Cases, Decrees and Judgments
Fed. Anti-Tr. Cas.
Federal Anti-Trust Decisions
F.A.D., Fed. Anti-Tr. Dec.
Federal Audit Guide, Commerce Clearing House
Fed. Audit Guide (CCH)
Federal Aviation Administration
FAA
Federal Aviation Administration Orders
F.A.A. Order
Federal Aviation Administrative Procurement Regulations
FAPR
Federal Aviation Regulations
F.A.R.
Federal Banking Law Reporter, Commerce Clearing House
CCH Fed. Banking L. Rep, Fed. Banking L. Rep. (CCH)
Federal Banking Law Reports, Commerce Clearing House
Fed. Banking L. Rep. (CCH)
Federal Bar Association
FBA

Federal Bar Association Journal
Fed. B.A. Jo., Fed. B.A.J.
Federal Bar Journal
Fed. B.J.
Federal Bar News
Fed. B. News, Fed. B.N.
Federal Bar News and Journal
Fed. B. News & J.
Federal Bureau of Investigation
FBI
Federal Capital Territory
F.C.T.
Federal Carrier Cases, Commerce Clearing House
F. Carrier Cas., C.C., Fed. Carr. Cas. (CCH), F. Carr. Cas.
Federal Carriers Reporter, Commerce Clearing House
Fed. Carr. Rep. (CCH), C.C.
Federal Case Number
Fed. Cas. No., F. Cas. No.
Federal Cases
Fed. Ca., F. Cas., F. Cas. No., Fed. Cas., Fed. Case., F.C.
Federal Chief Justice
F.C.J.
Federal Circuit Bar Journal
Fed. Ctr. B.J.
Federal Civil Defense Administration
FCDA
Federal Code Annotated
F.C.A.
Federal Communications Bar Journal
Fed. Com. B.J., Fed. Comm. B.J.
Federal Communications Commission
FCC
Federal Communications Commission Reports
F.C.C.

Federal Communications Com-
mission Reports, Second Series
  FCC 2d
Federal Communications Com-
mission Rulemaking Reports,
Commerce Clearing House
  FCC Rulemaking Rep. (CCH)
Federal Communications Law
Journal
  Fed. Com. L.J., Fed. Comm. L.J.
Federal Contracts Report, Bu-
reau of National Affairs
  Fed. Cont. Rep. (BNA)
Federal Court of Canada
  Can. F.C.
Federal Court Reporter, Canada
  Fed. R.
Federal Court Reports, Australia
  Fed. Ct. Rep.
Federal Court Reports, India
  F.C.R.
Federal Credit Union
  FCU
Federal Criminal Law Report
  Fed. Crim. L. Rep.
Federal Crop Insurance Corpora-
tion
  FCIC
Federal Data Processing Centers
  FDPC
Federal Deposit Insurance Corpo-
ration
  FDIC
Federal Disaster Assistance Ad-
ministration
  FDAA
Federal Election Campaign Fi-
nancing Guide, Commerce
Clearing House
  Fed. Election Camp. Fin. Guide
  (CCH)
Federal Election Commission
  FEC

Federal Emergency Management
Agency
  FEMA
Federal Emergency Relief Ad-
ministration
  FERA
Federal Employers' Liability and
Compensation Acts
  F.E.L.A.
Federal Energy Administration
  FEA
Federal Energy Regulatory Com-
mission
  F.E.R.C.
Federal Energy Regulatory Com-
mission Reports, Commerce
Clearing House
  Fed. Energy Reg. Comm'n Rep.
  (CCH)
Federal Estate and Gift Tax Re-
porter, Commerce Clearing
House
  Fed. Est. & Gift Tax Rep. (CCH)
Federal Estate and Gift Tax Re-
ports, Commerce Clearing
House
  Fed. Est. & Gift Tax Rep. (CCH)
Federal Estate Tax
  FET
Federal Excise Tax Reporter,
Commerce Clearing House
  Fed. Ex. Tax Rep. (CCH)
Federal Excise Tax Reports, Com-
merce Clearing House
  Fed. Ex. Tax Rep. (CCH)
Federal Executive Boards
  FEBs
Federal Farm Mortgage Corp.
  FFMC
Federal Food, Drug, and Cos-
metic Act
  F.D.C. Act

Federal Gift Tax
  FGT
Federal Grain Inspection Service
  F.G.I.S.
Federal Highway Administration
  FHWA
Federal Home Loan Bank
  F.H.L.B.
Federal Home Loan Bank Board
  FHLBB
Federal Home Loan Bank Board Journal
  Fed. Home Loan Bank Board J.
Federal Home Loan Mortgage Corporation
  FHLMC
Federal Housing Administration
  FHA
Federal Immigration Law Reporter
  Fed. Immigr. L. Rep.
Federal Income Gift and Estate Taxation
  Fed. Inc. Gift & Est. Tax'n
Federal Information Centers
  FIC
Federal Insurance Administration
  FIA
Federal Insurance Contribution Act
  FICA
Federal Insurance Counsel Quarterly
  Fed. Ins. Counsel Q.
Federal Insurance Tax
  FIT
Federal Inter-Agency Council on Energy Information
  FICEI
Federal Intermediate Credit Banks
  FICB

Federal Judicial Center
  F.J.C.
Federal Juror
  Fed. Juror
Federal Justice[s]
  F.J., F. JJ.
Federal Labor-Management Consultant
  F.L.M.C.
Federal Law Enforcement Training Center
  FLETC
Federal Law Journal
  Fed. L.J., F.L.J., F.L.J., Fed. L.J.
Federal Law Journal of India
  Fed. L.J. Ind.
Federal Law Quarterly
  Fed. L.Q.
Federal Law Reports
  Fed. L. Rep., F.L.R.
Federal Law Review
  Fed. L. Rev., F.L. Rev., F.L.R., Federal L. Rev.
Federal Maritime Board Reports, United States Maritime Administration, Department of Commerce
  F.M.B.
Federal Mediation and Conciliation Service
  FMCS
Federal Mine Safety and Health Review Decisions
  F.M.S.H.R.D.
Federal National Mortgage Association
  FNMA
Federal Parliament
  F.P.
Federal Personnel Manual
  F.P.M.

Federal Power Commission
FPC
Federal Power Commission Reports
FPC
Federal Power Service
Fed. Power Sev.
Federal Practice and Procedure
Fed. Prac.
Federal Preparedness Agency
F.P.A.
Federal Probate
Fed. Prob.
Federal Probation
Fed. Probation
Federal Probation Newsletter
Fed. Prob. N.L.
Federal Procurement Regulations
F. P. R.
Federal Public Housing Agency
FPHA
Federal Publications Inc.
FPI
Federal Radio Commission
FRC
Federal Railroad Administration
FRA
Federal Regional Councils
FRCs
Federal Register
F. R., Fed. Reg.
Federal Regulation of Employment Service
Fed. Reg. Empl. Serv., FRES
Federal Reporter
F. R., Fed. R., Fed. Rep., F, Fed.
Federal Reporter, 2d Series
F.2d, Fed.2d, F.2d
Federal Reports Act
FRA
Federal Republic
F. R.

Federal Republic of Germany
BDR, FRG, Germany (FR)
Federal Reserve Bulletin
Fed. Res. Bull., F.R.B.
Federal Reserve System
F.R.S.
Federal Revenue Forms, Prentice-Hall
Fed. Revenue Forms (P-H)
Federal Rules Decisions
Fed. R.D., Fed. Rules Dec.,
F.R.D.
Federal Rules of Appellate Procedure
Fed. R. App. P., FRAP
Federal Rules of Civil Procedure
Fed. R. Civ. P., Fed. R. Civil P.,
Fed. Rules Civ. Proc., F.R.C.P.,
FRCP
Federal Rules of Criminal Procedure
Fed. R. Crim. P., Fed. Rules Cr.
Proc., FR Crim P
Federal Rules of Evidence
Fed. Evid. R., Fed. R. Evid.,
Fed. R. Evid., FRE
Federal Rules of Evidence Service, Callaghan
Fed. R. Evid. Serv., Fed. R.
Evid. Serv. (Callaghan)
Federal Rules Service, Callaghan
Fed. Rules Serv.
Federal Rules Service, Second Series, Callaghan
Fed. R. Serv. 2d (Callaghan),
Fed. Rules Serv. 2d
Federal Savings and Loan Insurance Corp.
F.S.L.I.C.
Federal Securities Law Reporter, Commerce Clearing House
CCH Fed. Sec. L. Rep., Fed.
Sec. L. Rep. (CCH)

Federal Securities Law Reports, Commerce Clearing House
Fed. Sec. L. Rep. (CCH)
Federal Security Agency
FSA
Federal Sentencing Guidelines Handbook
FSG
Federal Service Impasses Panel
FSIP
Federal Statutes Annotated
Fed. Stat. Ann., F.S.A.
Federal Supplement
F. Supp., Fed. Sup., Fed. Supp., F.S.
Federal Supply Service
FSS
Federal Tax Coordinator, Tax Research Institute of America
Fed. Tax Coordinator 2d (Res. Inst. Am.)
Federal Tax Coordinator Second, Tax Research Institute of America
Fed. Tax Coordinator 2d (RIA)
Federal Tax Enforcement
Fed. Tax. Enf.
Federal Tax Forms, Commerce Clearing House
Fed. Tax Forms (CCH)
Federal Tax Guide Reports, Commerce Clearing House
Fed. Tax Guide Rep. (CCH)
Federal Tax Manual, Commerce Clearing House
Fed. Tax Manual (CCH)
Federal Taxation
Fed. Tax.
Federal Taxes, Prentice-Hall
Fed. Taxes (P-H), P-H Fed. Taxes, Fed. Taxes (P-H), P-H Tax.

Federal Taxes: Estate and Gift Taxes, Prentice-Hall
Fed. Taxes Est. & Gift (P-H)
Federal Taxes: Excise Taxes, Prentice-Hall
Fed. Taxes Excise (P-H)
Federal Taxes: Tax Ideas, Prentice-Hall
Fed. Taxes Tax Ideas (P-H)
Federal Taxes: Tax Treaties, Prentice-Hall
Fed. Taxes Treaties (P-H)
Federal Telecommunications System
FTS
Federal Tort Claims Act
Fed. Tort, F.T.C.A.
Federal Trade Commission
FTC
Federal Trade Commission Decisions
F.T.C.
Federal Trade Commission Statutes and Court Decisions
S. & D.
Federal Trade Reporter
Fed. Tr. Rep.
Federal Travel Regulations
F.T.R.
Federal Unemployment Tax Act
FUTA
Federal Utility Regulation Annotated
FURA
Federal Wage and Hour, Prentice-Hall
Fed. W. & H. (P-H), P-H Fed. Wage & Hour.
Federal Water Pollution Control Act
FWPCA
Federalist, by Hamilton
Ham. Fed.

Finch's Cases in Chancery Tempore, England
Ca. Temp. F., Rept. I. Fich., Cas. Temp. F., Cas. t. Finch (Eng.), Cas. t. F.

Finch's (H.) English Chancery Reports
Fin. H., N.Ch.R., Nel., Nels., Nels.Fol. Rep., Nelson (Eng.)

Florida Annual Report of the Attorney General
Fla. Ann. Rep. Att'y. Gen.

Foreign General Average
F.G.A.

Forsyth's Hortensius, (or the Duties of an Advocate)
For. Hort., Fors. Hor.

Forsyth's Trial by Jury
For. Jury Tr.

Fortescue's De Laudibus Legum Angliae
For., For. de Laud., Fortesc. de L. L. Angl., Fort. de Laud., Fortes. de Laud.

Fortescue's English King's Bench Reports
Fortesc., Fortescue (Eng.), Fortescue, Fort., Fortes. Rep., Fortes.

Fortnightly
Fort.

Fortnightly Law Journal
Fort. L.J., Fortn. L.J., Fortnightly L.J.

Fortune
Fortune

Fortune Telling
Fort. Tell.

Forum
F, Forum

Forum Law Journal
F.L.J.

Forum Law Review
Forum, Forum L.R.

Forum on Security Cooperation
FSC

Foss' Judges of England
Foss Judg., Fos.

Foster and Finlason's English Nisi Prius Reports
F. & F., Fost. & F., Fost. & F. (Eng.), Fost. & Fin.

Foster on Doctors' Commons
Fost. Doct. Com.

Foster on Federal Practice
Foster Fed. Pr.

Foster on Joint Ownership and Partition
Fost. Jt. Own.

Foster on the Writ of Scire Facias
Fost. on Sci. Fa., Fost. Sci. Fa., Fost. Sc. Fa.

Foster's Elements of Jurisprudence
Fost. El. Jur.

Foster's English Crown Law or Crown Cases
Fost. C.L., Foster, Fost. Cr. Law, Fost. Crown Law, Fost., Fost. C.L. (Eng.)

Foster's Legal Chronicle Reports, Pennsylvania
Fost., Foster (Pa.)

Foster's Reports (5, 6, and 8 Hawaii)
Fost., Fost. (Haw.)

Foster's Reports (21-31 New Hampshire)
Fost., Foster, Fost. (N. H.)

Foster's Treatise on Pleading and Practice in Equity in Courts of United States
Fost. Fed. Prac.

Foulke's Action at Law
Foulk. Act.

Foundation
Found., Fdn.
Foundation Law Review
Found. L. Rev.
Fountainhall's Decisions, Scotch Court of Session
Fount. Dec., Fount., Lauder
Fowler on Church Pews
Fowl. Pews
Fowler's Collieries and Colliers
Fowl. Col.
Fowler's Exchequer Practice
Fowl. Pr.
Fowler's Leading Cases on Collieries
Fowl. L. Cas.
Fox and Smith's Irish King's Bench Reports
Fox & Sm., Fox & S., Fox & S. (Ir.), Fox & S. Ir., F & S.
Fox and Smith's Registration Cases
Fox & Sm. R.C., Fox & Sm., Fox & S. Reg., F. & S.,
Fox's Digest of the Law of Partnership
Fox Dig. Part.
Fox's Federal Regulation of Energy
FRE
Fox's Patent, Trademark, Design and Copyright Cases, Canada
Fox, Fox Pat. C., Fox Pat. Cas., Fox P.C.
Fox's United States Circuit and District Court Decisions
Fox
Fox's Registration Cases
Fox. Reg. Ca., Fox
Fractional
Frac.
Fragment
Fr.

France
Fr.
France's Reports (3-11 Colorado)
France, France (Colo.)
Franchise[s]
Franch.
Franchise Law Journal
Franchise L.J.
Franchise Law Review
Franchise L. Rev.
Francillon's Lectures on English Law
Fran. Eng. Law
Francillon's County Court Judgments
Franc. Judg.
Francis' Common Law Precedents
Fran. Prec.
Francis' Maxims of Equity
Francis, Max., Fr. M. (or Fra.M.), Fran. Max., Fra.
Francis on Law of Charities
Fran. Char.
Franciso College Law Journal
Fran. Coll. L.J.
Frank on the United States Bankrupt Act of 1867
Fr. Bank.
Fraser on Master and Servant in Scotland
Fras. M. & S.
Fraser on Personal and Domestic Relations in Scotland
Fras. Dom. Rel.
Fraser's Conflict of Laws in Cases of Divorce
Fras. Div.
Fraser's Court of Session Cases
Fraser, F., F. Ct. Sess.
Fraser's English Cases of Controverted Elections
Fraser

Fraser's English Election Cases
Fr. E. C., Fras., Fras. Elec. Cas.

Fraser's House of Lords Reports
F.H.L.

Fraser's Husband and Wife
Fraser

Fraser's Justiciary Court Reports, Scotland
F.J.C., F

Fraser's Parent and Child
Fras. Par. & Ch.

Fraternal Orders and Benefit Societies
Frat.

Fraudulent Conveyances
Fraud. Conv.

Frazer's Admiralty Cases, Scotland
Fraz., Fraz. Adm.

Frederician Code of Prussia
Fred. Code

Free Alongside Ship
F.A.S.

Free From Capture and Seizure
F.C. & S.

Free From General Average
F.G.A.

Free From Particular Average
F.P.A.

Free of All Average
F.A.A.

Free of Charge
F.o.c.

Free of Damage
F.o.d.

Free of Income Tax
F.i.t.

Free on Board
F.o.b.

Free Representation Unit
FRU

Free Speech Yearbook
Free Speech Y.B.

Freedom of Information Act
FOIA

Freedom of Information Center Reports
F.O.I.C.R.

Freeman on Comparative Politics
Freem. Compar. Politics

Freeman on Cotenancy and Partition
Freem. Cot.

Freeman on Executors
Freem. Ex.

Freeman on Judgments
Freem. Judgm.

Freeman's English Chancery Reports
Fr. Ch., Fr. Chy., Fr., Free. Ch., Freem. Ch., Freem. Ch. (Eng.), Freem., Free.

Freeman's English King's Bench and Common Pleas Reports
Freem. K.B., Fr., Free. K.B., Free.

Freeman's Growth of the English Constitution
Freem. Eng. Const.

Freeman's Illinois Practice
Freem. Pr.

Freeman's Mississippi Chancery Reports
Fr. Ch., Freem. Ch. R., Freem. Chan., Freeman Ch. R., Freeman's (Miss.) Rep., Freem. (Miss.), Freem. C.C., Freem. Ch. (Miss.), Free. Ch., Fr. Chy.

Freeman's Mississippi Chancery Reports, (1839-43) Buckner's Decisions
Buck. Dec.

Freeman's Reports (31-96 Illinois)
Free., Freem. (Ill.)

French
F, Fr.

French Ordinances
Fr. Ord.
French's Reports (6 New Hampshire)
French, French (N.H.)
Frend and Ware's Precedents of Instruments Relating to the Transfer of Land to Railway Companies
Fr. & W. Prec., F. & W. Pr., Frend & W. Prec.
Frith's United States Attorney General's Opinion
Frith.
Fry on Lunacy
Fry Lun.
Fry on Specific Performance of Contracts
Fry, Fry Sp. Per.
Fry on the Vaccination Acts
Fry Vac.
Fulbecke's Study of the Law
Fulb. St. Law
Fulbeck's Parallel
Fulb. Par.

Full Bench Decisions for India
F.B.I.
Full Bench Rulings for Bengal, Edited by Goodeve and Woodman
F.B.R., Suth. Sp. N., Good. & Wood., Ben. F.B.
Full Bench Rulings for Northwest Provinces
F.B.R.N.W.P.
Full Court Judgments, Ghana
F.C.
Fuller's Church History
Full. Ch. Hist.
Fuller's Reports (59-105 Michigan)
Fuller
Fulton's Supreme Court Reports for Bengal
Fulton, Fult.
Funeral Directors and Embalmers
Funeral D.
Furlong on the Irish Law of Landlord and Tenant
Furl. L. & T.

G

Gabbett's Criminal Law
Gabb. Cr. Law.

Gabbett's Digest of the Statute Law
Gabb. Stat. L.

Gains and Ulpian by Adby and Walker
Adby & W. Gai., Add. Ecc., Add. Eccl., Addams, Ad., Add., Add. Eccl. Rep., Add. E.R., Adams Ecc. (Eng.)

Gaius' Institutes (Gaii Institutionum Commentarii)
Gaius, Inst., Gaii., Gaius, (See also Caii Institutions)

Galbraith and Meek's Reports (9-12 Florida)
Galb. & M., Galb. & M. (Fla.)

Galbraith's Reports (9-11 Florida)
Galb., Galbraith

Gale and Davidson's English Queen's Bench Reports
G. & D., Gale & Dav., Gale & D., Gale & D. (Eng.), Gal. & Dav.

Gale and Whatley on Easements
G. & Wh. Eas., Gale & Wh. Eas., Gale & Whatley Easem.

Gale on Easements
Gale Eas., Gale

Gales and Seaton's Register of Debates in Congress
Reg. Deb., Reg. Deb. (G. & S.), Gales, Reg. Deb. (Gales)

Gale's English Exchequer Reports
G., Gale

Gale's Statutes of Illinois
Gale's St., Gale Stat.

Gallaudet on International Law
Gall. Int. L.

Gallick's Reports
Gall. Cr. Cas.

Gallison's United States Circuit Court Reports
Gall. C.C.R., Gallison's Rep., Gal., Gall., Gallison

Gambia
Gam.

Gamble and Barlow's Irish Equity Digest
Gamb. & Barl, Gamb. & Bar. Dig.

Gambling
Gambl.

Gamboa's Introduction to Philippine Law
Gamboa, Gamboa, Philippine Law

Ganatra's Criminal Cases
Ganatra

Gantt's Digest of Arkansas Statutes
Gantts Dig., Gantt Dig.

Garde on Evidence
Gard. Ev.

Gardenhire's Reports (14-15 Missouri)
Garden., Gardenhire.

Gardenier's New York Reporter
Gard. N.Y. Rept., Gard. N.Y. Rep., Gard. N.Y. Rptr.

Garde's First Principles of Pleading
Gard. Pl.

Gardner's Institute of American
International Law
Gard. Int. Law
Gardner's Peerage Case, Re-
ported by Le Marchant
Gardn. P.C.
Gas and Oil
Gas & O.
Gaspar's Small Cause Court Re-
ports, Bengal, India
Gaspar.
Gavel, the State Bar Association
of North Dakota
Gavel
Gavin and Hord's Indiana Stat-
utes
G. & H.
Gavin and Hord's Revised Indi-
ana Statutes
Gav. & H. Rev. St.
Gayaree's Reports (25-28 Louisi-
ana)
Gayaree, Gay. (La.)
Gazette and Bankrupt Court Re-
porter, New York
Gaz. & B.C. Rep.
Gazette Law Reports, New Zea-
land
Gaz. L.R., G.L.R., G.L.R. (N.Z.)
Gazette Notice
G.N.
Gazette of Bankruptcy
Gaz. Bankr., Gaz. Bank.
Gazette of the Law Society of Up-
per Canada
Gaz. L. Soc. of Upper Can.
Gazzam's Digest of Bankruptcy
Decisions
Gaz. Bank. Dig.
Gear on Landlord and Tenant
Gear, Landl. & T.

Geldart and Maddock's English
Chancery Reports
Geldart., Geld. & M.
Geldert and Oxley's Nova Scotia
Decisions
N.S.D., Geld. & O., Geld. & Ox.
Geldert and Russel's Nova Scotia
Reports
Geld. & R., G. & R., N.S.R.G. & O.
Gender
Gender
General
Gen., Genl
General Abridgment of Cases in
Equity
Gen. Abr. Cas. Eq.
General Accounting Office
GAO
General Accounting Office Letter
Report
G.A.O. Let. Rep.
General Accounting Office Re-
view
G.A.O. Rev.
General Accounting Office, Re-
ports to
G.A.O. Rep.
General Acts of Arkansas
Ark. Acts
General Agreement on Privileges
and Immunities of the Council
of Europe
C. of E. Agr. P.I.
General Agreement on Tariffs
and Trade
GATT
General Agreement Tariffs and
Trade, Contracting Parties
GATT/CP
General and Special Laws of the
State of Texas
Tex. Gen. Laws

General Appraisers' Decisions
Ga.
General Assembly
Gen. Assem.
General Assembly Official Record, United Nations
GAOR
General Assembly Resolution, United Nations
G.A. Res.
General Assembly, United Nations
GA, G.A.
General Associations
Gen. Ass'ns.
General Business
Gen. Bus.
General Ceiling Price Regulation
G.C.P.R.
General City
Gen. City
General Code
G.C.
General Conference on Weights and Measures
C.G.P.M.
General Construction
Gen. Constr.
General Counsel
GC
General Counsel's, Assistant General Counsel's, or Chief Counsel's Memorandum, Internal Revenue Service
GCM, G.C.M.
General Digest
Gen. Dig.
General Digest of the United States
Gen. Dig. U.S.
General Digest, New Series, United States
Gen. Dig. N.S.

General Flight Rules
GFR
General International Agreement
GIA
General Land Office
GLO
General Laws
Gen. Laws, G.L.
General Laws of Mississippi
Miss. Laws
General Laws of Rhode Island
R.I. Gen. Laws
General Mortgage
Gen. Mtg.
General Municipal
Gen. Mun.
General Obligations
Gen. Oblig.
General Order Defense Transport Administration
GODPT
General Orders of the English High Court of Chancery
Gen. Ord. Ch.
General Orders, Ontario Court of Chancery
G.O., Gen. Ord.
General Overruling Regulation Office of Price Stabilization
GOR
General Provisions
Gen. Prov.
General Railroad Act
Gen. R.R. Act
General Railroad and Airline Stabilization Regulations
GRASR
General Register Office
G.R.O.
General Register Office for Births, Deaths and Marriages
G.R.O.B.D.M.

General Rules and Orders
India Gen. R. & O.
General Salary Order
GSO
General Salary Stabilization Regulations
GSSR
General Services Administration
GSA
General Services Administration Procurement Regulations
GSAPR
General Sessions
Gen. Sess.
General Statutes
Gen. St., G.S.
General Statutes Annotated
Gen. Stat. Ann.
General Statutes of Connecticut
Conn. Gen. Stat.
General Statutes of North Carolina
N.C. Gen. Stat.
General Term
Gen. T.
General Wage Stabilization Regulations
GWSR
Generalized System of Preferences
GSP
Geneva Arbitration
Gen. Arb.
Geopposserde (defendant) (Dutch)
Geopp.
George (King)
Geo., G.
George Mason Law Review
Geo. Mason L. Rev.
George Mason University Civil Rights Law Journal
Geo. Mason U. Civ. Rts. L.J.

George Mason University Law Review
Geo.Mason U. L. Rev., GMU L. Rev.
George on Partnership
George. Partn.
George Washington Journal of International Law and Economics
Geo. Wash. J. Int'l. L. & Econ.
George Washington Law Review
Geo. Wash. L. Rev., Geo. Wash. Law Rev., G.W., G.W.L.R.
George on Libel
Geo. Lib.
George's Mississippi Digest
Geo. Dig.
George's Reports (30-39 Mississippi)
George.
Georgetown
Geo.
Georgetown Immigration Law Journal
Geo. Immigr. L.J., Georgetown Immig L J
Georgetown International Environmental Law Review
Geo. Int'l Envtl. L. Rev.
Georgetown Journal of Legal Ethics
Geo J. Legal Ethics
Georgetown Law Journal
Geo. L.J., Georget. L.J., Gt. L.J., Geo.
Georgia
G., Ga., Geo.
Georgia Appeals Reports
Ga. App., Ga. A.
Georgia Appeals Reports, New Series
Ga. App. (N.S.)
Georgia Bar Association
Ga. B.A.

Georgia Bar Journal
   Ga. B.J., G.B.J., Georgia B.J.
Georgia Business Lawyer
   Ga. Bus. Law.
Georgia Code, by Clark, Cobb and Irwin
   Irwin's Code
Georgia Constitution
   Ga. Const.
Georgia Decisions
   Ga. Dec., Geo. Dec.
Georgia Journal of International and Comparative Law
   Ga. J. Int. & Comp. L., Ga. J. Int'l. & Comp. L., Georgia J. Int. Comp. L., Georgia J. Int'l. L. & Compl. L.
Georgia Journal of Southern Legal History
   Ga. J.S. Legal Hist.
Georgia Law Journal
   Ga. L.J.
Georgia Law Reporter
   Ga. L. Rep., Ga. Law Reporter
Georgia Law Review
   Ga. L., Ga. L. Rev., Geo. Rev., Georgia L. Rev., G.L.R.
Georgia Laws
   Ga. Laws
Georgia Lawyer
   Ga. L., Ga. Lawyer
Georgia Official Code Annotated
   O.C.G.A.
Georgia Official Compilation of the Rules and Regulations
   Ga. Admin. Comp.
Georgia Public Service Commission Reports
   Ga. P.S.C.
Georgia Railroad Commission
   Ga. R.C.

Georgia Reports
   Ga., Geo., Ga. Rep., Ga.R., Geo. R., Geo. Rep., Georgia, Georgia R., Georgia Rep., Georgia Reports, Georgia Reps.
Georgia Reports Annotated
   Ga. Rep. Ann., Michie's Ga. Repts. Ann.
Georgia Reports Supplement
   Ga. Supp., Ga. Supplement, Ga.Sup., Georgia (Supplement)
Georgia Sessions Laws
   Ga. L.
Georgia State Bar Journal
   Ga. St. B.J., Ga.S.B.J., Georgia St. B.J., G.S.B.
Georgia State University Law Review
   Ga. St. U.L. Rev.
Georgia Supreme Court Reports
   Ga.
Gerard's Titles to Real Estate
   Ger. Tit.
German
   G., Ger., Germ.
German Yearbook of International Law
   GYIL
   German Yb. Int'l. L.
Germany
   Ger.
Germany, Democratic Republic of
   G.D.R.
Germany, Federal Republic of
   F.R.G., FRG
Getz's Forms in Conveyancing
   Getz F.
Ghana Current Cases
   Ghana C.C.
Ghana Law Reform Commission
   Ghana L.R.C.
Ghana Law Reports
   G.L.R.

Ghose on Mortgages in India
Ghose Mort.
Giauque's Election Laws
Giauq. El.
Gibbon on Nuisances
Gibbon
Gibbon on the Civil Law
Gib. Civ. L.
Gibbons
Gibb.
Gibbons and Nathans' Equitable Jurisdiction of County Courts
Gib. & Na. Eq. Jur.
Gibbon's History of the Decline and Fall of the Roman Empire
Gibbon, Rom. Emp., Gibb. Rom. Emp.
Gibbons' Law of Dilapidations and Nuisances
Gib. Nui.
Gibbons' Lex Temporis (Limitation and Prescription)
Gib. Lim.
Gibbons on Contracts
Gib. Cont.
Gibbons on Dilapidations and Nuisances
Gib. Dil.
Gibbons on Law of Fixtures
Gib. Fix.
Gibbons' Reports, New York Surrogate Court
Gibbons, Gibbons (N.Y.), Gibb. Sur., Gibb. Surr., Gib.
Gibbs' Judicial Chronicle
Gibbs' Jud. Chr.
Gibbs' Practical Forms
Gibbs F.
Gibbs' Reports (2-4 Michigan)
Gibbs
Gibraltar
Gib.

Gibson's Aids to the Examinations
Gib. Aids
Gibson's [Edition of] Camden's Britannia
Gibs. Camd.
Gibson's Codex Ecclesiastia
Gibs. Code., Cod. Jur., Cod.
Gibson's Codex Juris Civilis
Cod.
Gibson's Codex Juris Ecclesiastical Angelicani
Gib. Cod.
Gibson's Decisions, Scotch Court of Session
Gibson., Gib. Dec.
Gibson's Law Notes
Gibs. L.N., Gib. L.N.
Gibson's Memoir of Lord Lyndhurst
Gib. Lynd.
Giffard and Hemming's English Chancery Reports
Giff. & H.
Giffard's English Vice-Chancellor's Reports
Gif., Giff., Giff. (Eng.)
Gift Tax
G.
Gift Tax Ruling
GT
Gilbart on Banking
Gilb. Bank.
Gilbert on Distress and Replevin
Gilb. Dis.
Gilbert on Ejectments
Gilb.Ej.
Gilbert on Replevin
Gilb.Repl.
Gilbert on Tenures
Gilb. Ten., Gilbert, Tenures

Gilbert on the Action of Debt (Appended to Gilbert's English Cases in Law and Equity)
Gilb. Debt

Gilbert on Uses and Trusts
Gilb. Uses

Gilbert's Cases in Equity Reports
Cas. Eq.

Gilbert's Cases in Law and Equity
Gilb. Cas. L. & Eq., Eq. Cas., Gilb. Cas. L. & Eq. (Eng.), Gilb. Eq. (Eng.), Gilb. Eq., Eq. R., Equity Rep., Eq. Rep., Gil., Gilb., Cas. L. & Eq., Gilb. K.B., Gilb. Cas., Gil., Gilb., Rep. Cas. Eq., Rep. Eq.

Gilbert's English Common Pleas
Gilb. Com. Pl., Gilb. C.P., Gilb. P.C., Gilb. Cas. L. & Eq. (Eng.)

Gilbert's English Equity or Chancery Reports
Gilb. Eq. (Eng.), Gilb. Eq., Eq. R., Eq. Rep.

Gilbert's English Exchequer Reports
Gilb. Exch.

Gilbert's Executions
Gilb. Ex.

Gilbert's Forum Romanum
Gilb. For. Rom., Gilb. Forum Rom.

Gilbert's History and Practice of the Exchequer
Gilb. Ch. Pr., Gilb. Exch. Pr.

Gilbert's History of Common Pleas
Gilb. Hist. C.P.

Gilbert's Law of Devises
Gilb. Dev.

Gilbert's Law of Evidence
Gilbert, Ev.

Gilbert's Lex Praetoria
Gilb. Lex Pr.

Gilbert's Railway Law of Illinois
Gilb. R.R.

Gilbert's Remainders
Gilb. Rem.

Gilbert's Treatise on Rents
Gilb. Rents

Gilbert's Uses and Trusts
Gilb. U.T.

Gilbert's Uses and Trusts by Sugden
Gilbert, Uses, by Sugd.

Gilchrist's Local Government Cases
Gilchr.

Gildersleeve's Reports (1-10 New Mexico)
Gildersleeve, N.M. (G.), Gildersleeve (N.Mex.), Gild.

Gilfillan's Reports (1-20 Minnesota)
Gilf., Gil. (Minn.), Gil., Gilfillan

Gill and Johnson's Maryland Reports
G. & Jo., G. & J. (Md.), G & John., Gill and J.(Maryland), Gill & J., Gill & J. (Md.), Gill & Johns., G. & J., Gill & Johnson, G.J., See also Maryland Reports

Gillett's Treatise on Criminal Law and Procedure in Criminal Cases
Gillett, Cr. Law

Gill's Maryland Reports
Gill, Gill (Md.)

Gill's Police Court Reports
Gill Pol. Rep.

Gilman's Illinois Digest
Gilm. Dig.

Gilman's Indiana Digest
Gilm. Dig.

Gilman's Reports (6-10 Illinois)
Gil., Gilman, Gilm., Gilm.(Ill.)

Gilmer's Reports (21 Virginia)
V.A., Gilmer, Gil., Gilm., Gilmer
(Va.), Va. R.

Gilmour and Falconer's Decisions, Scotch Court of Session
Pres. Fal., Gilm. & F., Gilm. &
Fal., Gilm. & Falc., Gil. & Fal.,
Gilm.

Gilpin's Opinions of the United States Attorneys-General
Gilp. Opin.

Gilpin's United States District Court Reports
Gilp.

Girard Will Case Report
Gir. W.C.

Givens on Advocacy
Advo

Givens on Business Torts and Competitor Litigation
BTCL

Givens on Demonstrative Evidence
DEVI

Givens on Legal Strategies for Industrial Innovation
SII

Givens' Manual of Federal Practice
MFP

Glanville's De Legibus et Consuetudinibus Angliae
Glan. llb., Glanvil., Glanv.

Glanville's English Election Cases
Glanv. El. Cas., Glan. El. Cas.

Glascock's Reports in all the Courts of Ireland
Glasc., Glascock, Glas.

Glassford on Evidence
Glassf. Ev.

Glen on Registration of Births and Deaths
Glen Reg.

Glen on the Public Health Laws
Glen Pub. H.

Glendale Law Review
Glendale L. Rev., Glendale L.R.

Glenn's Reports (16-18 Louisiana Annual)
Glenn

Glen's Highway Laws
Glen High.

Gloag and Henderson's Introduction to the Law of Scotland
Gloag & Henderson

Global System of Trade Preferences
GSTP

Glossa (a gloss or interpretation) (Lat.)
Gl.

Glover's Municipal Corporations
Glov. Mun. Cor.

Glyn and Jameson's English Bankruptcy Reports
Glyn & J., Glyn & J. (Eng.),
Glyn & Jam., Gl. & J., G. & J.

Glynn on Water Powers
Glynn Wat. Pow.

Gobert and Cohen on Rights of Prisoners
ROP

Godbolt's English King's Bench Reports
Godb. (Eng.)

Goddard on Easements
Godd. Easem., Godd. Ease., Goddard

Godefroi and Shortt's Law of Railway Companies
Godef. & Sh. R.C., G. & Sh. R.R.

Godefroi on Trusts and Trustees
Godefroi, Godef. Trust

Godolphin on Admiralty Jurisdiction
Godolph. Adm. Jur., Godo.

Godolphin's Ecclesiastical Law
Godo., Godolph. Ecc. Law, See also Godolphin's Repertorium Canonicum

Godolphin's Orphan's Legacy
Godo., Godol., Godolph. Orph. Leg.

Godolphin's Repertorium Canonicum
Godo., Godolph. Rep. Can., Godolph (or Godolph.Rep.Can.), See also Godolphin's Ecclesiastical Law

Godson on Patents
Gods. Pat.

Godson's Ontario Mining Commissioner's Cases
Godson

Goebel's Ohio Probate Reports
Go., Goeb., Goebel (Ohio), Goebel, Goebel's Rep., Ohio Prob.Ct., See also Ohio Probate Reports

Goff's Federal Income Taxation of Corporate Liquidations
TCL

Goguet's Origin of Laws
Gog. Or.

Goirand's French Code of Commerce
Goir. Fr. Co.

Gold Coast Divisional Court Reports
G.C.D.C.

Gold Coast Divisional Court Selected Judgment
D.Ct., G.C.Div.C.

Gold Coast Full Court Selected Judgments
G.C.F.C., G.C. Full. Ct.

Gold Coast Judgments and the Masai Case by King-Farlow
King-Farlow, K.F.

Gold Coast Judgments, by Earnshaw
Earnshaw, Earn.

Gold Coast Cases in Law
Danquah

Gold Coast Native Institutions, by Hayford
Hayford

Gold Coast Selected Judgments of the Divisional Courts
G.C. Div. Ct.

Goldbolt's English King's Bench, Common Pleas, and Exchequer Reports
Goldb.

Golden Gate Law Review
Golden Gate L. Rev., Golden Gate L. Review

Golden Gate University Advanced Legal Education Program
GGUALE

Golden Gate University Law Review
Golden Gate U. L. Rev.

Golden's Equitable Distribution of Property
EDP

Goldesborough's English King's Bench Reports
Goldes., Gold., See also Gouldsborough

Goldsmith and Guthrie's Reports (36-67 Missouri Appeals)
G. & G., G. & G. (Mo.), Gold. & G.

Goldsmith's Doctrine and Practice of Equity
Golds. Eq.

Gongwer's Ohio State Reports
G.S.R.

Gonzaga Law Review
Gonz. L. Rev., Gonzaga L. Rev.

Gonzaga Special Report: Public Sector Labor Law
Gonz. Pub. Lab. L. Rep.

Good Will
Good W.

Goodeve and Woodman's Full Bench Rulings for Bengal
Good. & Wood., See also Full Bench Rulings for Bengal

Goodeve on Railway Companies and Passengers
Good. Ry. C.

Goodeve on Real Property
Goodeve

Goodeve's Abstract of Patent Cases
Good. Pat.

Goodeve's Law of Evidence
Good. Ev.

Goodrich-Amram's Procedural Rules Service
Goodrich-Amram

Goodwin's Probate Practice
Good. Pr.

Gordon on the Law of Decedents in Pennsylvania
Gord. Dec.

Gordon's Digest of United States Laws
Gord. Dig.

Gordon's Reports (24-26 Colorado and 10-13 Colorado Appeals)
Gordon

Gordon's Treason Trials
Gord. Tr.

Gore-Brown on Companies
Gore-B. Comp.

Gosford's Manuscript Reports, Scotch Court of Session
Gosf.

Gottschall's Dayton (Ohio) Superior Court Reports
Gottschall

Goudsmit's Pandects
Goud. Pand.

Gould and Tucker's Notes on Revised Status of United States
Gould & T., G. & T.

Gould on the Principles of Pleading in Civil Actions
Gould, Pl.

Gould on Waters
Gould, Wat.

Gould's Digest of Arkansas Laws
Gould's Dig.

Gould's Stenographic Reporter
Gould Sten. Rep.

Gouldsborough's English King's Bench Reports
Gould., Gouldsb., Gouldsb. (Eng.), See also Goldesborough

Gourick's Patent Digest
Gour.

Gourlie on General Average
Gourl. Gen. Av.

Government
Gov't., Govt

Government Contracts Program, George Washington University Law Center
GCP

Government Contracts Reporter, Commerce Clearing House
Gov. Cont. Rep., Gov't. Cont. Rep.

Government Employee Relations Report, Bureau of National Affairs
G.E.R.R., Gov't. Empl. Rel. Rep. (BNA)

Government Furnished Property
GFP

Government Institutes, Inc.
  GII
Government National Mortgage Association
  GNMA
Government Printing Office
  GPO
Government Publications Review
  Govt. Pub. Rev., Govt. Pubns. Rev.
Government Research Management Consultants
  GORMAC
Government Statute of Local Governments
  Stat. Local
Government Union Review
  Gov't. Union Rev.
Governmental
  Govtl.
Governmental Affairs
  G.A.
Governor
  Gov.
Gow on Partnerships
  Gow Part.
Gow's English Nisi Prius Cases
  Gow., Gow N.P., Gow. N.P. (Eng.)
Grady on Fixtures
  Grad. Fix.
Grady's Hindu Law of Inheritance
  Grad. Hind. Inh.
Grady's Indian Codes
  Grad. Ind. Co.
Grady's Manual of Hindu Law
  Grad. Hind. L.
Graham and Waterman on New Trials
  G. & W. New Tr., Gra. & Wat. N.T., Grah. & W. New Trials

Graham on New Trials
  Gra. N. Tr.
Graham's Practice of the New York Supreme Court
  Gra. Pr.
Graham's Reports (98-107 Georgia)
  Gra.
Grand Jury
  Grand J.
Granger's Reports (22-23 Ohio)
  Granger
Grant
  Gra.
Grant of Elchies' Scotch Session Cases
  Grant
Grant on Banking
  Grant, Bank.
Grant on Corporations
  Grant, Corp.
Grant on Subchapter S Taxation
  SST
Granting
  Grant'g
Grant's Error and Appeal Reports for Ontario
  Grant Err, & App., E. & A.W.C., E. & A.U.C., Grant E. & A., Grant's, E. & A. R., Err. & App.
Grant's Jamaica Reports
  Grant, Grant, Jamaica, Gr., Gant's R.
Grant's Pennsylvania Cases
  Grant Cas., Gr., Gr. Ca., Grt., Grant (Pa.), Grant Cas. (Pa.), Grant Pa., Gr., Grant, Gr., Grant's R.
Grant's Upper Canada Chancery Reports
  Gr., Grant, Grant Ch., Grant Ch. (Can.), Grant U.C., Grant U.S., Grant

Grapel's Translation of the Institutes of Justinian
Grap. Just.
Grapel's Sources of the Roman Civil Law
Grap. Rom. Law
Grattan's Virginia Supreme Court Reports
Grat., Gratt. (Va.), Gratt.
Graves' Proceedings in King's Council
Graves
Gravina's De Jure Naturale Gentium, etc.
Grav. de Jur. Nat. Gent.
Gravina's Originum Juris Civilis.
Gravin.
Graya
Graya
Graydon's Forms of Conveyance
Gray. Forms
Gray's Country Attorney's Practice
Gray Att. Pr.
Gray's Massachusetts Reports (67-82 Massachusetts)
Gray, Gray (Mass.)
Gray's Nonprivate Foundations
NPF
Gray's Reports (112-22 North Carolina)
Gray
Gray's Rule Against Perpetuities
Gray, Perpetuities
Great Britain
G.B., Gr. Brit.
Great Britain Treaty Series
Gr. Brit. T.S.
Great Jurists of the World, by Sir John Macdonnel and Edward Manson
G.J.W.

Great Roll of Exchequer
Mag. Rot., Magna Rot. Pip.
Great Roll of the Pipe
Magna Rot. Pip.
Great War Prize Cases by Evans
Pr. Ca.
Greave's Edition of Russell on Crimes
Greav. Russ.
Greaves' Criminal Consolidation
Greav. Cr. L.
Greek
Gr.
Green and Long on Marriage and Family Law Agreements
MFLA
Green Bag, A Legal Journal
Green Bag
Green on Dissolution of Marriage
DOM
Greene's, C.E., New Jersey Equity Reports
C.E.Gr., C.E. Greene, Green. C.E.
Greene's Iowa Reports
Greene, Greene (Iowa), Greene G. (Iowa), G. Gr., G.
Greene's Outlines of Roman Law
Gre. Rom. Law, Green. Rom. Law
Greene's Reports (7 New York Annotated Cases)
Greene
Greenhood's Doctrine of Public Policy in the Law of Contracts
Greenh. Pub. Pol.
Greenhow's Law of Shipowners
Green. Ship.
Greenhow's Shipping Law Manual
Greenh. Sh.

Greening's Forms of Declarations, Pleadings, etc.
Green. Forms

Greenleaf on Evidence
Gr. Ev., Greenl. Ev., Green. Ev.

Greenleaf's Edition of Cruise's Digest of Real Property
Green. Cruise, Greenl. Cr., Greenl. Cruise, Greenl. Cruise Real Prop.

Greenleaf's Overruled Cases
Green. Ov. Cas., Greenl. Ov. Cas.

Greenleaf's Reports (1-9 Maine)
Gr., Greenl.

Greenleaf's Testimony of the Evangelists
Greenl. Test. Ev., Green. Test. Ev.

Green's Bankrupt Law
Green B.L.

Green's Criminal Cases, England
Green Cr. Cas., Green Sc. Cr. Cas. (See also Green's Criminal Reports)

Green's Criminal Law
Green Cr.

Green's Criminal Law Reports, England
Green Cr. L. Rep., Green, Cr. Law R., Crim. Law Reps. (Green), Green Cr. Rep., Green Crim. Reports (See also Green's Criminal Cases)

Green's Edition of Brice on Ultra Vires
Gr. Brice., Green Bri., Green's Brice, Ultra Vires.

Green's (J.S.) Reports
Green L., J.S.Gr. (N.J.), J.S.Gr.

Green's New Jersey Law and Equity Reports (13-15 New Jersey)
Green (NJ), Green C.E., Gr., Green L., Green, Green Ch., Green Eq., H.W. Gr., J.S. Gre.

Green's Reports (1-9 Maine or 1 Oklahoma)
Green

Green's Reports (11-17 Rhode Island)
Green, Green R.I., Green (R.I.)

Green's Scottish Trials for Treason
Green Sc. Tr.

Greenwood and Horwood's Conveyancing
Green. & H. Conv.

Greenwood and Martin's Magistrates' Police Guide
Greenw. & M. Mag. Pol.

Greenwood on Conveyancing
Greenw. Conv.

Greenwood on Courts
Green. Cts., Greenw. Cts.

Greenwood's Manual of Conveyancing
Green. Conv.

Greer's Irish Land Acts Leading Cases
Greer.

Gregg and Pond's Railroad Laws of the New England States
G. & P.R.R. Laws

Gregg on the Law of Bankruptcy
Gregg Bank.

Gregorowski's Reports of the High Court of the Orange Free State
Greg., G.

Gregory on Tours.
Greg. Turon.

Greiner's Ceylon Reports
Gren., Grenier

Greiner's Louisiana Digest
Grein. Dig.

Greiner's Louisiana Practice
Grein. Pr.

Grenada
Gren.

Gresley's Equity Evidence
Gr. Eq., Gres. Eq. Ev.

Grey's House of Commons De-bates
Grey Deb.

Griffin's Patent Cases
Grif. Pat. C., Griffin P.C., Grif.
P.C., Griff. Pat. Cas., Griffin
Pat. Cas.

Griffith on Arrangements with Creditors
Grif. Cr.

Griffith on Military Law and Courts-Martial
Grif. Ct. Mar. (or Mil.Law)

Griffith on the Judicature Acts
Grif. Jud. Acts

Griffith's English Poor Rate Cases
Grif. P.R. Cas., Grif. P.R.C.

Griffith's Institutes of Equity
Grif. Inst. (or Eq.)

Griffith's Law Register
Grif. L. Reg.

Griffith's London Poor Law Cases
Grif. P.L. Cas.

Griffith's Married Women's Property Act
Grif. Mar. Wom.

Griffith's Practice
Grif. Pr.

Griffith's Reports (1-5 Indiana Appeals and 117-132 Indiana)
Griffith

Griffith's Stamp Duties
Grif. St.

Grimke on Executors and Administrators
Grimke Ex.

Grimke's Justice
Grimke Jus.

Grimke's Public Laws of South Carolina
Grimke P.L.

Grimsey's Proceedings in Bankruptcy
Grim. Bank.

Griqualand High Court Reports, Cape Colony
G.W.R., H.C.G.

Griqualand West Reports, Cape Colony
Kitchen

Griswold's Fire Underwriter's Text-Book
Grisw. Und.

Griswold's Reports (14-19 Ohio)
Gris., Grisw., Griswold

Grosser Senat (German)
Gr. S.

Gross' Illinois Compiled Laws
Gross Laws (or St.), Gross St.,
Gross, St.

Gross National Product
GNP

Gross' Select Cases Concerning the Law Merchant (Selden Society)
Gro.

Grotius de Aequitate
Grot. de Acquit., Gro., Gro. B.P.,
Gro. de J.B.

Grotius on War and Peace by Barbeyrac
Barb. Gro.

Grotius Society Transactions
Grot. Soc'y.

Grounds and Maxims of English Law by William Noye
Noye
Group Legal Review
Group Legal Rev.
Guam
Gu.
Guam Administrative Rules and Regulations of the Government
Guam Admin. R.
Guam Civil Code
Guam Civ. Code
Guam Code of Civil Procedure
Guam Code Civ. Pro.
Guam Government Code
Guam Gov't. Code
Guam Probate Code
Guam Prob. Code
Guaranteed
Gtd.
Guaranteed Annual Wage
G.A.W
Guaranty
Gty., Guar.
Guardian
GDN.
Guardian and Ward
Guar. & W.
Guatemala
Guat.
Gude's Practice of the Crown Side of the Court of King's Bench
Gude Pr.
Guerin's Taxation of Real Estate Transactions
TRED
Guernsey on Key to Equity Jurisprudence
Guern. Eq. Jur.
Guernsey on Questions of Insanity
Guern. Ins.

Guernsey's Mechanics' Lien Laws of New York
Guern. Mech. L.
Guide to Computer Law, Commerce Clearing House
Guide to Computer L. (CCH)
Guild Lawyer
Guild Law.
Guild Practitioner
Guild Prac.
Guizot's History of Representative Government
Gulzot, Rep. Govt.
Gujarat Law Reporter, India
G.L.R.
Gujarat Law Times, India
Guj. L.T.
Gunby's Louisiana District Court Reports
Gunby's Dec., Gunby, Gunby(La.)
Gundry Manuscripts in Lincoln's Inn Library
Gundry.
Gunning on Tolls
Gunn. Tolls
Guterbock's Bracton
Gut. Brac.
Guthrie on Trade Unions
Guth. Tr. Un.
Guthrie's Landlord and Tenant
Guth. L. & T.
Guthrie's Principles of the Laws of England
Guth. Pr.
Guthrie's Reports (33-83 Missouri Appeals)
Guthrie
Guthrie's Sheriff Court Cases
Guth. Sh. Cas., Guth. Sher. Cas., Guthrie
Guy's Forensic Medicine
Guy For. Med.

Guy's Medical Jurisprudence
  Guy, Med. Jur.
Guyana
  Guy.
Guyot's Institutes Feodales.
  Guyot, Inst. Feod.

Gwillim's Tithe Cases
  Gwil., Gwill, Gwill. Bac. Abr.,
  Gwill. T. Cas., Gwill. Ti. Cas.,
  Gwil. Ti. Cas.
Gwilt's Encyclopedia of Architecture
  Enc. Arch.
Gwynne on Sheriffs
  Gw. Sh.

H

Habeas Corpus
Hab. Corp., H.C.
Habere Facias Possessionem (Lat.)
Hab. fa. poss.
Habere Facias Seisnam (Lat.)
Hab. fa. seis.
Habitual Criminals and Subsequent Offenders
Habit. Crim.
Hackett on the Geneva Award Acts
Hack. Gen. Aw.
Hackworth's Digest of International Law
D.I.L. (Hack.)
Haddan's Administrative Jurisdiction of the Court of Chancery
Had. Chy. Jur.
Haddington's Manuscript Reports, Scotch Court of Session
Hadd., Haddington, Had.
Hadley's Introduction to the Roman Law
Hadl. Rom. Law
Hadley's Reports (45-48 New Hampshire)
Had., Hadley, Hadl.
Hagan's Reports (1-2 Utah)
Hag., Hagan
Hagans' Reports (1-5 West Virginia)
Hag., Hagans
Haggard's English Admiralty Reports
Hag. Adm., Hag., Hagg. Adm., Hagg. Adm. (Eng.)

Haggard's English Consistory Reports
Hagg. Con., Hagg. Cons., Hagg. Consist., Hagg.Consist. (Eng.)
Haggard's English Ecclesiastical Reports
Hagg. Ecc., Hagg. Eccl. (Eng.), Hagg. Eccl., Hag. Ecc.
Hagner and Miller's Reports (2 Maryland Chancery)
Hagn. & M., Hagn. & Mill.
Hague Convention
H.C.
Hague Court Reports
Hague Ct. Rep.
Hague Court Reports, First Series
Hague Ct. Rep. (Scott)
Hague Court Reports, Second Series
Hague Ct. Rep. 2d (Scott)
Hailes' Annals of Scotland
Hailes' Ann.
Hailes' Decisions, Scotch Court of Sessions
Hailes Dec.
Haine's Illinois Justice of the Peace
Hain.J.P.
Halcomb's Mining Cases
Halc., Halc. Min. Cas.
Hale on Torts
Hale, Torts
Hale's Analysis of the Law
Hale, Anal., Hal. Anal.
Hale's De Jure Maris, Appendix to Hall on the Sea Shore
De Jure Mar., Hale, De Jure Mar.

Hale's De Portibus Maris
Hale de Port. Mar.

Hale's English Ecclesiastical Reports
Hale Ecc.

Hale's History of Parliament
Hale Parl.

Hale's History of Pleas of the Crown
H.H.P.C.

Hale's History of the Common Law
Hale C.L., H.H.C.L., Hale, Hale Com. Law, Hale, Hist. Eng. Law

Hale's Jurisdiction of the House of Lords
Hale Jur. H.L.

Hale's Pleas of the Crown
H.P.C., Hale P.C., Hale P.C. (Eng.)

Hale's Precedents in Ecclesiastical Criminal Cases
Hale Cr. Prec., Hale Prec., Hale's

Hale's Reports (33-37 California)
Hale

Hale's Sheriff's Account
Sh. Acc.

Hale's Suggestion on Courts-Martial
Hale Sug. C.M.

Hale's Summary of Pleas of the Crown
Sum., Hale Sum.

Halhed's Code of Gentoo Laws
Halh. Gent. L.

Halifax' Analysis of the Roman Civil Law
Halifax, Anal.

Halkerston's Compendium of Scotch Faculty Decisions
Halk., Halk. Comp.

Halkerston's Digest of the Scotch Marriage Law
Halk. Dig., Halk.

Halkerston's Latin Maxims
Halk., Halk. Lat. Max., Halk. Max.

Halkerston's Technical Terms of the Law
Halk. Tech. Terms

Hall and Twell's English Chancery Reports
Ha. & Tw., Hall & T., Hall & Tw., Hall & Tw. (Eng.), Hal. & Tw., H. & T., H. & Tw.

Hall (Jerome) on General Principles of Criminal Law
Hall, J. Criminal Law

Hall on International Law
Hall Int. Law

Hall's Admiralty Practice and Jurisdiction
Hall Adm.

Hall's American Law Journal
Hall A.L.J., Hall Am. L.J., Hall L.J., Hall's Am. L.J.

Hall's Essay on Maritime Loans from the French of Emerigon
Hall, Emerig. Mar. Loans, Hall, Marit. Loans

Hall's Laws of Mexico Relating to Real Property
Hall, Mex. Law

Hall's Journal of Jurisprudence
Jour. Juris.

Hall's Law Journal
L.J.

Hall's Legal Forms
H.L.F.

Hall's New York Superior Court Reports
Hall., Hall (N.Y.)

Hall's Reports (56-57 New Hampshire)
Hall N.H., Hall.

Hall's Rights and Duties of Neutrals
Hall, Neut.

Hall's Rights in the Sea Shores
Hall Shores

Hall's Tracts on Constitutional Law
Hall Const. L.

Hall's Treatise on the Law Relating to Profits a Prendre, etc.
Hall, Profits a Prendre

Hallam's Constitutional History of England
Hal. Const. Hist., Const. Hist., Hall. Const. Hist., Hallam., Hall. Hist.

Halleck's International Law
Hal. Int. Law, Hall Int. Law, Halleck, Int. law

Halleck's Law of War
Hall. Law of W.

Halleck's Mining Laws of Spain and Mexico
Hal. Min. Law

Hallett's Colorado Reports (1-2 Colorado)
Hall. (Col.), Hall., Hallet

Halliday's Elementary View of Chancery Proceedings
Hall. Ch. Pr.

Hallifax's Analysis of the Civil Law
Hallif. C.L., Hal. Civ. Law, Hall. Civ. Law, Hallifax, Anal. (or Civil Law)

Halsbury's Law of England
Halsbury L. Eng., Halsbury, Halsbury's Laws

Halsbury's Statutes of England
Halsbury, Halsbury's Statutes

Halsbury's Statutory Instruments
Halsbury's S.I.s.

Halsted's Digest of the Law of Evidence
Hal. Ev., Halst. Ev.

Halsted's New Jersey Chancery
Halst. Ch., Halst., Halsted (N.J.)

Halsted's Reports (5-8 New Jersey Equity)
Hals. Eq., Hals. Ch.

Halsted's Reports (6-12 New Jersey Law)
Hal. Law, Hals., Halst.

Hamel's International Law
Ham. Int.

Hamel's Laws of the Customs
Hamel, Cust., Ham. Cust.

Hamilton on Company Law
Hamilton

Hamilton's American Negligence Cases
Hamilton

Hamilton's Court of Session Reports
Ham.

Hamilton's Federalist
Ham. Fed.

Hamline Journal of Public Law and Policy
Hamline J. Pub. L. & Pol'y

Hamline Law Review
Hamline L. Rev.

Hamlin's Reports (81-93 Maine)
Hamlin

Hammerton, Allen and Otter's English Magistrates' Cases
Ham. A. & O.

Hammick's Marriage Laws
Ham. Mar. Laws

Hammon on Contracts
Ham. Cont.

**Hammond and Jackson's Reports
(45 Georgia)**
Ham. & J., Hammond & Jackson
Hammond on Fire Insurance
Ham. Ins.
Hammond on Insanity
Ham. Ins.
Hammond on Parties to Action
Ham. Parties, Ham. Part.
**Hammond's (Charles) Reports (1-
9 Ohio)**
Hammond, Ham., Ham. O.,
Ham. O.R.
**Hammond's India and Burma
Election Cases**
Ham.
**Hammond's Nisi Prius Reports,
England**
Ham. N.P.
**Hammond's Principles of Plead-
ing**
Ham. Pl.
**Hammond's Reports (36-45 Geor-
gia)**
Hammond
**Hampshire County Court Re-
ports**
Hamps. Co. Cas.
Hampson's Trustees
Hamp. Tr.
Hanbury-Jones on Uses
Hanb. Us.
**Hanbury's Judicial Error in the
Law of Patents**
Hanb. Pat.
**Hancock's System of Conveyanc-
ing**
Hanc. Conv.
Hand on Fines and Recoveries
Hand Fines
**Hand/Smith's Neighboring Prop-
erty Owners**
NPO

Handbook
Hdbk.
Handbook for Magistrates
Handb. Mag.
Handbook of Criminal Cases
Desai.
**Handelsgesetzbuch (Commercial
Code) (German)**
HGB
Hand's Chancery Practice
Hand Ch. P.
Hand's Crown Practice
Hand Cr. Pr.
Hands on Patents
Hand. Pat.
Hand's Reports (40-45 New York)
Hand.
**Handy's Cincinnati Superior
Court Reports**
Handy R.
**Handy's Ohio Reports (12 Ohio
Decisions)**
Han., Hand., Handy, Handy
(Ohio), H.
Hanes' English Chancery Reports
Hanes
**Hanes' United States Digest of
Criminal Cases**
Hane. Cr. Dig.
Hanford's Entries
Hanf.
**Hanhart on the Laws Relating to
Married Women**
Hanh. Mar. Wom., Han. Mar.
Wom.
**Hannay's Reports (12-13 New
Brunswick)**
N.B.R. Han., Han., Hann., Han.
(N.B.)
Hanover on the Law of Horses
Han. Hor.
Hansard on Aliens
Hans. Al.

Hansard's Parliamentary Debates
Han. Deb., Hansard, Hans.
Deb., Hans. Parl. Deb., Han.,
Han. Ent., Hans. Ent., Hans.
Deb.

Hansbrough's Reports (76-90 Virginia)
Hans., Hansb.

Hansell's Bankruptcy Reports
H.B.R., Han.

Hanson on the Probate and Legacy Acts
Hans. Pr., Han. Prob.

Haralambie on Handling Child Custody Cases
HCC

Harbors and Navigation
Har. & Nav.

Harbors and Navigation Code
Harb. & Nav. C.

Harcarse's Decisions, Scotch Court of Session
Harc.

Hardcastle on Election Petitions
Hard. El. Pet.

Hardcastle on Statutory Law
Hard. St. L.

Hardesty's Reports (Delaware Term)
Hard., Hardes.

Harding on Ecclesiastical Law
Hard. Eccl. L.

Hardingham on Trade Marks
Hard. Tr. M.

Hardin's Reports (3 Kentucky)
Hardin, Hardin (Ky.), Hard.

Hardres' English Exchequer Reports
Hard., Hardr. (Eng.), Hardres,
Hardr.

Hardwicke Cases Tempore by Lee and Hardwicke, England
Cas.t.Hard., Hardw. Cas.
Temp., Cas.t.Hardw., Cas.t.H.

Hardwicke Cases Tempore by Ridgeway, England
Hardw., Hardw. (Eng.)
Cas.t.Hardw., Cas.t.H.

Hardwicke Cases Tempore, England
Cas. Temp. Hardw., Ca. Temp. H.

Hardwicke Cases Tempore (W.Kelynge, English King's Bench Reports)
Cas.K.B.t.H., Cas.K.B.t.Hard.

Hardwicke King's Bench Cases Tempore by Annaly, England
Ca. temp. Hard., Ca. t. H.,
Ca.t.Hrd., Cas. temp. H.

Hardwicke's Cases in King's Bench Tempore, England
B.R.H.

Hardwicke's Note Books
Hardw. N.B.

Hare and Wallace's American Leading Cases
Hare & W.

Hare on Discovery of Evidence
Hare Disc. (or Ev.)

Hare on Elections
Hare Elec.

Hare's American Constitutional Law
Hare, Const. Law

Hare's English Vice-Chancellor's Reports
Hare, Hare (Eng.), H. (Ha.),
Ha., H., Hare App.

Hare's English Vice-Chancellor's Reports, Appendix to Vol. X
Har. App., Hare App., Ha. App.

Hargrave and Butler's Edition of Coke upon Littleton
Harg. & B. Co. Litt.

Hargrave and Butler's Notes on Coke on Littleton
Hargrave & Butlers Notes on Co. Litt.

Hargrave on the Thellusson Act
Harg. Th.

Hargrave's Collectanea Juridica
Harg. Coll. Jur., Har. Col. Jur.

Hargrave's Collection of Law Tracts
Harg. L.T.

Hargrave's Juridical Arguments and Collections
Harg. Jur. Arg.

Hargrave's Jurisconsult Exercitations
Harg. Exer., Harg. Coll. Jur.

Hargrave's Law Tracts
Harg. Law Tracts

Hargrave's Notes to Coke on Littleton
Harg. Co. Litt., Hargr. Co. Litt.

Hargrave's State Trials
Har. St. Tr., Harg. State Tr., Harg. St. Tr., Harg.

Hargrove's Reports (68-75 North Carolina)
Hargrove, Harg.

Harleian Collection, British Museum
Harl. C.B.M.

Harman's Upper Canada Common Pleas Reports
Harman, Harm.

Harmonized
H. (is used in Shepard's Citations)

Harmon's Manual of United States Pension Laws
Har. Pen. Man., Harm. Pens.

Harmon's Reports (13-15 California)
Harm.

Harper and James on Torts
Harper & James, Torts

Harper's Maryland Conspiracy Cases
Harp. Con. Cas., Harper

Harper's South Carolina Equity Reports
Harp., Harp. Eq., Equity Rep., Eq. Rep., Eq. R., Harper

Harper's South Carolina Law Reports (16 South Carolina)
Harper, Harp., Harp. L., Harp. L. (S.C.)

Harper's Reports (5 South Carolina Equity)
Harp. Eq. (S.C.), Eq. R., Harper

Harrigan and Thompson's Cases on the Law of Self-Defense
H. & T. Self-Def.

Harrington's Michigan Chancery Reports
Harring., Har., Harr., Har. Ch., Har. Chy., Harr Ch., Harr. Ch. (Mich.), Harr. Ch. R., Harring. Ch. (Mich.), Harr. (Mich.), Harrington

Harrington's Reports (1-5 Delaware)
Har. Del., Harrington, Harr., Harring.

Harrington's (W.W.) Reports (31-38 Delaware)
W.W.H., W.W. Harr., W.W. Harr. Del.

Harris and Clarkson on Conveyancing, & c.
Harr. & Cl. Conv.

Harris and Gill's Maryland Reports
Har. & G., Har. & G. Rep., Harris & Gill's Md. R., H. & G., Har. & Gill, Harr. & G., Har. & Gil., Harris & G.

Harris and Johnson's Maryland Reports
Har. & Johns. Md. Rep., Harris & J., Har. & John., Har. & J., Har. & J. (Md.), Harr. & J., Harr. & J. (Md.), H. & John.

Harris and McHenry's Maryland Reports
Har. and M'Hen., Harr. & McHen., Har. & McH., Harr. & McH., Harr. & McH. (Md.), Harr. & M'H., Md., Md, H. & McHenry, Harr. & M.

Harris and Simrall's Reports (49-52 Mississippi)
H. & S., Harr. & Sim., Harris & S., Harris & Sim., Harris & Simrall

Harris' Elements of Roman Law
Harr. Rom. Law

Harris' Georgia Digest
Har. Dig., Harris Dig., Harr. (Ga.)

Harris' Hints on Advocacy
Harr. Hints, Harr. Adv.

Harris' Modern Entries
Harr. Ent.

Harris on Titles to Mines
Harr. Min.

Harris' Principiae Primae Legum
Harr. Prin.

Harris' Principles of the Criminal Law
Harr. Cr. L.

Harris' Reports (13-24 Pennsylvania)
Harr., Harris, Har.

Harris' Translation of the Institutes of Justinian
Harr. Just., Har. Just.

Harrison and Hodgin's Upper Canada Municipal Reports
H. & H., Harr. & H., Harr. & Hodg.

Harrison and Rutherford's English Common Pleas Reports
Harr. & R., Har. & Ruth., Harr. & Ruth., H. & R.

Harrison and Wollaston's English King's Bench Reports
Harr. & W., Harr. & W. (Eng.), Harr. & Woll., Har. & Woll., H. & W., Har. & W.

Harrison on Probate and Divorce
Harr. Prob.

Harrison's Chancery Practice
Har. Ch. Pr., Harr. Ch., Harrison, Ch.

Harrison's Common Law Procedure Act, Canada
Har. Com. Proc., Harr. Proc.

Harrison's Compilation of the Laws of New Jersey
Har. Com.

Harrison's Condensed Louisiana Reports
Harr. Con. La. R.

Harrison's Digest of English Common Law Reports
Harr. Dig., Harrison Dig., Har. Dig.

Harrison's Municipal Law of Ontario
Harr. Mun. Law

Harrison's Practice of the Courts of King's Bench and Common Pleas
Harr. Pr. K.B.

Harrison's Reports (15-17, 23-29 Indiana)
Har., Harr., Harrison

Harrison's Reports (16-19 New Jersey)
Harr., Harrison, Harr. N.J.

Harsha's Medical Malpractice: Handling Orthopedic Cases
MMOC

Harston's California Practice and Pleading
Hars. Pr.

Hartley and Hartley's Reports (11-21 Texas)
Hartley & Hartley Rep., Hart. & H., Hartley & Hartley

Hartley's Digest of Texas Laws
Hart. Dig., Hart.

Hartley's Reports (4-10 Texas)
Hart., Hartley

Hart's Bankrupt Law and Practice
Hart. Bank.

Hart's United States Mining Statutes
Hart Min. Laws

Harvard
Harv.

Harvard Blackletter Journal
Harv. Blackletter J.

Harvard Business Review
Harv. Bus. Rev., H.B.R.

Harvard Business World
Harv. Bus. World

Harvard Civil Rights-Civil Liberties Law Review
Harv. Civ. Rights-Civ. Lib. L. Rev., Harv. C.R.-C.L. L. Rev., Harv. C.R.-C.L.L., Harvard Civil Rights L. Rev.

Harvard Computer-Aided Legal Instruction Project
HCLIP

Harvard Educational Review
Harv. Ed. Rev.

Harvard Environmental Law Review
Harv. Env. L. Rev., Harv Envir L Rev, Harv. Envt'l L. Rev., Harv. Envtl. L. Rev.

Harvard Human Rights Journal
Harv. Hum. Rts. J.

Harvard International Law Club Bulletin
Harv. Int'l L. Club Bull.

Harvard International Law Club Journal
Harv. Int'l. L. Club J.

Harvard International Law Journal
Harv. Int. L.J., Harv. Int'l. L.J., Harvard Int.L.J.

Harvard Journal of Law and Technology
Harv. J.L. & Tech.

Harvard Journal of Law and Public Policy
Harv. J.L. & Pub. Pol'y

Harvard Journal on Legislation
Harv. J. Legis., Harv. J. on Legis., Harvard J. on Legis.

Harvard Law Library Information Bulletin
Harv. L. Lib. Inf. Bull.

Harvard Law Review
Har. L.R., Harv. L. Rev., Harv LR, Harvard L. Rev., H.L.R.

Harvard Law School
H.L.S.

Harvard Law School Bulletin
Harv. L.S. Bull.

Harvard Law School Record
Harv. L.S. Rec.

Harvard Women Law Review
Harv. Women L.R.

Harvard Women's Law Journal
Harv. Women L.J., Harv.
Women's L.J.
Harvard World Tax Series
Harv. W. Tax Ser.
Harwood's Practice of United States Naval Courts-Martial
Har. Ct. Mar.
Hasbrouck's Reports, Idaho
Hasb.
Haskell's Reports for U.S. Courts in Maine (Fox's Decisions)
Hask.
Haslam's Medical Jurisprudence
Hasl. Med. Jur.
Hastings Center for Trial and Appellate Advocacy
HCTAA
Hastings Communications and Entertainment Law Journal
Hastings Comm. & Ent. L.J.
Hastings Constitutional Law Quarterly
Hast. Const. L.Q., Hastings Const. L.Q.
Hastings' International and Comparative Law Review
Hast. Int. & Comp. L. Rev., Hastings' Int'l. & Comp. L. Rev.
Hastings Law Journal
Hast. L.J. (Int'l), Hastings L.J., H.L.J.
Hastings' Reports (69-70 Maine)
Hast.
Hatcher's Kansas Digest
Hatcher's Kan. Dig., Kan. Dig.
Hatsell's Parliamentary Precedents
Hats. Pr., Hats., Hats. Prec.
Hague Yearbook of International Law
Hague Y.B. Int'l L.

Haviland's Prince Edward Island Chancery Reports, by Peters
Hav. Ch. Rep., Hav., Peters, Hav. P.E.I., Havil.
Hawaii
Ha., Haw., Hi.
Hawaii Appeals Reports
Hawaii App.
Hawaii Attorney General Report
Rep. Hawaii Att'y Gen.
Hawaii Bar Journal
Hawaii B.J.
Hawaii Bar News
Hawaii B.N.
Hawaii Constitution
Hawaii Const.
Hawaii Federal
Haw. Fed.
Hawaii Public Utilities Commission Decisions
Hawaii P.U.C. Dec.
Hawaii Reports
H., Haw., Hawaii, Hawaii Rep., Hawaiian Rep., Hi., Haw. Rep., Hawaiian Reports, Hawn.
Hawaii Revised Statutes
Haw. Rev. Stat., Hawaii Rev. Stat., H.R.S.
Hawaii Rules and Regulations
Hawaii Rules & Reg.
Hawaii Session Laws
Haw. Sess. Laws, Hawaii Sess. Laws
Hawaii Supreme Court Reports
Haw.
Hawaiian Federal
Hawaii. Fed.
Hawaiian Islands Reports
H.I. Rep.
Hawarde's Star Chamber Cases
Hawarde St. Ch., Haw., Hawarde

Hawes on Assignments
  Haw. Ass.
Hawes on Jurisdiction of Courts
  Hawes, Jur.
Hawes' Will Case
  Haw. W.C.
Hawkins' Abridgment of Coke Upon Littleton
  Hawk. Abr., Hawk. Coke Abr., Hawk. Co. Litt.
Hawkins' Construction of Wills
  Hawk. Wills
Hawkins' Louisiana Annual
  Hawk.
Hawkins' Pleas of the Crown
  H.P.C., Haw., Hawk. Pl. Cr., Hawk., Hawk. P.C.
Hawkins' Reports (19-24 Louisiana Annual)
  Haw., Hawkins
Hawks' North Carolina Reports (81 North Carolina)
  Hawks, Hawks (N.C.)
Hawley's American Criminal Reports
  Hawley's Crim. Rep., Haw. Cr. Rep., Hawl. Cr. R., Hawley
Hawley's Reports (10-20 Nevada)
  Haw., Hawl., Hawley
Hay and Marriott's Admiralty Reports
  Marr., Hay & Mar., H. & M., Hay & M., Hay & M. (Eng.), Hay & Marr.
Hay on Expatriation
  Hay Exp.
Hayes and Jarman's Concise Forms of Wills
  Hayes & J. Wills, H. & J., H. & J. Ir., Hay. & Jo., Hayes & J., Hayes & J.(Ir.), Hayes & Jo., Hayes & Jon., Hay & J., H. & J. Forms

Hayes' Concise Conveyancer
  Hayes Con. Conv.
Hayes' Dispositions to Heirs in Tail, etc.
  Hayes Heirs
Hayes' Introduction to Conveyancing
  Hayes Intr.
Hayes' Irish Exchequer Reports
  Hay. Exch., Hayes Exch. (Ir.), Hayes, Hayes Exch., Hay.
Hayes' Law of Uses, Devises, and Trust
  Hayes U.D. & T.
Hayes on Conveyancing
  Hayes, Conv.
Hayes on Crimes and Punishments
  Hayes Cr. & P.
Hayes on Limitations as to Heirs of the Body, etc.
  Hayes Lim.
Hayes' Real Estate
  Hayes R. Est.
Hayes' Reports, Calcutta
  Hay.
Haynes' Chancery Practice
  Hayn. Ch. Pr.
Haynes' Outlines of Equity
  Haynes, Eq., Hayn. Eq., Hay. Eq.
Haynes' Students' Leading Cases
  Hayn. Lead. Cas.
Hay's Decisions on Accidents and Negligence
  Hay Acc., Hay Dec.
Hay's High Court Appeals Reports, Bengal
  Hay., Hay (Calc.)
Hay's Poor Law Decisions
  Hay., Hay P.L.

Hayward and Hazelton's United
States Circuit Court Reports,
District of Columbia
 Hayw. & H.D.C., Hay. & Haz.,
 Hayw. & H., Hayw. & H., Hay.
 & H., H.H., Hay & H., U.S. Cir.
 Ct. Rep. D.C.
Hayward's Law Register
 Hayw. L.R.
Haywood's Manual of the Statute
Laws of North Carolina
 Hayw. Man.
Haywood's Reports (23 North
Carolina)
 Hay., Hayw., Hayw. N.C.
Haywood's Reports (4-6 Tennes-
see)
 Hayw., Hayw. Tenn., Haywood
 Tenn. Rep., Hay.
Hazard's Pennsylvania Register
 Haz. Pa. Reg., Haz. Pa. Reg.
 (Pa.), Haz. Reg.
Hazard's United States Register
 Haz. U.S. Reg.
Hazlitt and Roche's Bankruptcy
Reports
 H. & R. Bank.
Hazlitt and Roche on Maritime
Warfare
 Haz. & R. M. War.
Hazzard and Warburton's Prince
Edward Island Reports
 H. & W.
Headquarters
 Hdqrs., H.Q.
Headquarters, United States Air
Force
 JAEC
Head's Reports (38-40 Tennessee)
 Head (Tenn.), Head
Heale's Law of Church Pews
 Heal. Pews

Health
 Health
Health and Safety Code
 Health & S.C.
Health and Safety Executive
 H.S.E.
Health Care Financing Admini-
tration Rulings
 H.C.F. A.R.
Health Care Financing Review
 H.C.F. Rev., H.C.F.R.
Health Care Labor Manual
 H.C.L.M.
Health Law in Canada
 Health L. Can.
Health Lawyers News Report
 H.L.N.R.
Health Matrix
 Health Matrix
Health Resources Administration
 HRA
Health Service Commissioner
 H.S.C.
Health Services Administration
 HSA
Healy on Joint Stock Companies
 Heal. J.S. Comp.
Heard on Libel and Slander
 Heard Lib. & Sl.
Heard's Civil Pleading
 Heard Civ. Pl.
Heard's Criminal Pleading
 Heard Cr. Pl.
Heard's Curiosities of the Law
Reporters
 Heard Cur. Rep.
Heard's Edition of Shortt on Ex-
traordinary Legal Remedies
 Heard's Shortt, Extr. Rem.
Heard's Edition of Stephen on
Pleading
 Heard St. Pl.

Heard's Equity Pleading
Heard Eq. Pl.
Hearing
Hr'g
Hearing Examiner
Hear. Exam.
Heath's Maxims
Heath, Max.
Heath's Reports (36-40 Maine)
Heath
Hebrew
H.
Hecker's Cases on Warranty
Heck. Cas.
Hedges' Reports (2-6 Montana)
Hedges
Heineccius' Antiquitatum Romanarum
Heinecc. Ant. Rom.
Heineccius' Elementa Juris Cambialis
Heinecc. de. Camb., Heinec.Elem.Jur.Camb.
Heineccius' Elementa Juris Civilis
Heinecc. Elem., Heinec.Elem.Jur.Civ.
Heineccius' Elementa Juris Naturae et Gentium
Hein.
Heiskell's Reports (48-59 Tennessee)
Heisk. (Tenn.), Heisk.
Helm's Reports (2-9 Nevada)
Helm
Helsinki Accords, Conference on Security and Cooperation in Europe
CSCE
Hemingway's Reports (53-65 Mississippi)
Heming. (Miss.), Heming.

Hemmant's Select Cases in Exchequer Chamber (Selden Society Publications, 51)
Hemmant
Hemming and Miller's English Vice-Chancellors' Reports
H. & M. Ch., Hem. & Mill., Hem. & M., Hem. & M. (Eng.), H. & M.
Hempstead's Arkansas Reports
Hemp., Hempst.
Hempstead's United States Circuit Court Reports
Hemp., Hempst.
Hening and Munford's Reports (11-14 Virginia)
H. & M., Hen. & Mun., H. & M. (Va.), Hen. & M.
Hening's American Pleader
Hen. Am. Pl.
Hening's Maxims
Hen. Max.
Hening's Virginia Justice of the Peace
Hen. J.P.
Hening's Virginia Statutes
Hen. St.
Henley's Bankrupt Law
Hen. B.L.
Hennell's Forms
Hen. Forms
Hennen's Louisiana Digest
Hen. La. Dig.
Hennepin Lawyer
Hennepin Law, Henn. Law.
Henning CLE Reporter
Henning CLE Rep.
Henry (King)
H., Hen.
Henry I Laws
L.L. Hen. I, Leg. H.I.
Henry on Foreign Law
Hen. For. L.

Henry's Judgment in Ordwin v. Forbes
Henry Judg.

Henry's Manumission Cases
Hen. Man. Cas.

Hent's Forms and Use of Blanks in California
Hent Forms

Hepburn's Reports (3-4 California and 13 Pennsylvania)
Hepb.

Her Britannic Majesty
H.B.M.

Her Imperial Highness
H.I.H.

Her Majesty
H.M.

Her Majesty's Government
H.M.G.

Her Majesty's Stationery Office
H.M.S.O.

Herald
Herald

Herbert's Antiquities of the Inns of Court, etc.
Herb. Ant.

Here (in the same paragraph or title)
Hic

Herman on Chattel Mortgages
Her. Chat., Herm. Chat. Mortg.

Herman on Mortgages of Real Estate
Her. Mort.

Hermand's Consistorial Decisions
Herm., Hermand

Herman's Law of Estoppel
Her. Est., Herm. Estop.

Herman's Law of Executions
Herm. Ex'ns.

Herman's Law of Executors
Her. Ex.

Herne's Law of Charitable Uses
Her. Char. U., Her.

Herne's Precedents
Her. Prec.

Heron's Jurisprudence
Her. Jur.

Hertslet on Master and Servant
Hert. M. & Serv.

Hertslet's Map of Europe
Hert. Map Eur.

Hertslet's Treaties
Hert. Treat.

Hertzburg, Kaye and Plaia's International Trade Practice
ITP

Hertzog's Reports of Transvaal High Court
H., Hertzog

Hetley's English Common Pleas Reports
Hetl., Het. C.P., Het., Het. (Eng.)

Heyl's United States Import Duties
Heyl Imp. D.

Heywood and Massey's Court of Protection Practice
Heywood & Massey

Heywood on Elections
Heyw. Elec.

Heywood's County Courts Practice
Heyw. Co. Ct.

Heywood's Table of Cases, Georgia
Heyw. Ca.

Hibbard's Reports (67 New Hampshire)
Hibb.

Hibbard's Reports (20 Opinions of the Attorneys-General)
Hibb.

Hic (here, in the same paragraph)
H.
Hickman on Naval Courts-Martial
Hick. Ct. Mar.
Hicks on Materials and Methods of Legal Research
Hicks, Leg. Research
Hicks on Men and Books Famous in the Law
Hicks, Men & Books
Hicks' Organization and Ethics of Bench and Bar
Hicks, Ethics
Higgins' Digest of Patent Cases
Hig. Pat. Dig.
Higgin's Tennessee Civil Appeals Reports
Higgins, Tenn. C.C.A. (Higgins), Tenn. Civ. App. (Higgins)
Higgins' Pollution and Obstruction of Watercourses
Hig. Waterc.
High Commission Court
Burn.
High Commission Territories
H.C.T.
High Commission Territories Reports, Basutoland, Bechuanaland and Swaziland
H.C.T.R.
High Commission[er]
H.C.
High Commissioner for Germany, United States
HICOG
High Court
High Ct., H.C.
High Court of Admiralty in England
Adm.
High Court of Australia
H.C. A., H.C. of A.

High Court of Justice, England and Wales
High Court
High Court of Justiciary in Scotland
H.C.J.
High Court Reports for the Northwest Provinces of India
H.C.R., High Ct., H.C.R.N.W.F., H.C.R.N.W.P.
High Court Reports of Orange Free State
O.F.C., Gregorowski
High on Extraordinary Legal Remedies
High Ex. Rem., High, Extr. Leg. Rem.
High on Injunctions
High Inj.
High on the Law of Receivers
High Rec.
High Technology Law Journal
High Tech. L.J.
Higher Education Act
HEA
Highmore on Bail
High. Bail
Highmore on Lunacy
High. Lun.
Highmore on Mortmain
High. Mort.
Hight's Reports (57-58 Iowa)
Hight
Highway
High.
Highway Code
H.C.
Hilary Term
H., H. (Hil.), Hil., Hil. T.
Hilary Vacation
Hil. Vac.
Hildyard on Insurance
Hild. Ins.

Hildyard's Marine Insurance
Hild. Mar. Ins.

Hill and Denio's Supplement by Lalor
Hill & D. Supp.

Hill and Redman's Law of Landlord and Tenant
Hill & Redman

Hill on Trustees
Hill Tr.

Hill's Shepard's Florida Legal Filing Directory
SFLF

Hillard's Abridgment of Real Property Law
Hill. Abr.

Hilliard on Bankruptcy and Insolvency
Hill. Bank. (or B. & I.)

Hilliard on Contracts
Hill. Cont.

Hilliard on New Trials
Hill. New Trials

Hilliard on Real Property
Hill. Real Prop., Hilliard, R.P.

Hilliard on Remedies for Torts
Hill Rem.

Hilliard on Sales of Personal Property
Hill. Sales

Hilliard on the Law of Injunctions
Hill. Inj.

Hilliard on the Law of Mortgages
Hill. Mor.

Hilliard on the Law of New Trials
Hill. N.Tr.

Hilliard on the Law of Taxation
Hill. Tax.

Hilliard on the Law of Torts
Hil. Torts, Hill. Torts

Hilliard on the Law of Vendors
Hill. Vend.

Hilliard's American Jurisprudence
Hill. Am. Jur.

Hilliard's American Law
Hil. Abr., Hill. Am. Law

Hilliard's Elements of Law
Hil. Elem. Law, Hill. Elem. Law

Hill's Annotated Oregon Codes and General Laws
Hill's Ann. Codes & Laws, Hill's Code

Hill's Annotated Washington General Statutes and Codes
Hill's Ann. St. & Codes, Hill's Code

Hill's Chancery Practice
Hill Ch. Pr.

Hill's Illinois Chancery Practice
Hill Ill. Chy.

Hill's Illinois Common Law Jurisdiction and Practice
Hill Ill. Com. Law

Hill's Illinois Probate Jurisdiction and Practice
Hill Prob.

Hill's Law of Fixtures
Hill Fixt.

Hill's Law of South Carolina
Hill, Law

Hill's Liberty and Law
Hill Lib. & Law

Hill's New York Supreme Court Reports
Hill N.Y., H., Hill, Hill N.Y.R., Hill's Reports

Hill's South Carolina Law Reports
Hill, Hill Ch., HillEq., Hill Eq. (S.C.), Hill S.C.

Hillyer's Reports (20-22 California)
Hillyer

Hilton's New York Common Pleas Reports
Hilt., Hilt. (NY)

Hincmari Epistolae
Hincmar. Epist.

Hinde's Modern Practice of the High Court of Chancery
Hinde Ch. Pr.

Hindi
Hi.

Hindmarch on Patents
Hind. Pat.

Hind's Practice
Hind Pr.

Hindu Law Journal
Hind. L.J., H.L.J.

Hindu Law Quarterly
Hind. L.Q.

Hine and Nicholas' Insurance Digest
Hine & N. Dig.

Hine and Nicholas on Assignment of Life Policies
Hine & N. Ass.

Hines' Reports (83-96 Kentucky)
Hines

Hire Purchase
H.P.

Hirsh on Juries
Hirsh Juries

His Majesty
H.M.

His Britannic Majesty
H.B.M.

His Imperial Highness
H.I.H.

His Majesty's Government
H.M.G.

Historical
Hist.

History
Hist.

History and Jurisdiction of the Courts of Law
Aldridge

History of English Law, by W. Holdsworth
H.E.L., Holdsw. Hist. E.L.

Hitch's Practice and Procedure in the Probate Court of Massachusetts
Hitch, Pr. & Proc.

Hitotsubashi Journal of Law and Politics
Hitotsubashi J.L. & Pol.

Hittell's California Codes
Hitt. Cod.

Hittell's California General Laws
Hittell's Laws

Hobart's English Common Pleas Reports
Hob., Hob. R., Hub.

Hobart's English King's Bench Reports
Hobart, Hobart (Eng.), Hob. R., Hub., Hob.

Hoc Anno (this year) (Lat.)
H.A.

Hoc Titulo (this title) (Lat.)
H.T.

Hoc Verbo or Hac Voce (this word, under this word) (Lat.)
H.V.

Hodge on Presbyterian Law
Hodge, Presb. Law

Hodges' English Common Pleas Reports
Hod., Hodg., Hodges, Hodges (Eng.)

Hodges' Law of Railways
Hodg. Ry.

Hodgin's Canada Election Cases
Hodg. Can. Elec. Cas.

Hodgin's Ontario Election Cases
    H.E.C., Hodg. El. Cas., Hodg.
    El. Cas. (Ont.), Hodg. Ont.
    Elect., Hodg., Hodg. El.
Hoffman on Referees
    Hoff. Ref.
Hoffman's Course of Legal Study
    Hoff. Leg. St.
**Hoffman's Decisions, United
    States District Court**
    Hoff. Dec., Hoffm. Dec. (F.)
Hoffman's Ecclesiastical Law
    Hoff. Ecc. mL.
**Hoffman's Land Cases, United
    States District Court**
    Hoff., Hoff. Land Cas., Hoffm.
    Rep. Land Cases, Hoffm.,
    Hoffm. Ch., Hoff. L. Cas., Hoff.
    Land, Hoff. L.C., Hoffm. Land
    Cas. (F.)
Hoffman's Leading Cases
    Hoff. Lead. Cas.
Hoffman's Legal Outlines
    Hoff. Out.
Hoffman's Master in Chancery
    Hoff. Mast., Hoff. Mast. Ch.
**Hoffman's New York Chancery
    Reports**
    Hoff., Hoffm., Hoffm. Ch.,
    Hoffm. Ch. (N.Y.), Hoff. Ch. Pr.,
    Hoff. N.Y., Hoff. Ch., Hoff. C.R.,
    Hoffman Ch. R., Hoffman's Ch.
    R.
**Hoffman's Opinions, United
    States District Court**
    Hoff. Op., Hoffm. Ops. (F.)
**Hoffman's Provisional Remain-
    ders**
    Hoff. Pr. Rem.
**Hoffman's Public Papers for New
    York**
    Hoff. Pub. P.

Hofstra Labor Law Forum
    Hofstra Lab. L.F.
Hofstra Labor Law Journal
    Hofstra Lab. L.J.
Hofstra Law Review
    Hofstra L. Rev.
Hofstra Property Law Journal
    Hofstra Prop. L.J.
**Hog of Harcarse's Scotch Session
    Cases**
    Hog.
**Hogan's Irish Rolls Court Re-
    ports**
    Hog., Hogan, Hogan (Ir.)
**Hogan's State Trials, Pennsylva-
    nia**
    Hog. St. Tr.
**Hoge Raad (Dutch Supreme
    Court)**
    H.R.
Hogue's Reports (1-4 Florida)
    Hogue
Holcombe on Equity Jurisdiction
    Holc. Eq. Jur.
**Holcombe's Law of Debtor and
    Creditor**
    Holc. Debt. & Cr.
**Holcombe's Leading Cases of
    Commercial Law**
    Holc. L. Cas.
**Holdings and Decisions of Judge
    Advocate General Boards of Re-
    view and United States Court
    of Military Appeals**
    JAG (Def.Dept.)
**Holdsworth's History of English
    Law**
    Holdsw. Hist. E.L., H.E.L.
Holland
    Holl.
Holland on Composition Deeds
    Holl. Comp. Deeds

Holland's Elements of Jurisprudence
Holl. El. Jur., Holl. Jur.
Holland's Institutes of Justinian
Holl. Just.
Hollinshead's Reports (1 Minnesota)
Holl., Hollinshead
Holmes and Disbrow's Practice
H. & D. Pr.
Holmes on the Common Law
Holm. Com. Law
Holmes' Reports (15-17 Oregon)
Holmes, Holm.
Holmes' Statesman
Holm. Statesman
Holmes' United States Circuit Court Reports
Holm., Holmes
Holt on Libels
Holt Lib.
Holt on Navigation
Holt Nav.
Holt on Registration of Title
Holt Reg.
Holt on Shipping
Holt Sh., Holt, Shipp.
Holthouse's Law Dictionary
Holt. L. Dic., Holthouse (or Holthouse, Law Dict.)
Holt's Cases Tempore, (11 Modern Reports), England
Ca.t.H., Rept.t.Holt, Ca.t.Holt., Ca.t.Q.A.
Holt's English Admiralty Cases
Holt Adm. Ca., Holt Adm., Holt Adm. Cas.
Holt's English Equity Reports
Holt, Holt Eq.
Holt's English King's Bench Reports
Holt K.B., Holt

Holt's English King's Bench Reports, Cases Tempore
Cas.t.H., Cas.t.Holt., Ca.
Holt's English Nisi Prius Reports
Holt, Holt N.P.
Home Civil Service
H.C.S.
Home Loan Bank Board
HLBB
Home Office
H.O.
Home Owners' Loan Corporation
HOLC
Home's Decisions, Scotch Court of Session
Home (Clk.), C.Home, Home (Cl.), Cl. Home., ClerkHome
Home's Manuscript Decisions, Scotch Court of Session
Home, Home Ct. of Sess., Home H. Dec.
Homestead
Homstd.
Homicide
Homi.
Homosexual Law Reform Society
H.L.R.S.
Honduras
Hond.
Hong Kong
H.K.
Hong Kong Law Journal
H.K. L.J., Hong Kong L.J.
Hong Kong Law Reports
H.K. Law Reports, H.K. L.R., Hong Kong L.R.
Hong Kong University Law Journal
Hong Kong U. L.Jo.
Honorable
Hon.
Honorary
Hon.

Honorary Magistrate
Hon. Magist.
Hood on Executors
Hood Ex.
Hooker's Reports (25-62 Connecticut)
Hook., Hooker
Hoonahan's Sind Reports, India
Hoon., Hoonahan
Hope's Compendium of the Commercial Law of the Pacific
Hope Com. Law
Hope's Minor Practicks
Hop. Min.
Hope's (of Kerse) Manuscript Decisions, Scotch Court of Session
Hope Dec., Hope
Hope's (Sir T.), Major Practicks
Hop. Min. Pr., Hop. Maj. Pr.
Hopkins' New York Chancery Reports
Hop., Hopk, Hopk. C.C., Hopk. Chanc. Rep., Hopk. Rep., Hopk. Ch.
Hopkins on Average
Hopk. Av.
Hopkins on Marine Insurance
Hopk. Mar. Ins.
Hopkinson's Pennsylvania Admiralty Decisions
Hopk. Dec., Hopk. Adm. Dec., Hopk. W., Hopk. Adm., Hokp. Adm., Hopk. Judg.
Hopkinson's Works, Pennsylvania
Hopk. Works (Pa.), Hopk. Wks.
Hopwood and Coltman's English Registration Appeal Cases
Hopw. & C., Hopw. & Colt., Hop. & C., Hop. & Colt.

Hopwood and Philbrick's English Registration and Election Cases
Hop. & Ph., H. & P., Hopw. & P., Hopw. & Phil., Hop. & Ch., Hop. & Phil.
Horn and Hurlstone's English Exchequer Reports
H. & H., Horn & H.
Horne on Diplomacy
Horne Dip.
Horner's Annotated Revised Indiana Statutes
Horner's Ann. St., Horner's Rev. St.
Horner's Reports (11-23 South Dakota)
Horner
Horne's Mirror of Justice
Horne Mir., Horne, M.J., Mir., Mir. Just., Mirr.
Horowitz and Davidson's Legal Rights of Children
LRC
Horr and Bemis' Treatise on Municipal Police Ordinances
Horr & B. Mun. Ord.
Horrigan and Thompson's Cases on Self-Defense
Cas. Self Def., Hor. & Th.Cas., Horr. & T. Cas. Self-Def., Horr. & Th.
Horwood's Year Books of Edward I
Horw. Y.B.
Hosea's Ohio Reports
Hosea
Hoskins' Reports (2 North Dakota)
Hoskins
Hospital
Hosp.
Hospital Advisory Service
HAS

Hospitals and Asylums
    Hospit.
Hotomannus de Verbis Feudalibus
    Hotom. in Verb. Feud.
Houard's Anglo-Saxon Laws
    Houard, Ang. Sax. Laws, Hou.
    Ang. Sax. Law.
Houard's Dictionary of the Customs of Normandy
    Hou. Dict.
Houck on Merchanics' Lien Law
    Houck Mech. Lien
Houck on the Law of Navigable Rivers
    Houck Riv.
Hough's American Constitutions
    Hough Am. Cons.
Hough's Military Law and Courts-Martial
    Hough C.-M.Cas., Hough C.M.
Houghton's Reports (97 Alabama)
    Houghton
House Administration
    H.A.
House Armed Services Committee
    H.A.S.C.
House Bill
    H., H.B.
House Document
    H.R. Doc.
House of Commons
    H. of C., H.C.
House of Commons Journal
    Comm. Journ., H.C. Jour.
House of Commons Weekly Information Bulletin
    H.C. Wkly. Inf. Bull.
House of Delegates
    Ho. of Dels.
House of Keys
    H. of K.

House of Lords
    H. of L., H.L.
House of Lords Journal
    L.J., H.L. Jour.
House of Lords Record Office
    H.L.R.O.
House of Lords Reports
    H.L. Rep.
House of Lords Weekly Information Bulletin
    H.L. Wkly. Inf. Bull.
House of Representatives
    H. of R., Ho. of Reps.
House of Representatives Concurrent Resolution
    H. Con. Res., H.C.Res., H.R.
    Con. Res.
House of Representatives Document
    H.Doc.
House of Representatives Joint Resolutions
    H.R.J. Res.
House of Representatives Journal
    J.H.
House of Representatives Report
    H.R. Rept., H. Rept., H.R. Rep.
House of Representatives Resolution
    H. Res., H.R. Res.
House Roll
    H.R.
Houseman's Life Assurance
    Hous. Life Ass.
Houses of Parliament
    H.P.
Housing
    Hous.
Housing and Development Reporter, Bureau of National Affairs
    Hous. & Dev. Rep. (BNA), Housing & Devel. Rep.

Housing and Home Finance Agency
HHFA

Housing and Local Government
H.L.G.

Housing Centre
H.C.

Housing Improvement Association
H.I.A.

Housing Laws
Housing L.

Housman's Precedents in Conveyancing
Hous. Pr.

Houston Journal of International Law
Hous. J. Int'l.L., Houston J. Int'l. L.

Houston Law Review
Hou. L.R., Hous. L. Rev., Houst. L. Rev., Houston L. Rev., H.U.L.

Houston Lawyer
Hous. Law., Houston Law.

Houston's Delaware Criminal Reports
H.Cr., Houst. Cr. Cas., Houst. Crim. (Del.)

Houston's Delaware Supreme Court Reports (6-14 Delaware)
Hous., Houst., Hou., Houston

Houston's Law of Stoppage in Transitu
Houst. St. Tr.

Houston's Texas Public Service Commission
Houston, Tex. P.S.C.

Hoveden's Annals
Hov. Ann.

Hoveden's (Roger de) Chronica
Hoved., Rog. Hov.

Hovenden on Frauds
Hov., Hov. Fr.

Hovenden's Supplement to Vesey, Jr's English Chancery Reports
Hov. Supp., Ves. Supp., Ves. Jr. Suppl., Ves. Jun. Supp., Hov., Hov. Sup.

Howard and Hutchinson's Mississippi Statutes
How. & H. St.

Howard Irish Property Cases
How. Po. Cas., How. Cas., How. Po. Ca.

Howard Journal
How. J., Howard Journal

Howard Journal of Criminal Justice
How. J. Crim. Just.

Howard Journal of Penology and Crime Prevention
How. J. Pen., Howard Journal

Howard Law Journal
How. L.J., Howard L.J.

Howard Law Review
How. L. Rev.

Howard's Irish Chancery Practice
How. Ch., How. Ch. P., How. C., How. Ch. Pr.

Howard's Equity Exchequer, Ireland
How. Eq. Exch., How. Eq. Ex., How. E.E.

Howard's New York Court of Appeals Cases
How. App. Cas., How. App. Cases, How. Ct. App. Cas., How. A. Cas., How. App., How. Cas.

Howard's New York Practice Reports
How., How. Pr., How. N.S., N.Y. Spec. Term R., N.Y. Spec. Term. Rep., How. (N.Y.), How. P.R., How. Pr. Rep., How. Pr. Sup. C., How. Prac., How. Prac. Rep., Howard Pr., Howard Pr. Rep., Howard's Prac. Reports, Howard's Practice, Howard's Spec. Term Rep., H.P.R.

Howard's New York Practice Reports, New Series
H. Pr., How. Pra., How. Pr. N.S., How. Pr. N.S.

Howard's Reports (2-8 Mississippi)
How., Howard

Howard's United States Supreme Court Reports
How., How. S.C., How. U.S., H., Howard Rep.

Howell and Beatty's Reports (22 Nevada)
How. & Beat.

Howell and Norcross' Reports (23-24 Nevada)
How. & N., How. & Nor.

Howell's Annotated Michigan Statutes
How. Ann. St., How. St.

Howell's English State Trials
Howell, St. Tr., How. St. Tr., How. State Tr.

Howell's Michigan Nisi Prius Reports
Howell N.P., How. N.P. (Mich.)

Howell's Michigan Nisi Prius Reports or Cases by Brown
Mich.N.P.

Howell's Nisi Prius
How.N.P. (Mich.)

Howell's Probate Practice
How. Prob. Pr.

Howell's Reports (22-26 Nevada)
How.

Howe's Massachusetts Practice
Howe Pr.

Howison's Virginia Criminal Trials
How. Cr. Tr.

Howson on Patents
How. Pat., Hows. Pat.

Howson on Reissued Patents
Hows. Reis. Pat.

Hoyt's Compiled Laws of Arizona
Hoyt Comp. L.

Hubback's Evidence of Succession
Hub. Suc. (or Ev.), Hubb. Succ., Hub. Ev.

Hubbard's Reports (45-51 Maine)
Hubb., Hubbard.

Hubbell's Legal Directory
Hub. Leg. Dir., Hub. Leg. Direc.

Huber's Praelectiones Juris Civilis
Hub. Prael. J.C.

Hudson and Brooke's Irish King's Bench Reports
H. & B., Hud. & B., Hud. & Br., Hud. & Bro.

Hudson on Building Contracts
Hudson

Hudson on Wills
Hud. Wills

Hudson's Executor's Guide
Hud. Exec.

Hughes' Abridgment
Hugh. Abr.

Hughes' Edition of Van Heythuysen's Equity Draftsman
Hugh. Eq. D.

Hughes' Entries
Hugh. Ent.

Hughes' Federal Practice
Hughes Fed. Prac.
Hughes on Insurance
Hugh. Ins.
Hughes on Wills
Hugh. Wills
Hughes on Writs
Hugh.Wr.
**Hughes' Precedents in Convey-
ancing**
Hugh. Con., Hugh. Conv.,
Hugh. Prec.
Hughes' Reports (1 Kentucky)
Hughes', Hu., Hughes, Hugh.
**Hughes' United States Circuit
Court Reports**
Hu., Hughes
Hullock on Costs
Hull. Costs
Hulton on Convictions
Hult. Conv.
Human
Hum.
Human Immunodeficiency Virus
HIV
Human Life Review
Hum. Life Rev.
Human Resources
H.R.
Human Rights
Hum. Rts., Human Rts.
**Human Rights Convention, Coun-
cil of Europe**
H.R., H.R. Conv.
Human Rights in U.S.S.R.
Hum. Rts. U.S.S.R.
Human Rights Journal
Human Rts. J., H.R. L.J.
Human Rights Law Journal
Hum. Rts. L.J.
Human Rights Quarterly
Hum. Rts. Q.

Human Rights Review
Human Rights Rev., Human
Rts. Rev.
Human[ity, ities]
Human.
**Hume on Crimes, Bell's Supple-
mented Notes**
Bell No.
Hume's Commentaries on Crimes
Hume Com.
**Hume's Court of Session Deci-
sions**
Hume
Hume's History of England
Hume, Hist. Eng.
**Humphrey's Reports (20-30 Ten-
nessee)**
Humph., Humphr., Hum.
**Humphry's Common Precedents
in Conveyancing**
Humph. Prec.
Hungarian
Hu.
Hungarian Law Review
Hung. L. Rev.
Hungary
Hung.
**Hun's New York Appellate Divi-
sion Reports**
Hun
Hun's Supreme Court Reports
Hun
Hunt's Fraudulent Conveyances
Hunt Fr. Conv.
Hunter on Landlord and Tenant
H.L. & T., Hunt. L. & T.
Hunter on Roman Law
Hunt. Rom. L., Hunter, Rom.
Law.
**Hunter's Proceeding in a Suit in
Equity**
Hunter, Suit Eq., Hunt. Suit

Hunter's Torrens Cases
　Hunt. Torrens, Hunt.
Huntingdon's Trial for Forgery
　Hunt. Tr.
Hunt's Annuity Cases
　Hunt Cas., Hunt's A.C., Hunt.,
　Hunt Ann. Cas.
Hunt's Law of Boundaries and Fences
　Hunt, Bound.
Hunt's Merchant's Magazine
　Hunt Mer. Mag.
Hunt's Suit in Equity
　Hunt, Eq.
Hurd on Personal Liberty
　Hurd Pers. Lib.
Hurd on the Laws of Freedom and Bondage in the United States
　Hurd F. & B.
Hurd on the Writ of Habeas Corpus
　Hurd Hab. Cor.
Hurd's Illinois Statutes
　Hurd St.
Hurd's Revised Illinois Statutes
　Hurd's Rev. St.
Hurlstone and Coltman's English Exchequer Reports
　Hurl. & Colt., H. & C., Hurl.
　Colt., Hurlst. & C. (Eng.), Hurl.
　& C., Hurlst. & C.
Hurlstone and Gordon's English Exchequer Reports
　Hurlst. & G., Hurl. & Gord.,
　Hurl. & G., H. & G.
Hurlstone and Norman's English Exchequer Reports
　Hurl. & N., Hurl. & Nor.,
　Hurlst. & N. (Eng.), H. & N.

Hurlstone and Walmsley's English Exchequer Reports
　Hurlst. & W. (Eng.), Hurl. &
　W., Hurl. & Walm., Hurlst. &
　W., H. & W.
Hurlstone on Bonds
　Hurl. Bonds.
Husband and Wife
　Husb. & W.
Husband on Married Women
　Husb. Mar. Wom.
Husband's Forensic Medicine
　Husb. For. Med.
Hustings Court
　Hust.
Huston on Land Titles in Pennsylvania
　Hust. L. Tit.
Hutcheson's Justice of the Peace
　Hutch J.P.
Hutcheson's Reports (81-84 Alabama)
　Hutch.
Hutchinson on Carriers
　Hutch. Car., Hutch. Carr.
Hutchinson's Mississippi Code
　Hutch. Code., Hutch. Dig. St.
Hutton Wood's Decrees in Tithe Cases
　Wood H.
Hutton's Courts of Requests
　Hutt. Ct. Req., Hut. Ct. Req.
Hutton's English Common Pleas Reports
　Hutton (Eng.), Hut., Hutt.
Huxley's Second Book of Judgments
　Hux. Judg.
Hyatt's Condominiums and Home Owners Associations
　CHOA
Hyde's Bengal Reports
　Hyde

I

Ibidem (the same, in the same place) (Lat.)
Ibid., Ib.
ICC Practioner's Journal
I.C.C. Prac.J., P.J.
Iceland
Ice.
Icelandic
Ic.
Id Est (that is) (Lat.)
I.e.
Idaho
I., Id.
Idaho Code
Idaho Code
Idaho Constitution
Idaho Const.
Idaho Industrial Accident Board Reports
Ida. I.A.B.
Idaho Law Foundation
IDLF
Idaho Law Journal
Id. L.J., Idaho L.J.
Idaho Law Review
Id. L.R., Idaho L. Rev.
Idaho Public Utilities Commission
Ida. P.U.C.
Idaho Reports
Id., Ida., Idaho
Idaho Reports, New Series
Idaho N.S.
Idaho Session Laws
Idaho Sess. Laws
Idaho Supplement
Ida. Supp.

Idaho Supreme Court Reports
Idaho
Iddings' Dayton Term Reports, Ohio
Iddings T.R.D., Iddings D.R.B., Iddings D.R.D., Idding, IDD.T.R., Idings T.R.D., Dayton Term Rep., Dayton T.R.
Idea: The Journal of Law and Technology
Idea, Idea: J.L. Tech.
Idem (the same) (Lat.)
Id.
Illingsworth on Forestalling
Ill. Forest.
Illinois
I., Ill.
Illinois Appellate Court Reports
Il.A., IlA, Ill. App., Ill.A., App., Ill. Ap., Ill. App. Ct. Rep., Ill. Apps., Ills.App.
Illinois Appellate Court Reports, 2d Series
Ill. App 2d, IlA.2d
Illinois Appellate Court Reports, 3d Series
Ill. App.3d, Il.A.3d.
Illinois Attorney General's Opinion
Ill. Op. Att'y Gen., Op. Ill. Att'y Gen.
Illinois Bar Journal
I.B.J., Ill. Bar J., Ill. B.J.
Illinois Cahill's Statutes
Cahill's Ill. St.
Illinois Circuit Court
Ill. Cir.
Illinois Circuit Court Reports
Ill. Cir.Ct.

Illinois Commerce Commission Opinions and Orders
Ill.C.C.
Illinois Constitution
Ill. Const.
Illinois Continuing Law Education
Ill. Cont. L.Ed.
Illinois Continuing Legal Education
Ill. Cont. L.Ed., Ill. Cont. Legal Ed.
Illinois Court Commission Official Reports
Official Rep. Ill. Courts Commission
Illinois Court of Claims
Ill. Ct.Cl.
Illinois Court of Claims Reports
IlC.Cl., Ill. Ct.Cl.
Illinois Decisions
Ill. Dec.
Illinois Institute of Continuing Legal Education
IICLE
Illinois Law and Practice
I.L.P.
Illinois Law Bulletin
Ill. L.B.
Illinois Law Forum
Il. L.F.
Illinois Law Quarterly
Ill. L.Q.
Illinois Law Record
Ill. L.Rec.
Illinois Law Review
Ill. L. Rev.
Illinois Laws
Ill. Laws
Illinois Legislative Service
Ill. Legis. Serv.

Illinois Public Utilities Commission Opinions and Orders
Ill. P.U.C. Ops.
Illinois Railroad and Warehouse Commission Decisions
Ill. R. & W.C.D.
Illinois Railroad and Warehouse Commission Reports
Ill. R. & W.C.
Illinois Register
Ill. Admin. Reg.
Illinois Reports
Ill., Ill. R., Ill. Rep., Illinois Rep., Ills., Ills. R., Ills. Rep.
Illinois Reports, 2d Series
Ill.2d.
Illinois Revised Statutes
Ill. Rev. Stat.
Illinois State Bar Association Quarterly Bulletin
Ill. B.A. Bull., Ill. S.B.A. Q.B.
Illinois State Bar Association Reports
Ill. S.B.A.
Illinois Statutes by Cahill
Cahill's Ill. St.
Illinois Supreme Court Reports
Il.
Illinois Supreme Court Reports, 2d Series
Il.2d.
Illinois Workmen's Compensation Cases
Ill. W.C.C.
Illustrated Legal News
Ill. Leg.N.
ILSA (International Law Students Association) Journal of International Law
ILSA J. Int'l L.
Immediate Action Directive
IAD

Immigration
Immigr.
Immigration and Nationality Administrative Decisions
D.I.A.
Immigration and Nationality Decisions
I. & N., I. & N. Dec.
Immigration and Naturalization Service
INS, I. & N.S.
Immigration and Naturalization Service Decisions
I. & N. Doc.
Immigration Appeal Cases
I.A.C.
Immigration Appeal Reports
Imm. A.R.
Immigration Bar Bulletin
Immig. B. Bull.
Immigration Briefings
Immig. Brief
Immigration Journal
Immigr. J., Imm.J.
Immigration Law and Business News
Immig. L. & Bus. News.
Immigration Newsletter
Immig. Newsl.
Imperial
Imp.
Imperial Dictionary
Imp. Dict.
Imperial Federation
Imp. Fed.
Impey on Law and Practice of Mandamus
Imp. Man.
Impey on Modern Pleader
Imp. Pl.
Impey on Office of Sheriff
Imp. Sh.

Impey's Practice, Common Pleas
Imp. Pr. C.P.
Impey's Practice, King's Bench
Imp. Pr. K.B.
Implement[ed]
Imp.
Important
Impt.
Imported Food Regulations
IFR
Improvement[s]
Impt., Improv.
In Fine (at the end of a paragraph or title) (Lat.)
Inf.
In Propria Persona (in person) (Lat.)
I.P.P.
In the Matter of
In re, Re
In the Public Interest
In Pub. Interest
Inactive Insurance
I/Ins.
Included, [es, ing]
inc., Incl.
Income
Inc.
Income Tax
I.
Income Tax Decisions of Australia
I.T.D.A.
Income Tax Decisions of Australia, Ratcliffe and M'Grath
R. & McG.
Income Tax Division Ruling
I.T.
Income Tax Information Release
I.T. Info.
Income Tax Law Journal
Inc. Tax L.J., I.T. L.J.

Income Tax Reports
Inc. Tax R., I.T.R.
Income Tax Unit Order
ITU
Income Tax Unit Ruling
I.T.
Income Taxation of Natural Resources, Prentice-Hall
Income Tax'n Nat. Resources (P-H)
Incompetent Persons
Incomp. P.
Incorporated
Inc., incorp.
Incorporated Law Society
I.L.S.
Indebtedness
Indebt.
Indemnity
Indem., Indty.
Independent
I., Ind., Indep.
Independent Broadcasting Authority
I.B.A.
Independent Contractors
Indep. Contr.
Indermaur and Thwaites' Principles of the Common Law
Ind. Com. Law
Indermaur's Leading Cases in Common Law
Ind. L.C. Com. Law
Indermaur's Leading Cases in Conveyancing and Equity
Ind. L.C. Eq.
Indermaur's Practice in the Supreme Court of Judicature
Ind. Jud. Pr., Ind. Jur. Pr.
Inderwick on Wills
Ind. Wilis

Inderwick's Divorce and Matrimonial Causes Acts
Ind. Div.
Index
Ind.
Index to Canadian Legal Periodical Literature
Ind. Can. L.P. Lit.
Index to Current Legal Research in Canada
I.C.L.R. Can.
Index to Foreign Legal Periodicals
I.F.L.P.
Index to Indian Legal Periodicals
I.I.L.P., Ind. Ind. L.P.
Index to Legal Periodicals
I.L.P., Ind. Leg. Per.
Index to Legal Periodical Literature
I.L.P.L.
Index to Periodical Articles Related to Law
I.P.A.L.
India
Ind.
India Central Provinces, Select Cases
Sel. Cas.
India Supreme Court Reports
India S.Ct., S.C.R., Sup. Ct. R.
Indian
Indian
Indian Advocate
Ind. Advocate, Ind. Adv., Ind. Adv.
Indian Affairs
I.A.
Indian Appeals, Supplemental Law Reports
Ind. App. Supp.
Indian Cases
I.C., Ind. Cas.

Indian Civil and Criminal Law Series
Civ. & Cr.L.S.

Indian Claims Commission
Ind. Cl. Comm., ICC

Indian Code of Criminal Procedure, Curries' Edition
Cur. Cr. Proc.

Indian Council of Arbitration
I.C.A.

Indian Council Arbitration Quarterly
I.C. Arb.Q.

Indian Income Tax Decisions
Hari Rao

Indian Journal of International Law
I.J.I.L., Ind. J.Int.L., Indian J. Int. Law, Indian J. Int'l. L., Indian J. of Internat. L.

Indian Journal of Political Science
Ind. J. Pol. Sci.

Indian Journal of Public Administration
I.J.P.A., Ind. J. Pub. Admin., Indian J. Pub. Admin., Indian J. of Publ. Adm.

Indian Jurist
Ind. Jur.

Indian Jurist, New Series
Ind. Jur. N.S., I.J.

Indian Jurist, Old Series
Ind. Jur. O.S.

Indian Law Herald
Ind. L.H.

Indian Law Journal
Indian L.J.

Indian Law Magazine
Ind. L. Mag.

Indian Law Quarterly
I.L.Q., Ind. L.Q.

Indian Law Quarterly Review
I.L.Q.R., Ind. L.Q.Rev.

Indian Law Reporter
Ind. L.Rep., Indian L. Rep.

Indian Law Reports
I.L.R., Indian L.R., Ind. L.R.

Indian Law Reports, Allahabad Series
Indian L.R. Allahabad Ser., I.L.R. All., Ind. L.R. All., Ind. L.R. Alla., All.

Indian Law Reports, Andhra Series
And., I.L.R. And., Ind. L.R. And.

Indian Law Reports, Assam Series
I.L.R. Assam, Ind. L.R. Assam

Indian Law Reports, Bombay Series
I.L.R. Bom., Ind. L.R. Bomb., Bomb., Bomb. Ser., B

Indian Law Reports, Calcutta Series
C, Calc., I.L.R. Cal., I.L.R. Calc., I.L.R.C., Ind. L.R. Calc., Indian L.R. Calc.

Indian Law Reports, Hyderabad Series
Hyderabad, I.L.R. Hyderabad, Ind. L.R. Hyderabad

Indian Law Reports, Karachi Series
I.L.R. Kar., Ind. L.R. Kar., Kar.

Indian Law Reports, Kerala Series
I.L.R. Ker., I.L.R. Trav.-Cochin, Ind. L.R. Ker., Ker., Trav.-Cochin

Indian Law Reports, Lahore Series
I.L.R. Lah., Ind. L.R. Lah., Lah.

Indian Law Reports, Lucknow Series
I.L.R. Luck., Ind. L.R. Luck., Luck. Ser., Luck.

Indian Law Reports, Madhya Bharat Series
Madhya Bharat, I.L.R. Madhya Bharat, Ind. L.R. Madhya Bharat

Indian Law Reports, Madras Series
I.L.R. Mad., Ind. L.R. Mad., Indian L.R. Mad., L.R. Mad., M., Mad. Ser., Mad.

Indian Law Reports, Mysore Series
Ind. L.R. Mysore, I.L.R. Mysore

Indian Law Reports, Nagpur Series
Nag., I.L.R. Nag., Ind. L. R. Nag.

Indian Law Reports, Orissa Series
I.L.R. Cut., Ind. L.R. Or., Or., I.L.R. Or., Cut.

Indian Law Reports, Patiala Series
I.L.R. Patiala, Ind. L.R. Patiala, Patiala

Indian Law Reports, Patna Series
I.L.R. Pat., I.L.R.P., Ind. L.R. Pat., Pat., Pat. Ser.

Indian Law Reports, Punjab Series
Pun., I.L.R. Pun., Ind. L.R. Pun.

Indian Law Reports, Rajasthan Series
I.L.R. Rajasthan, Ind. L.R. Rajasthan, Rajasthan

Indian Law Reports, Rangoon Series
I.L.R. Ran., Ind. L.R. Ran.

Indian Law Review
I.L.R., Ind. L. Rev., Ind. L.R., Indian L. Rev.

Indian Law Times
Ind. L.T.

Indian Penal Code
India Pen. Code

Indian Privy Council Decisions
Priv. C.D.I.

Indian Reports
In.

Indian Reports, Allahabad Series
A

Indian Revenue Decisions
R.D.

Indian Rulings
Indian Rul., I.R.

Indian Rulings, Allahabad Series
I.R. All.

Indian Rulings, Bombay Series
I.R. Bom.

Indian Rulings, Calcutta Series
I.R. Cal.

Indian Rulings, Federal Court
I.R. Fed. Ct., Fed. Ct.

Indian Rulings, Journal Section
I. R. Jour.

Indian Rulings, Lahore Series
Lah., I. R. Lah.

Indian Rulings, Madras Series
Mad., I.R. Mad.

Indian Rulings, Nagpur Series
Nag., I.R. Nag.

Indian Rulings, Oudh Series
I.R. Oudh

Indian Rulings, Patna Series
Pat., I.R. Pat.

Indian Rulings, Peshawar Series
Peshawar, I.R. Pesh., I.R. Peshawar

Indian Rulings, Privy Council
I.R. Pr.C., I.R.P.C., P.C.

Indian Rulings, Rangoon Series
I.R. Ran.
Indian Rulings, Sind Series
Sind, I.R. Sind.
Indian Tax Journal
I.T.J.
Indian Territory
Ind. T., Ind. Terr.
Indian Territory Annotated Statutes
Ind. T. Ann. St.
Indian Territory Reports
Ind. Ter., Indian Terr., IT
Indian Weekly Reporter, Miscellaneous Appeals
Suth. Mis.
Indian Year Book of International Affairs
Ind. Y.B.I.A., Indian Yb. of Internat. Aff., Ind. Y.B. Int'l Aff.
Indiana
I., Ind.
Indiana Acts
Ind. Acts
Indiana Administrative Code
Ind. Admin. Code
Indiana Administrative Rules and Regulations
IND. Admin. R.
Indiana Annotated Statutes by Burns
Burns' Ann. St., Burns' Rev. St.
Indiana Appellate Court Reports
In.A., Ind. App. Ct.
Indiana Attorney General Annual Report and Official Opinions
Ind.Att'y.Gen.Ann. Rep. & Op.
Indiana Attorney General Reports
Rep. & Ops. Atty. Gen. Ind.
Indiana Cases
Indian Cas.

Indiana Code
Ind. Code
Indiana Constitution
Ind. Const.
Indiana Continuing Legal Education Forum
ICLEF
Indiana Court of Appeals Reports
Ind. App.
Indiana Decisions
Ind. Dec.
Indiana Decisions and Law Reporter
Ind. Dec.
Indiana International and Comparative Law Review
Ind. Int'l & Comp. L. Rev.
Indiana Journal of International Law
Ind. J.Int'l.L.
Indiana Judges Association
IJA
Indiana Judicial Center
IJC
Indiana Law Encyclopedia
I.L.E.
Indiana Law Journal
I.L.J., In. L.J., Ind. Law J., Ind. L.J., Indiana L.J.
Indiana Law Reporter
Ind. L.R., Ind. L.Rep.
Indiana Law Review
In. L.R., Ind. L. Rev., Ind. L.R., Indiana L.Rev.
Indiana Law Student
Ind. L. Stud., Ind. L.S.
Indiana Legal Forum
In. L.F., Ind. Leg. Forum, Ind. Legal F., Indiana Leg. Forum
Indiana Legal Register
Ind. L. Reg., Ind. L.R.

Indiana Public Service Commission
Ind. P.S.C.
Indiana Railroad Commission
Ind. R.C.
Indiana Reports
Ind., Ind. Rep., Ind. R., Indiana,
Indiana Sup. Ct. Rep.
Indiana State Bar Association
ISBA
Indiana State Bar Association Reports
Ind. S.B.A.
Indiana Statutes Annotated Code Edition by Burns
Ind. Code Ann.
Indiana Superior Court
Ind. S.C.
Indiana Supreme Court Reports
Ind.
Indiana Unemployment Compensation Division, Selected Appeal Tribunal Decisions
Ind. U.C.D.
Indictments and Information
Indict.
Individual Employment Rights
I.E.R.
Individual Retirement Account
I.R.A.
Individual Rights and Responsibilities Newsletter
I.R.R. Newsl.
Indonesia
Indon.
Indonesian
In
Industrial
Ind., Indus.
Industrial Accident Commission Decisions
IAC

Industrial and Intellectual Property in Australia
I.I.P., Ind. & Int. Prop. Aus.,
Ind. & Intell.Prop. Austl.
Industrial and Labor Relations Forum
Indus. & Lab. Rel. F.
Industrial and Labor Relations Review
I.L.R.R., Ind. & Lab. Rel. Rev.,
Ind. and Labor Rels. Rev., Indus. & Lab. Rel. Rev., Indust. &
L. Rel. Rev., ILR Rev., Ind. & L.
Rel. Rev.
Industrial Arbitration Cases
I.C.
Industrial Arbitration Reports, Australia
A. R., A. R. (Austrl.),
A.R.(N.S.W.)
Industrial Assurance Commissioner
I.A.C.
Industrial Awards Recommendations
Ind. Awards
Industrial Bulletin
Indust. Bull.
Industrial Cases Reports
Indus. Cas. R.
Industrial College of the Armed Forces
ICAF
Industrial Commission
Ind. Comm.
Industrial Court
I.C.
Industrial Court Awards
Ind. C. Aw., Indust. C. Aw., Ind.
Court Aw., Ind. Ct. Awards, Indust. Ct. Aw.
Industrial Court Reports
I.C.R.

Industrial Injuries Advisory Committee
  I.I.A.C.
Industrial Law Journal
  Indus. L.J., Indust. L.J.
Industrial Law Review
  Indus. L. Rev., Indust. L. Rev., Indust. Law Rev.
Industrial Law Review Quarterly
  Indust. L. Rev. Q.
Industrial Law Society
  Indust. L.Soc.
Industrial Law Society Bulletin
  Indust.L.Soc.Bull.
Industrial Property
  Ind. Prop., Indust. Prop.
Industrial Property Law Annual
  Indus. Prop. L.Ann.
Industrial Property Quarterly
  Ind. Prop. Q., Indust. Prop. Q., Industr. Prop'y.Q.
Industrial Property Yearbook
  Indust. Prop,y. Yb.
Industrial Relations
  Ind.Relations, Indus. Rel., I.R.
Industrial Relations, American Labor Arbitration, Prentice-Hall
  P-H Ind. Rel., Lab. Arb.
Industrial Relations Guide, Prentice-Hall
  Indus. Rel. Guide (P-H), Ind. Rel. Guide (P-H), Indus. Rel. Guide (P-H)
Industrial Relations: Journal of Economy and Society
  Ind. Rel. J. Econ. & Soc.
Industrial Relations Law Journal
  Ind. Rel. L.J., Indus. Rel. L.J., Indust. Rel. L.J.
Industrial Relations Legal Information Bulletin
  IRLIB

Industrial Relations, Prentice-Hall
  Ind. Rel.
Industrial Relations, Union Contracts and Collective Bargaining, Prentice-Hall
  P-H Ind. Rel., Union Conts.
Industry
  Ind., Indus.
Inequality in Education
  Inequal. Ed., Inequal. Educ.
Infants
  Inf.
Infant's Lawyer
  Inf. Law.
Inferior
  Inf.
Inflation Accounting Committee
  I.A.C.
Information
  Info.
Information Release
  I.R.
Infra (beneath or below) (Lat.)
  Inf.
Ingersoll on Habeas Corpus
  Ing. Hab. Corp.
Ingersoll's Digest of the Laws of the United States
  Ing. Dig.
Ingersoll's Edition of Roccus' Maritime Law
  Ing. Roc.
Ingraham on Insolvency
  Ing. Insolv.
Ingram's Compensation for Interest in Lands
  Ing. Comp.
Inheritance
  Inher.
Inheritance, Estate and Gift Taxes
  Inher. Tax.

Inheritance, Estate, and Gift Tax
Reporter, Commerce Clearing
House
    CCH Inh. Est. & Gift Tax Rep.,
    Inher. Est. & Gift Tax Rep.
Initiative and Referendum
    Init. & Ref.
Injunction
    Inj.
Injury
    Inj.
Inland Revenue Commissioners
    I. R. Comrs.
Innes on Easements
    Inn. Ease., Inn. Eas.
Innes' Scotch Legal Antiquities
    Inn. Sc. Leg. Ant.
Inns of Court Rifle Volunteers
    I.C.R.V.
Insolvency
    Ins., Insolv.
Inspection Laws
    Insp. L.
Institute
    Inst.
Institute for Continuing Legal
Education, New Jersey
    NJCLE
Institute for Court Management
    ICM
Institute for Criminal Justice,
University of Richmond
    ICJR
Institute for Improved Legal
Services
    IILS
Institute for Labor Relations Bul-
letin
    Inst. Lab. Rel. Bull.
Institute for Paralegal Training
    IPT

Institute for Shipboard Educa-
tion
    ISE
Institute of Advanced Law Study
    Ia. L. Rev.
Institute of Advanced Legal Stud-
ies Annual
    Inst. Ad. Legal Stud. Ann.
Institute of Arbitrators
    I. Arb.
Institute of Chartered Account-
ants
    I.C.A.
Institute of Continuing Legal
Education in Georgia, Univer-
sity of Georgia School of Law
    GICLE
Institute of Continuing Legal
Education, Louisiana State Uni-
versity Law Center
    LSU
Institute of Continuing Legal
Education, University of Michi-
gan
    MICLE
Institute of Estate Planning, Uni-
versity of Miami Law Center
    UMLC
Institute of Federal Taxation
    Inst. Fed. Tax
Institute of Information Scien-
tists
    I.Inf.Sc.
Institute of Judicial Administra-
tion, Birmingham
    Birmingham I.J.A.
Institute of Labor and Industrial
Relations, University of Illinois
    ILIR
Institute of Legal Executives
    Ilex.
Institute of Public Loss Assessors
    I.P.L.A.

Institute on Estate Planning
Inst. Estate Plan, Inst. on Est.
Plan.

Institute on Estate Planning, University of Miami
Inst. Est. Plan.

Institute on Federal Taxation
Inst. on Fed. Tax., Inst. on Fed.
Tax'n.

Institute on Mineral Law
Inst. Min. L.

Institute on Mineral Law, Louisiana State University
Inst. on Min. L.

Institute on Oil and Gas Law and Taxation
Inst. on Oil & Gas L. & Tax'n.

Institute on Planning and Zoning
Inst. Plan. & Zoning

Institute on Planning and Zoning and Eminent Domain
Inst. Plan. Zoning & E.D.

Institute on Planning, Zoning and Eminent Domain Proceedings, Southwestern Legal Foundation
Inst. on Plan. Zon. & Eminent
Domain Proc., Inst. on Plan.
Zoning & Eminent Domain

Institute on Private Investments and Investors Abroad Proceedings
Inst. on Priv. Invest. & Investors Abroad Proc., Inst. on Priv.
Inv. & Inv. Abroad

Institute on Securities Regulation, Practice Law Institute
Inst. on Sec. Reg., Inst. Sec.
Reg., Inst. Securities Reg.

Institutes of England, Sir Edward Coke (Commentary Upon Littleton)
Inst.

Institutes of Justinian
I., J., Jus. Inst., Institutes

Institution
Instn., Inst.

Institutions Juris Anglicani by Cowell
Inst. Jur. Angl.

Instruction
Instr.

Instructor Clericalis
Inst. Cler., Instr. Cler.

Insurance
Ins.

Insurance Code
Ins.C.

Insurance Counsel Journal
Ins. Couns. J., Ins. Counsel J.,
Insc. Counsel J., Insur. Counsel J.

Insurance Law Journal
Ins. Law J., Ins. L.J., Insur. L.J.

Insurance Law Reporter, Canada
Ins. L.R., I.L.R.

Insurance Law Reporter, Commerce Clearing House
Ins. L. Rep. (CCH), Insur. L.
Rep.

Insurance Law Reports, Commerce Clearing House
Ins. L. Rep. (CCH)

Insurance Liability Reporter
Ins. Liability Rep.

Insurance Litigation Reporter
InL

Insurance Monitor
Ins. Mon.

Insurance Reporter
Ins. Rep.

Insurrection
Insurr.

Intellectual
Intell.

Intellectual Property Law Review
Intell. Prop. L. Rev., Intellectual Property L. Rev.
Intelligence
Int.
Inter-Alia, Journal of the Nevada State Bar
Inter-Alia
Inter-Allied Reparation Agency
IARA
Inter-American Commercial Arbitration Commission
IACAC
Inter-American Commission on Human Rights Annual Report
Inter-Am.C.H.R.
Inter-American Defense Board
IABD, IADB
Inter-American Development Bank
IADB, IDB
Inter-American Law Review
Int.-Am. L. Rev., Inter-Am. L. Rev.
Inter-American Quarterly
Inter.Am.
Inter-Governmental Committee on Refugees
IGC
Inter-Governmental Maritime Consultative Organization
IMCO
Inter-Parliamentary Union
IPU
Intercontinental Ballistic Missile
ICBM
Interest
Int.
Interest and Usury
Interest & U.
Interference
Interfer.

Intergovernmental Committee on European Migration
ICEM
Intergovernmental Council of Copper Exporting Countries
CIPEC
Interim Commission for International Trade Organization
ICITO
Interior and Insular Affairs
IIA
Interior Board of Contract Appeals
I.B.C.A.
Interior Board of Indian Affairs
I.B.I.A.
Interior Board of Mine Operations Appeals
I.B.M.A.
Interior Board of Surface Mine Appeals
I.B.S.M.A.
Interior Department Decisions
I.D.
Internal Memoranda of the Internal Revenue Service, Prentice-Hall
IRS Mem. (P-H)
Internal Revenue Bulletin
Int. Rev. Bull., I.R.B.
Internal Revenue Bureau Committee on Appeals and Review, Memorandum
A. R. M.
Internal Revenue Bureau Committee on Appeals and Review, Recommendation
A.R.R.
Internal Revenue Bureau, Miscellaneous Tax Ruling
MT
Internal Revenue Circular
IR Circ.

Internal Revenue Code
Int. Rev. Code, I.R.C.
Internal Revenue Decisions
I.R.
Internal Revenue Manual
Int. Rev. Manual, IRM
Internal Revenue Manual Supplement
IRM Supp.
Internal Revenue Mimeograph
IR-Mim.
Internal Revenue News Release
IR News Release
Internal Revenue Record
Int. Rev. Rec.
Internal Revenue Service
IRS
Internal Revenue Service Announcements
Ann.
Internal Revenue Service Positions, Commerce Clearing House
IRS Pos. (CCH)
Internal Revenue Service Publication
IRS Pub.
International
Int., intern., Internat., Int'l
International Affairs
Int. Aff., Int'l. Aff., Int'l. Affairs, Int'l. Affairs (Moscow)
International African Law Association
I.A.L.A.
International Coffee Agreement
ICA
International and Comparative Law Bulletin
Int'l & Comp. L. Bull.

International and Comparative Law Quarterly
I. & C.L.Q., Int. & Comp., Int. & Compl. L.Q., L.Q., I.C.L.Q., Int. Comp. L.Q., Internat. Comp. L.Q., Int'l. & Comp. L.Q.
International Air Services Transit Agreement
IASTA
International Air Transport Agreement
IATA
International Air Transport Association
IATA
International Arbitration Journal
Int. Arb. J., Int'l. Arb. J.
International Association of Accident Boards and Commissions Newsletter
A.B.C. Newsl.
International Association of Democratic Lawyers
I.A.D.L.
International Association of Insurance Counsel
IAIC
International Association of Law Libraries
IALL
International Association of Law Libraries Bulletin
Int'l. Assoc. L. Lib. Bull., I.A.L.L.Bull.
International Atomic Energy Agency
IAEA
International Bank for Economic Cooperation
IBEC

**International Bank for Recon-
struction and Development
(World Bank)**
   Bank., I.B.R.D., IBRD
International Bar Association
   I.B.A., Internat. Bar Assoc.
**International Bar Association
Bulletin**
   Int'l. B.A. Bull., Bull.I.B.A.
International Bar Journal
   Int. BarJ., Int'l. Bar J., Int'l.
   B.J.
**International Broadcasting Con-
vention**
   I.B.C.
**International Brotherhood of
Electrical Workers**
   I.B.E.W.
**International Bulletin for Re-
search on Law in Eastern
Europe**
   Int. Bull. Res. E. Eur., Int'l.
   Bull. Research E. Eur.
**International Bulletin of Indus-
trial Property**
   Int. Bull. Indust. Prop.
**International Bureau for the Pro-
tection of Intellectual Property**
   BIRPI
**International Business and Trade
Law Reporter, Bureau of Na-
tional Affairs**
   Int'l Bus. & Trade L. Rep.
International Business Lawyer
   Int. Bus. Lawy., Int'l. Bus. Law.
**International Business Series,
Ernst & Ernst**
   Int'l Bus.Ser.
**International Centre for Settle-
ment of Investment Disputes**
   I.C.S.I.D., ICSID

**International Chamber of Com-
merce**
   ICC
**International Chamber of Com-
merce Arbitration**
   Int'l Comm. Arb.
**International Children's Emer-
gency Fund**
   ICEF
**International Civil Aviation Or-
ganization**
   ICAO
**International Civil Aviation Or-
ganization Bulletin**
   ICAO Bull.
**International Civil Service Advi-
sory Board**
   ICSAB
**International Classification of
Patents for Invention**
   I.P.C.
International Coffee Organization
   ICO
**International Commission for Air
Navigation**
   ICAN
**International Commission for
Northwest Atlantic Fisheries**
   ICNAF
**International Commission of Ju-
rists Review**
   Int'l. Comm. Jurists Rev.
**International Commission of Ju-
rists Bulletin**
   Bull.I.C.J.
International Conciliation
   Int. Concil., Int'l Concil.
**International Confederation of
Free Trade Unions**
   ICFTU
**International Construction Law
Review**
   Int'l Constr. L. Rev.

International Convention for the Carriage of Goods by Rail
CIM
International Cotton Advisory Committee
ICAC
International Council for Commercial Arbitration
ICCA
International Court of Justice Reports
ICJ
International Court of Justice Yearbooks
I.C.J. Y.B., Y.B.I.C.J.
International Criminal Police Organization
INTERPOL
International Criminal Police Review
Int'l Crim. Pol. Rev.
International Customs Tariff Bureau
ICTB
International Development Association
IDA
International Development Research Centre
IDRC
International Digest
Int. Dig., Intl. Dig.
International Digest of Health Legislation
Int'l Dig. Health Leg., Int'l Dig. Health Legis.
International Disarmament Organization
IDO
International Emergency Food Council
IEFC

International Encyclopedia of Comparative Law
Int. Enc. Comp. Law, Int'l Encycl. Comp. L.
International Energy Agency
IEA
International Environment Reporter, Bureau of National Affairs
Int'l Envt. Rep. (BNA), Int'l Envtl. Rep. (BNA)
International Faculty of Comparative Law
I.F.C.L.
International Federation of Consulting Engineers
FIDIC
International Federation of Freight Forwarders Associations
FIATA
International Federation of Law Students
I.F.L.S.
International Federation of Library Associations
IFLA
International Federation of Trade Unions
IFTU
International Federation of Women Lawyers
I.F.W.L.
International Finance Corporation
IFC
International Financial Law Review
IFL Rev., Int'l Fin. L. Rev.
International Franchise Association
IFA

International Fund for Agricultural Development
IFAD
International Hydrographic Organization
IHO
International Institute for the Unification of Private Law
UNIDROIT
International Institute for the Unification of Private Law, Yearbook
Unidroit Yb.
International Institute of Agriculture
IIA
International Institute of Labour Studies
IILS
International Institute of Space Law
I.I.S.L.
International Journal
Int'l. J.
International Journal of Comparative and Applied Criminal Justice
Int'l. J. Comp. & App. Crim. Just.
International Journal of Criminology and Penology
Int. J. Criminol., Int'l J. Crim. & Pen., Int'l. J. Crimin. & Penol.
International Journal of Environmental Studies
Int'l. J. Envir. Stud.
International Journal of Estuarine and Coastal Law
Int. J. Est. & Coast. L.
International Journal of Law and Psychiatry
Int'l. J.L. & Psych., Int'l J.L. & Psychiatry

International Journal of Law and the Family
Int'l J. L. & Fam.
International Journal of Law Libraries
IJLL, Int. J. Law Libs., Int'l. J. L. Lib., Int'l. J. L. Libr.
International Journal of Legal Information
Int'I. J. Legal Infor., Int'l. J. Legal lnfo.
International Journal of Legal Research
Int'l J. Legal Res., Internat. J. of Leg. Res.
International Journal of Offender Therapy and Comparative Criminology
Int'l. J. Offend. Ther. & Comp. Criminology, Int'l J. Off. Ther. & Comp. Crim.
International Journal of Politics
Int. J. Pol., Int'l. J. Pol.
International Journal of Refugee Law
Int'l J. Refugee L.
International Journal of the Sociology of the Law
Int'l. J. Soc. L.
International Journal on World Peace
Int'l J. World Peace
International Juridical Association Bulletin
Int. Jurid. Assn. Bull.
International Juridicial Association Monthly Bulletin
Int'l Jurid. Ass'n Bull.
International Juridicial Organisation for Developing Countries
I.J.O.

International Labour Office, Legislative Series
Int'l. Lab. Off. Leg. S.
International Labour Organisation
ILO
International Labour Reports
Int'l. Lab. Reports
International Labour Review
Int'l. Lab. Rev.
International Ladies' Garment Workers' Union
ILGWU
International Law
Intern. L., Int'l. Law.
International Law and Trade Perspective
Int'l L. & Trade Persp.
International Law Association
ILA
International Law Association Bulletin
Int. L. Bull., Int'l L.Ass'n.Bull.
Interational Law Association Transactions
Trans I.L.A., I.L.A. Trans.
International Law Commission, United Nations
Int'l L. Comm'n, ILC
International Law Commission Yearbook
Y.B. Int'l L. Comm'n, Y.B. Int. L. Comm.
International Law Documents
Int'l L. Doc.
International Law News
Int'l. L. News, Int. L.N., Internat. L.N., Int. L. Notes, Interna. L.N.
International Law Perspective
Int'l L. Persp.

International Law Quarterly
I.L.Q., Int. L.Q., Internat. L.Q., Int'l. L.Q.
International Law Reports
I.L.R., Int'l. L. Rep.
International Law Students Association
ILSA
International Law Studies, Naval War College
Int'l L. Stud.
International Law Tracts
Int. Law Tr.
International Lawyer
Int. Law, Int'l Law., Int'l. Lawyer, Internat. Lawyer
International Lead and Zinc Study Group
ICO
International Legal Aid Association
I.L.A.A.
International Legal Center Newsletter
I.I.L.C., I.L.C. Newl.
International Legal Education Newsletter
Int'l Legal Ed. Newsl.
International Legal Materials
Int. Legal Materials, Int'l. Legal Mat., Intl. Legal Materials, I.L.M.
International Legal Perspectives
Int'l Leg. Persp.
International Longshoremen's and Warehousemen's Union
ILWU
International Longshoremen's Association
ILA
International Mailers' Union
IMU

International Maritime Consult-
ation Organization
 IMCO
International Maritime Organiza-
tion
 IMO
International Market Letter:
East Europe
 East Europe
International Materials Confer-
ence
 IMC
International Meteorological Or-
ganization
 IMO
International Molders' and Allied
Workers' Union of North Amer-
ica
 IMAW
International Monetary Fund
 Fund, IMF, FUND
International Monetary Fund
Staff Papers
 IMF Staff Papers
International Non-Governmental
Organization
 INGO
International North Pacific Fish-
eries Commission
 INPFC
International Olive Oil Council
 IOOC
International Organization
 Int. Org., Int'l. Org., Int'l Org.
International Penal and Peniten-
tiary Commission
 IPPC
International Penal and Peniten-
tiary Foundation
 I.P.P.F.
International Perspectives
 Int. Persp.

International Planned Parent-
hood Federation
 I.P.P.F.
International Prisoners' Aid Asso-
ciation
 I.P.A.A.
International Property Invest-
ment Journal
 Int'l Prop. Inv. J.
International Publishing Corpo-
ration
 I.P.C.
International Red Cross
 IRC
International Refugee Organiza-
tion
 IRO
International Relations
 I.R.
International Revenue Record
 I.R.R.
International Review of Adminis-
trative Sciences
 Int'l Rev. Ad. Sci.
International Review of Criminal
Policy
 Int'l. Rev. Crim. Policy, Int.
 Rev. Crim. Pol.
International Review of Indus-
trial Property and Copyright
Law
 Int'l. Rev. Ind. Prop. & C'right
 L., IIC, Int'l. Rev. Ind. Prop'y. &
 Copyr.
International Review of Law and
Economics
 Int'l. Rev. L. & Econ.
International Road Transport Un-
ion
 IRV
International Shipping Federa-
tion
 I.S.F.

International Social Security Review
Int'l Soc. Sec. Rev.
International Society of Barristers Quarterly
Int'l Soc'y of Barr. Q.
International Standard Bibliographic Description
ISBD
International Sugar Organization
ISO
International Survey of Legal Decisions on Labour Law
I.S. L.R., I.S.L.L., Int'l Surv. L.D. L.L.
International Symposium on Comparative Law
Int'l Sym. Comp.L., Int'l. Symp. on Comp. L.
International Tax and Business Lawyer
Int'l Tax & Bus. Law
International Tax Institute, Inc.
ITII
International Tax Journal
Int. Tax Jour., Int'l. Tax J.
International Tax Planning Manual, Commerce Clearing House
Int'l Tax Planning Man. (CCH)
International Technical Committee of Aerial Legal Experts
CITEJA
International Telecommunication Union
ITU
International Telecommunications Satellite Consortium
INTELSAT
International Telephone & Telegraph Co.
IT & T
International Tin Council
ITC

International Trade Law and Practice
Int'l. Trade L. & Prac.
International Trade Law Journal
Int. Trade L.J., Int'l. Trade L.J.
International Trade Organization, United Nations
ITO
International Trade Reporter, Bureau of National Affairs
Int'l Trade Rep. (BNA)
International Trade Secretaries
I.T.S.
International Trading Service
ITS
International Union of Electrical, Radio and Machine Workers
IUE
International Union of Life Insurance Agents
L.I.A.
International Union of Local Authorities
I.U.L.A.
International Union of Official Travel Organizations
IUOTA
International Union of Railways
UIC
International Whaling Commission
IWC
International Wheat Council
IWC
International Woman Lawyer
Int. Woman L., Int'l Woman Law.
International Wool Textile Organization
IWTO
Interpleader
Interpl.

Interpretation
  Interp.
Interpretation Number
  Interp. No.
Interpretative Opinion
  Interp. Op.
Interrogatory
  Interrog.
Interstate and Foreign Commerce
  IFC
Interstate Commerce
  Inters. Com.
Interstate Commerce Commission
  Int. Com. Commn., Inters. Com.
  Com., ICC, Int. Com. Com.
Interstate Commerce Commis-
  sion Practitioners' Journal
  I.C.C. Pract.J.
Interstate Commerce Commis-
  sion Reports
  I.C.C. Rep., Int. Com. Rep., In-
  terst. Com. R., I.C.C.R.,
  I.C.Rep., Inst. Com. Com., In-
  ters. Com. Rep.
Interstate Commerce Commis-
  sion Reports, Motor Carrier
  Cases
  M.C.C., Val. R. (I.C.C.), ICC
  Valuation Rep.
Interstate Commerce Reports
  I.C., Interstate Com. R.
Interstate Oil Compact Commis-
  sion Bulletin
  I.O.C.C. Bull.
Intoxicating Liquor
  Intox. L.
Intramural
  Intra.
Intramural Law Journal
  Intramural L.J.
Intramural Law Review
  Intramural L. Rev.

Intramural Law Review, New
  York University
  Intra. L. Rev. (N.Y.U.)
Intramural Law Review, St.
  Louis University
  Intra. L. Rev. (St.L.U.)
Intramural Law Review, Univer-
  sity of California at Los Angeles
  Intra. L. Rev. (U.C.L.A.)
Introduction
  Int., Introd.
Investment[s]
  Inv.
Investment Companies and Advis-
  ers
  Inv. Co.
Investment Laws of the World
  I.L.W.
Investor[s]
  Inv.
Invitation for Bids
  IFB
Invoice
  Inv.
Involuntary Servitude and Peonage
  Invol. Serv.
Iowa
  I., Ia.
Iowa Acts and Joint Resolutions
  Iowa Acts
Iowa Administrative Bulletin
  Iowa Admin. Bull.
Iowa Administrative Code
  Iowa Admin. Code
Iowa Attorney General Biennial
  Report
  Biennial Rep. Iowa Att'y Gen.
Iowa Bar Review
  Ia. Bar Rev., Ia. B.Rev., Iowa B.
  Rev., Iowa Bar Rev.
Iowa Biennial Report of the State
  Attorney General
  Biennial Rep. Iowa Att'y Gen.

Iowa Board of Railroad Commission
Ia. R.C.
Iowa Code Annotated
I.C.A., Iowa Code Ann.
Iowa Constitution
Iowa Const.
Iowa Law Bulletin
Ia. L.Bull., Iowa L. Bull., Iowa L.B.
Iowa Law Review
Ia. L. Rev., I.L.R., Iowa L. Rev.
Iowa Law School Continuing Legal Education
ILSCLE
Iowa Lawyer
Iowa Law.
Iowa Legislative Service
Iowa Legis. Serv.
Iowa Railroad Commissioners Reports
Iowa R.C.
Iowa Reports
Ia., Iowa, Iow.
Iowa State Bar Association Quarterly
Iowa St. B.A. Q.
Iowa State Bar Association News Bulletin
Iowa St. B.A. News Bull.
Iowa State Bar Association Proceedings
Iowa S. B.A.
Iowa Supreme Court Reports
Iowa
Iowa University Law Bulletin
Iowa Univ. L. Bull.
Iowa Workmen's Compensation Commission Reports
Iowa W.C. S.
Iran-United States Claims Tribunal Reports
Iran-U.S. Cl. Trib. Rep.

Iredell's North Carolina Digest
Ired. Dig.
Iredell's North Carolina Law or Equity Reports
Ir., Ired. L. (NC)
Iredell's Reports (36-43 North Carolina Equity)
Ired. Eq., Ired., Ired. Eq. (N.C.), Ired. L.
Ireland
Ir., Ire.
Ireland Statutes Index by Ball
Ball Ind.
Irish
Ir.
Irish Chancery Reports
Ch. R., Ch. Rep., Ch. Rep. Ir., Ch. Repts., I.Ch.R., I.C.R., Ir. Ch. Rep., Ir. Ch.
Irish Circuit Cases
Ir. Circ. Cas.
Irish Circuit Reports
I.C.R., Ir. Cir., Ir. Circ. Rep., Ir.Cir.Rep.
Irish Common Law and Chancery Reports (New Series)
Ir. Law & Ch.
Irish Common Law Reports
Ir. Com. L. Rep., C.L., Ir. Law Rep. N.S., Ir. L.N.S., I.C.L.R., Ir. Com. Law Rep., Ir.C.L.
Irish Common Law Reports, 2nd Series
Ir. Com. Law Rep.
Irish Common Law Reports, New Series
Ir. Rep. N.S.
Irish Ecclesiastical Reports
Ir. Eccl.
Irish Equity Reports
I.E.R., Ir. Eq., Ir. Eq. Rep., I.Eq.R.

Irish Jurist
Irish Jur., I.J.

Irish Jurist, New Series
Ir. Jur. N.S., Ir. Jur. N.S., I.J.N.S.

Irish Jurist Reports
Ir. Jur. (Rep.), Ir. Jur., Ir. Jur. Rep.

Irish Land Purchase Cases
Maxwell

Irish Land Reports, Fitzgibbon
I.L.

Irish Law and Equity Reports
Ir. L. & Eq., Ir. Law & Eq.

Irish Law Journal
Ir. L.J.

Irish Law Recorder
Ir. Law Rec., Ir. L. Rec.

Irish Law Recorder, New Series
Ir. Law Rec. N.S., L.R. (N.S.), L.R.N.S.

Irish Law Reports
I.L.R., I.R., Ir. Law Rep., Ir. L.R., Ir.L., Ir. L.R., Ir. L.R., Ir. R.

Irish Law Times
Ir. Law T., Irish L.T., Ir. L.T., I.L.T.

Irish Law Times and Solicitors' Journal
I.L.T. & S.J., Ir. L.T., Ir. L.T. J., Ir. L.T. Journal, Ir. L. Times and Solicitors' J.

Irish Law Times, County Courts
Co. Ct. I.L.T.

Irish Law Times Journal
I.L.T. Jo., Ir. L.T. J., Ir. L.T. Jour.

Irish Law Times Reports
Ir. L.T. R., Ir. L.T. Rep., I.L.T.R.

Irish Patent Office
Ir. Pat. Off.

Irish Petty Sessions Journal
Ir. Pet. S.J.

Irish Reports, Chancery Series
Ir. Rep. Ch., Ir.R. Ch.

Irish Reports, Common Law Series
Ir. Rep. C.L., I.R.C.L., Ir.R. C.L.

Irish Reports, Equity Series
Ir. Rep. Eq., I.R. Eq., Ir. R. Eq.

Irish Reports, Registration Appeals
Ir. R. Reg. App.

Irish Reports, Registry and Land Cases
Ir. R. Reg. & L.

Irish Reports, Registry Appeals in Court of Exchequer Chamber, and Appeals in Court for Land Cases Reserved
I.R.R. & L.

Irish Reports, Verbatim Reprint
Ir. Rep. V.R.

Irish Selected Cases Tempore Napier
Sel. Cas. t. Napr.

Irish Society for Labor Law Journal
Ir. Soc'y for Lab. L.J.

Irish State Trials, Ridgeway's
Ir. St. Tr.

Irish Statutes
Ir. Stat.

Irish Statutes Index, by Ball
Ball.Ind.

Irish Term Reports, by Ridgeway, Lapp and Schoales
Ir. Term Rep., Ir. T.R., I.T.R., Ridg. L. & S.

Irish Weekly Law Reports
Ir. W.L.R.

Irish Workmen's Compensation Cases
Ir. W.C.C.

Irons on Police Law
Irons Pol. Law
Irons on Public Houses
Irons Pub. H.
Irregular
Irreg.
Irrigation
Irrig.
Irvine's Justiciary Cases, Scotland
I.J.C., Irvine Just.Cas.,
Irv.Just., I.J.Cas.
Irvine's Scotch Justiciary Reports
Irv.
Irving's Civil Law
Irv. Civ. Law, Irving, Civ. Law
Isaac Pitblado's Lectures on Continuing Legal Education
Pitblado Lect,
ISL Law Review
ISL L. Rev.
Island[s]
Is.
Isles
Is.
Israel
Isr.
Israel Law Review
Isr. L. Rev., Israel L. Rev., Is.
L.R.
Israel Studies in Criminology
Israel Stud. Criminol.

Israel Supreme Court Selected Judgments
S.C.Is.
Israel-Syrian Mixed Armistice Commission
I.S.M.A.C.
Israel Yearbook on Human Rights
Israel Yb. of Human Rights, Israel Y.B. Human Rights
Issue
Iss.
Issues in Criminology
Issues L. & Med.
Issues in Law and Medicine
Issues L. & Med.
Issuing Houses Association
I.H.A.
Italian
I., It., Ital.
Italian Yearbook of International Law
Italian Yb. of Int'l. L.
Italic
Ital.
Italy
It.
Ives on Military Law
Ives Mil. Law
Ivory's Notes on Erskine's Institutes
Iv. Ersk.

J

Jackson and Gross's Treatise on the Law of Landlord and Tenant in Pennsylvania
Jack & G. Landl. & Ten.

Jackson and Lumpkin's Reports (59-64 Georgia)
Jack. & L., Jackson & Lumpkin

Jackson's Index to the Georgia Reports
Jack. Geo. Ind.

Jackson's Pleadings
Jack Pl.

Jackson's Reports (46-58 Georgia)
Jackson, Jack.

Jackson's Reports (1-29 Texas Court of Appeals Reports)
Jack. Tex. App., Jackson

Jacob and Walker's English Chancery Reports
J. & W., Jac. & W., Jac. & W. (Eng.), Jac. & Walk.

Jacob's American Edition of Fisher's English Digest
Jac. Fish. Dig.

Jacob's English Chancery Reports
Jacob., Jac.

Jacob's Introduction to the Common, Civil, and Canon Law
Jac. Int.

Jacob's Law Dictionary
Jac., Jac. Dict., Jac. Law Dict., Jac. L.D., Jac. L.Dict., Jacob.

Jacob's Law Grammar
Jac. L.G.

Jacob's Lex Mercatoria, or the Merchants' Companion
Jac. Lex Mer.

Jacobsen's Law of the Sea
Jac. Sea Laws.

Jacobus (James)
JAC, Jac.

Jaeger's Cases and Statutes on Labor Law
Jaeger, Labor Law.

JAG Bulletin, United States Air Force
JAG Bull.

JAG Journal, United States Army
JAG J.

Jaggard on Torts
Jagg. Torts.

Jaipur Law Journal
Jaipur L.J.

Jamaica
Jam.

Jamaica Law Journal
Jam. L.J.

Jamaica Law Reform Committee
Jamaica L.R.C.

Jamaica Law Reports
J.L.R.

Jamaica Law Reports, Braithwaite
Braith.

Jamaica Statutes
Jam. St.

Jamaica Supreme Court Judgment Books
S.C.J.B.

Jamaica Supreme Court Judgments by Clark
Clark

James
Ja., Jas.

James' Bankrupt Law
James Bk. L.
James' Guide to Friendly Societies
James Fr. Soc.
James' Law of Joint Stock Companies
James J.S.
James on Courts-Martial
James Ct. Mar.
James on Merchant Shipping
James Sh.
James on Salvage
James Salv.
James' Opinions, Charges, etc.
James Op.
James' Reports (2 Nova Scotia)
James, James (N.Sc.)
James' Select Cases, Nova Scotia
James Sel. Cas., James Sel. Cases.
Jameson and Montagu's English Bankruptcy Reports
James. & Mont.
Jameson's Constitutional Convention
James. Const. Con.
Jani Anglorum facies Nova
Jan. Angl.
January
Ja., Jan.
Japan
Japan
Japan Annual of Law and Politics
Japan Ann. L. & Pol., Jap. Ann. of Law & Pol.
Japan Institute of Labour
J.I.L.
Japanese
J.
Japanese Annual of International Law
Jap. Ann. Intl. L.

Jardine's Criminal Trials
Jar. Cr. Tr.
Jardine's Index to Howell's State Trials
Jard. Ind.
Jarman and Bythewood's Conveyancing
Jar. & By. Conv.
Jarman on Wills
Jar. Wills.
Jarman on Wills by Bigelow
Big.Jarm.Wills
Jarman's Chancery Practice
Jar. Chy. Pr.
Jarman's Edition of Powell on Devises
Jar. Pow. Dev.
Jaywardine's Appeal Cases, Ceylon
Jay W.
Jeaffreson's Book About Lawyers
Jeaf.
Jebb and Bourke's Irish Queen's Bench Reports
Jebb. & B., Jebb. & B.(Ir.)
Jebb and Symes' Irish Queen's Bench Reports
Jebb & S.(Ir.), Jebb & Sym., Jebb. & S., J. & S.
Jebb's Irish Crown and Presentment Cases
Jebb Cr. & Pr. Cas.
Jebb's Irish Crown Cases
Jebb., Jebb. C.C., Jebb. C.C.(Ir.)
Jefferson's Manual of Parliamentary Law
Jeff. Man.
Jefferson's Reports, Virginia General Court
Jeff., Jeff.(Va.)
Jencken on Bills of Exchange
Jenck. Neg. B., Jenck. Bills

Jencken on Negotiable Securities
Jenck. Neg. S.
Jenkins' Clerk's Assistant
Jenk. Cl. Ass.
Jenkins' Eight Centuries of Reports, English Exchequer
Jenk., Jenk. Cent., Jenkins (Eng.)
Jenkinson and Formoy's Select Cases in the Exchequer of Pleas.(Selden Society Publication, 48)
Jenk. & Formoy
Jenks' Reports (58 New Hampshire)
Jenks
Jennett's Sugden Acts
Jenn. Sug. A.
Jennison's Reports (14-18 Michigan).
Jenn.
Jeremy on Carriers
Jer. Car.
Jeremy's Digest
Jer. Dig.
Jeremy's Equity Jurisdiction
Jer. Eq. Jur., Jeremy, Eq., Jeremy, Eq. Jur.
Jerrold on Copyright
Jerr. Copyr.
Jervis' New Rules
Jerv. N.R.
Jervis on Coroners
Jerv. Cor.
Jessel's (Sir George) Analysis and Digest of Decisions
Jes.
Jessel's (Sir George) Analysis and Digest of Decisions by A.P. Peter
Peter
Jevons on Criminal Law
Jev. Cr. Law

Jewish Yearbook of International Law
Jew. Y.B. Int'l L.
Jickling on Legal and Equitable Estates
Jick. Est.
Job Discrimination
Job Discrim.
Job Instruction Training
J.I.T.
Job Opportunities in the Business Sector
J.O.B.S.
Job Safety Training
J.S.T.
Jodah and Swan's Reports, Jamaica
Jud. & Sw.
John Kersey's English Dictionary
Kersey, Dict.
John Marshall
J. Mar.
John Marshall Journal of Practice and Procedure
J.M.J., J. Mar. J. Prac. & Proc., J. Marshall J., John Mar. J. Prac. & Proc., John Marshall Jr.
John Marshall Law Journal
J. Mar. L.J., John Marsh. L.J., John Marshall L.J.
John Marshall Law Quarterly
J. Mar. L.Q., John Marsh. L.Q., John Marshall L.Q.
John Marshall Law Review
J. Mar. L. Rev., J. Mar. L.R., John Marsh. L. Rev., J. Marshall L. Rev.
John Marshall Law School
JMLS
John's American Notaries
John. Am. Not.

Johnson and Hemming's English Chancery Reports
Johns. & H., Johns. & H.(Eng.), Johns, & Hem., J. & H., John. & H.

Johnson and Houghton's Institutes of Hindu Law
J. & H. Hind. L.

Johnson on Bills of Exchange
Johns. Bills

Johnson on Maritime Rights
Johns. Mar. R.

Johnson's Cases, New York
Johns. Cas., J., John., Johns. (N.Y.), Johns. Rep., John(s)., Johns. R., Johnson N.Y.R., Johnson R., Johnson, Johnson's Rep., Johns. Cas.(N.Y.), John. Cas., Johns. C., Johns. Cases, J.C.

Johnson's Chancery Reports, New York
Johns. Ch. Cas., Johns. Ch.(N.Y.), Joh. Ch. Rep., John. Ch. Rep., John. Chan., Johns. Ch., J. Ch., John(s)., John.

Johnson's Civil Law of Spain
Johns. Civ. L. Sp.

Johnson's Ecclesiastical Law
Johns. Eccl. L.

Johnson's English Chancery Reports
Johns. H.R.V., Johns. Eng. Ch.

Johnson's English Dictionary
John. Dict.

Johnson's English Vice Chancellors' Reports
Johnson., John., Johns Ch., John(s), Johns. V.C., Johns. V.C.(Eng.), John. Eng. Ch.

Johnson's Impeachment Trial
Johns. Tr.

Johnson's Maryland Chancery Decisions
Johns. Ch., John(s)., John., J. Rep., Md. Ch., See also Maryland Chancery Decisions, Johns. Dec., Johnson.

Johnson's New Mexico Reports
N.M. (J.)

Johnson's New Zealand Reports
Johns. N.Z.

Johnson's Patent Manual
Johns. Pat. Man.

Johnson's Quarto Dictionary
Johnson's Quarto Dict.

Johnson's Reports of Chase's United States Circuit Court Decisions
John[s.] U.S., J. Rep.

Johnson's Reports, New York Court of Errors
Johns. Ct. Err., Johnson's Cases in Error

Johnston's Institutes of the Laws of Spain
Johnst. Inst.

Johnston's New Zealand Reports
Johnst.(N.Z.)

Johore Law Reports, India
J.L.R.

Joint
Jt.

Joint Appendix
J.A.

Joint Chiefs of Staff
JCS

Joint Committee
Jt. Com.

Joint Committee on Atomic Energy
JCAE

Joint Committee on Continuing Legal Education of the Virginia State Bar and the Virginia Bar Association
VACLE

Joint Consultative Document
J.C.C.

Joint Financial Management Improvement Program
JFMIP

Joint Stock Company
Jnt. Stk. Co.

Joint Tenant With Right of Survivorship
J.T.R.S.

Joint Travel Regulations
J.T.R.

Joint Venture
Jnt. Ven.

Jones and Cary's Irish Exchequer Reports
J. & C., Jo. & Car., Jones Exch., Jon. & Car., Jones & C.

Jones and Haughton's Hindu Law
Jones & H. Hind. Law

Jones and La Touche's Irish Chancery Reports
Jo. & La.T., Jo. & Lat., J. & L., J. & La T., J. & Lat., Jon. & L., Jon. & La.T., Jones & L., Jones & L. (Ir.), Jones & La T.

Jones and McMurtrie's Pennsylvania Supreme Court Reports
Jones & McM., Jones & McM. (Pa.)

Jones and Spencer's Reports (33-61 New York Superior)
J. & S., J.S., Jones & S., Jones & Sp., Jones & Spen.

Jones and Varick's Laws of New York
J. & V., Jones & V. Laws.

Jones, Barclay, and Whittelsey's Reports (31 Missouri)
Jones, B. & W. (Mo.), Jones, Barclay & Whittelsey

Jones' Exchequer Proceedings Concerning Wales
Jo. Ex. Pro.W.

Jones' History of the French Bar
Jones Fr. Bar.

Jones' Institutes of Hindu Law
Jones Inst.

Jones' Introduction to Legal Science
Jones Intr.

Jones' Irish Exchequer Reports
Jon. Exch., Jo., Jo. Ex. Ir., Jon. Ex., Jones Exch., Jon. Ir. Exch., Jones Ir., Jones, Jon.

Jones' Law of Bailments
Jones B., Jones, Bailm.

Jones' Law of Salvage
Jones Salv.

Jones' Law of Uses
Jones Uses

Jones' North Carolina Law Reports (46-53 North Carolina Law)
Jones Law., Jones N.C.

Jones on Chattel Mortgages
Jones Ch. Mort.

Jones on Land and Office Titles
Jones L. Of. T.

Jones on Libel
Jones Lib.

Jones on Liens
Jones, Liens.

Jones on Litigating Private Antitrust Actions
LPAA

Jones on Mortgages
Jones Mort.

Jones on Pledges and Collateral Securities
Jones, Pledges.

Jones on Railroad Securities
Jones, Securities

Jones' North Carolina Equity Reports (54-59)
Jones Eq.(N.C.), Jones Eq., Jones

Jones' Railway Securities
Jones Ry. Sec.

Jones' Reports (43-48, 52-57, 61-62 Alabama)
Jones

Jones' Reports (22-30 Missouri)
Jones

Jones' Reports (11-12 Pennsylvania)
Jones, Jones Pa., Jones (Pa.)

Jones' (T.), English King's Bench Reports
Jones, Jones T., T. Jo., T. Jones, T. Jones (Eng.), Jo. T., Jon.

Jones' Treatise on Easements
Jones, Easem.

Jones' Upper Canada Common Pleas Reports
Jones

Jones' (W.), English King's Bench Reports
Jones, Jon.

Jordan and Gobert's Jury Selection
JuS

Jordan on Joint Stock Companies
Jord. Jt. St. Comp.

Jordan's Jury Selection
JuS

Jordan's Parliamentary Journal
Jord. P.J.

Jornandes de Rebus Geticis
Jornand. de Reb. Get.

Joseph and Beven's Digest of Decisions for Ceylon
Jos. & Bev.

Joseph's Reports (21 Nevada)
Jos.

Journal
J.

Journal, House of Representatives
J.H.

Journal of Accountancy
J. Account., J. Accountancy, J. Acct., J. of Account.

Journal of Administration Overseas
J. Admin. Overseas

Journal of African Administration
J.A.A.

Journal of African Law
J. Afr. L., J. African L., J. of Afr. L., J.A.L.

Journal of Agricultural Taxation and the Law
J. Agric. Tax'n & L.

Journal of Air Law
J. Air. L.

Journal of Air Law and Commerce
J. Air L. & Com., J. of Air L. & Commerce

Journal of American Academy of Matrimonial Lawyers
J. Am. Acad. Matrimonial Law., J. Am. Acad. Matrimonial Law

Journal of American Bankers Association
J. Am. Bankers' Assn.

Journal of American Institute of Criminal Law and Criminology
J. Crim. Law.

**Journal of American Judicature
Society**
Am. Jud. Soc'y., J. Am. Jud. Soc.
**Journal of American Society of
Chartered Life Underwriters**
J. Am. Soc. C.L.U., J. Am. Soc'y
C.L.U.
**Journal of American Trial Law-
yers Association**
JATLA
**Journal of American Trial Law-
yers Association Law Journal**
JATLA L.J.
**Journal of Arts Management and
Law**
J. Arts Mgmt. & L., J. Arts Mgt.
& L.
**Journal of Bar Association of
Kansas**
J.B.A. Kan.
**Journal of Bar Association of the
District of Columbia**
J.B.A.D.C.
Journal of Broadcasting
J. Broadcast., J. Broadcasting
**Journal of Broadcasting and Elec-
tronic Media**
J. Broadcasting & Electronic
Media
Journal of Business
J.of Business
Journal of Business Law
J. Bus. L, .J.B.L., J. of Bus. L.
Journal of Ceylon Law
J. Ceylon L., J. of Ceylon L.,
Journal of Chinese Law
J. Chin. L., J. Chinese L.
**Journal of Christian Jurispru-
dence**
J. Christ. Juris.
Journal of Church and State
J. Church & St., J. Church S.

**Journal of Collective Negotiation
in the Public Sector**
J.C.N.P.S., J. Collective Negot.
Pub. Sector
**Journal of College and Univer-
sity Law**
J. Coll. & U.L., J. Coll. & Univ.
L., J.C. & U.L.
Journal of Commerce
J. Commerce
Journal of Common Market Studies
J. Comm. Mt. Stud., J. Common
Market Stud., J. Common Mar-
ket Studies., J. Common Mkt.
Stud.
**Journal of Comparative Corpo-
rate Law and Securities Regu-
lation**
J. Comp. Corp. L. & Sec. Reg.
**Journal of Comparative Legisla-
tion and International Law**
J. Comp. Leg. & Int. Law,
J.C.L. & I.L., J. Comp. Leg. &
Int'l. L.
Journal of Conational Law
J. Conat. Law, Jour. Conat.
Law.
Journal of Conflict Resolution
J. Confl. Res., J. of Conflict
Resolution
**Journal of Constitutional and
Parliamentary Studies**
J. Const. & Parl. Stud., J.
Const. & Parliam. Stud.
Journal of Consumer Affairs
J. Cons. Affairs
**Journal of Contemporary Crimi-
nal Justice**
J. Contemp. Crim. Just.
**Journal of Contemporary Health
Law and Policy**
J. Contemp. Health L. & Pol'y

Journal of Contemporary Law
J. Contemp. L.
Journal of Contemporary Legal Issues
J. Contemp. Legal Issues
Journal of Contemporary Roman-Dutch Law
J. Contemp.R.D.L.
Journal of Contract Law
J. Cont. L.
Journal of Copyright Entertainment and Sports Law
J. Copyright Entertainment Sports L., J. Copyright, Ent. & Sports L.
Journal of Corporate Disclosure and Confidentiality
J. Corp. Disclosure & Confid.
Journal of Corporate Taxation
J. Corp. Tax., J. Corp. Tax'n
Journal of Corporation Law
J. Corp. L., J. Corpn. L.
Journal of Criminal Justice
J.Crim. Just.
Journal of Criminal Law
J. Crim. L., J. Crim. L. (Eng.), J. Crim. Law., J.C.L.
Journal of Criminal Law and Criminology
J Crim L & Criminal, J. Crim. L. & Crim., J. Crim. L. & Criminology, Jour. Crim. L.
Journal of Criminal Law, Criminology and Police Science
J. Crim. L., C. & P.S.
Journal of Criminal Science
J. Crim. Sci.
Journal of Development Planning
J. Dev. Planning
Journal of Dispute Resolution
J. Disp. Resol., J. Dispute Resolution

Journal of Drug Issues
J. Drug Issues
Journal of Economic Perspectives
J. Econ. Persp.
Journal of Education Finance
J. Educ. Fin.
Journal of Energy and Development
J. Energy & Devel.
Journal of Energy and Natural Resources Law
J. Energy & Nat. Resources L.
Journal of Energy Law and Policy
J. Energy L. & Pol'y.
Journal of Energy, Natural Resources and Environmental Law
J. Energy Nat. Resources & Envtl. L.
Journal of Environmental Law
J. Envtl. L.
Journal of Environmental Law and Litigation
J. Envtl. L. & Litig., J. Envir L & Litig
Journal of Ethiopian Law
J. Eth. L., J. of Ethiop. L.
Journal of Family
J. Family L., J. Fam. L.
Journal of Finance
J. Fin.
Journal of Forensic Medicine
J. For. Med.
Journal of Forensic Sciences
J. For. Sci., J. Forensic Sci.
Journal of Health and Hospital Law
J. Health & Hosp. L.
Journal of Health Politics, Policy and Law
J. Health Pol., J.Health Pol. Pol'y & L.

Journal of International and Comparative Law
J. Int'l & Comp. L.

Journal of International Affairs
J. Int'l Aff.

Journal of International Arbitration
J. Int'l Arb.

Journal of International Law and Diplomacy
J. Int'l L. & Dipl.

Journal of International Law and Economics
J. Int. L. & Econ., J. Int. Law & Econ., J. of Internat. L.and Econ.

Journal of International Law and Politics
J. Int. L. & Pol., J. Intl. L. & Pol.

Journal of International Money and Finance
J. Int'l Money & Fin.

Journal of Islamic and Comparative Law
J. Islam & Comp. L.

Journal of Jurisprudence
J. Jur., J. Juris., Jo. Jur., Journ. Jur., Jour. Jur.

Journal of Jurisprudence and Scottish Law Magazine
Jour. Jur. Sc.

Journal of Jurisprudence, Hall's
Hall Jour. Jur., Hall's J.Jur.

Journal of Juristic Papyrology
J. Jur. Papyrol.

Journal of Juvenile Law
J. Juv. L.

Journal of Kansas Bar Association
J. Kan.B.A.

Journal of Labor Research
J. Lab. Res.

Journal of Land and Public Utility Economics
J. Land & Pub. Util. Econ., J. Land & P.U. Econ.

Journal of Land Use and Environmental Law
J. Land Use & Envtl. L.

Journal of Law
J.L., Jour. Law

Journal of Law and Commerce
J. L. & Commerce, J.L. & Com.

Journal of Law and Economics
J. L. & Econ., J. L. & Econ., J. of L. and Econ.

Journal of Law and Economic Development
J.L. & Econ. Develop., J. L. & Econ. Dev., J.L. & Econ.

Journal of Law and Education
J. L. & Ed., J.L. & Educ.

Journal of Law and Health
J. L. & Health

Journal of Law and Information Science
J.L. & Info. Sci.

Journal of Law and Politics
J. Law & Pol., J.L. & Pol., J. of Law & Politics

Journal of Law and Religion
J.L. & Relig.

Journal of Law and Social Policy
J.L. & Soc. Pol'y

Journal of Law and Technology
J. L. & Tech.

Journal of Law, Economics and Organization
J. Law, Econ. & Org.

Journal of Law Reform
J. Law Reform
Journal of Law, Economi

Journal of Legal Education
J. Leg. Ed., J. Legal Ed., J. Legal Educ., J. of Leg. Educ.

Journal of Legal History
     J. Leg. Hist., J. Legal Hist.
Journal of Legal Medicine
     J. Leg. Med., J. Legal Med.
Journal of Legal Pluralism
     J. Legal Pluralism
Journal of Legal Studies
     J. Leg. Stud., J. Legal Stud., J.
     Legal Studies
Journal of Legislation
     J. Legis.
Journal of Malaysian and Comparative Law
     J. Mal. & Comp. L.
Journal of Maritime Law and Commerce
     J Marit L & Comm, J. Maritime
     L., J. Mar. L. & Com., J. Mar.
     Law & Com., J. of Marit. L. and
     Commerce
Journal of Medicine and Philosophy
     J. Med. & Phil.
Journal of Mineral Law and Policy
     J. Min. L. & Pol'y
Journal of Pension Planning and Compliance
     J. Pension Plan. & Compliance
Journal of Planning and Environment Law
     J. Plan. & Env. L., J. Plan. &
     Environ. L., J.P.E.L., J.P.L., J.
     Plan. & Envt'l L.
Journal of Planning and Property Law
     J. Plan. & Prop. L., J.P.P.L.
Journal of Planning Law
     J.Pl.L.
Journal of Planning Law Journal of Public Law
     J.P.L.

Journal of Police Science and Administration
     J. Pol. Sci. & Admin., J. Police
     Sci. & Ad.
Journal of Political Economy
     J. Pol. Econ.
Journal of Politics
     J.P.
Journal of Products Law
     J. Prod. L.
Journal of Products Liability
     J. Prod. Liab., J. Prod.Liability
Journal of Psychiatry and Law
     J. Psych. & L., J. Psych. &
     Law., J. Psychiatry & L.
Journal of Psychological Medicine and Medical Jurisprudence
     J. Psychological Medicine, Jour.
     Ps. Med.
Journal of Public Law
     J. of Publ. L., J. Pub. L.
Journal of Quantitative Criminology
     J. Quantitative Criminology
Journal of Radio Law
     J. Radio L., Jo. Radio Law
Journal of Real Estate Taxation
     J. Real Est. Tax'n
Journal of Reprints for Antitrust Law and Economics
     J. Reprints Antitrust L. & Econ.
Journal of Research in Crime and Delinquency
     J. Res. Crime & Del.
Journal of Social Welfare Law
     J. Soc. Welfare L.
Journal of Society of Comparative Legislation
     J. Comp. Leg.
Journal of Space Law.
     J. of Space L., J. Space L.

Journal of State Government
J. St. Gov't
Journal of State Taxation
J. St. Tax'n
Journal of Supreme Court History
J. Sup. Ct. Hist.
Journal of Taxation
J. Taxation, J. Tax'n, J.Tax.
Journal of Taxation of Investments
J. Tax'n Invest.
Journal of Taxation of S Corporations
J. Tax'n S Corp.
Journal of the American Academy of Matrimonial Lawyers
J. Am. Acad. Matrim. Law., J. Am. Acad. Matrim. Law
Journal of the American Judicature Society
J. Am. Jud. Soc'y., Jour. Am. Jud. Soc., Judicature
Journal of the American Medical Association
JAMA
Journal of the American Society of CLU (Chartered Life Underwriters)
J. Am. Soc'y C.L.U., J. CLU
Journal of the Association of Law Teachers
J. Ass'n. L. Teachers, J.A.L.T., J. Assoc. L. Teachers
Journal of the Association of Trial Lawyers of America
ATLA L.J.
Journal of the Bar Association of the District of Columbia
J.B. Ass'n D.C., J.B.A. Dist. Colum.

Journal of the Bar Association of the State of Kansas
J. of the B.A. of Kansas, J.B. Ass'n. St. Kan., J.B.K.
Journal of the Beverly Hills Bar Association
J. Bev. Hills B.A., J. Beverly Hills B. Ass'n, J. Beverly Hills B.A.
Journal of the Canadian Bar Association
J. Can. B. Ass'n., J. Can. B.A.
Journal of the Cincinnati Bar Association
J. Cin. B.A.
Journal of the Cleveland Bar Association
Clev. B.J.
Journal of the Copyright Society of the U.S.A.
J. Copr. Soc'y, J. Copyright Soc'y. U.S.A.
Journal of the Denning Law Society
J.Denning L.Soc'y, J.Denning L.S.
Journal of the Forensic Medicine Society
J. For. Med. Soc'y
Journal of the Forensic Science Society
J. For. Sci. Soc., J. For. Sci. Soc'y.
Journal of the House of Commons
C.J.
Journal of the Indian Law Institute
J. Ind. L. Inst., J.I.L.I.
Journal of the Indian Law Teachers Association Affairs
J.I.L.T.A.

Journal of the Institute of Arbitrators
J. of Ins. of Arbitrators, Arbitration Arbitration

Journal of the International Commission of Jurists
J. Int'l Comm. Jur., J.I.C.J.

Journal of the Irish Society for Labour Law
J. Ir. Soc. Lab. L.

Journal of the Kansas Bar Association
J. Kan. B. Ass'n

Journal of the Law and Commerce Society, Hong Kong
J.L. & Com. Soc.

Journal of the Law Society of Scotland `-
J. L. Soc. Scotland, J. L. Soc'y., J. L. Soc'y Scot., J. Law Soc. Sc., J.L.S., J.L.Soc., J. of the L. Soc. of Scotl.

Journal of the Legal Profession
J. Leg. Prof., J. Legal Prof.

Journal of the Missouri Bar
J. Mo. B., J. Mo. Bar

Journal of the National Association of Referees in Bankruptcy
J.N.A. Referees Bank., J.N.C. Referees Bank.

Journal of the Patent Office Society
J.P.O.S.

Journal of the Patent [and Trademark] Office Society
J. Pat. [& Trademark] Off. Soc'y.

Journal of the Society of Comparative Legislation
J. Soc'y Comp. Leg., Jour. Comp. Leg.

Journal of the Society of Public Teachers of Law
J. Soc. Pub. T. L., J. Soc. Pub. Teach. Law, J. Soc'y Pub. Tchrs L., J.S.P.T.L., J. of the Soc. of Publ.Teachers of L., J. Soc. Pub. Teach. Law N.S.

Journal of the State Bar of California
J. St. Bar Calif., J.B.C., S.B.J.

Journal of the Suffolk Academy of Law
J. Suffolk Acad. L.

Journal of Urban Law.
J. of Urban L., J. Urban, J. Urban L., J.U.L.

Journal of World Trade
J. World Trade, J. World Tr. L., J. World Trade L., J.W.T.L.

Journal, Oklahoma Bar Association
Okla. S. B. A., O.B.J.

Journals of the House of Commons
Com. Jour.

Journals of the House of Lords
Lords Jour.

Journal: The Canadian Bar Association
Can. Bar. A.J.

Jowitt's Dictionary of English Law
Jow. Dict.

Joy on Legal Education
Joy Leg. Ed.

Joy's Admissibility of Confessions
Joy Conf.

Joy's Evidence of Accomplices
Joy Acc., Joy Ev.

Joy's Peremptory Challenge of Jurors
Joy Chal.

Joyce on Injunctions
  Joyce
Joyce on Insurance
  Joyce, Ins.
Joyce on Limitations
  Joyce Lim.
Joyce's Doctrines and Principles of Injunctions
  Joyce Prin. Inj.
Joyce's Law and Practice of Injunctions
  Joyce Prac. Inj.
Joynes on Limitations
  Joyn. Lim.
Jacobus Rex (King James)
  J.R.
Judah and Swan's Jamaica Reports
  J. & S. Jam., J. & S.
Judd's Reports (4 Hawaii)
  Judd
Judge
  J., Judge
Judge Advocate
  J. Adv., J.A.
Judge Advocate General
  JAG
Judge Advocate General Compilation of Court Martial Order, Navy
  JAG COMPC.M.O.(Navy)
Judge Advocate General Court Martial Reports, Air Force
  JAG C.M.R.(A.F.)
Judge Advocate General, Army, Bulletin
  Bull.JAG
Judge Advocate General Digest of Opinions
  JAG Dig. Op.
Judge Advocate General, Navy, Manual
  JAG Man.

Judge Advocate General's Corps
  JAGC
Judge Advocate General's School
  JAGS
Judge Advocate Journal
  J.A.J., Judge Advo. J.
Judge Advocate of the Fleet
  J.A.F.
Judge of the Prize Court
  J.P.C.
Judges
  J.J.
Judge's Journal
  Judge's J.
Judges' Rules
  J.R.
Judgment
  J., Judgm.
Judgments in the Supreme Court, Lagos, Nigeria
  Lagos R.
Judgments of Divisional and Full Courts, Gold Coast
  D. & F.
Judgments of the Federal Supreme Court, Nigeria
  F.S.C. (Nig.)
Judgments of the Supreme Court of New South Wales for the District of Port Philip
  A'Beckett
Judgments of the Supreme Court of Nigeria
  S.C. (Nig.)
Judgments of the West Indian Court of Appeal
  W.I.C.A.
Judgments of the Windward Islands Court of Appeal
  Greaves
Judgments of Upper Bench
  Judg. U.B.

Judgments, Gold Coast Colony
Jud. G.C.C.
Judgments, Jamaica Supreme Court of Judicature
Clark (Jam.)
Judicature
Jud., Judicature, Judicature. J. Am. Jud. Soc'y
Judicature Quarterly Review
Jud. Q.R.
Judicial
Jud.
Judicial Assessor
J. As.
Judicial Chronicle
Jud. Chr.
Judicial Committee of the Privy Council
Jud. Com. P.C., P.C.
Judicial Conduct Reporter
Jud. Conduct Rep.
Judicial Council, New York, Annual Reports
Jud. Coun. N.Y.
Judicial Council Reports
J.C.R.
Judicial Counsils and Conferences
Jud. C.
Judicial District
JD, J.D.
Judicial District Court
JDC
Judicial Panel on Multidistrict Litigation
J.P.M.D.L., J.P.M.L.
Judicial Repositor[y, ies]
Jud. Repos.
Judicial Sale[s]
Jud. S.
Judiciary
J., Jud.

Jugemens d'Oleron
J. d'Ol.
Julius Frontinus
Jul. Frontin.
Julius Paulus, Sententiae Receptae
Paulus.
July
Jl., Jul.
Juncta Glossa
J. Glos.
Junior Judge
J.J.
June
Jn., Jun.
Jura Ecclesiatica
Jur. Eccl.
Juridical
Jur.
Juridical Review
Jur. Rev., Jurid. Rev., J.R.
Juridical Society Papers
Jur. Soc. P., Jurid. Soc'y Pap.
Juridical Styles
Jur. St.
Jurimetrics Journal
Jurimet J, Jurimetrics, Jurimetrics J.
Juris Canonici Bachelor
J.C.B.
Juris Canonici Doctor (Doctor of Canon Law)
J.C.D.
Juris Canonici Lector
J.C.L.
Juris Civilis Doctor (Doctor of Civil Law)
J.C.D.
Juris Doctor (Doctor of Law)
Jur. D., JD, J.D., Juris Dr.
Juris Utriusque Doctor: Doctor of Both (Canon and Civil) Laws
J.U.D.

Jurisconsultus
Jctus
Jurisdiction
Jurisd.
Jurisprudence
J., Jur., Juris., Jurispr.
Jurist
Jur., Jurist
Jurist, England
Jur., Jur. (Eng.)
Jurist, New Series
Jur. N.S., Jur. N.S. (Eng.)
Jurist, New Series, Exchequer
Jur. (N.S.)Ex.
Jurist, New York
Jur., Jur.N.Y.
Jurist Reports, England
Jur., Jur.R.
Jurist Reports, New Series, England
Jur. N.S., Jur. R.N.S.
Jurist Reports, New Series, New Zealand
J.R.N.S.
Jurist Reports, New Series, Court of Appeal, New Zealand
J.R.N.S.C.A.
Jurist Reports, New Series, Mining Law Cases, New Zealand
J.R.N.S.M.L., N.Z. Jur. Mining Law
Jurist Reports, New Series, Supreme Court, New Zealand
J.R.N.S.S.C.
Jurist Reports, New Zealand
J.R., Jur.
Jurum Baccalaureus (Bachelor of Laws)
J.B.
Jury Sittings (Faculty Cases, Scotland)
J.S.

Jus Navale Rhodiorum
Jus. Nav. Rhod.
Justice
J., Just.
Justice Court
Just. Ct.
Justice Court Act
Just. Ct. Act
Justice Itinerant or of Assize
Just. Itin.
Justice of Appeal
J.A.
Justice of the King 's Bench
J.K.B.
Justice of the Peace and Local Government Review, England
J.P., J.P. (Eng.), J.P.J., Just. P., Just. Peace, J.P.R.
Justice of the Peace, New South Wales
J.P.N.S.W.
Justice of the Peace, Weekly Notes of Cases, England
J.P.J., J.P., J.P. (Eng.), J.P. Jo.
Justice of the Peace, Western Australia
J.P.(W.A.)
Justice of the Peace's Court
J.P. Ct.
Justice of the Queen's Bench
J.Q.B.
Justice of the Upper Bench
J.U.B.
Justice of the United States Supreme Court
J.
Justice System Journal
Just. Sys. J.
Justices
J.J.
Justices' Code, Oregon
Jus. Code

Justices' Law Reporter, Pennsylvania
Just. L.R., Just., Justice's L.R. (Pa.)

Justices of Appeal
JJ.A.

Justices of the Supreme Court
JJ.S.C.

Justice's Sea Law
Just.S .L.

Justiciary
Just.

Justiciary Cases, in Session Cases, Scotland
Just. Cas., R.(J.), J.C., J.

Justiciary Reports, Scotland
Adam.

Justinian's Code
Cod. Jur. Civ.

Justinian's Institutes
Inst., Just. Inst., See also Institutes

Justinian's Institutes by Cooper
Coop.Inst., Coop. Inst. Just., Cooper, Just. Inst.

Juta's Daily Reporter, Cape Province
Juta.

Juta's Daily Reporter, Cape Provincial Division
J.D.R.

Juta's Prize Cases, South Africa
Juta.

Juta's Reports, Supreme Court, Cape of Good Hope
Juta.

Juta's South African Reports
J., S.C. Rep., S.C.R., S.C.

Juvenile
Juv.

Juvenile and Domestic Relations Court
Juv. & Dom. Rel. Ct.

Juvenile and Family Court Journal
Juv. & Fam. Ct. J., Juv. & Fam. Courts J.

Juvenile Court
Juv. Ct.

Juvenile Court Journal
Juv. Ct. J.

Juvenile Court Judges Journal
Juv. Ct. J.J., Juv. Ct. Judges J.

Juvenile Courts and Delinquent and Dependent Children
Juv. Cts.

Juvenile Justice
Juv. Just., Juv. Justice

K

Kames and Woodhouselee's Dictionary, Scotch Court of Session
F. Dict., Fol. Dict., Fol. Dic., K. & W., K. & W. Dic.

Kames' Dictionary of Decisions, Scotch Court of Session
Kam., Kames, Kames Dec., Kames Dict. Dec.

Kames' Elucidation of the Laws of Scotland
Kames Elucid., Kam. Eluc.

Kames' Essays
Kam. Ess

Kames' Principles of Equity
Kames, Eq., Kam. Eq.

Kames' Remarkable Decisions
Kames Rem. Dec., Kames Rem., Kam. Sel., Kam. Sel. Dec., Kames Sel. Dec., Kam. Rem. Dec., Kames, Kam., Kam. Rem.

Kansas
Kan.

Kansas, Administration Regulations
Kan Admin. Regs.

Kansas Appeals Reports
Ka. A., Kan. App., Kans. App.

Kansas Appellate Reports
Kan. Ct. App.

Kansas Appellate Reports, 2d Series
Kan Ap2d

Kansas Bar Association
KBA

Kansas Bar Association Journal
Kan. B. Ass'n. J., Kan. B.A.J.

Kansas City Bar Journal
Kans. B.A.

Kansas City Law Reporter
Kan. C.L. Rep.,Kan. City L. Rep.

Kansas City Law Review
Kan. City L. Rev., K.C.R.

Kansas City, Missouri, Bar Association
KCMOBA

Kansas City, Missouri, Public Utilities Commission Reports
K.C. Mo. P.U.C.

Kansas Commission of Labor and Industry Workmen's Compensation Department Reports
Kan. C.L. & I.W.C.

Kansas Constitution
Kan. Const.

Kansas Court of Appeals Reports
Kan. App.2d

Kansas Journal of Law and Public Policy
Kan. J.L. & Pub. Pol'y

Kansas Judicial Council Bulletin
J.C.B., Kan. Jud. Council Bul.

Kansas Law Journal
Kan. L.J., Kansas L.J.

Kansas Law Review
Ks. L.R., Kan. L. Rev.

Kansas Lawyer
Kan. Law.

Kansas Public Service Commission
Kan. P.S.C.

Kansas Public Utilities Commission
Kan. P.U.C.

Kansas Railroad Commission
Kan. R.C.
Kansas Reports
Kan., Kans., Ks., Kans. R., Kansas R., Kas., Kas.R.
Kansas Session Laws
Kan. Sess. Laws
Kansas State Bar Association
Kans. S.B.A.
Kansas State Corporation Commission Reports
Kan. S.C.C.
Kansas State Law Journal
Kan. St. L.J.
Kansas Statutes
Kan. Stat.
Kansas Statutes Annotated
Kan. Stat. Ann., K.S.A.
Kansas Supreme Court Reports
Kan.S.C.Rep.
Kansas University Lawyer
Kan. U. Lawy., Kan. Univ. Lawy.
Kanwit's Federal Trade Commission: Regulatory Manual
FTCR
Kappa Beta Phi Quarterly
KBPQ.
Karachi Law Journal
Kar. L.J., Karachi L.J.
Karp's Domestic Torts: Family Violence and Sexual Abuse
DTFV
Kashmir Law Journal
Kashmir L.J.
Kasner on Post Mortem Tax Planning
PMTP
Katchenovsky on Prize Law
Katch. Pr. Law
Kathiawar Law Reports, India
K.L.R.

Kaufmann's Edition of Mackeldey's Civil Law
Kauf. Mack., Kaufm. Mackeld. Civ. Law
Kay and Johnson's English Vice-Chancellors' Reports
K. & J., Kay & J., Kay & J. (Eng.), Kay & John., Kay & Johns.
Kay on Shipmasters and Seamen
Kay Ship.
Kay's English Vice Chancellors' Reports
Kay, Kay (Eng.)
Keane and Grant's English Registration Appeal Cases
K. & Gr., K. & G., K. & G.R.C., Keane & Gr., Keane & G.R.C.
Keating on Franchising Adviser
FRA
Keatinge on Family Settlements
Keat. Fam. Sett.
Keble's English King's Bench Reports
Keb., Kebl., Keble, Keble (Eng.)
Keble's Justice of the Peace
Keb. J.
Keble's Statutes
Keb. Stat.
Keener's Cases on Quasi Contracts
Keener, Quasi Contr.
Keen's English Rolls Court Reports
Ke., Keen, Keen Ch., Keen (Eng.)
Keilway's English King's Bench Reports
Cro., Keil., Keilw., Keilw. (Eng.), Keilway, Keyl., Croke
Keilway's Reports (Benloe or Bendloe)
Benl. inKeil.

Keio Law Review
Keio L. Rev.
Kelham's Norman French Law Dictionary
Kelham, Kelh., Kelh. Dict.
Kelke's Judicature Acts
Kelk. Jud. Acts
Kellen's Reports (146-55 Massachusetts)
Kellen
Kelley and Ludtke on Estate Planning for Farmers and Ranchers
EPFR
Kelley and Ludtke on Family Business Organization
FBO
Kelly and Cobb's Reports (4-5 Georgia)
Kelly & C., Kelly & Cobb.
Kelly on Contracts of Married Women
Kel. Cont.
Kelly on Life Annuities
Kel. Life Ann.,̇ Kel. An.
Kelly on Scire Facias
Kel. Sc. Fac.
Kelly on Usury
Kel. Us.
Kelly's Draftsman
Kel. Draft
Kelly's Reports (1-3 Georgia)
Kel. Ga., Kell. J.R., Kelly
Kelynge's English Chancery Reports
Kelynge, W., Kelynge, W. (Eng.), LW. Kel., W. Kelynge (Eng.), Kel. W., Rep. of Sel.Cas. in Ch., Rep. Sel. Cas. Ch.
Kelyng's English Crown Cases
Kelyng. J., Kelyng. J. (Eng.)
Kemble on The Saxons in England
Kemble, Sax.

Kenan's Reports (76-91 North Carolina)
Kenan
Kennedy on Courts-Martial
Kenn. C̈. M̈ar.
Kennedy on Juries
Kenn. Jur.
Kennedy's Chancery Practice
Kenn. Ch., Kenn. Pr.
Kennett Upon Impropriations
Kenn. Imp., Kennett
Kennett's Glossary
Kenn. Gloss., Kennett, Kennett, Gloss.
Kennett's Parochial Antiquities
Kennett, Par. Ant., Paroch. Ant., Kenn. Par. Antiq.
Kent and Radcliffs' Law of New York
K. & R., Kent & R. St.
Kent's Commentaries by Kinne, edited by Devereux
Dev.Kin.Kent
Kent's Commentaries on American Law
Kent's Commen., Kent, Kent, Com., Kent, Comm.
Kentucky
Ky.
Kentucky Acts
Ky. Acts
Kentucky Administration Regulations Services
Ky. Admin. Regs.
Kentucky Administrative Register
Ky. Admin. Reg.
Kentucky Bar Journal
Ky.B.J.
Kentucky Bench and Bar
Ky. Bench & B., K.B.B.
Kentucky Commentator
Ky. Comment'r.

Kentucky Constitution
Ky. Const.

Kentucky Court of Appeals Opinions
Ky. Op.

Kentucky Law Journal
Kentucky L.J., K.L.J., Ky. L.J.

Kentucky Law Reporter
Ken. L. Re., Ken. L.R., Ky. L.,
Ky. L. Rep., Ky. Law Rep., Ky.
L.R., R., K. Law Rep., K.L.R.,
Ky. L. Rptr.

Kentucky Law Review
Ky. L. Rev.

Kentucky Opinions
Ken. Opin., Ky. Opin.

Kentucky Opinions of Attorney General
Op. Ky. Att'y Gen.

Kentucky Railroad Commission
Ky. R.C.

Kentucky Reports
Ky., Ky. R.

Kentucky Revised Statutes
KRS, Ky. Rev. Stat.

Kentucky Revised Statutes and Rules Service
Ky. Rev. Stat. & Rules Serv.

Kentucky State Bar Association
Ky. S.B.A.

Kentucky State Bar Journal
Ky. S.B.J., Ky. St. B.J., K.B.J.

Kentucky Supreme Court Reports
Ky.

Kentucky Workmen's Compensation Board Decisions
Ky. W.C. Dec.

Kenya High Court Digest
K.H.C.D.

Kenya Law Reports
Kenya L.R., K.L.R., L.R.K.

Kenyon's English King's Bench Reports (1753-59), England
Keny., Ken., Ld. Ken., Ld. Kenyon, Ld. Kenyon (Eng.), K.

Kenyon's Notes of King's Bench Reports, Edited by Hanmer
Keny.

Kerala
Ker. Ind.

Kerala Law Journal
Kerala L.J.

Kerala Law Times
K.L.T., Ker. L.T.

Kerford and Box's Victorian Digest
K. & B. Dig.

Kernan's Reports (11-14 New York)
Kern.

Kern's Reports (100-116 Indiana)
Kern.

Kerr on Ancient Lights
Kerr Anc. L.

Kerr on Injunctions
Kerr, Inj.

Kerr on Inter-State Extradition
Kerr Ext.

Kerr on Receivers
Kerr, Rec.

Kerr's Actions at Law
Kerr. Act.

Kerr's Blackstone Commentaries
Kerr Black

Kerr's Discovery
Kerr Disc.

Kerr's Law of Fraud and Mistake
Kerr Fr., Kerr F. & M.

Kerr's New Brunswick Reports (3-5 New Brunswick)
Kerr (N.B.), N.B.R. Kerr., Kerr.

Kerr's Reports (18-22 Indiana)
Kerr

Kerr's Reports (27-29 New York Civil Procedure Reports)
Kerr

Kerr's Student's Blackstone Commentaries
Kerr Stu. Black

Kerr's Water and Mineral Cases
Kerr W. & M. Cas.

Kerse's Manuscript Decisions, Scotch Court of Session
Kerse

Kersey's English Dictionary
Kersey Dict.

Kestler on Questioning Techniques and Tactics
QTT

Key and Elphinstone on Conveyancing
Key & Elph. Conv., K. & E. Conv.

Keyes' Court of Appeals Reports (40-43 New York)
K., Key., Keyes

Keyes on Future Interest in Chattels
Key.Ch.

Keyes on Future Interest in Lands
Key. Lands

Keyes on Remainders
Key. Rem.

Keyser on Stock Exchange
Keys. St. Ex.

Keyword on Context
K.W.I.C.

Khairpur
Khairpur, Pak.

Khmer
Kh.

Kilburn's English Magistrates' Cases
Kilb.

Kilkerran's Scotch Court of Session Decisions
Kilkerran, Kilk.

King
K.

King Edward
E.R.

King Edmund's Laws
Leg. Edm.

King Ethelred's Laws
Leg. Ethel.

King-Farlow's Gold Coast Judgments and Masai Cases
KingFarlow, K.F.

King Henry I Laws
LL. Hen. I, Leg. H.I.

King Malcolm's Laws
L.L. Malcom, R. Scott

King's Bench
K.B.

King's Bench Court
K.B.C.

King's Bench Division
K.B.D.

King's Bench Divisional Court
K.B. Div'l. Ct.

King's Bench Reports, Upper Canada
K.B. (U.C.)

King's Civil Practice Cases, Colorado
King

King's Conflicting Cases, Texas
King's Con. Cs., King's Conf. Ca.

King's Counsel
K. Counsel, K.C.

King's Reports (5-6 Louisiana Annual)
King

King's Sergeant
K.S.

King's Tennessee Digest
King Dig.

Kingston Law Review
Kingston L. Rev., Kingston L.R.

Kinney's Law Dictionary and Glossary
Kinney, Law Dict. & Glos.

Kirby's Reports and Supplement, Connecticut
Kir., Kirb., Kirby, Kirby's Conn. R., Kirby's R., Kirby's Rep.

Kirtland on Practice in Surrogates' Courts
Kirt. Sur. Pr.

Kisbey on the Irish Land Law
Kisb. Ir. Land L.

Kitchin on Courts
Kitch. Cts.

Kitchin on Jurisdictions of Courts-Leet, Courts-Baron, etc.
Kitch., Kitch. Courts, Kit. Ct., Kit. Jur.

Kitchin on Road Transport Law
Kit. Rd. Trans.

Kitchin's Retourna Brevium
Kit.

Kluber's Droit des Gens
Kluber, Dr. des Gens.

Knapp and Ombler's English Election Cases
K. & O., Kn. & Omb., Knapp & O., Kn. & O.

Knapp's Privy Council Cases
Kn. A.C., Kn., Kn. P.C., Rep., Knapp., Knapp P.C. (Eng.)

Knapp's Privy Council Reports
Kn. & Moo.

Knight
Kt.

Knight's American Mechanical Dictionary
Knight, Mech.Dict.

Knight's Industrial Reports
K.I.R., Knight's Ind.

Knight's Local Government Reports
K.L.G.R., L.G.R., Kn. L.G.R.

Knowles' Reports (3 Rhode Island)
Knowles

Knox and Fitzhardinge's New South Wales Reports
Knox & Fitz., Knox & F., K. & F.N.S.W.

Knox on Civil Procedure in India
Kn. Civ. Proc.

Knox Supreme Court Reports, New South Wales
Knox (N.S.W.)

Knox's Bengal Criminal Law
Kn. Cr. Law

Knox's New South Wales Reports
Knox, Knox (N.S.W.), Kn. N.S.W.

Kobe University Law Review
Kobe U.L. Rev., Kobe Univ. L. Rev.

Koch's Supreme Court Decisions
Koch

Konstam and Ward's Rating Appeals
Konst. & W. Rat. App.

Konstam's Rating Appeals
Konst. Rat. App.

Korea
Korea

Korea and World Affairs: A Quarterly Review
Korea & World Aff.

Korea Law Review
Korea L.R.

Korean
K.

Korean Journal of Comparative Law
Korean J. Comp. L.

Korean Journal of International Law
Korean J. Int'l L., Korean J. of Internat. L.
Korean Law
Korean L.
Korngold's Private Land Use
PLU
Kotze and Barber's Transvaal Reports
K. & B., Kotze & B., Kotze & Barb., K.
Kotze's Transvaal High Court Reports
Kotze
Kreider's Reports (1-23 Washington)
Kreider
Kress's Reports (166-194 Pennsylvania State)
Kress
Kress's Reports (2-12 Pennsylvania Superior)
Kress

Ku Klux Klan
K.K.K.
Kulp's Luzerne Legal Register Reports, Pennsylvania
Culp, Kulp
Kushner's Fair Housing; Discrimination in Real Estate, Community Development and Revitalization
DRE
Kwansei Gaknin Law Review
Kwansei Gak. L. Rev.
Kyd on Awards
Kyd Aw.
Kyd on Bills of Exchange
Kyd, Kyd Bills
Kyd on Corporations
Kyd Corp.
Kyoto Law Review
Kyoto L. Rev.
Kyshe's Malaya Reports
Kyshe

L

La Raza Law Journal
   La Raza L.J.
La Themis
   Them.
Labatt's District Court Reports,
   California
   Lab.
Labor
   Lab.
Labor and Automation Bulletin
   Lab. & Auto. Bull.
Labor and Employment Law
   Lab. & Empl. L.
Labor Arbitration
   Lab. Arb.
Labor Arbitration and Dispute
   Settlements
   Lab. Arb. & Disp. Settl.
Labor Arbitration Awards, Com-
   merce Clearing House
   A. R. B., Arb., CCH Lab. Arb.
   Awards, Lab. Arb. Awards
   (CCH)
Labor Arbitration Reports, Bu-
   reau of National Affairs
   L.A., Lab. Arb. Rep. (BNA),
   Lab. Arb., L.A.R.
Labor Arbitration Service
   Lab. Arb. Serv.
Labor Cases, Commerce Clearing
   House
   Lab. Cas. (CCH), L.C., CCH
   Lab.Cas.
Labor Code
   Labor C.
Labor Dispute
   L.D.

Labor Law Journal
   Lab. L.J., Labor Law J., Labor
   L.J., L.L.J.
Labor Law Reporter, Commerce
   Clearing House
   CCH Lab. L. Rep., CCH L.L.R.,
   Lab. L. Rep. (CCH)
Labor Law Reports, Commerce
   Clearing House
   Lab. L. Rep. (CCH)
Labor Lawyer
   Lab. Law.
Labor Management Relations Act
   L.M.R.A.
Labor-Management Reporting
   and Disclosure Act
   LMRDA
Labor Management Services Ad-
   ministration
   LMSA
Labor Relations and Employ-
   ment News
   Lab. Rel. & Empl. News
Labor Relations Guide, Prentice-
   Hall
   Lab. Rel. Guide (P-H)
Labor Relations Law Letter
   Lab. Rel. L. Letter
Labor Relations Reference Man-
   ual, Bureau of National Affairs
   L.R.M., L.R.R.M. (BMA)
Labor Relations Reporter, Bu-
   reau of National Affairs
   Lab. Rel. Rep. (BNA), L.R.R.
Labor Studies Journal
   Lab. Stu. J.
Laboratory[ies]
   Lab.

Labour
Lab.
Labour Appeal Cases
Lab. A.C.
Labour Arbitration Cases
L.A.C.
Labour Gazette
Lab. Gaz.
Labour Law Journal
Labour L.J.
Lacey's Digest of Railway Decisions
Lac. R.R. Dig., Lacey Dig.
Lackawanna Bar
Lackawanna B., Lack. Bar.
Lackawanna Bar Reporter, Pennsylvania
Lack. Bar. R.
Lackawanna County Reports, Pennsylvania
Lack. Co.(Pa.)
Lackawanna Jurist, Pennsylvania
Lac. Jur., Lack. Jur., Lack. Jurist
Lackawanna Legal News, Pennsylvania
Lack. Leg. News (Pa.), Lack. Leg. N., Lack. L.N., Lacka. Leg. News
Lackawanna Legal Record, Pennsylvania
Lack. Leg. R., Lack. Leg. Rec., Lack. L.R.
Ladd's Reports (59-64 New Hampshire)
Ladd.
Lagos High Court Reports, Nigeria
Lagos H.C.R.
Lahore Cases, India
Lah. Cas.
Lahore Law Journal, India
Lah. L.J., L.L.J.

Lahore Law Times, India
Lahore L. Times, Lah. L.T., L.L.T.
Lalor's Cyclopaedia of Political Science, Political Economy, etc.
Lalor, Pol. Econ.
Lalor's Law of Real Property
Lal. R.P.
Lalor's Supplement to Hill and Denio's New York Reports
H. & D., Lalor., Lalor, Supp., Hill & D., Hill & Den., Hill & Den. Supp., Lalor's Supp. (Hill & Denio), Lalor's Suppl., L.Sup.H.& D.
Lamar's Reports (25-40 Florida)
Lamar.
Lambard's Archainomia
Lamb., Lamb. Arch., Lamb. Archaion., Lamb.
Lambard's Duties of Constables, etc.
Lamb. Const.
Lambard's Eirenarcha
Eir., Lamb. Eir., Lamb. Eiren., Lamb.
Lambard's Explication
Lamb., Lamb. Explic.
Lambert's Law of Dower
Lamb. Dow.
Lamb's Reports (103-105 Wisconsin)
Lamb.
Lancaster Bar, Pennsylvania
L. Bar., Lanc. Bar
Lancaster Law Review, Pennsylvania
Lanc. L. Rev., Lanc. Law Rev., L. Bar., L.L.R.
Lancaster Review, Pennsylvania
Lanc. Rev.
Land
Land

Land and Concessions Bulletin
L.C.B.
Land and Valuation Court Reports, New South Wales
L.V.R. (N.S.W.), L.V.R.
Land and Water Law Review
Land & Water L. Rev., L.W.R.,
L.W.L.R., Land & Water L.R.
Land Appeal Court Cases
L.A.C.C., Land App. Ct. Cas.
Land Conservation and Development Commission
L.C.D.C.
Land Court
L.C.
Land Court Cases, New South Wales
L.C.C., L.C.C.N.S.W.
Land Decisions
Land Dec.
Land Development Law Reporter
L.D.L.R.
Land Grant
L/G
Land Office Decisions, United States
L. Dec., L.D.
Land Registry
L.R.
Land Title Trust
L.T.T.
Land Transfer Committee
L.T.C.
Land Use and Environment Law Review
Land Use & Env. L. Rev., Land Use & Env't L. Rev.
Land Use Planning Reports
Land U. Pl. Rep.
Landed Estate Court
Land. Est. C.

Landed Estates Courts Commission
LEC
Landlord and Tenant
L. & T.
Lands Tribunal Rating Appeals
L.T.R.A.
Lane's English Exchequer Reports
La., Lane
Langdell's Cases in Equity Pleading
Lang. Eq. Pl.
Langdell's Cases on Contracts
Lang. Cont., Langd. Cont.,
Lang. Ca. Cont., L.C.Cont.
Langdell's Cases on Law of Sales
Lang. Ca. Sales., Lang. Sales,
L.C. Sales
Langdell's Summary of Equity Pleading
Lang. Eq. Pl.
Langdell's Summary of the Law of Contracts
Lang. Cont., Lang. Sum. Cont.
Langley's Trustees' Act
Lang. Tr.
Language
Lang.
Lanham Housing Act
LHA
Lansing's Select Cases in Chancery, New York
L., L., Lans. Ch., Lans. Sel. Cas.
Lansing's Supreme Court Reports, New York
Lans., L.
Laotian
L.
Laperriere's Speaker's Decisions
Lap. Dec.
Larceny
Larc.

Laritz's Attorney Guide to Social Security Disability Claims
AGSS

Lascelles on Juvenile Offenders
Lasc. Juv. Off.

Lascelles on Horse Warranty
Lasc. H. War.

Last-In, First-Out Inventory Method
LIFO

Last Law
Leg. Ult.

Latch's English King's Bench Reports
Latch, Lat.

Latham on the Law of Window Lights
Lath. Wind. L.

Lathrop's Reports (115-145 Massachusetts)
Lath., Lathrop.

Latin American Economic System
SELA

Latin American Free Trade Association
LAFTA

Latin American Journal of Politics, Economics and Law
L.A.J.P.E.L.

Latrobe's Justice
Lat. Jus.

Lattey's Privy Council Practice
Latt. Pr. C. Pr.

Laurence on Primogeniture
Laur. Prim.

Laurence's Reports of the High Court of Griqualand
Laurence

Lauren's High Court Cases, South Africa
Laur. H.C. Ca.

Laussat's Equity Practice in Pennsylvania
Lauss. Eq.

Law
L., Law

Law (a periodical published in London)
Law.

Law Advertiser
L. Advertiser, Law Advert.

Law Almanac
Law Alm.

Law Amendment Journal
Law Am. Jour., Law Amdt. J.

Law and Communication
L. & Comm.

Law and Computer Technology
L. & Comp. Technol., L. & Computer Tech., Law & Comput. Tech., Law & Computer Tech.

Law and Contemporary Problems
L. & Contemp. Prob., Law & Contemp. Probs., Law & Contemp. Problems, L & Contemp Probs, L & CP, L. and Contemp. Probl., L. Comment'y, L.C.P.

Law and Equity Reporter, New York
Law & Eq. Rep., L. & Eq. Rep.

Law and History Review
Law & Hist. Rev.

Law and Housing Journal
Law & Housing J.

Law and Human Behavior
L & Human Beh, L. & Human Behav., Law & Hum. Behav., Law & Human Behavior

Law and Inequality
Law & Ineq.

Law and Inequality Journal
Law & Ineq. J.

Law and International Affairs, Bangladesh
Law & Int. Aff.

Law and Justice
L. & Just., L. & Justice, Law & Just.

Law and Legislation in the German Democratic Republic
L. & Leg. GDR, L. & Legis. in G.D.R., Law & Legisl. in the German Dem. Rep.

Law and Liberty
L. & Lib., Law & Lib.

Law and Order
L. & Order

Law and Philosophy
Law & Phil.

Law and Policy in International Business
L. & Pol. Int'l. Bus., L. and Policy in Internat. Bus., Law & Pol'y. Int'l. Bus.

Law and Policy Quarterly
Law & Pol'y. Q.

Law and Psychology Review
L. & Psych. Rev., L. & Psychol. Rev., Law & Psych. Rev., Law & Psychology Rev.

Law and Sexuality
Law & Sex.

Law and Social Change
Law & Soc.,

Law and Social Inquiry: Journal of the American Bar Foundation
L. & Soc. Inquiry: J. Am. B. Found., Law & Soc. Inquiry

Law and Social Problems
Law & Soc. Probs.

Law and Society Review
Law & Soc'y. Rev.

Law and State
Law & State

Law and the Social Order
L. & Soc. Order

Law and the Social Order, Arizona State Law Journal
Law & Soc. Ord.

Law Book Adviser
L. Book Adviser

Law Book Company's Land Laws Services, New South Wales
Land L. Serv.

Law Book Review Digest and Current Legal Bibliography
Law Bk. Rev. Dig.

Law Bulletin
Law Bul., Law Bull.

Law Bulletin and Brief
Law Bul. & Br.

Law Bulletin, State University of Iowa
Law Bul. Ia.

Law Cases, William I to Richard I (Placita Anglo-Normannica)
Law Cas. Wm.I., Law Cases

Law Centres Federation
LCF

Law Chronicle
L. Chron., L. Chr., L. Chr.

Law Chronicle and Auction Record
Law Chr. & Auct. Rec.

Law Chronicle and Journal of Jurisprudence
Law Chr. & Jour. Jur.

Law Chronicle and Law Students' Magazine
L. Chron. & L. Stud. Mag.

Law Chronicle and Law Student's Magazine, New Series
L. Chron. & L. Stud. Mag., (N.S.)

Law Clerk
Law Cl.

Law Clerk Record
  Law Cl. Rec.
Law Coach
  L. Coach, Law Coach
Law Commentary
  L. Comment., L. Comment'y
Law Commission
  Law Com., L.C.
Law Commission of India
  India L.C.
Law Commission Report
  Law Com.
Law Commission Working Paper
  L.C.W.P.
Law Court[s]
  Law Ct., L.C.
Law Court Division
  L. Ct., Div.
Law Department Bulletin, Union Pacific Railroad Co.
  Law Dept. Bull.
Law Dictionary
  L. Dict., L.D.
Law Digest
  Law Dig.
Law Division
  Law Div.
Law Enforcement Assistance Administration
  LEAA
Law Examination Journal
  Law Ex. J.
Law Examination Reporter
  Law Ex. Rep.
Law French
  L. Fr., L.F.
Law French Dictionary
  Law Fr. Dict.
Law Gazette
  L. Gaz., Law Gaz.
Law Glossary
  L.G.

Law Guardian
  L. Guard.
Law in American Society
  L. Am. Soc., L. Am. Soc'y
Law in Context
  Law in Context
Law in Eastern Europe
  L. East. Eur., L.I.E.E., L. in Eastern Eur.
Law in Japan
  L. Japan, L. in Japan
Law in Society
  L. in Soc'y
Law in Transition Journal
  L. In. Trans. J.
Law in Transition Quarterly
  L. in Trans. Q., L. Trans. Q.
Law Institute Journal
  Law Inst. J., L. Inst. J.
Law Institute Journal of Victoria
  L. Inst. J. Vict.
Law Intelligencer
  L. Intell., Law Int.
Law Journal
  L.J., Law Jour.
Law Journal, Common Pleas, Old Series, England
  L.J.C.P. (O.S.)
Law Journal, County Courts Reporter, England
  L.J.C.C.
Law Journal, Exchequer in Equity, England
  L.J. Ex. Eq.
Law Journal, Ireland
  L.J.Ir.
Law Journal, Irish Free State
  L.J.I.F.S.
Law Journal, King's Bench, Old Series, England
  L.J.K.B.O.S.
Law Journal Law Tracts
  L.J.L.T.

Law Journal, Lower Canada
L.J.L.C.

Law Journal, Magistrates Cases, New Series, England
L.J. Mag.

Law Journal Newspaper, England
L.J. News (Eng.), L. Jo., L.J. News., L.J. Newsp.

Law Journal Newspaper County Court Appeals, England
L.J.C.C.A., L.J.N.C.C.A.

Law Journal Newspaper County Court Reports, England
L.J.N.C.C.R.

Law Journal, Notes of Cases, England
L.J.N.C., L. Jo. N.C., L.J.N.C. (Eng.)

Law Journal of Student Bar Association, Ohio State University
O.S.L.J.

Law Journal of the Marut Bunnag International Law Office, Bangkok, Thailand
L.J. of the Marut Bunnag Internat. L. Off.

Law Journal of Upper Canada
L.J.U.C.

Law Journal, Old Series, England
L.J.O.S.

Law Journal Privy Council, New Series, England
L.J.P.C.N.S.

Law Journal Probate and Matrimonial, England
L.J. Prob. & Mat., L.J. Prob. (Eng.), L.J.P. & M.

Law Journal Reports, Admiralty, New Series, England
L.J. Adm. N.S., L.J.Adm.N.S. (Eng.), L.J.Adm.

Law Journal Reports, Appeals, New Series, England
L.J. App.

Law Journal Reports, Bankruptcy, England
L.J. Bank., L.J. Bankr., L.J. Bk., L.J.Bcy.

Law Journal Reports, Bankruptcy, New Series, England
L.J. Bank. N.S., L.J.Bankr.N.S. (Eng.), L.J.Bcy.N.S.

Law Journal Reports, Chancery, England
L.J. Ch., Law J. Ch., L.J. Ch. (Eng.), L.J. Ch. N.S. (Eng.), L.J.Eq.

Law Journal Reports, Chancery, Old Series, England
L.J. Ch. (O.S.)

Law Journal Reports, Common Pleas, England
L.J.C.P., L.J.C.P. (Eng.), L.J.C.P.D., L.J.C.P.N.S.

Law Journal Reports, Common Pleas, New Series, England
L.J.C.P.N.S. (Eng.), L.J.C.

Law Journal Reports, Crown Cases Reserved, New Series, England
L.J.C.C.R., L.J.C.C.R. (N.S.)

Law Journal Reports, Divorce and Matrimonial, New Series, England
L.J.D. & M., L.J. Mat. Cas.

Law Journal Reports, Ecclesiastical Cases, New Series, England
L.J. Ecc., L.J. Eccl.

Law Journal Reports, England
Law J., Law Jour., L.J. Rep., L.J.R. (Eng.), L.J.R.

Law Journal Reports, Exchequer Division, New Series, England
L.J. Ex., L.J. Ex. D., L.J. Exch., L.J. Exch. (Eng.), L.J. Exch. N.S. (Eng.)

Law Journal Reports, Exchequer, New Series, England
L.J. Exch. N.S., Law J. Exch.

Law Journal Reports, Exchequer, Old Series, England
L.J. Exch. (O.S.)

Law Journal Reports, House of Lords, New Series, England
L.J.H.L.

Law Journal Reports, King's Bench, England
L.J.K.B., L.J.K.B. (Eng.)

Law Journal Reports, King's Bench, New Series, England
L.J.K.B.N.S., L.J.K.B.N.S. (Eng.), L.J.K.B. (N.S.)

Law Journal Reports, Magistrates' Cases, England
L.J. Mag. Cas. (Eng.), L.J. Mag. Cas., L.J. Mag. Cas. N.S. (Eng.), L.J. Mag. Cas. N.S.

Law Journal Reports, Magistrates' Cases, New Series, England
L.J.M. Cas., L.J.M.C.

Law Journal Reports, Magistrates' Cases, Old Series, England
L.J.M.C.O.S.

Law Journal Reports, Matrimonial, England
L.J. Mat., L.J. Mat. (Eng.)

Law Journal Reports, Matrimonial, Probate and Admiralty, England
L.J.M.P.A.

Law Journal Reports, New Series, England
L.J. Rep. N.S., L.J.N.S.

Law Journal Reports, Old Series, Chancery, England
L.J.O.S. Ch.

Law Journal Reports, Old Series, Common Pleas, England
L.J.O.S.C.P.

Law Journal Reports, Old Series, Exchequer, England
L.J.O.S. Ex.

Law Journal Reports, Old Series, King's Bench, England
L.J.O.S.K.B.

Law Journal Reports, Privy Council, England
L.J.P.C., L.J.P.C. (Eng.)

Law Journal Reports, Privy Council, New Series, England
L.J.P., L.J.P.C. (N.S.)

Law Journal Reports, Probate and Matrimonial, New Series, England
L.J. Prob., L.J.Prob.N.S.

Law Journal Reports, Probate, Divorce, Admiralty, England
L.J.P., L.J. Prob. N.S. (Eng.)

Law Journal Reports, Probate, Divorce and Admiralty, New Series, England
L.J.P.D. & A., Law J.P.D. & A., L.J.P.D. & Adm., L.J.P.M. & A.

Law Journal Reports, Queen's Bench, New Series, England
L.J.Q.B.N.S., Law J. R., Q. II., Law J. Q. B., L.J.Q.B., L.J.Q.B. (Eng.), L.J.Q.B.N.S. (Eng.)

Law Journal Reports, Queen's Bench Division, New Series, England
L.J.Q.B.D., L.J.Q.B.D.N.S.

Law Journal, (Smith)
   Sm. L.J.
Law Judge
   L.J.
Law Latin
   L. Lat., L.L.
Law Latin Dictionary
   Law Lat. Dict.
Law Librarian
   Law Lib., Law Libn., L. Lib.
Law Library
   L.L.
Law Library Journal.
   L. Lib. J., L. Libr. J., Law Lib.
   J., Law Libr. J., L.L.J.
Law Library News
   Law Lib. N.
Law Library, New Series
   Law Lib. N.S., L.L.N.S.
Law Magazine
   Law Mag., L. Mag., L.M.
Law Magazine and Law Review
   Law Mag. & Law Rev., L. Mag.
   & L.R., L.M. & L.R.
Law Magazine and Review
   Law Mag. & R., Law Mag. &
   Rev.
Law, Medicine and Health Care
   Law, Med. & Health Care
Law News, St. Louis
   Law N.
Law Notes
   Law N., Law Notes, L.N., L.N.,
   L. Notes, L.N., Law Notes, New
   York, L. Notes (N.Y.)
**Law Notes for the General Practi-
tioner**
   L. Notes Gen. Pract.
Law Observer
   L.O.
Law of the Sea
   L. Sea

**Law of the Sea Institute Proceed-
ings**
   Law Sea Inst. Proc.
**Law Office Economics and Man-
agement**
   L. Off. Econ. & Man., L. Off.
   Econ. & Mgt., Law Off. Econ. &
   Mgt.
Law Office Information Service
   Law Off. Information Service
Law on Church Building Societies
   Law Ch. Bdg. Soc.
Law on Church Wardens
   Law Ch.Ward.
Law Opinions
   I.O., O.
Law Practice Management
   L. Prac. Mgmt.
Law Quarterly
   L.Q.
Law Quarterly Review
   Law Q. Rev., L.Q. Rev., L.Q.R.,
   Law Quar. Rev., Law Quart.
   Rev.
Law Record
   L.R.
Law Recorder
   L. Record., Law Rec., L.R., L.
   Rec.
Law Recorder, 1st or Old Series
   IR. L. Rec. lst ser., Law Rec.
   (O.S.), L. Rec. O.S., Ir. L. Rec.
   N.S., Law Rec. (O.S.), L. Rec.
Law Recorder, New Series
   L. Rec.N.S., Ir. L. Rec. N.S.,
   Law Rec. (N.S.)
**Law Reform Commission of Can-
ada**
   L.R.C. Canada
Law Reform Committee
   Law Ref. Com., Law Ref. Cttee.,
   L.R.C.

Law Reform Committee, Bermuda
Bermuda L.R.C.

Law Register
L.R., Law Reg.

Law Reporter , England
L.R., Law Rep.

Law Reporter, Boston
Month. Law Rep., Law Rep.

Law Reporter, Ramsey and Morin, Montreal
L. Rep. Mont., R. & M., Law Repr., Law Rep.

Law Reporter, Toronto
Law Rep. (Tor.)

Law Reports
Law Rep., L.R.

Law Reports, Admiralty and Ecclesiastica, England
L.R. Adm. & Eccl. (Eng.), L.R. Adm. & Ecc., L.R. Adm. & Eccl., Law Rep. A. & E.

Law Reports, Appeal Cases, England
A.C., L.R. App. Cas., App. Cas.

Law Reports, Appeal Cases, Second Series, England
App. Cas.2d

Law Reports, Appeal Cases, Third Series, England
A.C.

Law Reports, Bankruptcy and Probate, New South Wales
L.R. (N.S.W.) B. & P.

Law Reports, British Burma
L.R.B urm., L.R. Burma.

Law Reports, British Guiana
L.R.B.G.

Law Reports, Chancery, England
Ch.

Law Reports, Chancery Appeal Cases, England
Law Rep. Ch., Law Rep. Ch. App., L.R. Ch., L.R. Ch. (Eng.), Ch.App.Cas.

Law Reports, Chancery Division, England
Law Rep. Ch. D., L.R. Ch. D. (Eng.), L.R. Ch. Div. (Eng.)

Law Reports, Common Pleas, England
Law Rep. C.P., C.P., L.R.C.P. (Eng.), L.R.C.P.

Law Reports, Common Pleas Division, England
Law Rep. C.P.D., L.R.C.P. Div., C.P.D.

Law Reports, Court of Appeals, New Zealand
L.R.C.A.

Law Reports, Crown Cases, England
Law Rep. C.C.

Law Reports, Crown Cases Reserved, England
L.R. Cr. Cas. Res., L.R.C.C.R.

Law Reports Digest
Law Rep. Dig., L.R. Dig.

Law Reports, Divorce, New South Wales
L.R. (N.S.W.) D.

Law Reports, East Africa
L.R.E.A.

Law Reports, Eastern Africa Court of Appeal
E. Afr. Ct. App., E.A.C.A.

Law Reports, Equity Cases, England
Law Rep. Eq.

Law Reports, Equity, New South Wales
L.R. (N.S.W.) Eq.

Law Reports, Exchequer, England
Law Rep. Ex.

Law Reports, Exchequer Division, England
Law Rep. Ex. D., Ex. D., Ex. Div., L.R. Exch. Div., L.R. Ex. D.

Law Reports, House of Lords, English and Irish Appeals
Eng. & Ir. App., L.R. Eng. & Ir. App., Eng. Ir. App., L.R.E. & I. App., H.L., Law Rep. H.L., E. & I. App.

Law Reports, House of Lords, English and Irish Appeals and Peerage Claims
L.R.H.L., L.R.H.L. (Eng.)

Law Reports, House of Lords, Scotch and Divorce Appeal Cases
L.R.H.L. Sc. App. Cas., Law Rep.H.L. Sc., Sc. & Div., L.R.S. & D. App.

Law Reports, Indian Appeals
Ind. App., Law Rep. Ind. App.

Law Reports, Ireland
IR., Ir., L.R. Ir., Law Rep. Ir.

Law Reports, Miscellaneous Division, England
Law Rep. Misc. D., L.R. Misc. D.

Law Reports, New York
Law Rep., Law Rep. (N.Y.)

Law Reports, New York, New Series
Law Rep. N.S.

Law Reports, New South Wales Supreme Court
L.R.N.S.W.

Law Reports, New South Wales, Vice-Admiralty
L.R. (N.S.W.) Vice-Adm.

Law Reports, New Zealand
L.R.N.Z.

Law Reports, New Zealand Supreme Court
L.R.S.C.

Law Reports, Privy Council Appeals, England
P.C. App., Law Rep. P.C.

Law Reports, Probate, England
Law Rep. P.

Law Reports, Probate and Divorce, England
P. & D., Pr. & Div., Law Rep. P. & D.

Law Reports, Probate and Matrimonial Cases, England
P. & M., L.R.P. & M.

Law Reports, Probate Division, England
Prob., P. Div., L.R.P.D., Prob. (1891), Pr. Div.

Law Reports, Probate Divorce and Admiralty Division, England
P.D., P.

Law Reports, Queen's Bench, England
Law Rep. Q.B.

Law Reports, Queen's Bench Division, England
Law Rep. Q.B.D.

Law Reports, Restrictive Practices Cases, England
L.R.R.P.

Law Reports, Sarawak, North Borneo and Brunei Supreme Court
S.C.R.

Law Reports, Scotch Appeals
L.R. Sc. App., L.R. Sc. Div. App.

Law Reports, Sierra Leone Series
L.R.S.L.

Law Reports, South Australia
L.R.S.A.

Law Repository
L. Repos.
Law Review
Law Rev., L.R.
Law Review and Quarterly Journal
L. Rev. & Quart. J., Law Rev. &
Qu. J.
Law Review Digest
L. Rev. Dig.
Law Review Journal
Law Rev. J.
Law Review, Manila
L. Rev.
Law Review Quarterly
Law Rev. Qu.
Law Review University of Detroit
Law Rev. U. Det., L. Rev. U. Detroit
Law Revision Commission
Law Rev. Comm.
Law Revision Committee
Law Rev. Com., Law Rev.
Cttee., L.R.C.
Law Revision Committee, Bahamas
Bahamas L.R.C.
Law School Record
Law School Rec.
Law School Review
Law School Rev.
Law Society Gazette
Gazette, Law Soc'y. Gaz.,
L.S.G., L. Soc'y Gaz.
Law Society Journal
L. Soc. J., L. Soc'y J., Law Soc'y.
J., Law Soc. J.
Law Society of Massachusetts, Journal
Law Soc. Jo.
Law Society of Scotland
J. Law Soc'y, Scotland, Law
Soc'y. Scotl.

Law Society of Western Australia Brief
Brief
Law Society's Gazette
L. Soc. Gaz., L.S. Gaz., Law Soc.
Gaz.
Law Student
Law Stu., L.S., Law Stud.
Law Students' Helper
L. Stud. H., L. Stud. Helper,
Law Stud. H., Lw Stu. H., L.
Stud. J.
Law Students' Magazine
Law Stud. Mag., L. Stu. Mag.,
Law Stu. Mag.
Law Students' Magazine, New Series
Law Stud. Mag. N.S.
Law Teacher
L. Teach., Law Tcher, Law
Tchr., L. Teacher
Law-Technology
Law-Tech.
Law Times, England
L.T. Jo., L.T., Law Times, L.T.
Jour., L.T. Newsp.
Law Times Bankruptcy Reports, England
A.L.T.B.R., L.T.B.
Law Times Journal, England
L.T., L.T. Jo. (Eng.), L.T.J., L.T.
(Eng.)
Law Times Newspaper, England
L.T.
Law Times Reports, England
Law T., L.T.R., L.T.
Law Times Reports, New Series, England
Law T. Rep. N.S., Law T., N.S.,
L.T. Rep., L.T.R.N.S., L.T. Rep.
N.S., L.T.N.S.

Law Times Reports, Old Series, England
Law T. Rep. O.S., L.T. (O.S.), Law Times (O.S.), L.T.O.S.

Law Times, New Series, England
L.T.N.S. (Eng.), L.T.(N.S.), Law Times (N.S.), L.T.N.S., Law T., N.S., L.T. (O.S.), Law Times (O.S.), L.T.

Law Tracts
Law Tr.

Law Weekly
Law W., L.W.

Lawasia Law Journal
Lawasia L.J., Lawasia

Lawes on Charter-Parties
Lawes Ch., Law. Ch. P.

Lawes on Pleading
Lawes, Pl.

Lawes on Pleading in Assumpsit
Law. Pl.

Lawes on Pleading in Civil Actions
Law. Pl.

Lawrence Law Journal
Law. L.J.

Lawrence's Edition of Wheaton on International Law
Law. Wheat., Lawr. Wh.

Lawrence's First Comptroller's Decisions
Lawrence Comp. Dec., Lawrence, Compt. Dec.

Lawrence's High Court Reports for Griqualand, South Africa
Lawr.

Lawrence's Reports (20 Ohio)
Lawrence

Lawrence's Visitation and Search
Law. V. & S.

Law[s]
L., Law, St.

Law's Digest of United States Patent Cases
Law Pat. Dig.

Law's Ecclesiastical Law
Law Ecc. Law

Law's Forms of Ecclesiastical Law
Law Forms

Law's Jurisdiction of the Federal Courts
Law Jur.

Laws of Alfred
LL. Aluredi., Leg. Alfred.

Laws of Athelstan
LL. Athelst.

Laws of Burgundians
LL. Burgund

Laws of Delaware
Del. Laws

Laws of Edmund
Leg. Edm.

Laws of Edward the Confessor
LL. Edw. Conf.

Laws of Ethelred
Leg. Ethel.

Laws of Florida
Fla. Laws

Laws of Henry I
LL. Hen. I., Leg. H.I.

Laws of Illinois
Ill. Laws

Laws of King Canute
LL. Canuti R., Leg. Canuti, Leg. Cannt., Leg.Canut., LL. Canuti

Laws of Malcolm, King of Scotland
LL. Malcom, R. Scott.

Laws of Maryland
Md. Laws

Laws of Minnesota
Minn. Laws

Laws of Missouri
Mo. Laws

Laws of Montana
  Mont. Laws
Laws of Naples
  LL. Neapolit.
Laws of New Jersey
  N.J. Laws
Laws of New Mexico
  N.M. Laws
Laws of New York
  L.N.Y., N.Y. Laws
Laws of North Dakota
  N.D. Sess. Laws
Laws of Oleron
  Leg. Oler.
Laws of Puerto Rico
  P.R. Laws
Laws of Puerto Rico Annotated
  L.P.R.A., P.R. Laws Ann.
Laws of Rhodes
  Leg. Rhod.
Laws of the Alemanni
  L. Alem, L.All.
Laws of the Australian Capital Territory
  Austl.Cap.Terr. Laws, Laws
  Austl. Cap. Terr., A.C.T. Laws
Laws of the Bavarians
  L. Baivar., L. Boior, L.Bai.
Laws of the Canal Zone
  L.C.Z.
Laws of the General Assembly of the Commonwealth of Pennsylvania
  Pa. Laws
Laws of the Lombards
  LL. Longobard
Laws of the Ripuarians
  L. Ripuar.
Laws of the State of Maine
  Me. Laws
Laws of the State of New Hampshire
  N.H. Laws

Laws of the United States
  L.U.S.
Laws of the Visigoths
  LL. Wisegotho.
Laws of Utah
  Utah Laws
Laws of Vermont
  Vt. Acts
Laws of Virginia
  L.V.
Laws of Washington
  Wash. Laws
Laws of William the Bastard
  LL. Wm. Noth.
Laws of William the Conqueror
  LL. Wm. Conq.
Laws of Visby
  Leg. Wisb., Wisb.
Laws of Wisconsin
  Wis. Laws
Laws of Women
  Laws Wom.
Law's Practice in United States Courts
  Law Pr., Law U.S. Cts.
Law's United States Patent Cases
  Law Pat.
Lawson on Contracts
  Law. Con., Laws. Cont.
Lawson on Expert and Opinion Evidence
  Lawson, Exp. Ev.
Lawson on Presumptive Evidence
  Lawson, Pres. Ev.
Lawson on Rights, Remedies and Practice
  Lawson, Rights, Rem. & Pr.
Lawson on the Law of Usages and Customs
  Lawson, Usages & Cust.
Lawson's Notes of Decisions, Registration
  L.

Lawson's Registration Cases
Lawson's Reg. Cas., Law Reg.
Cas., Laws. Reg. Cas.

Lawting Court Acts, Scotland
Act.Lawt.Ct.

Lawyer[s, s', 's]
Law, Lawy., Law.

Lawyer and Banker
L. & Bank., Law. & Bank.

**Lawyer and Banker and Central
Law Journal**
Law & Banker, Lawyer &
Banker

Lawyer and Law Notes
Lawy. & L.N., Law. & L.N.

Lawyer of the Americas
Law. Am., Law. Americas

Lawyers'and Bankers' Quarterly
Law. & Bank.

**Lawyer's and Magistrate's Maga-
zine**
Law. & Magis. Mag., Law. &
Mag.

Lawyers Committee News
Law. Committee News

**Lawyers Cooperative Publishing
Co.**
Lawyers Co-op

**Lawyers' Edition, United States
Supreme Court Reports**
L.Ed., L.Ed. (U.S.), Law. Ed.,
L.E., U.S. L. Ed.

**Lawyers' Edition, United States
Supreme Court Reports, Sec-
ond Series**
L.E.2d, U.S.L. Ed. 2d

Lawyers' Guild Monthly
Law. Guild M.

Lawyers' Guild Review
Law. Guild Rev.

Lawyers' Magazine
Lawy. Mag.

**Lawyers' Manual on Professional
Conduct**
Laws. Man. on Prof. Conduct
(ABA/BNA)

Lawyers Medical Journal
Law. Med. J., Lawy. Med. J.,
Lawyers' Med. J.

Lawyers' Reports Annotated
L.A., Lawy. Rep. Ann., Lawyers'
Rep. Ann., Lawyers' Rep. Annotated, Lawyers' Reports Annotated, L.R. Ann., L.R.A.

**Lawyers' Reports Annotated,
New Series**
Lns, L.R.A. (N.S.), L.R.A.N.S.

**Lawyers' Review, Seattle, Wash-
ington**
Lawy. Rev., Lawyer's Rev.

**Lawyers Title Guaranty Funds
News**
Law. Title Guar. Funds News

**Lawyers' Title Guaranty Funds
Newsletter**
L.T.G.F. Newl.

Lay's English Chancery Reports
Lay

**Lee and Murphy's Sales and
Credit Transactions Handbook**
SCT

**Le Marchant's Gardner Peerage
Case**
Le Mar.

Leach's Club Cases
Leach Cl. Cas.

Leach's English Crown Cases
L.C.C., Leach C.L., Leach C.C.,
Leach, Cr. Cas., Leach.

**Leadam and Baldwin's Select
Cases before the King's Council**
L. & B.

Leadam's Select Cases before King's Council in the Star Chamber (Selden Society Publications, 16 and 25)
Leadam
Leadam's Selected Cases in the Couret of Requests (Selden Society Publications, 12)
Leadam Req.
Leader Law Reports, Ceylon
Lead.
Leader Law Reports, South Africa
Lead. L.R., L.L.R.
Leading Cases
L.C.
Leading Cases Annotated
L.C.A.
Leading Cases in Equity by White and Tudor
Lead. Cas. Eq., Lead. Cas. in Eq., Lead Cas. In. Eq. (Eng.)
Leading Cases on Buddhist Law
Chan Toon.
League of Conservation Voters
L.C.V.
League of Nations
L.N., Lo N
League of Nations Official Journal
League of Nations Off. J., League of Nations O.J.
League of Nations Official Journal, Special Supplement
League of Nations O.J., Spec.Supp.
League of Nations Treaty Series
L.N.T.S.
League of Nations Yearbook
Y.B. League
League of Red Cross Societies
LICROSS
League of Women Voters
LWV

Leake and Bullen's Precedents of Pleading
L. & B. Prec.
Leake on Contracts
Leake, Cont., Leake
Leake's Digest of the Law of Property in Land
Leake, Leake Land
Leaming and Spicer's Laws, Grants, Concessions and Original Constitutions
Leam. & Spic.
Leapingwell on the Roman Civil Law
Leap. Rom. Civ. L.
Learning and the Law
Learn. & L., Learn. & Law
Lea's Tennessee Reports
B.J. Lea, Lea.
Leasehold
L/H
Lebanon
Leb.
Lebanon County Legal Journal
Lebanon, Lebanon Co. L.J.(Pa.)
Lecture
Lect.
Lee and Hardwicke's Cases Tempore, England
Cas.t.Hard., Hardw. Cas. Temp., Cas.t.Hardw., Cas.t.H.
Lee on Captures
Lee Cap.
Leembruggen and Asirvatham's Appeal Court Reports, Ceylon
L. & A.
Lee's Abstracts of Title
Lee Abs.
Lee's Cases Tempore, England
Ca.t.Lee, Cas.temp.Lee

Lee's Cases Tempore Hardwicke
Hardw., Hardw. (Eng.),
Cas.t.Hard. (by Lee),
Cas.t.Hardw., Cas.& H.
Lee's Dictionary of Practice
Lee, Dict.
Lee's English Ecclesiastical Reports
Lee Eccl., Lee
Lee's English King's Bench Reports Tempore Hardwicke, Annaly Edition
Annaly
Lee's English King's Bench Reports Tempore Hardwicke
Lee & H., Lee t. Hardw., Lee t.
Hard., Rep.t.Hard.,
Rep.t.Hardw.
Lee's Law and Practice of Bankruptcy
Lee Bank.
Lee's Laws of Shipping
Lee Ship.
Lee's Reports (9-12 California)
Lee
Leese's Reports (26 Nebraska)
Leese
Lefevre's Parliamentary Decisions, by Bourke
Lef. Dec.
Lefroy and Cassel's Practice Cases
Lef. & Cas., L. & C.
Lefroy's English and Canal Cases
Lefroy
Lefroy's Irish Criminal Law
Lef. Cr. L.
Legal
Legal
Legal Action Group
L.A.G.
Legal Action Group Bulletin
L.A.G. Bull.

Legal Administrator
Legal Ad.
Legal Advertiser
Legal Adv.
Legal Adviser
L.A., Legal Adv., Leg. Adv.
Legal Aid Review
Leg. Aid Rev., Legal Aid Rev.
Legal and Insurance Reporter
Leg. & Ins. Rept., Leg. & Ins.
Rep., Leg. & Ins. R.
Legal Aspects of Medical Practice
Legal Asp. Med. Prac., Legal Aspects Med. Prac.
Legal Bibliography
Leg. Bib., Leg. Bibl.
Legal Chronicle
Leg. Chron.
Legal Chronicle Reports, Edited by Foster
Foster, Leg. Chron. Rep.
Legal Corporation
LC
Legal Economics
Leg. Econ., Legal Econ.
Legal Education Institute, United States Civil Service Commission
LEICSC
Legal Education Newsletter
Legal Educ. Newsl.
Legal Education Review
Legal Educ. Rev.
Legal Examiner
Leg. Exam.
Legal Examiner and Law Chronicle
Leg. Exam. & L.C.
Legal Examiner Medical Jurist
Leg. Exam. & Med. J.
Legal Examiner, New Series
Leg. Exam. N.S.

Legal Examiner Weekly Reporter
Leg. Exam. W.R.
Legal Exchange
Leg. Exch.
Legal Executive
Leg. Exec.
Legal Gazette, Pennsylvania
Leg. Gaz., Legal Gazette, Ph.
Leg. Gaz., Pa. Leg. Gaz., Pa.
L.G., Pa. Leg. Gaz., Pa. L.G., Legal Gaz. (Pa.)
Legal Gazette Reports, Pennsylvania
Leg. Gaz., Legal Gazette, Ph.
Leg. Gaz., Pa. Leg. Gaz., Pa.
L.G., Pa. Leg. Gaz., Pa. L.G., Legal Gaz. (Pa.)
Legal Guide
Leg. G.
Legal Historian
Leg. Hist.
Legal History
Leg. Hist.
Legal Information Bulletin
Leg. Inf. Bul.
Legal Inquirer
Leg. Inq.
Legal Intelligence
L.I., Intelligencer, Leg. Intel.,
Leg. Intell., Leg. Inti., Legal
Int., Legal Intel., Legal Intell.,
Legal Intelligencer, Leg. Int.
Legal Maxims with Observations by George Frederick Wharton
Whart.
Legal Medical Quarterly
Legal Med. Q., L.M.Q.
Legal Medicine
Leg. Med.
Legal Medicine Annual
Legal Med. Ann.

Legal Member of the Town Planning Institute
L.M.T.P.J.
Legal Miscellany
Leg. Misc.
Legal Miscellany and Review
Leg. Misc. & Rev.
Legal Monthly Digest
Leg. M. Dig., L.M.D.
Legal News
L.N., Leg. News
Legal Notes and Viewpoints Quarterly
Leg. Notes & View. Q.
Legal Notes on Local Government
Leg. Notes
Legal Notification
L.N.
Legal Observer
Legal Obser., L.O., Leg. Obs.
Legal Observer and Solicitor's Journal
Leg. Obs.
Legal Opinion[s]
L.O., Leg. Op., Leg. Ops.
Legal Opinions of the Office of General Counsel of the Law Enforcement Assistance Administration
L.E.A.A. Legal Op.
Legal Practitioner and Solicitors' Journal
Leg. Pract. & Sol. J.
Legal Record
Leg. Rec.
Legal Record Reports
Leg. Rec. Rep., Leg. R.
Legal Reference Services Quarterly
Legal Reference Services Q.
Legal Reformer
Leg. Ref.

Legal Remembrancer
Leg. Rem.
Legal Reporter
Leg. Rep., Leg. Rep.
Legal Reporter, Irish Courts
Leg. Rep. (Ir.), Leg. Rep.
Legal Reporter, Parallel to Shannon Cases, Tennessee
Leg. R. (Tenn.)
Legal Reporter, New Series, Tennessee
Legal Rep.
Legal Research Journal
Leg. Res. J., Legal Res. J., Legal Research J.
Legal Response: Child Advocacy and Protection
Legal Resp. Child Adv. Protection
Legal Review
Leg. Rev.
Legal Service Bulletin
Leg. Serv. Bull.
Legal Service Bulletin, American Bankers' Association
Leg. Serv. Bull.
Legal Services Bulletin
Legal Services Bull.
Legal Studies
Legal Stud.
Legal Studies Forum
Legal Stud. Forum
Legal Tender Cases
Leg. T. Cas.
Legal Times
Legal Times
Legal Video Review
Legal Video Rev.
Legal World
Leg. W.
Legal Yearbook
Leg. Y.B.

Leges (laws) (Lat.)
Ll.
Leges Fluviorum
Leg. Fluv.
Leges Portuum
Leg. Port.
Legge on Outlawry
Leg. Out., Legg. Out.
Legge's Supreme Court Cases, New South Wales
Legge.
Leggett on Bills of Lading
Legg. Bills L.
Leggett's Reports, India
Legg.
Leggo's Chancery Forms
Leg. Ch. Forms
Leggo's Chancery Practice
Leg. Ch. Pr.
Legislat[ion, ive]
Leg., Legis.
Legislative Assembly
L.A.
Legislative Studies Quarterly
Legis. Stud. Q., Leg. Stud. Q.
Legislature
Leg., Legis.
Leguleian, The
Legul.
Lehigh County Law Journal, Pennsylvania
Leh. Co. L.J. (Pa.), Leh. L.J., Leh., Lehigh Co. L.J., Lehigh L.J.
Lehigh Valley Law Reporter, Pennsylvania
Leh. V.L.R. (Pa.), Lehigh, Lehigh Val. L. Rep., Lehigh Val. Law Rep., Lehigh Val. L.R., L.V. Rep.
Leiby's Florida Construction Law Manual
FCLM

Leicester Records, by Bateson
  Bateson
Leicester's Straits Law Reports
  S.L.R.Leicester, S.L.R.Leic.
Leiden Journal of International Law
  Leiden J. Int'l L.
Leigh and Cave's English Crown Cases Reserved
  L. & C.C.C., L. & C., Leigh & C.C.C., Le. & Ca., Leigh & C.
Leigh and Dalzell on Conversion of Property
  Leigh & D. Conv., L. & D. Conv.
Leigh and Le Marchant on Elections
  L. & LeM., Leigh & L.M. Elec.
Leigh's Abridgment of the Law of Nisi Prius
  Leigh Abr., Leigh N.P.
Leigh's Game Act
  Leigh G.A.
Leigh's Virginia Supreme Court Reports
  Leigh, Leigh (Va.)
Leith's Blackstone on Real Property
  Leith Black.
Leith's Real Property Statutes, Ontario
  Leith R. Pr.
Lely and Foulkes on Elections
  Lely & F. Elec.
Lely and Foulkes on Judicature Acts
  Lely & F. Jud. Acts
Lely and Foulkes on Licensing Acts
  Lely & F. Lic. Acts
Lely on Regulation of Railway Acts
  Lely Railw.

Lending Law Forum
  Lending L.F.
Leonard's English King's Bench, Common Pleas and Exchequer Reports
  Leo., Leon.
Leonard's Louisiana Digest of United States Cases
  Leon. La. Dig.
Leonard's Precedents in County Courts
  Leon. Prec.
Les Cahiers de Droit
  C. de D.
Les Jugemens d'Oleron
  J.d'Ol.
Les Termes de la Ley
  Term. de la L.
Lesotho Law Journal
  Lesotho L.J.
Lester and Butler's Supplement to Lester's Georgia Reports
  Lester & B., Lest. & But., Lester Supp.
Lester's Decisions in Public Land Cases
  Lest. P.L.
Lester's Reports (31-33 Georgia)
  Lester.
Letter of Authority
  L/A
Letter of Credits
  Letter Cred.
Levi on International Commercial Law
  Levi Com. L.
Levi on Mercantile Law
  Levi Merc. L.
Levinge's Irish Justice of the Peace
  Lev. J.P.
Levinz's Entries
  Lev. Ent.

**Levinz's King's Bench and Com-
mon Pleas Reports**
    Lev.
Lewin on Apportionment
    Lew. App.
Lewin on Trusts
    Lewin, Lew. Tr.
**Lewin's English Crown Cases Re-
served**
    Lewin C.C. (Eng.), Lew. Tr., Le-
    win C.C., Lew. C.C., Lewin, Cr.
    Cas., Lew.
Lewis' Criminal Law
    Lew. C.L.
**Lewis' Digest of United States
Criminal Law**
    Lew. Dig. Cr. L., Lew. U.S. Cr.
    L.
Lewis' East India Penal Code
    Lew. Ind. Pen.
Lewis' Election Manual
    Lew. Elec.
Lewis' Kentucky Law Reporter
    Lewis
Lewis' Law of Perpetuity
    Lewis, Perp.
**Lewis' Leading Cases on Public
Land Law**
    Lew. L. Cas.
Lewis on Bonds and Securities
    Lew. B. & S.
Lewis on Eminent Domain
    Lewis, Em. Dom.
Lewis on Equity Drafting
    Lew. Eq. Dr.
**Lewis on Land Titles in Philadel-
phia**
    Lew. L.T.
Lewis on Stocks, Bonds, & c.
    Lew. St.
**Lewis' Principles of Conveyanc-
ing**
    Lew. Conv.

Lewis' Reports (1 Nevada)
    Lewis, Lew.
**Lewis' Reports (29-35 Missouri
Appeals)**
    Lewis, Lew.
Lewis's Law of Perpetuities
    Lew. Perp.
Lex Custumaria
    Lex Cust.
**Lex et Scientia. Official Organ of
the International Academy of
Law and Science**
    Lex et Scientia, Lex & Sci.
Lex Maneriorum
    Lex Man.
Lex Mercatoria Americana
    Lex Mer. Am.
**Lex Mercatoria Rediviva, by
Beawes**
    Lex Merc. Red.
Lex Parliamentaria
    Lex Parl.
Ley on Wards and Liveries
    Ley Wards
Ley's Court of Star Chamber
    Ley
Ley's Court of Wards Reports
    Ley
**Ley's King's Bench Reports, Eng-
land**
    Leigh, Ley
Liability
    Liab.
Libel and Slander
    Lib. & Sl.
Liber
    L.
**Liber Assisarum or Pleas of the
Crown, Book of Assizes (Pt. 5 of
Yearbooks)**
    Lib. Ass., Ass.

Liber Feudorum (at the end of the Corpus Juris Civilis)
Lib. Feud.
Liber Intrationum (Old Book of Entries)
Entries, Old Book of, Lib. Int., Lib. Intr.
Liber Niger Scaccarii (Black Book of the Exchequer)
Lib. Nig. Scacc., L.N., Lib. Nig.
Liber Placitandi (Book of Pleading)
Lib. Pl.
Liber Ramesiensis (Book of Ramsey)
Lib. Rames.
Liber Ruber Scaccarii (Red Book of the Exchequer)
Lib. Rub. Scacc., Lib. Rub.
Liberal Party
Lib.
Liberia
Lib.
Liberian Law
Liberian L.
Liberian Law Journal
Liberian L.J.
Liberties
Lib.
Librarian
Lib., Libr.
Library[ies]
Libr., Lib., Libr.
Library Association
L.A.
Library Journal
L.J.
Library of Congress
LC, L.C.
Library of Congress Quarterly
Lib. Cong. Q.
Library of Law and Equity
Lib. L. & Eq.

Licenses and Permits
License & P.
Licensing Act
L.A.
Licensing Law and Business Report
Licensing L. & Bus. Rep.
Licentiate of Laws
LL. L.
Lieber on Civil Liberty and Self Government
Lieber Civ. Lib.
Lieber's Hermeneutics
Lieb. Herm.
Liechtenstein
Liech.
Life Cases, Including Health and Accident (Insurance Case Series), Commerce Clearing House
Life C.
Life (Health and Accident) Cases, Commerce Clearing House
Life Cas.
Life (Health and Accident) Cases, Commerce Clearing House, Second Series
Life Cas.2d, Life Health & Accid. Ins. Cas. 2d (CCH)
Life Insurance Trust
L.I.T.
Life Tenants and Remainderman
Life Ten.
Ligon's Alabama Digest
Lig. Dig.
Lilly's Abridgment, or Practical Register
Lil. Abr., L. Abr., Lilly, Abr.
Lilly's Conveyancer
Lil. Conv.
Lilly's English Assize Reports
Lil., Lib. Plac., Lilly Assize, Lilly Assize (Eng.), Lilly

Lilly's Entries
Lill. Ent.
Lilly's Practical Register
Lil. Reg., L.P.R.
Limitation of Action
Lim. Act.
Limited
L., Ltd.
Limited Partnership
L.P.
Lincoln Law Review
Lincoln L. Rev.
Lincoln's Inn Library
L.I.L.
Lindewoode's Provinciales
Lind. Pr.
Lindley on Companies
Lindl. Co., Lindley Comp., Lindley.
Lindley on Partnerships
Lindley P., Lindley Part., Lindl. Partn., Lind. Part.
Lindley's Study of Jurisprudence
Lind. Jur.
Lindsay on Probates
Lind. Prob.
Linn on the Laws of the Province of Pennsylvania
Linn, Laws Prov. Pa.
Linn's Index of Pennsylvania Reports
Linn Ind.
Lipenius' Bibliotheca Juridica
Lip. Bib. Jur.
Lippitt's Massachusetts Criminal Law
Lipp. Cr. L.
Liquor Control Law Reports, Commerce Clearing House
Liquor Cont. L. Rep. (CCH)
Liquor Control Law Service, Commerce Clearing House
Liquor Cont. L. Serv.(CCH)

Liquor Liability Journal, Commerce Clearing House
Liquor Liab. J.
Lis Pendens (pending case or matter) (Lat.)
Lis Pen.
Litigation
Litig.
Littell and Swigert's Digest of Kentucky Statute Law
Litt. & S. St. Law
Littell's Kentucky Statute Law
Litt. Comp. Laws
Littell's Reports (11-15 Kentucky)
Littell., Litt., Lit., Litt. (Ky.)
Littell's Select Kentucky Cases
Litt. Sel. Cas., Lit. Sel. Ca.
Littleton and Blatchley's Insurance Digest
L. & B. Ins. Dig., Lit. & Bl. Dig.
Littleton's English Common Pleas and Exchequer Reports
Lit., Litt., Litt. Rep., Littleton.
Littleton's Tenures
Lit., Litt. Ten.
Livermore on Principal and Agent
Liverm. Ag., Livermore, Ag., Liv. Ag.
Livermore's Dissertation on the Contrariety of Laws
Liv. Dis.
Liverpool Law Review
Liverpool L. Rev.
Livingston's Cases in Error, New York
Liv. Cas.
Livingston's Judicial Opinions, New York
Liv. Jud. Op. (or Cas.), Liv. Judic. Op.
Livingston's Law Magazine
Liv. L. Mag., Liv. Law Mag.

Livingston's Law Register, New York
Liv. L. Reg.
Livingston's Louisiana Criminal Code
Liv. La. Cr. Code
Livingston's Mayor's Court Reports, New York
Liv.
Livingston's Monthly Law Magazine
Livingston's M.L. Mag.
Livingston's System of United States Penal Laws
Liv. U.S. Pen. Co.
Lizar's Scotch Exchequer Cases
Liz. Sc. 'Exch., Lizars
Lloyd
Ll.
Lloyd and Goold's Irish Chancery Reports Tempore Plunkett
Lloyd & Goold (t.Plunkett) (Ir.), Cas. t. Plunk., L. & G. temp. Plunk., L. & G.t.P., Ll. & G.t. Pl., L. & G.t. Plunk., Ll. & G.t.P.
Lloyd and Goold's Irish Chancery Reports Tempore Sugden
L. & G. temp. Sugd., L. & G.t.S., Lloyd & Goold (t.Sugden) (Ir.), L. & G.t. Sug., Ll. & G.t.S.
Lloyd and Welsby's Commercial and Mercantile Cases, England
Ll. & Weis., L. & Welsb., Lloyd & W., Ll. & W., L. & W.
Lloyd on Prohibition
Ll. Pr.
Lloyd on Succession Laws
Ll. Suc.
Lloyd on Trade-Marks
Ll. Tr. M.
Lloyd's Compensation for Lands
Ll. Comp

Lloyd's County Courts Practice
Ll. C.C. Pr.
Lloyd's Law Reports, England
Lloyd's L. Rep., Lloyd, L.R.
Lloyd's List
Lloyd's List., Lloyd List
Lloyd's List Law Reports, England
Ll. Rep., Ll. L.L.R., Ll. L.R., Ll. L. Rep., Ll. List. L.R., Lloyd's List L.R., Lloyd's Rep.
Lloyd's List Prize Cases Reports, England
Ll. Pr. Cas.Ll. L. Pr. Cas., Lloyd's Pr. Cas., Lloyd's Prize Cas., Lloyd Pr. Cas.
Lloyd's List Prize Cases, New Series, England
Ll. Pr. Cas. N.S.
Lloyd's List Prize Cases Reports, 2nd Series, England
Ll. R. Pr. Cas., Lloyd Pr. Cas. N.S., LL. Pr. Cas. N.S.
Lloyds Maritime and Commercial Law Quarterly
Lloyds Mar. & Com. L.Q., LMCLQ
Lloyd's Maritime Law Newsletter
Ll. Mar. L.N., Lloyd's Mar. L.N.
Lloyd's Statutes of Practical Utility
Ll. St.
Lloyd's Supreme Court of Judicature Acts
Ll. Jud. Act
Lobingier's Extraterritorial Cases, United States Court for China
Exter. Ca., Extra. Ca., Lobin.
Local
Loc.
Local Acts
Loc. Acts

Local Advisory Board Procedural Regulation, Office of Rent Stabilization. Economic Stabilization Agency
LABPR
Local Authority
L.A.
Local Code
Loc. Code
Local Courts and Municipal Gazette
Local Ct. & Mun. Gaz., Loc. Ct. Gaz.
Local Finance
Local Fin.
Local Government
Loc. Gov.
Local Government and Magisterial Reports, England
Local Gov., Local Gov't
Local Government Appeals Tribunal Reports, New South Wales
L.G.A.T.R. (NSW)
Local Government Board
L.G.B.
Local Government Bulletin
L.G.B.
Local Government Chronicle
L.G.C., Loc. Gov. Chron.
Local Government Chronicle and Magisterial Reporter, England
Loc. Govt. Chr. & Mag. Rep.
Local Government Reports, England
L.G.R., L.G.R. (Eng.)
Local Government Reports, New South Wales
L.G.R. (N.S.W.), L.G.R.A., Local Gov. R. Aust., Local Govt. R. Austl., Local Govt. R. (N.S.W.), L.G.R.

Local Government Reports, New Zealand
N.Z.L.G.R.
Local Government Reports of Australia
L.G.R.A., Local Gov. R. Aust., Local Govt. R. Austl.
Local Government Review
L.G. Rev., Loc. Gov. Rev., Loc. Govt. Rev.
Local Laws
Loc. Laws.
Loccenius' de Jure Maritimo et Navali
Locc. de Jur. Mar., Locc.
Locke on Foreign Attachment
Lock. For. At.
Locke's Game Laws
Lock. G.L.
Lockwood's Reversed Cases, New York
Lock. Rev. Ca. Lock. Rev. Cas.
Loco Citato (in the place cited) (Lat.)
Loc. cit.
Locus Sigilli (the place of the seal) (Lat.)
L.S.
Locus Standi Reports
L.S.R., Locus Standi
Lofft on the Law of Libels
Lofft Lib.
Lofft's Elements of Universal Law
Lofft Un. L.
Lofft's English King's Bench Reports
Lofft's Rep; Loft., Lofft.
Lofft's Maxims, Appended to Lofft's Reports
Lofft, Append., Lofft Max.
Logan's Compendium of Ancient Law
Log. Comp.

Lois Recentes du Canada
  Log. Comp.
Lomas's City Hall Reporter, New York City
  Lom. C.H. Rep., C.H.Rep., City H.Rep., City Hall Rep., City Hall Rep.(NY)
Lomax on Executors
  Lomax, Ex'rs., Lom. Ex.
Lomax's Digest of Real Property
  Lom. Dig.
London County Council
  L.C.C.
London Encyclopedia
  Lond.
London Gazette
  Lond.Gaz.
London Jurist, New Series
  Lond. Jur. N.S.
London Jurist Reports
  Lond. Jur.
London Law Magazine
  Lond. L. Mag., Lond. L.M.
Long and Russell's Election Cases, Massachusetts
  Long & R.
Long Beach Bar Bulletin
  Long Beach B. Bull.
Long on Irrigation
  Long, Irr.
Long on Sales of Personal Property
  Long S.
Long Quinto (Yearbooks, Part X)
  Long.Q.
Long-Range Navigation
  LORAN
Longfield and Townsend's Irish Exchequer Reports
  Longf. & T., L. & T., Longf. & T., Long. & T.

Longfield on Distress and Replevin
  Longf. Dist.
Longfield on Ejectment
  Longf. Ej.
Longshoremen's and Harbor Worker's Compensation Act
  L.H.C.A.
Longworth House Office Building
  L.H.O.B.
Lonsdale's Statute Criminal Law
  Lons. Cr. L.
Lord Advocate
  L. Adv.
Lord Advocate of Scotland
  L.A.
Lord Birkenhead's Judgments, House of Lords
  Ld. Birk.
Lord Brougham's Speeches
  Ld. Br. Sp.
Lord Chancellor
  C., L.C.
Lord Chancellor's Department
  L.C.D.
Lord Chancellor's Legal Aid Advisory Committee
  L.A.A.C.
Lord Chancellor's Office
  L.C.O.
Lord Chief Baron
  L.C.B.
Lord Chief Justice
  L.C.J., C.J.
Lord Great Chamberlain
  L.G.C.
Lord High Chancellor
  L.H.C., L.C.
Lord Justice[s]
  L.J.
Lord Justice-General of Scotland
  L.J.G.

Lord Keeper of the Great Seal
　L.K.
Lord President of the Court of Session, Scotland
　L.P.
Lords of the Privy Council
　L.P.C.
Lorenz's Appeal Reports, Ceylon
　Lorenz. App. R.
Lorenz's Ceylon Reports
　Lorenz
Lorimer's Handbook of Scotch Law
　Lor. Sc. L.
Lorimer's Institutes of Law
　Lor. Inst.
Loring and Russell's Massachusetts Election Cases
　Mass. Election Cases, Lor. &
　Russ., Loring & Russell, L. &
　R., L. & R. Election Cases,
　Loring & Russel El. Cases,
　Mass. E.C., L. & R.
Los Angeles
　L.A.
Los Angeles Bar Association Bulletin
　Los Angeles B.A.B.,
　B.A.Bull.L.A.
Los Angeles Bar Bulletin
　L.A.B., L.A.B. Bull., Los Angeles B. Bull., Los Angeles Bar Bull.
Los Angeles Bar Journal
　L.A.B.J.
Los Angeles Board of Public Utilities
　Los Angeles Bd. P.U.
Los Angeles Law Review
　Los Angeles L. Rev.
Los Angeles Lawyer
　L.A. Law

Loss and Damage Review
　Loss & Dam. Rev.
Loss' Security Regulations
　Loss, Sec. Reg.
Lost and Destroyed Instruments
　Lost Instr.
Loughborough's Digest of Kentucky Statute Law
　St. Law
Louisiana
　La., Lou.
Louisiana Acts of the Legislature
　La. Acts
Louisiana Administrative Code
　La. Admin. Code
Louisiana Administrative Register
　La. Admin. Reg.
Louisiana Annual Reports
　La. Ann., La. A., Annual R., L.
　Ann., La. An. R., La. An. Rep.,
　La. Ann. Reps., Louisiana Ann.,
　Louisiana Ann.Rep.
Louisiana Annuals
　A
Louisiana Bar
　La. B., La. Bar.
Louisiana Bar Association
　La. B.A.
Louisiana Bar Journal
　La. Bar J., La. B.J.
Louisiana Civil Code
　Code La.
Louisiana Constitution
　La. Const.
Louisiana Court of Appeals (Parish of Orleans)
　La. A. (Orleans)
Louisiana Courts of Appeals Reports
　La. A., L. Ap., La. App., La. A.

Louisiana Law Journal
Lou. L. Jour., Lou. L.J., La. L.J., La. L.J.

Louisiana Law Review
La. L. Rev., La. L.R., Lou. L. Rev., Louisiana L. Rev.

Louisiana Legal News
Lou. Leg. N.

Louisiana Public Service Commission Reports
La. P.S.C.

Louisiana Railroad Commission
La. R.C.

Louisiana Reports
L., La., La. R., La. Rep., La. Reports, Law Rep., Lou. R., Lou. Reps., Louis. Rep., Louisiana Rep., L.R.

Louisiana Session Law Service
La. Sess. Law Serv.

Louisiana State Bar
LSB

Louisiana State Bar Association
La. S.B.A.

Louisiana State University Quarterly
La. S.U.Q.

Louisiana Statutes Annotated
L.S.A.

Louisiana Statutes Annotated, Civil Code
L.S.A.C.R.

Louisiana Statutes Annotated, Code of Civil Procedure
L.S.A.C.C.P.

Louisiana Statutes Annotated, Code of Criminal Procedure
L.S.A.C.Cr.P.

Louisiana Statutes Annotated, Revised Statutes
L.S.A.R.S.

Louisiana Supreme Court Condensed Reports
Cond. Lou'a. Reps., Condensed Rep.

Louisiana Supreme Court Reports
La.

Louisiana Term Reports (3-12 Martin's Louisiana)
La. T.R.

Louisiana Term Reports, New Series
La. T.R. (N.S.)

Louisville Lawyer
Louisville Law

Lovelass on Wills
Lov. W.

Lovesy on Arbitration
Love. Arb.

Lovesy on Bankruptcy Act
Love. Bank.

Lowell's Decisions
Low. Dec. (F)

Lowell's United States District Court Reports
Low., Lowell, Low. Dis.

Lower Burma Printed Judgments
P.J.L.B.

Lower Burma Rulings
L.B.R.

Lower Burma Selected Judgments
S.J.L.B.

Lower Canada
L.C.

Lower Canada Civil Code
L.C.C.C.

Lower Canada Civil Procedure
L.C.C.P.

Lower Canada Jurist
L.C. Jur., Low. Can. Jurist, Lower Can. Jur., Low. Can. Jur., J., L.C.J.

Lower Canada Law Journal
L.C.L. Jo., Low. Can. L.J.,
L.C.L.J., L.J.

Lower Canada Reports
Low. Can., Low. Can. R., Lower
Can., L.C.R., Low. Can. Rep.

Lower Canada Reports, Seig-
norial Questions
L.C. Rep. S. Qu., Lower Can.
S.Q., Low. Can. Rep. S.Q.,
Seign. Rep., Low. C. Seign.

Lower Courts and Municipal Ga-
zette
L.C. & M. Gaz.

Lower Courts Gazette
L.C.G.

Lower Provinces Code, India
Low. Pr. Code

Lowndes and Maxwell's English
Bail Court Reports
Bail Cr. Rep., Bail Ct. Cas., Bail
Ct. Rep., Lowndes & M., Lownd.
& M., Lowndes & M. (Eng.),
Lown. & M., L. & M.

Lowndes on Collisions at Sea
Lownd. Col.

Lowndes on Copyright
Lownd. Cop.

Lowndes on General Average
Lownd. Av.

Lowndes on Insurance
Lownd. Ins.

Lowndes on Legacies
Lown. Leg, Lownd. Leg.

Lowndes, Maxwell and Pollock's
English Bail Court Reports
Lowndes, M. & P., Pr. Rep.
B.C., Lownd. M. & P., Lown. M.
& P., L.M. & P.

Loyalty Review Board
LRB

Loyola
Loy.

Loyola Consumer Law Reporter
Loy. Consumer L. Rep.

Loyola Consumer Protection
Journal
Loy. Con. Prot. J., Loy. Cons.
Prot. J.

Loyola Digest
Loy. Dig., Loyola Dig.

Loyola Law Journal
Loyola L.J., Loy. L.J.

Loyola Law Review
Lo. L.R., Loyola L. Rev., Loy. R,
Loy. L. Rev.

Loyola Lawyer
Loy. Law.

Loyola of Los Angeles Entertain-
ment Law Journal
Loy. L.A. Ent. L. J., Loy. Ent.
L.J.

Loyola of Los Angeles Interna-
tional and Comparative Law
Journal
Loyola Los. Ang. Int'l & Comp.
L. Ann., Loy. L.A. Int'l & Comp.
L.J., Loy. L.A. Int'l & Comp. L.
Ann.

Loyola of Los Angeles Law Re-
view
Loy. L. A. Rev., Loyola of Los
Angeles L. Rev.

Loyola University Consumer Law
Reporter
Loy. Consumer L. Rep.

Loyola University Law Journal
Loyola U.L.J. (Chicago), Loy.
U.L.J.

Loyola University of Chicago
Law Journal
Loyola Univ. L. Rev., Loy. Chi.
L.J., Loy. U. Chi. L.J., Loyola U.
Chi. L.J., Loyola Univ. of Chi-
cago L.J.

Loyola University of Los Angeles Law Review
Loy. L.A. L. Rev., Loyola U.L. Rev. (LA), Loyola U.L.A.L. Rev.

Loyola University School of Law
LUSL

Lube on Equity Pleading
Lube Eq. (or Pl.)

Lucas' Reports (Modern Reports)
Lucas., Luc.

Ludden's Reports (43-44 Maine)
Ludd., Ludden.

Luder's English Election Cases
Luders Elec. Cas. (Eng), Lud. El. Cas., Luder Elec. Cas., Lud.E.C.

Ludlow and Jenkyns on the Law of Trade-Marks
L. & J. Tr. Mar., Lud. & J. Tr. M.

Lumley on Bastardy
Lum. Bast.

Lumley on Bye-Laws
Lum.B.L.

Lumley on the Law of Annuities
Lum. Ann.

Lumley on the Law of Settlements
Lum. Sett.

Lumley's Public Health Acts
Lum. Pub. H.

Lumley's Parliamentary Practice
Lum. Parl. Pr.

Lumley's Poor Law Cases
Lumley P.L.C., Lum.P.L.Cas., Lum.P.L.C.

Lumpkin's Reports (59-77 Georgia)
Lumpkin

Lund on Patents
Lund Pat.

L'Unification du droit Annuaire/ Unification of Law Yearbook
Ann. Unidroit

Lushington on Prize Law
Lush. Pr. L.

Lushington's English Admiralty Reports
Lush., Lush. Adm.

Lush's Common Law Practice
Lush. Pr.

Lutwyche's Election Cases
Lut. Elec. Cas.

Lutwyche's (Nelson) English Common Pleas Reports
Lutw. E., N.L.

Lutwyche's English Registration Appeal Cases
Lut. R.C.

Lutwyche's Entries
Lut. Ent.

Lutwyche's Entries and Reports, Common Pleas, England
Lut.E., Lut., Lutw.

Lutwyche's Registration Cases
Lutw. Reg. Cas., Lutw.

Luxembourg
Lux.

Luzerne Law Journal, Pennsylvania
Luzerne L.J. (Pa), Luz. L.J.

Luzerne Law Times, New Series, Pennsylvania
Luz. L.T. (N.S.).

Luzerne Law Times, Old Series, Pennsylvania
Luz, L.T. (O.S.)

Luzerne Law Times, Pennsylvania
Luz. Law T., Luz. L.T.

Luzerne Legal Observer, Pennsylvania
Luzerne Leg. Obs. (Pa.), Luz. Leg. Obs., Luz. L.O.

**Luzerne Legal Register, Pennsyl-
vania**
   Luzerne Leg. Reg. (Pa), L.L.R.,
   Luz. Leg. Reg., Luz. L.R.
**Luzerne Legal Register Reports,
Pennsylvania**
   Luzerne Leg. Reg. R. (Pa),
   Luzerne Leg. Reg. R. (PH), Luz.
   L. Reg. Rep., Luz. Leg. Reg. Rep.
**Lycoming Reporter, Pennsylva-
nia**
   Lycoming R. (Pa.), Lycoming
Lyndwood's Provinciales
   Lynd., Lyndw. Prov., Lynd.
   Prov.

Lyne on Leases for Lives
   Lyne Lea.
Lyne on Renewals
   Lyne on Renew.
Lyne's Irish Chancery Cases
   Lyne
Lyon and Redman on Bills of Sale
   Lyon & R.B.S.
Lyon on the Laws of India
   Lyon Ind. L.
Lyon's Institutes of Justinian
   Lyon Just.

M

Macalpin on Money Lenders
Macalp.Mon.L.

MacArthur and Mackey's District of Columbia Supreme Court Reports.
MacAr. & M., MacArth. & M., MacAr. & Mackey., MacArthur & M., MacArth. & M., McArth. & M.

MacArthur on Courts-Martial
MacArth. Ct. Mar.

MacArthur's Patent Cases
MacAr., MacArth., MacArthur, Mac. A. Pat. Cas., MacAr.Pat.Cas., MacArth. Pat. Cas.

MacArthur's Reports (8-10 District of Columbia)
MacAr., MacArthur, MacArth.

Macaskie on Executors, etc.
Macask. Ex.

Macassey's New Zealand Reports
Mac. N.Z., Macas., Mac.

Macaulay's History of England
Macaulay, Hist. Eng.

Maccala's Breach of Promise Cases
Macc.Cas.

Maccala's Reports (10 Modern Reports) England
Maccl.

MacCarthy's Irish Land Cases
MacCarthy

Macclesfield's Cases in Law and Equity (10 Modern Reports), England
Mccl.

Macclesfield's Trial (Impeachment)
Maccl.Tr.

MacDevitt's Irish Land Cases
MacDev.

Macdevitt's Irish Land Commissioner's Reports
Macd.

Macdonald's Scotch Criminal Law
Macd. Cr. L.

Macdonell and Manson's Great Jurists of the World
GJ.W.

Macdonell's State Trials
St. Tr. N.S.

MacDouall's (Lord Bankton) Institutes of Laws of Scotland
Bankt.

Macdougall's Jamaica Reports
Macd. Jam., Mac.R.

Macfarland's Digest of Mining Cases
Macf. Min.

MacFarlane's Jury Trials
MacF., MacFarl., Macfarlane

MacFarlane's Practice of the Court of Sessions
Macf. Pr.

Macfarlane's Reports, Jury Courts, Scotland
Macf., Mac. F., M'F.R., Macfar.

Macfie on Copyright
Macf. Cop.

MacGillivray and Parkington's Insurance Law
MacGillivray & Parkington

MacGillivray's Copyright Cases
MacG.C., M.C.C., Mac.G.C.C.

Machine[ry]
  Mach.
Machine Readable Cataloging
  MARC
Mackay's Law of Property
  Mack. Law of Prop.
Mackeldey on Modern Civil Law
  Mack. C.L., Mackeld., Mackeld.
  Civil Law
Mackeldey on Roman Law
  Mackeld., Mackeld. Rom. Law,
  Rom. Law
Mackenzie on Bills of Lading
  Mack. B.L.
**Mackenzie's Institutes of the Law
  of Scotland**
  Mack. Inst., Mack.
**Mackenzie's Observations on
  Acts of Parliament**
  Mack. Obs.
**Mackenzie's Studies in Roman
  Law**
  Mack. Rom. Law
**MacKenzie's Treatise on Crimi-
  nal Law**
  Mack. Crim.
**Mackeson and Forbes' Judica-
  ture Acts**
  Mack. & F. Jud. A.
**Mackey's Court of Session Prac-
  tice**
  Mack. Ct. Sess.
**Mackey's District of Columbia Re-
  ports**
  Mackey
**Mackintosh on Law of Nature
  and Nations**
  Mack. Nat.
**Maclachian on Merchant Ship-
  ping**
  Macl. Shipp., Macl. Sh.

**Maclaren on Wills and Succes-
  sions**
  Macl. Wills
Maclaurin's Remarkable Cases
  Macl. Rem. Cas.
**Maclaurin's Scotch Criminal De-
  cisions**
  Macl.
**Maclean and Robinson's Scotch
  Appeal Cases**
  Macl. & R., Macl. & Rob.,
  Maclean & R. (Sc.), M. & R.,
  M.& Rob., Mac. & Rob.,
  Maclean & R., Mac. & R.
**Macleod's Theory and Practice of
  Banking**
  Macl. Bank.
**Macnaghten and Gordon's Eng-
  lish Chancery Reports**
  M. & G., M. & Gord., Mac. & C.,
  Macn. & G. (Eng.), Macn. & G.
Macnaghten on Courts-Martial
  Macn.C. M.
MacNaghten on Hindu Law
  F. Mac. N.
Macnaghten's Criminal Evidence
  Macn.Cr. Ev.
**Macnaghten's Elements of Hindu,
  etc., Law**
  Macn. El. Hind. L.
**Macnaghten's English Chancery
  Reports**
  Mac.
**Macnaghten's (Francis) Bengal
  Reports**
  Macn.Fr.
Macnaghten's Hindu Law Cases
  Macn.
**Macnaghten's Nizamut Adawlut
  Reports, Bengal**
  Macn., Macn. N. A. Beng.

Macnaghten's Select Cases in Chancery Tempore King, England
C.t.K., McNagh., Macn., See also Select Cases in Chancery

Macnaghten's Select Cases, Sudder Dewanny Adawlut, Bengal
Macn., Macn. S.D.A.

Macnally's Rules of Evidence on Pleas of the Crown
McNal. Ev., Macn. Ev.

Macnamara on Nullities and Irregularities in Law
Macn. Nul.

Macomb on Courts-Martial
Mac.C.M., Macomb C.M.

Macpherson, Lee and Bell's Session Cases, Scotland
Macph. L. & B., Macph.

Macpherson on Infancy
Macph. Inf.

Macpherson, Shirreff and Lee's Session Cases, Scotland
Macph. S. & L.

Macpherson's Court of Session Cases, Scotland
Macph.

Macpherson's House of Lords Appeals, Scotland
M. (H.L.)

Macpherson's Practice of the Judicial Committee of the Privy Council
Macph. Pr. C., Macph. Jud. Com.

Macpherson's Privy Council Practice
Macph. Priv. Counc.

Macqueen on Divorce
Macq. Div.

Macqueen on Marriage, Divorce and Legitimacy
Macq. Mar.

Macqueen on Rights and Liabilities of Husband Wife
Macq. H. & W.

Macqueen's Debates on Life-Peerage Question
Macq.D.

Macqueen's Scotch Appeal Cases, House of Lords
Macq. H.L. Cas., Marq. Sc. App. Cas., Macq. Sc. App. Cas., Macq., McQ.

Macrae and Hertslet's English Insolvency Cases
Macr. & H., Mac. & I.

Macrory's Patent Cases, England
Mac. P.C., Macr. P.Cas., Mac. Pat.Cas., Macr., Macr. Pat. Cas.

MacSweeney on Mines, Quarries and Minerals
MacS.

Madagascar
Madag.

Madden on Registration of Deeds
Mad. Reg.

Maddock and Geldart's English Chancery Reports
M. & G., M. & Gel., Madd. & Gel., Mad. & Gel., Madd. & G.

Maddock's English Chancery Practice
Mad. Ch. Pr., Madd. Ch. (Eng.), Madd. Ch. Pr.

Maddock's English Chancery Reports
Mad., Madd. Ch., Madd. Ch. (Eng.), Mad., Madd.

Maddock's Reports (9-18 Montana)
Mad., Madd., Mad. & B., Madd. & B.

Made Perpetual
Made p.

Madhya Bharat Law Reports, India
M.B.L.R.

Madhya Pradesh, India
M.P.Ind.

Madison's (James) Papers
Mad. Papers

Madox's Barona Anglia
Mad. Bar.

Madox's Firma Burgi
Mad. Fir. Burg.

Madox's Formulare Anglicanum
Madox, Mad. Form., Mad.
Form. Angl.

Madox's History of the Exchequer
Mad. Exch., Madox, Mad. Hist.
Exch.

Madras, India
M., Madr.

Madras Code, India
Mad. Co.

Madras Criminal Cases, India
M. Cr. C.

Madras High Court Reports, India
Mad., Mad. H.C., M.H.C.,
M.H.C.R., M.J., Mad. Jur.

Madras Law Journal, India
Madras L.J., Mad. L.J., M.L.J.

Madras Law Journal and Reports, India
Madras L.J.

Madras Law Journal, Criminal, India
Madras L.J. Crim.

Madras Law Reporter, India
Mad. Law Rep., Mad. L.Rep.

Madras Law Times, India
Mad. L.T., M.L.T.

Madras Law Weekly, India
Mad. L.W., M.L.W.

Madras Sadr Diwani Adalat Reports, India
Mad. S.D.A.R.

Madras Select Decrees, India
Mad. Sel. Dec.

Madras Sudder Dewanny Adawlut Reports, India
S.A.D.Mad.

Madras Weekly Notes, India
Mad. W.N., M.W.N.

Madras Weekly Notes, Criminal Cases, India
Mad.W.N.C.C., M.W.N.C.C.

Magazine
Mag.

Magen on Insurance
Mag. Ins.

Magisterial Cases
Mag. Cas.

Magistrate
M., Mag

Magistrate and Constable
Magis. & Const. (Pa.), Mag. &
Con., Mag. & Const.

Magistrate and Municipal and Parochial Lawyer
Mag. & M. & P.L., Mag. Mun.
Par. Law, Mag.

Magistrates Appeal Cases, Malaya
M.A.C.

Magistrates' Association
M.A.

Magistrates' Cases
M.C., Mag. Cas.

Magistrates' Court
Mag. Ct., Magis. Ct., M.C.

Magistrates' Court Reports, New Zealand
M.C.D., M.C.R.

Magna Carta (or Charta)
Mag. Char., Magna Cart.,
Magna Chart.

Magnus and Estrin on Companies
Mag. & E. Comp.
Magnus Rotulus Pipae (the Great Roll of the Exchequer)
Magna Rot. Pip., Mag. Rot.
Magrath's South Carolina Digest
Mag. Dig.
Magruder's Reports (1-2 Maryland)
Mag., Mag. (Md.), Magruder
Mahaffy and Dodson's Road Traffic
Mah. & D.R.T.
Maharashtra Law Journal
Maharashtra L.J., Mah.L.J.
Maine
Me., Mai.,M.
Maine Acts, Resolves and Constitutional Resolutions
Me. Acts
Maine Bar Journal
Me. B.J.
Maine Constitution
Me. Const.
Maine Law Review
Maine L. Rev., Me. L. Rev.
Maine Legislative Service
Me. Legis. Serv.
Maine Public Utilities Commission
Me. P.U.C.
Maine Public Utilities Commission Reports
Maine P.U.R.
Maine Railroad Commissioners
Me. R.C.
Maine Reports
Maine, Me., Maine R., Mai., Maine Rep.
Maine Revised Statutes
Me. Rev. Stat.

Maine Revised Statutes Annotated
Me. Rev. Stat. Ann., M.R.S.A.
Maine State Bar Association
Maine S.B.A.
Maine State Bar Association Reports
Maine Bar
Maine Supreme Judicial Court Reports
Me.
Maine's Ancient Law
Mai. Anc. L., Maine Anc.Law
Maine's History of Institutions
Mai. Inst.
Maine's Village Communities
Mai.VII.Com.
Maintenance
Maint.
Maitland's Manuscript Session Cases
Maitland
Maitland's Pleas of the Crown
Maitland
Maitland's Pleas of the Crown, County of Gloucester
Mait. Gl.
Maitland's Select Pleas of the Crown
Mait., Maitland
Major Peace Treaties of Modern History
M.P.T.M.H.
Major Tax Planning
Major Tax Plan.
Makere Law Journal
M.L.J., Mak. L.J., Makerere L.J.
Malabar Law Quarterly
M.L.Q.
Malay
Ma.
Malaya
Mal.

Malaya Law Review
Mal. L. Rev., Malaya L.R., Malaya L. Rev.
Malayan
Mal.
Malayan Cases
M.C.
Malayan Law Journal
Mal. L.J., Malayan L.J., M.L.J.
Malayan Law Journal, Supplement
M.L.J. Supp.
Malayan Law Reports
M.L.R.
Malaysia
Mal., Malay.
Malcolm on Legal and Judicial Ethics
Malcolm, Ethics
Male
M.
Male's Law of Elections
Male El.
Malicious Mischief
Mal. Misch.
Malicious Prosecution
Mal. Pros.
Mallory's Irish Chancery Reports
Mallory
Mallory's Modern Entries
Mall. Ent.
Malone (6, 8-10 Heiskell's Tennessee Reports)
Malone
Maltbie's Appellate Procedure
Conn. App. Proc.
Maltby on Courts-Martial
Malt. C.M.
Malyne's Ancient Law Merchant
Mal. Law M.
Malyne's Lex Mercatoria
Mal. Lex Merc., Malynes

Management
Mgmt., Mgt
Manby on Fines
Manb. Fines
Manby's Abridgment of Coke's Reports
Manb. Coke
Manchester Court Leet Records
Harland
Manchester Law Students' Chronicle
Man. L.S. Chron.
Manchester Law Students' Journal
Man. L.S.J.
Mandamus
Mand.
Manhattan
Man.
Manitoba
Man.
Manitoba and Saskatchewan Tax Reporter, Commerce Clearing House
Man. & Sask. Tax Rep. (CCH)
Manitoba Bar News
Man. B. News, Man. Bar News
Manitoba Gazette
Man. Gaz.
Manitoba Law Journal
M.L.J., Man. L.J., Manitoba L.J.
Manitoba Law Reform Commission
Man. L.R.C., M.L.R.C.
Manitoba Law Reports
Man. L.R., Manitoba, Manitoba L. (Can.), M.L.R., Man., Man. R., M.R.
Manitoba Public Utilities Commission
Man. P.U.C.

Manitoba Queen's Bench Tempore Wood, by Armour
Armour
Manitoba Reports
Carey. M.R.
Manitoba Reports Tempore Wood
Rep.t.Wood, R.t.W., Temp.
Wood., Man. R.t. Wood, Man. T.
Wood
Manitoba Revised Statutes
Man. Rev. Stat.
Manitoba Statutes
Man.Stat.
Manning and Granger's English Common Pleas Reports
Mann. & G. (Eng.), M. & G.
Manning and Ryland's English King's Bench Reports
Mann. & R. (Eng.), Man. & Ry.,
Man. & R., Mann. & R., M. & R.
Manning and Ryland's English Magistrates' Cases
Man. & Ry., Man. & R., Man. &
Ry. Mag. Cas., Man. & Ry.
M.C., Mann. & R., M. & R.M.C.,
Man. & Ry. Mag.
Manning and Scott's English Common Bench Reports, Old Series
Man. & S., Man. & Sc., M. & S.
Manning, Granger and Scott's English Common Bench Reports
Comb.B. (N.S.), Comm.B.,
Com.B.
Manning, Granger and Scott's English Common Bench Reports, New Series
Mann. G & S., C.B. (N.S.),
C.B.N.S., Com. B.N.S., C.B.N.S
(Eng.), M.G. & S.

Manning, Granger and Scott's English Common Bench Reports, Old Series
Man. Gr. & S., Man., G. & S.,
Mann. G. & S. (Eng.), C.B., C.B.
(Eng.)
Manning on Bills and Notes
Mann. Bills
Manning's Commentaries on the Law of Nations
Mann. Com.Man. Int. Law,
Mann. Nat.
Manning's Digest of the Nisi Prius Reports
Mann.
Manning's English Election Cases, Court of Revision
Man. El. Cas., Mann. E.C.
Manning's English Revision Court Reports
Man., Mann.
Manning's Exchequer Practice
Mann. Ex. Pr., Man. Exch. Pr.
Manning's Reports (1 Michigan)
Man., Manning, Mann.
Manning's Unreported Cases, Louisiana
Man. Unr. Cases, Mann. Unrep.
Cas., Manning La., Manning's
U.C., Manning's Unrep.Cases,
Man.Unrep.Cas. (La.), Man. Unrep. Cas., Manning
Mansel on Costs
Mans. on C.
Mansel on Demurrer
Man. Dem., Mans. Dem.
Mansel on Limitations
Mans. Lim., Man. Dem., Man.
Lim.
Mansfield's Decisions, by Evans
Evans

Mansfield's Digest of Arkansas Statutes
Mansf., Mansf. Dig.

Mansfield's Reports (49-52 Arkansas)
Mans., Mansf.

Manson's Bankruptcy and Companies' Winding-Up Cases
Mans., Manson, Bankr. Cas., Manson, Man., Manson (Eng.)

Manual for Courts-Martial
M.C.M.

Manual of Patent Examining Procedure
M.P.E.P.

Manual of the Judge Advocate General, Navy
JAG Man.

Manufacturer
Mfr.

Manufacturing
Mfg., Mfr.

Manuscript[s]
Ms., (Mss.)

Manuscript Cases, Scotch Court of Session
Auch. Auchinleck's

Manuscript Decisions, Commissioner of Patents
Ms.D.

Manuscript Decisions, Comptroller General
Ms.D.

Manuscript, Inner Temple
Ms.I.T.

Manuscript, Lincoln's Inn
Ms.L.I.

Manuscript, Middle Temple
MS.M.T.

Manuscript Reports
M.S.

Manuscript Reports or Decisions
Ms.

Manwood's Forest Laws
Manw. For. Law, Manw., Manwood

Marans, Williams, Griffin and Pattison's Manual of Foreign Investment in the United States
MFI

March
Ma., Mar.

March's Action for Slander and Arbitrament
Ma.

March's English King's Bench and Common Pleas Reports
March., Mar.

March's New Cases, English King's Bench
Mar. N.R., March N.C., March N.R., March N., Mar. N.C.

March's Translation of Brooke's New Cases, English King's Bench
March., Mar. Br., Mar. (N.C.), March N.C.

Marcy on Conveyancing Statutes
Mar. Conv.St.

Marcy on Epitome of Conveyancing
Mar. Conv.

Marijuana Review
Marijuana Rev.

Marine Court Reporter (McAdam's)
Marine Ct. R.

Marine Safety Manual, Coast Guard
M.S.M.

Maritime
M., Mar., Marit.

Maritime Administration
M.A.

Maritime Administration Reports
MA

Maritime, Aviation and Transport (Insurance)
MAT
Maritime Labor Board
MLB
Maritime Law Association of Australia and New Zealand Newsletter
M.L.A.A.N.Z. Newsletter
Maritime Lawyer
Mar.Law
Maritime Notes and Queries
Mar. N. & Q.
Maritime Provinces Reports
Mar. Prov., M.P.R.
Maritime Subsidy Board
MSB
Maritimes Law Reporter, Commerce Clearing House
Maritimes L. Rep. (CCH)
Marius on Bills of Exchange
Mar. Bills, Marius
Markby's Elements of Law
Mark. El.
Market[s]
Mkt(s).
Marketing
Mktg
Markets and Marketing
Mark. & M.
Marks and Sayre's Reports (108 Alabama)
Mark's & Sayre's, Marks & Sayre
Marquess
M.
Marquette
Marq.
Marquette Business Review
Marquette Bus. Rev.
Marquette Law Review
Marq. L.Rev., Marquette L. Rev., Mq.L., Mq.L.R.

Marquette Sports Law Journal
Marq. Sports L. J.
Marrack's European Assurance Cases
Marr.
Marriage
Marr.
Marriage Certificate
M.C.
Marriage License
Mar. lic.
Marriage Settlement
Marr. settl.
Married
M.
Marriott's English Admiralty Reports
Marr. Adm.
Marriott's Formulare Instrumentorum (Admiralty Court)
Marr. Form.
Marsden on Collisions at Sea
Mars. Coll.
Marsden's Admiralty
Mars. Adm.
Marsden's Select Pleas in the Court of Admiralty (Selden Society Publications, 6 and 11)
Mars.
Marshaling Assets
Marsh. A.
Marshall and Sevestre's Bench Appeals, Bengal
Mar., Marsh.
Marshall and Wood's Abridgment
M. & W. Abr.
Marshall on Marine Insurance
Marsh. Ins.
Marshall on Railways as Carriers
Marsh. Car. (or Ry.)
Marshall on the Federal Constitution
Marsh. Dec.

Marshall on the Law of Costs
Marsh. Costs
Marshall's (A.K.) Reports (8-10 Kentucky)
A.K. Marsh., Marsh. A.K.
Marshall's Bengal Reports
Mar., Marsh. Beng., Marshall, Marsh. Calc.
Marshall's Ceylon Reports
Marsh. Ceylon, Mar., Marsh.
Marshall's Constitutional Opinions
Marsh. Op.
Marshall's Duties and Obligations of Railway Companies
Marsh. Ry.
Marshall's English Common Pleas Reports
Marsh. C.P., Marsh. (Eng.), Marsh.
Marshall's High Court Reports, Bengal
Marsh.
Marshall's (J.J.) Reports (24-30 Kentucky)
J.J.Mar., J.J. Marsh., Marsh. J.J., J.J.Marsh.(Ky.), Mar.
Marshall's Reports (4 Utah)
Marsh., Marsh., Marsh. (Ky.)
Marshall's United States Circuit Court Reports
Marsh., Marsh. Dec., Mar.
Martens' Law of Nations
Mart. Law Nat.
Martin and Yerger's Tennessee Reports (8 Tennessee)
M. & Y., M. & Y.R., Mar. & Yer., Mart. & Y., Mart. & Y. (Tenn.), Mart. & Yer., Mart. & Yerg., M. and Yerger's Rep.
Martin on Executors
Mart. Ex.

Martin's Arkansas Chancery Decisions
Martin's Chy., Mart. Ark.
Martin's Circuit Court Reports (1 North Carolina)
Mart. U.S.C.C., Mart., Mar., Mart. N.C., Mar. N.C., Martin
Martin's Condensed Louisiana Reports
Mart. Cond. La.
Martin's Index to Virginia Reports
Martin Index.
Martin's Louisiana Reports
Mar. La., Mart. Rep., Martin's La. Rep., Martin's Louisiana R.
Martin's Louisiana Reports, New Series
Mar. N.S., Lou. Rep. N.S., Mart. Rep. N.S., Martin (Lou.) N.S., Martin's La. Rep. N.S., Martin's N.S., Martin's R.N.S., M.N.S., New Series, Mart. N.S. (La.), Mart. N.S., Martin, Mart. La.
Martin's Louisiana Reports, Old Series
Mart. O.S. (La.)
Martin's Mining Cases, British Columbia
M.C.C., Mart. M.C., Martin Mining., M.M.C., M.M. Cas.
Martin's Practice of Conveyancing
Mart. Conv.
Martin's Recital Book
Mar. Rec. B.
Martin's Reports (21-30 Georgia)
Mart. Ga., Martin, Martin
Martin's Reports (54-70 Indiana)
Mart. Ind.
Martin's Reports of Mining Cases, Canada
M.M.C., M.M.Cas.

Marvel's Reports (15-16 Dela-ware)
Marv., Marv.(Del.), Marvel, Mar.
Marvin on General Average
Mar. Av., Marv. Av.
Marvin on Wreck and Salvage
Mar. Wr. & S., Marv. Wr. & S.
Marvin's Legal Bibliography
Mar. Leg. Bib., Marv. Leg. Bib.
Mary
Mar.
Maryland
Md., Md, M.
Maryland Annotated Code
Md.Ann.Code, Md.Code Ann.
Maryland Annual Report and Official Opinions of the Attorney General
Md. Ann. Rep. & Op. Att'y. Gen.
Maryland Appellate Reports
Md. A., Md. App.
Maryland Bar Journal
Mar. B.J., Md. B.J.
Maryland Chancery Decisions
Maryland Ch.Dec., Maryland Ch.Rep., Md. Ch. D., Md. Ch. Dec., Md. Chan., Md. Chan. Dec., Md. Ch., See also Johnson's Maryland Chancery Decisions
Maryland Constitution
Md. Const.
Maryland Court of Appeal Proceedings (1 American Legal Records)
Bond Md. App.
Maryland Institute for Continuing Professional Education of Lawyers, Inc.
MICPEL
Maryland Journal of Contemporary Legal Issues
Md. J. Contemp. Legal Issues

Maryland Journal of International Law and Trade
Md. J.Int'l L. & Trade
Maryland Law Encyclopedia
M.L.E.
Maryland Law Forum
Md. L.F.
Maryland Law Journal and Real Estate Record
Mar. L.J.
Maryland Law Record
Mar. L.Rec., M.L.R., Md. L.Rec.
Maryland Law Reporter
Md. L.Rep.
Maryland Law Review
Mar. L.Rev., Mary. L. Rev., Maryland L. Rev., Md. L.R., Md. L.Rev.
Maryland Laws
Md. Laws
Maryland Public Service Commission
Md. P.S.C.
Maryland Public Utility Commission
Md. P.U.R.
Maryland Register
Md. Admin. Reg.
Maryland Reports
Maryland, Md., Md, Gill & Johnson, Mary., Md. R., Md.Rep.
Maryland State Bar Association, Report
Mr.S.B.A.
Maryland Supreme Court Reports
Md., Md
Maryland Workmen's Compensation Cases
Md.W.C.C.
Mascardus de Probationibus
Mascard.de Prob.

Mason's New England Civil Practice
    Mas. N.E.Pr.
Mason's United States Circuit Court Reports
    Mas., Mason R., Mason, Mason C.C.R., Mason Circt. Ct. R., Mason U.S., Mason U.S. Cir.Ct. Rep., Mason U.S.R., Mason's R., Mason's Rep.
Mason's United States Code Annotated
    Mason's Code
Massachusetts
    Mass.
Massachusetts Acts and Resolves
    Mass. Acts
Massachusetts Advance Legislative Service
    Mass. Adv. Legis. Serv.
Massachusetts Advance Sheets
    Mass. Adv. Sh., Mass. Adv. Sheets
Massachusetts Annotated Laws
    Mass. Ann. Laws
Massachusetts Appeals Court Reports
    Mass. App. Ct., Ma.A., Mass. App. Rep.
Massachusetts Appellate Court Advance Sheets
    AS, ASA, Mass. App.Ct. Adv. Sh.
Massachusetts Appellate Decisions
    Mass. App. Dec., Mass. A.D.
Massachusetts Appellate Division Reports
    App. Div. Rep., Mass. App. Div., Mass. A.D.R.
Massachusetts Appellate Reports
    Mass Ap

Massachusetts Attorney General Reports
    O.A.G.Massachusetts, Rep. Mass. Att'y Gen.
Massachusetts Board of Conciliation and Arbitration Reports
    Mass. B.C. & A.
Massachusetts Board of Gas and Electric Light Commissioners
    Mass.G. & E.L.C.
Massachusetts Board of Railroad Commissioners
    Mass. R.C.
Massachusetts Board of Tax Appeals
    Mass. B.T.A.
Massachusetts Constitution
    Mass. Const.
Massachusetts Continuing Legal Education, New England Law Institute, Inc.
    MCLNEL
Massachusetts Controverted Election Cases
    Mass. Cont. Election, Cushing, S. & J.
Massachusetts Department of Industrial Accidents Bulletin
    Mass. D.I.A.
Massachusetts Digest (Bennett and Heard)
    B.&H.Dig., Benn. & H.Dig.
Massachusetts Division of Unemployment Compensation Digest of Board of Review Decisions
    Mass. U.C. Dig.
Massachusetts Division of Unemployment Compensation Opinions
    Mass. U.C. Ops.
Massachusetts Election Cases
    Mass. Elec. Ca., Mass. Elec. Cas.

Massachusetts General Laws
    Mass. Gen. Laws
Massachusetts General Laws Annotated
    Mass. Gen. Laws Ann. (West),
    M.G.L.A.
Massachusetts Highway Commission
    Mass. High. Com.
Massachusetts Industrial Accident Board Reports of Cases
    Mass. I.A.B.
Massachusetts Institute of Technology
    MIT
Massachusetts Labor Relations Commission
    MLRC
Massachusetts Labor Relations Commission Decisions
    Mass. L.R.C. Dec.
Massachusetts Land Court Decisions
    Davis L. Ct. Cas.
Massachusetts Law Quarterly
    Mass. L.Q., M.Q.
Massachusetts Law Review
    Mass. L. Rev., Mass. L.R.
Massachusetts Public Service Commission
    Mass. P.S.C.
Massachusetts Public Utility Commission Reports
    Mass. P.U.R.
Massachusetts Register
    Mass. Admin. Reg.
Massachusetts Reports
    Ma., Mas., Mass., Mas. R., Mas. Rep., Mass. R., Mass. Rep.
Massachusetts State Board of Conciliation and Arbitration Reports
    Mass. St.B.C. & A.

Massachusetts Supreme Judicial Court Reports
    Mass.
Massachusetts Unemployment Compensation Commission Opinions
    Mass. U.C.C. Op.
Massachusetts Workmen's Compensation Cases
    Mass. W.C.C.
Masse on Le Droit Commercial
    Mass. Dr. Com.
Master and Servant
    M. & S.
Master of Arts in Law and Diplomacy
    M.A.L.D.
Master of Business Administration
    M.B.A.
Master of Civil Law
    M.C.L.
Master of Comparative Jurisprudence
    M.C.J.
Master of Comparative Law
    M.C.L.
Master of Comparative Laws
    LL. C.M.
Master of Juridical Science
    M.J.S.
Master of Jurisprudence
    J.M.
Master of Law
    LL. M.
Master of Laws
    M.L.
Master of Library Science
    M.L.S.
Master of Patent Law
    M.P.L.
Master of Public Law
    MPL

Master of Science in Law and Society
    M.S.L.S.
Master of Science in Library Service
    M.S.L.S.
Master of the Rolls
    M.R.
Master of the Science of Law
    J.S.M.
Masterman on Parliamentary Elections
    Mast. El.
Master's Patents Decisions
    M.D.
Master's Reports (25-28 Canada Supreme Court)
    Mast.
Matara Cases, Ceylon
    M.C.
Materials Transportation Bureau
    MTB
Mathews on Landlord and Tenant
    Mat. L. & T.
Mathews on Presumptive Evidence
    Math. Pres. Ev.
Mathews on the Law of Partnership
    Mat. Part.
Mathews on the Law of Portions
    Mat. Por.
Mathieu's Quebec Reports
    Math.
Mathieu's Quebec Revised Reports
    R.J.R., R.J.R.Q.
Matrimonial Causes Rules
    M.C.R.
Matsons' Reports (22-24 Connecticut)
    Mats., Matson

Matthew and Bangs' Illinois Circuit Court Reports
    Ill.C.C.
Matthew Bender and Company
    M.B., Bender
Matthew Paris on Historia Minor
    Mat. Par., Mat. Paris.
Matthews' Digest of Criminal Law
    Matth. Cr.L.
Matthews, Executors and Administrators
    Matth. Exe.
Matthews' Guide to Commissioner in Chancery
    Matth. Com.
Matthews on Partnership
    Matth. Part.
Matthews on Presumptive Evidence
    Matth. Pr.Ev.
Matthews' Reports (75 Virginia)
    Matthews
Matthews' Reports (6-9 West Virginia)
    Matthews, Math.
Maturity
    Mat.
Maude and Pollock's Law of Merchant Shipping
    M. & P. Sh., Maude & P. Mer. Shipp., Maude & P. Shipp., Maude & P., Mau. & Pol.Sh.
Maudsley on Mental Responsibility
    Maud. Ment. Res.
Maugham on Attorneys, Solicitors and Agents
    Maug. Att.
Maugham on Literary Property
    Maugh. Lit. Pr.
Maugham's Outlines of Criminal Law
    Maug. Cr. L.

Maugham's Outlines of Law
Maug. Law
Maugham's Outlines of Real Prop-erty Law
Maugh. R.P., Maug. R.P.
Maugham's Outlines of the Juris-diction
Maug. Jur.
Maugham's Statutes Relating to Attorneys, etc.
Maug. Att.
Maule and Selwyn's English King's Bench Reports
Maul. & Sel., Maule & S., M. & S., Mau. & Sel.
Mauritius Decisions (or Reports)
Maur. Dec., M.R.
Mauritius Law Reporter
M.L.R.
Mauritius Reports by Bruzard
Bruzard
Maxim[s]
Max.
Maxims of the Laws of England by William Noye
Noye's Max.
Maxwell on the Interpretation of Statutes
Maxw. Interp. St., Maxwell, Max. Int. Stat.
Maxwell's Law Dictionary
Max. L. D.
Maxwell's Marine Law
Max. Mar. L.
Maxwell's Nebraska Digest
Max. Dig.
Maxwell's Treatise on Criminal Procedure
Maxw. Cr. Proc.
May
Ma.

May on Fraudulent Conveyances
May Fr. Conv.
May on Insurance
May, Ins.
Mayhew on Action at Law
May. Act.
Mayhew on Merger
May. Merg.
Maynard's Reports, (Exchequer Memoranda of Edward I, and Year Books of Edward II)
Mayn.
Maynard's Yearbooks
Y.B., Yearb.
Mayne on the Law of Damages
May. Dam.
Mayo and Moulton's Pension Laws
Mayo & Moul.
Mayor's Court
M.C.
Mayo's Justice
May. Just., Mayo Just.
May's Constitutional History of England
May Const. Hist.
May's Criminal Law
May Crim. Law
May's Parliamentary Law
May, Parl. Law.
May's Parliamentary Practice
May, Parl. Pr., May. P.L.
Mayurbhani Law Report, India
May. L.R.
McAdam on Landlord and Tenant
McAdam, Landl. & T., McA.L. & Ten.
McAdam's Marine Court Practice
McA. Mar. Ct.
McAdam's Marine Court Reporter
Marine Ct. R.

McAllister's United States Circuit Court Reports
Macall., McAl., McAll.,
McAll.(Cal.), Macal., McAll.,
McAllister U.S. Circ. Court R.

McArthur's District of Columbia Reports
McAr.

McBride's Reports (1 Missouri)
McBride

McCafferty and Meyer on Medical Malpractice: Bases of Liability
MMBL

McCahon's Reports (Kansas 1858-68)
McCah., McCahon.

McCall's Clerk's Assistant
McC.Cl.Ass.

McCall's Forms
McC.F.

McCall's New York Justice
McC.Just.

McCall's Precedents (Forms)
McCall Pr.

McCanless' Tennessee Reports
McCanless

McCarter's Reports (14-15 New Jersey Equity)
McCarter, McCar., McCart.

McCartney's New York Civil Procedure Reports
McCartney, McCarty, McCarty, Civ.Proc., McCart.

McClain's Annotated Iowa Code and Statutes
McClain's Code.

McClain's Criminal Law
McClain, Cr. Law

McClain's Iowa Code
McCl. Ia. Co.

McCleland and Younge's English Exchequer Reports
M'Cl. & Y., McCl. & Y., McCle. & Yo., McClell. & Y.

McCleland's English Exchequer Reports
McCl., M'Cl., M'Clel. (Eng.), McClell., McCle., McClel.

McClelland on Civil Malpractice
McCl. Mal.

McClellan's Florida Digest
McCl. Dig., McClel. Dig.

McClellan's Manual for Executors
McCl. Ex.

McClellan's Probate Practice
McCl. Pr.

McCook's Reports (1 Ohio State)
McCook

McCord's South Carolina Chancery Reports
McCord Eq., McCord Ch., McCord.

McCord's South Carolina Law Reports
McCord., see also M'Cord's South Carolina Law Report and M'Cord's South Carolina Equity Reports

McCorkle's Reports (65 North Carolina)
McCork., McCorkle

McCrary's American Law of Elections
McCr. Elect., McCrary, Elect.

McCrary's United States Circuit Court Reports
McCr., McCrary, McCrary's Rep.

McCulloch's Political Economy
McCul. Pol. Econ.

McCullough's Commerical Dictionary
McCul. Dict.

McDermot Irish Land Laws
    McDer. Land L.
McDevitt's Irish Land Commissioner's Reports
    McDevitt.
McDonald's Justice
    McDon. Jus.
McDonnell's Sierra Leone Reports
    McDonnell
McDowall's Institutes of the Law of Scotland
    McDow. Inst.
McFarlane's Jury Court Reports, Scotland
    McFar.
McGill Law Journal
    McGill L.J.
McGill's Manuscript Decisions, Court of Session, Scotland
    McGill
McGlashan's Aliment
    McGl. Al.
McGlashan's Sheriff Court Practice
    McGl. Sh.
McGloin's Louisiana Courts of Appeal Reports
    McG., McGl., McGloin., McGl. (La), McGloin Rep. (La.)
McGrath's Michigan Mandamus Cases
    McGrath
McIntyre and Evans' Judicature Practice
    McIn. & E. Jud.Pr.
McKelvey on Evidence
    McKelvey, Ev.
McKinney's Consolidated Laws of New York
    McK. Consol. Laws, N.Y. Law (McKinney)

McKinney's Justice
    McKin. Jus.
McKinney's Unconsolidated Laws of New York
    N.Y. Unconsol. Laws
McKinnon's Philosophy of Evidence
    McKin. Phil. Ev.
McLaren on Law of Wills in Scotland
    McLar. W.
McLaren on Trusts in Scotland
    McLar. Tr.
McLean and Robinson's Appeal Cases
    McL. & R.
McLean's United States Circuit Court Reports
    Mc.L., Macl., McLean, McLean's C.C.R., McLean's Rep., M'Lean's R.
M'Cleland and Younge's English Exchequer Reports
    M'Clel. & Y., M'Cle. & Yo., M'Clel. & Y. (Eng.), M'Clel., M'Cle., M'Cl. & Yo.
McMaster's Commercial Cases
    McM. Com. Cas.
McMaster's Commercial Decisions
    McM. Com. Dec.
McMaster's New York Railroad Laws
    McMas. R.R.
McMullan, South Carolina Equity Reports
    McMull. Eq. (S.C.), McMul. Eq.
McMullan, South Carolina Law Reports
    McMull. L. (S.C.), McMul.
McNamara's Constitutional Limitations on Criminal Procedure
    CLCP

M'Cord's South Carolina Equity Reports
   M'Cord. Eq. (S.C.), See also McCord's South Carolina Equity Reports

M'Cord's South Carolina Law Reports
   M'Cord. L. (S.C.)

McPherson, Lee, and Bell's Session Cases, Scotland
   McPherson

McQueen and Crestol on Federal Tax Aspects of Bankruptcy
   FTAB or TAB

McQuillin on Municipal Corporations
   McQuillin Mun.Corp.

McVey's Ohio Digest
   McVey Dig.

McWillie's Reports (73-76 Mississippi)
   McWillie

Mean's Kansas Reports
   Means.

Mears' Edition of Justinian and Gaius
   Mears Just.

Meat and Poultry Inspection Regulations
   M.P.I. Regulations

Meawes' Lex Mercatoria
   Beawes' Lex Merc.

Mechanics' Liens
   Mech. L.

Mechem on Agency
   Mechem., Mechem, Ag.

Mechem on Partnership
   Mechem.

Mechem on Public Offices and Officers
   Mechem, Pub. Off.

Meddaugh's Reports (13 Michigan)
   Medd., Meddaugh.

Media
   Media

Media Law and Practice
   Media L. & P., Med. L. & P.

Media Law Notes
   Media L. Notes

Media Law Reporter, Bureau of National Affairs
   Media L. Rep. (BNA)

Mediation
   Mediation

Mediator
   Med.

Medicaid
   M.A.

Medical Devices Reports, Commerce Clearing House
   Med. Devices Rep. (CCH)

Medical Jurisprudence
   Med. Jur.

Medical Liability Reporter
   MeLR

Medical Literature and Analysis and Retrieval System
   MEDLARS

Medical Literature On-Line
   MEDLINE

Medical, Medicine
   Med.

Medical Trial Technique Quarterly
   Med. Tr. T.Q., Med. Trial Tech. Q.

Medicine and Law
   Med. & L.

Medicine, Law and Public Policy
   Med. L. & Pub.Pol

Medicine, Science and the Law
   Med. Sci. & L.

Medico-Legal and Criminological Review
Med. Leg. & Crim. Rev., Med.-Legal Crim. Rev.

Medico-Legal Bulletin
Med. Leg. Bul.

Medico-Legal Journal
Med. Leg. J., Med.-Legal J., Medico-Legal J., Med.L.J.

Medico Legal News
Med. Leg. N., Med. L.N.

Medico-Legal Papers
Med. Leg. Pap., Med. L.P.

Medico-Legal Society Transactions
Med.-Legal Soc'y Trans.

Meeson and Roscoe's English Exchequer Reports
Mees. & Ros.

Meeson and Welsby's English Exchequer Reports
Mees. & W., Mees. & Wels.

Megarry on the Rent Acts
Megarry

Meggison on Assets in Equity
Megg. Ass.

Megone's Company Acts Cases
Meg., Megone

Meigs' Digest of Decisions of the Courts of Tennessee
Meigs, Dig.

Meigs' Tennessee Supreme Court Reports
Meigs'R., Meigs

Melanesian Law Journal
Melanesian L.J.

Melbourne
Melb.

Melbourne University Law Review
Melbourne U. L.R., Melb.U. L. Rev., Melb.Univ. L.R., M.U.L.R., Melb.Univ. L. Rev., Melbourne Univ. L. Rev.

Mell's Parliamentary Practice
Mell Parl.Pr.

Melvill's Trial (Impeachment)
Melv. Tr.

Member of Parliament
M.P.

Memorandum
Mem., Memo.

Memorandum Opinions, Judge Advocate General of the Army
MO-JAGA

Memorandum or Memoranda in the Exchequer
Mem.in Scacc.

Memphis
Mem.

Memphis Law Journal
M.L.J., Mem. L.J., Memp. L.J., Memphis L.J.

Memphis State University Law Review
Mem. St. U. L. Rev., Memphis State U. L. Rev., Memphis State Univ. L. Rev., Memphis St.U. L. Rev.

Mence on Law of Libel
Mence Lib.

Menken's Reports (30 New York Civil Procedure Reports)
Menken.

Mental and Physical Disability Law Reporter
Mental & Physical Disab.L.Rep.

Mental Disability Law Reporter
Mental Disab. L.Rep.

Mental Hygiene
Mental Hyg.

Menzie's Cape Colony Supreme Court Reports
M., Men., Menz., Menzies

Menzies' Conveyancing
Menz. Conv.

Mercantile Adjuster and the Lawyer and Credit Man
Merc. Ad. & Law. & Credit Man, M.A.L.C.M.

Mercantile Law Journal
Mer. L.J., Merc.L.J.

Mercer Beasley Law Review
Mercer B.L. Rev., Mercer, Beasley L. Rev.

Mercer County Law Journal
Mercer

Mercer Law Review
Mercer L. Rev., Mercer Law Rev., Mer.

Merchandise
Mdse.

Merchant Marine and Fisheries
M.M.F.

Merchantile Cases
Merc. Cas.

Merchants' Dictionary
Merch. Dict.

Meredith's (W.C.J.) Memorial Lectures
Meridith Lect.

Merewether and Stephen's Municipal Corporations
Mer. & St.Corp.

Mergers and Acquisitions
Merg. & Acq.

Merivale's English Chancery Reports
Mer., Meriv., Meriv. (Eng.)

Merlin's Repertoire
Merlin, Repert.

Merrifield on Attorneys
Merr. Att.

Merrifield's Law of Costs
Merr. Costs

Merten's Law of Federal Income Taxation
Mert.

Metcalf on the Law of Contracts
Metc. Cont.

Metcalf's Edition of Yelverton
Metc. Yelv.

Metcalfe's Reports (58-61 Kentucky)
Metc., Metc. Ky., Met.

Metcalf's Reports (42-54 Massachusetts)
Metc. Mass., Metc., Met.

Metcalf's Reports (3 Rhode Island)
Met., Metc.

Methodist Church Cases Report
Meth. Ch. Ca.

Metropolis
Metrop.

Metropolitan
Met., Metro., Metrop.

Metropolitan District Council
M.D.C.

Mews' Digest of English Case Law
Mews, Mews Dig.

Mew's Supplement to Fishers' English Digest by Chitty
Chit. & M. Dig.

Mexico
Mex.

Miami Law Quarterly
Miami L.Q.

Miami Law Review
Miami L. Rev.

Michaelmas Term
M., Mich., Mich. T.

Michaelmas Vacation
Mich.Vac.

Michie's Jurisprudence of Virginia and West Virginia
Michie's Jur.

Michigan
Mich., M., Mi.

Michigan Administrative Code
Mich. Admin Code

Michigan Attorney General Biennial Report
Mich.Att'y Gen. Biennial Rep.
Michigan Bar Journal
Mich. B.J.
Michigan Biennial Report of the State Attorney General
Mich. Att'y Gen. Biennial Rep.
Michigan Business Law Journal
Mich. Bus. L.J.
Michigan Circuit Court Reporter
Mich. C.C.R., Mich. Cr. Ct. Rep.
Michigan Civil Jurisprudence
M.C.J.
Michigan Compiled Laws
Mich. Comp. Laws
Michigan Compiled Laws Annotated
M.C.L.A., Mich. Comp. L. Ann., Mich. Comp. Laws Ann.
Michigan Constitution
Mich. Const.
Michigan Corporate Finance and Business Law Journal
Mich. Corp. Finance & Bus. L.J.
Michigan Court of Appeals Reports
Mich. App.
Michigan Court of Claims Reports
Mich. Ct. Cl.
Michigan Digest by Binmore
Bin.Dig.
Michigan Employment Relations Commission
MERC
Michigan Industrial Accident Board, Workmen's Compensation Cases
Mich. W.C.C.
Michigan Journal of International Law
Mich. J. Int'l L.

Michigan Jurisprudence
Mich. Jur.
Michigan Labor Mediation Board
Mich. LMB
Michigan Law and Practice
M.L.P.
Michigan Law Journal
Mich. L.J.
Michigan Law Review
McL, Mi. L., Mich. L. Rev., Mich LR
Michigan Lawyer
Mich. L., Mich. Lawyer
Michigan Legal News
Mich. Leg. News
Michigan Legislative Service, West
Mich. Legis. Serv. (West)
Michigan Political Science Association
Mich. Pol. Soc.
Michigan Public and Local Acts
Mich. Pub. Acts
Michigan Public Utilities Commission Orders and Opinions
Mich. P.U.C. Ops.
Michigan Railroad Commission Decisions
Mich. R.C. Dec.
Michigan Reports
Mch., Mi., Mich. R., Mich. Supr. Ct. Rep., Mich.
Michigan Reports Advanced Sheets
Mich. Adv.
Michigan Reports Index Digest by Binmore
Binm.Ind.
Michigan State Bar Association Journal
Mich. S.B.A. Jo.

Michigan State Bar Journal
M.B.J., Mich. S.B.J., Mich. St.B.J.

Michigan State University Business Topics
M.S.U. Business Topics

Michigan Statutes Annotated
Mich. Stat. Ann.

Michigan Supreme Court Reports
Mich.

Michigan Unemployment Compensation Commisson
M.U.C.C.

Michigan Yearbook of International Legal Studies
Mich. Y.B.Int'l.Legal Stud.

Mid-West Nigeria Legal Notice
M.W.N.L.N.

Middle District
M.D.

Middle East Executive Reports
Middle E. Executive Rep.

Middle East Law Review
Mid. East L. Rev.

Midwest Practice Institute
MPI

Mifflin County Legal Journal, Pennsylvania
M.C.L.J.

Milbank Quarterly
Milbank Q.

Miles' District Court Reports, Philadelphia, Pennsylvania
Miles

Miles' Pennsylvania Reports
M., Mil., Miles (Pa.), Mill., Miles R., Miles Rep.

Miles' Rules and Orders (Common Pleas)
Miles R. & O.

Military
Mil., Milit.

Military Affairs Division
CSJAGA

Military Affairs Division, Office of Judge Advocate General, United States Army
JAGA

Military Airlift Command
MAC

Military and Civil Defense
Mil.

Military and Veterans Code
Mil. & Vet. C.

Military Assistance Program
M.A.P.

Military Inspection Service Manual, United States Navy
MIS

Military Jurisprudence, Cases and Materials
Mil. Jur., Cas. & Mat.

Military Justice Reporter
M.J.

Military Law Journal
Military L.J.

Military Law Reporter
Mil. L. Rep.(Pub.L.Educ.Inst.), Mil. L.Rep.

Military Law Review
Mil. L. Rev., Milit. L.R.

Military Laws of the United States
ML

Military Orders issued by the President as Commander in Chief of the Armed Forces
M.O.

Military Staff Committee, United States
MSC

Military Standards
Mil. Std.

**Military Standard Transporta-
tion and Movement Procedures**
MILSTAMP

**Military Traffic Management and
Terminal Service**
MTMTS

Militia Reporter
Mil. Rep.

Miller and Collier on Bills of Sale
M. & C. Bills, Mill. & C. Bills

**Miller and Field's Federal Prac-
tice**
Mill. & F.Pr.

Miller on Partition
Mill. Part.

**Miller on the Constitution of the
United States**
Miller, Const.

Miller's Civil Law of England
Mill. Civ.L.

**Miller's Elements of the Law of
Insurances**
Mill.Ins. (or El.)

Miller's Equitable Mortgages
Mill. Eq. M.

Miller's Iowa Code
Mill. Code

**Miller's Iowa Pleading and Prac-
tice**
Mill. Pl. & Pr.

**Miller's Iowa Revised and Anno-
tated Code**
Miller's Code.

Miller's Reports (1-5 Louisiana)
Mil., Mill., Mill. La., Miller

Miller's Reports (3-18 Maryland)
Mil., Mill., Mill. Md., Miller

**Miller's United States Circuit
Court Decisions**
Mill.Op., Mill. Dec.

**Miller's United States Supreme
Court Decisions**
Mill. Dec.

**Milliken and Vertrees' Tennessee
Code**
Mill. & V.Code

**Mills' Annotated Colorado Stat-
utes**
Mills Ann. St.

Mill's Logic
Mill, Log.

Mills on Eminent Domain
Mills Em.D., Mills, Em. Dom.

**Mills' New York Surrogate Court
Reports**
Mills., Mills (N.Y.), Mills' Surr.
Ct., Mil., Mill.

Mill's Political Economy
Mill, Pos. Ec.

**Mills' South Carolina Constitu-
tional Reports**
Mil., Mill Const., Mill, Const.
(S.C.), Mill.

Milner's Questions de Droit
M.Q.D.

**Milward's Irish Ecclesiastical Re-
ports**
Milw., Milw. Ir. Ecc. Rep.

Milwaukee Bar Association Gavel
Gavel, Milw.B.A.G.

Milwaukee Lawyer
Milwaukee Law.

Mimeographed Letter
Mim.

**Mine Safety and Health Re-
porter, Bureau of National Affairs**
Mine Safety & Health Rep.
(BNA)

Mineral
Min.

**Mineral Order (Defense Minerals
Exploration Administration,
United States Department of
the Interior)**
M.O.

Minimum Lending Rate
M.L.R.
**Minimum Property Standards,
Housing and Urban Development**
M.P.S.
Mining and Water Cases Annotated
M. & W. Cas.
**Mining Commissioner's Cases,
Canada**
M.C.C.
**Mining Enforcement and Safety
Administration**
MESA
Minister
Min.
Minister of National Revenue
MNR
Ministry
Min.
Ministry of Agriculture, Fisheries and Food
M.A.F.F.
Minnesota
Minn., Mn.
Minnesota Code Annotated
Minn. Code Ann.
Minnesota Code of Agency Rules
Minn. Code Agency
Minnesota Constitution
Minn. Const.
Minnesota Continuing Legal Education
Minn. Cont. L. Ed., Minn. Cont.
Legal Ed., MNCLE
Minnesota Court Reporter
Minn. Ct. Rep.
**Minnesota Department of Labor
and Industries, Compilation of
Court Decisions**
Minn. D.L. & I. Comp.

Minnesota General Laws
Minn. Gen. Laws
Minnesota Law Journal
Minn. Law J., Minn.L.J.
Minnesota Law Review
Minn. L. Rev., Minn LR, Minnesota L. Rev., Mn. L.R., MnL
Minnesota Laws
Minn. Laws
Minnesota Railroad and Warehouse Commission
Minn. R. & W.C.
**Minnesota Railroad and Warehouse Commission. Auto Transportation Company Division
Reports**
Minn. R & W.C.A.T. Div.
Minnesota Reports
Min., Minn., Min. Rep., Minn.
Rep., Minn. Reps., Min.R.
Minnesota Reports (Gilfillan Edition)
Minn. (Gil.), Minn. (Gill.)
Minnesota Session Law Service
Minn. Sess. Law Serv. (West)
Minnesota State Bar Association
Minn. S.B.A.
Minnesota State Register
Minn. Admin. Reg.
Minnesota Statutes
Minn. Stat.
Minnesota Statutes Annotated
Minn. Stat. Ann., M.S.A.
Minnesota Statutes by Bissell
Biss.Stat.
Minnesota Supreme Court Reports
Minn.
Minnesota Workmen's Compensation Decisions
Minn. W.C.D.
Minor
Min.

Minority Enterprise Small Business Investment Companies
MESBIC
Minority Rights Group
MRG
Minor's Alabama Reports
Ala., Minor, Minor (Ala.), Minor's Ala. R., Minor's Ala. Rep., Minor's Alabama Rep., Minor's R., Minor's Rep., Minor's Reports, Min.
Minor's Institutes of Common and Statute Law
Min. Inst., Minor, Inst.
Minot's Massachusetts Digest
Min. Dig.
Minute[s]
Min(s).
Minutes of Evidence
Min. Ev.
Mirchall's Doctor and Student
Mirch. D. & S.
Mirehouse on Advowsons
Mireh. Advow.
Mirehouse on Tithes
Mireh. Ti.
Mirror of Parliament
Mir. Parl.
Mirror of the Patent Office
Mir.Pat.Off.
Miscellaneous
Misc.
Miscellaneous Branch, Internal Revenue Bureau
M.B.
Miscellaneous Oregon Laws
Misc. Laws
Miscellaneous Personal Property
M.P.P.
Miscellaneous Reports, New York
Misc., Misc. (N.Y.), Misc. Rep., Miscel.

Miscellaneous Reports, Second Series, New York
Misc.2d
Mississippi
Mis., M., Miss., Ms.
Mississippi Code Annotated
M.C.A., Miss. Code Ann.
Mississippi College Law Review
Miss. C.L. Rev.
Mississippi Constitution
Miss. Const.
Mississippi Decisions
Miss. Dec.
Mississippi General Laws
Miss. Laws
Mississippi Institute of Continuing Legal Education
MSCLE
Mississippi Law Journal
Miss. L.J., M.L.J., Ms.L.J.
Mississippi Law Review
Miss. L. Rev., Miss. Law. Rev.
Mississippi Lawyer
Miss. Law., Miss. Lawyer
Mississippi Railroad Commission Reports
Miss. R.C.
Mississippi Reports
Mis., Miss., Miss. R., Miss. Rep.
Mississippi State Bar Association
Miss. S.B.A.
Mississippi Supreme Court Reports
Miss.
Missouri
Miss., Mo., Mo
Missouri Appeal Reports
Mo. App., Mo. App. Rep., Mo. Ap., Mo. App. (St.L.), Mo. Appeals, Mo. App.(K.C.), Mo. Apps., M.A.
Missouri Appellate Reporter
Mo. A.R.

Missouri Bar
Mo. Bar, MOB
Missouri Bar Journal
Mo. Bar J., Mo. B.J., Mo. St.B.J.
Missouri Code of State Regulations
Mo. Admin. Code
Missouri Constitution
Mo.Const.
Missouri Decisions
Mo. Dec.
Missouri Digest by Barclay
Barc.Dig., Barc.Mo.Dig.
Missouri Law Review
Mo. L. Rev., Mo. L. Rev., Mo. L. Rev.
Missouri Laws
Mo. Laws
Missouri Legislative Service
Mo. Legis. Serv.
Missouri Public Service Commission Reports
Mo. P.S.C.R.
Missouri Public Utility Reports
Mo. P.U.R.
Missouri Railroad and Warehouse Commission
Mo.R. & W.C.
Missouri Railroad Commissioners
Mo. R. C.
Missouri Register
Mo. Admin. Reg.
Missouri Reports
Mo., Mo, Mis., Mis. R., Mis. Rep., Misso., Misso. R., Misso. Rep., Missour. Rep., Missouri, Missouri R., Missouri Rep., Missouri Reports, Mo. R., Mo. Rep.
Missouri Revised Statutes
Mo. Rev. Stat.
Missouri State University Continuing Legal Education
MSUCLE

Missouri Statutes Annotated
Mo.St.Ann.
Missouri Supreme Court Reports
Mo., Mo
Mister's Reports (17-32 Missouri Appeals)
Mister
Mitchell's Bills, Notes, etc.
Mitch. B. & N.
Mitchell's Maritime Register, England
M.M.R., Mar. Reg., Mitchell's Mar.Reg., Mitch. M.R.
Mitchells' Modern Geography
Mitch. Mod. Geog.
Mitford on Equity Pleading
Mitf. Eq. Pl., Mit. Ch. Pl.
Mittermaier's Effect of Drunkenness on Criminal Responsibilty
Mit. Drunk
Mixed Claims Commission
M.C.C.
M'Laurin's Judiciary Cases
M'Laur.
M'Mullan's South Carolina Equity Reports
M'Mul.Ch.S.C., M'Mul.L.S.C.
Moak's Edition of Underhill on Torts
Moak Und., Moak, Underh.Torts.
Moak's Edition of Van Santvoord's Equity Pleading
Moak Van S.Pl.
Moak's English Reports
Moak, Eng., Eng. Rep., Moak & Eng. Rep., Moak (Eng.), Moak Eng. Rep., Moak, Eng. R.
Mobile Homes, Trailer Parks and Transit Camps
Mobil H.

Mobley's Contested Election Cases, United States House of Representatives
Mob., Mobl.
Model Secondary School for the Deaf
MSSD
Modern
Mod.
Modern American Law
M.A.L., Mod. Am. Law
Modern Cases
Mod. Cas.
Modern Cases at Law and Equity
Mod. Cas. L. & Eq.
Modern Cases Tempore Holt, by Farresley (7 Modern Reports)
Mod. Cas. Per. Far., Mod. Cas.t.Holt., Mod. Cas. per Far. (t.Holt), Farr., Farresley, Far.
Modern Entries
Mod. Ent.
Modern Federal Practice Digest
M.F.P.D.
Modern Law and Society
Mod.L. & Soc'y
Modern Law Review
M.L.R., Mod. L. Rev., Modern L. Rev., Modern L.R.
Modern Practice Commentator
Mod. Pract. Comm.
Modern Practice of the Exchequer
M.P. Ex.
Modern Reports, English King's Bench
Mod. Rep., Mo., Mo, Mod.
Modification[s]
Mod(s)., Modif.
Modified
M., Mod., Modif., m. (used in Shepard's Citations)

Modified Accelerated Cost Recovery System
MACRS
Modified in
Mod.
Modifying
Mod., Mod'g
Moile's Precedents
Mo. Prec.
Moir on Capital Punishment
Moir Cap. Pun.
Molloy's de Jure Maritimo et Navali
Mol. J. M., Mol.de Jure Mar., Jur. Mr., Mol., Moll.
Molloy's Irish Chancery Reports
Molloy, Mol., Moll.
Molyneaux's Reports, Tempore Car. I., England
Moly.
Monaghan's Reports (147-165 Pennsylvania)
Mona., Monaghan., Monag., Monaghan (Pa.), Monag., Monaghan (Pa.)
Monaghan's Unreported Cases, Pennsylvania Superior Court
Mon.
Monahan's Method of the Law
Mon. Meth.
Monash University Law Review
Mon. L. R., Monash U. L. Rev., Monash Univ. L. Rev.
Monasticon Anglicanum
Mon. Angl.
Moncrieff on the Liability of Innkeepers
Monc. Rev., Monc. Inn.
Money Lenders and Pawn Brokers
Money Lend.
Mongolia
Mong.

Mongolian
M.
Monopolies, Restraints of Trade and Unfair Trade Practices
Mon., Monop.
Monroe Legal Reporter
Mon. Leg. R. (Pa.), Monroe, Monroe L.R.
Monroe's Kentucky Reports (40-57 Kentucky)
Mon., Mon.B., (See also Ben Monroe's Kentucky Reports and T. B. Monroe's Reports
Monroe's (T.B.) Reports (17-23 Kentucky)
T.B.Mon., Mon., T.B. Mon.(Ky.), Mon.T.B.
Monro's Acta Cancellariae
Monro. A.C., Monro.
Montagu and Ayrton on the Bankrupt Law
M. & A.B.L., Mont. & Ayr. B.L.
Montagu and Ayrton's English Bankruptcy Reports
Mont. & Ayr. Bankr., Mont. & Ayr. Bankr. (Eng.), M. & Ayr., M. & A., Mont. & A., Mont. & Ayr.
Montagu and Bligh's English Bankruptcy Reports
Mont. & B. Bankr., Mont. & B., Mont. & B. Bankr.(Eng.), Mont. & Bl.
Montagu and Chitty's English Bankruptcy Reports
M. & Chit. Bankr., Mont. & C. Bankr., M. & Cht. Bankr., Mont. & C. Bankr. (Eng.), Mont. & Ch., M. & C., Mont. & Chitt., Mont. & C.

Montagu and Macarthur's English Bankruptcy Reports
M. & M., M. & Mc.A., M.McA., M. & M'A., M. & B., M.& C., Mont. & MacA., Mont.& M. Bankr. (Eng.), Mont. & M.
Montagu on Bankrupt Law
Mont. Bk. L.
Montagu on Composition
Mont. Comp.
Montagu, Deacon, and DeGex's English Bankruptcy Reports
Mont. D. & DeG., M.D. & DeG., M.D. & D.
Montagu on Liens
Mont. Liens
Montagu on Set-Off
Mont. S.O.
Montagu's Digest of Pleadings in Equity
Mont. Dig., Mont. Eq. Pl.
Montagu's Digest of the Law of Partnership
Mont. Part.
Montagu's English Bankruptcy Reports
Mont. Bank. Rep., Mont., Mont. Bankr. (Eng.), Mont. B.C.
Montana
Mon., Mont., Mt.
Montana Administrative Register
Mont. Admin. Reg.
Montana Administrative Rules
Mont. Admin. R.
Montana Code Annotated
M.C.A., Mont. Code Ann.
Montana Constitution
Mont. Const.
Montana Digest by Bishop
Bishop Dig.
Montana Law Review
Mont. L.Rev., Montana L. Rev., M.R.

Montana Lawyer
Mont. Law.
Montana Railroad Commission
Mont. R.C.
Montana Railroad and Public Service Commission
Mont. R. & P.S.Co.
Montana Reports
Mon., Mont., Mt., Montana Reports
Montana Revised Code Annotated
Mont. Rev. Code Ann.
Montana Supreme Court Reports
Mon., Mont.
Montana Territory
Mon.
Montana Utilities Reports
M.U.R.
Montefiore's Synopsis of Mercantile Law
Mont. Merc. Law
Montesquieu's Esprit des Lois
Montesq., Montesq. Esprit des Lois.
Montesquieu's Spirit of Laws
Mont. Sp. L., Sp. Laws
Montgomery County Law Reporter
Mont. Co. L. Rep., Mont. Co. L.R., Montg., Montg. Co. L. R. (Pa.), Mont'g. Co. L. Rep., Montg. Co. L. Rep'r., Montg. Co. Law Rep'r., Mont'g. L. Rep., Montg.Co., Montg.(Pa.), Montg. Co. L.R.
Monthly
Mo., Mo, Mon., Monthly, Mthly., Mt.
Monthly Bulletin of Decisions of the High Court of Uganda
M.B.
Monthly Digest of Tax Articles
Month. Dig. Tax Articles

Monthly Index to Reporters
Mont. Ind.
Monthly Journal of Law
Month. J.L., Month. L.J.
Monthly Jurist
Mo. Jur., Month. Jur.
Monthly Labor Review
M.L.R., Mo Labor R, Mo. Labor Rev., Mo. Lab.R ev., Month. Lab. Rev., Monthly Lab. Rev.
Monthly Law Bulletin
Month. L. Bull. (N.Y.), Month. Law Bul.
Monthly Law Digest and Reporter
M.L. Dig. & R.
Monthly Law Magazine
Mon. Law Mag., Mo. L. Mag., Month. L.M., Month. L.Mag.
Monthly Law Reporter
Mo. Law Rep., Mon. Law Rep., Month. L. Rep., Law Rep.
Monthly Law Reports
Month. L. Rep.
Monthly Law Review
Month. L. Rev.
Monthly Law Review of University of Detroit
Mon. L. Rev., Univ.of Detroit
Monthly Legal Examiner
Month. Leg. Ex., Mo. Leg. Exam., Month. Leg. Exam. (N.Y.), Month. Leg. Exam.
Monthly Review
Mo. Rev.
Monthly Western Journal
Month. West. J.
Monthly Western Jurist
Mon. W.J., Month. West. Jur., Mo.W.Jur.
Montreal Condensed Reports
M.C.R., Montr. Cond. Rep., Mont. Cond. Rep.

Montreal Law Reports
M.L.R.
Montreal Law Reports, Queen's Bench
M.L.R.Q.B., Montr. Q.B., Mont. L.R., Mont. L.R.Q.B., Montreal L.Q.B. (Can.), Montreal L.R.Q.B., M.L.R., C.B.R.
Montreal Law Reports, Superior Court
Mont. L.R., Mont. L.R.S.C., Montr. Super., M.L.R., C.S., M.L.R.S.C., Montreal L.R.S.C., Montreal L.S.C. (Can.)
Montreal Legal News
Mont. Leg. News, Montr. Leg. N.
Montriou's Cases in Hindu Law
Mont. Cas.
Montriou's Institutes of Jurisprudence
Mont. Inst.
Montriou's Reports, Bengal
Montr., Mont., Mont. Rep.
Montriou's Supplement to Morton's Reports
Montr.
Moody and Mackin's English Nisi Prius Reports
Moody & M. (Eng.), Moody & M., Moody & M., Mood. & Mack., Mood. & M., Mood & Malk., Moo. & Mal., M. & M.
Moody and Robinson's English Nisi Prius Reports
Mo. & R., Mood. & R., Mood. & Rob., Moody & R., Moody & R. (Eng.), Moo. & R., Moo. & Rob., M. & R., M.& Rob.

Moody's English Crown Cases Reserved
Moody., Moody C.C. (Eng.), Moody Cr.C., Mood. C.C., Moody, Cr.Cas., Moo., Moo. Cr. C., Moo. C.C., Mood., M.C.C.
Moon's Reports (133-144 Indiana and 6-14 Indiana Appeals)
Moon.
Moore and Payne's English Common Pleas Reports
Moo. & P., Moo. & Pay., M. & P., Mo. & P., Moore & P., Moore & P. (Eng.)
Moore and Scott's English Common Pleas Reports
M. & Sc., M. & S., M. & Scott., Moore & S., Moore & S. (Eng.), Mo. & S., Moo. & S., Moo. & Sc.
Moore and Walker's Reports (22-24 Texas)
Moore & W., Moore & Walker.
Moore's (A.) Reports, (1 Bosanquet and Puller)
A. Moor, Moore.A., Moo.A.
Moore's Abstracts of Title
Moore. Abs.
Moore's Criminal Law and Procedure
Moore, Cr. Law.
Moore's Digest of International Law
Moore Int. L., D.I.L. (Moore)
Moore's Divorce Trials
Moo. Tr.
Moore's East Indian Appeals
Moore E.I.
Moore's (B.) English Common Pleas Reports
Moo. C.P., Moo. J.B., Mo. J.B.

Moore's English King's Bench Reports
Moo. K.B., F. Moore, Moor., Moo. F., Moore K.B., Moore, Mo., Mo, Moo.

Moore's English King's Bench Reports (Arguments of Moore)
Arg. Mo.

Moore's English Privy Council Cases
Moore P.C.C., Moore P.C., Moore P.C.C. (Eng.), Moore P.C.C.N.S. (Eng.)

Moore's English Privy Council Reports, New Series
Moore P.C.N.S., M.P.C., Moo. P.C.C., Moo. P.C. (N.S.), Moore P.C.C.N.S., Moo. N.S., Moo. P.C.C.N.S., Moo. P.C.Cas.N.S., Moo. P.C., Moore, Mo.P.C., Mo., Mo

Moore's English Queen's Bench Reports
Moore Q.B., B.M., B. Monr.

Moore's Federal Practice
Moore, Fed. Practice

Moore's Gorham Case (English Privy Council)
Moore G.C., Moo. G.C.

Moore's Indian Appeal Report
Mo., Mo, Moore Ind. App. (Eng.), Mo.I.A., Moo. Ind. App., Moore Indian App., M.I.A., Moore Ind. App.

Moore's Presbyterian Digest
Moore, Presby. Dig.

Moore's Reports (67 Alabama)
Moore

Moore's Reports (28-34 Arkansas)
Moore

Moore's Reports (22-24 Texas)
Moore

Moore's Separate Report of Westerton v. Liddell
Moo. Sep. Rep.

Morawetz on Private Corporations
Mor. Corp., Mor. Priv. Corp.

Moreau-Lislet and Carleton's Laws of Las Siete Partidas in Force in Louisiana
M. & C. Partidas., Mor. & Carl., Moreau & Carleton's, Partidas.

Morehead and Brown's Digest of Kentucky Statute Laws
Ky. St. Law.

Morehead's Practice
Mor. Pr.

More's Lectures on the Law of Scotland
More. Lect.

More's Notes on Stair's Institutions of Scotland
More St., M. St.

Morey's Outlines of Roman Law
Morey Out. Rom. Law.

Morgan and Chute on the Judicature Acts
Morg. & Ch. Jud. Acts

Morgan and Williams' Law Journal
L.J.M. & W., Law Jour. (M. & W.), Morg, & W.L.J.

Morgan on the Law of Literature
Mor. Lit., Morg. Lit.

Morgan on the United States Tariff
Morg. Tar.

Morgan's Chancery Acts and Orders
Mor. Chy. Acts, Morg. Ch., Morg.

Morgan's Digest for Ceylon
Morgan.

Morgan's Legal Miscellany, Ceylon
    Morgan L. M.
Morice's English and Roman Dutch Law
    Mor. E. & R. D. Law
Morison's Dictionary, Court of Session Decisions, Supplement
    Mor. Supp.
Morison's Dictionary of Decisions, Scotch Court of Session
    Mor. Dic., Mor. Dict., Mor., Morr. Dict., M. Dict., M.
Morison's Synopsis, Scotch Session Cases
    Mor. Syn.
Morley's Digest of the Indian Reports
    Mor. Dig.
Morley's East Indian Digest
    Morl. Dig.
Morrell on the Law of Horses
    Mor. Hors.
Morrell on the Law of Wills
    Mor. Wills
Morrell's English Bankruptcy Cases
    Morrell B.C., Morr. Bankr. Cas., Morr., M.B., Morr. B.C., Morrell (Eng.), Morrell, Bankr. Cas.
Morris and Harrington's Reports, Bombay
    Morris & Har.
Morris' Iowa Reports
    Morris (Ia.), Morris (Iowa), Mor. Ia., Morr., Morris.
Morris' Jamaica Reports
    Morr. Jam., Morris R., Morr., Morris.
Morris' Law of Replevin
    Mor. Rep.
Morris' Mississippi State Cases
    Miss. St. Ca., Miss. St. Cas.

Morris on Compensations
    Mor. Comp.
Morris on Dilapidations, 2ed. (1871)
    Mor. Dil.
Morris on Railway Compensations
    Mor. Ry. Com.
Morris on Replevin
    Morr. Repl., Morris Repl.
Morris on the Law of Easements
    Mor. Eas.
Morris' Reports (5 California)
    Morr., Morr. Cal., Morris.
Morris' Reports (23-26 Oregon)
    Morr., Morris.
Morris' Reports (43-48 Mississippi)
    Mor. Miss., Morr. Miss., Morris.
Morris' Reports, Bombay
    Morr. Bomb., Morr., Morris.
Morris' State Cases, Mississippi
    Morr. St. Cas., Morris St. Cas., Mor. St. Ca., Mor. St. Cas.
Morrison's Dictionary of Decisions in the Scotland Court of Session, Brown's Supplement
    Bro.Sup. to Mor., Brown Supp. or Brown Sup. Dec., Br. Sup., B.S., Bro.Supp.
Morrison's Dictionary, Scotch Court of Sessions, Supplement
    Morr. Supp.
Morrison's Digest of Mining Decisions
    Morr. Dig., Morr. Mines.
Morrison's Mining Reports
    Mor. Min. Rep., M.R., Morr. Min. Rep., Morr. M. R., Morr. Min. R., Morrison Min. Rep.
Morrison's New Hampshire Digest
    Mor. Dig., Morr. Dig.

Morrison's Transcript of United States Supreme Court Decisions
Mor. Tran., Morr. Trans.

Morrissett's Reports (80, 98 Alabama)
Morris.

Morse on the Law of Arbitration and Award
Morse Arb.

Morse on the Law of Banks and Banking
Morse Bk., Morse, Banks.

Morse's Exchequer Reports, Canada
Morse Exch. Rep.

Morse's Famous Trials
Morse Tr.

Mortgage
M., Mort., Mtg.

Mortgage Guaranty Insurance Corporation
MGIC

Mortgagee
Mtgee.

Mortgagor
Mtgor.

Morton's Medical Malpractice: Handling Urology Cases
MMUC

Morton on Vendors and Purchasers
M.V. & P., Mort. Vend.

Morton's Reports, Calcutta Superior Court
Morton.

Moseley on Contraband of War
Mos. Cont.

Moseley on Elementary Law
Mos. El. L.

Moseley's English Chancery Reports Tempore King
Moseley, Mosely (Eng.), Mos.

Moses on the Law of Mandamus
Mos.Man.

Motion
Mot.

Motion for Mandamus Overruled
M.O.

Motor Carrier Cases
M.C.C.

Motor Vehicle Department
M.V.D.

Motor Vehicle Reports
M.U.R.

Moulton's New York Chancery Practice
Moult. Ch., Moult. Ch. P.

Mowbray's Styles of Deeds
Mow. St.

Moyle's Criminal Circulars
Moyle

Moyle's Entries
Moyle

Mozambique
Mozam.

Mozley and Whitley's Law Dictionary
M. & W. Law Dic., Mozley & Whiteley., Moz. & W., Mozley & W.

Muchall's Doctor and Student
Much. D. & S.

Muirhea's Institutes of Gaius
Muir. Gai.

Mulford's Nation
Mulford, Nation

Multilateral Investment Guarantee Agency
MIGA

Multiple
Mult.

Multiple Dwelling
Mult. Dwell.

**Multiple Independently Tar-
getable Reentry Vehicles**
  MIRV
Multiple Listing Service
  M.L.S.
Multiple Residence
  Mult.Resid.
**Multnomah Bar Association Com-
mittee on Continuing Legal
Education**
  MBACLE
**Mundy's Abstracts of Star Cham-
ber Proceedings**
  Mundy
Mumford's Jamaica Reports
  Mum. Jam., Mumf.
**Munford's Reports (15-20 Vir-
ginia)**
  Mun., Munf. (Va.), Munf.
**Munger on Application of Pay-
ments**
  Mung. Pay.
Municipal
  Mun., Munic.
Municipal and Election Cases
  Mun. & El. Cas.
Municipal and Parish Law Cases
  Munic. & P.L.
**Municipal and Planning Law Re-
ports**
  Mun. Plan. L. Rep., M.P.L.R.
**Municipal Association Reports,
New South Wales**
  M.A.R.
Municipal Attorney
  Mun. Att'y., Mun. Atty.
Municipal Code
  Mun. Code
**Municipal Code of the Province
of Quebec**
  M.C.P.Q.

Municipal Corporation Cases
  Mun. Corp. Cas., M.C.Cas., Mu.
  Corp. Ca.
Municipal Corporation Circular
  Mu. Corp. Cir.
**Municipal Corporation's Chron-
icle**
  M.C.C.
Municipal Court
  Mun. Ct.
**Municipal Court of Appeals for
the District of Columbia**
  Mun. Ct. App. Dist. Col., D.C.
  Mun. App.
Municipal Court of Montreal
  M.C.M.
Municipal Finance Journal
  Mun. Fin. J.
Municipal Home Rule
  Mun. Home Rule
Municipal Law Court Decisions
  Mun. L. Ct. Dec.
Municipal Law Journal
  Mu. L.J., Mun. L.J.
**Municipal Law Reporter, Penn-
sylvania**
  Mun., Munic. L. R. (Pa.), Mun.
  L.R.
Municipal Law Reports
  Mun., Mun. L.R., Mun.
Municipal Ordinance Review
  Mun. Ord. Rev.
Municipal Reports
  Mun. Rep.
**Municipal, School and State Tort
Liability**
  Mun. Tort Lib.
Munitions Appeal Reports
  Mun., Mun. App., Mun. App.
  Rep.
Munitions Board
  M.B.

Munitions of War Acts, Appeal Reports, Scotland
Mun. App. Sc.

Munitions Tribunals Appeals, Great Britain High Court of Justice
M.A.

Munkman's Employer's Liability at Common Law
Munk. Emp. Liab.

Muratori's Antiquitates Medii Aevi
Murat. Antiq. Med. Aevi.

Murdoch's Epitome Canada
Murd. Epit.

Murfree on Official Bonds
Murfree, Off. Bonds

Murphey's Reports (5-7 North Carolina)
Mur., Murph., Murph. (N.C.)

Murphy and Hurlstone's English Exchequer Reports
Murph. & H., Mur. & Hurl., M. & H., Mur. & H.

Murphy's Creditors' Rights in Bankruptcy
CRB

Murray on Usury
Murr. Us.

Murray's Ceylon Reports
Murr., Murray (Ceylon)

Murray's English Dictionary
Murray's Eng. Dict.

Murray's History of Usury
Mur. Us.

Murray's Jury Court Cases
Mur., Murray, Murray (Scot.), Murr.

Murray's Laws and Acts of Parliament
Murr.

Murray's New South Wales Reports
Murr.

Murray's Overruled Cases
Murr. Over. Cas.

Murray's Proceedings in the United States Courts
Mur. U.S. Ct.

Murray's Table of United States Cases
Mur. Tab. Cas.

Mutual
Mut.

Mutual Atomic Energy Liability Underwriters
MAELU

Mutual Atomic Energy Reinsurance Pool
MAERP

Mutual Funds Guide, Commerce Clearing House
Mut. Funds Guide (CCH)

Mutual Security Agency
M.S.A.

Mutukisna's Ceylon Reports
Mutukisna, Mut.

Myer's Federal Decisions
Myer Fed. Dec., Myer's Fed. Dec.

Myer's Texas Digest
Myer Dig.

Myers on Debtor Creditor Relations
DCR

Mylne and Craig's English Chancery Reports
My. & C., My. & Cr., Myl. & C., Myl. & C. (Eng.), Myl. & Cr.

Mylne and Keen's English Chancery Reports
M. & K., My. & K., Myl. & K., Myl. & K. (Eng.), Mylne & K.

Myrick's California Probate Court Reports
Myr., Myr. Prob., Myrick (Cal.), Myrick Prob. (Cal.), Myr. Cal. Prob., Myr. Prob. Rep., Myrick's Prob. Rep.

Mysore Chief Court Reports, India
Mys. Ch. Ct.

Mysore High Court Reports, India
Mys. H.C.R.

Mysore Law Journal , India
My. L. J., Mys. L.J., Mysore, L.J.

Mysore Law Reports, India
Mys. L.R., Mysore

Mysore Reports (Reprint), India
Mys.R.(R.)

Mysore Weekly Notes , India
Mys. W.N.

N

Naar on Suffrage and Elections
Naar Elec.
NACCA Law Journal (National
Association of Claimants' Compensation Attorneys)
NACCA L.J., Nacca L.J.
Nachmias/Nasuti on Joint Ventures
JV
Nagpur Law Journal, India
Nag. L.J., N.L.J.
Nagpur Law Notes, India
Nag. L.N.
Nagpur Law Reports, India
Nag. L.R., N.L.R.
Nagpur University College of
Law Magazine, India
Nag. U.C.L. Mag.
Nahmod's Civil Rights and Civil
Liberties Litigation
CRCL
Nalton's Collection of State Papers
Nal. St. P.
Namibia
Namib.
Napton's Reports (4 Missouri)
Napt., Napton.
NARAS Journal
NARAS J.
Narcotics Control Digest
Narcotics Control Dig.
Narcotics Law Bulletin
Narcotics L. Bull.
Nares on Penal Convictions
Nar. Conv.

Narrationes Modernae (Style's
English King's Bench Reports)
Narr. Mod.
Nash's Ohio Pleading and Practice
Nash Pl.
Nasmith's Institutes of English
Private Law
Nas. Inst. Priv., Nas. Inst. Pub.,
Nas. Inst.
Nassau Lawyer
Nassau L.
Natal Law Journal
Nat. L.J., Natal L.J.
Natal Law Magazine
Nat. L.M., Natal L.M.
Natal Law Quarterly
Natal L.Q., Nat. L.Q.
Natal Law Reports
Natal L.R., N.L.R.
Natal Law Reports, Old Series
N.L.R. (O.S.)
Natal Native High Court Reports
N.N.H.C.
Natal Reports
N.R.
Natal University Law Review
Nat. U.L. Rev., Natal U.L. Rev.
Nathan Bailey's English Dictionary
Bailey, Dict.
Nathan's Common Law of South
Africa
Nathan
National
Nat., Nat'l
National Academy of Arbitrators
NAA

National Academy of Arbitrators: Proceedings of the Annual Meeting
  Nat'l Acad. Arb. Proc. Ann. Meeting

National Academy of Science
  NAS

National Academy of Sciences-National Research Council
  NAS-NRC

National Advisory Committee for Aeronautics
  NACA

National Aeronautics and Space Administration Procurement Regulations
  NASAPR

National Aeronautics and Space Agency
  NASA

National Alliance of Businessmen
  N.A.B.

National Archives and Records Service
  NARS

National Association for the Advancement of Colored People
  NAACP

National Association of Businessmen
  N.A.B.

National Association of Claimants' Compensation Attorneys
  NACCA

National Association of Claimants' Compensation Attorneys Law Journal
  NACCALJ

National Association of Manufacturers Law Digest
  N.A.M.L. Dig.

National Association of Railway Commissions Annual Proceedings
  Nat.Asso.R.Coms.Ann.Proc.

National Association of Securities Dealers
  NASD

National Automobile Theft Bureau
  NATB

National Bank Cases
  Nat. B.C.

National Bankruptcy Law
  Nat. Bankr. Law.

National Bankruptcy News and Reports
  Nat. Bankr. N. & R., N.B.N. Rep., N.B.N.R.

National Bankruptcy Register
  Bankr. Reg., Nat. Bankr. R., Nat. Bankr. Reg., Nat. B.R.

National Bankruptcy Register Reports
  Bk. Reg., N. Bk. R., N. Bkpt. R., N. Bkpt. Reg., Nat. Bank. Reg., Nat. Bankr. Rep., N.B.R.

National Bar Bulletin
  Nat. Bar Bull.

National Bar Journal
  Nat. Bar. J., Nat. B.J., N.B.J.

National Black Law Journal
  Nat'l Black L. J.

National Board of Trial Advocates
  NBTA

National Bureau of Standards
  N.B.S.

National Center for Administrative Justice
  NCAJ

National Civic Review
  Nat. Civ. Rev., Nat'l Civic Rev., Nat. Civic Rev.

National Civil Service League
NCSL
National College of Criminal Defense Lawyers and Public Defenders
NCCDL
National College of District Attorneys
NCDA
National College of Juvenile Justice
NCJJ
National College of the State Judiciary
NCSJ
National Consumers' Finance Association Law Bulletin
N.C.F.A.
National Corporation Reporter
Nat. Corp. Rep.
National Council of Juvenile Court Judges
NCJCJ
National Council on Crime and Delinquency
NCCD
National Credit Union Administration
NCUA
National Crime Information Center
NCIC
National Defense Act
N.D.A.
National Defense University
NDU
National Democratic Party of Alabama
N.D.P.A.
National District Attorneys Association
NDAA

National Economic and Legislative Report, Commerce Clearing House
A. N. R.
National Economic Development Council
N.E.D.C.
National Environment Research Council
N.E.R.C.
National Environmental Policy Act
N.E.P.A.
National Farm Loan Association
NFLA
National Farmers' Union
NFU
National Federation of Federal Employees
NFFE
National Fire Protection and Control Association
NFPCA
National Fire Protection Association
NFPA
National Guard Regulation
NGR
National Health Insurance (Ministry of Health Decisions)
Min. H.M.D.
National Highway Transportation Safety Administration
N.H.T.S.A.
National Housing Act
N.H. Act
National Income Tax Magazine
Nat. Inc. Tax Mag., Nat'l Income Tax Mag., N.I.T.M., T.M.
National Industrial Equipment Reserve
NIER

National Industrial Recovery Act
  N.I.R.A.
National Industrial Relations
  Court National Labour Tribu-
  nal
  N.I.R.C.
National Institute for Occupa-
  tional Safety and Health
  NIOSH
National Institute for Trial Advo-
  cacy
  NITA
National Institute of Education
  NIE
National Institute of Law En-
  forcement and Criminal Justice
  NILECJ
National Institute of Mental
  Health
  NIMH
National Institutes of Health
  NIH
National Insurance Commis-
  sioner
  Nat. Ins. Commiss.
National Insurance Law Review
  Nat. Ins. L.R.
National Jewish Law Review
  Nat'l Jewish L. Rev.
National Journal of Criminal De-
  fense
  Nat. J. Crim. Def., Nat'l J.Crim.
  Def.
National Journal of Legal Educa-
  tion
  Nat. J. Leg. Ed.
National Labor Relations Act
  N.L.R.A.
National Labor Relations Board
  N.L.R.B.

National Labor Relations Board
  Advice Memorandum Case
  Number
  NLRB Advice Mem. Case No.
National Labor Relations Board
  Annual Report
  NLRB Ann. Rep.
National Labor Relations Board
  Decisions
  N.L.R.B. Dec.
National Labor Relations Board
  Decisions and Orders
  N.L.R.B.
National Labor Relations Board
  Decisions, Commerce Clearing
  House
  CCH NLRB
National Law Enforcement Tele-
  type System
  LETS
National Law Foundation
  NLF
National Law Journal
  Nat'l L.J.
National Law Record
  Nat. L. Rec.
National Law Reporter
  Nat. L. Rep.
National Law Review
  Nat. L. Rev.
National Lawyers' Guild Practi-
  tioner
  Nat'l Law Guild Prac.
National Lawyers' Guild Quar-
  terly
  Guild Q., Nat. L. Guild Q., Nat.
  Law Guild Q., N.L.G.Q.
National Legal Center for the
  Public Interest
  NLCPI
National Legal Magazine
  Nat. Legal Mag., Nat'l Legal
  Mag.

National Liberation Council De-
cree, Ghana
N.L.C.D.
National Liberation Front
N.L.F.
National Library of Medicine
NLM
National Medication Board
NMB
National Municipal Review
Nat. Mun. Rev., Nat. Munic.
Rev., Nat'l Mun. Rev.
National Oceanic and Atmos-
pheric Administration
NOAA
National Organization on Legal
Problems of Education
NOLPE
National Patents Appeal Tribu-
nal
P.A.T.
National People's Congress
N.P.C.
National Petroleum Council
N.P.C.
National Pollutant Discharge
Elimination System, Adjudica-
tory Hearings Proceedings
N.P.D.E.S.
National Production Authority
N.P.A.
National Public Employment Re-
porter
Nat'l Pub. Empl. Rep.
(Lab.Rel.Press)
National Quarterly Review
Nat. Q. Rev.
National Railroad Adjustment
Board Awards
N.R.A.B.
National Railroad Passenger Cor-
poration
Amtrak

National Recovery Administra-
tion
N.R.A.
National Redemption Council De-
cree, Ghana
N.R.C.D.
National Register
Nat. Reg.
National Reporter System
Nat. Rept. Syst., Natl. Rep. Sys.
National Research Council
NRC
National Research Development
Corporation
N.R.D.C.
National Resource Center for
Consumers of Legal Services
NRCLS
National Review
Nat. Rev.
National School Law Reporter
Nat. School L. Rptr., Nat'l
School L. Rptr.
National Science Foundation
NSF
National Security Agency
NSA
National Security Council
NSC
National Security Index of the
American Security Council
N.S.I.
National Security Resources
Board
N.S.R.B.
National Student Volunteer Pro-
gram
N.S.V.P.
National Tax Association Bulletin
Bull.N.T.A., Bull. Nat. Tax As-
soc.

National Tax Association Proceedings
N.T.A. Proceedings
National Tax Journal
Nat. Tax. J., Nat'l Tax J.
National Tax Magazine
Nat. Tax Mag.
National Technical Information Service
NTIS
National Transportation Safety Board
N.T.S.B.
National Transportation Safety Board Decisions
N. Trans. S. Dec., N.T.S.B.
National University Law Review
Nat. U.L. Rev.
National War College
NWC
National War Labor Board
N.W.L.B.
National Youth Administration
NYA
Native Appeal Courts
N.A.C.
Native Authority Legal Notice
N.A.L.N.
Native Court
N.Ct.
Native High Court Reports
N.H.C.
Native Tribunals' Reports
Al.Kada
Natural
Nat.
Natural Gas Lawyer's Journal
Nat. Gas Law. J.
Natural Law Forum
Nat. L.F., Natural L.F.
Natural Resources
Nat. Res.

Natural Resources and Environment
Nat. Resources & Env't
Natural Resources Journal
Nat. Res. J., Nat. Resources J., Natural Resources J., N.R.J.
Natural Resources Law Institute
NRLI
Natural Resources Law Newsletter
Nat. Resources L. Newsl.
Natural Resources Lawyer
Nat. Res. Lawyer, Nat. Resources Law, Natural Resources Lawy.
Naval Courts and Boards
N.C. & B.
Naval Law Review
Naval L. Rev.
Naval Material Command
NMC
Naval Supplement, Manual for Courts-Martial
N.S.M.C.M.
Naval War College Review
Nav. War C. Rev.
Navigation
Nav.
Navy Department Bulletin
N.D.B.
Navy Judge Advocate General Manual
JAG Man.
Navy Regulations
N.R.
North Dakota Journal of Legislation
N.D. J. Legis.
Ne Exeat (Lat.)
Ne. Ex.
Nebraska
N., Nb., NE, Neb.

Nebraska Administrative Rules and Regulations
Neb. Admin. R.

Nebraska Attorney General Reports
Rep. Neb. Att'y Gen.

Nebraska Board of Railroad Commissioners
Neb. Bd. R.C.

Nebraska Board of Transportation
Neb. Bd. Trans.

Nebraska Constitution
Neb. Const.

Nebraska Continuing Legal Education, Inc.
NCLE

Nebraska Law Bulletin
N.B.L.B., Neb. L. Bull., Neb. L.B., Nebr. L.B.

Nebraska Law Review
Nb. L., Nb. L.R., Neb. L. Rev., Nebr. L. Rev., Nebraska L. Rev.

Nebraska Laws
Neb. Laws

Nebraska Legal News
Neb. Leg. N.

Nebraska Railway Commission Reports
Neb. R.C.

Nebraska Reports
Neb., Nebr.

Nebraska State Bar Journal
Neb. S.B.J., Neb. St. B.J., Nebr. B.A.

Nebraska State Railway Comm.
Neb. S.R.C.

Nebraska Supreme Court Journal
Neb. Sup. Ct.J., S.C., J.

Nebraska Supreme Court Reports
Neb.

Nebraska Unofficial Reports
Neb. (Unof.), N.U., Neb. Unoff.

Nebraska Workmen's Compensation Court Bulletin
Neb. W.C.C.

Needham's Annual Summary of Tax Cases
Need.

Negligence
Negl.

Negligence and Compensation Cases Annotated
Negl. & Comp. Cas. Ann., N.C.C.A.

Negligence and Compensation Cases Annotated, New Series
Negl. & Comp. Cas. Ann. (N.S.), N.C.C.A.N.S.

Negligence and Compensation Cases Annotated, Third Series
Negl. & Comp. Cas. Ann.3d.. N.C.C.A.3d

Negligence Cases, Commerce Clearing House
Neg. C., Negl. Cas.

Negligence Cases, Second Series, Commerce Clearing House
Negl. Cas.2d, Negligence Cases (2d)

Negotiable Instrument
Neg. Inst.

Negotiable Instruments Law
N.I.L., Neg. Inst. Law

Negotiation Journal
Negotiation J.

Neighborhood Youth Corps
NYC

Nell's Reports, Ceylon
Nell

Nelson's Abridgment of the Common Law
Nels. Abr.

Nelson's English Chancery Reports
Nels., Nelson (Eng.), Nel., N.
Ch. R., Nel. C.R., Nels.

Nelson's Finch's English Chancery Reports, tempore Finch
Nelson's Rep., Ca. & F., Nels.
F., Fin., Nels. F.t.

Nelson's Lex Maneriorum
Nels. Lex Man.

Nelson's Lutwyche English Common Pleas Reports
N.L.

Nelson's Rights of the Clergy
Nels. Cler.

Nemine Contra Dicente (no one dissenting) (Lat.)
N.C.D.

Nemine Contradicente (nobody contradicting) (Lat.)
Nem. con.

Nemine Dissentiente (nobody dissenting) (Lat.)
Nem. dis.

Nepal
Ne.

Nepalese
Ne.

Net operating Loss
NOL

Netherlands
Neth.

Netherlands Arbitration Institute
N.A.I.

Netherlands International Law Review
Neth. Int'l L. Rev., N.I.L. Rev.,
NILR, N.I.L.R.

Netherlands Yearbook of International Law
Neth. Y.B. Int'l Law, N.Y.I.L.,
Nederl. Yb. of Internat. L., Netherl. Int'l L. Rev.

Nevada
N., Nev., Nv.

Nevada Administrative Code
Nev. Admin. Code

Nevada Attorney General Official Opinions
Op. Nev. Att'y Gen.

Nevada Constitution
Nev. Const.

Nevada Public Service Commission
Nev. P.S.C.

Nevada Public Service Commission Opinions
Nev. P.S.C. Op.

Nevada Railroad Commission
Nev. R.C.

Nevada Reports
Nev., Nevada Rep., Nevada
Repts., Nevada State Reports

Nevada Revised Statutes
Nev. Rev. Stat., N.R.S.

Nevada State Bar Journal
Nev. S.B.J., Nev. St. Bar J.,
Nev. St. B.J.

Nevada Supreme Court Reports
Nev.

Nevile and Macnamara's English Railway & Canal Cases
N. & Macn.

Nevile and Manning's English King's Bench Reports
N. & Ma., N. & M., Nev. &
Man., Nev. & M.K.B., Nev. &
Man. Mag. Cas., Nev. & M.M.C.

Nevile and Manning's English Magistrates' Cases
Nev. & M. (Eng.), Nev. & Man.
Mag. Cas., N. & M.M.C., N. &
M. Mag.

Nevile and Perry's English King's Bench Reports
N. & P., Nev. & P.K.B., Nev. & P.

Nevile and Perry's English Magistrates' Cases
N. & P. Mag., Nev. & P. Mag. Cas., Nev. & P.M.C., Nev. & P., N. & P.M.C.

Neville and Macnamara' s English Railway and Canal Cases
Nev. & Mac., Nev. & Macn., N. & McN., Nev. & MacN., Nev. & McN.

New Annual Register
New Ann. Reg.

New Benloe's English King's Bench Reports
N.B., New Benl., N. Benl., N. Ben.

New Brunswick
N.B.

New Brunswick Board of Public Utilities Commission
N.B. Bd. P.U.C.

New Brunswick Equity Cases
N.B. Eq. Ca., New B. Eq. Ca., New Br. Eq. Cas. (Can.)

New Brunswick Equity Reports
N.B. Eq., New Br. Eq. (Can.), N.B. Eq. R., N.B. Eq. Rep., New B. Eq. Rep.

New Brunswick Reports
N.B. Rep., New Br., N. Bruns., N.B.R., New Br. R., N.B.

New Brunswick Reports, Second Series
N.B.2d., N.B.R.2d.

New Brunswick Revised Statutes
N.B. Rev. Stat.

New Brunswick Statutes
N.B. Stat.

New Brunswick Vice Admiralty Reports
N.B.V. Ad.

New Cases (Bingham's New Cases)
New Cas., N.C., See also Bingham's New Cases

New Cases in Equity (8-9 Modern Reports)
New Cas. Eq.

New Chancery Cases (Younge and Collyer)
N.C.C., see also Younge & Collyer's Chancery Reports

New Community
New Commun.

New Edition
N.E.

New England
N.E.

New England Historical and Genealogical Register
New Eng. Hist.

New England Journal of Medicine
New Eng. J. Med.

New England Journal of Prison Law
New Eng. J. Prison, New Eng. J. Prison L., N. Eng. J. Prison L.

New England Journal on Criminal and Civil Confinement
New Eng. J. Crim. & Civil Confinement, New Eng. J. on Crim. & Civ. Confinement

New England Law Review
N. Eng. L. Rev., N. Engl. L. Rev., New Eng. L. Rev., New England L. Rev.

New England Reporter
N. Eng. Rep., N.E. Rep., N.E.R., New Eng., New Eng. R., New Eng. Rep.

New Hampshire
N.H.

New Hampshire Bar Journal
New Hamp. B.J., N.H.B.J.,
N.H.J.

New Hampshire Board of Railroad Commissioners
N.H.R.C.

New Hampshire Code of Administrative Rules
N.H. Admin. Code

New Hampshire Constitution
N.H. Const.

New Hampshire Judicial Council
N.H. Judicial Council

New Hampshire Law Reporter
N.H.L. Rep.

New Hampshire Laws
N.H. Laws

New Hampshire Public Service Commission Reports
N.H.P.S.C.R.

New Hampshire Reports
N.H., N.H.R., New Hamp. R.,
New Hamp. Rep., N. Hamp., N.
Hamp. R., N. Hampshire Rep.,
New Hamp., New Hampshire
Rep., N.H. Rep., N.H. Reports,
Roc., Rock., N. Hamp. Rep.

New Hampshire Revised Statutes
N.H.R.S.

New Hampshire Revised Statutes Annotated
N.H. Rev. Stat. Ann.

New Hampshire Rulemaking Register
N.H. Rulemaking Reg.

New Hampshire State Bar Association
N. Hamp. S.B.A.

New Hampshire Supreme Court Reports
N.H.

New Irish Jurist
N.I.J.

New Irish Jurist and Local Government Review
New Ir. Jur.

New Irish Jurist Reports
N.I.J.R.

New Jersey
N.J.

New Jersey Administrative Code
N.J. Admin. Code

New Jersey Administrative Register.
N.J. Admin. Reg.

New Jersey Advance Reports and Weekly Review
Adv. Rep. N.J.

New Jersey Board of Railroad Commissioners Annual Reports
N.J.R.C.

New Jersey Constitution
N.J. Const.

New Jersey Equity Reports, New Jersey
New Jersey Eq., New Jersey Equity, N.J. Ch., N.J. Eq., N.J. Eq.
R., N.J. Equity, N.J.E.

New Jersey Juvenile and Domestic Relations Court
N.J. Jur. & Dom. Rel. Ct.

New Jersey Law Journal
New Jersey L.J., N.J. Law J.,
N.J.L.J.

New Jersey Law News
N.J. Law N.

New Jersey Law Reports
N.J. Law., N.J.L., N. Jersey R.,
New Jersey, N.J. Law Rep., N.J.
Rep., N.J. Reports, N.J.L. Rep.

New Jersey Law Review
New Jersey L. Rev., N.J.L. Rev.

New Jersey Laws
N.J. Laws

New Jersey Lawyer
N.J. Law., N.J. Lawy.
New Jersey Legal Record
New Jersey Leg. Rec., N.J. Leg.
Rec.
New Jersey Miscellaneous Reports
N.J. Mis. R., N.J. Misc., NJM,
N.J. Mis.
New Jersey Municipal Court
N.J. Mun. Ct.
New Jersey Public Utility Commission Reports
N.J.P.U.C.
New Jersey Realty Title News
N.J. Re. Tit. N.
New Jersey Register
N.J.R.
New Jersey Reports
N.J.
New Jersey Revised Statutes
N.J. Rev. Stat.
New Jersey Session Law Service
N.J. Sess. Law Serv.
New Jersey State Bar Association
N.J.S.B.A.
New Jersey State Bar Association Quarterly
New Jersey S.B.A. Qu.,
N.J.S.B.A.Q.
New Jersey State Bar Journal
N.J. St. B.J., N.J.S.B.J.
New Jersey State Board of Tax Appeals Opinions
N.J.S.B.T.A. Ops.
New Jersey Statutes Annotated
N.J. Stat. Ann. (West), N.J.S.A.
New Jersey Superior Court Reports
N.J. Super., N.J.S., N.J. Sup.
New Jersey Supreme Court Reports
N.J.

New Jersey Tax Court Reports
N.J. Tax
New Law Journal
New L.J.
New Law Reports, Ceylon
N.L.R.
New Library of Law
N.L.L.
New Library of Law and Equity
N.L.L.
New Mexico
N.M.
New Mexico Constitution
N.M. Const.
New Mexico Court of Appeals
N.M., N.M. App.
New Mexico Law Review
N. Mex. L. Rev., New Mex. L.
Rev., New Mexico L. Rev.,
N.M.L., N.M.L. Rev., N.M.L.R.
New Mexico Reports
N.M.
New Mexico Reports (Gildersleeve)
N.M. (G.), Gildersleeve,
Gildersleeve (N.Mex.), Gild.
New Mexico Reports (Johnson)
N.M. (J.)
New Mexico State Bar Association
N.M. St. Bar Assn., N.M.S.B.A.,
New Mex. B.A., New Mex. S.B.A.
New Mexico State Corporation Commission
N.M.S.C.C.
New Mexico Statutes
N.M.S.
New Mexico Statutes Annotated
N.M. Stat. Ann.
New Mexico Supreme Court Reports
N.M.

New Mexico Territorial Court
  N.M., N. Mex
New Natura Brevium
  New Nat. Brev.
New Practice
  N. P.
New Practice Cases, England
  New Pract. Case., New Pr.
  Cases., N.P.C.
New Reports, England
  New Rep.
New School of Social Research
  NSSR
New Senate Office Building
  NSOB
New Series
  N.S., (n.s.)
New South Wales
  N.S. Wales, N.S.W.
New South Wales Arbitration Reports
  N.S.W.A.R.
New South Wales Bankruptcy
  Cases
  B.C. (N.S.W.), B.C.
New South Wales Court of Review Decisions
  N.S.W.C.R.D.
New South Wales Equity Reports
  N.S.W. Eq.
New South Wales Incorporated
  Acts
  N.S.W. Inc. Acts
New South Wales Industrial Arbitration Cases
  N.S.W. Ind. Arbtn., N.S.W. Ind.
  Arbtn. Cas.
New South Wales Industrial Arbitration Reports
  N.S.W. Indus. Arb. R.
New South Wales Land Appeal
  Court Cases
  N.S.W. Land App.

New South Wales Land Appeal
  Courts
  N.S.W. Land App. Cts.
New South Wales Land Valuation
  Reports
  N.S.W.L.V.R.
New South Wales Law
  N.S. Wales L.
New South Wales Law Reports
  New So. W.L., N.S.W.L.R.
New South Wales Law Reports
  Equity
  N.S. Wales L.R. Eq., N.S.W. Eq.
  Rep.
New South Wales Local Government Reports
  N.S.W. Local Gov't R.
New South Wales, Port Phillip
  District Judgments
  R.J.
New South Wales Public Acts
  N.S.W. Pub. Acts, Pub. Acts
  N.S.W.
New South Wales Public Statutes
  N.S.W. Pub. Stat.
New South Wales Regulations, By
  Laws and Ordinances
  N.S.W. Regs., B. & Ords.
New South Wales Reports
  N.S.W.R., N.S.W.
New South Wales Reports, Admiralty
  N.S.W. Adm.
New South Wales Reports, Bankruptcy Cases
  N.S.W. Bktcy. Cas., N.S.W.B.
New South Wales Reports, Equity
  N.S.W.C. Eq.
New South Wales Reports, (1-3)
  Ow.
New South Wales Reserved Equity Decisions
  R.E.D.

New South Wales State Reports
New So. W. St., St. Rep. N.S.W.,
N.S.W. St. R., N.S.W.S.R., S.R.,
S.R.N.S.W.
**New South Wales State Reports,
Bankruptcy and Probate**
S.R. (N.S.W.) B. & P.
**New South Wales State Reports,
Equity**
S.R. (N.S.W.) Eq.
**New South Wales Supreme Court
Cases**
N.S.W.S. Ct. Cas.
**New South Wales Supreme Court
Reports**
N.S.W.S.C.R., S.C.R.N.S.W.,
N.S.W.S. Ct. R.
**New South Wales Supreme Court
Reports, Equity**
S.C.R. (N.S.W.) Eq., S.C.R.
(NSW) Eq.
**New South Wales Supreme Court
Reports, Law**
S.C.R. (N.S.W.) L.,
N.S.W.S.C.R. (L.)
**New South Wales Supreme Court
Reports, New Series**
N.S.W.S.C.R.N.S., S.C.R. (N.S.)
(N.S.W.)
New South Wales Weekly Notes
New So. W.W.N., Week. No.,
N.S.W.W.N., W.N.N.J.W.
**New South Wales Worker's Com-
pensation Reports**
N.S.W. Worker's Comp. R.,
N.S.W.W.C.R.
New Style
N.S., (n.s.)
New Term Reports, England
New Term Rep., N.T. Repts.,
N.T. Rep.
New Trial
New Tr.

New York
N.Y.
**New York Advance Digest Serv-
ice, Commerce Clearing House**
N.Y.C.C.H.
New York Annotated Cases
Ann. Cas., N.Y. Ann. Ca., N.Y.
Ann. Cas., N.Y. Anno. Cas.
New York Annotated Code by
Bliss
Bliss N.Y.Code
New York Annotated Digest
N.Y. Anno. Dig., N.Y. Annot.
Dig.
**New York Appellate Division Re-
ports**
Ap.
**New York Appellate Division Re-
ports, Second Series**
Ap. 2d
**New York Attorney General Opin-
ions**
Op. N.Y. Atty. Gen.,
Atty.Gen.Op.N.Y.
**New York Attorney General Re-
ports**
New York Att'y Gen. Annual
Rep.
New York Banking Law
N.Y. Bank. Law
New York Chancery Sentinel
N.Y. Ch. Sent.
New York City
NYC
**New York City Bar Association
Bulletin**
N.Y.C.B.A., N.Y.C.B.A.Bull.,
New York City B.A.Bul.
New York City Civil Court Act
City Civ. Ct. Act.

New York City Committee on Criminal Courts Law and Procedure, Association of the Bar, Bulletin
C.C.C.Bull
New York City Court
N.Y. City Ct.
New York City Court Reports
N.Y. City Ct. Rep.
New York City Court Reports Supplement
N.Y. City Ct. Supp.
New York City Criminal Court Act
City Crim. Ct. Act.
New York City Hall Recorder
N.Y. City H. Rec., City H. Rec.
New York Civil Practice
Civ. Prac. (NY)
New York Civil Practice Law and Rules
N.Y. Civ. Prac. Law & R.
New York Civil Procedure
Civ. Proc. (NY), N.Y. Civ. Pro., N.Y. Civ. Proc.
New York Civil Procedure Reports
N.Y. Civ. Pr. Rep., N.Y. Civ. Proc. R.
New York Civil Procedure Reports, New Series
N.Y. Civ. Proc. R., N.S., N.Y. Civ. Proc. (N.S.)
New York Code by Bliss
Bliss N.Y.Co.
New York Code Remedial Justice
N.Y. Co. Rem.
New York Code Reporter
N.Y. Code R., N.Y. Code Rep., N.Y. Code Report., N.Y. Code Reptr.

New York Code Reporter, New Series
N.Y. Code Reptr. N.S., N.Y. Code Report. N.S., Code Rep. N.S., N.Y. Code R. N.S., N.Y. Code Rep. N.S., N.Y. Code Reports, N.S.
New York Codes, Rules and Regulations
N.Y.C.R.R.
New York Condensed Reports
N.Y. Cond.
New York Consolidated Law Services
N.Y. Law (Consol.)
New York Consolidated Laws (McKinney)
McK. Consol. Laws
New York Constitution
N.Y. Const.
New York Continuing Legal Education
N.Y. Cont. L. Ed., N.Y. Cont. Legal Ed.
New York County Lawyers Association Bar Bulletin
N.Y. County B. Bull., N.Y. County Law. Assn. B. Bull., N.Y. County Law Ass'n. B. Bull.
New York County Lawyer's Bar Bulletin
Bar Bull. (N.Y. County L.A.)
New York Court of Appeals
N.Y. Ct. App.
New York Court of Appeals Decisions
N.Y. App. Dec.
New York Court of Appeals Reports
N.Y., N.Y. Rep., New York R., New York Rep., N.Y. Reps, N.Y.C.A., N.Y.R.

New York Court of Appeals Reports, Second Series
N.Y.2d
New York Criminal Reports
N. Cr., N.Y. Cr. R., N.Y. Cr.
Rep., N.Y. Cr., N.Y. Crim., N.Y.
Crim. R., N.Y. Crim. Rep.
New York Current Court Decisions
N.Y.C.C.D.
New York Daily Law Gazette
N.Y. Daily L. Gaz.
New York Daily Law Register
N.Y. Daily L. Reg.
New York Daily Register
Dai. Reg., N.Y. Daily Reg., N.Y.
Reg.
New York Daily Transcript
Daily Transc., Daily Trans.,
N.Y. Daily Tr.
New York Department Reports
N.Y. Dept. R., N.Y. Dep't R.,
N.Y.D.R.
New York Election Cases
N.Y. El. Cas., N.Y. Elec. Cas.,
N.Y. Elect. Cas., El. Cas., El.
Cas. (NY), Elect. Cas. N. Y., See
also Armstrong's Contested
Election Cases
**New York Estate Power and
Trust Law**
EPTL
**New York Estate Tax Reports,
Prentice-Hall**
N.Y.E.T.R.
New York International Law Review
N.Y. Int'l L. Rev.
New York Intramural Law Review
N.Y.U. Intra. L. Rev.

New York Judicial Repository
Jud. Rep., N.Y. Jud. Rep., N.Y.
Jud. Repos.
New York Jurisprudence
N.Y. Jur.
New York Jurist
N.Y. Jur.
New York Law Forum
N.Y. Law Forum, N.Y.F.,
N.Y.L.F.
New York Law Gazette
N.Y. Law Gaz., N.Y.L. Gaz.
New York Law Journal
L.J., N.Y. Law, N.Y.L.J.
New York Law Record
N.Y.L. Rec.
New York Law Review
N.Y. Law Rev., N.Y.L. Rev.
New York Laws
L.N.Y., N.Y. Laws
New York Law School International Law Society Journal
N.Y.L. Sch. Int'l. L. Soc'y. J.
**New York Law School Journal of
Human Rights**
N.Y.L. Sch. J. Hum. Rts.
**New York Law School Journal of
International and Comparative
Law**
N.Y.J. Intl & Comp. L., N.Y.L.
Sch. J. Int'l. & Comp. L., N.Y.L.
Sch. J. Intl. & Comp. L.
New York Law School Law Review
N.Y.L. Sch. L. Rev., N.Y.L.
School Rev.
New York Law School Review
N.Y.L.S. Rev.
**New York Law School Student
Law Review**
N.Y.L.S. Stud. L. Rev.
New York Leading Cases
N.Y.L. Cas.

New York Leading Cases Annotated
N.Y.L.C. Ann.

New York Legal News
N.Y. Leg. N.

New York Legal Observer
Legal Observer, N.Y. Legal Observer, N.Y.L.O., N.Y. Leg. Obs.

New York Legal Register
N.Y. Leg. Reg.

New York Miscellaneous Reports
N.Y. Misc., Delehanty, M., Msc., Mis., Misc. Reports, Misc. Repts.

New York Miscellaneous Reports, Second Series
Msc2d, N.Y. Misc.2d.

New York Monthly Law Bulletin
N.Y. Mo. L. Bul., N.Y. Month. L. Bull., N.Y. Month. L. But., N.Y. Mo. Law Bul., Monthly L. Bul., N.Y. Law Bul., N.Y. Monthly Law Bul.

New York Monthly Law Record
N.Y. Mo. L. Rec., N.Y. Monthly Law Record

New York Monthly Law Reports
N.Y. Mo. L.R., N.Y. Month. L. Rep., N.Y. Month. L.R.

New York Municipal Gazette
N.Y. Mun. Gaz.

New York Official Compilation of Codes, Rules and Regulations
N.Y. Admin. Code

New York Official Department Reports
N.Y. Off. Dept. R.

New York Practice Reports
N.Y. Pr., N.Y.P.R., N.Y.Pr. Rep.

New York Public Service Commission, First District
N.Y.P.S.C.(1st D.)

New York Public Service Commission, Second District
N.Y.P.S.C.(2d D.).

New York Railroad Commission Reports
N.Y.R.C.

New York Record
N.Y. Rec.

New York Reporter
N.Y. Reptr.

New York Reports
N.Y.

New York Revised Laws
N.Y.R.L.

New York Revised Statutes
N.Y.R.S.

New York Sea Grant Law and Policy Journal
N.Y. Sea Grant L. & Pol'y J.

New York Senate Journal
N.Y. Sen. J.

New York State
N.Y.S.

New York State Bar Association
NYSBA

New York State Bar Association Antitrust Law Symposium
N.Y. St. B.A. Antitrust L. Symp.

New York State Bar Association Bulletin
N.Y. St. Ba. A., N.Y.S.B.A. Bull.

New York State Bar Journal
N.Y. St. B.J., N.Y. State Bar J., N.Y.S.B.J.

New York State Commission on Administration of Justice Report
CAJR

New York State Department of Labor, Court Decisions of Workmen's Compensation
N.Y.D.L.W.C. Dec.

New York State Department Reports
N.Y. St. Dept. Rep., N.Y.S.D.R., S.D.R.

New York State Department Reports, Unofficial
Dept. R. Un.

New York State Labor Relations Board
N.Y.L.R.B.

New York State Labor Relations Board Decisions
N.Y.SLRB

New York State Labor Relations Board Decisions and Orders
N.Y.L.R.B. Dec.

New York State Register
N.Y. St. Reg.

New York State Reporter
N.Y. St., N.Y.S., N.Y.S.R., S.R., N.Y. St. R., N.Y. St. Rep., N.Y. St. Repr., N.Y. State R., N.Y. State Rep., State R., State Rep., State Reporter

New York Statutes by Birdseye
Birds. St.

New York Stock Exchange
N.Y.S.E.

New York Stock Exchange Guide, Commerce Clearing House
N.Y.S.E., N.Y.S.E. Guide (CCH)

New York Superior Court Reports
N.Y. Super, N.Y. Super. Ct., N.Y. Supr. Ct. Rep., N.Y. Super. Ct. R., N.Y. Super. Ct. Rep., N.Y. Supr., N.Y. Supr. Ct., N.Y. Supr. Ct. R., N.Y.S. Ct.

New York Supplement
New York Supp., N.Y. Supp., N.Y.S., S., N.Y. Supl., N.Y. Suppl., Supp.

New York Supplement Second Series
N.Y.S.2d, N.Y. Supp.2d, S.2d., N.Y. Supplement 2d Series

New York Supreme Court, Appellate Division
App. Div.

New York Supreme Court, Appellate Division Reports
App. Div., App. Div. (NY), A.D., Ap., N.Y. App. Div., App. Div. N. Y. Sup. Ct., App. Div. R., A.D.2d

New York Supreme Court, Appellate Division Reports, Second Series
App. Div. 2d

New York Supreme Court Reports
Hun, N.Y. Sup. Ct., N.Y. Suprm. Ct., Sup. Ct. R. (N.Y.)

New York Supreme Court Reports by Thompson and Cook
N.Y. Supr. Ct. Repts. (T. & C.)

New York Supreme Court Reports, Lansing
Lansg., Lansing

New York Tax Cases, Commerce Clearing House
N.Y. Tax Cas.

New York Term Reports (Caines' Reports)
N.Y.T.R.

New York Themis
N.Y. Them.

New York Times
N.Y. Times

New York Transcript
N.Y. Trans.

New York Transcript Appeal
N.Y. Trans. App.

New York Transcript Appeals Reports
    Trans. Appeal R., Transcript Appeals

New York Transcript, New Series
    N.Y. Trans. N.S.

New York Transcript Reports
    N.Y. Trans. Rep.

New York Unconsolidated Laws (McKinney)
    N.Y. Unconsol. Laws

New York University
    NYU

New York University Annual Conference on Labor
    N.Y. Cn.

New York University Conference on Charitable Foundations Proceedings
    N.Y.U. Conf. Charitable

New York University Conference on Labor
    N.Y.U. Conf. Lab., N.Y.U. Conf. on Lab.

New York University Institute of Federal Taxation
    N.Y.U. Inst. Fed. Taxation, N.Y.U. Inst. Fed. Tax., N.Y.U. Inst. on Fed. Tax.

New York University Intramural Law Review
    N.Y.U. Intramur. L. Rev.

New York University Journal of International Law and Politics
    N.Y. Univ. J of Internat. L. and Polit., N.Y.U.J. Int. Law & Pol., N.Y.U.J. Int'l L. & Pol., N.Y.U.J. Intl Law & Pol.

New York University Law Center Bulletin
    N.Y.U.L. Center Bull.

New York University Law Quarterly Review
    N.Y.U. L. Q. Rev., N.Y.U. L. Qu. Rev.

New York University Law Review
    N.Y.L., N.Y.U. L. Rev., N.Y.U. L.R., N.Y. Univ. L. Rev.

New York University Review of Law and Social Change
    N.Y.U. Rev. L. & Soc. Change, N.Y.U. Rev. L. & Soc., N.Y.U. Rev. Law & Soc., N.Y.U. Rev. Law & Soc.C.

New York University School of Continuing Education, Continuing Education in Law and Taxation
    NYU LT

New York University Tax Institute
    N.Y.U. T.I.

New York Weekly Digest
    N.Y. Week. Dig., N.Y. Wkly. Dig., Wkly. Dig., Week. Dig., Week. Dig. (N.Y.), N.Y. Weekly Dig., W.Dig.

New Yugoslav Law
    New Yugo. L.

New Zealand
    New Zeal., N.Z.

New Zealand Appeal Court Reports
    App.Ct.Rep.

New Zealand Appeal Reports
    N.Z. App. Rep., App.N.Z.

New Zealand Appeal Reports, Second Series
    App.N.Z.2d

New Zealand Awards, Recommendations, Agreements, etc.
    N.Z. Awards.

New Zealand Colonial Law Journal
   N.Z. Col. L.J.

New Zealand Contracts and Commercial Law Reform Committee
   N.Z.C.C.L.R.C.

New Zealand Court of Appeals
   N.Z. Ct. App.

New Zealand Court of Arbitration
   N.Z. Ct. Arb.

New Zealand Criminal Law Reform Committee
   N.Z.C.L.R.C.

New Zealand Foreign Affairs Review
   N.Z. Foreign Aff. Rev.

New Zealand Gazette Law Reports
   Gaz. L.R. (N.Z.), N.Z. Gaz. L.R., N.Z.G.L.R.

New Zealand Industrial Arbitration Awards
   N.Z. Ind. Arb.

New Zealand Journal of Public Administration
   N.Z.J. Pub. Admin., N.Z.J. Pubi. Adm.

New Zealand Jurist
   N.Z. Jur.

New Zealand Jurist, New Series
   N.Z. Jur. N.S.

New Zealand Jurist Reports
   New Zeal. Jur. R.

New Zealand Justice of the Peace
   N.Z.J.P.

New Zealand Law Journal
   New Zeal. L.J., N.Z.L.J., NZLJ

New Zealand Law Journal, Magistrates' Court Decisions
   N.Z.L.J.M.C.

New Zealand Law Reports
   Law Rep., L.R., New Zeal L., New Zeal. L.R., N.Z.L.R.

New Zealand Law Reports, Court of Appeal
   N.Z.L.R.C.A.

New Zealand Law Revision Commission
   N.Z.L.R.C.

New Zealand Law Society Newsletter
   N.Z. Law Soc. N.

New Zealand Legal Research Foundation
   N.Z.L.R.F.

New Zealand Privy Council Cases
   N.Z.P.C. Cas., N.Z.P.C.C.

New Zealand Property Law and Equity Reform Committee
   N.Z.P.L.E.R.C.

New Zealand Public and Administrative Law Reform Committee
   N.Z.P.A.L.R.C.

New Zealand Recent Law Review
   N.Z. Recent L. Rev.

New Zealand Reports
   N.Z.

New Zealand Reports, Court of Appeals
   N.Z. Rep.

New Zealand Rules, Regulations and Bylaws
   N.Z.R., Regs. & B.

New Zealand Statutes Reprint
   N.Z. Repr. Stat., Repr. Stat. N.Z.

New Zealand Statutory Regulations
   N.Z. Stat. Regs., Stat. Reg. N.Z.

New Zealand Supreme Court
   N.Z.S.C.

New Zealand Taxation Board of Review Decisions
   N.Z.T.B.R.

New Zealand Torts and General Law Reform Committee
   N.Z.T.G.L.R.C.

New Zealand Treaty Series
N.Z.T.S.
New Zealand Universities Law Review.
N.Z. Univ. L.R., N.Z.U.L. Rev.,
N.Z.U.L.R., N.Z. Univ. L. Rev.
New Zealand Workers Compensation Cases
W.C.C.(N.Z.)
Newberg on Attorney Fee Awards
AFW
Newberg on Class Actions
NOCA
Newberry's United States District Court, Admiralty Reports
Newberry, Newberry's Ad. Rep.,
Newb., Newb. Adm., Newberry
Adm. (F.)
Newbon's Private Bills Reports
Newbon
Newbyth's Manuscript Decisions, Scotch Session Cases
Newbyth
Newell on Defamation
Newell, Defam.
Newell on Slander and Libel
Newell, Sland. & L.
Newell's Reports (48-90 Illinois Appeals)
New., Newell
Newell's Treatise on Malicious Prosecution
Newell, Mal. Pros.
Newell's Treatise on the Action of Ejectment
Newell, Eject.
Newfoundland
N., Nd., Newf., Newfoundl.,
N.F., Nfld.
Newfoundland and Prince Edward Island Reports
N. & P.E.I.R., Nfld. & P.E.I.R.,
Nfld. & P.E.I.R.

Newfoundland Law Reports
Newfld. L.R., Newfoundl. L.R.,
Nfld. L.R., N.L.R., Newf. L.R.
Newfoundland Reports
Nd., Newfoundl. R., N.F., Nfld.
R.
Newfoundland Revised Statutes
Nfld. Rev. Stat.
Newfoundland Select Cases
Newfoundl. Sel. Cas., Newf. Sel.
Cas., Sel. Cas. N.F.
Newfoundland Statutes
Nfld. Stat.
Newfoundland Supreme Court Decisions
Newf. S. Ct., Nfld.
Newland's Chancery Practice
Newl. Ch. Pr., Newl. Ch. Pprac.
Newland on Contracts
Newl. Cont.
Newman on Conveyancing
Newm. Conv.
News Media and the Law
News Media & L.
News' Tariff Index
Tarrif Ind., New.
Newsletter
Newsl.
Newsletter on Legislative Activities, Council of Europe
Newsl. Leg. Act.
Newspapers, Periodicals and Press Associations
Newsp.
Newton's International Estate Planning
IEP
Nicaragua
Nicar.
Nicholas on Adulterine Bastardy
Nich. Adult. Bast.

Nicholl, Hare and Carrow's English Railway and Canal Cases
Nic. Ha. C., Nich. H. & C., R.C., Nicholl H. & C.

Nicholls and Stops' Reports, Tasmania
N. & S.

Nichols-Cahill's Annotated New York Civil Practice Acts
Nichols-Cahill

Nicholson's Manuscript Decisions, Scotch Session Cases
Nicholson

Nicolas on Adulterine Bastardy
Nic. Adult. Bast. (See also Nicholas on Adulterine Bastardy)

Nicolas' (Sir Harry) Proceedings and Ordinances of the Privy Council
Nicolas

Nicoll and Flaxman on Registration
Nic. & Fl. Reg.

Nicolson's Elections in Scotland
Nic. Elec.

Niebuhr on Roman History
Niebh. Hist. Rom.

Nient Culpable (not guilty) (Lat.)
Nient cul.

Nigeria
Nig.

Nigeria Federal Supreme Court Selected Judgments
F.S.C.

Nigeria Law Quarterly Review
N.L.Q.R.

Nigeria Law Reports
Nig. L.R., Nigeria L.R., N.L.R.

Nigeria Lawyers' Quarterly
Nig. Lawy. Q., N.L.Q.

Nigerian
Nig.

Nigerian Annual of International Law
Nig. Ann. Int'l L., Nigerian Ann. Int'l L.

Nigerian Bar Journal
Nig. B.J.

Nigerian Bar Journal, Annual Journal of the Nigeria Bar Association. Lagos, Nigeria
Nigeria Bar J., Nig. Bar. J.

Nigerian Journal of Contemporary Law
Nig. J. Contemp.L.

Nigerian Law Journal
Nig. L.J., Nigerian L.J.

Nigerian Law Quarterly Review
Nig. L.Q.R.

Nigerian Monthly Law Reports
N.M.L.R.

Night Law School Bulletin, University of Omaha
U. of Omaha Bull.

Niles' Weekly Register
Nil. Reg., Niles Reg.

N.I.M.L.O. Institute of Municipal Law Officers
N.I.M.L.O. Mun. L. O.

Nisbet of Dirlecton's Scotch Session Cases
Nisbet.

Nisi Prius
N. P.

Nisi Prius and General Term Reports
Nisi Prius & Gen. T. Rep., N.P. & G.T. Rep.

Nisi Prius Cases
N.P.C.

Nisi Prius Reports
N.P.R.

Nixon's Digest of New Jersey Laws
Nix. Dig.

Nixon's Forms
Nix. F.
Nizamut Adalut Reports, India
N.A., NA.
NLADA Briefcase
NLADA Brief.
NLRB Decisions, Commerce Clearing House (National Labor Relations Board)
NLRB Dec. (CCH)
No coupons attached
N.C.A.
No Date
N.D.
No Place
N.p.
No Value
N/V
Noble's Current Court Decisions
Noble
Noise Regulation Reporter, Bureau of National Affairs
Noise Reg. Rep. (BNA)
Nokes on Mortgages and Receiverships
Nok. Mort.
Nolan on the Poor Laws
Nolan, Nol. P.L.
Nolan's English Magistrates' Cases
No. Sett. Cas., Nol.(Just.), Nol., Nol. Mag., Nolan
Nolan's English Settlement Cases
Nol.
Nolle Prosequi (Lat.)
Nol-pros
NOLPE School Law Journal (National Organization on Legal Problems of Education)
NOLPE, NOLPE Sch. L.J., NOLPE School L.J.
NOLPE School Law Reporter
NOLPE School L. Rep.

Nomos, Yearbook of the American Society of Political and Legal Philosophy
Nomos
Non Allocatur (Lat.)
N.A., NA.
Non Callable
N.C.
Non-Contributory Pension Scheme
N.C.P.S.
Non Culpabilis (not guilty) (Lat.)
Non cul.
Non Est Inventus (he is not found) (Lat.)
N.E.I.
Non-Governmental Organization
NGO
Non Obstante Veredicto (the judgment notwithstanding) (Lat.)
N.O.V.
Non Prosequitur (delay or neglect in prosecuting) (Lat.)
Non pros.
Non Sequitur (it does not follow) (Lat.)
Non seq.
Nonacquiescence
N.A., NA.
Nonacquiescence by Commissioner in a Tax Court or Board of Tax Appeals Decision
Nonacq.
Norcross' Reports (23-24 Nevada)
Norc.
Norman French
Nor. Fr.
Norman on Letters Patent
Nor. Pat.
Norris and Leach on Rule Against Perpetuities
Norris & L, Perpetuities

Norris' Edition of Peake's Law of Evidence
Norr. Peake
Norris' Law of Seamen
Norris Seamen
Norris Reports (82-96 Pennsylvania)
Norris, Norr.
North[ern]
N.
North America
N. Am.
North American Bar News
Am. Bar
North American Review
N. Am. Rev.
North Atlantic Regional Business Law Review
N. Atlantic Reg. Bus. L. Rev.
North Atlantic Treaty Organization
NATO
North Borneo Law Reports
N.B.L.R.
North Carolina
N. Car., N.C.
North Carolina Administrative Code
N.C. Admin. Code
North Carolina Advance Legislative Service
N.C. Adv. Legis. Serv.
North Carolina Appellate Reports
NC App
North Carolina Attorney General Reports
Rep.N.C. Att'y Gen.
North Carolina Bar
N.C.B.
North Carolina Bar Foundation
NCBF

North Carolina Board of Railroad Commissioners
N.C.R.C.
North Carolina Central Law Journal
N.C. Cent. L.J., North Carolina Cent. L.J., N. Car. Central L.J.
North Carolina College Law Journal
North Carolina College L.J.
North Carolina Conference Reports
N.C. Conf., N.C. Conf. Rep. (N.C.), N.C. Conf. Rep.
North Carolina Constitution
N.C. Const.
North Carolina Corporation Commission
N.C.C.C.
North Carolina Court of Appeals Reports
N.C. App., N.C.A.
North Carolina Digest by Battle
Bat.Dig.
North Carolina General Statutes
N.C. Gen. Stat.
North Carolina Industrial Commission Advance Sheets
N.C.I.C. Ops.
North Carolina Journal of International Law and Commercial Regulation
N.C.J. Int'l L. & Com. Reg., North Car. J. Int'l. L. & Comm.
North Carolina Journal of Law
N.C.J. of L.
North Carolina Law Journal
N.C.L.J.
North Carolina Law Repository
N.C. Law Repos., N.C.L. Rep.

North Carolina Law Repository (Reprint)
N.C. Law Repository, N.C.L. Reps.

North Carolina Law Review
N.C.L., N.C.L. Rev., N.C.L. Review, N.C.L.R.

North Carolina Reports
N.C., N. Car., N. Car. Rep., N. Carolina Cases, N.C. Rep., N.C. Reports

North Carolina Reports, Appendix
N.C. Rep. Appendix

North Carolina Revisal of Public Statutes by Battle
Bat.Rev.St., Battle's Revisal

North Carolina Revised Statutes by Battle
Bat.Stat.

North Carolina Session Laws
N.C. Sess. Laws

North Carolina State Bar Association
N. Car. S.B.A.

North Carolina State Bar Newsletter
N.C. St. B. Newsl.

North Carolina State Bar Quarterly
N.C. St. B.Q.

North Carolina Supreme Court Reports
N.C.

North Carolina Term Reports
N.C.T. Rep., N.C. Term R., N.C. Term Rep.

North Carolina Utilities Commission Reports
N.C.U.C.

North Central School Law Review
N. Cent. School L. Rev.

North Dakota
N.D.

North Dakota Administrative Code
N.D. Admin. Code

North Dakota Bar Brief
N.D.B.B.

North Dakota Board of Railroad Commissioners
N.D.R.C.

North Dakota Century Code
N.D. Cent. Code

North Dakota Commissioners of Railroads
N.D.C. of R.

North Dakota Constitution
N.D. Const.

North Dakota Laws
N.D. Sess. Laws

North Dakota Law Review
N.D.L. Rev., N.D.L.R., N.D.R., North Dakota L. Rev.

North Dakota Reports
N.D., N. Dak.

North Dakota Supreme Court Reports
N.D.

North Guthrie's Reports (68-80 Missouri Appeals)
North & G.

North Ireland
N. Ir.

Northampton County Reporter, Pennsylvania
Northam. Law Rep., North. Co. R. (Pa.), North, North. Co., North. Co. Rep., Northamp. Co. Repr., Northampton Co. Rep.

Northampton Law Reporter, Pennsylvania
Northam., Northam. L. Rep.

Northeast
N.E.

Northeastern Law Review
N.L. Rev.
Northeastern Reporter
N.E., N.E. Reporter., N.E.
Repr., N.E. Rep., N.E.R.
Northeastern Reporter, Second Series
N.E. 2d
Northern
N.
Northern District
N.D.
Northern Illinois University Law Review
N. Ill. U.L. Rev.
Northern Ireland
N. Ir., N.I.
Northern Ireland Law
N. Ir.
Northern Ireland Law Reports
N., N. Ir., N. Ir. L.R., N.I.,
N.I.L.R.
Northern Ireland Legal Quarterly
N. Ir. Legal Q., N. Ir. L.Q.,
N.I.L.Q., No. Ire. L.Q., North.
Ireland L.Q.
Northern Ireland Public General Acts
N. Ir. Pub. Gen. Acts
Northern Ireland Statutes
N. Ir. Stat.
Northern Ireland Statutory Rules and Orders
Stat. R. & O. N. Ir., Stat. R. &
O. N.I.
Northern Kentucky Law Review
N. Ky. L. Rev., North. Ky. L.R.
Northern Kentucky State Law Forum
N. Ky. St. L.F.

Northern Kentucky State Law Review
North. Ken'y. S.L. Rev.
Northern Nigeria Case Notes
N.N.C.N.
Northern Nigeria Law Reports
N.N.L.R.
Northern Nigeria Legal Notes
N.N.L.N.
Northern Region of Nigeria Law Reports
N.N.L.R., N.R.N.L.R.
Northern Regional Legal Notice, (Nigeria)
N.R.L.N.
Northern Rhodesia Gazette
N.R.G.
Northern Rhodesia Law Reports
N.R.L.R.
Northern Territorial Ordinances, Australia
N.Terr. Austl. Ord.
Northern Territory Law Review Committee, Australia
N.T.L.R.C.
Northington Case Tempore (Eden's English Chancery Reports)
C.t.N., Cas.t.Northington
Northrop University Law Journal of Aerospace, Business and Taxation
Northrop U.L.J. Aerospace Bus.
& Tax'n, Northrop U.L.J. Aero.
Energy & Envt., Northrop
U.L.J. Aerospace Energy and
Env.
North's Illinois Probate Practice
North Pr., Nor. Pro. Pr.
North's Study of the Laws
North St. L.

Northumberland County Legal News, Pennsylvania
Northum. Co. Leg. N.,
Northum. Leg. N. (Pa.),
Northum., Northumb. Co.,
Northumb. Co. Leg. News

Northumberland Legal Journal, Pennsylvania
Northum Leg. J. (Pa.),
Northumb.Legal J., Northumb.
L.J., Northum. Leg. J.,
Northumb. L.N., Northumber-
land Co. Leg. Jour., Northum-
berland L.J.

Northwest
N.W.

Northwest Provinces, India
Northw. Pr.

Northwest Provinces Code, India
N.W.P.C.

Northwest Provinces, High Court Reports, India
N.W.P.H.C.

Northwest Provinces Select Cases, India
Sel. Cas. N.W.P.

Northwest Territories, Canada
N.W.T.

Northwest Territories Law Reports, Canada
N.W.T.L.R., N.W.T.R.

Northwest Territories Ordinances, Canada
N.W.T. Ord.

Northwest Territories Reports, Canada
N.W.T., N.W. Terr. (Can.),
N.W.T. Rep.

Northwest Territories Revised Ordinances, Canada
N.W.T. Rev. Ord., N.W. Rev.
Ord.

Northwest Territories, Supreme Court Reports, Canada
N.W. Terr.

Northwestern
Nw.

Northwestern Journal of International Law and Business
Nw. J. Int'l. L. & Bus., North-
west. J. Int'l. L. & Bus.

Northwestern Law Journal
North. W. L.J., Northw. L.J.

Northwestern Law Review
N.W. Law Rev., N. WLR,
N.W.L. Rev.

Northwestern On-Line Total Integrated System
NOTIS

Northwestern Provinces Circular Orders
Cir.Ord.N.W.P.

Northwestern Provinces High Court Reports
N.W.P., N.W.

Northwestern Reporter
N.W. Repr., N.W., N.W.R., N.W.
Rep., N., Northw. Rep., No.
West. Rep.

Northwestern Reporter, Second Series
N.W.2d.

Northwestern School of Law of Lewis and Clark College
Northw. SL of L & C Coll.

Northwestern University Law Review
North U.L. Rev., Northw. L.
Rev., Northwestern U.L. Rev.,
Northwestern Univ. L. Rev.,
N.U.L.R., Nw. U.L. Rev.,
N.W.L., Nw.L., N.W.U.L. Rev.

Northwestern University Law Review, Supplement
Nw. L.S.

Northwestern University School of Law
NWU

Norton's Cases on Hindu Law of Inheritance
Norton

Norton's Leading Cases on Inheritance
Nort. L.C.

Norway
Nor.

Norwegian
N.

Not-for Profit Corporation
Not-For-Profit Corp.

Not Otherwise Indexed By Name (Used Under Terms of Tariffs, Filed With Interstate Commerce Commission)
N.O.I.B.N.

Nota Bene (Lat.)
N.B.

Notaries Journal
Not. J.

Notcutt on Factories and Workshops
Notc. on Fac.

Note[s]
N., nn., Nts., n.

Notes from Hume's Lectures
N.H.L.

Notes of Cases at Madras, by Strange
N. of Case., N.C., See also Strange's Notes of Cases, Madras, No. of Cas. Madras., Not. Cas. Madras., Not. Cas.

Notes of Cases (Australian Jurist)
N.C.

Notes of Cases in Ecclesiastical and Maritime Courts, England
N.C., No. Ca. Ecc. & Mar., N.C. Ecc., Not. Cas. Ecc. & M., Not. Cas., Ec. & Mar., Notes of Cas., Notes of Cases, N. of Case.

Notes of Cases, England
Notes of Ca.

Notes of Cases in Smoult's Collection of Orders, Calcutta, India
Smoult

Notes of Cases, Law Journal, England
No. Cas. L.J.

Notes of Decisions (Martin's North Carolina Reports)
Not. Dec.

Notes of Decisions of Appeal Court of Registration at Inverness
Inv. Reg. Cas.

Notes of Ecclesiastical Cases , England
N.E.C.

Notes of Unreported Cases, Supreme Court of Canada (Coutlee)
Cout. S.C.

Nothstein's Toxic Torts
TT

Notice of Judgment
N.J.

Notices of Judgment Under the Federal Insecticide, Fungicide and Rodenticide Act
N.J.I.F.R.

Notices of Judgment, United States Food and Drug Administration
N.J.F.D.

Notre Dame Annual Estate Planning Institute
Ann.Notre Dame Est. Plan. Inst.

Notre Dame Estate Planning Institute Proceedings
 Notre Dame Est. Plan. Inst.,
 Notre Dame Est. Plan. Inst.
 Proc.

Notre Dame Institute on Charitable Giving Foundations and Trusts
 Found. & Tr., Notre Dame Inst.
 on Char. Giving Foundations &
 Tr.

Notre Dame Journal of Laws, Ethics, and Public Policy
 Notre Dame J.L. Ethics & Pub.
 Pol'y

Notre Dame Journal of Legislation
 Notre Dame J. Leg.

Notre Dame Law Review
 Notre Dame L. Rev.

Notre Dame Lawyer
 N.D.L., Notre Dame L., Notre
 Dame Law.

Nott and Hopkins' Reports (8-15 United States Court of Claims)
 Nott & Hop., N. & H., N. & Hop.

Nott and Huntington's Reports (1-7 United States Court of Claims)
 N. & H., N. & Hunt., Nott &
 Hunt.

Nott and McCord's South Carolina Reports
 N. & Mc., N. & McC., Nott &
 McC., Nott & M'C. (S.C.)

Nott on the Mechanics' Lien Law
 Nott Mech. L.

Nova Law Journal
 Nova L.J.

Nova Law Review
 Nova L. Rev., N.Sc.

Nova Scotia
 N.S., Nov.Sc.

Nova Scotia Board of Commissioners of Public Utilities
 Nov. Sc. P.U.C.

Nova Scotia Decisions
 N. Sc. Dec., N.S. Dec., Nov. Sc.
 Dec.

Nova Scotia Decisions by Geldert and Oxley
 Geld. & O., Geld. & Ox.

Nova Scotia Law News
 N.S.L. News

Nova Scotia Law Reform Advisory Commission
 Nova Scotia L.R.A.C.

Nova Scotia Law Reports
 L.R. (N.S.), L.R.N.S., N.S.L.R.

Nova Scotia Reports
 N.S. Rep., N.S.R.

Nova Scotia Reports, Geldert and Russell
 N.S.R.G. & R., Gold. & R., G. &
 R.

Nova Scotia Reports, Geldert and Oxley
 N.S.R.G. & O.

Nova Scotia Reports (James)
 N.S.R.J., N.S.R. (James)

Nova Scotia Reports, Old Right
 N.S.R.(Old.)

Nova Scotia Reports, 2d Series
 N.S.R.2d.

Nova Scotia Revised Statutes
 N.S. Rev. Stat

Nova Scotia Supreme Court Reports
 Nov. S.C.R., Nov. Sc. C.R.

Nova Scotia Statutes
 N.S. Stat.

Novae Narrationes (Lat.)
 No.N.

Novation
 Nov.

Novellae, The Novels or New Constitutions
Nov.
Novellae (the Novels of Justinian)
N.
Novels (Roman Law)
Nov.
November
No., Nov., Nv.
Novisima Recopilacion
Nov. Recop.
Now Known As
nka
Noyes on Charitable Uses
Noy. Ch. U.
Noy's English King's Bench Reports
Noy, Noy (Eng.)
Noy's Maxims of the Law of England
Noy, Max., Noye's Max.

Nuclear Law Bulletin
Nuclear L. Bull.
Nuclear Regulation Reporter, Commerce Clearing House
Nuclear Reg. Rep. (CCH)
Nuclear Regulatory Commission
NRC
Nuclear Regulatory Commission Issuances
NRCI
Nuisances
Nuis
Nulla Bona (Lat.)
N.B.
Number[s]
No., nos.
Nyasaland
Ny.
Nyasaland Law Reports
N.L.R., Ny. L.R.
Nye's Reports (18-21 Utah)
Nye

O

Obiter Dicta
O.D., obiter
O'Brien's Lawyer's Rule of Holy Life
O'Bri. Lawy.
O'Brien's Military Law
O'Bri. M. L.
O'Brien's Upper Canada Reports
O'Brien
Observations
Observ.
Observer
Obs.
Obstructing Justice
Obst. Jus.
O'Callaghan's History of New Netherland
O'Callaghan, New Neth.
Occasional Notes, Canada Law Times
Occ. N.
Occupation
Occ.
Occupational Safety and Health Administration
OSHA
Occupational Safety and Health Cases, Bureau of National Affairs
O.S.H. Cas. (BNA)
Occupational Safety and Health Decisions
O.S.H.D.
Occupational Safety and Health Decisions, Commerce Clearing House
O.S.H. Dec. (CCH)

Occupational Safety and Health Reports, Commerce Clearing House
OSHR, OSHR (CCH)
Occupational Safety and Health Reporter, Bureau of National Affairs
O.S.H. Rep. (BNA)
Occupational Safety and Health Review Commission
OSAHRC, OSHRC
Occupations and Professions
Occ. & Prof.
Occupations, Trades and Professions
Occup.
Ocean Development and International Law
Ocean Dev. & Int. L.
Ocean Development and International Law Journal
Ocean Dev. & Intl. L.J.
Octavo
Oct.
Octavo Strange, Select Cases on Evidence
Oct. Str.
October
Oc., Oct.
O'Dea's Medical Experts
O'Dea Med. Exp.
O'Dedy's Principal and Accessory
O'D. Pr. & Acc.
Odeneal's Reports (9-11 Oregon)
Odeneal
Odger on Libel and Slander
Odg. Lib., Odgers

Odgers's Principles of Pleading
Odg. Pl.

O'Donnell and Brady's Irish Equity Digest
O'D. & Br. Eq. Dig.

O'Dowd's Merchant Shipping Act
O'Dowd Sh.

OFCCP Federal Contract Compliance Manual, Commerce Clearing House (Office of Federal Contract Compliance and Procurement)
OFCCP Fed. Cont. Compl. Man. (CCH)

Offender Rehabilitation
Offend. Rehab.

Office
off.

Office Decision, United States Internal Revenue Bureau
O.D.

Office for Democratic Institutions and Human Rights
ODIHR

Office for Emergency Management
OEM

Office for Handicapped Individuals
OHI

Office of Alien Property
OAP

Office of Child Development
O.C.D.

Office of Child Support Enforcement
OCSE

Office of Collective Bargaining
O.C.B.

Office of Contract Compliance and Procurement
OFCCP

Office of Contract Settlement, Appeal Board Decisions
App. Bd. O. C. S.

Office of Contract Settlement Decisions
O.C.S.

Office of Defense Mobilization
ODM

Office of Domestic Commerce
ODC

Office of Drug Abuse Policy
ODAP

Office of Economic Opportunity
OEO

Office of Economic Opportunity Procurement Regulations
OEOPR

Office of Education
OE

Office of Emergency Preparedness
OEP

Office of Employment Development Programs
OEDP

Office of Energy Information and Analysis
OEIA

Office of Energy Research and Development Policy
OEP

Office of Federal Contract Compliance
OFCC

Office of Federal Contract Compliance and Procurement
OFCCP

Office of Federal Procurement Policy
OFPP

Office of Foreign Direct Investments
OFDI

Office of Free Elections
   OFE
Office of General Counsel
   OGC
Office of Hazardous Materials Operations
   OHMO
Office of Human Development
   OHD
Office of International Trade
   OIT
Office of Management and Budget
   OMB
Office of Military Government, United States Zone, Germany
   OMGUS
Office of Minority Business Enterprise
   OMBE
Office of Native American Programs
   ONAP
Office of Naval Research
   O.N.R.
Office of Oil and Gas
   OOG
Office of Personnel Management
   OPM
Office of Pipeline Safety Operations
   OPSO
Office of Price Administration
   OPA
Office of Price Stabilization
   OPS
Office of Rent Stabilization
   ORS
Office of Rural Development
   ORD
Office of Strategic Services
   OSS
Office of Technology Assessment
   OTA

Office of Telecommunications
   OT
Office of Telecommunications Policy
   OTP
Office of the Attorney General, State of Washington Opinions
   Op. Wash. Att'y Gen.
Office of the Comptroller of the Currency
   OCC
Office of the Director of Law Reform, Northern Ireland
   N.I.D.L.R.
Office of the Federal Register
   OFR
Office of the General Sales Manager
   OGSM
Office of Thrift Supervision Journal
   Off. Thrift Supervision J.
Office of War Mobilization
   OWM
Office of Water Research and Technology
   OWRT
Office of Youth Development
   OYD
Office, Chief of Finance, United States Army
   OCF
Officer of the Order of the British Empire
   O.B.E.
Officer's Reports (1-9 Minnesota)
   Officer
Official
   Off.
Official Bulletin, International Commission for Air Navigation
   O.B.

Official Circular
O.C.
Official Code of Georgia Annotated
O.C.G.A.
Official Commonwealth Statutory Rules
Austl. Stat. R.
Official Compilation of Codes, Rules and Regulations of the State of New York
N.Y. Admin. Code
Official Compilation of the Rules and Regulations of the State of Georgia.
Ga. Admin.Comp.
Official Compilation Rules and Regulations of the State of Tennessee
Tenn. Admin. Comp.
Official Gazette of the United States Patent and Trademark Office: Trademarks
O.G.TM
Official Gazette Reports, British Guiana
O.G.B.G.
Official Gazette, United States Patent Office
Off. Gaz. Pat. Off., Off. Gaz., Off. Gaz. Pat. Office, O.G., O.G. Pat. Off., Pat. Off. Gaz., P.O.G.
Official Journal of Industrial and Commercial Property
Official J. Ind. Comm. Prop.
Official Journal of Patents
Off. Jl. Pat.
Official Journal of the European Communities
E.E.C.J.O., J.O., O.J., O.J. Eur. Comm., O.J. Spec. Ed.

Official Opinions of the Attorney General of Nevada
Op. Nev. Att'y Gen.
Official Opinions of the Solicitor for the Post Office Department
Op. Solic. P.O. Dep't.
Official Public Service Reports
O.P.S.
Official Receiver
O.R.
Official Referee
O.R.
Official Reporter of New York State Labor Relations Board Decisions
N.Y. SLRB
Official Reports of the High Court of the Transvaal
Off. Rep.
Official Reports: Illinois Courts Commission
Official Rep. Ill. Courts Commission
Official Reports, South Africa
O.R.
Official Reports, South African Republic
O.R.S.A.R.
Official Reports, United States Court of Military Appeals
USCMA
Officina Brevium
Off. Brev., Off. Br.
Officium Clerici Pacis
Of. Cl. Pac.
Offtrack Betting
OTB
Ogden's Reports (12-15 Louisiana)
Ogd., Ogden
Ogilvie's Imperial Dictionary of the English Language
Ogilvie, Dict.

Ogston's Medical Jurisprudence
Ogs. Med. Jur.
OHA Law Journal, Office of Health Administrtion
OHA L. J.
O'Hara on Wills
O'Hara Wills
O'Hara, Durst, Griffith and Shurtz on Corporate Taxation
CT
Ohio
O., Oh., Ohio
Ohio Administrative Code
Ohio Admin. Code
Ohio Appellate Reports
O. App., O.A., O.A.R., Oh. A.,
Ohio App., App., Oh. Ap., Ohio
Appellate Reports, Ohio Apps.
Ohio Appellate Reports, Second Series
O. App. 2d, O.A. 2d, Oh. A. 2d,
Ohio App. 2d
Ohio Board of Tax Appeals Reports
Ohio B.T.A.
Ohio Circuit Court Decisions
O.C.D., Ohio C.C.Dec., Ohio Cir.
Ct., O.A. & C.
Ohio Circuit Court Decisions, New Series
C.D. (N.S.), Ohio Circuits
Ohio Circuit Court Reports
C.C., Oh. Cir. Ct., Ohio C.C.,
Ohio C.C.R., Ohio Cir. Ct. R.,
Cir. Ct. Ohio
Ohio Circuit Court Reports, New Series
C.C. (N.S.), CCns, C.C.N.S.,
O.C.C.N.S., Oh. Cir. Ct. N.S.,
Ohio C.C. (n.s.), Ohio C.C.N.S.,
Ohio C.C.R.N.S., Ohio Cir. Ct.
(N.S.), Ohio Cir. Ct. R. N.S.

Ohio Circuit Decisions
C.D., O.D.C.C., Oh. Cir. Dec.,
Ohio C.D., Ohio C.Dec., Ohio
Cir. Dec., Circ. Dec., Ohio Circ.
Dec., O.C.C.
Ohio Commissioners of Railroads and Telegraphs
Ohio C. of R. & T.
Ohio Constitution
Ohio Const.
Ohio Court of Appeals
Oh.
Ohio Courts of Appeal Reports
O.C.A., Ohio C.A., Ohio Ct. App.
Ohio Decisions
Dec. O., O.D., O.D.N.P.,
Oh.Dec., Ohio Dec., Sup. & C.P.
Dec.
Ohio Decisions Nisi Prius
Ohio Dec. N.P.
Ohio Decisions Reprint
D. Rep., D. Repr., O.Dec. Rep.,
Oh. Dec. (Reprint), Ohio Dec.
Repr., Dec. R., Dec. Re., Dec.
Repr., O.D. Re., O.D. Rep., O.D.
Reprint, Oh. Dec. Rep., Ohio
Dec. R., Ohio Dec. Re., Ohio
Dec. Rep., Re., Ohio Dec. Reprint, Dec. Rep.
Ohio Department Reports
O.Dep. Rep., Ohio Dep't.
Ohio Digest by Bates
Bates' Dig.
Ohio Federal Decisions
O. F. D., Oh. F. Dec., Ohio F.
Dec., Ohio Fed. Dec., Ohio F. D.
Ohio Government Reports
Ohio Gov't.
Ohio Jurisprudence
O. Jur., Oh. Jur., Ohio Jur.
Ohio Jurisprudence, Second Series
Ohio Jur. 2d

Ohio Law Abstract
Abs., O. L. A., O. L. Abs., Ohio
Abs., Ohio L. Abs., Ohio Law
Abst., Ohio Abstract, Ohio Law
Abstract, Ohio Law Abs.

Ohio Law Bulletin
O. L. B., Oh. L. Bul., Oh. L.
Bull., Ohio L. Bull.

Ohio Law Journal
O. L. Jour., Oh. L.J., Ohio Law
J., Ohio L.J., O.L.J.

Ohio Law Reporter
Law Rep., L.R., O. L. Rep., Oh.
L. Rep., Ohio L. Rep., Ohio Law
R., Ohio Law Rep., Ohio L.R.,
O.L.R., Ohio Law Repr.

**Ohio Law Reporter and Weekly
Bulletin**
Ohio L. R. & Wk. Bul.

Ohio Laws
O. L.

Ohio Legal Center Institute
OLCI

Ohio Legal News
O. Legal News, Oh. Leg. N.,
Ohio Leg. N., Ohio Leg. News,
Ohio Legal N., O.L.N.

Ohio Legislative Acts
Ohio Laws

Ohio Legislative Bulletin
Ohio Legis. Bull.

Ohio Legislative Service
Ohio Legis. Serv.

Ohio Lower Court Decisions
L.C.D., Lower Ct. Dec., Oh.
L.Ct. D., Ohio Low. Dec., Ohio
Lower Dec., O.L.D., O. Lower D.

**Ohio Miscellaneous Decisions,
Gottshall**
OM, Ohio Misc. Dec., Misc. Dec.

Ohio Miscellaneous Reports
M., O. Misc., Oh. Misc., Ohio
Misc.

Ohio Miscellaneous Reports, Second Series
Ohio Misc. 2d

**Ohio Miscellaneous Reports,
Third Series**
Ohio Misc. 3d

Ohio Monthly Record
Ohio Monthly Rec.

Ohio Nisi Prius Reports
Oh. N.P., NP, N.P. Ohio, Ohio
N.P., O.N.P., Nisi Prius Rep.,
Ohio Nisi Prius

Ohio Nisi Prius Reports, New Series
Oh. N.P. (N.S.), Ohio N.P.N.S.,
O.N.P.N.S., NPns, N.P.N.S.,
Ohio Nisi Prius (N.S.)

Ohio Northern University Intramural Law Review
Oh. N. U. Intra. L. R., O.N.U.
Intra. L. R.

**Ohio Northern University Law
Review**
Oh. N. U. L. R., Ohio North. L.
Rev., Ohio North Univ. L. Rev.,
Ohio Northern U. L. Rev., Ohio
N.U.L.Rev., O.N.U.L.R.

Ohio Opinions
Ohio O., Ohio Op., Ohio Ops.,
O.O.

Ohio Opinions Annotated
Ohio O., Ohio Opinions

Ohio Opinions, Second Series
Ohio O.2d, Ohio Op.2d, O.O. 2d

Ohio Opinions, Third Series
Ohio Op.3d

Ohio Probate Reports by Goebel
Oh. Prob., Ohio Prob.

Ohio Public Defenders Association
OHPA

Ohio Public Service Commission
Ohio P.S.C.

Ohio Public Utilities Commission
Ohio P.U.C.
Ohio Railroad Commission
Ohio R.C.
Ohio Reports
O. Rep., O., Ohio, Ohio R., Ohio
Rep.
Ohio Reports Condensed
Ohio R.Cond.
Ohio Revised Code Annotated
Ohio Rev. Code Ann.
**Ohio Revised Code Annotated,
Anderson**
Ohio Rev. Code Ann. (Anderson)
**Ohio Revised Code Annotated,
Baldwin**
Ohio Rev. Code Ann. (Baldwin)
**Ohio Revised Code Annotated,
Page**
Ohio Rev. Code Ann. (Page)
**Ohio Revised Statutes Anno-
tated, Bates**
Bates' Ann.St.
Ohio State Bar Association
Ohio S.B.A., O. Bar, OSBA
**Ohio State Bar Association Bulle-
tin**
Ohio S.B.A. Bull., OSBA Bull.
**Ohio State Bar Association Re-
port**
Ohio Bar, O. Bar, Ohio St. B. A.
Rep.
**Ohio State Journal on Dispute
Resolution**
Ohio St. J. on Disp. Resol.
Ohio State Law Journal
L.J., Oh. S. L.J., Ohio S.L.J.,
Ohio St. L.J., Ohio State L.J.

Ohio State Reports
O. St., Oh. St., Ohio St., O.S., O.
St. R., O. St. Rep., O. State,
Ohio (New Series), Ohio N.S.,
Ohio S., Ohio S. Rep., Ohio S.R.,
Ohio St. R., Ohio St. Rep., Ohio
St. Report, Ohio St. R.(N.S.),
Ohio State, Ohio State R. (N.S.),
Ohio State Rep., O.S. Rep.,
O.S.R.
Ohio State Reports, New Series
Ohio St. (N.S.)
Ohio State Reports, Second Series
O.S. 2d, Oh. St. 2d.
Ohio State Reports, Third Series
Ohio St. 3d
Ohio Statutes at Large, Chase
Chases' St.
**Ohio Superior and Common
Pleas Decisions**
Ohio S. & C. P., Oh.S. & C.P.,
Ohio S. & C. P. Dec., O.S. &
C.P. Dec., Ohio Sup. & C. P. Dec.
Ohio Supplement
O. Su., O. Supp., Ohio Supp.
Ohio Supplement Court Reports
OSu, Ohio
**Ohio Supreme Court Decisions
(Unreported Cases)**
Oh. S.C. D., Ohio S. U., Ohio
Unrept. Cas., O.S.C.D., O.S.U.
**Ohio Unreported Judicial Deci-
sions**
Pollack
Ohlinger's Federal Practice
Ohlinger, Fed. Practice
Oil and Gas Compact Bulletin
Oil & Gas Compact Bull.
Oil and Gas Institute
Oil & Gas Inst.
Oil and Gas Journal
Oil & Gas J.

Oil and Gas Law Review
Oil & Gas. L.R.
Oil and Gas Law and Taxation Institute, Southwestern Legal Foundation
Oil & Gas L. & Tax. Inst.
(S.W.Legal Fdn.)
Oil and Gas Natural Resources, Prentice-Hall
Oil & Gas.-Nat.Resources (P-H)
Oil and Gas Reporter
Oil & Gas, Oil & Gas Reptr., Oil
& Gas Rptr., Oil and Gas Reporter
Oil and Gas Tax Quarterly
Oil & Gas Tax Q.
Oke's Fisher Laws
Oke Fish.L.
Oke's Game Laws
Oke Game L.
Oke's Magisterial Formulist
Oke Mag. Form.
Oke's Magisterial Synopsis
Oke Mag. Syn.
Oke's Turnpike Laws
Oke Turn.
O'Keefe's Order in Chancery, Ireland
O'Keefe Ord.
Oklahoma
O., Ok., Okl., Okla.
Oklahoma Appellate Court Reporter
Okla. Ap. Ct. Rep.
Oklahoma Bar Association Journal
Okla. B. Assn. J., Okla. B.
Ass'n. J.
Oklahoma Bar Journal
Okla. B.J.

Oklahoma City University Law Review
Okl. City U. L. Rev., Okla. C. U.
L. R., Okla. City U. L. Rev.
Oklahoma Constitution
Okla. Const.
Oklahoma Corporation Commission
Okla.C.C.
Oklahoma Court of Appeals
Okl. App.
Oklahoma Court on the Judiciary
Okl. Jud.
Oklahoma Criminal Reports
O. Cr., Okl. Cr., Okla., Okla.
Cr., Okla. Crim., Okl. Car., Okl.
Cr. R.
Oklahoma Gazette
Okla. Gaz.
Oklahoma Industrial Commission Reports
Okla. I. C. R.
Oklahoma Law Journal
Okl. L.J., Okla. L.J.
Oklahoma Law Review
Ok. L. R., Okla. L. Rev., Oklahoma L. Rev., O.R.
Oklahoma Lawyer
Okla. Lawy.
Oklahoma Reports
Okla., Okl., Oklahoma, Oklahoma Reports
Oklahoma Session Law Service
Okla. Sess. Law Serv.
Oklahoma Session Laws
Okla. Sess. Laws
Oklahoma State Bar Journal
Okla. S. B. J.
Oklahoma Statutes
Okla. Stat.
Oklahoma Statutes Annotated
Okl. St. Ann., Okla. Stat. Ann.
(West), O.S.A.

Oklahoma Statutes Supplement
O.S. Supp.

Oklahoma Supreme Court Reports
Okla.

Olcott's United States District Court Reports, Admiralty
Olcott Adm. (F.), Olc. Adm. Olcott, Olcott, Olcott's Adm., Olc., Olc. Adm.

Old Age and Survivors Insurance, Trust Fund
OASI

Old Age Assistance
OAA

Old Age, Survivors, and Disability Benefits
OASDI

Old Bailey
O.B.

Old Bailey Chronicle
Old Bailey Chr.

Old Bailey Session Papers
Sess. Pap. O. B., O.B.S.P., O.B.S.

Old Benloe's Reports, English Common Pleas
O.B., O.Ben., O.Benl.

Old Books of Entries
Lib. Ent.

Old Code (Louisiana Code of 1808)
O.C.

Old Natura Brevium
Old Nat. Brev., O.N.B., Vet. N. Br., Vet. Na. B.

Old Select Cases, Oudh, India
Old S.C.

Old Senate Office Building
OSOB

Old Series
O.S.

Old Style
O.S.

Oldham and White's Digest of Texas Laws
O. & W. Dig.

Oldnall's Sessions Practice
Oldn. Pr.

Oldright's Nova Scotia Reports
N.S.R. Old., Oldr. N.S., Old., Oldr.

Oleck's Modern Corporation Law
Oleck, Corporations

Oleron Jugemens
J.d'Ol.

Oliphant on the Law of Horses
Oliph. Hor., Ol. Horse

Oliver, Beavan and Lefroy's English Railway and Canal Cases
Oliv. B. & L.

Oliver's Conveyancing
Ol. Conv., Oliv. Conv.

Oliver's Precedents
Oliv. Prec., Ol.Prec.

Ollennu's Principles of Customary Land Law in Ghana
P.C.L.L.G.

Ollivier, Bell and Fitzgerald's New Zealand Reports
Olliv. B. & F., Oll. B. & F., O.B. & F.N.Z., O.B. & F. (C.A.), O.B. & F. (S.C.), O.B. & F.

Olmsted's Privy Council Decisions
Olmsted

Olwine's Law Journal, Pennsylvania
Olwine's L.J. (Pa.)

O'Malley and Hardcastle's English Election Cases
O'M. & H. El. Cas., O'M. & H., O'Mal. & H.

Omnibus Budget Reconciliation Act of 1990
OBRA
Omond on the Law of the Sea
Om. Sea
Omond on the Merchant Shipping Acts
Om. Mer. Sh.
On
On
On-the-Job Training
O.J.T.
O'Neal's Negro Law of South Carolina
O'Neal Neg. L.
Online Computer Library Center
OCLC
Onslow's Nisi Prius Reports, England
Onsl.N.P.
Ontario
O., Ont.
Ontario Appeal Reports
A. R., App. Rep. Ont.,
A.R.(Ont.), O.A.R., Ont. App.,
App. Rep.
Ontario Appeals
Ont. A.
Ontario Chancery Chambers' Reports
Chamb.Rep.
Ontario Consolidated Regulations
Ontario Cons. Reg.
Ontario Election Cases
Ont. Elec. C., Ont. El. Cas., Ont.
Elec., Ont. Elect., E.C., O.E.C.
Ontario Judicature Act
O.J. Act
Ontario Labour Relations Board Monthly Report
O.L.R.B.

Ontario Law Journal
Ont. L.J.
Ontario Law Journal, New Series
Ont. L.J. (N.S.)
Ontario Law Reform Commission
Ont. L.R.C., Ontario L.R.C.
Ontario Law Reporter
O.L.R.
Ontario Law Reports
O.L.R., Ont. L., Ont. L. Rep.
Ontario Municipal Board Reports
O.M.B.R.
Ontario Practice
Ont. Pr.
Ontario Practice Reports
Ont. P. R., Ont. Pr. Rep., O.P.R.
Ontario, Province of
P.O.
Ontario Railway and Municipal Board
Ont. Ry. & Mun. Bd.
Ontario Regulations
Ont. Regs., Ont. Reg.
Ontario Reports
O., Ont. R., O.R., Ont., Ont. L.R.
Ontario Reports and Weekly Notes
Ont. R. & W.N.
Ontario Reports, Second Series
Ont. 2d.
Ontario Revised Regulations
Ont. Rev. Regs.
Ontario Revised Statutes
Ont. Rev. Stat.
Ontario Statutes
Ont.Stat.
Ontario Tax Reporter, Commerce Clearing House
Ont. Tax Rep. (CCH)
Ontario Weekly Notes
Ont. Week N., O.W.N., Ont.
Wkly. N., Ont. W.N.

Ontario Weekly Reporter
Ont. Week R., Ont. Wkly. Rep.,
Ont. W.R., O.W.R., Ont.W.R.

**Ope Consilio (by aid and counsel)
(Lat.)**
O.C.

Operations
Ops

Opinion[s]
Op.[s.]

Opinion Letter
Op. Let.

**Opinion's of Chief Counsel,
United States Coast Guard**
Op. CCCG

**Opinion's of General Counsel,
United States Treasury Depart-
ment**
Op. GCT

**Opinion's of Judge Advocate Gen-
eral, United States Air Force**
Op. JAGAF.

**Opinion's of Judge Advocate Gen-
eral, United States Army**
CSJAG, Ops. J.A.C.

**Opinion's of Judge Advocate Gen-
eral, United States Navy**
Op. JAGN.

**Opinions and Orders of the Rail-
road Commission of California**
Cal. R. Com.

Opinions of Attorney General
Ops. Atty. Gen.

Opinion's of the Attorney General
Op. A. G., Op. Att. Gen., Op. At-
tys. Gen., Ops. A.G., Opin.,
OAG, Op. Att'y. Gen.

**Opinions of the Attorney General
and Report to the Governor of
Virginia**
Op. Va. Att'y Gen.

**Opinions of the Attorney General
of California**
Op. Cal. Att'y Gen.

**Opinions of the Attorney General
of New York**
N.Y. Ops. Atty. Gen., N.Y. Op.
Att. Gen., Op. N.Y. Atty. Gen.

**Opinions of the Attorney General
of Ohio**
Op. Ohio Att'y Gen.

**Opinions of the Attorney General
of Oklahoma**
Op. Okla. Att'y Gen.

**Opinions of the Attorney General
of Oregon**
Op. Or. Att'y Gen.

**Opinions of the Attorney General
of Pennsylvania**
Op. Pa. Att'y Gen.

**Opinions of the Attorney General
of Tennessee**
Op. Tenn. Att'y Gen.

**Opinions of the Attorney General
of Texas**
Op. Tex. Att'y Gen.

**Opinions of the Attorney General
of the State of Wisconsin**
Op. Wis. Att'y Gen.

**Opinions of the Attorney General
of Wyoming**
Op. Wyo. Att'y Gen.

**Opinions of the Attorney Gen-
eral, State of Georgia**
Op. Ga. Att'y Gen.

**Opinions of the Attorney Gen-
eral, State of Kansas**
Op. Kan. Att'y Gen.

**Opinions of the Attorney General
of the State of Louisiana**
Op. La. Att'y Gen.

**Opinions of the Attorney Gen-
eral, State of Minnesota**
Op. Minn. Att'y Gen.

Opinions of the Attorney General, State of North Dakota
Op. N.D. Att'y Gen.

Opinions of the Office of Legal Counsel
Op. Off. Legal Counsel

Opinions of the Solicitor for the United States Department of Labor Dealing With Workmen's Compensation
Op. Sol. Dept. Labor

Opinions of the Solicitor for the United States Post Office Department
Op. Sol. P.O.D.

Opinions of the Solicitor, United States Department of Labor
Op. Sol. Dept.

Oppenheim's International Law
Opp. Int. L.

Opposition
Opp'n

Optional County Government
Opt.County Gov't.

Orange County Bar Association Journal
Orange County B. J.

Orange Free State
O.F.S.

Orange Free State Reports
DeVitliers Reports

Ord on Usury
Ord.Us.

Order[s]
O., o., Ord.

Order in Council
O. in C., O.C., OIC

Order in Chancery
Ord. Ch.

Order of Court
Ord. Ct.

Orders, Lord Clarendon's
Ord. Cla.

Ordinance
O., Ord.

Ordinance of Amsterdam
Ord. Amst.

Ordinance of Antwerp
Ord. Antw.

Ordinance of Copenhagen
Ord. Copen.

Ordinance of Florence
Ord. Flor.

Ordinance of Genoa
Ord. Gen.

Ordinance of Hamburg
Ord. Hamb.

Ordinance of Konigsberg
Ord. Konigs.

Ordinance of Leghorn
Ord. Leg.

Ordinance of Portugal
Ord. Port.

Ordinance of Prussia
Ord. Prus.

Ordinance of Rotterdam
Ord. Rott.

Ordinance of Sweden
Ord.Swe.

Ordinance Procurement Instructions
OPI

Ordinances of Bilboa
Bilb. Ord.

Ordinances of the Australian Capital Territory
Austl. Cap. Terr. Ord., Ord. Austl. Cap. Terr.

Ordinances of the Legislative Council of New Zealand
N.Z. Ords., Ords. N.Z.

Ordronaux on Judicial Aspects of Insanity
Ordr. Jud. Ins.

**Ordronaux's Medical Jurispru-
dence**
Ord. Med. Jur., Ordr. Med. Jur.
Oregon
O., Or., Ore., Oreg.
Oregon Administrative Rules
Or. Admin. R.
**Oregon Administrative Rules Bul-
letin.**
Or. Admin. R. Bull.
**Oregon Annotated Codes and
Statutes by Billinger and Cot-
ton**
B.& C.Comp., Ann. Codes & St.
Oregon Appellate Reports
Ore Ap
Oregon Bar Bulletin
Or. Bar Bull.
Oregon Constitution
Or. Const.
Oregon Court of Appeals Reports
Or. A., Ore. App.
Oregon Law Review
O.L.R., Or. L. R., Or. L. Rev.,
Ore. L. Rev., Oreg. L. Rev.
Oregon Law School Journal
Or. L. S. J.
Oregon Laws Advance Sheets
Or. Laws Adv. Sh.
Oregon Laws and Resolutions
Or. Laws, Or. Laws Spec. Sess.
**Oregon Office of Public Utilities
Commissioner, Opinions and
Decisions**
Or. P.U.C. Ops.
**Oregon Public Service Commis-
sion Reports**
Or. P.S.C.
Oregon Railroad Commission
Or. R. C.
Oregon Reports
O., Or., Oreg., Or. Rep., Oregon

Oregon Reports, Court of Appeal
Or. App.
Oregon Revised Statutes
Or. Rev. Stat., Ore. Rev. Stat.,
Oreg. Rev. Stat.
Oregon State Bar
OSB
Oregon State Bar Bulletin
Or. St. B. Bull., Ore. St. B.
Bull., Oreg. S.B. Bull.
**Oregon Supreme Court Advance
Sheets**
Or. Ad. Sh.
Oregon Supreme Court Reports
Or., Ore
Oregon Tax Court Reports
Ore. Tax Ct.
Oregon Tax Reporter
Or. T. R.
Oregon Tax Reports
O.T.R.
**O'Reilly's Administrative Rule-
making**
ARm
**O'Reilly's Federal Information
Disclosure**
FID
**O'Reilly's Federal Information
Disclosure, Second Edition**
FID(2)
**O'Reilly's Federal Regulation of
the Chemical Industry**
FRCI
Orfila's Medicine Legale
Orf. M. L.
Organiz[ation, ing]
org.
**Organization for Economic Coop-
eration and Development**
OECD

**Organization for Trade Coopera-
tion of the General Agreement
on Tariffs and Trade (GATT)**
O.T.C.

Organization Management, Inc.
OMI

Organization of African Unity
OAU

Organization of American States
OAS

**Organization of Arab Petroleum
Exporting Countries**
OAPEC

**Organization of Central Ameri-
can States**
OCAS, O.D.E.C.A.

**Organization of European Eco-
nomic Cooperation**
OEEC

**Organization of Petroleum Ex-
porting Countries**
OPEC

**Organized Crime and Racketeer-
ing Section of the Department
of Justice**
O.C.R.

**Orlando Bridgman's English Com-
mon Pleas Reports**
O.B., O.Bridgm., O.Bridg.,
O.Bridg. (Eng.), Orl. Bridg., Orl.
Bridgman

Orleans Court of Appeals
Orleans App.

**Orleans Term Reports (1-2 Mar-
tin, Louisiana)**
Or. T. Rep., Orl. T. R., Orleans
T.R.

**Ormond's Reports (19-107 Ala-
bama)**
Ormond

Orphans' Court
O.C., Orphans' Ct.

**Ortolan's History of the Roman
Law**
Ort. Rom. Law, Ort. Hist.

Ortolan's Institute de Justinian
Ort. Inst.

Osaka University Law Review
Osaka U. L. R., Osaka U. L.
Rev., Osaka Univ. L. Rev.

Osgoode Hall Law Journal
O.H.L.J., Osgoode Hall L.J.

Osgoode Hall Law School Journal
Osgoode Hall L.S.J.

**OSHA Compliance Guide, Com-
merce Clearing House (Occupational Safety and Health
Administration)**
OSHA Compl. Guide (CCH)

Otago Law Review
Otago L. R., Otago L. Rev.

Otago Police Gazette
Otago Pol. Gaz.

Ottawa Law Review
Ottawa L. R., Ottawa L. Rev.

**Otto's United States Supreme
Court Reports (vols. 91-107
United States Reports)**
O., Ott's. U.S. Sup. Ct. R., Ot.,
Ott., Otto

Oudh Appeals, India
O.A.

Oudh Cases, India
O.C.

Oudh Code , India
Oudh.C., Oud.C.

Oudh Criminal Cases, India
O. Cr. C.

Oudh Law Journal, India
Oudh L.J., O. L. Jour., O.L.J.

Oudh Law Reports, India
O.L.R., Oudh L. R.

Oudh Select Cases, India
S.C., S.C. Oudh.

Oudh Weekly Notes, India
Oudh W.N., Oudh Wkly. N.,
O.W.N.
Oughton's Ordo Judiciorum
Ought.
Oulton's Index to Irish Statutes
Oult. Ind.
Oulton's Laws of Ireland
Oult. Laws Ir.
Outer Continental Shelf
O.C.S.
Outer House of the Court of Session, Scotland
Outer House
Outerbridge's Reports (97-98 Pennsylvania State)
Outerbridge, Out.
Overdose of Narcotics
O.D.
Overruled
O.
Overruled in
Overr.
Overruled; Ruling in Cited Case Expressly Overruled
O (used in Shepard's Citations)
Overruling
Overr.
Overseas Countries and Territories
OCT

Overseas Education Association
OEA
Overseas Private Investment Corporation
OPIC
Overton's Iowa and Wisconsin Practice
Overt.Pr.
Overton's Reports (1-2 Tennessee)
Over., Overt.
Owen on Bankruptcy
Owen Bankr.
Owen's English Common Pleas Reports
Ow.
Owen's English King's Bench Reports
Owen, Ow.
Oxford Journal of Legal Studies
Oxford J. Legal Stud.
Oxford Lawyer
Oxford Law, Oxf. Lawy.
Oxford Quarter Sessions Records
Gretton
Oxley's Railway Cases
Oxley
Oyer and Terminer
O. & T.

P

Pace Environmental Law Review
Pace Envtl. L. Rev., Pace Envtl.
L. Rev.

Pace Law Review
Pace L. Rev.

Pace Yearbook of International Law
Pace Y.B. Int'l L.

Pacific
Pac

Pacific Coast International
P.C. Int.

Pacific Coast Law Journal
P. Coast L.J., Pac. Coast L.J.,
P.C.L.J., Pacific C.L.J.

Pacific Law Journal
Pac. L.J., Pacific L.J.

Pacific Law Magazine
Pac. Law Mag., Pacific Law
Mag., P.L.M.

Pacific Law Reporter
P.L. Rep., P.L.R., Pac. Law
Reptr.

Pacific Legal Foundation
PLF

Pacific Legal News
Pac. Leg. N.

Pacific Reporter
P., Pac, Pac. Rep., Pac. Repr.,
Pacif. Rep., Pacific Rep., Pac.R.,
P.R.

Pacific Reporter, Second Series
Pac.2d, P.2d

Page
P.

Page and Adams' Code
P. & A.

Page on Contracts
Page Contr.

Page on Divorce
Page Div.

Page on Wills
Page, Wills

Page's Three Early Assize Rolls, County of Northumberland (Selden Society Publications, 88)
Page

Paget's Judicial Puzzles
Pag. Jud. Puz.

Paige's New York Chancery Reports
Paige Ch. Rep., Paige's Ch.,
Pai., Pai. Ch., Paige., Paige Ch.

Paine and Duer's Practice
Paine & D. Pr.

Paine on Elections
Paine, Elect.

Paine's United States Circuit Court Reports
Pa., Pai., Paine., Paine C.C.,
Paine C.C.R., Paine Cir. Ct. R.

Pakistan
Pak.

Pakistan Bar Journal
Pak. Bar J.

Pakistan Criminal Law Journal
Pak. Crim. L.J.

Pakistan Law Reports
P.L.R., Pak. L.R.

Pakistan Law Reports, Dacca Series.
Dacca, P.L.R. Dacca

Pakistan Law Reports, Karachi Series
Kar., P.L.R. Kar.

Pakistan Law Reports, Lahore Series
Lah., P.L.R. Lah.

Pakistan Law Reports, West Pakistan Series
P.L.R.W.P., W.P.

Pakistan Law Review
Pak. L. Rev., P.L.R.

Pakistan Supreme Court Law Quarterly
Pak. Sup. Ct. Q.

Paley on Principal and Agent
Paley, Ag., Paley, Prin. & Ag., Paley Princ. & Ag., Pal. Ag.

Paley's Moral Philosophy
Paley. Mor. Ph.

Paley's Summary Convictions
Pal. Conv.

Palgrave's Proceedings in Chancery
Palg. Ch., Palgrave.

Palgrave's Rise and Progress of the English Commonwealth
Palg. Rise, etc., Palg. Rise & Prog., Palgrave.

Palmer's Assizes at Cambridge
Pal., Palm., Palmer

Palmer's Company Law
Palm. Comp. L.

Palmer's Company Precedents
Palm. Comp. Prec., Palmer Co. Prec.

Palmer's English King's Bench Reports
Pal., Palm., Palmer

Palmer's Law of Wreck
Palm.Wr.

Palmer's Practice in the House of Lords
Palm. Pr. Lords

Palmer's Private Companies
Palm. Pr. Comp.

Palmer's Reports (53-60 Vermont)
Pal., Palm., Palmer

Palmer's Shareholders
Palm. Sh.

Pamphlet
Pamph., Pmph.

Pamphlet Laws
P.L., Pamph. Laws, Pamphl. Laws

Pan American Health Organization
PAHO

Pan American Sanitary Organization
PASO

Pan American Treaty Series
Pan-Am. T.S.

Pan American Union
PAU

Panama
Pan.

Pandects
Pand.

Pandects of Justinian
Ff.

Panel, Association of Grand Jurors of New York County Bar
Panel

Panel Publishers
PANPUB

Panjab (or Punjab) Code, India
Panj. C.

Pankhurst's Jurisprudence
Pank. Jur.

Paper Book of Laurence, J., in Lincoln's Inn Library
L.P.B.

Papua and New Guinea Law Reports
P. & N.G.L.R., Papua & N.G.

Papua New Guinea
Papua N.G.
Papua New Guinea Law Reform Commission
P.N.G.L.R.C.
Papua New Guinea Law Reports
P.N.G.L.R.
Papy's Reports (5-8 Florida)
Papy
Par Value
Pv.
Paragraph
Par., Para.
Paraguay
Para.
Parent and Child
Par. & C.
Paris and Fonblanque's Medical Jurisprudence
Par. & Fonb. Med. Jur.
Paris Topics, France
Paris Topics
Paris Union Committee for International Co-operation in Information Retrieval Among Patent Offices
ICEREPAT
Parish Court
Parish Ct.
Parish Will Case
Par. W.C.
Park on Dower
Park, Dow.
Parke on Real Property
Park. R.P.
Parker on Arbitration
Park. Arb.
Parker on Shipping and Insurance
Park. Sh., Parker
Parker's California Digest
Park. Dig.

Parker's Chancery Practice
Park. Ch.
Parker's Criminal Reports, New York
Park. Crim. (N.Y.), P.C.R.,
Park. Cr., Park. C.R., Park. Cr.
Rep., Park. Crim. L., Park.
Crim. R., Park. Crim. Rep.,
Parker's Cr. R., Parker's Crim.
R., Parker's Crim. Rep. (N.Y.),
P.Cl. R., Parker, Cr. R., Park.
Cr. Cas., Parker, Park., Par.
Parker's English Exchequer Reports
Par., Parker, Park. Exch., Park.
Rev. Cas., Park.
Parker's Insurance
Park. Ins.
Parker's New Hampshire Reports
Park., Parker, Park. N.H.
Parker's Practice in Chancery
Park. Pr. Ch.
Parkes on the History of Court of Chancery
Park. Hist. Ch.
Parks and Recreation
Parks & Rec.
Parks and Wildlife
Parks & Wild.
Park's Trial Objections Handbook
TOH
Parliament
Parl.
Parliament House Book
P.H.B.
Parliamentary
Parly.
Parliamentary Affairs
Parliam. Aff.
Parliamentary Cases
P.C.

**Parliamentary Cases, House of
Lords Reports**
Parl. Cas.
Parliamentary Debates
P.D., Parl. Deb.
Parliamentary History of England
Parl. Hist. Eng.
Parliamentary Law
Parl. L.
Parliamentary Papers
P.P.
Parliamentary Question
P.Q.
Parliamentary Register
Parl. Reg.
Parliamentary Reports
P.R.
Parliamentary Secretary
P.S.
Parochial Antiquities
Par. Ant.
Parole Board
P.B.
Parry's Consolidated Treaty Series
Consol. T.S.
**Parsons' Answer to the Fifth Part
of Coke's Reports**
Pars. Ans.
Parson's Commentaries on American Law
Par. Am. Law, Par. Am. Law
Comm.
Parsons' Decisions (2-7 Massachusetts)
Pars. Dec., Par. Dec.
Parsons' Essays on Legal Topics
Par. Ess.
Parson's Law by Hughes
Par. L.
Parsons' Laws of Business
Par. Laws Bus.

Parsons on Bills and Notes
Par. N. & B., Par. Bills & N.,
Pars. Bills & N.
Parsons on Contracts
Par. Cont., Pars. Cont.
Parsons on Costs
Par. Costs
**Parsons on Marine Insurance
and General Average**
Pars. Mar. Ins., Par. Mar. Ins.
Parsons on Maritime Law
Par. Mar. L., Pars. Mar. Law
Parsons on Mercantile Law
Par. Merc. Law, Pars. Merc. Law
Parsons on Partnership
Par. Part.
Parsons on Shipping and Admiralty
Par. Sh. & Adm., Pars. Shipp. &
Adm., Par. Adm.
Parsons on the Rights of a Citizen of the United States
Par. Rights Cit.
Parsons on Wills
Par. Wills
**Parsons' Reports (65-66 New
Hampshire)**
Par.
**Parsons' Select Equity Cases,
Pennsylvania**
Pars. Sel. Eq. Cas. (Pa.), Par.
Eq. Cases, Par. R., Pars. S. Eq.
Cas., Parsons', Pars. Eq. Cas.,
Par. Eq. Cas., Pars.
Part[s]
P., Pt.
Participating
Part., Partic.
Participation
Part., Partic.
Particles
P.

Partition
Partit.
Partner[s]
Part., Ptnr
Partnership
Partn.
Party Wall
Party W.
Paschal or Easter Term
Pasc., Pasch., Pas.
**Paschal's Reports (Supp. to 25; 28-
31 Texas)**
Pasc., Paschal.
**Paschal's Texas Digest of Deci-
sions**
Pasch. Dig.
**Paschal's United States Constitu-
tion Annotated**
Paschal's Ann. Const.
Passive Activity Loss
PAL
Passport
Passp.
Past and Present
Past & Present
Patch on Mortgages
Pat. Mort.
Patent
Pat.
Patent and Trademark Review
Pat. & T.M. Rev., Pat. & Tr.
Mk. Rev.
Patent and Trademark Office
PTO
**Patent and Trademark Office, Of-
ficial Gazette: Trademarks**
O.G.TM
Patent Cases
P.C.
**Patent, Copyright and Trade
Mark Cases**
Pat. Copyright & T.M. Cas.

**Patent, Design and Trade Mark
Review**
Pat. Des. & T.M. Rev.
**Patent Examining Procedure
Manual**
M.P.E.P.
**Patent Journal, including Trade-
marks and Models**
Pat. J.
Patent Law Annual
Pat. L. Ann.
Patent Law Review
Pat. L. Rev., Pat. Law Rev., Pat.
L.R., P.L.R.
Patent Office
Pat. Off., P.O.
Patent Office Journal
Pat. Off. J., P.O.J.
Patent Office, Official Gazette
Off. Gaz. Pat. Off., Off. Gaz.,
Off. Gaz. Pat. Office, O.G., O.G.
Pat. Off., Pat. Off. Gaz., P.O.G.
Patent Office Reports
Pat. Off. Rep., P.O.R.
Patent Office Society Journal
Pat. Off. Soc. J.
**Patent, Trademark and Copy-
right Journal**
Pat. T.M. & Copy. J., Pat. Trade-
mark & Copyright J.
**Patent, Trademark and Copy-
right Journal of Research and
Education**
Pat. T.M. & Copyr. J. of R. &
Educ., Idea
Patent World
Pat. World
Patents Cooperation Treaty
P.C.T.
**Patents, Decisions of the Commis-
sioner and of United States
Courts**
Dec. Comm'r Pat.

Paterson and Murray's Supreme Court Reports, New South Wales
Pat. & Mr., Pat. & Mur.

Paterson on Game Laws
Pat. Game L.

Paterson on the Game Laws
Paterson.

Paterson on the Liberty of the Subject
Paterson.

Paterson's Abridgment of Poor Law Cases
Pat. Abr.

Paterson's Compendium of English and Scotch Law
Pat. Comp., Paters. Comp., Paterson.

Paterson's Law and Usages of the Stock Exchange
Paterson.

Paterson's Licensing Acts Annual
Pat. Licens.

Paterson's New South Wales Reports
Pater., Paterson.

Paterson's Scotch Appeal Cases
Pat.H.L.Sc., Paterson Sc. App. Cas., Pat. App. Cas., Pater., Paterson., Pat., Pater. Ap. Cas., Pater. App.

Patna Law Journal, India
Pat. L.J.

Patna Law Reporter, India
Pat. L. Reptr.

Patna Law Reports, India
P.L.R., Pat. L.R.

Patna Law Times, India
Pat. L.T., P.L.T.

Patna Law Weekly, India
P.L.W., Pat. L.W.

Paton on Insurance
Pat. Ins.

Paton on Stoppage in Transitu
Pat. St. Tr.

Paton's Scotch Appeal Cases
Paton App. Cas., Paton Sc. App. Cas., Pat. App. Cas., Pat., Pat.H.L.Sc.

Patrick's Elections Cases, Ontario, Canada
Patr. Elec. CA., Patr. Elect. Cas., Patrick El. Cas.

Pattison's Missouri Digest
Pat. Dig.

Patton, Jr. and Heath's Reports, Virginia Special Court of Appeals
P. & H., Patton & H., Pat. & H., P. Jr. & H., Patton & H. (Va.), Patt. & H., Patt. & H. (Va.), Patt. & Heath R., Patton & Heath

Paying Agent
PA

Payment
Paym.

Payne and Ivamy on Carriage by Sea
Pay. & Iv. Carr.

Peabody Law and Review
Peab. L. Rev.

Peace and Freedom Party
PF

Peachey on Marriage Settlements
Pea. M.S.

Peake Cases, England
Peake

Peake on the Law of Evidence, England
Peake Ev.

Peake's Additional Nisi Prius Cases, England
Peake Add. Cas., Peake N.P. Add. Cas., Peake N.P. Add. Cas. (Eng.), Pea.

Peake's English Nisi Prius Cases
  Peake N.P., Peake N.P. Cas.
  (Eng.), P.N.P., Peake N.P. Cas.,
  Pea., Peake's Nisi Prius Reports
  (v. 2 of Peake), Pea. Add. Cas.
**Pearce's Reports in Dearsley's
  Crown Cases, England**
  Pearce C.C.
Pearson on Common Pleas
  Pearson
Pearson's Reports, Pennsylvania
  Pears., Pears. (Pa.)
Peck's Reports (24-30 Illinois)
  Peck., Peck (Ill.)
Peck's Reports (7 Tennessee)
  Peck., Peck (Tenn.)
Peck's Trial (Impeachment)
  Peck Tr.
**Peckwell's English Election
  Cases**
  Peck. Elec. Cas., Peck., Peck.
  El. Cas., Peckw.
**Peeples and Stevens' Reports (80-
  97 Georgia)**
  Peeples & Stevens
Peeples' Reports (77-97 Georgia)
  Peeples.
**Pelham's South Australia Re-
  ports**
  Pelham.
**Peltier's Orlean's Appeals Deci-
  sions**
  Pelt., Plt.
**Pemberton on Judgments and Or-
  ders**
  Pemb. Judg.
Penal
  Penal
**Penal and Correctional Institu-
  tions**
  Penal Inst.

Penal Code
  P.C., Pen. C., Pen. Code., Pen.
  Laws
**Penal Reform League Monthly
  Record**
  Pen. Ref. League M. Rec.
**Penal Reform League Quarterly
  Record**
  Pen. Ref. League Q. Rec.
Penal Reformer
  Pen. Ref.
Penault's Prerosti de Quebec
  Pen. P.
**Pennell and Postlewaite on Part-
  nership Taxation**
  PT
Pennewill's Delaware Reports
  Pen., Penn., Penn. Del., Penne.,
  Pennewill., Pe. R., Pennew.
**Pennington's Reports (2-3 New
  Jersey Law)**
  Penn., Pen., Pen. N.J., Penning.
Pennsylvania
  P., Pa., Penn., Penna.
**Pennsylvania Administrative
  Code**
  Pa. Admin. Code
Pennsylvania Bank Cases
  Pa. Bk. Cas.
Pennsylvania Bar Association
  Penn. B.A.
**Pennsylvania Bar Association
  Quarterly**
  Pa. B. Assn. Q., Pa. B. Ass'n. Q.,
  Pa. B.A.Q., Pa. Bar Asso. Q.,
  Penn. B.A.Q.
**Pennsylvania Bar Association Re-
  ports**
  Pa. B.A.
Pennsylvania Bar Brief
  Pa. B. Brief
Pennsylvania Bar Institute
  PBI

Pennsylvania Bulletin
Pa. Admin. Bull.
Pennsylvania Common Pleas Reporter
Pa. Com. Pl., Pa. C.P., Pa. C. Pl.
Pennsylvania Commonwealth Court Reports
Pa C., Pa. Cmwlth., Pa. Commw., Pa. Commw. Ct.
Pennsylvania Consolidated Statutes
Pa. Cons. Stat.
Pennsylvania Consolidated Statutes Annotated
Pa. Cons. Stat. Ann., Pa. C.S.A.
Pennsylvania Consolidated Statutes Annotated, Purdon
Pa. Cons. Stat. Ann. (Purdon)
Pennsylvania Constitution
Pa. Const.
Pennsylvania Corporation Reporter
Corp., Corp. Rep. (Pa.), Pa. Corp., Pa. Corp. R., Pa. Corp. Rep., P.C.R., Penn. Corp. Rep., Corp. Rep.
Pennsylvania County Court Reports
Co. Ct. Rep., Pa. C.C., Pa. Co. Ct., Pa. Co. Ct. R., Pa. County Ct., P.C.R., Penn. Co. Ct. Rep., Co. C.R., County Court, County Court R., County Court Rep., Pa. C.C. Reps., Pa. C.C.R., Pa. C.R.
Pennsylvania County Courts
Pa. Co.
Pennsylvania Courts, Decisions in Workmen's Compensation Cases
Pa. C. Dec. W.C.C.

Pennsylvania Department of Labor and Industry Decisions
Pa. Dep. L. & I. Dec.
Pennsylvania Department Reports
Pa. Dep. Rep.
Pennsylvania District and County Reports
Pa. D. & C., Penn. Dist. & Co. Rep., Pa. Dist. & Co., D. C., Pa. Dist. & C. Rep., D. & C.C., Dist. & Co. Rep., Pa. D. & C. Rep., Pa. Dist. & Co. R., Pa. Dist. & Co. Repts.
Pennsylvania District and County Reports, Fourth Series
DC4th
Pennsylvania District and County Reports, Second Series
D. C. 2d, Pa. D. & C.2d, Pa. Dist. & Co.2d
Pennsylvania District and County Reports, Third Series
DC3d, Pa. D. & C.3d
Pennsylvania District Reporter
Pa. Dist., Pa. Dist. R.
Pennsylvania District Reports
Penn. Dist. Rep., Dist. R., Dist. Reports, Dist. Reps., District, District Reps., Pa. Dist. Rep., Pa. D.R.
Pennsylvania Fiduciary Reporter
Pa. Fid., Pa. Fid. Reporter, Pa. Fiduc.
Pennsylvania General Assembly Laws
Pa. Laws
Pennsylvania Labor Relations Board
PLRB

Pennsylvania Law Journal
Pa. Law J., Pa. L.J., Penn. Law
Jour., Penn. L.J., P.L.J., Penna.
Law Journal, Penna. L.J., Pa.
Law Jour.

Pennsylvania Law Journal Reports
Pa. L.J., Penn. L.J.R., Clark

Pennsylvania Law Record
Pa. L. Rec., Penn. L. Rec., P.L.R.

Pennsylvania Law Review
Penn. L. Rev.

Pennsylvania Law Series
Pa. L. Ser., Pa. Law. Ser., Pa.
L.S.

Pennsylvania Lawyer
Pa. Law.

Pennsylvania Legal Gazette
Penn. L.G.

Pennsylvania Legal Gazette Reports
Penn. L.G.

Pennsylvania Legislative Service
Pa. Legis. Serv.

Pennsylvania Miscellaneous Reports
Pa. Misc.

Pennsylvania Public Service Commission Annual Report
Pa. P.S.C.

Pennsylvania Public Service Commission Decisions
Pa. P.S.C. Dec.

Pennsylvania Record
Pa. Rec.

Pennsylvania Reports
Pa. Rep., P.R.

Pennsylvania State Railroad Commission
Pa. S.R.C.

Pennsylvania State Reports
Pa., Pa. State, Penn. St. Rep.,
Pa. St., Penn., Penn. Rep.,
Penn. St., P.S.R., Pa. St. R., Pa.
State R., Pen. St. R., Penn. R.,
Penn. Stat., Penn. State Rep.,
Penna. R., Penna. S.R., Penna.
St., Penna. State Rep

Pennsylvania State Trials
Pa. St. Tr.

Pennsylvania Statutes Annotated
Pa. Stat. Ann.

Pennsylvania Summary of Jurisprudence
Pa. Summary

Pennsylvania Superior Court Reports
Pa. S., Pa. Super., Pa. Super.
Ct., Pa. Superior Ct., Penn. Super., Supr. Ct.

Pennsylvania Supreme Court Cases
Pa. Cas., Pa.

Pennsylvania Workmen's Compensation Board Decisions
Pa. W.C. Bd. Dec.

Pennypacker's Pennsylvania Colonial Cases
Penny., Penny. Col. Cas., Pennyp. Col. Cas.

Pennypacker's Reports, Pennsylvania
Pen

Pennypacker's Unreported Pennsylvania Cases
Pennyp., Pennyp. (Pa.), Penn.,
Penny.

Penology
Penol.

Penrose and Watts' Pennsylvania Reports
Penn. Rep., Penr. & W., P. &
W., Pen. & W., PW

Penruddocke's Short Analysis of Criminal Law
  Penr. Anal.
Pension Agency
  PA
Pension and Bounty, United States Department of Interior
  P.D.
Pension and Profit Sharing, Prentice-Hall
  Pens. & Profit Sharing (P-H)
Pension Benefit Guaranty Corporation
  PBGC
Pension Benefit Guaranty Corporation Opinions
  PBGC Op.
Pension Decisions, U.S. Interior Department
  Pen. Dec.
Pension Plan Guide, Commerce Clearing House
  Pens. Plan Guide (CCH)
Pension Reporter, Bureau of National Affairs
  Pension Rep., Pens. Rep. (BNA)
Pension Review Board Reports
  P.R.B.
Pension Trust, Profit-Sharing, Stock Bonus, or Annuity Plan Ruling
  P.S.
Pension Trustee
  P.T.
Pensions and Retirement Funds
  Pens.
People's Legal Advisor
  Peo. L. Adv.
People's Republic of China
  China (PR), PRC

Pepper and Lewis' Digest of Pennsylvania Laws
  P. & L. Dig. Laws, Pepper & L. Dig., Pepper & L. Dig. Laws
Pepperdine Law Review
  Pepp. L. Rev., Pepperdine L. Rev., Pepperdine L.R.
Pepperdine University School of Law
  PEPUSL
Per Power of Attorney
  P.p.a.
Per Procurationem (by proxy) (Lat.)
  Per pro.
Perera's Select Decisions, Ceylon
  Per.
Performing Arts Review
  Perf. Arts Rev., Performing Arts Rev.
Perjury
  Perj.
Perkins on Conveyancing
  Perk.
Perkins on Pleading
  Perk.
Perkins' Profitable Book (Conveyancing)
  Perk., Perk. Pr. Bk.
Permanent
  Perm.
Permanent Central Opium Board
  PCOB
Permanent Court of International Justice
  PCIJ
Permanent Court of International Justice Annual Reports
  P.C.I.J. Ann. R.
Permanent Court of International Justice Cases
  PCIJ

Perpetual
Perp., Perpet.
Perpetuities and Restraints on Alienation
Perp.
Perrault's Prevoste de Quebec
Per. P., Perrault
Perrault's Quebec Reports
Perrault
Perry and Davison's English King's Bench Reports
Perry & D., Perry & D. (Eng.), Per. & Dav.
Perry and Davison's English Queen's Bench Reports
P. & D.
Perry and Knapp's English Election Cases
Perry & K., Perry & Kn., P. & K., Per. & Kn.
Perry on Trusts
Per. Tr., Perry, Trusts
Perry's Insolvency Cases, England
Perry Ins.
Perry's Oriental Cases
P.O.Cas., Per. Or. Cas., Perry O.C., Perry
Persian
P.
Personal
Pers.
Personal Finance Law Quarterly Report
Pers. Finance L.Q.
Personal Injury Annual
Pers. Inj. Ann.
Personal Injury Commentator
Pers. Inj. Comment., Pers. Inj. Comment'r.
Personal Injury Deskbook
Pers. Inj. Deskbook

Personal Injury Law Journal
Pers. Inj. L.J.
Personal Property
Pers. Prop.
Personnel Administration
Personnel Admin.
Personnel Board
Pers.
Personnel Management, Prentice-Hall
Personnel Mgmt. (P-H)
Perspectives
Persp.
Perspectives: The Civil Rights Quarterly
Perspectives: Civ. Rights Q.
Peters' Admiralty Decisions, United States
Pet. Adm. App., Pet. Ad. Dec., Pet. Ad. R., Peters' Ad., Peters' Adm. R., Peters Adm. Rep., Peters' Admiralty Dec., P.A.D., Pet., Peters Adm.
Peters' Analysis and Digest of the Decisions of Sir George Jessel
Peter
Peters' Reports Volume 11, Appendix by Baldwin (United States Reports)
Bald.App. 11 Pet.
Peters' Condensed United States Circuit Court Reports
Pet. Cir. C.R., Pet. Cond. Rep., Pet.
Peters' Condensed United States Supreme Court Reports
Condensed Rep., Pet. Cond., Cond. Rep. U.S., Cond. R., Cond. Rep., U.S. Cond. Rep.
Peters' Prince Edward Island Reports
Pet.

Peters' United States Circuit Court Reports
P.C.C., Pet. C.C., Peters C.C.

Peters' United States Digest
Pet. Dig.

Peters' United States District Court Reports, Admiralty Decisions
Pet. Ad., Peters' Adm. Dec., Pet. Adm. See also: Peters' Admiralty Decisions

Peters' United States Reports, Appendix to Volume 11 by Baldwin
Bald.App.

Peters' United States Supreme Court Reports
P.S.C.U.S., Peters, P., Pet., Pet. S.C.

Petersdorff's Abridgment of Cases
Pet. Ab., Petersd. Ab., Pet. Abr.

Petersdorff's Abridgment, Supplement
Pet. Suppl.

Petersdorff's Bail
Pet. Bail

Petersdorff's Law of Nations
Pet. L. Nat.

Petersdorff's Master and Servant
Pet. M. & S.

Petgrave on Principals and Agents
Petg. Pr. & Ag.

Petheram on Discovery by Interrogations
Peth. Dis.

Peticolas' Texas Digest
Pet. Dig.

Petition
Pet., Petn.

Petition to U.S. Supreme Court for Writ of Certiorari Granted
Cert. granted

Petitioner
Pet'r

Petroleum Economist
Petroleum Econ.

Petroleum Revenue Tax
P.R.T.

Petronius' (Titus) Arbiter, Satyricon, etc.
Petron. Satyric.

Petty Session Division
P.S.D.

Petty Sessions
P.S.

Petty Sessions Cases, Ireland
Millin

Phalen's Criminal Cases
Phal. C.C.

Pharmacy Board
Phar.

Phear on Rights of Water
Phear Wat.

Pheney's New Term Reports, England
Pheney Rep.

Philadelphia
Phila.

Philadelphia Law Journal
Phila. L.J.

Philadelphia Law Library
Phila. Law Lib.

Philadelphia Legal Intelligencer
Philadelphia Leg. Int., Phila. Leg. Int.

Philadelphia Reports
Phil., Ph. Rep., Phil. (Pa.), Phil. R., Phil. Rep., Phila. Reports, Philad., Philada. R., Philada. Rep., Philadelphia Rep., P.R., Phila., Phila. (Pa.)

Philanthropist
Philanthrop

Philip and Mary
Ph. & M., Phil. & Mar., Phil. &
M.

Philippine Code
Philippine Co.

**Philippine International Law
Journal**
Phil. I.L.J., Phil. Int. L.J., Phil.
Int'l L.J., Philippine Int'l. L.J.,
Philippine Internat. L.J.

**Philippine Islands Public Service
Commission Reports**
P.I.P.S.C.R., P.I.P.U.C.R.

Philippine Islands Reports
P.I. Rep., P.R., Phil.

**Philippine Journal of Public Ad-
ministration**
Phil. J. Pub. Admin., Philippine
J. Pub. Admin.

**Philippine Labour Relations
Journal**
Phil. Lab. Rel. J.

Philippine Law Journal
Philippine L.J., Phil. L.J.

Philippine Law Review
Phil. L. Rev., Philippine L. Rev.

Philippine Reports
Philippine.

Philippine Studies
Phil. Stud.

**Philippine Yearbook of Interna-
tional Law**
Phil. Yb. Int'l. L.

Philippines
Phil.

Phillimore on the Law of Domicil
Phillim. Dom., Phil. Dom.

Phillimore's Civil and Canon Law
Phil. Civ. & Can. Law

**Phillimore's Ecclesiastical Cases
Tempore Lee, England**
Cas. t. Lee

**Phillimore's Ecclesiastical Judg-
ments, England**
Phil. Jud., Phil. Ecc., Phil.
Judg., Phill. Ecc. Judg., Phillim.
Eccl., Phil. Ecc. Judg., Phill.
Eccl. Judg., Phillim.

Phillimore's Ecclesiastical Law
Phillim. Ecc. Law, Phil. Ecc.
Law, Phil. Ecc.

**Phillimore's Ecclesiastical Re-
ports, England**
Phil. Ecc. R., Phillim. Eccl.,
Phill. Ecc. R., Phillim. Eccl.,
Ph., Phil., Phil. Ecc.

Phillimore's International Law
Phil. Int. Law, Phillim. Int. Law

**Phillimore's Introduction to the
Roman Law**
Phil. Int. Rom. Law

**Phillimore's Private Law Among
the Romans**
Phil. Rom. Law

**Phillipps' Famous Cases in Cir-
cumstantial Evidence**
Phil. Fam. Cas., Fam. Cas. Cir.
Ev.

Phillipps' State Trials
Ph. St. Tr.

**Phillips' English Chancery Re-
ports**
Ph. Ch., Ph., Phil., Phill., Phillips, Phill. Ch. (Eng.), Phill. Ch.

Phillips' English Election Cases
Phil. El. Cas., Ph., Phil., Phill.,
Phillips

**Phillips' Equity Reports, North
Carolina**
Phil. Eq., Phill., Phill. Eq.
(N.C.), Phillips

Phillip's Grandeur of the Law
Phil. Grand.

Phillips' Illinois Reports (152-245 Illinois)
Phil., Phill., Phillips
Phillips' Law of Copyright Designs
Phil. Cop.
Phillips' Law Reports (61 North Carolina)
Phill., Phill.L. (N.C.), Phillips, Phil. Law, Phl. N.C., Phil.
Phillips on Evidence
Phil. Ev., Ph. Ev.
Phillips' on Evidence, Notes by Cowen, Hill and Edwards
Phil. Ev. Cow. & H. & Edw. Notes
Phillips on Insurance
Phil. Ins., Phil., Phill. Ins.
Phillips on Lunatics
Phil. Lun., Phil. Luna.
Phillips on Mechanics' Liens
Phil. Mech. Liens.
Phillips on Patents
Phil. Pat.
Phillip's Studii Legalis Ratio
Phil. St. Leg. R.
Phillips' United States Supreme Court Practice
Phil. U.S. Pr.
Philosophical
Phil.
Philosophical Quarterly
Phil. Q.
Philosophical Research
Phil. Res., Philos. Res.
Philosophical Review
Phil. Rev., Philos. Rev.
Philosophy
Phil., Philosophy
Philosophy and Phenomenlogical Research
Phil. & Phenom. Res.

Philosophy and Public Affairs
Phil. & Publ. Aff., Philos. & Publ. Aff.
Philosophy Today
Philos. Today
Phipson on Evidence
Phip. Ev.
Phipson's Digest, Natal Reports
Phip.
Phipson's Reports, Natal Supreme Court
Phip.
Phoenix (a journal published in Toronto, Canada)
Phoenix
Photoduplicated Reprint
Photo. reprint
Physicians, Surgeons and Other Healers
Phys. & S.
Pickering's English Statutes
Pick. Stat.
Pickering's Reports (18-41 Massachusetts)
Pick., P., Pick. (Mass.)
Pickle's Reports (85-108 Tennessee)
Pickle
Pierce on Railroad Law
Pierce, R.R.
Pierce's Perpetual Code
P.P.C.
Piggott's Common Recoveries
Pig.
Piggott's Foreign Judgments
Pig. Judg.
Pigott and Rodwell's English Common Pleas Report
P. & R.
Pigott and Rodwell's English Registration Appeal Cases
Pig. & R.

Pigott's Recoveries
Pig. Rec.
Pike and Fischer's Administrative Law Reporter
P & F, P.& F., Pike & F. Adm. Law, Pike & Fischer, Admin. Law
Pike and Fischer's Administrative Law, Second Series
P & F Ad. L.2D
Pike and Fischer's Federal Rules Service
P.& F., Pike & F. Fed. Rules Ser., Pike & F. Fed. Rules Service
Pike and Fischer's OPA Price Service (Office of Price Administration)
P.& F.
Pike and Fischer's Radio Regulations
R.R., P. & F. Radio Reg.
Pike and Fischer's Radio Regulations, Second Series
R.R. 2d
Pike's History of the House of Lords
Pike. H. of L.
Pike's Reports (1-5 Arkansas)
Pike.
Pim on Feudal Tenures
Pim Ten.
Pingrey's Treatise of Chattel Mortgages
Ping. Chat. Mortg.
Pinney's Wisconsin Reports
Pinn., Pin. (Wis.), Pinney., Pinney (S.U.), Pin.Wis. R., Pin.
Pipelines
Pipe.
Pipon and Collier on Military Law
Pip. & C. Mil. L.

Piston's Mauritius Reports
Pist., Piston.
Pitcairn's Ancient Criminal Trials, Scotland
Pitc. Tr., Pitc. Crim. Tr., Pitc.
Pitisci's Lexicon
Pitisc. Lex.
Pitman on Principal and Surety
Pitm. Prin. & Sur.
Pitman on Suretyship
Pitm. Sur., Pit. Sur.
Pitt's Bankruptcy Acts
Pitt Bank.
Pitt's County Court Practice
Pitt C.C. Pr.
Pittsburgh
Pitt., Pittsb., Pitts.
Pittsburgh Law Review
Pittsb. L. Rev.
Pittsburgh Legal Journal
Pitt. L.J., Pitts. L.J., Leg. J., Leg. Jour., P. Leg. J., P. Leg. Jour., Pgh. Leg. Journal, Pitts. Leg. J., Pitts. Leg. Jour., Pittsb. Leg. J., Pittsb. Leg. J. (Pa.), Pittsb. L.J., Pittsburgh Leg. J., Pittsburgh Leg. Journal, Pittsburgh Legal Journal, P.L.J.
Pittsburgh Legal Journal, New Series
Pittsb. Leg. J.N.S., P.L.J.N.S., Pitts. Leg. J. (N.S.), Pitts. L.J. (N.S.)
Pittsburgh Legal Journal, Old Series
Pittsb. Leg. J. (O.S.)
Pittsburgh Reports
Pittsb. R. (Pa.), Pitts., Pitts. Rep., Pitts. R., Pitts. Rep. (Pa.), P.R., Pittsb.
Pittsburgh Reports, Edited by Crumrine
Crumrine

Pixley on Auditors
Pix. Aud.

Placita Anglo-Normannica Cases, Bigelow
Plac. Angl. Nor., Pl. Ang.-Norm.

Placita Coronae (Pleas of the Crown)
Pl. C.

Placita de Quo Warranto (English Records Commission)
P.Q.W.

Placita Parliamentaria
Pl. Par., Pla. Par.

Placitorum Abbreviatis (Record Commissioner)
Plac. Abbrev., Abbrev. Plac.

Placitum or Placita (subdivision) (Lat.)
P., Pla., Pl.

Plaintiff[s]
Pl., plf., P, Pls.

Plan Canada
Plan. Can.

Planned Unit Development
PUD

Planning
Plan.

Planning and Compensation Reports
P.& C.R., Plan & Comp.

Planning, Zoning and Eminent Domain Institute
Plan., Zoning & E.D. Inst.

Plant and Job Safety — OSHA and State Laws
Plant Saf.

Platt on Leases
Pl. L., Platt. Leas., Platt.

Platt on the Law of Covenants
Platt,Cov., Platt.

Plaxton's Canadian Constitutional Decisions
Plaxton.

Pleading
Plead.

Pleading and Practice Cases, England
Pl. & Pr. Cas.

Pleas of the Crown (Placita Coronae)
P.C.

Plebiscite
Pleb.

Plowden on Usury
Pl. U.

Plowden's Criminal Conversation Trials
Pl. Cr. Con. Tr.

Plowden's English King's Bench Commentaries or Reports
Plowd., Pl., Pl. Com., Plow., Plow.

Plumtree on Contracts
Plum. Contr.
Plunkett Cases in Chancery Tempore, England
Ca.t.Plunk.

Pocock on Costs
Poc. Costs

Poe on Pleading and Practice
Poe, Pl.

Points and Authorities
P. & A.

Polamerican Law Journal
Polam. L.J.

Poland
Pol.

Poland's Digest of the Military Laws of the United States
Pol. Mil. Dig.

Poland's Law of Trade Marks
Pol. Tr. Mar.

Police
Pol., Police

Police Court
Po. Ct.

Police Department
PD
Police Federation Newsletter
Pol. Fedn. Newsl.
Police Journal
Police J.
Police Justice's Court
Police J. Ct.
Police Law Quarterly
Pol. L.Q., Police L.Q.
Policy
Pol., Pol'y.
Policy Proof of Interest
P.P.I.
**Policy Statements of the Austra-
lian Broadcasting Tribunal**
Po S
Polish
Pol.
Polish Perspectives
Polish Perspectives
Polish Social Research
Polish Soc. Res.
**Polish Yearbook of International
Law**
Pol. Yb. of Internal. L., Pol. Y.B.
Int'l L.
Political
Pol.
Political Code
Pol. C., Pol. Code
**Political-Economic Association of
Ivory Coast, Dahomey, Niger,
Upper Volta, and Togo**
ENTENTE
Political Quarterly
Pol. Q.
Political Science Quarterly
Pol. Sci. Q., P.S.Q.
Political Science Review
Pol. Sci. Rev.
Political Studies
Pol. Studies

Political Theory
Pol. Theory
Politics
Pol.
Politics and Society
Pol. & Soc'y
**Pollack's Ohio Unreported Judi-
cial Decisions**
Ohio Unrep. Jud. Dec., Poll.
**Pollard and Burton's Guide to Ef-
fective Bankruptcy Litigation**
GEBL
**Pollexfen's English King's Bench
Reports**
Pollexf., Poll., Pol., Pol., Pollex.
**Pollock and Maitland's History of
English Law**
P. & M., P. & M.H.E.L., Pollock
& Maitl.
Pollock on Contracts
Pol. Cont.
**Pollock on the Power of Courts
to Compel the Production of
Documents**
Pol. Prod. Doc.
**Pollock on the Production of
Documents**
Poll. Prod.
**Pollock's Digest of the Laws of
Partnership**
Pol. Dig. Part., Pol. Part.
Pollution Abstracts
Pollution Abs.
Pollution Control
Poll. Const.
**Pollution Control Guide, Com-
merce Clearing House**
Pollution Cont. Guide (CCH),
Poll. Contr. Guide
**Polson's Principles of the Law of
Nations**
Pols. Nat., Pol. Law of Nat.

Poly Law Review
Poly. L. Rev.
Pomeroy on Civil Remedies and Remedial Rights
Pom. Rem., Pom. Rem. & Rem. Rights
Pomeroy on Code Remedies
Pom. Code Rem.
Pomeroy on Contracts
Pom. Contr.
Pomeroy on Municipal Law
Pom. Mun. Law
Pomeroy on Specific Performance of Contracts
Pom. Spec. Perf.
Pomeroy's Constitutional Law of the United States
Pom. Const. Law
Pomeroy's Equity Jurisprudence
Pom. Eq. Jur., Pom. Eq. Juris.
Pomeroy's Reports (73-128 California)
Pomeroy
Poor Law
P.L.
Poor Law and Local Government Magazine
Poor L. & Local Gov't
Poor Law Board
P.L.B.
Poor Law Commissioner
P.L. Com.
Poor Law Magazine
P.L.M., P.L. Mag.
Poore's Federal and State Constitutions
Poore Const.
Pope on Customs and Excise
Pope Cust.
Pope on Lunacy
Pope, Lun.

Popham's English King's Bench Reports
Pop., Poph., Popham
Popham's Insolvency Act of Canada
Poph. Insol.
Popular Government
Pop. Govt.
Popular Monthly Law Tracts
Pop. Mo. L. Tr.
Popular Science Monthly
Pop. Sci. Mo.
Porter's Alabama Reports
Port. (Ala.), Porter, Port., Port. Ala. R., Port. Ala. R., Porter (Ala.), Porter R., Porter's Ala. R., Porter's R., Porter's Repts.
Porter's Indiana Reports (3-7 Indiana)
Port., Porter
Porter's Laws of Insurance
Port. Ins.
Portia Law Journal
Portia L.J.
Portland University Law Review
Port. U.L. Rev., Portland U.L. Rev.
Porto Rico Federal Reports
Porto Rico Fed. Rep., Pr. R. Fed.
Porto Rico Reports, Spanish Edition
D. P. R.
Portugal
Port.
Portuguese
Po
Posey's Unreported Texas Cases
Posey, Unrep. Cas., Posey U.C., Posey's U.C., Tex. Unrep. Cas.
Post (after) (Lat.)
Post
Post Meridiem (afternoon) (Lat.)
P.M.

Post Office
P.O., Post. Off.
Post Office and Civil Service
POCS
Post Office Department Procurement Regulations
PODPR
Post Office Department Solicitor's Official Opinions
Op. Solic. P.O. Dep't., Op. Sol. P.O.D.
Postage and Registration
Post. & Reg.
Postal Rate Commission
P.R.C.
Postal Regulations
P.R.
Poste's Translation of Gaius
Poste Gai., Poste's Gaius Inst.
Postlethwaite's Dictionary of Trade and Commerce
Postl. Dict.
Postlewaite's International Corporate Taxation
ICT
Postmaster
P.M.
Post's Reports (23-26 Michigan)
Post
Post's Reports (42-64 Misssouri)
Post
Pothier on Partnership
Poth. Part.
Pothier on the Law of Obligations
Poth. Ob., Poth. Obl., Poth. Oblig.
Pothier's Pandectae Justinianeae, etc.
Pothier, Pand., Poth. Pand.
Pothier's Treatise on Maritime Contracts
Poth. Mar. Cont.

Pothier's Treatise on the Contract of Sale
Poth. Cont. Sale, Poth. Contr. Sale, Poth. Cont.
Potomac Law Review
Potomac L. Rev.
Potter on Corporations
Pott. Corp.
Potter's Edition of Dwarris on Statutes
Pot. Dwar., Pott. Dwarris
Potter's Reports (4-7 Wyoming)
Potter
Pott's Law Dictionary
Pot. L.D., Potts L.D.
Poverty Law Reporter, Commerce Clearing House
Pov. L. Rep.
Powell on Contracts
Pow. Cont.
Powell on Conveyancing
Pow. Conv.
Powell on Evidence
Pow. Ev.
Powell on Mortgages
Pow. Mortg., Pow. Mort.
Powell on Powers
Pow. Pow.
Powell on the Law of Inland Carriers
Pow. Inl. Car., Pow. Cas.
Powell's Analysis of American Law
Pow. An. Law
Powell's Essay upon the Learning of Devises, etc.
Pow. Dev.
Powell's Law of Appellate Proceedings
Pow. App. Proe.
Powell's Precedents in Conveyancing
Pow. Pr.

Power of Attorney
P/ A, PA

Power, Rodwell and Dew's English Election Cases
P.R. & D. El. Cas., Pow. R. & D., P.R. & D.

Powers' Reports, New York Surrogate Court
Pow. Surr., Powers, Power's Sur.

Poynter on Marriage and Divorce
Poynt. M. & D.

Practical
Prac.

Practical Approach to Patents, Trademarks and Copyrights
Prac. Appr. Pat. T.M. & Copyright

Practical Lawyer
Prac. Law., Pract. Law.

Practical Litigation
Prac. Litig.

Practical Real Estate Lawyer
Prac. Real Est. Law.

Practical Register in Chancery
Pr. Reg. Ch., P.R. Ch.

Practical Register in Common Pleas
P.R.C.P., Pr. Reg. C.P., Pract. Reg.

Practical Register in the Bail Court
Pr. Reg. B.C.

Practical Tax Lawyer
Prac. Tax Law.

Practice
Prac.

Practice Act
Prac. Act.

Practice Cases
P.C.

Practice Cases, King's Bench
Pr. C.K.B.

Practice Notes of the Australian Broadcasting Tribunal
PRN

Practice of the High Court of Chancery
Pr.H.C.Ch.

Practice Reports
Prt. Rep., P.R.U.C., Pr. Rep., Pr. Rep., Pr.R., Pr.R., Pr., Pr.R.

Practicing Law Institute
PLI

Practitioner[s]
Pract., Prac.

Prater on Husband and Wife
Pra. H. & W.

Prater's Cases on Conflict of Laws
Pra. Cas.

Pratt and Mackenzie on Highways
Pratt. High.

Pratt on Contraband of War
Pr. Cont.

Pratt on Friendly Societies
Pratt. Fr. Soc.

Pratt on Savings Banks
Pratt Sav. B.

Pratt on Sea Lights
Pratt S.L.

Pratt on the Property Tax Act
Pratt Prop. T.

Pratt's Contraband of War Cases
Pratt, Pratt Cont.

Pratt's Edition of Bott on the Poor Laws
Pratt P.L., Pratt., Pratt's Bott

Pratt's Law of Benefit Building Societies
Pratt B.S.

Pratt's Statutes Establishing Courts of Request
Pratt Cts. Req.

Praxis Almae Curiae Cancel-
lariae, Brown
    Prax. Can.
Preble's Digest of Patent Cases
    Preb. Dig., Preb. Pat. Cas.
Precedents in Chancery, Edited
by Finch
    Ch. Prec., P.C., Ch. Pre., Prec.
    Ch., Prec. in Ch. (Eng.), Prec. in
    Ch., Pre. Ch., Pr. Ch., Finch
    Prec., See also Finch's Prece-
    dents in Chancery
Precedents of Private Acts of Par-
liament
    P.P.A.P.
Preference
    Pref
Preferred
    Pfd.
Preliminary (Incorporated Law
Society), England
    Prelim.
Premises Liability
    Prem. Liab.
Premium
    Prem.
Prentice-Hall
    P-H
Prentice-Hall New York Estate
Tax Reports
    P.-H.N.Y.E.T.R.
Prentice-Hall Unreported Trust
Cases
    P.-H.Unrep. Tr. Cas.
Prentice's Proceedings in an Ac-
tion
    Pren. Act.
Preparation
    Prep.
Preparing for Settlement and
Trial
    PST

Prerogative Court
    Pr. Co., Prer.
Prerogative Court of Canterbury
    P.C.C.
Prerogative Court, New Jersey
    Prerog. Ct.
President
    Pres.
Presidential Executive Order
    E.O., Exec. Order
Presiding Judge
    P.J.
Press Release
    P.R.
Preston on Abstracts of Title
    Pres. Abs.
Preston on Conveyancing
    Prest. Conv., Pres. Conv.
Preston on Estates
    Prest. Est., Pres. Est.
Preston on Legacies
    Pres. Leg.
Preston on Merger
    Pres. Mer., Prest. Merg.
Pretrial Conference
    Pretrial Conf.
Preventive Law Reporter
    Prev. L. Rep.
Preview of United States Su-
preme Court Cases
    Preview
Price and Stewart's Trade Mark
Cases
    Price & St.
Price Control Cases
    P.C.
Price Decontrol Board
    PDC
Price on Acts Relating to Real Es-
tate
    Price R. Est.
Price on Maritime Liens
    Price Liens

Price Procedural Regulation
PPR
Prices and Incomes Board
P.I.B.
Price's English Exchequer Reports
Pr., Pr. Exch., Pri., Price
Price's English Practice Cases
Price, P.C., Price Pr. Cas.
Price's General Practice
Price Gen. Pr.
Price's Mining Commissioners' Cases
Price Min. Cas., Pri., Price
Price's Notes of Points of Practice, English Exchequer Cases
Price Notes P.P., Price Notes P.C.
Prickett's Idaho Reports
Prickett
Prideaux and Cole's English Reports
Prid. & C., P. & C., Prid. & Co.
Prideaux and Whitcomb's Precedents in Conveyancing
Prid. Conv.
Prideaux's Directions to Churchwardens
Prid. Ch. W.
Prideaux's Forms and Precedents in Conveyancing
Prid. Conv.
Prideaux's Judgments and Crown Debts
Prid. Judg.
Prime Minister
P.M.
Prince Edward Island
P.E.I., Pr. Edw. Isl.
Prince Edward Island Law Reform Commission
P.E.I.L.R.C.

Prince Edward Island Reports
Pr. Edw. Isl., Pr. Edw. I., P.E.I., P.E.I. Rep.
Prince Edward Island Revised Statutes
P.E.I. Rev. Stat.
Prince Edward Island Statutes
P.E.I. Stat.
Prince's New Mexico Laws
Prince N.M.L.
Principal
Prin.
Principal and Interest
P. & I.
Principal Clerk of Session
P.C.S.
Principal Probate Registry
P.P.R.
Printed Judgments of Sind by Candy and Birdwood, Ceylon
Candy.
Printed Minutes of Evidence
Pr. Min.
Printing
Prtg.
Prior
Pr.
Prison Law Reporter
Prison L. Rptr.
Prison Officers' Association
P.O.A.
Prison Service Journal
Prison Serv. J.
Pritchard's Divorce and Matrimonial Causes
Pritch. M. & D.
Pritchard's English Admiralty Digest
Pritch. Adm. Dig., Pr. Adm. Dig.
Pritchard's Quarter Sessions
Pritch. Quar. Sess.
Privacy Journal
Priv. J.

Privacy Report
Priv. R.
Private
Pr., Pvt.
Private Acts of the State of Tennessee
Tenn. Priv. Acts.
Private Agency Trust (Agency Accounts)
PA
Private and Local Laws
P. & L. Laws
Private and Special Laws
Sp. St.
Private Foundations Reporter, Commerce Clearing House
Priv. Found. Rep.
Private Franchise Contracts
Priv. Fran. Cont.
Private Housing Finance
Priv. Hous. Fin.
Private International Law
Int. Private Law
Private Investments Abroad
Priv. Inv. Abroad
Private Laws
Pr. L., Priv. L., Priv. Laws
Private Legislation Reports
P.L.R.
Private Statutes
Pr. Stat., Priv. St.
Private Trust (including testamentary, investment, life insurance, holding title, etc.)
P., P. Tr.
Privilegia Londini (Customs of Privileges of London)
Priv. Lond.
Privy Council
P.C.
Privy Council Acts
Act.P.C., Acts P.C.

Privy Council Acts, New Series
Act. P.C.N.S.
Privy Council Appeals
Priv. C. App., Priv. Counc. App.
Privy Council Cases
P.C.C.
Privy Council Decisions
P.C.I., Priv. Counc. D.I.
Privy Council Judgments
Pershad, P.C. Judg.
Privy Council Reports
P.Cl. R.
Privy Seal
P.S.
Prize Cases
Pr. C., P. Cas., P. Cas.
Prize Court
P.C.
Prize Court Reports
Prize C.R.
Pro Defendente (for on behalf of defendant) (Lat.)
P.d.
Pro Hac Vice (for this purpose or occasion) (Lat.)
P.H.V.
Pro Querente (for or on behalf of plaintiff) (Lat.)
P.q., Pro quer.
Probate
Prob.
Probate and Admiralty Division Law Reports, England
Prob. & Adm. Div.
Probate and Divorce
P. & D.
Probate and Divorce Cases, England
L.R.P. & D.
Probate and Divorce, English Law Reports
Prob. & Div.

Probate and Matrimonial Cases, England
Prob. & Mat.
Probate and Property
Prob. & Prop.
Probate Code
Prob. C.
Probate Court
P. Ct., P.C., Prob. Code.
Probate Court Act
P.C. Act
Probate Court Reporter
Prob. Ct. Rep.
Probate, Divorce, and Admiralty
P.D.A.
Probate, Divorce, and Admiralty Division or Divisional Court
P.D. Div'l Ct.
Probate Division, English Law Reports
Prob. Div.
Probate Law Journal (National College of Probate Judges and Boston University School of Law)
Prob. L.J.
Probate Lawyer
Prob. Law.
Probate Practice Act
Prob. Pr. Act.
Probate Practice Reporter
PPR
Probate Reports
P.R., Prob. R., Prob. Rep.
Probate Reports Annotated
Prob. Rep. Ann.
Probation
Prob., Probation
Probation and Parole Law Reports
Probation & Parole L. Rep.

Probation and Parole Law Summaries
Probation & Parole L. Summ.
Probation Journal
Prob. J.
Problems
Prob., Probs.
Problems of Accountancy
P. of Accountancy
Problems of Communism
Probs. Communism
Probyn on Land Tenure
Prob. L.T.
Procedendo (order to proceed) (Lat.)
Proced.
Procedure[s]
Proc.
Procedure Civile
P.C.
Proceedings
Proc.
Proceedings, American Society of International Law
Proc. Amer. Soc. of Internat. L., ASIL Proc.
Proceedings of Cambridge Philological Society
Proceed. of the Cambridge Philol. Soc.
Proceedings of Conference, Indian Society of International Law
Proc. Indian Soc. of Internat. L.
Proceedings of the Fordham Corporate Law Institute
Fordham Corp. Inst.
Proceedings of the Uniform Law Conference of Canada
Unif. L. Conf.

Processing Tax Board of Review Decisions, United States Internal Revenue Bureau
P.T.B.R.
Processing Tax Division, United States Internal Revenue Bureau
P.T.
Proclamation
Proc.
Proctor's Bench and Bar of New York
Proc. B. & B.
Proctor's Practice
Proc. Pr., Proc. Prac.
Procurement Division, Judge Advocate General, United States Army
JAGT.
Produce
Produc.
Product
Prod.
Product Liability International
Prod. Liab. Int., Prod. Liab. Int'l
Product Safety and Liability Reporter, Bureau of National Affairs
Prod. Safety & Liab. Rep. (BNA)
Production
Prod., Produc.
Production and Marketing Administration
PMA
Products Liability
Prod. Liab.
Products Liability Reporter, Commerce Clearing House
Prod. Liab. Rep. (CCH), Prod. Liab. Rep. (CCH)

Proeme (Introduction) to (A Designated Part or Volume of Coke's Institutes)
Inst. Proem.
Profession[al]
Prof.
Professional Administration
Prof Admin
Professional Administrator
Prof Admin
Professional Administrator (Official Journal of the Australian Division of the Institute of Chartered Secretaries and Administrators)
PA
Professional Association
P.A.
Professional Corporation
P.C.
Professional Corporation Guide, Prentice-Hall
Prof. Corp. Guide (P-H)
Professional Development Program, State Bar of Texas
SBT
Professional Legal Corporation
P.L.C.
Professional Liability Reporter
P.L.R.
Professions (free quarterly insert with Business Review Weekly)
(The) Professions
Proffatt on Notaries
Prof. Not.
Proffatt on Private Corporations in California
Prof. Corp.
Proffatt on Trial by Jury
Prof. Jur.
Proffatt on Wills
Prof. Wills

Profit-Sharing Trustee
PST
Program of Advanced Professional Development, University of Denver College of Law
PADUD
Prohibition
Prohib.
Prolonged
Prolong
Promissory
Prom.
Property
Prop.
Property and Compensation Reports
P.& C.R., Prop. & Comp., Prop. & Comp. R.
Property Law Bulletin
Prop. Law Bull.
Property Lawyer
Prop. Law.
Property Lawyer, New Series
Prop. Law.N.S.
Property Management and Disposal Service
PMDS
Property Press
PROPRE
Prosecuting Attorney
Pros. Atty.
Prosecutor, Journal of the National District Attorneys Association
Pros. J. Nat'l Dist. Att'y. A.
Prospectively
Prosp.
Prostitution
Prostit.
Protocol
Prot.

Protocol on Privileges and Immunities
Prot. P.I.
Protocol on Privileges and Immunities of the European Economic Community
E.E.C. Prot. P.I.
Protocol on the Statute of the European Communities Court of Justice
Prot. C.J.
Proudfit's United States Land Decisions
Proudf. Land Dec.
Proudhon's Domaine Public
Proud. Dom. Pub.
Prouty's Reports (61-68 Vermont)
Prouty
Province
Prov.
Province Laws
Pro. L.
Province of Ontario
P.O.
Province of Quebec
P.Q.
Provincial Inheritance and Gift Tax Reporter, Commerce Clearing House
Prov. Inher. & Gift Tax Rep. (CCH)
Provincial Judges Journal
P.J.J.
Provisional International Civil Aviation Organization
P.I.C.A.O.
Provisions
Provns.
Psychiatry
Psych.
Psycholog[y, ical]
Psychol., Psych.

Psychological and Medico-Legal Journal
Psych. & M.L.J.
Public
Pub.
Public Acts
Pub. Acts
Public Acts of New South Wales
N.S.W. Pub. Acts, Pub. Acts N.S.W.
Public Acts of Queensland
Queensl. Pub. Acts, Pub. Acts Queensl.
Public Acts of the State of Tennessee
Tenn. Pub. Acts
Public Administration
Pub. Admin.
Public Administration and Development
Publ. Adm. & Dev.
Public Administration in Israel and Abroad
Pub. Admin. in Israel & Abroad
Public Administration Review
P.A.R., Pub. Ad. Rev., Pub. Adm. Rev., Pub. Admin. Rev.
Public and Local Acts of the Legislature of the State of Michigan
Mich. Pub. Acts
Public and Local Laws
Pub. & Loc. Laws
Public Authorities
Pub. Auth.
Public Bargaining Cases, Commerce Clearing House
Pub. Bargaining Cas.(CCH)
Public Buildings
Pub. Bldgs.
Public Buildings Service
P.B.S.

Public Contract Law Journal
Pub. Cont. L.J., Pub. Contract L.J.
Public Contract Newsletter
Pub. Cont. Newsl.
Public Documents
Pub. Doc.
Public Employee Bargaining Reports, Commerce Clearing House
Pub. Employee Bargaining (CCH), Pub. Employee Bargaining Rep. (CCH)
Public Employee Relations Reports
Pub. Employee Rel. Rep.
Public Employment Program
P.E.P.
Public Employment Relations Board
P.E.R.B.
Public Finance/Finances Publiques
Publ. Finance
Public Finance Quarterly
Publ. Finance Q
Public Funds
Pub. F.
Public General Acts of South Australia
Pub. Gen. Acts S. Austl., S. Austl. Pub. Gen. Acts
Public General Laws
Pub. Gen. Laws.
Public Health Service
PHS
Public Housing
Pub. Hous.
Public Housing Administration
PHA
Public Information Bulletin
PIB

Public Interest
Publ. Interest, Pub. Interest
Public International Law
Pub. Int'l L.
Public Land and Resources Law Digest
Pub. Land & Res. L. Dig.
Public Land Law Review
Pub. Land L. Rev.
Public Land Order
P.L.O.
Public Lands
Pub. Lands
Public Law[s]
P.L., Pub. L., Pub. Laws
Public Law Boards
P.L. Boards
Public Law Forum
Pub. L.F.
Public Laws of Rhode Island
R.I. Pub. Laws
Public Local Laws
Pub. Loc. Laws
Public Management
Pub. Manag.
Public Officer[s]
P.O., Pub. Off.
Public Papers of the President
Pub. Papers
Public Personnel Review
Publ. Pers. Rev.
Public Record Office
P.R.O.
Public Relations Bulletin
Pub. Rel. Bull.
Public Resources
Pub. Res.
Public Safety
Pub. Safety
Public Securities and Obligations
Pub. Sec.
Public Service
Pub. Serv.

Public Service Commission
P.S.C., Pub. Ser. Comm.
Public Service Commission Reports
P.S.C.R.
Public Service Commission Reports, Montana
Mo. P.S.C.
Public Service Commission Reports, New Series, Montana
Mo. P.S.C. (N.S.)
Public Service Stops Relations Board
P.S.S.R.B.
Public Statutes
P.S., Pub. St.
Public Studies
Publ. Stud.
Public Trustee
P.T.
Public Trustee Office
PTO
Public Utilities
Pub. Util.
Public Utilities Code
Pub. Util. C.
Public Utilities Commission
Pub. Util. Comm., P.U.C.
Public Utilities Fortnightly
P.U. Fort., Pub. Util. Fort.
Public Utilities Law Anthology
Pub. Util. L. Anthol.
Public Utilities Reports
Pub. Util. Rep., P.U.R., Pub. U. Rep.
Public Utilities Reports, New Series
P.U.R. (N.S.)
Public Utilities Reports, Third Series
P.U.R.3d
Public Welfare
P.W.

Public Works
P.W.
Public Works Administration
PWA
Public Works and Contracts
Pub. Wks.
Publication
Pub., Pub., Publ.
Publications of the Pipe Roll Society
Pipe Roll Soc'y
Publications of the Pipe Roll Society, New Series
Pipe Roll Soc'y (N.S.)
Publications Reference File
PRF
Publish
Pub.
Published
Pub.
Published Internal Revenue Mimeograph
I.R.-M.I.M.
Publisher
Pub.
Publishers' Association
PA
Publishing
Pub.
Publishing, Entertainment, Advertising and Allied Fields Law Quarterly
P.E.A.L.Q., Pub. Ent. Advert. & Allied Fields L.Q., PEAL, Pub. Ent. Adv. L.Q.
Puerto Rico
P.R.
Puerto Rico Decisiones (Spanish)
P.R.D.
Puerto Rico Federal Reports
P.R. Fed., P.R.F., P.R.H., Puerto Rico F., Puerto Rico Fed.

Puerto Rico Industrial Commission Decisions
P.R.I.C. Dec.
Puerto Rico Laws
P.R. Laws
Puerto Rico Laws Annotated
L.P.R.A., P.R. Laws Ann.
Puerto Rico Reports
P.R.R., Puerto Rico
Puerto Rico Reports, Spanish Edition
S.P.R.
Puerto Rico Supreme Court Reports
P.R., P.R.R., P.R.S.C.R., Puerto Rico Rep.
Puerto Rico Tax Court Decisions
P.R.T.C.D.
Puffendorf's Law of Nature and Nations
Puf., Puffendorf.
Pugsley and Burbidge's New Brunswick Reports (17-20 New Brunswick)
Pugs. & Bur., Pugs. & Burb., N.B.R.P. & B., P. & B.
Pugsley and Trueman 's New Brunswick Reports
Pugs. & T., P. & T., N.B.R.P. & T., Pugs. & Tru.
Pugsley's New Brunswick Reports (14-16 New Brunswick)
N. B. R. Pug., N.B.R. Pugs., Pug(s).
Pulling's Attorneys and Solicitors
Pull. Att.
Pulling's Law of Mercantile Accounts
Pull. Accts., Pull. Acc.

**Pulling's Treatise on the Laws,
Customs, and Regulations of
the City and Port of London**
Pull. Laws & Cust. Lond., Pull.
Port of London
Pulsifer's Reports (35-68 Maine)
Pulsifer (Me.)
Pulton de Pace Regis
Pult.
**Pulton's Abridgment of the Stat-
utes**
P. Abr.
Pump Court
Pump Ct.
Punjab Code, India
Punj. C.
Punjab High Court Cases, India
P.H.C.C.
Punjab Law Reporter, India
P.L.J., P.L.R.
**Punjab Law Reporter, Jammu
and Kashmir Section, India**
P.L.R.J. & K.
Punjab Law Times, India
P.L.T.
Punjab Record, India
P.R., Punj. Rec.
Punjab, India
Punj. Ind.
Punjab, Pakistan
Punj. Pak.

Purchase
Pur.
Purchase Money
P.M.
Purchase Tax
P.T.
**Purdon's Digest of Pennsylvania
Laws**
Purd. Dig. Laws., Purd. Dig.
Purdon's Digest of Pennsylva-
nia Laws, Brightly's Edition
Bright.Pur.Dig., Bright. Purd.
Purdon's Pennsylvania Statutes
P.S.
**Purple's Statutes, Scates' Compi-
lation**
Purple's St.
**Purvis' Collection of the Laws of
Virginia**
Purv. Coll.
**Puterbaugh's Illinois Chancery
Pleading**
Puter Ch.
**Puterbaugh's Illlinois Common
Law Pleading**
Puter.Pl.
**Putnam's Proceedings before the
Justices of the Peace**
Putnam.
**Pyke's Lower Canada Reports,
King's Bench**
Pyke, Py. R., Pyke, P.R., Pyke

Q

Quadragesms (Year Books, Part IV)
Quadr.
Quail on Real Property Practice and Litigation
RPL, RPPL
Qualified Products List
QPL
Qualified Terminable Interest Property
QTIP
Quare Executionem Non (wherefore execution should not be issued) (Lat.)
Q.E.N.
Quarles' Tennessee Criminal Digest
Quar. Crim. Dig.
Quarter Sessions
Q.S.
Quarterly
Q.
Quarterly Journal
Q. J.
Quarterly Journal of Inter-American Relations
Qu. Jour. Int-Amer. Rel.
Quarterly Law Journal
Qu. L.J., Quart. L.J., Quar. Law Journal
Quarterly Law Review
Q.L. Rev., Qu. L. Rev., Quart. L. Rev., Quar. L. Rev.
Quarterly Newsletter, American Bar Association
Q.N., Quart. Newsl.

Quarterly Newsletter-Special Committee on Environmental Law
Q. Newl.-Spec. Comm. Env.L.
Quarterly of the Japan Commercial Arbitration Association
Q. Japan Com'l. Arb. Ass'n.
Quarterly Review of Jurisprudence
Q. Rev. Juris.
Quebec
Q., Que.
Quebec Civil Code Revision Office
Quebec C.C.R.O.
Quebec King's Bench Reports
Q.R.K.B.
Quebec Law
Q.L., Que. L.
Quebec Law Reports
Q.L.R., Quebec L. (Can.), Que. L.R.
Quebec Official Reports
Q.O.R., Q.R.
Quebec Official Reports, King's Bench
Que. K.B., Queb. K.B.
Quebec Official Reports, Queen's Bench
Que. Q.B.
Quebec Official Reports, Superior Court
Que. S.C., Que. Super., S.C.
Quebec Practice
Que. Pr., Quebec Pr. (Can.)
Quebec Practice Reports
Q.P.R., Que. P.R., Que. Prac., Queb. Pr.

Quebec, Province of
P.Q.
Quebec Reports, Queen's Bench
Q.R.Q.B., L.R.Q.B
Quebec Reports, Superior Court
Q.R.S.C., S.
Quebec Reports, Supreme Court
C.S.
Quebec Revised Judicial Acts
Que. Rev. Jud.
Quebec Revised Statutes
Que. Rev. Stat.
Quebec Society of Criminology Bulletin
Bull. Que. Soc. Crim.
Quebec Statutes
Que. Stat.
Quebec Tax Reporter, Commerce Clearing House
Que. Tax Rep. (CCH)
Queen Elizabeth
El., E.R., Eliz.
Queen Elizabeth II
E.R. II
Queen Mary
M.
Queen Victoria
Vic.
Queens Bar Bulletin
Queens B. Bull.
Queen's Bench
Q.B., Q.B. (Eng.)
Queen's Bench Division, English Law Reports
Q.B. Div.
Queen's Bench Divisional Court, England
Q.B. Div'l Ct.
Queen's Bench Reports, England
Q.B., Q.B.R.
Queen's Bench Reports, Lower Canada
Q.B.L.C.

Queen's Bench Reports, Quebec
Q.B.
Queen's Bench Reports, Upper Canada
Q.B., Q.B.U.C.
Queen's Counsel
Q.C.
Queens County Bar Association Bulletin
Queens C.B.A. Bull.
Queen's Intramural Law Journal
Queen's Intramural L.J.,
Queens Intra. L.J.
Queen's Law Journal
Q.L.J., Queen's L.J.
Queensland
Q., Qld., Queensl.
Queensland Acts
Queensl. Acts
Queensland Criminal Reports
Q.C.R.
Queensland Justice of the Peace
Queensl. J.P. (Austr.)
Queensland Justice of the Peace and Local Authorities' Journal
Queens J.P. & Loc. Auth. Jo.
Queensland Justice of the Peace, Magisterial Cases
Q.J.P. Mag. Cus.
Queensland Justice of the Peace Reports
Q.J.P.R., Queensl. J.P. Rep.,
Queensl. J.P.R., Q.J.P.
Queensland Land Court Reports
Q.L.C.R., Queensl. Land Ct. R.
Queensland Law
Queensl. L.
Queensland Law Journal
Queensl. L.J. (Austr.), Q.L.J.
Queensland Law Journal and Reports
Queensl. L.J. & R.

Queensland Law Journal and State Reports
Queensl. L.J. & St. R.

Queensland Law Journal (Notes of Cases)
Q.L.J. (N.C.)

Queensland Law Reform Commission
Q.L.R.C.

Queensland Law Reporter and Weekly Notes
Queensl. W.N.

Queensland Law Reports
Q.L.R., Beor., Queensl. L.R., Queens. L.R.

Queensland Law Reports by Beor
Q.L.R. (Beor).

Queensland Law Society
Queensl. L.S.J.

Queensland Law Society Journal
Q.Law Soc. J., Queens. L. Soc'y J., Queensl. L. Soc'y J., Queensland L. Soc'y J.

Queensland Lawyer
Queensl. Law, Q.L.

Queensland Reports
Queensl. R., Queensl., Qd. R.

Queensland State Reports
Queens. St. R., S.Q.R., S.R.Q., S.R. Queen. C., Queensl. St. (Austr.), Queensl. St. Rep., S.Q.T., St. Rep. Queensl. (Austr.), Queensl. St. R., Q.S.R., St. R. Q., St. R. Qd.

Queensland Statutes
Queensl. Stat.

Queensland Supreme Court Reports
Queensl. S.C., Queensl. S.C.R., Q.S.C.R., Queensl. S.Ct. R., S.C.R. (Q)

Queensland University Law Journal
Q.U.L.R.

Queensland University of Technology Law Journal
Queensl. U. Tech. L.J.

Queensland Weekly Notes
Queensl. W.N. (Austr.), Q.W.N.

Queensland Worker's Compensation Report
W.C.R. (Qn.)

Questioned; Soundness of Decision or Reasoning in Cited Case Questioned (used in Shepard's Citations)
Q., q.

Qui Tam (Lat.)
Q.t.

Quieting Title and Determination of Adverse Claims
Quiet T.

Quin on Banking
Quin Bank.

Quincy's Massachusetts Reports
Quin., Quincy, Quincy (Mass.)

Quis Custodiet (Lat.)
Quis Cust.

Quo Warranto
Q. War., Quo War.

Quod Vide (to which, refer) (Lat.)
Q.V.

Quoniam Attachiamenta (Lat.)
Q. Att., Quo. Attach.

Quorum
Q.

Quotation
Quot.

Quoted in
Quot.

Quoting
Quot.

R

Rabin's Medical Malpractice: Handling Ophthalmology Cases
MMO

Rabkin and Johnson's Federal, Income, Gift and Estate Taxation
R.& J.

Race Relations Law Reporter
Race Rel. L. Rep.

Race Relations Law Survey
Rac. Rel. L. Survey

Racketeering Influenced and Corrupt Organizations
RICO

Rader's Reports (138-163 Missouri)
Rader

Radical Alternatives to Prison
RAP

Radio Free Europe
RFE

Radio Liberty
RL

Radio Regulations, Pike and Fisher
Rad. Reg. (P & F)

Radio Regulations, Second Series, Pike and Fischer
Rad. Reg. 2d (P & F)

Raff's Pension Manual
Raff Pens. Man.

Rafique and Jackson's Privy Council Decisions
R.& J.

Ragland's California Superior Court Decisions
Rag., Rag. Super. Ct. Dec. (Calif.)

Railroad
R., R.R.

Railroad and Public Service Commission of Montana
Mont. R. & P.S. Co.

Railroad Commission for the State of Florida
Fla. R.C.

Railroad Labor Board Decisions
R.L.B. Dec.

Railroad Reports
R.R.Rep., R.R.R.

Railroad Retirement Board
R.R.B.

Railway
R., Rwy, Ry.

Railway and Canal Cases, England
Ry. & Can. Traffic Cas., R. & C.C., Rail. Ca., Ry. & Can. Cas., R.R. & Cn. Cas., N.H. & C., R. & C. Cas., R. & Can. Cas., R. & C.Ca., R.R. & Can. Cas.

Railway and Canal Traffic Cases, England
R. & Can. Tr. Cas., Rail. & Can. Cas., Ry. & Can. Traf. Ca., Rye & C. Traffic Cas. (Eng.), R. & C. Tr. Cas., R. & Can. Tr.

Railway and Corporation Law Journal
Railway & Corp. Law J., Ralw. & Corp. L.J., Ry. & Corp. Law J., Ry. & Corp. Law. Jour., Ry. Corp. Law Jour.

Railway, Canal and Road Traffic Cases, England
Traff. Cas.

Railway Cases, England
Rail (or Railw.) Cas., Railw.
Cas., Railway Cas., R.C.

Railway Commission of Canada
Can. R.C.

Railway Labor Act
RLA

Raithby's Statutes at Large
Raith. St.

Raithby's Study of the Law
Raith. St.

Rajaratam's Revised Reports, Ceylon
Raj.

Rajasthan, India
Raj. Ind.

Rajasthan Law Weekly, India
R.L.W.

Ram on Assetts, Debts and Incumbrances
Ram Ass.

Ram on Facts
Ram F.

Ram on Exposition of Wills of Landed Property
Ram. W.

Ram on Science of Legal Judgment
Ram Leg. J.

Ramachandrier's Cases on Adoption, India
Ramachandrier A.

Ramachandrier's Cases on Dancing Girls, India
Ramachandrier D.G.

Ramachandrier's Cases on Hindu Marriage Law
Ramachandrier H.M.L.

Ramanathan's Reports, Supreme Court, Ceylon
Ram. S.C.

Ramos on California Land Use Procedure
CLUP

Ram's Cases of Pleading and Evidence
Ram Cas. P. & E.

Ram's Science of Legal Judgment, Notes by Townshend
Ram Leg. Judgm. (Towns.Ed)

Ramsay's Appeal Cases, Canada
Ramsay App. Cas. (Can.), Ramsay, App. Cas., R.A.C.

Ramsey and Morin's Montreal Law Reporter
Ram. & Mor.

Ramsey's Quebec Appeal Cases
Rams. App., Ram.

Rand and Furness on Poisons
Rand & Fur. Poi.

RAND Journal of Economics
RAND J. Econ.

Randall on Perpetuities
Rand. Perp.

Randall's Edition of Peake on Evidence
Rand. Peak.

Randall's Reports (62-71 Ohio)
Rand.

Randolph and Barrandall's Virginia Colonial Decisions
Va. Col. Dec.

Randolph on Commercial Paper
Rand. Com. Paper

Randolph on Eminent Domain
Rand. Em. Dom.

Randolph's Annual, Louisiana
Rand. Ann.

Randolph's Reports (21-56 Kansas)
Rand.

Randolph's Reports (7-11 Louisiana)
Rand.

Randolph's Reports (22-27 Virginia)
Rand.
Raney's Reports (16-20 Florida)
Raney
Range
R.
Rangoon Criminal Law Journal
Rang. Cr. L.J.
Rangoon Law Reports
Rang. L.R.
Rankin on Patents
Rank. P.
Ranking and Spicer on Company Law
Rank. & S. Comp. L.
Ranking, Spicer and Pegier on Executorship
Rank. S. & P. Exec.
Rao's Decisions on Hindu Law
Rao D.H.L.
Rapalje and Lawrence's American and English Cases
Rap. & Law., Rap. & L., Rapal. & L.
Rapalje and Lawrence's Law Dictionary
Rapalje & L., Rap. & L. Law. Dict.
Rapalje and Mack's Digest of Railway Law
R.M. Dig.
Rapalje on Contempt
Rap.Contempt
Rapalje on Larceny
Rap. Lar.
Rapalje's Federal Reference Digest
Rap. Fed. Ref. Dig.
Rapalje's New York Digest
Rap. N.Y. Dig.
Rapalje's Treatise on Witnesses
Rap.Wit.

Rapid Transit
Rapid Trans.
Rapp on the Bounty Laws
Rapp Bount.
Rastell's Abridgment of the Statutes
Rast. Abr.
Rastell's Entries and Statutes
Ent., Rast. Ent., Entries, Antient., Entries, New Book of, Rast.
Rastell's Old Entries
Old Ent.
Ratanlal's Unreported Criminal Cases, India
Rat. Unrep. Cr.
Ratcliffe and M'Grath's Income Tax Decisions of Australia
R. & McG.
Rating and Income Tax Reports
R. & I.T.
Rating and Valuation Reports
R. & V. R.
Rating Appeals
R.A.
Ratio Juris
Ratio Juris
Rattigan's Leading Cases on Hindu Law
Ratt. L.C.
Rattigan's Roman Law of Persons
Ratt. R.L.
Rattigan's Select Law Cases in Hindu Law
Rat. Sel. Cas., Rattigan
Rawle on Covenants for Title
Raw. Cov., Rawle Cov.
Rawle on Equity in Pennsylvania
Raw. Eq.
Rawle on the Constitution of the United States
Rawle Const. U.S., Raw. Const.

**Rawle, Penrose and Watts' Penn-
sylvania Reports**
  R.P.W., Rawle Pen. & W., R.P.
  & W.
**Rawle's Pennsylvania Supreme
Court Reports**
  Rawle, R., Raw.
**Rawlinson on Municipal Corpora-
tions**
  Rawl. Mun. Corp.
**Ray' Medical Jurisprudence of In-
sanity**
  Ray, Med. Jur.
Rayburn House Office Building
  RHOB
Rayden on Divorce
  Rayden
Raymond (Lord) Entries
  Raym. Ent., Ra. Ent.
Raymond on Bills of Exceptions
  Ray. B. Ex., Raym. B. Ex.
**Raymond's Digested Chancery
Cases**
  Raym. Ch. Dig.
Raymond's Reports (81-89 Iowa)
  Raymond
**Raymond's (Sir T.) English King's
Bench Reports**
  Raym., Raym. Ld., Ld. Raym.,
  Ld. Ray., Sir T. Ray.
Rayner on the Law of Libels
  Rayn. Lib.
Rayner's English Tithe Cases
  Rayn., Rayn. Ti. Cas., Ray. Ti.
  Cas.
**Ray's Medical Jurisprudence of
Insanity**
  Ray Ins. (or Med.Jur.)
Ray's Mental Pathology
  Ray Men. Path.

**Reading of Robert Callis on the
Statute of Sewers, 23 Hen. 8. c.
5., Delivered by Him at Gray's
Inn, August 1622**
  Callis
Reading on Statute Law
  R.S.L.
**Read's Declarations and Plead-
ings**
  Read Dec. (or Pl.)
Reaffirmed
  Reaf.
Real
  Real
Real Estate Brokers' Board
  R.E.B.
Real Estate Commission
  Real Est. Comm'n.
Real Estate Investment Trust
  REIT
Real Estate Law Journal
  Real Est. L.J., Real Estate L.J.
Real Estate Law Report
  Real Est. L. Rep.
**Real Estate Mortgage Investment
Conduit**
  REMIC
Real Estate Record
  Real Est. Rec.
Real Estate Review
  Real Est. Rev.
Real Estate Securities Journal
  Real Est. Sec. J.
**Real Estate Settlement Proce-
dures Act**
  RESPA
Real Estate Time Sharing
  Real Estate Time Shar.
Real Property
  Real Prop.
**Real Property Actions and Pro-
ceedings**
  Real Prop. Acts

Real Property Cases
Real Prop.Cas., R.P.C., Real Pr.
Cas.

**Real Property Commissioner's
Report**
R.P.C., R.P.C. Rep.

**Real Property, Probate and Trust
Journal**
Real Prop.Prob. & Tr. J., Real
Prop.Prob. & Trust J.

Real Property Reports
Real Prop. Rep., R.P.R.

Real Property Tax
Real Prop. Tax

Realtor
Rlt.

Realty
Rlty.

Reappraisement Decisions
R.D.

Receipt
Rec.

Received
Recd.

Receivers
Receiv.

**Receiving and Transporting Sto-
len Property**
Rec. St. P.

Recent Law
Rec. L.

Recent Laws in Canada
Rec. Laws

Reconsideration
Recons.

**Reconstruction Finance Corpora-
tion**
RFC

Record[s]
R., Rec.

Record Commission
Rec. Com., Rec. Comm.

Record Commissioners
R.C.

**Record of the Association of the
Bar of the City of New York**
Rec. A. B. City N. Y., Rec. Ass'n.
Bar City of N.Y., Record of
N.Y.C.B.A., Record

Recorder
Rec.

**Records of the Court of Justici-
ary, Scotland**
Adjournal, Books of

Red Book of the Exchequer
Lib. Rub. Seace.

Reddie on Science of Law
Red. Sc. L.

**Reddie's Inquiries in Interna-
tional Law**
Red. Int. L.

**Reddie's Law of Maritime Com-
merce**
Red. Mar. Com.

**Reddie's Researches in Maritime
International Law**
Red. Mar. Int. L.

Reddie's Roman Law
Red. R. L.

Redemption
Redem.

**Redesdale's Treatise upon Equity
Pleading**
Redes. Pl.

**Redfield and Bigelow's Leading
Cases on Bills and Notes**
R. & B. Cas., Red. & Big. Cas.
B. & N., Redf. & B.

**Redfield on Carriers and Bail-
ments**
Red. Bail., Red. Car., Redf. Carr.

Redfield on the Law of Railroads
Redf. Railways, Red. R.R.

Redfield on the Law of Wills
Red. Wilis

Redfield's Leading American Cases on Wills
Red. Cas. Wills, Redf. Wills

Redfield's Leading American Railway Cases
Red. Am. R.R. Cas., Red. Cas. R.R., Red. R.R. Cas., Red. Am. R. Cas., Redf. Am. Railw. Cas.

Redfield's New York Practice
Red. Pr.

Redfield's New York Surrogate Court Report
Redf. Surr. (N.Y.), Redf. Sur. (N.Y.), Redf., Redf. (N.Y.), Redf. Surr., Red.

Redfield's Railway Cases, England
Redf. R. Cas.

Redington's Reports (31-35 Maine)
Red., Redington

Redman and Lyon on Landlord and Tenant
R. & L.L. & T.

Redman on Arbitration
Redm. Arb.

Redman on Landlord and Tenant
Redman

Reduction in Force
RIF

Redwar's Comments on Ordinances of the Gold Coast
Redwar, Red.

Reed on Bills of Sale
Reed, Reed B.S.

Reed on Railways as Carriers
Reed Car.

Reed's American Law Studies
Reed Am. L.S.

Reed's Leading Cases on Statute of Frauds
Reed Fraud.

Reed's Pennsylvania Blackstone
Reed Pa. Black

Reed's Practical Suggestions for the Management of Lawsuits
Reed Pr. Sug.

Reeve on Descents
Reeve Des.

Reeve on Domestic Relations
Reeve Dom. Rel.

Reeve's English Law
Reeve Eng. L.

Reeves' History of the English Law
Reeves H.E.L., Reeve, Eng. Law, Reeve, Hist. Eng. Law, Reeves Hist. Eng. Law

Reeves on the Law of Shipping
Reeve Sh.

Refer to
cf.

Referee[s]
Ref.

Referee Tribunal
Ref. Trib.

Referee's Decision
Ref. Dec.

Referees' Journal (Journal of National Association of Referees in Bankruptcy)
Ref. J.

Reference
Ref.

Referred
Ref.

Refining
Ref.

Reform
Ref.

Reformation of Instruments
Reform. Inst.

Refunding
Ref.

Refusal To Extend Decision of Cited Case Beyond Precise Issues Involved (used in Shepard's Citations)
    L.

Refused, Not Reversible Error
    Ref.n.r.e.

Refused, Want of Merit
    Ref. w.m.

Regent University Law Review
    Regent U. L. Rev., Regent Univ. L. Rev.

Regina (queen) (Lat.)
    Reg.

Regio Decreto (royal decree) (Lat.)
    R.D.

Register
    Reg.

Register Book[s]
    Reg. Lib., Lib. Reg.

Register of Debates in Congress, Gales
    Reg. Deb. (Gales)

Register of Judicial Writs (Registrum Judiciales)
    Reg.Jud.

Register of Writs
    Reg. Brev., Reg.Writ.

Registered
    Reg., Regd.

Registered Designs Appeal Tribunal
    R.D.A.T.

Registered in Name of
    N/O

Registered Trademark
    Reg. T.M.

Registrar
    Reg.

Registrar's Book, Chancery
    Reg. Lib.

Registrar's Book, Keith's Court of Chancery, Pennsylvania
    Keith Ch. Pa.

Registration
    Reg.

Registration Appeals
    R.A., Reg. App.

Registration Board of Architects and Professional Engineers
    A/E

Registration Cases
    R.C., Reg. Cas., Reg.

Registration of Land Titles
    Regis. L. T.

Registrum Judiciales (Register of Judicial Writs)
    Reg. Jud.

Registrum Omnium Brevium
    Reg. Om. Brev.

Registrum Originale
    Reg. Orig.

Registry
    Reg.

Regna (queen) (Lat.)
    R.

Regula Generalis (general rule or order of court)
    R.G.

Regula Placitandi
    Reg. Pl., Plac., Reg. Plac.

Regulae Generales
    Reg. Gen.

Regulated Investment Company
    RIC

Regulation[s]
    Reg., Regs.

Regulation Appeals
    R.A.

Regulations of Connecticut State Agencies
    Conn. Agencies Reg.

Regulatory
    Reg.

Regulatory Information System
RIS
Rehabilitation Services Administration
R.S.A.
Rehearing
Reh'g.
Rehearing Allowed (used in Shepard's Citations)
Reh. allowed
Rehearing Denied (used in Shepard's Citations)
Reh. den.
Rehearing Denied by U.S. Supreme Court
U.S.reh.den.
Rehearing Dismissed (used in Shepard's Citations)
Reh. dis.
Rehearing Dismissed by U.S. Supreme Court
U.S.reh.dis.
Reid's Digest of Scotch Poor Law Cases
Reid P.L. Dig.
Reilly's English Arbitration Cases
Reilly
Reilly's European Arbitration, Lord Westbury's Decisions
Reilly, E.A.
Rein's Thermographic Evidence of Soft Tissue Injuries
TE
Reinstated; Regulation or Order Reinstated (used in Shepard's Citations)
Rein.
Relations
Rel.
Religion and the Public Order
Rel. & Pub. Order
Religious Corporations
Relig. Corp.

Religious Societies
Relig. Soc.
Remainder
Rmdr.
Remand[ed, ing]
Remd., Rem'd, Rem'g.
Remarkable Criminal Trials
Rem. Cr. Tr.
Remington and Ballinger's Code, Washington
R. & B.
Remington and Ballinger's Code, Supplement, Washington
R. & B. Supp.
Remington on Bankruptcy
Remington, Bankruptcy
Remington's Code, Washington
R.C.
Remington's Compiled Statutes, Washington
R.C.S.
Remington's Compiled Statutes, Supplement, Washington
R.C.S. Supp.
Remington's Revised Statutes
R.R.S.
Remit[tance, ted]
Rem., Remitt.
Remys' Reports (145-162 Indiana and 15-33 Indiana Appellate)
Remy
Renaissance Studies
Renaissance Stud.
Renegotiation Board
RB
Renegotiation Board Regulations
R.B.R.
Renegotiation Bulletins
R.B.
Renegotiations Rulings
R. Rul.
Renner's Gold Coast Reports
R.G.C.R., Ren.

Renner's Reports, Notes of Cases Gold Coast Colony and Colony of Nigeria
Renn.
Rent Law Reports
Rt. Law Rep.
Rent Procedural Regulation, Office of Price Stabilization, Economic Stabilization Agency
RPR
Rent Regulation, Office of Price Stabilization, Economic Stabilization Agency
R.P., R.R.
Renumbered; Existing Article Renumbered (used in Shepard's Citations)
Rn.
Reorganization Plans
Reorg. Plan No. of year
Reorganization[s]
Reorg.
Repeal[ed, ing]
r., Rep., R., Rep.
Repertoire
Rep.
Repertorium Juridicum
Rep. Jur.
Replacement
Repl.
Replevin
Replev.
Report[s]
R., Rep.
Report by the Scottish Land Court
Sc. La. Rep.
Report of Bellingham's Trial
Bellingh. Tr.
Report of Commercial Cases
Rep. Com. Cas.

Report of Methodist Church Cases
Meth. Ch. Ca.
Report of Mining Cases Decided by the Railway and Canal Commission
Bamber.
Report of the "Alexandra" Case by Dudley
Alex. Cas.
Report of the Chesapeake Case, New Brunswick
Ches. Ca.
Report of the Girard Will Case
Gir. W.C.
Report of the Tichborne Trial
Tichb. Tr.
Reports of the Attorney General of the State of Nebraska
Rep. Neb. Att'y Gen.
Reports of the Attorney General, State of Massachusetts
Rep. Mass. Att'y Gen.
Reporter
Rep.
Reporter (Boston, Los Angeles, New York or Washington)
Reptr.
Reporter on Human Reproduction and the Law
Human Reprod. & L. Rep. (Legal Medical Studies)
Reporter, Phi Alpha Delta
The Rep.
Reporter (New York or Washington)
Rep.
Report[s]
R., Rep.
Reports, Mews, England
Mews

Reports of Bankruptcy and Companies Winding up Cases, England
 B. & C. R.

Reports of Cases Decided in the Supreme Court of South Africa, Griqualand West Local Division, by Kitchin
 G.W.L.

Reports of Cases in the Supreme Court of Natal
 Phipson.

Reports of Cases on Income Tax
 Inc. Tax Cas.

Reports of Cases Relating to Income Tax
 Rep. Cas. Inc. Tax

Reports of Cases - Supreme Court of Victoria
 S. Ct. Vict., Vict. S. Ct.

Reports of Certain Judgments of the Supreme Court, Vice-Admiralty Court and Full Court of Appeal, Lagos
 R.C.J.

Reports of Criminal Law Commissioners
 Rep. Cr. L. Com.

Reports of Family Law
 Rep. Fam. L., R.F.L.

Reports of Family Law, Second Series
 R.F.L. (2d)

Reports of Inland Revenue Commissioners
 I.R. Rep.

Reports of International Arbitral Awards
 Int'l Arb. Awards

Reports of Irish Cases, by Sir John Davis
 Dav.

Reports of Irish Circuit Cases
 Ir. Cir. Rep.

Reports of Municipal Corporations
 Rep. M.C.

Reports of Patent Cases, England
 R.P.C., R.P.D. & T.M. Cas., R. Pat. Cas., Pat. Cas., Rep. Pat. Des & Tr. Cas., Rep. Pat. Cas.

Reports of Patent, Design and Trade Mark Cases, England
 R.P.C., R.P.D. & T.M. Cas., R. Pat. Cas., Pat. Cas., Rep. Pat. Des & Tr. Cas., Rep. Pat. Cas.

Reports of Restrictive Practices Cases
 Restric. Prac.

Reports of Tax Cases
 T.C.

Reports of the High Court of Griqualand
 Laur., G., H.C.

Reports of the High Court of South-West Africa
 S.A. Law Reports, S.W.A., S.W.A.

Reports of the High Court of the Orange River Colony
 O.R.C.

Reports of the International Law Association
 Int'l. L. Ass'n.

Reports of the Subversive Activities Control Board
 SACB

Reports of the United States District Court of Hawaii
 D. C. H.

Reports of the Witwatersrand High Court, Transvaal Colony
 T.H., T.L.

Represent[ative, ing]
 Rep., Repr.

Reprint[ed]
Rep., Repr.
Reprint of the Statutes of New Zealand
N.Z. Repr. Stat., Repr. Stat. N.Z.
Reprinted Acts of Western Australia
Repr. Acts W. Austl., W. Aust. Repr. Acts
Reproduct[ion, ive]
Reprod.
Republic[an]
Rep., Repub.
Republicana
R.
Republic of China
China (Rep.)
Republic of Korea
Korea (Rep.)
Request
Req.
Request for Proposal
R.F.P.
Res Gestae
Res Gestae
Res Ipsa Loquitur
Res Ipsa
Res Judicatae
Res Judic., Res. Jud.
Rescinded
R.
Rescript of Gamma Eta Gamma
Res. Gamma Eta Gamma
Rescriptum
Rc.
Research
Res.
Research and Development
R. & D.
Research and Development Board
R.D.B.

Research in Law and Economics
Res. L. & Econ., Research L. & Econ.
Research in Law and Sociology
Res. L. & Soc.
Research in Law, Deviance and Social Control
Res. L. Deviance & Soc. Control
Research Institute of America
R.I.A.
Research Institute of America Tax Coordinator
R.I.A. Tax.
Research Libraries Information Network (bibliographic utility network)
RLIN
Reserve
Res.
Reserve Officers Training Corps
ROTC
Reserved and Equity Judgments, New South Wales
Res. & Eq. Judgm., Res. & Eq. J., Res. & Eq. Jud.
Reserved Cases, Ireland
Reserv. Cas., Res. Cas.
Residence
Res.
Resigned
Res.
Resolution
Resol.
Resolution of a Legislative Body
Res.
Resolved
R., Res.
Resources
Res., Resources
Respectively
Resp.
Respondent
Resp., Resp't

Responsa Meridiana
 Resp.Merid.
Responsibility
 Resp.
Restatement of the Law
 Rest
Restatement of the Law Second
 Rest. 2d
Restitution
 Restit.
Restricted
 Restr.
Restrictive Practices Cases
 L.R.R.P.C.
Restrictive Practices Court
 R.P.C.
Retired Senior Volunteer Program
 RSVP
Retirement and Social Security
 Retire. & Soc. Sec.
Retorna Brevium
 Ret. Brev.
Retrospectively
 Retrosp.
Rettie, Crawford and Melville's Court of Session Cases, Scotland
 Rettie, J.C. Rettie, RC (J), R. (Ct. of Sess.)
Rettie, Scotch Sessions Cases, House of Lords
 R.H.L.
Rettie's Court of Session Cases, Scotland
 Rett.,Sess. Cas., Rettie, R.
Revenue and Taxation
 Rev. & Tax.
Revenue Cases
 Rev. Cas.

Revenue, Civil and Criminal Reporter, Calcutta
 R.C. & C.R., Rev. C. & C. Rep., R.J. & P.J.
Revenue Decisions
 R.D.
Revenue Decisions, Supplement
 R.D. Sup.
Revenue, Judicial, and Police Journal, Calcutta
 Rev. J. & P.J., Rev., Jud., & Police J.
Revenue Procedure, United States Internal Revenue Service
 Rev. Proc.
Revenue Reconciliation Act
 REVRA
Revenue Release
 R.R.
Revenue Reports of Upper Provinces, India
 Behari
Revenue Ruling
 Rev. Rul.
Reversed
 Rev'd.
Reversed on Rehearing, or Reversing on Rehearing (used in Shepard's Citations)
 Rev. reh.
Reversed, Revoked or Rescinded; Exisiting Order Aborgated (used in Shepard's Citations)
 R.
Review
 rev.
Review of Central and East European Law
 Rev. C.E.E. Law, Rev. CEE Law
Review of Contemporary Law
 Rev.Contemp.L., Rev.Cont.L.

Review of Ghana Law
Rev. Ghana L., R.G.L., Rev. of Ghana L.

Review of Law and Social Change
Rev. L. & Soc. Change

Review of Litigation
Rev. Litig., Rev. Litigation

Review of Polish Law
Rev. Pol. L.

Review of Polish Law and Economics
Rev. of Polish Law and Econ.

Review of Securities Regulation
Rev. Sec. Reg.

Review of Selected Code Legislation
Rev. Sel. Code Leg.

Review of Socialist Law
Rev. Socialist L., Rev. Soc. L.

Review of Taxation of Individuals
Rev. Tax. Indiv., Rev. Tax'n Indiv.

Review of the International Commission of Jurists
I.C.J. Rev., Rev.Int'l Comm.Jur., Rev. Intl Comm. Jurists

Revised
Rev., Rev'd.

Revised and Expurgated Law Reports
R.E.L.R.

Revised Cases, India
Rev. Cas. (Ind.)

Revised Civil Code
Rev. Civ. Code

Revised Civil Statutes
Rev. Civ. St.

Revised Code
R.C., Rev. Code

Revised Code of Civil Procedure
Rev. Code Civ.Proc.

Revised Code of Criminal Procedure
Rev. Code Cr.Proc.

Revised Code of Montana
R.C.M.

Revised Code of Washington
Wash. Rev. Code

Revised Code of Washington Annotated
R.C.W.A.

Revised Codes of Montana Annotated
Mont. Rev. Codes Ann.

Revised Collection of Selected Cases Issued by Chief Commissioner and Financial Commissioner of Oudh, India
Oudh Rev. Sel. Cas.

Revised Criminal Code
Rev.Cr. Code

Revised Edition
Rev.ed.

Revised General Regulation, General Accounting Office
Rev.Gen.Reg.

Revised Laws
Rev. L., Rev. Laws, R.L.

Revised Laws, New York
N.R.L.

Revised Municipal Code
Rev. Mun. Code

Revised Ordinances
Rev. Ord.

Revised Ordinances, North West Territories
R.O.N.W.T., Rev. Ord. N.W.T.

Revised Penal Code
Rev. Pen. Code

Revised Political Code
Rev. Pol. Code

Revised; Regulation or Order Revised (used in Shepard's Citations)
Rv.

Revised Reports
Revised R. (Eng.), Rev. R., Rev. Rep., Revised Rep., R.R.

Revised Reports, Criminal Rulings
R.R.Cr.R.

Revised Rules of the Supreme Court of the United States
S Ct Rule

Revised Rules of the United States Court of Military Appeals
Ct Mil App Rule

Revised Statutes
Rev. St., Rev. Stat., R.S.

Revised Statutes Annotated
R.S.A.

Revised Statutes of Alberta
R.S.A.

Revised Statutes of Canada
Can. Rev. Stat., R.S.C.

Revised Statutes of Manitoba
R.S.M.

Revised Statutes of Nebraska
Neb. Rev. Stat.

Revised Statutes of New Brunswick
R.S.N.B.

Revised Statutes of Newfoundland
R.S.N.

Revised Statutes of Nova Scotia
R.S.N.S.

Revised Statutes of Ontario
R.S.O.

Revised Statutes of Quebec
R.S.Q.

Revised Statutes of Saskatchewan
R.S.S.

Revision
R., Rev.

Revision of Swift's Digest of Connecticut Laws
Rev. Sw. Dig.

Revision of the Statutes Revised
Rev.

Revista de Derecho Puertorriqueno
Rev. D.P.

Revista del Colegio de Abogados de Puerto Rico
Rev. Col. Ab. P.R.

Revista Juridica de la Universidad de Puerto Rico
Rev. Jur. U.P.R.

Revoked
R.

Revoked or Rescinded in Part; Existing Regulation or Order Abrogated in Part (used in Shepard's Citations)
Rp.

Revue Critique de Droit International Private
R.C.D.I.P.

Revue de Droit International et de Droit Compare
R.D. Int'l. & D. Comp.

Revue de Droit, Universite de Sherbrooke
R.D.U.S.

Revue Generale de Droit
Rev. Gen.

Revue Internationale de Droit Compare
R.I.D.C.

Revue Juridique Themis
R.J.T.

**Revue Legale Reports, Queen's
Bench, Canada**
  R.L.Q.B.
**Revue Legale Reports, Supreme
Court, Canada**
  R.L.S.C.
**Revue Quebecoise de Droit Inter-
national**
  R. Q. D. I.
Rex (king) (Lat.)
  R.
**Reynold's Edition of Stephens on
Evidence**
  Reyn. Steph.
Reynold's Life Insurance
  Reyn. L. Ins.
**Reynold's Spanish and Mexican
Land Laws**
  Reynolds' Land Laws
**Reynold's Reports (40-42 Missis-
sippi)**
  Reyn., Reynolds
RFE/RL Research Report
  RFE/RL Res. Rep.
Rhode Island
  R.I.
Rhode Island Bar Journal
  R.I. B.J.
**Rhode Island Board of Railroad
Commission Reports**
  R.I.Bd. R.C.
Rhode Island Clerk's Magazine
  Clk. Mag.
**Rhode Island Compilation of
Rules of State Agencies**
  R.I. Comp. of Rules of St. Agen-
cies
Rhode Island Constitution
  R.I. Const.
Rhode Island Court Records
  R.I. Ct. Rec.
Rhode Island Decisions
  R.I. Dec.

Rhode Island General Laws
  R.I. Gen. Law
Rhode Island Public Laws
  R.I. Pub. Laws
**Rhode Island Public Utilities
Commission**
  R.I. P.U.C.
**Rhode Island Railroad Commis-
sion**
  R.I.R.C.
Rhode Island Reports
  Rh.I., R.I., Rhode Island Rep.,
R.I. Rep.
Rhode Island Superior Court
  Super. Ct. (R.I.)
**Rhode Island Supreme Court Re-
ports**
  Rh.I.
**Rhodesia and Nyasaland Court of
Appeal Law Reports**
  R.N.C.A.
**Rhodesia and Nyasaland Law
Journal**
  R. N. L.J.
**Rhodesia and Nyasaland Law Re-
ports**
  R. & N., R. & N.L.R.
**Rhodesian Court of Appeal Law
Reports**
  Rh. C.A.
Rhodesian Law Journal
  Rh.L.J., Rhodesian L.J., R.L.J.
Rhodian Law
  Leg. Rhodes, Rho. L.
**Rice's Digest of Patent Office De-
cisions**
  Rice Dig.
Rice's Code of Colorado Practice
  Rice's Code
Rice's Law of Evidence
  Rice, Ev.

Rice's South Carolina Equity Reports
Rice Ch., Rice Eq.
Rice's South Carolina Law Reports
Rice, Rice L. (S.C.)
Richard (King)
Ric., Rich.
Richardson and Hook's Street Railway Decisions
Rich. & H.
Richardson and Sayles' Select Cases of Procedure Without Writ (Selden Society Publications, 60)
Rich. & S.
Richardson and Woodbury's Reports (2 New Hampshire)
Rich. & W.
Richardson on Establishing a Law Practice
Richardson, Law Practice
Richardson's Attorney's Practice in the Court of King's Bench, England
Rich. Pr.K.B.
Richardson's Court of Claims Reports
Rich. Ct. Cl.
Richardson's English Chancery Practice (1838)
Rich. Ch. Pr.
Richardson's (J.S.G.) Equity Reports, South Carolina
Richd. E. Repts., Rich. Cas. (S.C.), Rich. Ch., Rich. Eq. Cas., lRic. Eq. Ch., Rich. Eq.
Richardson's (J.S.G.) Law Reports, South Carolina
Richardson's S. Ca. Rep., Rich. Cas., Rich., Rich. Law (S.C.), Rich. L. (S.C.), Rich'd. Law R.

Richardson's Law of Testaments and Last Wills
Rich. Wills
Richardson's New Dictionary of the English Language
Rich. Dict.
Richardson's Practical Register of Common Pleas
Rich. P.R.C.P., Rich. Pr.Reg., Rich. C.P.
Richardson's Reports (2-5 New Hampshire)
Rich. N.H., Rich.
Richardson's South Carolina Reports, New Series
Rich. N.S.
Richey's Irish Land Act
Rich. Land A.
Rickards and Michael's Locus Standi Reports, England
Rick. & M.
Rickards and Saunders' Locus Standi Reports, England
Ric. & S., Rick. & S.
Rickard's English Statutes
Rick. Eng. St.
RICO Business Disputes Guide, Commerce Clearing House (Racketeering Influenced and Corrupt Organizations)
RICO Bus. Disp. Guide (CCH)
Riddle's Lexicon
Riddle's Lex.
Riddle's Supplementary Proceedings, New York
Rid. Sup. Proc.
Ridgeway, Lapp and Schoales' Irish King's Bench Reports
R.L. & S.
Ridgeway, Lapp, and Schoales' Irish Term Reports
Ridg. L. & S., Ir. Term. Rep., Ir. T.R., I.T.R., Ridgew. L. & S. (Ir.)

Ridgeway's Irish Appeal or Parliamentary Cases
Ridg. Ap., Ridgw. Ir. P.C., Ridg. Parl. Rep., Ridgew. Ir. P.C., Ridg. P.C., Ridg. Pr. Rep., Ridg. App.
Ridgeway's Reports of State Trials in Ireland
Ridg. St. Tr., Ridg. Rep.
Ridgeway's Report Tempore Hardwicke, English Chancery and King's Bench
Ridg. & Hard., Ridgew. t. Hardw., Ridg., Ridg. Cas., Ridg. Temp. H., Ridgew., Ridgew.t.Hardw., Ridg.t.H., Ridg.t.Hard., Ridg.t.Hardw., R.t.H.
Ridley's Civil and Ecclesiastical Law
Ridley, Civil & Ecc. Law
Riedell's Reports (68-69 New Hampshire)
Ried.
Riffer's Sports and Recreational Injuries
SRI
Rigg's Selected Pleas, Starrs and Other Records from the Rolls of the Exchequer of the Jews (Selden Society of Publications, 15)
Rigg.
Right[s]
Rt., Rt(s).
Riley's Edition of Harper's South Carolina Reports
Ril. Harp.
Riley's Federal Contracts Grants and Assistance
CGA

Riley's Reports (37-42 West Virginia)
Riley, Ril(ey)
Riley's South Carolina Chancery Reports
Riley, Ril.
Riley's South Carolina Equity Reports
Ril., Riley Ch., Riley Eq., Riley Eq. (S.C.)
Riley's South Carolina Law Reports
Riley, Riley L. (S.C.)
Riner's Reports (2 Wyoming)
Rin., Riner
Ringwood's Principles of Bankruptcy
Ring. Bank.
Risk
Risk
Risk, Issues in Health and Safety
Risk Issues Health & Safety
Ritchie's Cases Decided by Francis Bacon
Ritch.
Ritchie's Equity Decisions, Nova Scotia
Ritchie, Ritch. Eq. Dec., R.E.D.
Ritchie's Equity Reports, Nova Scotia
Ritch. Eq. Rep., Ritch.
Ritso's Introduction to the Science
Rits. Int.
Ritson's Jurisdiction of Courts-Leet
Rits. Cts. Leet
Rivington's Annual Register
Riv. Ann. Reg.
Road Haulage Cases
R.H.C.
Road Traffic Act
R.T.A.

Road Traffic Reports
R.T.R.

Robards and Jackson's Reports (26-27 Texas)
Robards & Jackson, Rob. & J.

Robards' Conscript Cases, Texas
Rob. Cons. Cas. (Tex.), Ro. Rep., Robards, Rob.

Robard's Reports (12-13 Missouri)
Rob. (Mo.), Rob., Rob. Mo., Robards

Robards' Texas Conscript Cases
Rob. Consc. Cas.

Robbery
Rob.

Robbins' New Jersey Equity Reports (67-70 New Jersey Equity)
Robb. (N.J.), Robb.

Robb's United States Patent Cases
Robb., Robb Pat. Cas.

Robert
Robt.

Robert's Digest, Lower Canada
Rob. Dig.

Robert's Digest of Vermont Reports
Rob. Dig.

Roberts, Leaming, and Wallis' County English Court Reports
Rob. L. & W., R.L. & W.

Roberts on Admiralty and Prize
Rob. Adm. & Pr.

Roberts on Federal Liabilities of Carriers
Roberts Emp. Liab.

Roberts on Frauds
Rob. Fr.

Roberts on Fraudulent Conveyances
Rob. Fr. Conv.

Roberts on Wills
Rob. W.

Roberts on the Law of Personal Succession
Rob. Succ.

Roberts' Principles of Equity
Rob. Eq.

Roberts' Reports (29-31 Louisiana Annual)
Rob., Roberts

Robertson and Jacob's New York Marine Court Reports
Rob. Mar. (N.Y.)

Robertson's English Ecclesiastical Reports
Robt. Eccl., Rob., Robertson, Robt. Eccl. (Eng.), Rob. E., Rob. Ecc., Rob. Eccl.

Robertson's Handbook of Bankers' Law
Rob. Bank., Robs. Bankr.

Robertson's History of the Reign of the Emperor Charles V.
Rob. Car. V.

Robertson's House of Lords Appeals
Robert. App., Robert. App. Cas.

Robertson's Law of Personal Succession
Rob. Per. Suc.

Robertson's Law of Priority of Incumbrances
Rob. Prior.

Robertson's Legitimation by Subsequent Marriage
Rob. Leg.

Robertson's New York Marine Court Reports
Robertson

Robertson's Reports (1 Hawaii)
Rob., Robertson

Robertson's Reports (24-30 New York Superior Court)
Robertson, Rob., Rob. Super. Ct., Rob. Sr. Ct., Robertson's Rep., Rob. (N.Y.), Robt. (N.Y.)

Robertson's Sandwich Island Reports (1 Hawaii)
Rob. S.I.

Robertson's Scotch Appeal Cases
Robt. Sc. App. Cas., Rob., Robert., Robertson

Robinson and Harrison's Ontario Digest
R. & H. Dig.

Robinson and Joseph's Ontario Digest
R. & J. Dig.

Robinson on Patents
Rob. Pat.

Robinson's Common Law of Kent, or Custom on Gavelkind
Rob. Gav.

Robinson's Justice of the Peace
Rob. Jus.

Robinson's Appeal Cases
Robin. App. Cas.

Robinson's Book of Entries
Rob. Ent.

Robinson's Elementary Law
Rob. El. Law

Robinson's English Admiralty Reports
Rob., Robinson Chr., Ch. Rob., Rob. A., Rob., C. Rob. Adm., C. Rob., Rob. Adm., Chr. Rob., Robinson, Robinson Chr. C. Rob. Adm., Ch. Rob., Rob. A., Rob Wm. Adm., Rob. Ch., W. Robinson, W. Rob. Adm., Wm. Rob., Wm. Rob. Adm.

Robinson's English Ecclesiastical Reports
Rob., Robinson.

Robinson's House of Lords Appeals, England
Robin. App., Robinson.

Robinson's Louisiana Reports (1-4 Louisiana Annual)
Rob.

Robinson's Practice
Rob. Pr.

Robinson's Reports (38 California)
Robinson Chr., Rob., Rob. Cal., Robinson.

Robinson's Reports (17-23 Colorado Appeals)
Robinson Chr., Robinson., Rob. Colo., Rob. Chr., Rob.

Robinson's Reports (1 Hawaii)
Rob. Hawaii

Robinson's Reports (1-12 Louisiana)
Rob. Louis., Robinson Chr., Robinson.

Robinson's Reports (1 Nevada)
Robinson Chr., Rob. (Nev.), Rob., Rob. Nev., Robinson.

Robinson's Reports (1-8 Ontario)
Rob., Robinson Chr., Rob. Ont.

Robinson's Reports (40-41 Virginia)
Robinson Chr., Robinson., Rob. Va., Rob.

Robinson's Upper Canada Reports
Robinson., Rob., Robinson Chr., Rob. U.C.

Robinson's Scotch Appeal Cases
Rob. Sc. App., Rob., Rob. App., Rob. Cas., Robin. Sc. App., Robinson Sc. App. Cas.

Robinson's Virginia Forms
Rob. Forms

Robinson's Virginia Practice
Rob.Va. Prac.

Robson on Bankruptcy
Robson., Robs. Bank., Rob. Bank.

Roccus' de Navibus et Naulo
Rocc. de Nav.et Nau., Rocc.

Roccus on Insurance
Roc. Ins., Roccus. Ins.

Roche and Hazlitt on Bankruptcy Practice
Roche & H. Bank., R. & H. Bank.

Roche, Dillon, Kehoe's Irish Land Reports
Roche D. & K., Land Com. Rep., Land Comp. Rep.

Rockwell on Mines
Rock. Min.

Rockwell's Spanish and Mexican Law Relating to Mines
Rock. Sp. Law

Rocky Mountain
Rocky Mtn.

Rocky Mountain Law Review
R.M.R., Rocky Mt. L. Rev., Rocky Mtn. L. Rev., R.M.L.R.

Rocky Mountain Mineral Law Institute
RMMLF, Rocky. Mt. M. L. Inst., Rocky Mt. Min. L. Inst., Rocky Mtn. Min. L. Inst.

Rocky Mountain Mineral Law Institute Proceedings
Rocky Mt. Min. L. Inst. Proc.

Rocky Mountain Mineral Law Newsletter
Rocky Mt. Min. L. Newsl.

Rocky Mountain Mineral Law Review
R.M.M.L.R., Rocky Mt. Miner. L. Rev.

Roddy on RICO in Business and Commercial Litigation (Racketeering, Influenced and Corrupt Organizations)
RICO

Rodman's Reports (78-82 Kentucky)
Rodm., Rodman.

Roelker's Manual for Notaries and Bankers
Roelk. Man.

Roe's Manual for United States Commissioners
Roe U.S. Com.

Roger de Hovenden's Chronica
Rog. Hov.

Rogers' Ecclesiastical Law
Rog. Ecc. Law, Rog. Ecc. L.

Rogers' New City Hall Recorder
Rog. Rec., Rog. C.H.R.

Rogers on Elections and Registration
Rogers., Rog. Elec.

Rogers on Mines and Minerals
Rog. Min.

Rogers on the Judicature Acts
Rog. Jud. Acts

Rogers' Reports (47-51 Louisiana Annual)
Rogers.

Rogers' Wrongs and Rights of a Traveller
Rog. Trav.

Roll of the Term
Roll.

Rolle's Abridgment of the Common Law
Rol., Ro., Rol. Ab., Roll. Abr., Rolle, Abr., Rolle, Roll.

Rolle's English King's Bench Reports
Roll. Rep., Rolle R., Ro. Rep., Rol., Roll., Rolle.

Rolls
R.
Roll's Court
M.R.
Rolls' Court Reports
Rolls Ct. Rep.
Rolls of Court
R.C.
Rolls of the Assizes in Channel Islands
Ch. Is. Rolls.
Rolls Series
R.S.
Rolls Series, Yearbooks
Y.B. (R.S.), Y.B. (Rolls Ser.)
Roman Law
R.L.
Romania
Rom.
Romanian
Ro.
Romilly's Observations on the Criminal Law
Rom. Cr. Law
Romilly's Notes of English Chancery Cases
Romilly N.C. (Eng.), Rom., Rom. Cas.
Root's Digest of Law and Practice in Bankruptcy
Root Bt. Laws
Root's Connecticut Supreme Court Reports
Root., Root R., Roots, Root's Rep., Root's Reports, Root.
Roper on Husband and Wife
Rop. Husb. & Wife
Roper on Law of Property Between Husband and Wife
Rop. H. & W., Rop. Prop.
Roper's City Hall Recorder, New York City
City Hall Rec. (NY)

Roper on Legacies
Rop. Leg., Rop.
Roper on Revocation of Wills
Rop. Rev.
Rorer on Inter-State Law
Ror. Int. St. L.
Rorer on Railways
Rorer, R.R.
Rorer on Void Judicial Sales
Ror. Jud. Sal., Rorer, Jud. Sales.
Roscoe on Real Actions
Rosc. R.A.
Roscoe on Stamp Duties
Rosc. St.D.
Roscoe's Actions
Rosc. Act.
Roscoe's Admiralty Jurisdiction and Practice
Rosc. Adm.
Roscoe's Bills of Exchange
Rosc. Bills
Roscoe's Cape of Good Hope Eastern District Reports
R., E.D.R.
Roscoe's Digest of Building Cases
Rosc. Bdg. Cas., Roscoe, Bldg. Cas., Roscoe's B.C.
Roscoe's English Prize Cases
Eng. Pr. Cas., Rosc. P.C., E.P.C.
Roscoe's Jurist
Rosc. Jur., Jur. Ros.
Roscoe's Law of Evidence at Nisi Prius
Rosc. N.P., Rosc. Ev., R.N.P.
Roscoe's Law of Evidence in Criminal Cases
Rosc. Cr., Rosc. Crim. Ev., Roscoe, Cr. Ev.
Roscoe's Law of Light
Rosc. Light
Roscoe's Outlines of Civil Procedure
Rosc. Civ. Pr.

Roscoe's Pleading
Rosc. Pl.

Roscoe's Reports of Supreme Court of Cape of Good Hope
Roscoe., Rosc.

Rose Will Case, New York
Rose W.C.

Rosenberger's Pocket Law Journal
Rosenberger Pock. L.J.

Rosenblum's Medical Malpractice: Handling Cardilogy and Cardiovascular Surgery Cases
MMCC

Rose's English Bankruptcy Reports
Rose Bankr., Rose., rose Bankr. (Eng.), Rose B.C.

Rose's Digest of Arkansas Reports
Rose Dig.

Rose's Notes on United States Reports
Rose Notes., Rose's Notes (U.S.)

Ross' Leading Cases
Ross Lead. Cas.

Ross' Lectures on Conveyancing, etc.
Ross, Conv.

Ross on Contracts
Ross, Cont.

Ross on Vendors and Purchasers
Ross V. & P.

Ross's Leading Cases in Commercial Law
Ross L.C., Ross Ldg. Cas.

Ross's Leading Cases in the Law of Scotland (Land Rights)
Ross L.C., Ross Lead. Cas., Ross Ldg. Cas.

Rotae Florentine (Rota of Florence)
Rot. Flor.

Rothstein on Rights of Physically Handicapped Persons
RPHP

Rotulae Parliamentariae
Rot. Parl.

Rotuli Clause (Close Roll)
Rot. Claus.

Rotuli Curiae Regis
Rot. Cur. Reg., Rotuli Curiae Reg.

Rotuli Hundredorum, Record Commission
R.H.

Rotuli Parliamentorum
R.P.

Rotuli Patenes
Rot. Pat.

Rotuli Placitorum
Rot. Plac

Rotulus Chartarum (The Charter Roll)
Chart., Chart. (or Rot. Chart), Rot. Chart.

Rotulus Clausarum (Close Roll)
Cl.

Round on Law of Domicil
Roiund Dom.

Round on Law of Lien
Round Lien

Round on Right of Light and Air
Round L. & A.

Rouse's Copyhold Enfranchisement Manual
Rouse Cop.

Rouse's Practical Conveyancer
Rouse Conv.

Rouse's Precedents and Conveyances of Mortgaged Property
Rouse Pr. Mort.

Rowell's Contested Election Cases, United States Congress, House of Representatives
Rowell, El. Cas.

Rowell's Interesting Cases, England and Ireland
Int. Cas., Int. Case, Rowe
Rowell's Reports (45-52 Vermont)
Rowell.
Rowe's English Reports
Rowe's Rep.
Rowe's Interesting Parliamentary and Military Cases, England
Rowe.
Rowe's Irish Reports
Rowe Rep.
Rowe's Scintilla Juris
Rowe Sci. Jur.
Rowland's Manual of the English Constitution
Row. Eng. Const.
Royal Canadian Mounted Police Quarterly
R.C.M.P.Q.
Royal Commission on Historical Manuscripts
H.M.C.
Royal Commission on Non-Muslem Marriage and Divorce Laws in Malaysia
Malaysia R.C.
Royall's Digest of Virginia Reports
Roy. Dig.
Royle on the Law of Stock Shares, & c.
Royle Stock Sh.
Rubinstein on Conveyancing
Rub. Conv.
Rubric
Rub.
Rucker's Reports (43-46 West Virginia)
Rucker
Ruegg on Employer's Liability
Ruegg Emp. L.

Ruffhead's Edition of the Statutes by Serjeant Runnington
Ruff.
Ruffhead's English Statutes
Ruff. (or Ruffh.)St.
Ruffin and Hawks' Reports (8 North Carolina)
Ruff., Ruff. & H.
Rule
R.
Rules and Administration
R.A.
Rules for Admission to Practice
R.A.P.
Rules for the Discipline of Attorneys
R.D.A.
Rules for the Municipal Courts
Municipal Court Rule
Rules of Bankruptcy and Official Forms
Bankr. R.
Rules of Pleading, Practice, and Procedure
R.P.P.P.
Rules of Practice in Patent Cases
R. Prac. Patent Cases
Rules of Procedure
R.P.
Rules of Procedure, Judicial Panel on Multi-District Litigation
RP Jud Pan Mult Lit
Rules of Procedure of the Court of Justice
R.P.
Rules of the American Stock Exchange
Am. Stock Exch. Rules
Rules of the Supreme Court
Rules Sup.Ct., R.S.C.

Rules of the Tax Court of the United States
T Ct Rule

Rules of the United States Court of Customs and Patent Appeals
Cust & Pat App Rule

Rules on Appeal
R.A.

Rules Peculiar to the Business of the Supreme Court
R.P.B.S.C.

Rules, Regulations and By-Laws Under New Zealand Statutes
N.Z.R., Regs. & B.

Ruling Case Law
R.C.I., R.C.L.

Ruling Cases
R.C.

Rulings of the Judicial Panel on Multidistrict Litigation
Jud. Pan. Mult. Lit.

Runnell's Reports (38-56 Iowa)
Runn., Runnell.

Runnington on Ejectment
Runn. Eject.

Runnington on Statutes
Runn. Stat.

Rural Development Service
R.D.S.

Rural Electric Cooperative
Rural Elec. Coop.

Rural Electrification Administration
REA

Rural Electrification Bulletin
R.E.A. Bull.

Rural Environmental Assistance Program
REAP

Rural Environmental Conservation Program
RECP

Rural Free Delivery
RFD

Rural Municipality
R.M.

Rural Rehabilitation
R.R.

Rural Telephone Bank
RTB

Rushworth's Historical Collections
Rushw.

Russell and Chesley's Equity Reports, Nova Scotia
Russ. & Eq., Rus. & C. Eq. Cas., Russ. & Ches. Eq., Russ. & C. Eq. Cas.

Russell and Chesley's Nova Scotia Reports
N.R.R. & C., R. & C., N.S.R.R. & C., R. & C. N. Sc., Russ. & Ches.

Russell and Geldert's Nova Scotia Reports
N.S.R.R. & G., R. & G., Russ. & G., Russ. & Geld., R. & G. N. Sc.

Russell and Mylne's English Chancery Reports
Russ. & M., R. & My., R. & M., Russ. & My.

Russell and Ryan's English Crown Cases Reserved
R. & R., Russ. & R.C.C., Russ. & Ry., R. & R.C.C., Russ. & R., Russ. & R.C.C. (Eng.), R. & Ry. C.C., Russ. & R. Cr. Cas.

Russell on Arbitrators
Russ. Arb.

Russell on Crimes and Misdemeanors
Russ. Crim, Russ. Cr., Russ. Crimes.

Russell on Factors and Brokers
Russ. Fact.

Russell on Mercantile Agency
Russ. Merc. Ag.
Russell Senate Office Building
RSOB, OSOB
Russell's Contested Election Cases, Massachusetts
Mass. Election Cases, Rus. E.C., Russ., Russ. Con. El. (Mass.), Russ. Elect. Cas.
Russell's Election Cases, Nova Scotia
Rus., Rus. Elec. Rep., Rus. E. R., Russ., Russ. Elect. Cas., Russ. El. Cas., Rus. E.C.
Russell's English Chancery Reports
Rus., Russ., Russ. Ch.
Russell's English Chancery Reports Tempore Elden
Russ.t.Eld.
Russell's Nova Scotia Equity Decisions
R.E.D., Russ. Eq., Russ. Eq. Cas., Russ. N.Sc., Rus. Eq. Rep., Russ. Eq. Rep., Russell., Russell N.S.
Russian
R.
Russian and Japanese Prize Cases
Russ. & Jap. P.C.
Russian Federation
R.F., Russ. Fed.
Russian Politics and Law
Rus. Pol. & L.
Rusian Politics and Law: A Journal of Translations
Rus. Pol. & L.
Russian Review
Russian Rev.
Russian Soviet Federative Socialist Republic
R.S.F.S.R.

Russo's Regulation of the Commodities Futures and Options Markets
RCF
Rutger-Waddington Case, New York City
Rutg. Cas.
Rutgers-Camden
Rut.-Cam.
Rutgers-Camden Law Journal
Rut.-Cam. L.J., Rutgers-Camden L.J.
Rutgers Computer and Technology Law Journal
Rutgers Computer & Tech. L. J.
Rutgers Journal of Computers and the Law
Rutgers J. Comp. & L., Rutgers J. Computers & Law
Rutgers Journal of Computers Technology and the Law
Rutgers J. Computer Tech. & L.
Rutgers Law Journal
Rutgers L.J.
Rutgers Law Review
RLR, Rutg. L. Rev., Rutgers L. Rev.
Rutgers University Law Review
Rutgers U. L. Rev.
Rutherford's Institutes of Natural Law
Ruth. Inst.
Ryan and Moody's English Crown Cases Reserved
Ry. & Moo., Ry. M.C.C., R.M.C.C., R.M.C.C.R., R. & M.C.C.
Ryan and Moody's English Nisi Prius Reports
R. & M., R. & M.N.P., Ry. & M., Ry. & M.N P., Ry & M. C.C., Ryan. & M., Ryan. & M. (Eng.)

Ryan's Medical Jurisprudence
Ry. Ed. Jur., Ry. Med. Jur.
Ryde and Konstam's Reports of Rating Appeals, England
Ryde & K. Rat. App., Ryde & K.
Ryde's Rating Appeals, England
Ryde., Ryde Rat. App.

Ryde's Rating Cases, England
R.R.C.
Ryley's Placita Parliamentaria
Ryl. Plac. Parl.
Rymer's Fodera
Ry. F., Rym. F.

S

Sachse's Minutes, Norwich Mayoralty Court, England
Sachse N.M.
Sadler's Cases, Pennsylvania
Sadler (Pa.), Sad., Sadler, Sad.
Pa. Cas., Sad. Pa. Cs.
Sadr Diwani Adalat Court, Bengal
S.D.
Sadr Diwani Adalat Selected Cases, Bengal
S.A.D. Bengal, Sel. Cas. S.D.A.,
Sel. Cas. D.A.
Sadr Diwani Adalat Selected Cases, Bombay
Sel. Cas. Bomb.
Sadr Diwani Adalat Selected Cases, Madras
Sel. Cas. Madr.
Safe Drinking Water Act
SDWA
Saft's Commercial Real Estate Forms
CREF
Saft's Commercial Real Estate Leasing
CREL
Saft's Commercial Real Estate Transactions
CRET
Saft's Commercial Real Estate Workouts
CREW
Saint Lawrence Seaway Development Corporation
SLS

Saint Louis University Law Journal
Saint Louis Univ. L.J., S.L.U.
L.J., St. Louis U. L.J.
Saint Louis University Public Law Review
St. Louis U. Pub. L. Rev.
Saint's Digest of Registration Cases, England
Saint.
Salaman on Liquidation and Composition with Creditors
Sal. Comp. Cr.
Salary Stabilization Board
SSB
Sales and User Taxes
Sales T.
Sales Tax Branch, United States Internal Revenue Bureau
S.T.
Sales Tax Cases
S.T.C.
Sales Tax Rulings, United States Internal Revenue Bureau
S.T.
Salic Law
L. Sal., L. Salic.
Salinger's Reports (88-117 Iowa)
Sal.
Salkeld's English King's Bench Reports
Salk., Salk. (Eng.)
Salmon's Abridgment of State Trials
Salm. Abr., Salm. St. R.
Salsich's Land Use Regulation
LUR

Salvage
    Salv.
**Same Case; Same Case As Case
    Cited (used in Shepard's Cita-
    tions)**
    s.
Samoan Pacific Law Journal
    Samoan P. L.J., Samoan Pac.
    L.J.
San Diego Law Review
    San. D. L.R., San. Diego L. Rev.
San Fernando Valley
    San. Fern. V.
San Fernando Valley Law Review
    San. Fern. V. L. Rev.
San Francisco
    S.F.
San Francisco Bar Association
    BASF
San Francisco Law Bulletin
    San Fr. L.B., San Fran. Law
    Bull.
San Francisco Law Journal
    San. F. L.J., San Fr. L.J., San
    Fran. L.J., S.F. L.J.
**Sanborn and Berryman's Anno-
    tated Wisconsin Statutes**
    Sanb. & B. Ann. St.
**Sandels and Hill's Digest of Ar-
    kansas Statutes**
    Sand. & H. Dig.
**Sanders' Edition of Justinian's In-
    stitutes**
    San. Just., Sand. Inst. Just. In-
    trod., Sandars, Just. Inst.
Sanders on Uses and Trusts
    Sand. Uses and Trusts.
**Sanders' Essays on Uses and
    Trusts**
    Sand. Essays
**Sandford on Heritable Succes-
    sion in Scotland**
    Sandf. Suc.

**Sandford's New York Chancery
    Reports**
    San. Ch., Sand. Ch. R., Sandf.
    Ch. Rep., Sands. Ch., Sanford's
    Ch. R., Sandf. Ch., Sandf.,
    Sandf. Ch. (N.Y.), Sand. Chy.,
    Sand. Ch.
**Sandford's New York Superior
    CourtReports (3-7 New York
    Superior)**
    Sand., Sand. R., Sand. S.C.,
    Sand. S.C.R., Sand. Sup. Ct.
    Rep., Sand. Supr. Ct. R., Sandf.
    C., Sandf. (N.Y.)R., Sandf. R.,
    Sandf. S.C.R., Sandf. Sup. C.R.,
    Sandf. Sup. Ct., S.S.C., Sandf.
    Superior Court R., Sandford,
    Sandford's S.C.R., Sandford's
    Sup. Ct. R.
Sandler's State Papers
    Sandl. St. Pap.
**Sandwich Islands Reports (Ha-
    waii)**
    Sand. I. Rep.
Sanford's Reports (59 Alabama)
    San., Sanf.
**Santa Clara Computer and High
    Technology Law Journal**
    Santa Clara Computer & High
    Tech. L. J.
Santa Clara Law Review
    Santa Clara L. Rev.
Santa Clara Lawyer
    Santa Clara L., Santa Clara
    Law., Santa Clara Lawyer,
    S.C.L.
**Santerna de Asse Curationibus et
    Sponsionibus Mercatorum**
    Santerna de Ass.
**Sanyal's Criminal Cases Between
    Natives and Europeans, India**
    Sanyal

Saratoga Chancery Sentinel, New York
  Sarat. Ch. Sent., Sar. Ch. Sen.
Sarawak Supreme Court Reports
  S.S.C.
Sarbah's Fanti Customary Law, Ghana
  F.C.L., Sar. F.C.L., Sarbah F.C.
Sarbah's Fanti Law Cases, Ghana
  Sarbah, Sar. F.L.R.
Sarbah's Fanti National Constitution, Ghana
  Sar. F.N.C.
Sarswati's Indian Privy Council Judgments
  Sar.
Saskatchewan
  S., Sask.
Saskatchewan Bar Review
  Sask. B. Rev., Sask. Bar Rev., Sask. B.R.
Saskatchewan Gazette
  Sask. Gaz.
Saskatchewan Law
  Sask. L.
Saskatchewan Law Reform Commission
  Sask. L.R.C.
Saskatchewan Law Reports
  S.L.R., Sask., Sask. R., Sask. L.R.
Saskatchewan Law Review
  Sask. L. Rev., Sask. Law Rev., Saskatchewan L. Rev.
Saskatchewan Revised Statutes
  Sask. Rev. Stat.
Saskatchewan Statutes
  Sask. Stat.
Saunders and Austin's English Locus Standi Reports
  Saund. & Aust., S. & A., Saund. & A.

Saunders and Bidder's English Locus Standi Reports
  Saund. & B., S. & B.
Saunders and Cole's English Bail Court Reports
  Saund. & Cole, Bail Ct. Rep., Saund. B.C., S. & C., B.C.R., B.C.Rep., B.C.C., Bail Ct.R.
Saunders and Macrae's English County Court Cases
  Saund. & M., Saund. & Mac.
Saunders' King's Bench Reports
  Saund.
Saunders on Affiliation and Bastardy
  Saund. Bast.
Saunders on Assault and Battery
  Saund. Ass.
Saunders on Magistrates' Courts Practice
  Saund. Mag. Pr.
Saunders on Militia Law
  Saund. Mil. L.
Saunders on Municipal Registration
  Saund. Mun. Reg.
Saunders on Negligence
  Saund. Neg.
Saunders on Warranties and Representations
  Saund. War.
Saunders' Pleading and Evidence
  Saund. Pl. & Ev.
Saunders' Precedents of Indictments
  Saund. Prec.
Saunders' (Sir Edmund) Reports, Edited by Williams, England
  Wms. Saund. (Eng.)
  Wms. Saund.
Saurastra Law Reports, India
  Sau. L.R.

Sausee and Scully's Irish Rolls Court Reports
Sau. & Sc., Sausse & Sc., S. & Sc., S. & S.

Savigny's Conflict of Laws
Sav. Conf. Law

Savigny's History of the Roman Law
Savigny, Hist. Rom. Law

Savigny's Possessions
Sav. Pos.

Savile's English Common Pleas Reports
Savile, Sav., Savile (Eng.)

Savings
Sav.

Sawyer's United States Circuit Court Reports
Saw., Sawy., Sawyer Circt., Sawyer U.S. Ct. Rep.

Saxton's New Jersey Chancery Reports
Saxt. Ch., Sax., Saxt.

Sayer's English King's Bench Reports
Say., Sayer (Eng.), Sayer

Sayles' Annotated Texas Civil Statutes
Sayles' Ann. Civ. St.

Sayles' Annotated Texas Civil Statutes, Supplement
Sayle's Supp.

Sayles' Revised Texas Civil Statutes
Sayles' Civ. St., Sayles' St., Sayles' Rev. Civ. St.

Sayre's Cases on Admiralty
Sayre, Adm. Cas.

Scaccaria Curia (Court of Exchequer)
Scac.

Scaccaria (Exchequer)
Sc.

Scammon's Reports, (2-5 Illinois)
Sc., Scam.

Scandalum Magnatum
Scan. Mag.

Scandinavia[n]
Sc.

Scandinavian Studies in Criminology
Sc. St. Crim., Scand. Stud. Criminol., Sc. Stud. Criminol.

Scandinavian Studies in Law
Sc. St. L., Sc. Stud. Law, Scand. Stud. Law, Scand. Stud. in L.

Schafler's Medical Malpractice: Handling Dental Cases
MMDC

Schalk's Jamaica Reports
Schalk

Scheiffer's Practice
Scheif. Pr.

Scherer's New York Miscellaneous Reports
Scher.

Schmidt's Civil Law of Spain and Mexico
Schm. Civil Law, Schmidt,Civ. Law

Schmidt's Law Journal, New Orleans
Schm. L.J.

Schneider and Hoelschen on Federal Tax Aspects of Corporate Reorganizations
FTAC

Schoales and Lefroy's Irish Chancery Reports
Sch. & Lef., S. & L., Schoales & L.

Schomberg's Treatise on the Maritime Laws of Rhodes
Schomberg, Mar. Laws Rhodes

School
Sch.

School Code
School C.
School Law Bulletin
Sch. L. Bull.
School Law Reporter
School L. Rep.(Nat'l Org.on Legal Probs.in Educ.)
School of Advanced International Studies Review
School of Advanced Studies Rev.
School of Law Review
S.O.L. Rev., School of L.R., U. of T. School of L.R.
School[s]
Sch.
Schouler
Schoul.
Schouler on Bailment
Sch. Bailm., Schouler, Bailm.
Schouler on Domestic Relations
Sch. Dom. Rel., Schouler, Dom. Rel.
Schouler on Husband and Wife
Sch. H. & W.
Schouler on Personal Property
Schouler, Pers. Prop., Sch. Per. Prop.
Schouler on Wills
Schouler, Wills
Schouler's History of the United States Under the Constitution
Schouler, U.S. Hist.
Schultes on Aquatic Rights
Sch. Aq. R.
Schuylkill Legal Record
Schuy. Leg. Rec. (Pa.), Sch. Leg. Rec., Sch. L.R., Schuyl. L. Rec., Schuyl. Leg. Rec., Schuyl. Legal Rec., Schuyl. Leg. Rec.
Schuylkill Register
Schuy. Reg. (Pa.), Sch. Reg.
Schwartz's Engineering Evidence
EE

Schwartz, Lee and Kelly's Guide to Multistate Litigation
GMS
Schwarzenberger's International Law
Schwarz. Int. L.
Science and Technology
S.T.
Science[s]
Sci.
Scientific
Sci.
Scientific American
Sci. Am.
Scilicet (that is to say, to wit) (Lat.)
Scil., s.
Scire Facias (revival of judgment) (Lat.)
Sci. Fa.
Scire Facias Ad Disprobandum Debitum (Lat.)
Sci. fa. ad dis. deb.
Scotch
Sc.
Scotch and Divorce Appeals, English Law Reports
L.R. Sc. & Div., Sc. & Div. App., L.R.Sc. & D.App.
Scotch Court of Session Cases
Sc. Sess. Cas., Sess. Ca., Sess. Cas., Sess. Cas. Sc.
Scotch Court of Session Cases, Decided by English Judges
Eng. Judg.
Scotch Court of Sessions Cases, 1st Series
Ct. Sess. 1st Ser., Sess. Cas. S.
Scotch Court of Session Cases, 2d Series, by Dunlop
Sess. Cas. D.

Scotch Court of Session Cases, 3d Series, by Macpherson
Sess. Cass. M.

Scotch Court of Session Cases, 4d Series
Sess.Cas. (4 Ser.)

Scotch Court of Session Cases, 5th Series, by Fraser
Fraser (Scot.), Sess. Cas. F.

Scotch Court of Session Cases, 6th Series, by Rettie
Sess. Cas. R., Sess. Cas. (6 Ser.)

Scotch Court of Session Cases, New Series
S.C. (Scot.)

Scotch Munitions Appeals Reports
Sc. Mun. App. Rep.

Scotch Session Cases
S.S.C.

Scotland
S., Sc., Scot.

Scotland, Acts of Parliament (1124-1707) (1814-1875)
A.P.S., Scot. Parl. Acts

Scotland Acts of the Lords of Council in Public Affairs
Act. Ld. Co. Pub. Aff.

Scots
Sc., Scot.

Scots Law Times
Sc. L. T., S.L.T., Scot. L.T., Scots L.T.

Scots Law Times Lyon Court Reports
S.L.T. (Lyon Ct.)

Scots Law Times Notes of Recent Decisions
S.L.T. (notes)

Scots Law Times Reports
Scots L.T.R.

Scots Law Times Sheriff Court Reports
S.L.T. (Sh.Ct.)

Scots Revised Reports
Scots R.R., Sc. Rev. Rept., S.R.R., Sc.R.R.

Scott and Jarnigan on the Law of Telegraphs
Sco. & J. Tel.

Scott on Costs in the High Court
Sco. Costs

Scott on Naturalization of Aliens
Sco. Nat.

Scottish
S., Sc., Scot.

Scottish Appeal Reports
Scot. App. Rep.

Scottish Consumer Council
S.C.C.

Scottish Council of Social Service
S.C.S.S.

Scottish Courts
Sc. Cts.

Scottish Jurist
Sc. Jur., Scot. Jur., J., S.J., Jur. (Sc.)

Scottish Land Court Reports
L.C., S.L.C., S.L.C.R., S.L.R., Sc. La. R., Sc. La. Rep.

Scottish Land Court Reports Appendices
Sc.La.Rep.App.

Scottish Land Courts
S.L.C.

Scottish Law Commission
Scot. Law. Com., S.L.C.

Scottish Law Gazette
S.L.G.

Scottish Law Journal and Sheriff Court Record
Scot. L.J., Sc. L.J., Scot. Law J., S.L.J.

Scottish Law Magazine
Scot. L. Mag.
Scottish Law Magazine and Sheriff Court Reporter
Scot. L. M., Sc. L. M.
Scottish Law Reporter
Sc. L.R., Scot. L. Rep., Scot. L.R., Sc. L. Rep., S.L.R.
Scottish Law Review
Scot. L.R.
Scottish Law Review and Sheriff Court Reports
S. L. Rev., Scot. L. Rev., S.L.R., Sc. L.R.
Scottish Legal Action Group
SCOLAG
Scottish Legal Action Group Bulletin
SCOLAG Bull.
Scottish Trades Union Congress
S.T.U.C.
Scott's A.B.C. Guide to Costs
Sc. Costs
Scott's English New Common Pleas Reports
Scott N.R., Sc. N.R., Sco. N. R.
Scott's Intestate Laws
Sco. Int.
Scott's (John) English Common Pleas Reports, New Series
Scott, J. Scott, N.S., Sco., Scott., Scott (Eng.), Sc.
Scott's Reports (25-26 New York Civil Procedure)
Scott
Scranton Law Times, Pennsylvania
Scr. L.T.
Scratchley and Brabook on Building Societies
Scrat. & Bra.
Scratchley on Building Societies
Scrat. Bdg. Soc.

Scratchley on Life Assurance
Scrat. Life Ass.
Scribes Journal of Legal Writing
Scribes J. Legal Writing
Scribes, the American Society of Writers on Legal Subjects
SCRIBES
Scribner on the Law of Dower
Scrib. Dow.
Scriven on Law of Copyholds
Scriv. Cop., Scriven
Scrutton on Charterparties
Scrutton, Scrut.Charter
Sea Grant Law and Policy Journal
Sea Grant L. & Pol'y J.
Sea Grant Law Journal
Sea Grant L.J.
Seaborne on Vendors and Purchasers
Seab. Vend., Sea.Vend.
Seager on Parliamentary Registration
Seag. Parl. Reg.
Search and Seizure Bulletin
Search & Seizure Bull.
Search and Seizure Law Report
Search & Seizure L. Rep.
Searle and Smith's English Probate and Divorce Reports
Searle Sm., S. & S., Searle & Sm., S. & Sm., Sea. & Sm.
Searle's Cape of Good Hope Reports
S., S., Searle
Searle's Minnesota Digest
Searle Dig.
Seaton's Forms in Chancery
Seat. F. Ch.
Sebastian on Trade Marks
Seb. Tr. M., Seb. Trade-marks

SEC Accounting Rules, Commerce Clearing House
SEC Accounting R. (CCH)
Second Book of Judgments (Huxley), England
Sec. Bk. Judg.
Secretary
Secy
Secretary of State
Sec. of State
Secretary of the Interior
Sec. Int.
Section[s]
S., Sec., Sect., s., sec., secs., ss.
Secundum (Lat.)
Sec.
Secundum Legum (according to law) (Lat.)
Sec.leg.
Secundum Regulam (according to rule) (Lat.)
Sec. reg.
Secured Transactions
Secured Trans.
Secured Transactions Guide, Commerce Clearing House
Secured Transactions Guide (CCH)
Securities
Sec.
Securities and Exchange Commission
S.E.C., Sec. & Ex. C.
Securities and Exchange Commission Judicial Decisions
S.E.C. Jud. Dec.
Securities and Exchange Commission Compliance, Prentice-Hall
SEC Compl. (P-H)
Securities and Exchange Commission Decisions and Reports
S.E.C.

Securities and Exchange Commission Docket
S.E.C. Docket
Securities and Federal Corporate Law Report
Sec. & Fed. Corp. L. Rep. (Clark Boardman)
Securities Law Review
Sec. L. Rev.
Securities Regulation and Law Report, Bureau of National Affairs
BNA Sec. Reg., Sec. Reg. & L. Rep. (BNA)
Securities Regulation — Federal
Secur. Reg. Fed.
Securities Regulation Guide, Prentice-Hall
Sec. Reg. Guide (P-H)
Securities Regulation Law Journal
Sec. Reg. L.J.
Securities Regulation — State
Secur. Reg. St.
Securities Regulations and Transfer Report
Sec. Reg. & Trans.
Security Council Official Records
SCOR
Secus (otherwise) (Lat.)
Sec.
Sedgwick and Wait on the Trial of Title to Land
Sedg. & W. Tit., Sedg. & W. Tr. Title Land
Sedgwick on Statutory and Constitutional Law
Sedg. St. & Const. Law, Sedg. Stat. Law
Sedgwick on the Measure of Damage
Sedg. Dam.

Sedgwick's Leading Cases on Damages
Sedg. L. Cas.
Sedgwick's Leading Cases on Real Property
Sedg. L. Cas.
Sedition, Subversive Activities and Treason
Sedit.
Seduction
Seduc.
See
S.
Selden Society
Seld. Soc., S.S.
Selden Society Yearbook
Seld. Soc. Yrbk.
Selden on Office of Lord Chancellor
Sel. Off. Ch., Seld. Off. Ch.
Selden's Dissertatio ad Fletam
Diss. ad Flet., Seld. Fl.
Selden's (Henry R.) Court of Appeals Reports, New York
Seld. R., Selden
Selden's (Henry R.) New York Court of Appeals Notes of Cases
Selden Notes, Seld. Notes
Selden's Judicature in Parliaments
Seld. J.P.
Selden's Mare Clausum
Seld. Mare Claus., Seld. Mar. Cl.
Selden's Titles of Honor
Seld. Tit. Hon.
Select Bills in Eyre (Selden Society Publications, 30)
Bolland
Select Cases (37-39 Alabama)
Shep.
Select Cases for Central Provinces, India
Sel. Cas.

Select Cases in Chancery, England
Cas. in C., Cas. Ch., Cases in Ch., Sel. Cas. Ch.
Select Cases in Chancery tempore King, Edited by Macnaghten, England
Sel. Ch. Cas., Macn. Sel. Cas., Sel. Ca.t.King, S.C.L.
Select Cases in Chancery tempore King, England
Sel. Cas. Ch. (t.King), Sel. Cas.t.King, S.C.C., King Cas. temp., Cas. t. King, Cas. t. K., King
Select Cases in Evidence, by Strange, England
Sel. Cas. Ev., S.C.E.
Select Cases in King's Bench under Edward I, edited by Sayles, England
Sel. Cas. K.B. Edw.I.
Select Cases in the Court of Requests, edited by Leadam (Selden Society Publications, 12), England
Leadam Req.
Select Cases Sadr Diwani Adalat, Bengal
Sel. Cas. S.D.A., Sel. Cas. D.A., S.A.D. Bengal, Sel. App. Beng.
Select Cases Sadr Diwani Adalat, Bombay
Sel. Dec. Bomb.
Select Cases tempore Napier, Ireland
Sel. Cas.t.Nap.
Select Cases, Newfoundland
Sel. Cas. N.F.
Select Cases, Northwest Provinces, India
Sel. Cas. N.W.P.

Select Cases, Oudh, India
S.C.

Select Cases with Opinions, by a Solicitor, England
Sel. Cas. with Opin.

Select Collection of Cases, England
Sel. Col. Cas.

Select Committee
Sel. Com.

Select Decrees, Sadr Diwani Adalat, Madras
Sel. Dec. Madr.

Select Law Cases, England
Sel. L. Cas.

Select Pleas, Starrs, and Other Records from the Rolls of the Exchequer of the Jews, edited by J.M. Riggs (Selden Society Publication, 15)
Rigg

Selected Cases, Yearbooks, England
Y.B.S.C.

Selected Decisions by Umpire for Northern Ireland, Respecting Claims to Benefit
U.I.D.

Selected Decisions of the Board of Revenue, Bihar and Orissa, India
B. & O. Bd. of Rev.

Selected Decisions of the Native Appeal Court, Central Division, South Africa
N.A.C. (C.)

Selected Decisions of the Native Appeal Court, Transvaal and Natal, South Africa
N.A., T. & N.

Selected Judgments, Federal Supreme Court, Nigeria
F.S.C.

Selected Judgments, Lower Burma
S.J.L.B.

Selected Judgments of the Divisional Courts, Gold Coast
D. Ct., G.C. Div. C.

Selected Judgments of the Full Court, Accra and Gold Coast
F.C.

Selected Judgments of the Supreme Court of Israel
S.C.Is.

Selected Judgments of Zambia
S.J.Z.

Selection of Cases Decided in the Native Appeal and Divorce Court, Cape and Orange Free State, South Africa
N.A. & D., C. & O.

Selective Service Law Reporter
Sel. Serv. L. Rep., Sel. Serv. L. Rptr.

Selective Service System
SSS

Selective Temporary Employment Programme
STEP

Selfridge's Trial
Self. Tr.

Sellon's Practice in the King's Bench
Sel. Pr., Sell. Pr., Sell. Prac.

Selwyn's Law of Nisi Prius
Selw. N.P., Sel. N.P., Selw.

Selz and Simensky's Entertainment Law
EL

Semble (it seems) (Lat.)
Sem. (or Semb.)

Senate
S.

Senate Bill
S., S.B.

Senate Concurrent Resolution
S. Con. Res., S.C. Res.

Senate Document
S.Doc., Sen. Doc.

Senate Executive Document
S. Exec. Doc.

Senate Executive Report
S. Exec. Rep.

Senate-House Joint Reports
S.H. J.R.

Senate Journal
Sen. J., Sen. Jo.

Senate Report[s]
Sen. Rep., S. Rep.

Senate Resolution[s]
S.R.

Senate Treaty Document[s]
S. Treaty Doc.

Senator
Sen.

Senegal
Sen.

Senior Counsel
S.C.

Senior Magistrate
S.M.

Sentencis Arbitrales de Griefs, Quebec
S.A.G.

Seoul Law Journal
Seoul L.J.

September
Se., Sep., Sept.

Sequstration
Seques.

Sergeant and Rawle's Pennsylvania Reports
Serg. & R., Serg. & Raw., S. & R., Serg. & Rawl.

Sergeant on Attachment
Serg. Att.

Sergeant on Mechanics' Lien Law
Serg. Mech. L.

Sergeant on the Land Laws of Pennsylvania
Serg. Land Laws Pa., Serg.L.L.

Sergeant Wilson's English King's Bench Reports
Wils. K.B.

Sergeant's Constitutional Law
Serg. Const. L.

Series, serial[s]
Ser.

Service
Serv.

Service and Regulatory Announcement, United States Department of Agriculture
SRA

Service Corps of Retired Executives
SCORE

Service Employees' International Union (AFL-CIO)
S.E.I.U.

Session
Sess.

Session Acts
Sess. Acts

Session Cases
Ct. of Sess., S.C., Sess. Cas.

Session Laws
Sess. Laws, S.L.

Session Laws of Colorado
Colo. Sess. Laws.

Session Laws of Hawaii
Haw. Sess. Laws, Hawaii Sess. Laws

Session Laws of Idaho
Idaho Sess. Laws

Session Laws of Kansas
Kan. Sess. Laws

Session Laws of North Carolina
N.C. Sess. Laws
Session Laws of Wyoming
Wyo. Sess. Laws
Session Notes
Sess. N., S.N.
Sessions Settlement Cases English King's Bench
Sess. Ca., Sess. Cas., Sess. Cas. K.B.
Seton Hall Constitutional Law Journal
Seton Hall Const. L. J.
Seton Hall Journal of Sport Law
Seton Hall J. Sport Law
Seton Hall Law Review
Seton Hall L. Rev.
Seton Hall Legislative Journal
Seton Hall Leg. J., Seton Hall Legis. J.
Seton on Decrees
Seton, Seton Dec.
Settlement and Removals Cases in English Kings Bench
Sett. & Rem., Sett., Sett. Cas.
Sevestre and Marshall's Bengal Reports
App. Cas. Beng.
Sevestre's Bengal High Court Reports
Sev. App. Cas., Sev. H.C.
Sevestre's Sadr Diwani Adalat Reports, Bengal
Sev. S.D.A.
Sewell on the Law of Coroners
Sew. Cor.
Sewell on the Law of Sheriffs
Sewell, Sheriffs, Sew. Sh.
Sex Problems Court Digest
Sex Prob. Ct. Dig.
Sexual Law Reporter
Sex. L. R., Sex. L. Rep.

Seychelles
Sey.
Seychelles Law Reports
Seych. L. R., S.L.R.
Seymour on Merchant Shipping Acts
Sey. Merch. Sh.
Shadforth's Reports
Shad.
Shadforth's Reserved Judgments
Sh.
Shale's Decisions and Judgments in Federal Anti-Trust Cases
Shale
Shand's Practice, Court of Sessions, Scotland
Shand Pr.
Shand's Reports (11-41 South Carolina)
Sh., Shand
Shankland's Tennessee Public Statutes
Shankland's St.
Shannon's Tennessee Annotated Code
Shannon's Code
Shannon's Tennessee Cases
Ten. Cas., Shan. Cas., Tenn. Cas. (Shannon)
Shannon's Unreported Tennessee Cases
Shan., Tenn. Cas., Shannon Cas. (Tenn.)
Shareholder
Shrhldr
Sharkey's Practice of Election Committees
Shark. Elec.
Sharp on Congregational Courts
Sharp. Cong. Ct.
Sharpstein's Insurance Digest
Sharp. Ins. Dig.

Sharswood and Budd's Leading Cases of Real Property
Shars. & B. Lead. Cas. Real Prop., Am. L. C. R. P.

Sharswood's Commercial Law
Shars. Comm. L.

Sharswood's Edition of Blackstone's Commentaries
Shars. Black., Shars. Bl. Comm.

Sharswood's Lectures on the Profession of the Law
Shars. Law Lec.

Sharswood's Legal Ethics
Shars. Leg. Eth.

Sharswood's Table of Cases, Connecticut
Shars. Tab. Ca.

Shaw and Dunlop's Scotch Court of Session Reports, 1st Series
Shaw & D., Shaw & Dunl., Sh. & Dunl.

Shaw and Maclean's Scotch Appeal Cases
S. & M., Sh. & Macl., Shaw & M., Shaw & M. Sc. App. Cas. (Scot.), Shaw & Macl., Shaw & M. Sc. App. Cas.

Shaw, Dunlop and Bell's Scotch Court of Sessions, 1st Series
Shaw, D. & B., Shaw, Dunl. & B., S., S. & D., S.D. & B.

Shaw, Dunlop, and Bell's Supplement, containing House of Lords Decisions for Scotland
S.D. & B. Sup., S.D. & B. Supp., Shaw, D. & B. Supp.

Shaw, Wilson and Courtenay's Scotch Appeals Reports, House of Lords
Sh.W. & C., Shaw, W. & C.

Shaw's Appeal Cases, House of Lords, Appeals from Scotland
Sh., Shaw App., Shaw, H.L., Shaw Sc. App. Cas., Shaw, Sh. App., S. App., S.

Shaw's Criminal Cases, Justiciary Court, Scotland
Shaw Crim. Cas.Sh. Crim. Cas.

Shaw's Digest of Decisions, Scotland
Shaw Dig., Sh Dip.

Shaw's Ellis on Insurance
Shaw Ell. Ins.

Shaw's (G.B.) Reports (10-11 Vermont)
Sh., Shaw., Shaw (G.B.), Shaw (Vt.)

Shaw's (John) Justiciary Reports, Scotland
J.Shaw, Shaw Jus.J., J.Shaw Just.

Shaw's Justiciary Cases, Scotland
Sh. Jus., Shaw, S.Just., Sh. Just., Shaw. P., P. Shaw, Sh.

Shaw's Parish Law
Shaw P.L.

Shaw's Scotch Appeals, House of Lords
Sh. Sc. App.

Shaw's Scotch Court of Session Cases, 1st Series
S., Sh., Sh. Ct. of Sess., Shaw, Shaw Dec.

Shaw's Scotch Teind Court Reports
Shaw T. Cas., Shaw T.C., S. Teind., Shaw Teind, Sh. Teind Ct., Sh., Shaw

Shaw's (W.G.) Reports (30-35 Vermont)
Sh., Shaw, Shaw (W.G.), Shaw (Vt.)

Shearman and Redfield on the Law of Negligence
Sh. & R. Neg., Shearm. & Red. Neg., S. & R. Neg., S. & R. on Neg., Shear. & R. Neg.

Shearwood on Contracts
Shear. Cont.

Shearwood on Personal Property
Shear. Pers. Pr.

Shearwood on Real Property
Shear. R. Pr.

Shearwood's Bar Examinations
Shear. Bar Ex.

Shearwood's Student's Guide to the Bar
Shear. St. G.

Sheil's Cape Times Law Reports, South Africa
Sh., Sheil., (See also Shiel's Cape Colony Reports)

Sheil's Sketches of the Irish Bar
Sheil Ir. Bar

Sheldon on Real Property Statutes
Shel. R. Pr. St.

Sheldon on Subrogation
Sheld. Subr.

Sheldon's Reports, Superior Court of Buffalo, New York
Sh., Sheld., Sheldon, Buff. Super. Ct., Buff. Super. Ct. (N.Y.)

Shelford on Bankrupt and Insolvency Law
Shel. Bank.

Shelford on Highways
Shel. High.

Shelford on Joint Stock Companies
Shelf. J. St. Cos., Shel. J. St. Com.

Shelford on Lunacy
Shelf. Lun., Shel.Lun.

Shelford on Marriage and Divorce
Shelf. Mar. & Div., Shel. M. & D.

Shelford on Mortmain and Charitable Uses
Shel. Mort.

Shelford on Probate, Legacy etc.
Shel. Prob.

Shelford on Railways
Shel. Ry.

Shelford on Wills
Shel. Wills, Shel. Will

Shelley's Cases, (1 Coke's Reports)
Shel. Ca.

Sheneman's California Foreclosure: Law and Practice
CF

Shepherd's Alabama Reports
Shepherd, Sh., Shep.

Shepherd's Alabama Select Cases
Shep. Sel. Cas., Shep. Touch., Sheph. Sel. Cas.

Shepley's Reports (13-18 and 21-30 Maine)
Shepley, Sh., Shep.

Sheppard's Abridgment
Shep. Abr.

Sheppard's Action on the Case
Shep. Act.

Sheppard's Cases of Slander, etc.
Shep. Cas.

Sheppard's Precedent of Precedents
Shep. Prec.

Sheppard's Touchstone
Touch.

Sheppard's Touchstone, by Preston
Prest. Shep. T.

Sheridan's Practice, King's Bench
Sher. Pr.

Sheriff
Sh.

Sheriff Court District Court, Scotland
Sh. Ct.

Sheriff Court Reports, Scotland
Sh. Ct. Rep., Sher. Ct. Rep.

Sheriff's Court
Sh. C.

Sherman's Marine Insurance
Sher. Mar. Ins.

Sherman's Products Liability
PL

Shiel's Cape Colony Reports, South Africa
Shiel. (See also Sheil's Cape Times Law Reports)

Shiffman's Medical Malpractice: Handling General Surgery Cases
MMGS

Shillman's Workmen's Compensation Cases, Ireland
Shill. W.C.

Shingle, Philadelphia Bar Association
Shingle

Shinn's Treatise on American Law of Replevin
Shinn, Repl.

Ship Repairs Maintenance Order, National Shipping Authority Maritime Administration
SRM

Shipping
Ship.

Shipping Gazette
Ship. Gaz.

Shipping Regulations, Pike and Fisher
Shipping Reg. (P & F)

Shipp's Reports (66-67 North Carolina)
Sh., Shipp

Shirley's Dartmouth College Case
Shir. D.C. Ca.

Shirley's Leading English Crown Cases
Shirl. L.C.

Shirley's Magisterial Law
Shir. Mag. L.

Shirley's Reports (49-55 New Hampshire)
Sh.,Shirley, Shirl.

Shirley's Sketch of the Criminal Law
Shir. Cr. L.

Shoenfield's Legal Negotiations
LN

Shome's Law Reporter, India
Shome L. R.

Shortt on Informations, Criminal, Quo Warranto, Mandamus, and Prohibition
Shortt, Inform., Shortt. Inf.

Shortt on Works of Literature
Sh. Lit., Shortt Lit., Sh. Litt.

Shortt's Law of Copyright
Shortt Copy.

Shower's English King's Bench Reports
Shower K.B., Shower K.B. (Eng.), Sh., Show., Show. K.B.

Shower's English King's Bench Reports, Butts' edition
Butts Sh.

Shower's Parliamentary Cases, England
Show., Show. Parl. Cas., Show. P.C, Shower P.C. (Eng.), Sh.

Shrady on Suicide and Intemperance in Life Insurance
Shr. Sui.

Shumaker and Longsdorf's Cyclopedic Dictionary
Cyclop. Dict.

Shuman's Psychiatric and Psychological Evidence
PPE
Si De Ka Quarterly
S.D.K.
Sickels' Opinions of the New York Attorneys-General
Sick. Op.
Sickels' Reports (46-85 New York)
Sick.
Sickels' United States Mining Laws and Decisions
Sick. Min. Dec.
Siderfin's English King's Bench Reports
Sid., Sid. (Eng.)
Sidney on Government
Sid. Gov.
Sierra Leone Full Court Reports
S.L.F.C.
Sierra Leone Law Recorder
S.L.L.R.
Signs
Signs
Sill on Composition in Bankruptcy
Sill Comp.
Silver Tax Division, Internal Revenue Bulletin
Sil.
Silvernail's New York Citations
Silv. Cit., Silv.
Silvernail's New York Court of Appeals Reports
Silv. Ct. App., Silvernail's N.Y.Rep., Sil. (Ct. of Ap.), Silv. A., Silv. App., Silv., Silv. Ct. App. (N.Y.)
Silvernail's New York Supreme Court Reports
S.S., Silv., Silv. Sup., Sil. (Sup. Ct.), Silv. (Sup. Ct.)

Silvernail's Reports (9-14 New York Criminal Reports)
Silv.
Silvernail's Unreported Cases, New York
Silv. Unrep.
Simeon on Elections
Sim. Elect.
Simes and Smith on the Law of Future Interests
Simes & S., Future Interests
Simmons and Conover's Reports (99-100 Wisconsin)
Sim. & C.
Simmons on Courts-Martial
Sim.Ct.M.
Simmons' Reports (95-97 and 99 Wisconsin)
Sim.
Simmons' Wisconsin Digest
Sim. Dig.
Simon on Law Relating to Railway Accidents
Sim. Ry. Acc.
Simonds's Digest of Patent Office Decisions
Sim. Dig. Pat. Dec.
Simonds' Law of Design Patents
Sim. Des. Pat.
Simond's Patent Law
Sim. Pat. L.
Simons and Stuart's English Chancery Reports
Sim. & S., Sim. & St., Sim. & Stu. (Eng.), Sim. & Stu., S. & S., Sim.
Simons' English Reports
Sim. (Eng.)
Simons' English Vice-Chancery Reports, New Series
Sim. N.S., Sim. N.S. (Eng.)
Simons' Law of Interpleader
Sim. Int.

Simon's Tax Cases, England
Simon's T.C.
Simplified Employee Pension
SEP
Simpson on Infants
Simp. Inf.
Sinclair's Manuscript Decisions, Scotch Session Cases
Sinclair
Sind Law Reporter, India
S.L.R.
Sind Sudder Court Reports, India
S.S.C.R.
Sind, Pakistan
Sind, Pak.
Sine Fraude Sua (without fraud on his part) (lat.)
S.f.s.
Singapore
Sing.
Singapore Law Reports
S.L.R.
Singapore Law Review
Sing. L.R., Singapore L. Rev.
Singer's Probate Cases, Pennsylvania
Singer Prob. Cas. (Pa.), Singers
Sinking Fund
S.F.
Sittings for Middlesex at Nisi Prius
Middx.Sit.
Skene's de Verborum Significatione
Skene de Verb.Sign.
Skidmore's Mining Statutes
Skid. Min.
Skillern on Environmental Protection: The Legal Framework
EP

Skillman's New York Police Reports
Burlesque Reps., Skill. Pol. Rep.
Skinker's Reports (65-79 Missouri)
Skinker
Skinner's English King's Bench Reports
Skinner, Skinner (Eng.), Skin.
Slade's Compilation of the Statutes of Vermont
Sl.St., Slade's St.
Slade's Reports (15 Vermont)
Slade
Slip Opinions
Slip op.
Sloan on Landlord and Tenant
Sloan L. & T.
Sloan's Legal Register
Sloan Leg. Reg.
Slovene
Sl
Smale and Giffard's English Chancery Reports
Sm. & G., Sma. & Giff., Smale & G., S. & G.
Small Business
S.B.
Small Business Administration
SBA
Small Business Investment Companies
SBIC
Small Cause Court
S.C.C.
Small Defense Plants Administration
S.D.P.A.

Smedes and Marshall's Chancery Reports, Mississippi
S. & Mar. Ch., S. & M., S. & M. Ch. Rep., S. & M. Ch. R., Smeade & Marshall Ch., Smedes & M. Ch., Smedes and Marshall's Chy.-Repts., S. & M. Ch., S. & M. Chy., Smed. & M. Ch., Smed. & M., Smedes & M. (Miss.), S. & Mar., Sm. & M., Sm. & M. Ch., S. & M., Sme. & M.

Smethurst on Locus Standi
Smeth.L.S.

Smith
Sm.

Smith and Bates' American Railway Cases
Sm. & B.R.R. Cas., Smith & B., Smith & B.R.R.C., Smith & B.R.C.

Smith and Batty's Irish King's Bench Reports
Smi. & Bat., Smith & Bat., Smith & B., Sm. & Bat., S. & B.

Smith and Guthrie's Missouri Appeal Reports (81-101 Missouri Appeals)
Smith & G., Sm. & G.

Smith and Heiskell's Tennessee Reports
Smith & H.

Smith and Sager's Drainage Cases
Sm. & S.

Smith and Soden's Landlord and Tenant
Sm. & Sod. L. & T.

Smith-Hurd's Illinois Annotated Statutes
S.H.A., Ill. Ann. Stat., Smith-Hurd Ann.St., Smith-Hurd

Smith on Constitutional and Statutory Construction
Sm. Const. Cons.

Smith on Contracts
Smith, Cont., Sm. Con.

Smith on Conveyancing
Sm. Conv.

Smith on Ecclesiastical Courts
Sm. Ecc. Cts.

Smith on English Registration
Smith

Smith on Executory Interest
Sm.Ex.Int., Smith, Ext. Int.

Smith on Forensic Medicine
Sm.For.Med.

Smith on Joint-Stock Companies
Sm. J. St. Comp.

Smith on Mercantile Law
Smith, Merc. Law, Sm. Merc. L.

Smith on the Law of Real and Personal Property
Sm. R. & P.Prop.

Smith on the Laws of Patents
Smith Pat., Sm. Pat.

Smith (Sir Thomas), De Republica Anglica (The Commonwealth of England and the Manner of Government Thereof)
Smith de Rep. Angl.

Smith's Actions at Law
Smith, Act., Sm.Act.

Smith's Admiralty Practice
Sm. Adm. Pr.

Smith's, (C.L.), Registration Cases, England
Smith, Smith Reg., Smith Reg. Cas.

Smith's Chancery Practice
Sm. Ch. Pr., Smith, Ch. Pr.

Smith's Chancery Rules
Smith Rules

Smith's Circuit Courts- Martial Reports, Maine
Sm.C.C.M., Smith, C.C.M.

Smith's Condensed Alabama Reports
Sm. Cond. Ala., Smith Cond., Smith Cond. Rep.

Smith's Dictionary of Greek and Roman Antiquities
Smith, Dict. Antiq.

Smith's (E.B.) Reports (21-47 Illinois Appeals
Smith

Smith's (E.D.) New York Common Pleas Reports
E.D. Smith's R., E.D. Smith, E.D.S., E.D. Smith R., E.D. Smith's C.P.R., Sm. E.D., Smith C. P., E.D. Smith (N.Y.), Smith, E.D.

Smith's (E.H.) New York Reports (147-162 New York Court of Appeals)
Smith E.H.

Smith's (E.P.) Reports (15-27 and 147-162 New York Court of Appeals)
Smith N.Y.

Smith's Education for the English Bar
Sm.Ed.

Smith's Election Cases, United States
Smith Cong. Election Cases

Smith's Elements of Law
Sm.El.

Smith's English King's Bench Reports
Smith K.B., Sm. K.B., Sm.Eng.

Smith's Forms of Procedure
Sm. Forms

Smith's Indiana Reports
Smith, Sm. Ind., Smith Ind., Smith's (Ind.) R., Smith's R.

Smith's Inquiry into the Nature and Causes of the Wealth of Nations
Smith, Wealth Nat.

Smith's (J.P.), English King's Bench Reports
J.P. Smith, J.P. Smith (Eng.), Smith, J.P. Sm.

Smith's (J.W.) Manual of Equity
Sm.Eq.

Smith's Landlord and Tenant
Sm. L. & T.

Smith's Law Journal, London, England
Smith, L.J., L.J. Sm.

Smith's Law of Receivers
Smith Rec.

Smith's Law of Reparation
Smith Repar.

Smith's Laws of Pennsylvania
Smith, Laws Pa., Smith's Laws

Smith's Lawyer and His Profession
Sm. Lawy.

Smith's Leading Cases
S.L.C., Sm. L.C., Smith L.C., Smith, Lead. Cas., Smith's Lead. Cas.

Smith's Leading Cases on Commercial Law
Sm.L.Cas.Com.L.

Smith's Manual of Common Law
Smith, Com. Law, Sm.Com.L.

Smith's Manual of Equity
Sm. Man. Eq.

Smith's Manual of Equity Jurisprudence
Smith, Man. Eq. Jur.

Smith's Master and Servant
Sm. M. & S.

Smith's Medical Malpractice: Psychiatric Care
MMPC
Smith's Negligence
Sm. Neg.
Smith's New Hampshire Reports
Smith, Smith N.H., Cheshire, Grafton, Merrimack., Rock., Rockingham, Strafford, Sullivan
Smith's (P.F.) Pennsylvania State Reports
Smith, Smith Pa., Smith P.F., P.F. Smith, P.F.S.
Smith's Principles of Equity
Sm. Pr. Eq., Sm.Eq.
Smith's Probate Law and Practice
Sm. Prob. L.
Smith's Reporter (7 and 12 Heiskell's Tennessee Reports)
Smith
Smith's Reports (54-62 California)
Smith
Smith's Reports (61-84 Maine)
Sm. Me., Smith Me., Smith
Smith's Reports (81-83 Missouri Appeals)
Smith
Smith's Reports (2-4 South Dakota)
Smith
Smith's Reports (1-11 Wisconsin)
Smith, Smith Wis.
Smith's Scotch Poor Law
Sm. Poor L.
Smith's Statute Law
Sm. Stat. Law
Smithsonian Institution Traveling Exhibition Service
S.I.T.E.S.
Smithsonian Science Information Exchange, Inc.
SSIE

Smoult's Collection of Orders, Notes of Cases, India
Smoult
Smyth on the Law of Homestead and Exemptions
Sm.Homest., Smy. Home.
Smythe and Bourke's Irish Marriage Cases
Smy. & B.
Smythe's Irish Common Pleas Reports
Smy., Smythe
Sneed's Kentucky Decisions (2 Kentucky) (also known as Printel Decisions)
Ky. Dec., Ken. Dec., Pr. Dec., Prin. Dec., Sneed, Sneed Dec.
Sneed's Reports (33-37 Tennessee)
Sneed, Sneed Tenn., Sneed (Tenn.) Rep.
Snell's Principles in Equity
Snell, Eq.
Snow and Winstanley's Chancery Practice
Sn. & W. Ch.
Snow's Reports (3 Utah)
Snow
Snyder on Mines and Mining
Snyder, Mines
Snyder on Religious Corporations
Sny. Rel. Corp.
Snyder's Notaries' and Commissioners' Manual
Sny. Not. Man.
Social
Soc.
Social Action and the Law
Soc. Act. & L., Soc. Action & L.
Social and Economic Statistics Administration
SESA
Social and Labour Bulletin
Soc. & Lab. Bull.

Social and Rehabilitation Service
  SRS
Social Economisch Wetgeving Tijdschrift Voor Europees en Economisch Recht, Netherlands
  Soc. Econ. Wetgeving
Social Economist
  Soc. Econ.
Social Justice
  Soc. Just.
Social Responsibility
  Soc. Resp., Soc. Sci.
Social Security
  Soc. Sec., S.S.
Social Security Act
  S.S.A.
Social Security Acts Amendments
  S.S.A.A.
Social Security Administration
  S.S.A.
Social Security and Medicare
  Soc. Sec.
Social Security Board
  SSB
Social Security Board Ruling
  SSB
Social Security Bulletin
  Soc. Sec. Bull.
Social Security Ruling on Old-age, Survivors, and Disability Insurance Benefits, United States Internal Revenue Bureau
  SSR
Social Security Tax Ruling, Internal Revenue Bulletin
  S.S.T.
Social Security Taxes, Prentice-Hall
  P.-H Soc. Sec. Taxes
Social Service Review
  Soc. Serv. Rev.

Social Services
  Soc. Ser.
Socialist
  Socialist
Society
  Soc., Soc'y
Society for Computers and Law
  S.C.L.
Society for the Prevention of Cruelty to Animals
  SPCA
Society of Conservative Lawyers
  S.C.L.
Society of Labour Lawyers
  S.L.L.
Society of Local Government Barristers
  S.L.G.B.
Society of Public Teachers of Law
  S.P.T.L.
Sociological
  Soc.
Sociology
  Soc.
Software Law Journal
  Software L. J.
Soil and Water Conservation Districts
  Soil & Water Conserv. Dist.
Soil Conservation Service
  S.C.S.
Solar Law Report
  Solar L. Rep.
Solicitor[s]
  Sol., Solic., Solr(s).
Solicitor General
  S.G., Sol. G., Sol. Gen.
Solicitor Quarterly
  Sol. Q.
Solicitors' Clerks' Gazette
  Sol. Cl. Gaz.

Solicitor's Journal
  Sol. J.,S.J., Solic. J., Sol. Jo.
  (Eng.), Solicitor's J.
Solicitors' Journal and Reporter
  Sol. J. & R.
**Solicitor's Law Opinion, United
States Internal Revenue Bu-
reau**
  L.O., Sol. Op.
**Solicitor's Law Opinion, United
States Internal Revenue Serv-
ice**
  O., Sol. Op.
**Solicitor's Managing Clerks' Ga-
zette**
  Sol. Man. Cl. Gaz.
**Solicitor's Memorandum, United
States Internal Revenue Bu-
reau**
  S.M.
Solicitor's Opinion
  S., Sol. Op.
**Solicitor's Recommendation,
United States Internal Reve-
nue Bureau**
  S.R.
Solid Waste Disposal Act
  SWDA
Solomon Islands
  Solom.
**Soloman's Court of Request Ap-
peals, Ceylon**
  Sol.
**Soma's Computer Technology
and the Law**
  CTL
Somalia
  Somal.
Somalia Law Reports
  Som. L. R.

Somerset Legal Journal
  Somerset L.J., Som., Som. Leg.
  J. (Pa.), Som. L.J., Somerset Le-
  gal Journal
**Somersetshire Pleas (Civil and
Criminal) edited by Chadwyck,
Healey and Landon (Somerset
Record Society Publications,
11, 36, 41, 44)**
  Sm. Pl., Som. Pl.
Somner on Gavelkind
  Somn.on Gav.
**Soule's Dictionary of English
Synonymes**
  Soule, Syn.
South[ern]
  S., So.
South Africa
  S. Afr., S.A.
**South Africa Law Reports, Appel-
late Division**
  App. D.
**South Africa Law Reports, Gri-
qualand West Local Division**
  G.W.L.D.
South Africa Official Reports
  O.R.
**South Africa, Selected Decisions
of the Native Appeal Court for
the Central Division**
  N.A.C. (C.)
**South African Bankers, Journal,
Cape Town, South Africa**
  S. Afr. Bankers J.
**South African Journal of Crimi-
nal Law and Criminology**
  S. Afr. J. Crim. L.
South African Law Journal
  S. Afr. L.J., South Afr. L.J., S.A.
  L.J., So. Afr. L.J., So. African
  L.J.

South African Law Reports
S. Afr. L.R., S.A., S.A.L.R., So. Afr. L. R.
So. African L.

South African Law Reports Appellate Division
S. Afr. L. R. App., A.D.

South African Law Reports, Cape Provincial Division
S.A. Law Reports, C.P., S.A. Law Reports, C.P.D., S.A.L.R.C.P., C.P.D.

South African Law Reports, Eastern Districts Local Division
E.D.L.

South African Law Reports, Griqualand West Local Division
G.W.D.

South African Law Reports, Natal Province Division
N., N.L.R., S.A. Law Reports, N.P.D., N.P.D.

South African Law Reports, Orange Free State Provincial Division
O.P.D., O., S.A. L. Reports,O.P.D.

South African Law Reports, South West African Reports
S.A.L.R., S.W.A.

South African Law Reports, Transvaal Provincial Division
T.P.D.

South African Law Reports, Witwatersrand High Court
W.H.C.

South African Law Reports, Witwatersrand Local Division
W.L.D.

South African Law Review
S. Afr. L. Rev.

South African Law Review (Butterworth's)
Butt.S.A. Law Rev., Butterworth's S.A.Law Review, Butterworth's South Afr. L.Rev.

South African Law Times
S. Afr. L. T., S.A.L.T., So. Afr. L.T.

South African Prize Cases
So. Afr. Prize Cas.

South African Reports, High Court
Sth. Afr. Rep.

South African Republic High Court Reports
H.C.R.S.A.R., S.A.R.

South African Republic Official Reports
O.R.S.A.R.

South African Supreme Court Appellate Division Reports
A.D.

South African Tax Cases
S. Afr. Tax, S. Afr. Tax Cas., S.A. Tax Cas., S.A.T.C.

South African Yearbook of International Law
S. Afr.Y.I. L.

South America
S. Am.

South Australia
S. Aust., S. Austl., S. Austr., S.A.

South Australian Acts
S. Austl. Acts, Acts S. Austl.

South Australian Acts and Ordnances
S.Austl.Acts & Ord., Acts S. Austl.

South Australian Criminal Law Reform Committee
S.A.C.L.R.C.

South Australian Industrial Reports
I.R., S.A.I.R., Aust. Indus. R.

South Australian Law
S. Aust. L., S. Austr. L.

South Australian Law Reform Committee
S.A.L.R.C.

South Australian Law Reports
S. Aust. L.R., S.A.L.R., So. Aust. L.R., So. Austr. L., Sou. Aus. L. R., South Aus. L. R., So. Aus. L.R., S. Austl. L.R.

South Australian Licensing Court Reports
S.A.L.C.R.

South Australian Planning Reports
S.A.P.R., S. Austl. St. R., S. Austl.

South Australian Public General Acts
Pub. Gen. Acts S. Austl., S. Austl. Pub. Gen. Acts

South Australian Reports
S.A.R., S.Austl. St. R., S. Austl.

South Australian State Reports
S.A.S.R., So. Austr. St.

South Australian Statutes
S. Austl. Stat., S.Austl.Sess.Stat.

South Carolina
S.C., S.Car., So. Car., South Car.

South Carolina Acts and Joint Resolutions
S.C.Acts

South Carolina Annual Report for the Attorney General
S.C.Ann.Rep.Att'y.Gen.

South Carolina Bar
SCB

South Carolina Bar Association
S.C. Bar Assn.

South Carolina Bar Association Reports
So. Car. B. A. Rep.

South Carolina Constitution
S.C. Const.

South Carolina Constitutional Court Reports (by Treadway, by Mill, or by Harper)
Rep. Const. Ct., So. Car. Const., See also: Treadway's South Carolina Constitutional Reports, Mill's South Carolina Constitutional Reports, and Harper's South Carolina Law Reports.

South Carolina Digest of the Public Statute Law
Brev.Dig.

South Carolina Equity Reports
S.C.Eq.

South Carolina Law Journal
S.C. L.J., So. Car. L.J.

South Carolina Law Quarterly
S.C. L.Q., So. Car. L.Q.

South Carolina Law Reports
S.C.L., S.Car. R., So. Car. R.

South Carolina Law Review
S.C. L. Rev., S.C. L.R., So. Car. L. Rev., South Carolina L. Rev.

South Carolina Public Service Commission Reports
S.C.P.S.C.

South Carolina Reports
S.C., S.Car., S.C.R., So. Car., So.C., South Car., S.Ca.

South Carolina Unemployment Compensation Commission Decisions
S.C.U.C.C.Dec.

South Carolina Unemployment Compensation Commission Reports of Hearings
S.C.U.C.C.R.

South Dakota
    S.D., S. Dak.
South Dakota Administrative
    Rules
    S.D. Admin. R.
South Dakota Attorney General
    Biennial Report
    Biennial Rep. S.D. Att'y Gen.
South Dakota Bar Journal
    S.D. B. Jo., So. Dak. B. Jo.
South Dakota Biennial Report of
    the State Attorney General
    Biennial Rep.S.D.Att'y Gen.
South Dakota Board of Railroad
    Commissioners Opinions
    S.D.R.C. Ops.
South Dakota Codified Laws
    S.D. Codified Laws
South Dakota Codified Laws An-
    notated
    S.D. Codified Laws Ann.
South Dakota Compiled Laws
    SDCL
South Dakota Compiled Laws An-
    notated
    S.D., S.D. Comp. Laws Ann.,
    S.D.Compiled Laws Ann.
South Dakota Constitution
    S.D. Const.
South Dakota Law Review
    S.D. L. Rev., So. Dak. L. Rev.,
    South Dak. L. Rev., South Da-
    kota L. Rev.
South Dakota Railroad Commis-
    sion
    S.D.R.C.
South Dakota Register
    S.D. Admin. Reg.
South Dakota Reports
    S. Dak., S.D.
South Dakota Session Laws
    S.D. Sess. Laws

South Dakota State Bar Journal
    S.D. St. B.J.
South Dakota Uniform Probate
    Code
    S.D. Uniform Prob. Code
Southeast
    S.E.
Southeastern Reporter
    Southeastern Rep., S.E., S., So.
    East. Rep.
Southeastern Reporter, Second
    Series
    S.E. 2d
South Georgia and the South
    Sandwich Islands
    S. Georg. & S. Sandwich Is.
South Jersey Law School Dictum
    So. Jersey L.S. Dictum.
South Pacific Commission
    SPC
South Pacific Law Review
    S. Pac. L. Rev., S. Pac. L.R.
South Texas Law Journal
    S. T. L.J., S. Tex. L.J., S. Texas
    L.J., So. Tex. L.J., South Texas
    L.J.
South Texas Law Review
    S. Tex. L. Rev.
Southampton Court Leet Records
    Hearnshaw
Southard's New Jersey Law Re-
    ports
    Southard
Southeast Asia Treaty Organiza-
    tion
    SEATO
Southeastern Bankruptcy Law In-
    stitute
    SBLI
Southern California Law Review
    S. Calif. Law Rev., S. Ca.L.R.,
    S.Cal. L. Rev., So. Cal. L.R., So.
    Calif. L. Rev., South Calif. Rev.

Southern California Review of Law and Women's Studies
S. Cal. Rev. L. & Women's Stud.

Southern California Tax Institute
S. Cal. Tax Inst.

Southern District
S.D.

Southern Illinois University Law Journal
S. Ill. U. L.J., So. Ill. L.J., So. Ill. U. L.J., South. Ill. U. L.J.

Southern Law Journal
South. L.J., South. Law J.

Southern Law Journal and Reporter
So. L.J., South. L.J. & Rep., South. Law J. & Rep., South. Law J.

Southern Law Quarterly
So. L.Q.

Southern Law Review
South. L. Rev., South. Law Rev., So. L. R., So. L. Rev., So. L. Rev., S.L.R.

Southern Law Review, New Series
South. L. Rev. N.S., So. L. Rev. N.S., South. Law Rev. N.S., So. L. R. N.S.

Southern Law Times
So. L. T., So. Law T.

Southern Lawyer
So. Law

Southern Legislative Conference
SLC

Southern Methodist University
SMU

Southern Methodist University Law Review
SMU L. Rev.

Southern Reporter
S., S. Rep., So. Rep., So. Repr., Southern, Southern Rep., South., So.

Southern Reporter, Second Series
So. 2d

Southern Rhodesia
S.R.

Southern Rhodesia High Court Reports
S.R., S.R., H.C.R.

Southern Rhodesia Native Appeal Court Reports
N.A. So. Rhod.

Southern Rhodesia Reports
Burns-Begg

Southern University Law Review
So. U. L. Rev., So. Univ. L. Rev., South. U. L. Rev., S.U. L. Rev.

Southwest[ern]
Sw.

Southwestern Law Journal
S.L.J., So. West. L.J., Southwestern L.J., S.W. Law J., Sw. L.J.

Southwestern Law Journal and Reporter
Southw. L.J., S.W. L.J.

Southwestern Law Review
S.W. L. Rev.

Southwestern Legal Foundation
SLF

Southwestern Legal Foundation Institution on Oil and Gas Law and Taxation
Sw. Legal Found. Inst. on Oil & Gas L. & Tax.

Southwestern Political Science Quarterly
S.W. Pol. Sci. Q.

Southwestern Reporter
S. W. Repr., So. West Rep., S.W. R., S.W. Rep., S.W.

Southwestern Reporter Second Series
S.W.2d

Southwestern University Law Review
Southwest. U. L. Rev., Southwestern U. L. Rev., Southwestern Univ. L. Rev., Sw. U. L. Rev.

Southwestern University School of Law
SWUSL

Soviet Jewry Law Review
Soviet Jewry L. Rev.

Soviet Law and Government
Soviet L. & Govt., Soviet Law & Gov't

Soviet Socialist Republic
S.S.R.

Soviet Statutes and Decisions
Sov. Stat. & Dec., Soviet Stat. & Dec.

Soviet Studies
Soviet Stud.

Soviet Yearbook of International Law
Soviet Y. B. Int'l L.

Space Law
Space L.

Spalding on Copyright
Spald. Cop.

Spanish
S.

Sparks' Rangoon Decisions, British Burmah
Rang. Dec.

Sparks' Reports, British Burmah.
Sparks.

Spaulding's Reports (71-73 Maine)
Spaulding.

Spearman on Highways
Spear. High.

Spear's Law of Extradition
Spear Ext.

Spears' (or Speers') South Carolina Equity and Law Reports
Sp. Ch., Spear Ch., SP. Eq., Spear Eq., Spears Eq., Speers Eq., Spear or Speer, Speers., sp., Spears, Speers Eq. (S.C.), Spears L. (S.C.)

Special
Spec.

Special Acts
Sp. Acts

Special and Selected Law Cases
Sp. & Sel. Cas.

Special Appeal
Sp.A.

Special Bulletin
S.B.

Special Commissioner
Sp.C.

Special Committee
Sp. Com.

Special Court-Martial, United States Air Force
A.C.M.S.

Special Court-Martial, United States Coast Guard
CGCMS

Special Court-Martial, United States Navy
Sp. CM

Special Court Regional Railroad Reorganization Act
Regional Rail Reorg. Ct., Sp. Ct. R.R.R.A.

Special Criminal Court
Sp. Cr. Ct.

Special Disbursing Agent, United States Bureau of Indian Affairs
S.D.A.

Special Lectures of the Law Society of Upper Canada
Lect. L.S.U.C., Lectures L.S.U.C.

Special or Local Assessments
Spec. A.
Special Regulation, United States Army
S.R.
Special Ruling
Sp. Rul.
Special Session
Sp. Sess.
Special Tax Ruling, United States Internal Revenue Service
Sp. Tax. Rul.
Special Term
Sp. T.
Specific Performance
Spec. Perf.
Specification
Spec.
Speculum Juris, Forte Hare, South Africa
Speculum Juris
Spelling on Extraordinary Relief in Equity and in Law
Spell. Extr. Rel.
Spelling on Injunctions and Other Extraordinary Remedies
Spell. Extr. Rem.
Spelman on Feuds
Spel. Feuds.
Spelman's Glossarium Archailogicum
Spelm., Spelman.
Spelman's Glossary
Sp. Glos., Spel. Gl.
Spelman's Law Tracts
Spel. L.T.
Spelman's Reports, Manuscript, English King's Bench
Spel. Rep
Spence on Copyright of Designs
Spence Cop.
Spence on Patentable Inventions
Spence Pat. Inv.

Spencer's Reports (10-20 Minnesota)
Spenc., Spencer
Spencer's Reports (20 New Jersey Law)
Spen. (N.J.), Spenc., Spencer
Spence's Equitable Jurisdiction of the Court of Chancery
Spence, Ch., Spence, Eq. Jur.
Spence's Origin of Laws
Spence Or. L.
Spens' Select Cases, Bombay
Spens Sel. Cas.
Spike on Master and Servant
Spike M. & S.
Spinivasan's Reports of Income Tax Cases, India
I.T.C.
Spinks' Admiralty Prize Cases, England
Spinks Prize Cas. (Eng.), Spinks, Prize Cas., Spinks, P.C., Sp. Pr. Cas.
Spinks' English Ecclesiastical and Admiralty Reports
Sp., Eccl. & Adm., E. & A., Eccl. & Ad., Ecc. & Ad., Sp. Ecc. & Ad., Spinks, Spinks Eccl. & Adm. (Eng.)
Spirit of the Laws by Montesquieu
Sp. Laws
Spooner's Reports (12-15 Wisconsin)
Spoon., Spooner.
Spottiswoode's English Common Law and Equity Reports
Spottis. C.L. & Eq., Spott.C.L. & Eq.
Spottiswoode's English Common Law Reports
Com.Law R., Com. Law Rep., Com.L.R.

Spottiswoode's English Equity Reports
Spott. Eq. Rep., Eq. Rep., Spottis. Eq., Spottisw., Spottisw. Eq.

Spottiswoode's Practicles
Spottis. Pr.

Spottiswoode's Styles
Spottis. St.

Spragens and Fleming's Tax Aspects of Forming and Operating Closely Held Corporations
TAFO

Sprague on International Law
Spr. Int. L.

Sprague's United States District Court (Admiralty) Decisions
Spr., Sprague.

Squibb, on Auctioneers
Squibb Auc.

St. Armand on the Legislative Power of England
St. Arm. Leg. Pow.

St. Christopher (Kitts) - Nevis
St. Chris.-Nevis

St. Clement's Church Case, Philadelphia
St. Clem

St. German's Doctor and Student
St. Ger. D. & S.

St. John's Journal of Legal Commentary
St. John's J. Legal Comment., St. John's J. Legal Comment.

St. John's Law Review
S.J. L. R., St. John's L. Rev.

St. Joseph, Missouri, Public Utilities Commission Reports
St.J. Mo. P.U.C.

St. Louis Bar Journal
St. Louis B.J.

St. Louis Law Review
St. Louis L. Rev.

St. Louis Metropolitan Bar Association Bankruptcy Reporter
BAMSL

St. Louis University Intramural Law Review
St. L. U.Intra. L. Rev.

St. Louis University Law Journal
St. Lou. U. L.J.

St. Mark's Church Case, Philadelphia
St. Mark.

St. Mary's Law Journal
S.M.L.J., St. Mary's L.J.

St. Mary's Law Review
St. Mary's L. Rev.

St. Thomas Law Review
St. Thomas L. Rev.

Stabilization
Stab.

Stafford's Reports (69-71 Vermont)
Stafford.

Stair's Decisions, Court of Session, Scotland
Stair., St., Stair Rep.

Stair's Institutes, Scotland
St., Stair I., Stair. Inst.
Stair's Institutions, Notes and Supplement by Brodie
Bro.St., Bro.Stair, Brod.Stair.

Stair's Principles of the Laws of Scotland
Stair Prin.

Stalman on Election and Satisfaction
Stal. Elect.

Stand's Georgia Practice
Ga. Prac.

Standard Dictionary
Stand. Dict.

Standard Excess Profits Tax Reporter, Commerce Clearing House
Stand. Ex. Prof. Tax. Rep.

Standard Federal Tax Reporter, Commerce Clearing House
CCH Stand. Fed. Tax Rep.,
Stand. Fed. Tax. Rep. (CCH)

Standard Federal Tax Reports, Commerce Clearing House
Stand. Fed. Tax. Rep. (CCH)

Standard Form
S.F.

Standard Georgia Practice
Stand. Ga. Prac.

Standard International Tariff Classification
S.I.T.C.

Standard Metropolitan Statistical Area
SMSA

Standard Pennsylvania Practice
Pa. Prac., Stan. Pa. Prac.,
Stand. Pa. Prac.

Standards of Official Conduct
S.O.C.

Standing Committee
S.C.

Standing Committee of Commonwealth and State Attorneys-General
S.C. of A.G.

Stanford
Stan.

Stanford Environmental Annual
Stan. Env't. Ann.

Stanford Environmental Law Annual
Stan. Envt'l L. Ann., Stan.
Envt'l L. J., Stan. Envtl. L.J.

Stanford Journal of International Law
Stan. J. Int'l L., Stan. J.Intl. L.

Stanford Journal of International Studies
Stanford J. Int'l. Stud., Stan. J.
Int'l. Stud.

Stanford Journal of Law, Gender and Sexual Orientation
Stan. J.L. Gender & Sex Orient.

Stanford Law and Policy Review
Stan. L. & Pol'y Rev.

Stanford Law Review
S.L.R., Stan. L. R., Stan. L.
Rev., Stanford L. Rev., Stn. L.

Stanford Lawyer
Stan. Law.

Stanford's Pleas of the Crown
Stanford

Stanton's Kentucky Digest
Stan. Dig.

Stanton's Reports (11-13 Ohio)
Stanton.

Stanton's Revised Kentucky Statutes
Stanton's Rev. St.

Star Chamber Cases by Crompton, England
Crompt., Cromp.

Star Chamber Cases, England
Star Ch. Ca., St. Ch. Cas., Star
Ch. Cas.

Star Chamber Proceedings
Burn.

Star's Session Cases, Scotland
Star. S.C.

Starkie on Evidence
Stark. Ev., Starkie, Ev.

Starkie on Libel
Stark. Lib.

Starkie on Slander and Libel
Starkie, Sland. & L., Stark. Sl.
& L.

Starkie on Trial by Jury
Stark. Jury Tr.

Starkie's Criminal Law
  Stark. C.L.
Starkie's Criminal Pleading
  Stark. Cr. Pl.
Starkie's English Nisi Prius Reports
  Star., Stark. N.P., Starkie.,
  Starkie's, Starkie (Eng.), Stark.
Starling's East India Criminal Law and Procedure
  Starl. I. Cr. Law
Starr and Curtis' Annotated Illinois Statutes
  Starr & C. Ann. St.
State
  St., State
State Aeronautics Commission
  Aer
State and Local Tax Service, Prentice-Hall
  St. & Loc. Tax Serv. (P-H)
State and Local Taxation
  State Tax.
State and Local Taxes, Bureau of National Affairs
  State & Loc. Taxes, St. & Loc.
  Taxes (BNA)
State and Local Taxes, Prentice-Hall
  P-H State & Local Taxes
State Athletic Commission
  Ath.
State Bar Journal of California
  S. Bar J.
State Bar of Arizona
  SBA
State Bar of Montana
  SBM
State Bar of South Dakota
  SDB
State Bar of Wisconsin Advanced Training Seminars
  WATS

State Bar Review
  St. Bar. Rev.
State Board of Medical Examiners
  Med.
State Court Journal
  St. Ct. J., State Court J.
State Department (for a state)
  S.D., St. Dept.
State Finance
  State Fin.
State Government
  State Gov't
State Income Taxes, Prentice-Hall
  St. Income Taxes (P-H)
State Labor Relations Board
  S.L.R.B.
State, Local and Urban Law Newsletter
  State Locl & Urb. L. Newsl.
State Motor Carrier Guide, Commerce Clearing House
  State Mot. Carr. Guide, St. Mot.
  Carr. Guide (CCH)
State of Louisiana: Acts of the Legislature
  La. Acts
State of Ohio: Legislative Acts Passed and Joint Resolutions Adopted
  Ohio Laws
State of Utah Bulletin
  Utah Admin. Bull
State Papers
  St. P.
State Planning Agency
  SPA
State Printing
  State Print.
State Reporter
  St. Rep.
State Reports
  St. Rep.

State Tax Cases, Commerce Clearing House
St. Tax Cas. (CCH), State Tax Cas., S.T.C.

State Tax Cases Reporter, Commerce Clearing House
St. Tax Cas. Rep. (CCH), CCH State Tax Cas.Rep., State Tax Cas. Rep.

State Tax Cases Reports, Commerce Clearing House
St. Tax Cas. Rep. (CCH)

State Tax Guide, Commerce Clearing House
State Tax Guide (CCH), St. Tax Guide (CCH)

State Tax Reporter, Commerce Clearing House
St. Tax Rep. (CCH)

State Tax Reports, Commerce Clearing House
St. Tax Rep. (CCH)

State Tax Review, Commerce Clearing House
CCH State Tax Rev.

State Teachers Retirement Board
TR

State Trials
S.T., St. Tri., State Tr.

State Trials, New Series
State Tr. N.S.

Statement
Stmt.

Statement of Procedural Rules
S.P.R.

Statham's Abridgment, England
St. Ab., Stath. Abr.

Statistical
Stat.

Statistical Annals
Stat. An.

Statistical Reporting Service
SRS

Statistic[s, al]
Stat.

Statute[s]
S., St., Stat.

Statute Book
S.B.

Statute Law Committee
S.L.C., State. Law. Cttee.

Statute Law Review
Stat. L.R., Statute L. Rev.

Statute Law Revision
S.L.R.

Statute Law Society
S.L.S., Stat. Law Soc.

Statute Modus Levandi Fines
St. Mod. Lev. Fin., Stat. Mod. Lev. Fin.

Statute of Frauds
Stat. F.

Statute of Glocester
St. Gloc., Stat. Glo.

Statute of Limitations
St. Lim.

Statute of Marlbridge
St. Marlb., Stat. Marl.

Statute of Merton
St. Mert., Stat. Mer., Stat. Merl.

Statute of the International Court of Justice
Stat. I.C.J.

Statute of Westminster
St. Westm., Stat. Westm.

Statute of Winchester
Stat. Winch.

Statutes and Amendments to the Code of California
Cal. Stat.

Statutes and Court Decisions, Federal Trade Commission
S. & D.

Statutes and Decisions: Laws of the USSR and its Successor States
Stat. & Dec.

Statutes at Large, England
St.at Large

Statutes at Large, Ruffhead's Edition, England
Ruff.

Statutes at Large, Runnington Ed., England
Runn.

Statutes, Laws, of the Province of Massachusetts
Prov. St.

Statutes of British Columbia
S.B.C.

Statutes of California
Cal. Stats.

Statutes of Canada
Can. Stat., S. of C.

Statutes of Connecticut
R.S. Comp.

Statutes of Nevada
Nev. Stats.

Statutes of New South Wales
N.S.W. Stat., Stat. N.S.W.

Statutes of New Zealand
N.Z. Stat., Stat. N.Z.

Statutes of Province of Quebec (Reign of Victoria)
Q. Vict., Q. Vic.

Statutes of the Province of Canada
Prov. Can. Stat.

Statutes of the Realm
Stat. Realm

Statutes of Western Australia
W. Austl. Stat.

Statutes Revised
S.R., Stat., Stat. Rev.

Statutory Committee
S.C.

Statutory Definition[s]
Stat. Def.

Statutory Instruments
S.I., Stat. Inst., St. Inst.

Statutory Orders and Regulations, Canada
Can. Stat. O. & Regs., Stat. O. & R., S.R. & O.

Statutory Regulations, New Zealand
Stat. Reg. N.Z.

Statutory Rules and Orders and Statutory Instruments Revised, England
S.R. & O. and S.I. Rev., Stat. R. & O. & Stat. Inst. Rev.

Statutory Rules and Orders, England
Stat. R. & O., S.R. & O.

Statutory Rules and Orders of Northern Ireland
Stat. R. & O.N.Ir., Stat. R. & O.N.I.

Statutory Rules, Consolidation, Australia
Austl. Stat. R. Consol.

Staundeforde's King's Prerogative
St. Pr., Staunf. Pr., Staundf. Prerog., Staundef.

Staundeforde's Pleas of the Crown
Staunf. P.C., Staundeforde, Staundef.P.C.

Staundford's Placita Coronae
Staundf. Pl. Cor.

Steamship
S.S.

Stearns on Real Actions
Stearns R.A., Stearns, Real Act.

Stecher's Cases on Agency and Partnership
Stecher, Agency & Partnership

Steer's Parish Law
Steer P.L.

Stein's Cable Television: Handbook and Forms
CTHF

Stephen on Pleading
Steph. Pl.

Stephens' Commentaries on the Laws of England
Steph. Com, St. C., Steph. Comm.

Stephen's Digest of Evidence by Chase
Chase, Steph. Dig. Ev.

Stephen's Digest of the Criminal Law
Steph. Cr., Dip. Crim. Proc., Steph. Crim. Dig., Steph. Dig. Cr. L., Steph. Dig. Cr. Law

Stephen's Digest of the Law of Evidence
Steph. Dig. Ev., Steph. Ev.

Stephen's Digest, New Brunswick Reports
Steph. Dig.

Stephen's General View of the Criminal Law
Steph. Cr. Law., Gen. View Cr. L., Steph. Cr. L., Steph. Gen. View

Stephen's History of Criminal Law
Stephen, H.C.L.

Stephen's Law of Nisi Prius
Steph. N.P.

Stephen's Lectures on History of France
Steph. Lect.

Stephens on Clergy
Steph. Cl.

Stephens on Elections
Steph. Elect.

Stephens on Procurations
Steph. Proc.

Stephens on Slavery
Steph. Slav.

Stephens on the English Constitution
Steph. Const.

Stephens' Supreme Court Decisions, Jamaica
Steph., Stephens

Steph's Joint-Stock Companies in Canada
Steph J. St. Comp.

Stern and Felix-Retzke's Practical Guide to Preventing Legal Malpractice
PLM

Stetson Law Review
Stet. L. Rev., Stetson L. Rev.

Stetson University College of Law
SUCL

Stevens and Benecke on Average
Ben. Av.

Stevens and Benecke on Insurance
Stev. & Ben. Ins.

Stevens and Graham's Reports (98-139 Georgia)
Stev. & G., Stevens & G.

Stevens' New Brunswick Digest
Stev. Dig.

Stevens on Arbitration
Stev. Arb.

Stevens on Average
Stev. Av.

Stewart and Porter's Alabama Supreme Court Reports
Stew. & P., S. & P. (Ala.) Rep., St. & P., St. and Port., Stev. and Porter, Stew. & P. Rep., Stuart & Por., Stuart & Porter, Stur. & Porter

Stewart-Brown's Lancashire and Cheshire Cases in the Court of Star Chamber, England
St. Brown, Stewart-Brown.

Stewart's Alabama Reports
Stew. (Ala.), Stewart (Ala.), Stewart R., Stewt. Rep., Stew., Stewart.

Stewart's Answers to Dirleton's Doubts
Stew. Ans.

Stewart's Digest of Decisions of Law and Equity, New Jersey
Stewart Vice-Adm. (Nov.Sc.), Stew. Dig.

Stewart's Nova Scotia Admiralty Reports
Stew., Stew. Admr., Stew. N.Sc., Stewart., Stew. Adm., Stew. Admr., Stew. V.A.

Stewart's Reports (28-45 New Jersey Equity)
Stew., Stewart., Stew. Eq.

Stewart's Reports (1-10 South Dakota)
Stew., Stewart.

Stiles' Reports (22-29 Iowa)
Stiles., Stiles (Ia.)

Stillingfleet's Discourse on Ecclesiastical Law
Still. Ecc. Law

Stillingfleet's English Ecclesiastical Cases
Still. Eccl. Cas, St. Eccl. Cas., St. Cas., Stil.

Stimson's Law Glossary
Stim. Gloss., Stim. L. Gl., Stim. Law Gloss., Stimson

Stiness' Reports (20-34 Rhode Island)
Stiness.

Stipendiary Magistrate
S.M.

Stipulation[s]
Stip.

Stock
Stk.

Stock and Commodity Exchange
Stock. Ex.

Stock Corporation Law
S.C.L.

Stock on Non Compotes Mentis
Stock Non Com.

Stock Transfer Guide, Commerce Clearing House
Stock Transfer Guide (CCH)

Stockett's Reports (27-53 Maryland)
Stockett

Stockton's New Jersey Equity Reports (9-11 N.J. Equity)
Stock., Stockt., Stockt. Ch.

Stockton's Vice-Admiralty Reports, New Brunswick
Stockt. Vice-Adm., Stockton., Stock.

Stokes on Lien of Attorneys and Solicitors
Stokes L. of Att., Sto. Att. Lien

Stone and Graham's Court of Referees Reports, England
S. & G.

Stone and Graham's Private Bills Reports, England
S. & G., Sto. & G.

Stone and Liebman's Testimonial Privileges
TP

**Stone on Benefit Building Socie-
ties**
Stone Ben. Bdg. Soc.
Stone's Justices' Manual (Annual)
Stone Just. Man., Stone.
Stone's Justices' Practice
Stone Just. Pr.
**Storer and Heard on Criminal
Abortion**
St. & H. Abor., Sto. & H. Cr.
Ab., Stor. & H. Abor.
Storey's Delaware Reports
Sto.
**Stormouth's Dictionary of the
English Language**
Stor. Dict.
Story on Agency
Sto. Ag., Story, Ag.
Story on Bailment
Sto. Bailm., Story, Bailm.
Story on Bills
Sto. Bills, Story, Bills.
Story on Conflict of Laws
Sto. Conf. Law., Story, Confl.
Laws
Story on Contracts
Sto. Con., Sto. Cont., Story,
Cont.
Story on Equity Jurisprudence
Story., Sto. Eq. Jur., Story Eq.
Jur.
Story on Equity Pleadings
Sto. Eq. Pl.
Story on Partnership
Sto. Part., Story, Partn.
**Story on Prize Courts, edited by
Platt**
Sto. Pr.
Story on Promissory Notes
Sto. Pr. Notes, Story, Prom.
Notes

**Story on Sales of Personal Prop-
erty**
Sto. Sales, Story, Sales
**Story's Abridgment of the Consti-
tution**
Sto. Abr. Const.
Story's Civil Pleading
Sto. Pl.
**Story's Commentaries on the Con-
stitution of the United States**
Sto. Comm., Sto. Const., Story,
Comm. Const., Story, Const.
Story's Constitutional Class Book
Sto. Const. Cl. B.
Story's Equity Planning
Story, Eq. Pl.
Story's Miscellaneous Writings
Sto. Miscel. Writ.
**Story's United States Circuit
Court Reports**
Sto., Sto. C.C., Story., Story's
Rep., Story's Circit C.R., St.,
Story Laws., Story U.S. Laws,
William W. Story's Rept., Story
R.
Story's United States Laws
Sto. Laws, Sto. U.S. Laws,
Story's Laws
Stovins' Law Respecting Horses
Stov. Hors.
Strahan's Domat's Civil Law
Strah. Domat
Strahan's Reports (19 Oregon)
Strahan
Straits Law Journal
S.L.J.
Straits Law Journal and Reporter
Straits L.J. & Rep.
Straits Law Reports, New Series
S.L.R.N.S.
Straits Settlements Law Reports
S.S.L.R.

Straits Settlements Law Reports, Supplement
S.S.L.R. Supp.
Strange's Cases of Evidence
Stra., Stran., Str., Str. Ev., Str. Cas. Ev.
Strange's English King's Bench Reports
Str.
Strange's Hindu Law
Str. H.L.
Strange's Notes of Cases, Madras
Strange, Madras, N.C. Str., N. of Cases, N. of Case., No. of Cas. Madras, Not. Cas. Madras, Not. Cas.
Strange's Reports, England
Strange., Strange (Eng.)
Strange's Select Cases in Evidence
Sel. Cas. Ev., S.C.E.
Strategic Air Command
S.A.C.
Strategic Arms Limitation Talks
S.A.L.T.
Stratton's Reports (12-14 Oregon)
Stratton.
Street
St.
Street Railway Law
Rosenberger
Street Railway Reports
Street Ry. Rep., St. Ry. Rep.
Streets and Highways
Sts. & Hy.
Streets and Highways Code
Str. & H.C.
Strickland on Evidence
Strick. Ev.
Stringfellow's Reports (9-11 Missouri)
Stringf., Stringfellow

Strobhart's South Carolina Equity Reports
Strob. Ch., Strob. Eq., Strobh. Eq. (S.C.)
Strobhart's South Carolina Law Reports
Strob., Strobh. L. (S.C.)
Stroud on Slavery
Stroud Sl.
Struve's Reports, Washington Territory
Struve
Stuart, Milne and Peddie's Scotch Court of Sessions Reports
St.M. & P., Stu. Mil. & Ped., Stuart., Stuart M. & P., Stu. M. & P., St.
Stuart's Appeals, Lower Canada
St. R., S.L.C., LS.L.C. App.
Stuart's Kings Bench Reports, Quebec
Stuart K.B.
Stuart's Lower Canada King's Bench Reports
Stuart L.C.K.B., Stu. K.B., Stuart K.B. (Quebec), Stu. L.C., Stuart's R., Stu. Ap.
Stuart's Lower Canada Reports
S.R.C., Stuart.
Stuart's Lower Canada Vice-Admiralty Reports
Stu. Adm., Stu. Adm.V.A., Stuart L.C.V.A., Stuart Vice-Adm., Stuart Adm. N.S., Stuart., Stuart's Adm., S.V.A.R.
Stuart's Lower Canada Vice-Admiralty Reports, New Series
St. Adm. N.S., Stu. Adm. N.S.
Stuart's Select Cases, Bengal
Stuart Beng.
Stubb's Constitutional History
Stubbs, C. H.

Stubb's Select Charters
Stubbs Sel. Ch.
Student Law Review
Student L. Rev.
Student Lawyer
Student Law.
Student Lawyer Journal
Student Law. J.
Student Nonviolent Coordinating Committee
SNCC
Students' Pocket Law Lexicon
Stud. Law Lex.
Studia et Documenta Historiae et Juris, Rome, Italy
Stud. & Doc. His. Jur.
Studies
Stud.
Studies in Comparative Local Government
Stud. in Comp. Local Govt.
Studies in Criminal Law and Procedure
Studies Crim. L.
Studies in History, Economics and Public Law
Stud. Hist.
Studies in Law and Economic Development
Stud. L. & Econ. Dev.
Studies on International Fiscal Law
Stud. Int'l Fiscal L.
Sturgeon's Insolvent Debtors Act
Sturg. Ins. D.
Style's English King's Bench Reports
Style., Sty., Mod., Mod. Rep.
Style's Practical Register
Style, Pr. Reg., Sty. Pr. Reg., St. Pr. Reg.
Subcommittee
Sub., Subcomm

Subdivision
Subd.
Subordinated
Sub.
Subparagraph
Subpar.
Subrogation
Subrog.
Subscription
Subsc.
Subsection
Subsec.
Subsidiary Legislation
India Subs. Leg.
Subsidiary Legislation of the Australian Capital Territory
Austl. Cap. Terr. Subs. Leg., Subs. Leg. Austl. Cap. Terr.
Successor
Suc.
Sudan Law Journal and Reports
S.L.J.R., Sudan L.J. & Rep.
Sudder Dewanny Adawlut Cases, Madras
Chetty
Sudder Dewanny Adawlut Cases, North West Frontier, India
S.A.D.N.W.F., Sud.Dew.Rep.
Sudder Dewanny Adawlut Reports, Bombay
S.A.D. Bom.
Sudder Dewanny Adawlut Reports, India
Sud. Dew. Ad., S.D.A.
Sudder Foujdaree Adawlut Reports, India
S.F.A.
Sudder Nizamut Adawlut Reports, Bengal
S.N.A. Beng.
Sudder Nizamat Adawlut Reports, India
S.N.A.

Sudder Nizamut Adawlut Reports, New Series, Bengal
S.N.A. Beng. (N.S.)
Suffolk Transnational Law Journal
Suffolk Transnat'l L.J.
Suffolk University Law Review
Su. L.R., Suffolk U. L. Rev., Suffolk Univ. L. Rev.
Sugden on Powers
Sugd., Sugd. Powers., Sug. Pow.
Sugden on Property Statutes
Sug. Pr. St.
Sugden on the Law of Estates
Sug. Est.
Sugden on the Law of Property
Sug. Pr., Sug. Prop.
Sugden on Vendors and Purchasers
Sug. Vend., Sugd. Vend., Sug. V. & P.
Sugden's Hand-Book of Property Law
Sug. Hd. Bk.
Sugden's Irish Chancery Cases Tempore
Cas.t.Sugd.
Sullivan's Land Titles in Massachusetts
Sull. Ld. Tit.
Sullivan's Lectures on Constitution and Laws of England
Sull. Lect.
Summary
Summ.
Summary Court-Martial
S.C.M.
Summary Decisions
Summ. Dec., Sum. Dec.
Summary Judgment[s]
Sum. Judg.

Summary of Pennsylvania Jurisprudence
Pa. Summary
Summary of the Law of Nisi Prius
Summ. N.P.
Summerfield's Reports (21 Nevada)
Summerfield, Summerfield, S.
Summers on Oil and Gas
Summers, Oil & Gas
Sumner's Edition of Vesey's Reports, England
Sum. Ves., Sumn. Ves.
Sumner's United States Circuit Court Reports
Sumn., Sum., Sumner., Sum. Rep., Sum. U.C.C.R.
Sundays and Holidays
Sun. & H.
Superintendent of Documents, United States Government Printing Office
SuDoc
Superior
Sup, Supr.
Superior Court
S.C., Su., Super., Super. Ct.
Superior Court Appellate Division
Super. Ct. App. Div.
Superior Court Chancery Division
Super. Ct. Ch. Div.
Superior Court Law Division
Super. Ct. Law. Div.
Superior Court Reports
Super., Super. Ct. Rep.
Superseded in Part; New Matter Substituted For Part of an Existing Regulation or Order (used in Shepard's Citations)
Sp.

Superseded; New Regulation or Order Substituted For an Existing One (used in Shepard's Citations)
S.

Supersonic Transport
S.S.T.

Supervised Agency
S/Ag

Supplement[al]
Supp., Suppl.

Supplement to Code
Supp. Code, Code Supp.

Supplement to Compiled Statutes
C.S. Supp.

Supplement to General Statutes
Supp. Gen. St.

Supplement to Morrison's Dictionary, Scotch Court of Session
Morr. Supp.

Supplement to Petersdorff's Abridgment
Pet. Suppl.

Supplement to Revised Code
Supp. Rev. Code

Supplement to Revised Statutes
Supp. Rev. St., R.J.Supp.

Supplement to Revision
Supp. Rev.

Supplement to Sayles' Annotated Texas Civil Statutes
Sayles' Supp.

Supplemental Indian Appeals, Law Reports
Ind. App. Supp.

Supplementary
Suppl.

Supplementing; New Matter Added to an Existing Regulation or Order (used in Shepard's Citations)
Sg.

Support
Supp.

Support of Persons
Support Per.

Supreme
Sup., Supr.

Supreme Bench
S.B.

Supreme Commander, Allied Powers
SCAP

Supreme Court
S.C., S.Ct., Sup.Ct.

Supreme Court Appeals
Sup. Ct. App.

Supreme Court Appellate Term
App. T., App. Term

Supreme Court Appendix Case
US Appx.

Supreme Court Cases
S.C. Cas., S.C.C.

Supreme Court, Ceylon
Su. Ct. Cir.

Supreme Court Decisions, St. Vincent
S.C.D. (St.V.)

Supreme Court Historical Society Quarterly
Sup. Ct. Hist. Soc'y Q.

Supreme Court Historical Society Yearbook
Sup. Ct. Hist. Soc'y Y.B.

Supreme Court in Banco
S.C. in Banco

Supreme Court Journal, India
S.C.,J., Sup. Ct. J.

Supreme Court Judgments by Clark, Jamaica
Clark
Supreme Court Law Review
Sup. Ct. L. Rev.
Supreme Court Law Review, Second Series
Sup. Ct. L. Rev. 2d
Supreme Court Monthly Review
Sup. Ct. M.R.
Supreme Court of Canada
S.C.C.
Supreme Court of Errors
Sup. Ct. Err.
Supreme Court Practice
Sup. Ct. Pr.
Supreme Court Reporter
S., SC, S.Ct., Sup. Court Rep., Sup. Ct. Rep., Sup. Ct. Repr., Supr. Ct. Rep., U.S. Sup. Ct. Reps., S.C., Sup.Ct.
Supreme Court Review
S. Ct. Rev., Sup. Ct. Rev.
Supreme Headquarters, Allied Powers in Europe
SHAPE
Supreme Judicial Court
S. Jud. Ct., Sup. Jud. Ct.
Supreme Military Council Decree
S.M.C.D.
Supreme Tribunal
Sup. Trib.
Surety
Sur.
Suretyship
Surety
Suriname
Surin.
Surrogate
Surr.
Surrogate's Court
Sur. Ct., Surr. Ct.

Surrogate's Court Procedure Act
Surr. Ct. Proc. Act
Survey
Surv.
Survey of California Law
Survey Calif. L.
Survivorship Agreement
S/A
Suspended
Susp.
Suspended in Part; Regulation or Order Suspended in Part (used in Shepard's Citations)
Sdp.
Suspended; Regulation or Order Suspended (used in Shepard's Citations)
Sd.
Susquehanna Legal Chronicle, Pennsylvania
Susq. L. C., Sus. Leg. Chron., Susq. Legal Chron., Susquehanna Leg. Chron. (Pa.), Susq. Leg. Chron., Susq. L. Chron
Sutherland on Statutes and Statutory Construction
Suth. St. Const., Suth. Stat. Const.
Sutherland on the Law of Damages
Suth. Dam.
Sutherland's Appeals Reports, Small Causes Court, Bengal
Suth. App.
Sutherland's Bengal Full Bench Reports
Suth. F.B.R.
Sutherland's Bengal High Court Reports
Suth. Bengal
Sutherland's Calcutta Reports
Suth.

Sutherland's Privy Council Appeals (or Judgments), India
Suth, P.C.A., Suth. P.C.J.

Sutherland's Special Number of Weekly Reports, India
Suth. Sp. N.

Sutherland's Weekly Reporter, Calcutta
W.R., W.R. Calc., Suth. W.R.

Sutherland's Weekly Reports, Miscellaneous Appeals, India
Suth. W.R. Mis.

Sutton on Personal Actions at Common Law
Sutton.

Svensk Juristtidning, Sweden
Svensk Jur.-Tidn., SvJT

Swabey and Tristram's English Probate and Divorce Reports
Swabey & T. (Eng.), Sw. & Tr., Swab. & T., Swab. & Tr., S. & T.

Swabey's English Ecclesiastical Reports
Sw., Swab.

Swabey's English Divorce and Matrimonial Causes
Swab. Div.

Swabey's English Admiralty Reports
Swabey Adm. (Eng.), Swabey Adm., Sw., Swab. Admr.

Swan and Critchfield's Revised Ohio Statutes
S. & C., Swan C. R. St., S. & C. Rev. St.

Swan and Sayler's Revised Statutes of Ohio
S. & S.

Swan and Sayler's Supplement to the Revised Statutes of Ohio
Swan & S. St.

Swan, on Ecclesiastical Courts
Swan. Eccl. C.

Swan's Ohio Justice
Swan Just.

Swan's Ohio Pleading and Practice
Swan. Pl. & Pr.

Swan's Ohio Practice
Swan Pr.

Swan's Ohio Statutes
Swan's St.

Swan's Reports (31-32 Tennessee)
Sw., Swan's, Swan's R.

Swan's Tennessee Supreme Court Reports
Swan

Swan's Treatise on Ohio Law
Swan Tr.

Swanston's English Chancery Reports
Swan, Sw., Swan. Ch., Swans., Swanst., Swanst. (Eng.)

Swaziland
Swaz

Sweden
Swed.

Swedish
Sw.

Swedish and International Arbitration
Swed. & Int'l Arb.

Sweeney, New York Superior Court Reports, (31-32 New York Superior)
Sweeney (N.Y.), Swen., Sweeny., Sw., Sween.

Sweet on the Limited Liability Act
Sweet., Sweet L.L.

Sweet on Wills
Sweet., Sweet Wills

Sweet's Dictionary of English Law
Sweet L.D., Sweet.

Sweet's Marriage Settlement Cases
Sweet., Sweet M. Sett. Cas.
Sweet's Precedents in Conveyancing
Sweet., Sweet Pr. Conv.
Swift on Evidence
Swift Ev.
Swift's Connecticut Digest
Swift, Dig.
Swift's System of the Laws of Connecticut
Swift Sys.
Swinburne on Descents
Swinb. Desc.
Swinburne on Married Women
Swinb. Mar.
Swinburne on Spousals
Swinb. Spo.
Swinburne on Wills
Swinb. Wills, Swin.
Swinton's Scotch Justiciary Cases
Swint., Swin., Sw., Swin. Jus. Cas.
Swinton's Scots Registration Appeal Cases
Swin. Reg. App.
Switzerland
Switz.
Sworn statement
S.s.
Sydney Law Review
Syd. L.R., Sydney L. Rev.
Sydney Morning Herald
S.M.H.

Syllab[i, us]
Syl.
Syme's Justiciary Reports
Syme.
Symposium
Symp.
Symposium l'Association de jeune Barreau de Montreal
Symposum Jun. Bar
Symposium. Private Investors Abroad
Symp. Priv. Invest. Abroad
Syms' Code of English Law
Sym. Code
Synonym
Syn.
Synopsis
Syn., Synop.
Synopsis Decisions, United States Treasury
S.T.D.
Synopsis Series of the United States Treasury Decisions
Syn. Ser., S.S.
Syracuse Journal of International Law and Commerce
Syracuse J. Int'l L., Syr. J.Int'l L. & Com., Sy. J. Int. L., Syracuse J. Int'l L. & Com.
Syracuse Law Review
Sy. L.R., Syracuse L. Rev.
Syracuse University College of Law
SYRUCL
System
Sys.

T

Tait on Evidence
Tait Ev.
Tait's Index to Morison's Dictionary
Tait.
Tait's Index to Scotch Session Cases
Tait Ind., Tait.
Tait's Justice of the Peace
Tait J.P., T.J.
Tait's Manuscript Decisions, Scotch Session Cases
Tait.
Taken and Adjudged Cases in English Chancery
Cas. Tak. & Adj. Cases
Talbot's Cases in Chancery Tempore
Ca.Temp.Talb.
Talbot's Cases in Equity, England
Tal., Talb.
Talbot's Cases Tempore, England
Cas.temp.Talb., Ca.temp.Talbot, Cas.t.Talb., Ca.t.Talb., C.t.T., Tal, Talb., Cas.t.Tal.
Tambyah's Ceylon Reports
Tamb.
Tamlyn on Evidence in Chancery
Taml. Ev.
Tamlyn on Terms of Years
Taml. T.Y.
Tamlyn's English Rolls Court Reports
Tam., Taml., Tamlyn., Tamlyn Ch., Tamlyn (Eng.)
Tancred on Quo Warranto
Tanc. Q.W.

Taney's United States Circuit Court Reports
Taney, Tan., Taney's C.C. Dec., Taney's Dec. (U.S.C.C.)
Tang Thanh Trai Le on Protecting Consumer Rights
PCR
Tanganyika Law Reports
T.L.R.
Tanganyika Law Reports (Revised)
T.L.R. (R.)
Tanganyika Territory Law Reports
Tan. L.R., T.T.L.R.
Tanner's Reports (8-14 Indiana)
Tann., Tanner
Tanner's Reports (13-17 Utah)
Tann., Tanner
Tanzania
Tanz.
Tanzania Gazette Law Reports
T.L.R.
Tapp on Maintenance and Champerty
Tapp. M & Ch.
Tappan's Ohio Common Pleas Reports
T., Tappan's Ohio Rep., Tappan's R., Tap., Tapp., Tappan., Tappan (Ohio)
Tapping on the Writ of Mandamus
Tapping, Tap. Man.
Tapping's Copyholder's Manual
Tap. C.M.

Tariff Schedules of the United States
T.S.U.S.
Tariff Schedules of the United States, Annotated
T.S.U.S.A.
Tarl Town Reports, New South Wales
T.T.R.
Tarleton Term Reports, New South Wales
Tarl., Tarl. Term R.
Taschereau's Criminal Law Acts of Canada
Can.Cr.Acts, Tasch. Cr. Acts
Tasmania
Tas.
Tasmania Acts
Acts Tasm.
Tasmanian Acts of Parliament
Tasm. Acts
Tasmanian Building Appeal Reports
Tas. Bldg. App. R.
Tasmanian Law Journal Reports
T.L.R.
Tasmanian Law Reform Commission
Tas. L.R.C.
Tasmanian Law Reports
Tas. L.R., Tasm. L.R., Tas. L.R.
Tasmanian State Reports
Tas. R., Tasm., Tasm. St. L., Tas. S.R., Tasm. S.R.
Tasmanian Statutes
Tasm. Stat., Tasm. Sess. Stat.
Tasmanian Statutory Rules
Tasm. Stat. R.
Tasmanian University Law Review
Tasm. U.L. Rev., Tasmania U.L. Rev., Tas.U.L.R., Tas. Univ. L. Rev., Tasmanian Univ. L. Rev.

Taswell-Langmead's English Constitutional History
Tasw. Lang. Hist.
Tate's Digest of Virginia Laws
Tate's Dig.
Tate's Virginia Analytical Digested Index
Tate Dig. Ind.
Taunton's English Common Pleas Reports
Taun., Taut., Taunt. (Eng.)
Tax
Tx., Tax
Tax Administrators News
Tax Adm'rs. News
Tax Adviser
Tax Adviser, T. Ad.
Tax Board Memorandum, Internal Revenue Bulletin
T.B.M.
Tax Cases
Tax Cas.
Tax Cases Leaflets
L.(T.C.)
Tax Conference
Tax. Conf.
Tax Convention
T. Cv.
Tax Counselor's Quarterly
Tax. Coun. Q., Tax Counselor's Q., T.C.Q.
Tax Court Memorandum Decisions, Commerce Clearing House or Prentice-Hall
CCH Tax Ct. Mem., TCM, T.C.M. (CCH), T.C. Memo., Tax Ct. Mem. Dec. (CCH) [or (P-H)], P-H Tax Ct. Mem., TCM, T.C.M. (P-H)
Tax Court of the United States
T.C., T. Ct.

Tax Court of the United States Reports
    T. Ct. Rep.

Tax Court of the United States Memorandum
    T.Ct. Mem.

Tax Court Reported and Memorandum Decisions, Prentice-Hall
    P-H Tax Ct. Rep. & Mem. Dec., Tax Ct. Rep. & Mem. Dec.(P-H)

Tax Court Reported Decisions, Prentice-Hall
    Tax Ct. Rep. Dec. (P-H)

Tax Court Reporter, Commerce Clearing House
    CCH Tax Ct. Rep., Tax Ct. Rep. (CCH)

Tax Court Reports, Commerce Clearing House
    Tax Ct. Rep. (CCH)

Tax Equity and Fiscal Responsibiity Act of 1982
    TEFRA

Tax Executive
    Tax Exec.

Tax-Exempt Organizations, Commerce Clearing House
    Tax-Exempt Orgs.

Tax-Exempt Organizations, Prentice-Hall
    Tax-Exempt Org. (P-H)

Tax Law Reporter
    Tax. L.R., Tax. L.Rep.

Tax Law Review
    Tax L. Rev., T.L.R.

Tax Lawyer
    T. Lwyr., Tax Law.

Tax Lax & Reporter
    Tax Law Rep.

Tax Magazine
    Tax Mag., Tax Magazine, T.M.

Tax Management
    Tax Man., T.M.

Tax Management, Bureau of National Affairs
    Tax Mgmt.(BNA), Tax Mngm't.

Tax Management International Journal
    Tax Management Int'l., Tax Mgmt. Int'l J., TMIJ

Tax Management Memorandum, Bureau of National Affairs
    Tax Management Memo, T.M.M.

Tax Memo
    T.M.

Tax Notes
    Tax Notes

Tax Planning
    T.P.

Tax Planning Ideas
    T.P.I.

Tax Planning Ideas, Institute for Business Planning
    Tax Plan. Ideas (IBP)

Tax Planning, Institute for Business Planning
    Tax Plan. (IBP)

Tax Planning International
    Tax Pl. Int.

Tax Planning Review
    Tax Pl. Rev.

Tax Practitioners Forum
    Tax Pract. Forum

Tax Reform Act of 1984
    TRA '84

Tax Reform Act of 1986
    TRA '86

Tax Review
    Tax Rev.

Tax Treaties, Commerce Clearing House
    Tax Treaties (CCH)

Tax Value Added
    T.V.A.

Taxation
Tax, Tax., Tax'n.
Taxation and Revenue
Tax. & Rev.
Taxation Board of Review Decisions
T.B.R.D.
Taxation Board of Review Decisions, New Series
C.T.B.R. (N.S.)
Taxation for Accountants
Tax. Acct., Tax'n for Acct.
Taxation for Lawyers
Tax. for Law., Tax'n for Law.
Taxation Reports, England
Tax. R., T.R.
Taxes
T.
Taxes: The Tax Magazine
Taxes
Taxpayer Identification Number
TIN
Taxpayers' Actions
Taxp. Act.
Tayler's Precedents of Wills
Tay. Pr., Tay. Wills
Taylor
Tay.
Taylor and Bell's Bengal Reports
Tay. & B.
Taylor and Bell's Calcutta Supreme Court Reports
T. & B.
Taylor on Civil Law
Tayl. Civil Law
Taylor on Equity Jurisprudence
Tay. Eq. Jur.
Taylor on Evidence
Tayl. Ev., T. Ev., Tay. Ev.
Taylor on Government
Tay. Gov.
Taylor on Private Corporations
Tayl. Corp., Tayl. Priv. Corp.

Taylor on Poisons
Tay. Poi.
Taylor on the Bankruptcy Law
Tay. Bank. L.
Taylor on Tithe Commutation
Tay. Tit.
Taylor's Book of Rights
Tay. Bk. R.
Taylor's Customary Laws of Rembau, Maylaya
Taylor, Taylor (Malaya)
Taylor's Elements of Civil Law
Tay. Civ. L.
Taylor's Landlord and Tenant
Tay. L. & T., Tayl. Landl. & Ten.
Taylor's Law Glossary
Tay. L. Gl., Tayl. Gloss., Tay.Glos.
Taylor's Medical Jurisprudence
Tayl. Med. Jur., Tay.Med.Jur.
Taylor's North Carolina Term Reports
N.C.T.R., Term R. (N.C.), Taylor, Term N.C
Taylor's Reports (1 North Carolina)
Tay. Rep., Tay. J.L., Tayl. N.C., Tay. N.C., Taylor., Tay.
Taylor's Reports, Bengal
Taylor., Tay.
Taylor's Revised Wisconsin Statutes
Tayl. St.
Taylor's (Silas) History of Gavelkind
Tayl. Hist. Gav.
Taylor's Upper Canada King's Bench Reports
Taylor K.B. (Can.), Tay. U.C., Taylor, Taylor U.C., Tay.
Taylor's Wisconsin Statutes
Tay. Wis. Stat.

Tea Inspection Service
T.I.S.
Teacher[s]
Tchr(s).
Technical
Tech.
Technical Advice Memorandum
TAM
Technical and Miscellaneous Revenue Act of 1988
TAMRA
Technical Assistance Board
TAB.
Technical Information Release, Internal Revenue Service
T.I.R.
Technical Manual, United States Army
T.M.
Technical Memorandum
TM
Techn[ique, ology])
Tech.
Teisser's Court of Appeal, Parish of Orleans Reports, Louisiana
Teiss., Teissler
Tel-Aviv University Studies in Law
Tel-Aviv U. Stud. L., Tel-Aviv Univ. Stud. L.
Telecommunications
Telecom.
Tele[gram, graph]
Tel.
Telephone
Tel.
Templar (1788-79), London
Tem.
Temple
Tem.

Temple and Mew's English Crown Cases
Temple & M., Temple & M. (Eng.), Temple & M., T. & M., Temp. & M.
Temple and Mew's English Criminal Appeal Cases
T. & M.
Temple Environmental Law and Technology Journal
Temp. Envtl. L. & Tech. J.
Temple International and Comparative Law Journal
Temp. Int'l & Comp. L.J.
Temple Law Quarterly
Temp. L.Q., Temple L. Quart., Temple L.Q., T.L.Q.
Temple Law Review
Temp. L. Rev.
Temple University Law Quarterly
Temp. Univ. L.Q.
Temporary
Tem., Temp.
Temporary Emergency Court of Appeals
Temp. Emer. Ct. App.
Temporary International Council for Educational Reconstruction
TICER
Temporary National Economic Committee
T.N.E.C.
Temporary Restraining Order
T.R.O.
Temporary Unemployment Compensation
T.U.C.
Tempore (in the time of) (Lat.)
T., Tem., Temp.
Tempore Regis (in the time of the reign) (Lat.)
T.R.

Tennessee
Ten., Tenn., TN, Tn.

Tennessee Administrative Register
Tenn. Admin. Reg.

Tennessee Appeals
Tenn. App.

Tennessee Appeals Reports
Tn. A., Ten. App., Tenn. App. R., Tenn. Appeals

Tennessee Appellate Bulletin
Tenn. App., Tenn. App. Bull.

Tennessee Bar Association
TBA, Tenn. B.A.

Tennessee Bar Journal
Tenn. Bar J., Tenn. B.J.

Tennessee Chancery Appeals
Tenn. Chancery App., Tenn. Ch. App., Tenn. Ch. A.

Tennessee Chancery Appeals Decisions
Tenn. Ch. App. Dec.

Tennessee Chancery Reports
Tenn. Ch. R., Tenn. Chancery

Tennessee Civil Appeals
Tenn. Civ. A., Tenn. Civ. App.

Tennessee Civil Appeals Reports
Tenn. App.

Tennessee Code Annotated
T.C.A., Tenn. Code Ann.

Tennessee Constitution
Tenn. Const.

Tennessee Court of Civil Appeals
Tenn. C.C.A.

Tennessee Criminal Appeals
Tenn. Cr. App.

Tennessee Criminal Appeals Reports
Tenn. Crim. App., Tn. Cr.

Tennessee Jurisprudence
Tenn. Jur., Tenn. Juris.

Tennessee Law Review
Tenn. L. Rev., Tenn. L. Rev., Tenn. L.R., Tn. L., Tn. L.R.

Tennessee Law Revision Commission
Tenn. L.R.C.

Tennessee Lawyer
Tenn. Law.

Tennessee Legal Reporter
Tenn. Leg. Rep.

Tennessee Legal Reporter, New Series
Tenn. Legal Reporter

Tennessee Official Compilation of Rules and Regulations
Tenn. Admin. Code

Tennessee Private Acts
Tenn. Priv. Acts

Tennessee Public Acts
Tenn. Pub. Acts

Tennessee Railroad and Public Utilities Commission Board
Tenn. R. & P.U.C.

Tennessee Railroad Commission
Tenn. R.C.

Tennessee Reports
Tenn., Tn., Law Tenn. Rep., Tenn. R., Tenn. Rep., Tennessee R., Tennessee Rep.

Tennessee Supreme Court Reports
Tenn.

Tennessee Valley Authority
T.V.A.

Tentative
Tent.

Term
T.

Term Reports (6 North Carolina)
Term., Term. N.C.

Term Reports, English King's Bench (Durnford and East's Reports)
Term., Term R., T.R.(Eng.), Term. Rep., T.R., See also Durnford & East's Reports

Term Reports, English King's Bench, New Series (East's Reports)
T.R.N.S., See also East' Reports

Termes de la Ley
T.L., Term. de ler L.

Terminus Paschae (Easter Term)
Pas.

Terms of the Common Laws and Statutes Expounded and Explained by John Rastell
Termes de la Ley

Terrell and Walker's Reports (38-51 Texas)
Terr. & Wal., Terr. & Walk.

Terrell's Reports (38-71 Texas)
Terr.

Territorial Laws
Ter. Laws.

Territorial Sea Journal
Terr. Sea J.

Territor[y, ies]
T., Terr., Ty.

Territories Law, Northwest Territories, Canada
Terr. L.

Territories Law Reports, Canada
Terr. L. (Can.), Terr. L.R., Can. Terr.

Terry's Delaware Reports
Ter.

Teruvenkatachariar's Railway Cases, India
Teruv.

Testamentary, Testator, Testimonial, Testimony
Test.

Texas
Tex., Tx.

Texas Administrative Code
Tex. Admin. Code

Texas Bar Journal
Tex. B.J., Texas B.J.

Texas Business Corporation Act Annotated
Tex. Bus. Corp. Act Ann.

Texas Business Review
Texas Bus. Rev.

Texas Civil Appeals Cases
Tex. App., CATx.

Texas Civil Appeals Reports
Civ., Tex. Civ. App., Tex. Civ. Rep., Tx. Ci., Texas Civ., Texas Civ. App.

Texas Civil Cases
App. C. C., App. C. C. (White & W.), App. C. C. (Willson), App. Civ. Cases, Ct. App.C.C., Tex. Ct. App. Civ., Tex. Ct. App. Dec. Civ., Texas Ct. App. Civ. Cas., W.Con. Rep., White & W. Civil Cases Ct. App., White & Willson, Will. Con. Rep., Willson's C.C.

Texas Code of Criminal Procedure Annotated
Tex. Code Crim. Proc. Ann.

Texas Codes Annotated
Tex. Code Ann.

Texas Commission of Appeals
Tex. Com. App.

Texas Constitution
Tex. Const.

Texas Court of Appeals
Tex. A.

Texas Court of Appeals Reports
Tex. Ct. App. R., Tex. App.,
App., Court Appeals, Ct.
App.C.C., Ct. Apps., Tex. Ct.
App., Texas Cr. App., Texas Ct.
App., Texas Ct. of App.

Texas Court Reporter
Tex. Ct. Rep., Tex. Court Reporter, Texas Ct. Rep.

Texas Criminal Appeals Reports
Tex. Cr., Cr., Tex. Cr. App., Tex.
Cr. R., Tx. Cr., Texas Crim. App.

Texas Criminal Reports
Cr., Tex. Crim. Rep., Tex. Cr.
Rpts., Texas Cr. Rep., Texas
Crim., Texas Crim. Rep., Tex.
Crim.

Texas Decisions
Tex. Dec.

Texas Digest
Texas Dig.

Texas Election Code Annotated
Tex. Elec. Code Ann.

Texas General and Special Laws
Tex. Gen. Laws

Texas Insurance Code Annotated
Tex. Ins. Code Ann.

Texas International Law Forum
Tex. Int. L. Forum, Texas Internat. L. Forum, Texas Int'l L.F.

Texas International Law Journal
Tex. Int. L.J., Tex. Int'l L.J.,
Texas Internat. L.J., Texas Int'l
L.J.

Texas Jurisprudence
Tex. Jur.

Texas Jurisprudence, 2d Edition
Tex. Jur.2d

Texas Law and Legislation
Tex. Law & Leg.

Texas Law Journal
Tex. L.J., Tx. L.J.

Texas Law Reporter
Tex. L. Rep.

Texas Law Review
Tex. L. Rev., Texas L. Rev.,
Texas LR, Tx. L., Tx. L.R.

Texas Lawman
Tex. Law.

Texas Probate Court Annotated
Tex. Prob. Code Ann.

Texas Railroad Commission
Tex. R.C.

Texas Register
Tex. Admin. Reg.

Texas Reports
Tex., Tx., Texas R., Texas Rep.

**Texas Revised Civil Statutes An-
notated**
Tex. Rev. Civ. Stat. Ann. (Vernon)

**Texas Revised Civil Statutes An-
notated (Batt)**
Batt's Ann.St., Batt's Rev.St.

Texas Session Law Service
Tex. Sess. Law Serv.

**Texas Southern Intramural Law
Review**
Tex. So. Intra. L. Rev.

**Texas Southern University Law
Review**
Tex. So. U.L. Rev., Tex. S.U.L.
Rev., Texas South. U.L. Rev.

Texas Statutes Annotated
Tex. Stat. Ann.

Texas Supplement
Tex. Supp., Tex. Suppl.

Texas Supreme Court Reporter
Tex. S. Ct.

Texas Supreme Court Reports
Tex.

**Texas Supreme Court Reports,
Supplement**
Tex. S.

Texas Tax-General Annotated
Tex. Tax-Gen. Ann.
Texas Tech Law Review
Tex. Tech L. Rev., Texas Tech
L. Rev.
Thacher Criminal Cases, Massachusetts
Thacher Crim. Cas. (Mass.),
Thach. Cr., Thacher Cr.,
Thacher Cr. Cas., Th. C.C.,
Thac. Cr. Cas.
Thai
Th
Thailand
Thail.
Thayer's Preliminary Treatise on Evidence
Thayer, Prelim. Treatise Ev.
Thayer's Reports (18 Oregon)
Thayer
Theobald's Act for the Amendment of the Law
Theo. Am. A.
Theobald on Principal and Surety
Theo. Pr. & S.
Theobald on Wills
Theobald, Theo. Wills
Theory of Presumptive Proof
Theo. Pres. Pr.
Thesaurus Brevium
Thes. Brev., Th. br.
Thesawaleme, Ceylon
Thes.
Third World Legal Studies
Third World Legal Stud.
Thomas
Tho., Thos.
Thomas and Franklin's Reports (1 Maryland Chancery)
Thomas & Fr., Thom. & Fr.

Thomas' Edition of Coke upon Littleton
Thom. Co. Lit., Thom. Co. Litt.,
Thos. Co. Lit.
Thomas' Leading Cases in Constitutional Law
Th. C. Const. Law., Th. Ca.
Const. Law, Thom. Const. L.,
Thom. L.C.
Thomas' Leading Statutes Summarized
Thom. St. Sum.
Thomas M. Cooley Law Review
Thomas M. Cooley L. Rev.
Thomas on Mortgages
Thom. Mort., Thomas, Mortg.
Thomas on Negligence
Thomas,Negl.
Thomas' Reports (1 Wyoming)
Thom., Thomas
Thomas's Universal Jurisprudence
Thom. Un. Jur.
Thompson
Tho.
Thompson and Cook's New York Supreme Court Reports
N.Y. Sup. Ct. Rep., N.Y. Sup.
Ct. (T. & C.), N.Y.S.C., S.C. (T.
& C.), Thomp. & Cook,
Thompson & C., T. & C.,
Thomp. & C., Th. & C.
Thompson and Merriam on Juries
Thomp. & M. Jur.
Thompson and Steger's Tennessee Code
Thomp. & St., T. & S., Thomp.
& St. Code.
Thompson on Benefit Building Societies
Thom. B.B.S.

Thompson on Carriers
Thomp. Car.

Thompson on Charging the Jury
Thomp. Ch. Jur.

Thompson on Homesteads and Exemptions
Thomp. H. & Ex.

Thompson on Liability of Officers of Corporations
Thomp. Liab. Off.

Thompson on Liability of Stockholders
Thomp. Liab. St., Thomp. Liab. Stockh.

Thompson on the Law of Highways
Thomp. High.

Thompson on Trials
Thomp. Trials.

Thompson's Cases on Negligence
Thomp. Neg.

Thompson's Cases, Tennessee
Thomps. Cas., Thomp. Cas.

Thompson's Citations, Ohio
Thomp. Cit.

Thompson's Commentaries on Law of Private Corporations
Thomp. Corp.

Thompson's Digest of Laws, Florida
Dig. Fla., Thomp. Dig., Fla. Dig., Thompson's Fla. Dig.

Thompson's Entries
Thomp. Ent.

Thompson's Law of the Farm
Thomp. Farm

Thompson's National Bank Cases
Thomp. N.B. Cas.

Thompson's Nova Scotia Reports
Thompson

Thompson's Patent Laws of all Countries
Thomp. Pat.

Thompson's Provisional Remedies
Thomp. Prov. Rem.

Thompson's Reports (39-40 California)
Thomp. Cal., Thompson

Thompson's Unreported Cases, Tennessee
Thompson Unrep., Tenn. Cas. (Shannon), Ten. Cas., Thomp. Tenn. Cas.

Thoms' Judicial Factors
Thoms Jud. Fac.

Thomson
Tho.

Thomson on Bills
Thom. Bills

Thomson on Bills and Notes
Thom. B. & N.

Thomson's Nova Scotia Reports
Thom. Rep., Thom., N.S.R. Thom., Thomson, Thom. N. Sc.,Thomson

Thomson's Select Decisions, Nova Scotia
Thom. Sel. Dec., Thom. Dec.

Thomson's Scotch Acts
Thom. Sc. Acts

Thorborn on Bankers' Law
Thor. Bank.

Thorington's Reports (107 Alabama)
Thor.

Thorne Ecological Institute
TEI

Thornton and Blackledge's Law Relating to Building and Loan Associations
Thornt. & Bl. Bldg. & Loan Ass'ns.

Thornton on Gifts and Advancements
Thornton, Gifts.

Thornton's Notes of Ecclesiastical and Maritime Cases, England
Thorn.

Thornton's Conveyancing
Thorn. Conv.

Thorpe's Ancient Laws of England
Thorpe Anc. L.

Thorpe's Reports (52 Louisiana Annual)
Thorpe.

Thring on Joint Stock Companies
Thring J. St. Com.

Thring on Land Drainage Act
Thring. L.D.

Throop on the Validity of Verbal Agreements
Thr. Verb. Agr.

Throop's Treatise on Public Officers
Throop, Pub. Off.

Thrupp's Historical Law Tracts
Thr. Hist. Tr.

Thurgood Marshall Law Review
Thur. Marsh. L.J., TMLJ, T. Marshall L. Rev., Thur. Mar. L. Rev., T.M.L. Rev.

Tidd's Costs
Tidd., Tidd. Co.

Tidd's Practice
Tidd., Tidd Pr., Tidd, Prac., Tidd's Pract.

Tidd's Practice Appendix
Tidd App.

Tiedeman on Real Property
Tiedeman, Real. Prop.

Tiedeman's Treatise on Municipal Corporations
Tied. Mun. Corp.

Tiedeman's Treatise on the Limitations of Police Power in the United States
Tied. Lim. Police Power.

Tiffany and Bullard on Trusts and Trustees
Tif. & Bul. Tr., Law of Trusts, Tiff. & Bul.

Tiffany and Smith's New York Practice
Tif. & Sm. Pr.

Tiffany on Government and Constitutional Law
Tif. Gov.

Tiffany on Landlord and Tenant
Tiffany, Landlord & Ten., Tiffany Landl. & T.

Tiffany on Real Property
Tiffany Real Prop.

Tiffany's Reports (28-39 New York Court of Appeals)
Tiff., Tiffany

Tigar's Federal Appeals: Jurisdiction and Practice
FAP

Tillinghast and Shearman's New York Practice and Pleading
Til. & Sh.Pr., T. & S. Pr.

Tillinghast and Yates on Appeals
Till. & Yates App.

Tillinghast's Precedents
Til. Prec.

Tillman's Reports (68, 69, 71, 73, 75 Alabama)
Tillman.

Tilsley on Stamp Laws
Tils. St. L.

Timber Tax Journal
Timber Tax J.

Time and Materials
T & M

Times Law Reports, England
Times L. (Eng.), T.L.R., Times
L. Rep., Times L.R.,
Tinwald's Reports, Scotch Court of Session
Tinw.
Title[s]
T., Tit.(s)
Title Certificate Book
T.C.B.
Tobacco Branch, United States Internal Revenue Bureau
Tob.
Tobacco Tax Ruling Term, United States Internal Revenue Bureau
T.T.
Tobacco Tax Ruling, United States Internal Revenue Bureau
T.
Tobey's Reports (9-10 Rhode Island)
Tobey
Toledo
Tol.
Toller on Executors
Toll. Ex., Toller.
Tolstoy on Divorce and Matrimonial Causes
Tolst. Div.
Tomkins and Jenckens' Compendium of Modern Roman Law
Tomkins & J. Mod. Rom. Law.,
Tom. & J. Comp.
Tomkins and Lemon's Translation of Gaius
Tom. & Lem. Gai.
Tomkins' Institutes of Roman Law
Tom. Inst.
Tomlin
Tom.

Tomlin's Criminal Law
Toml. Cr. L.
Tomlins' Election Cases, England
Toml., Toml. Cas.
Tomlins' Law Dictionary
Toml. Law Dict., Tomlins.,
Tom., Toml. L.D.
Tomlins' Supplement to Brown's Parliamentary Cases, England
Toml. Supp. Br.
Toronto University Faculty Law Review
Toronto U. Faculty L. Rev.
Tort and Insurance Law Journal
Tort & Ins. L.J.
Torts and Insurance Practice Section of American Bar Association
TIPS
Total Disability Benefit
T.D.B.
Tothill's English Chancery Reports
Toth., Tot., Tothill (Eng.)
Tothills Transactions in Chancery
Tot., Tothill (Eng.), Tr. Ch.
Tourgee's North Carolina Digest
Tourg. Dig.
Touro Journal of Transnational Law
Touro J. Transnat'l L.
Touro Law Review
Touro L. Rev.
Towle's Analysis of the United States Constitution
Towle Const.
Town Clerk
T.C.
Town Council[lor]
T.C.
Townsend on Commercial Law
Town. Com. Law

Townsend's Judgment
Town. Jud.
Townsend's Modern State Trials
Town. St. Tr.
Townshend
Towns.
Townshend on Slander and Libel
Town. Sl. & Lib., Town. St. &
Lib., Townsh. Sland. & L.
Townshend's Code
Town. Co.
Townshend's Pleading
Town. Pl., Townsh. Pl.
Townshend's Practice, New York
Town. Pr.
**Townshend's Precedents of
Pleading**
Town. Pr. Pl.
**Townshend's Summary Landlord
and Tenant Process**
Town. Sum. Proc.
Township
Twp.
Toxic Substances Control Act
TSCA
**Tracewall and Mitchell's United
States Comptroller's Decisions**
Trace. & M.
**Tracewell, Bowers, and Mitchell's
United States Comptroller's De-
cisions**
T.B. & M.
Tracey's Cases on Evidence
Tracey, Evidence
Trade
Trade
Trade and Development Board
TDB
**Trade and Development Board of
the Conference on Trade and
Development**
TDBOR

**Trade Cases, Commerce Clearing
House**
T.C., Trade Cas. (CCH)
Trade Expansion Act of 1962
T.E.A.
**Trade Practices Reporting Serv-
ice**
T.P.R.S.
**Trade Regulation Reporter, Com-
merce Clearning House**
T.R.R., Trade Reg. Rep. (CCH)
Trade Regulation Review
Trade Reg. Rev.
Trademark
T.M., Trademark
**Trademark Bulletin, Bulletin of
United States Trademark Asso-
ciation, New Series**
Trademark Bull. (N.S.)
Trademark Bulletin, New Series
T.M. Bull.
**Trademark Manual of Examining
Procedure**
T.M.E.P.
Trademark Record
T.M. Rec.
Trademark Reporter
Trademark Rep., Trademark
Rptr., T.M. Rep., T.M.R., Trade
Mark R.
Trademark Rules of Practice
T.M.R. Prac.
**Trademark Trial and Appeal
Board**
TMT & App. Bd.
Trademark World
Trademark World
Trademarks and Tradenames
Trademark
Trademarks Journal
T.M.J.
Trading As
T.A.

Traffic Cases
  T.
Traill on Medical Jurisprudence
  Traill Med. Jur.
Train and Heard's Precedents of Indictment
  Tr. & H. Prec. Ind.
Transaction
  Tr., Trans.
Transactions of the Grotius Society
  Grot. Soc'y
Transactions of the International Law Association
  Trans. I.L.A., I.L.A. Trans.
Transcript
  Tr., Trans.
Transcript Appeals, New York
  Transc. A., Transcr. A., Trans. App., Tr. App., Trans. Ap.
Transfer[red]
  Trans., Trf.
Transferred From, [To]
  Transf.
Transit Commission Reports
  T.C.R.
Transit Law Review
  Transit L. Rev.
Transitional
  Transtl.
Translat[or, ed, ion]
  Tr., Transl., Trans., Transl.
Translation of Brook's New Cases
  March N.C.
Transnational
  Transnat'l.
Transnational Law and Contemporary Problems
  Transnat'l L. & Contemp. Probs.
Transnational Lawyer
  Transnat'l Law
Transnational Reporter
  Transnat'l. Rep.

Transport[ation]
  Transp.
Transportation Corporations
  Transp. Corp.
Transportation Journal
  Transp. J.
Transportation Law Journal
  Transp. L.J.
Transportation Law Seminar
  Transp. L. Sem.
Transportation Practitioners Journal
  Transp. Prac. J.
Transvaal
  Tvl.
Transvaal and Natal Native Appeal and Divorce Court Decisions
  N.A. & D.T. & N.
Transvaal and Natal Native Appeal Court, Selected Decisions
  N.A., T. & N.
Transvaal and Witswatersrand Reports
  Trans. & Wit.
Transvaal Colony, Witwatersrand High Court Reports
  T.H., T.L.
Transvaal Court Reports
  Kotze & Barber
Transvaal High Court Official Reports
  Off. Rep.
Transvaal Provincial Division Reports
  T.
Transvaal Reports by Kolze
  Kolze
Transvaal Supreme Court Reports
  T.P., T.S.
Travancore
  Trav.

Tranvancore Law Journal, India
 T.L.J., Trav. L.J.
Travancore Law Reports, India
 T.L.R., Trav. L.R.
Travancore Law Times, India
 T.L.T., Trav. L.T.
Travers and Twiss on Law of Nations
 Trav. & Tw. L. of N.
Trayner's Latin Maxims and Phrases, etc.
 Tray. Lat. Max.
Treadway's South Carolina Constitutional Reports
 Tread., Tread. Const., Treadway Const. (S.C.), Rep. Const. Ct., So. Car. Const.
Treadway's South Carolina Law Reports
 Tread.
Treasur[er, y]
 Treas.
Treasury Decisions
 T.D.
Treasury Decisions Under Customs and Other Laws
 Treas. Dec.
Treasury Decisions Under Internal Revenue Laws
 Treas. Dec. Int. Rev.
Treasury Department Circular
 Circ., TDC, Treas. Dept. Cir., D. C.
Treasury Department Orders, United States
 TDO
Treasury Department, United States
 Treas. Dept.
Treasury Regulations
 Treas. Reg.

Treat, Scates and Blackwell's Compiled Illinois Statutes
 Scates' Comp. St.
Treaties and Other International Agreements of the United States of America
 T.I. Agree.
Treaties and Other International Agreements of the United States of America 1776-1949, Compiled Under Direction of Charles I. Bevans
 Bevans
Treaties and Other International Agreements Series, United States
 T.I.A.S., TIAS
Treaties in Force, United States
 T.I.F., TIF
Treatise on Trover and Conversion
 Treat. Tro.
Treaty[ies]
 Tr., Treat.
Treaty on Conventional Armed Forces in Europe
 CFE
Treaty Series, United States
 Tr. Ser., T.S., TS
Treaty Setting Up the European Atomic Energy Community
 E.A.E.C.
Tredgold's Cape Colony Reports
 Tred.
Trehearn and Grant's English Prize Cases
 P. Cas., Pr. C., Treh. & Gr. Pr. C.
Tremaine's Pleas of the Crown
 Trem., Trem. P.C.
Trent Law Journal
 Trent L.J.

Trespass
  Tresp.
Trevor's Taxes on Succession
  Trev. Tax. Suc.
Trial
  Tr., Trial
Trial Advocate Quarterly
  Trial Advoc. Q.
Trial and Tort Trends
  Tr. & T.T.
Trial Diplomacy Journal
  Trial Diplomacy J.
Trial Judges' Journal
  Tr. Judge J.
Trial Lawyers Forum
  Trial Law. Forum
Trial Lawyer's Guide
  Tr. Law Guide, Trial Law. Guide
Trial Lawyer's Quarterly
  Tr. Law Q., Trial Law Q.
Trial of John Fries
  Fries Tr.
Trial of Professor Webster for Murder
  Web. Tr.
Trial of the Earl of Coventry
  E. of Cov., Tri. E. of Cov.
Trial of the Rebels, etc. (Foster's Crown Cases)
  Fost. Tr. Reb.
Trial of the Savannah Privateers
  Sav. Priv.
Trial of the Seven Bishops
  Tri. Bish.
Trial of Warren Hastings
  Hast. Tr.
Trials Per Pais
  Tri. per. P.
Tribun[e, al]
  Trib.
Trinidad
  Tr.

Trinidad and Tobago
  Trin. & Tobago
Trinidad and Tobago Supreme Court Judgments
  T. & T. Sup.
Trinidad Law Reports
  Tr. L.R., Trinidad L.R.
Trinity
  T.
Trinity Term
  Trin., T.T., Trin. T., Trint.T.
Tripp's Reports (5-6 Dakota)
  Tripp
Tristram's Consistory Judgments, England
  Tristram, Tr. Consist. J., Tr., Trist.
Tristram's Probate Practice
  Tris. Pr. Pr., Tristram
Tristram's Supplement to 4 Swabey and Tristram Reports, England
  Tristram, rist.
Troubat and Haly's Pennsylvania Practice
  Troub. & H. Pr., Tr. & H. Pr., Troub. & H. Prac., T. & H. Prac.
Troubat and Haly's Practice, Brightly's Edition
  Bright.Tr. & H.Pr.
Troubat on Limited Partnership
  Troub. Lim. Partn.
Trower's Debtor and Creditor
  Trow. D. & Cr.
Trower's Manual of the Prevalance of Equity
  Trow. Eq.
Trueman's New Brunswick Equity Cases
  Tru., Truem. Eq. Cas., Trueman Eq. Cas.

Trueman's New Brunswick Reports
N.B.R. Tru., True.

Truman's American Railway Reports
Tru. Railw. Rep.

Trust Bulletin, American Bankers Association
Trust Bull.

Trust Companies Magazine
Trust Co. Mag.

Trust Investment Committee
TIC

Trust Investment Committee Memorandum
T.I.C.M.

Trust Officers Committee Minutes
T.O.C.M.

Trust Territor[ies, y]
TT, Trust Terr.

Trust Territory of the Pacific Islands
TTPI

Trust Territory Reports
Trust Terr. Rep.

Trust Territory Reports of Pacific Island
T.T.R.

Trustee
Tr.

Trustee Under Agreement
T/U/Ag, T.A.

Trustee Under Will
T.U.W., T.W.

Trusteeship Council
TC

Trusteeship Council Resolution
T.C. Res.

Trust[s]
Tr.

Trusts and Estates
Tr. & Est., Trusts & Es., Trusts & Est.

Trye's Jus Filizarii
Trye

Tucker and Clephane's Reports (21 District of Columbia)
Tuck. & C., Tuck., Tuck. & Cl., Tuck. Dist. of Col.

Tucker's Blackstone's Commentaries
Tuck. Bl. Com., Tucker's Blackstone

Tucker's District of Columbia Reports
Tuck.

Tucker's Lectures
Tuck. Lect.

Tucker's New York Surrogate's Court Reports
Tucker, Tuck., Tuck. Sur., Tuck. Surr.

Tucker's Pleadings
Tuck. Pl.

Tucker's Reports (156-175 Massachusetts)
Tuck.

Tucker's Select Newfoundland Cases
Tuck., Nfld. Sel. Cas., Tuck. Sel. Cas., Tuck. Sur., Tuck. Surr.

Tudor on Charitable Trusts
Tud. Char. Tr., Tud. Char. Trusts

Tudor's Leading Cases on Mercantile Law
Tudor's L.C.M.L., Tud. Cas. Merc. Law

Tudor's Leading Cases on Real Property
Tudor, Lead. Cas. Real Prop., Tudor's L.C.R.P., Tud. Cas. R.P.

Tulane
  Tul.
Tulane Civil Law Forum
  Tu. Civ. L.F.
Tulane Environmental Law Journal
  Tul. Envtl. L.J.
Tulane Law Review
  T.L.R., Tu. L.R., Tul. L. Rev.,
  Tulane L. Rev., Tu. L.
Tulane Maritime Law Journal
  Tul. Mar. L.J.
Tulane Tax Institute
  T.T.I., Tul. Tax Inst.
Tulsa Law Journal
  Ts. L.J., Tulsa L.J.
Tunisia
  Tunis.
Tupper' Upper Canada Practice Reports
  Tupper, Tupp.
Tupper's Reports, Ontario Appeals
  Tupp. App., Tup. App., Tupp.,
  Tupper
Turk[ey, ish]
  T., Tur., Turk.
Turks and Caicos Islands
  Turks & Caicos Is.
Turley on Aviation Litigation
  AL
Turley and Rooks' Firearms Litigation: Law, Science and Practice
  FL
Turnbull's Practice, New York
  Turn. Pr.
Turner and Phillips' English Chancery Reports
  T. & P., Turn. & P., Turn. & Ph.

Turner and Russell's English Chancery Reports
  Tu. & Rus., T. & R., Tur. & R.,
  Tur. & Ru., Tur. & Rus., Turn.
  & Rus., Turn. & Russ., Turn. &
  R., Turn. & R. (Eng.)
Turner on Copyright in Designs
  Turn. Cop.
Turner on Irrevocable Trusts
  IT
Turner on Patents
  Turn. Pat.
Turner's Practice of the Court of Chancery
  Turn. Ch. Pr.
Turner on Quieting Titles
  Turn. Qui. Tit.
Turner on Revocable Trusts
  RT
Turner's History of the Anglo Saxon
  Turn. Anglo. Sax.
Turner's Insurance Coverage of Construction Disputes
  ICCD
Turner's Reports (35-48 Arkansas)
  Turner, Tur., Turn.
Turner's Reports (99-101 Kentucky)
  Tur., Turn., Turner
Turner's Select Pleas of the Forest (Selden Society Publication, 13)
  Tur., Turn.
Tuttle & Carpenter's Reports (52 California)
  Tutt. & C., Tutt. & Carp., Tuttle, Tuttle & Carpenter
Twiss' Black Book of the Admiralty
  Black Bk. Adm., Bl.B. Adm.

Twiss' Law of Nations in Time of Peace
Tw. Nat. P., Tw. Nat. W.

Tydskrif vir Hedendaagse Romeins-Hollandse Reg (Journal of Contemporary Roman- Dutch Law), Netherlands
THR-HR

Tyler on Boundaries, Fences, etc.
Tyl. Boun.

Tyler on Ejectment and Adverse Enjoyment
Tyl. Eject., Tyler, Ej.

Tyler on Fixtures
Tyl. Fix.

Tyler on Infancy and Coverture
Tyl. Inf.

Tyler on Partnership
Tyl. Part.

Tyler on Usury, Pawns and Loans
Tyl. Us.

Tyler's American Ecclesiastical Law
Tyl. Eccl. L.

Tyler's Edition of Mitford's Equity Pleading
Mitf. & Ty. Eq. Pl.

Tyler's Edition of Stephen on the Principles of Pleading
Tyler, Steph. Pl., Tyl. St. Pl.

Tyler's Vermont Supreme Court Reports
Tyler, Tyl.

Tyng's Reports (2-17 Massachusetts)
Tyng

Tyre's Jus Filizarii
Tyre, Jus Filiz.

Tyrwhitt and Granger's English Exchequer Reports
Tyr. & G., T. & G., Tyr., Tyrw., Tyr. & Gr., Tyrw. & G., Tyrw. & G. (Eng.)

Tytler on Military Law and Courts-Martial
Tytler, Mil. Law, Tyt. Mil. L.

U

U.C.L.A.-Alaska Law Review
U.C.L.A.-Alaska L. Rev.
U.C.L.A. Intramural Law Review
U.C.L.A. Intra. L. Rev.
UCLA Journal of Environmental Law and Policy
UCLA J.Envtl. L. & Pol'y.
UCLA Law Review
UCLA L. Rev.
UCLA Pacific Basin Law Journal
UCLA Pac. Bas. L.J., UCLA Pac. Basin L.J.
Udal's Fiji Law Reports
UDAL
Uganda Journal
U.J.
Uganda Law Focus
Ug. L.F., Uganda L. Foc., Uganda L.F.
Uganda Law Reports
ULR, Ug. L. R.
Uganda Legal Focus
Uganda Leg. Focus
Uganda Protectorate Law Reports
Uganda L.R., U.L.R., U.P.L.R., Ug. Pr. L.R.
Ulman's Law Record
Ulm. L. Rec.
Ulpiani Fragmenta
Ulp.
Umfreville's Office of Coroner
Umfrev. Off. Cor.
UMKC Law Review
UMKC L. Rev.
Umpire Decisions, Benefit Claims
O.U.U.I.D.

UN Chronicle
UN Chron.
UN Monthly Chronicle
UN Mo.Chron., UN Monthly Chron.
Unauthorized
Unauth.
Unauthorized Practice News
Un. Prac. News., Unauth. Prac. News, U.P. News
Unconsolidated Laws
Unconsol. Laws
Under Agreement
U/A
Under Sheriff
Und.Sher.
Under the Name
sub.nom.
Under Trust
U/T
Under Will
U/W
Underhill on Evidence
Underhill, Ev.
Underhill on Torts
Und.Torts
Underhill on Trusts and Trustees
Und.Tr.
Underhill's Chancery Procedure
Und. Ch. Pr.
Underhill's New Conveyancing
Und. Conv.
Underhill's Partnership
Und.Part.
Underwood on Art Copyright
Und. Art Cop.
Underwriters
U/wrs

Undivided
Und.
Unemployment Benefit
UB
Unemployment Compensation
Unempl. C.
Unemployment Compensation Agency
UCA
Unemployment Compensation and Placement Division
UCPD
Unemployment Compensation Board
UCB
Unemployment Compensation Bureau
UCB
Unemployment Compensation Commission
UCC
Unemployment Compensation Division
UCD
Unemployment Compensation Interpretation Service
UCIS
Unemployment Compensation Interpretation Service, Benefit Series
U.C.I.S.
Unemployment Compensation Interpretation Service, Federal Series
U.C.I.S.
Unemployment Compensation Interpretation Service, State Series
U.C.I.S.
Unemployment Insurance
Unemp. Ins.
Unemployment Insurance Code
Un. Ins. Co.

Unemployment Insurance Commission
UIC
Unemployment Insurance Division
UID
Unemployment Insurance Reports, Commerce Clearing House
Unempl. Ins Rep. (CCH), Unempl. Ins. Rep-(CCH)
Unemployment Insurance Service
UIS
Unemployment Reserves Commission
URC
UNESCO Copyright Bulletin
Copyright Bull.
UNESCO Regional Office for Education in Asia and Oceania
UROEA
Unified
Unif.
Uniform
Unif.
Uniform Capitalization Rules
UNICAP
Uniform City Court Act
Uniform City Ct. Act.
Uniform Code of Military Justice
UCMJ
Uniform Commercial Code
U.C.C., UCC
Uniform Commercial Code Law Journal
UCC L.J.
Uniform Commercial Code Law Letter
U.C.C. Law Letter
Uniform Commercial Code Reporting Service, Callaghan
U.C.C. Rep. Serv. (Callaghan)

Uniform Consumer Credit Code
UCCC
Uniform District Court Act
Uniform Dist. Ct. Act
Uniform Law Conference of Canada
Unif. L. Conf. Can.
Uniform Law Review
U.L.R., Uniform L. Rev., U.L.R.
Uniform Laws Annotated
U.L.A.
Uniform Partnership Act
UPA
Uniform Probate Code
UPC
Uniform Probate Code Practice Manual
UPC Practice Manual
Uniform System of Citation
Unif. Sys. Citation
Union Labor Report, Bureau of National Affairs
Union Lab. Rep. (BNA)
Union Law Review
U.L.R.
Union of South Africa Water Courts Decisions
W.Ct. S.A.
Union of Soviet Socialist Republics
U.S.S.R.
Union Pacific Law Department Bulletin
Union Pac. L.D.B.
United Arab Emirates
U.A.E.
United Auto Workers
UAW
United Kingdom
U.K.
United Kingdom Immigrants Advisory Service
UKIAS

United Kingdom NATO Air Defense Region
UKADR
United Nations
UN
United Nations Appeal for Children
UNAC
United Nations Association International Service
UNAIS
United Nations Bulletin
U.N. Bull.
United Nations Capital Development Fund
UNCDF
United Nations Centre for Regional Development
UNCRD
United Nations Commission for India and Pakistan
UNCIP
United Nations Commission for Relief and Rehabilitation of Korea
UNCURK
United Nations Commission on International Trade Law
UNCITRAL
United Nations Commission on International Trade Law Yearbook
U.N. Comm. Int'l Trade L.Y.B., UNCITRAL Y.B.
United Nations Commission on Korea
UNCOK
United Nations Committee on the Peaceful Use of Outer Space
UNCOPUOS
United Nations Conference on International Organization
UNCIO

United Nations Conference on International Organization Documents
UNCIO Doc.

United Nations Conference on the Law of the Sea
UNCLOS

United Nations Conference on Trade and Development
UNCTAD

United Nations Development Advisory Team
UNDAT

United Nations Development Cooperation Cycle
UNDCC

United Nations Development Program
UNDP

United Nations Disaster Relief Office
UNDRO

United Nations Document Index
UNDI

United Nations Documents
UNDoc.

United Nations Economic and Social Commission for Asia and the Pacific
UNESCAP, ESCAP

United Nations Economic and Social Commission for Western Asia
UNESCWA

United Nations Economic and Social Council
ECOSOC

United Nations Economic and Social Council Official Record
UNESCOR

United Nations Economic and Social Office at Beirut
UNESOB

United Nations Economic and Social Records
U.N.ECOSOC

United Nations Economic Commission for Africa
UNECA

United Nations Economic Commission for Asia and the Far East
UNECAFE, ECAFE

United Nations Economic Commission for Europe
UNECE

United Nations Economic Commission for Latin America
UNECLA, ECLA

United Nations Economic Commission for Latin America and the Caribbean
UNECLLAC

United Nations Economic Development Administration
U.N.E.D.A.

United Nations Educational, Scientific and Cultural Organization
UNESCO

United Nations Emergency Force
UNEF

United Nations Environment Program
UNEP

United Nations Force in Cyprus
UNFICYP

United Nations Fund for Population Activities
UNFPA

United Nations General Assembly
U.N.G.A.

United Nations General Assembly Official Record
UNGAOR

United Nations Headquarters
U.N.H.Q.

United Nations High Commission for Refugees
UNHCR

United Nations High Commissioner for Refugees
UNCHR

United Nations Industrial Development Organization
UNIDO

United Nations Institute for Training and Research
UNITAR

United Nations International Children's Emergency Fund
UNICEF

United Nations Juridical Yearbook
U.N. Juridical Y.B., U.N. Jur. Y.B.

United Nations Korean Reconstruction Agency
UNKRA

United Nations Law of the Sea (Conference)
UNLOS

United Nations Law Reports
U.N.L.R.

United Nations League of Lawyers
U.N.L.L.

United Nations Military Observer Group for India and Pakistan
UNMOGIP

United Nations Multilateral Treaties
U.N.M.T.

United Nations Organization
U.N.O.

United Nations Relief and Rehabilitation Administration
UNRRA

United Nations Relief and Works Agency
UNRWA

United Nations Relief and Works Agency for Palestine Refugees in the Near East
UNRWAPRNE, UNRWAPR

United Nations Relief for Palestine Rufugees
UNRPR

United Nations Relief Operation in Dacca
UNROD

United Nations Reports of International Arbitral Awards
R. Int'l Arb. Awards, R.I.A.A., UNRIAA

United Nations Research Institute for Social Development
UNRISD

United Nations Resolutions
U.N. Res.

United Nations Review
U.N. Rev.

United Nations Scientific Conference on the Conservation and Utilization of Resources
UNSCCUR

United Nations Secretary General
U.N.S.G.

United Nations Security Council
S.C.

United Nations Security Council Official Records
U.N. SCOR

United Nations Social Defense Research Institute
UNSDRI

United Nations Social Development Division
UNSDD

United Nations Special Committee on Palestine
UNSCOP

United Nations Special Committee on the Balkans
UNSCOB

United Nations Temporary Commission on Korea
UNTCOK

United Nations Temporary Executive Authority
UNTEA

United Nations Treaty Series
UNTS, U.N.T.S.

United Nations Truce Supervision Organization
UNTSO

United Nations Trust for Development Planning and Projections
UNTFDPP

United Nations Trust Fund for Social Development
UNTFDS

United Nations Trust Territory
U.N.T.T.

United Nations Trusteeship Council
U.N.T.C.

United Nations Trusteeship Council Official Record
UNTCOR

United Nations University
UNU

United Nations Yearbook
U.N.Y.B., Y.B.U.N.Y.U.N.

United Provinces Law Reports, India
U.P.L.R.

United Provinces Law Times, India
U.P.L.T.

United States
U.S.

United States Air Force
USAF

United States Air Force Judge Advocate General Law Review
JAG L. Rev.

United States Air Force Judge Advocate General Opinions
Op. JAGAF

United States Air Force Reserve
USAFR

United States and Canadian Aviation Reports
U.S. & C. Av. R., United States & C. Avi. Rep., United States & Can. Av., U.S. & Can. A.R.

United States Annual Law Register
Ann.Law Reg., Ann.L.Reg.U.S.

United States Appeal Cases
App.Cas.

United States Appeals Reports
U.S. Ap., U.S. App.

United States Arbitration Act
USAA

United States Armed Services Board of Contract Appeals Decisions
ASBCA

United States Army Air Force
USAAF

United States Army, Judge Advocate General Opinions
CSJAG, Op. J.A.G.

United States Attorney General's Reports
Att'y. Gen. Rep., Op. A.G., Op. Att. Gen., Op. Attys. Gen., Ops. A.G.

United States Attorney's Manual
U.S.A.M.
United States Aviation Quarterly
Aviation Q.
United States Aviation Reports
U.S. Av., U.S. Av. R., U.S. Aviation Rep., U.S.Avi.Rep.
United States Bankruptcy Court
B.C.
United States Board of Tax Appeals Reports
B.T.A.
United States Bureau of Animal Industry, Monthly Record
B.A.I.M.R.
United States Circuit Court
U.S.C.C.
United States Circuit Court of Appeals Reports
U.S.C.C.A.
United States Claims Court Rules
Cl. Ct. R.
United States Coast Guard
USCG
United States Coast Guard Chief Counsel's Opinions
Op. CCCG.
United States Code
U.S.C.
United States Code Annotated
U.S.C.A., USCA
United States Code Annotated Appendix
U.S.C.A. app.
United States Code Appendix
U.S.C.App.
United States Code Congressional and Administrative News
U.S. Code Cong. & Ad. News
United States Code Service
U.S.C.S.

United States Code Service Appendix
U.S.C.S. app.
United States Code Supplement
U.S.C. Supp.
United States Commerce Court Opinions
Com.
United States Compiled Statutes
U.S. Comp. St.
United States Compiled Statutes Supplement
U.S. Comp. St. Supp.
United States Constitution
U.S. Const.
United States Congress, House of Representatives
H.R.
United States Congress, Senate
S.
United States Congressional and Administrative Service
U.S. Cong. & Adm. Serv.
United States Court of Appeals
C.A., US Ct App
United States Court of Appeals for District of Columbia
U.S.App.D.C.
United States Court of Appeals for the Federal Circuit
CAFC
United States Court of Claims
U.S.C.C., U.S.Ct.Cl., Cls. Ct., Ct.Cla., Ct. of Cls.
United States Court of Claims Reports
Court Cl., Ct. Cl.
United States Court of Customs and Patent Appeals
U.S.C.C.P.A.
United States Court of Military Appeals
Ct Mil App

United States Court of Military Appeals, Advance Opinions
U.S.C.M.A., Adv. Op.

United States Court of Military Appeals, Official Reports
UJCMA

United States Customs Appeals
Cust. A., Cust. App.

United States Customs Bureau, Digest of Customs and Related Laws
C.B.Dig.

United States Customs Court Reports, Reappraisement Decision
Reap. Dec., Reapp. Dec.

United States Customs Service
Customs

United States Daily
U.S.Daily

United States Decisions in Martin's North Carolina Circuit Court Reports
Mart. Dec.

United States Department of Agriculture
USDA

United States Department of Commerce, Bureau of Foreign and Domestic Commerce, General Legal Bulletin
U.S. Dept. of Commerce, Bureau of Foreign and Domestic Commerce, Gen. Leg. Bull.

United States Department of Interior
U.S. Dept. Int.

United States Department of Justice
US Dep't of Justice

United States Department of State
US Dep't of State

United States Department of State, Bulletin
Dept. of State Bull.

United States Department of the Treasury
U.S.Treas.Dept.

United States Digest
U.S. Dig.

United States District Court
D. C., U.S. Dist. Ct., U.S.D.C.

United States District Court for the Central District of California
C.D. Cal.

United States District Court for the District of Alaska
D. Alaska

United States District Court for the District of Arizona
D. Ariz.

United States District Court for the District of Colorado
D. Colo.

United States District Court for the District of Columbia
D.C. Dist. Col., DC DC

United States District Court for the District of Connecticut
D. Conn.

United States District Court for the District of Delaware
D. Del.

United States District Court for the District of Guam
D. Guam

United States District Court for the District of Hawaii
D. Hawaii, D.Haw., U.S. Dist. Ct. Haw., H. Dist. Ct., U.S.D.C. Hawaii, H. Dist. Ct., U.S.D.C. Hw., U.S. D.C. Haw., U.S. D.C. Hawaii

United States District Court for
the District of Idaho
D. Idaho
United States District Court for
the District of Kansas
D. Kan.
United States District Court for
the District of Maine
D. Me.
United States District Court for
the District of Maryland
D. Md.
United States District Court for
the District of Massachusetts
D. Mass.
United States District Court for
the District of Minnesota
D. Minn.
United States District Court for
the District of Montana
D. Mont.
United States District Court for
the District of Nebraska
Neb.
United States District Court for
the District of Nevada
D. Nev.
United States District Court for
the District of New Hampshire
D. N.H.
United States District Court for
the District of New Jersey
D. N.J.
United States District Court for
the District of New Mexico
D. N.M.
United States District Court for
the District of North Dakota
D. N.D.
United States District Court for
the District of Oregon
D. Or.

United States District Court for
the District of Puerto Rico
D. P. R.
United States District Court for
the District of Rhode Island
D. R. I.
United States District Court for
the District of South Carolina
D. S. C.
United States District Court for
the District of South Dakota
D. S. D.
United States District Court for
the District of the Virgin Is-
lands
D. V. I.
United States District Court for
the District of Utah
D. Utah, D.Utah
United States District Court for
the District of Vermont
D. Vt.
United States District Court for
the District of Wyoming
D. Wyo.
United States District Court for
the Eastern and Western Dis-
tricts of Arkansas
E.D. Ark.
United States District Court for
the Eastern District of Califor-
nia
E.D. Cal.
United States District Court for
the Eastern District of Illinois
E.D. Ill.
United States District Court for
the Eastern District of Ken-
tucky
E.D. Ky.

United States District Court for
the Eastern District of Louisiana
   E.D. La.

United States District Court for
the Eastern District of Michigan
   E.D. Mich.

United States District Court for
the Eastern District of Missouri
   E.D. Mo.

United States District Court for
the Eastern District of New
York
   E.D.N.Y.

United States District Court for
the Eastern District of North
Carolina
   E.D.N.C.

United States District Court for
the Eastern District of Oklahoma
   E.D. Okla.

United States District Court for
the Eastern District of Pennsylvania
   E.D. Pa.

United States District Court for
the Eastern District of Tennessee
   E.D. Tenn.

United States District Court for
the Eastern District of Texas
   E.D. Tex.

United States District Court for
the Eastern District of Virginia
   E.D. Va.

United States District Court for
the Eastern District of Washington
   E.D. Wash.

United States District Court for
the Eastern District of Wisconsin
   E.D. Wis.

United States District Court for
the Middle District of Alabama
   M.D. Ala.

United States District Court for
the Middle District of Florida
   M.D. Fla.

United States District Court for
the Middle District of Georgia
   M.D. Ga.

United States District Court for
the Middle District of Louisiana
   M.D. La.

United States District Court for
the Middle District of North
Carolina
   M.D.N.C.

United States District Court for
the Middle District of Pennsylvania
   M.D. Pa.

United States District Court for
the Middle District of Tennessee
   M.D. Tenn.

United States District Court for
the Northern District of Alabama
   N.D. Ala.

United States District Court for
the Northern District of California
   N.D. Cal.

United States District Court for
the Northern District of Florida
   N.D. Fla.

Bieber's Reversed Dictionary

United States District Court for the Northern District of Georgia
    N.D. Ga.

United States District Court for the Northern District of Illinois
    N.D. Ill.

United States District Court for the Northern District of Indiana
    N.D. Ind.

United States District Court for the Northern District of Iowa
    N.D. Iowa

United States District Court for the Northern District of Mississippi
    N.D. Miss.

United States District Court for the Northern District of New York
    N.D.N.Y.

United States District Court for the Northern District of Ohio
    N.D. Ohio

United States District Court for the Northern District of Oklahoma
    N.D. Okla.

United States District Court for the Northern District of Texas
    N.D. Tex.

United States District Court for the Southern District of Alabama
    S.D. Ala.

United States District Court for the Southern District of California
    S.D. Cal.

United States District Court for the Southern District of Florida
    S.D. Fln.

United States District Court for the Southern District of Georgia
    S.D. Ga.

United States District Court for the Southern District of Illinois
    S.D. Ill.

United States District Court for the Southern District of Indiana
    S.D. Ind.

United States District Court for the Southern District of Iowa
    S.D. Iowa

United States District Court for the Southern District of Mississippi
    S.D. Miss.

United States District Court for the Southern District of New York
    S.D. N.Y.

United States District Court for the Southern District of Ohio
    S.D. Ohio

United States District Court for the Southern District of Texas
    S.D. Tex.

United States District Court for the Southern District of West Virginia
    S.D. W.Va

United States District Court for the Western District of Kentucky
    W.D.Ky.

United States District Court for
the Western District of Louisi-
ana
  W.D.La.
United States District Court for
the Western District of Michi-
gan
  W.D.Mich.
United States District Court for
the Western District of Mis-
souri
  W.D.Mo.
United States District Court for
the Western District of New
York
  W.D.N.Y.
United States District Court for
the Western District of North
Carolina
  W.D.N.C.
United States District Court for
the Western District of Okla-
homa
  W.D.Okla.
United States District Court for
the Western District of Pennsyl-
vania
  W.D.Pa.
United States District Court for
the Western District of Tennes-
see
  W.D.Tenn.
United States District Court for
the Western District of Texas
  W.D.Tex.
United States District Court for
the Western District of Virginia
  W.D.Va.
United States District Court for
the Western District of Wash-
ington
  W.D.Wash.

United States District Court for
the Western District of Wiscon-
sin
  W.D.Wis.
United States District of Colum-
bia
  U.S.D.C.
United States Economic Commis-
sion for Africa
  ECA
United States Employment Serv-
ice
  USES
United States Equity Digest
  U.S. Eq. Dig.
United States Executive Agree-
ment Series
  E.A.S., EAS
United States Federal Labor Re-
lations Council Decisions and
Interpretations
  F.L.R.C.
United States Federal Maritime
Board
  F.M.B.
United States Federal Power
Commission Opinions and Deci-
sions
  F.P.C.
United States Food and Drug Ad-
ministration. Notices of Judg-
ment: Foods
  F.N.J. , F.D.C.
United States High Commis-
sioner for Germany, Informa-
tion Bulletin
  U.S. High Comm. for Germany
  Inf. Bull.
United States House of Repre-
sentatives Joint Resolution
  H.J.Res.

United States Housing Authority
USHA
United States Immigration and Naturalization Service Monthly Review
Immig. & Naturalization Serv. Mo. Rev.
United States Indian Affairs Office Digest of Decisions
Ind. A.Dig.
United States Indian Service
USIS
United States Information Agency
USIA
United States Information Agency Procurement Regulation
IAPR
United States Internal Revenue Bureau, Commissioner's Mimeographed Published Opinions
Mim.
United States International Trade Commission Publication
U.S.I.T.C.Pub.
United States Interstate Commerce Commission Reports
U.S.I.C.C. Rep.
United States Interstate Commerce Commission Valuation Reports
U.S.I.C.C. V.R.
United States Judge-Advocate General (Navy) Compilation of Court-Martial Orders
C.M.O.
United States Jurist
U.S. Jur.

United States Land Decisions by Proudfit
Proudf. Land Dec.
United States Law Intelligencer and Review
U.S. Law Int.
United States Law Journal
U.S. Law Jour., U.S.L.J.
United States Law Magazine
U.S. L. Mag., U.S. Law Mag.
United States Law Review
U.S. L. Rev.
United States Law Week
U.S.L. Week, U.S.L.W.
United States Laws
U.S.L., L.U.S.
United States Marine Corps
USMC
United States Marine Corps Reserve
USMCR
United States Maritime Commission
USMC
United States Monthly Law Magazine
U.S. Month. Law Mag., U.S.M.L.Mag.
United States National Railroad Adjustment Board Awards, First Division
N.R.A.B. (1st D.)
United States National Railroad Adjustment Board Awards, Fourth Division
N.R.A.B. (4th D.)
United States National Railroad Adjustment Board Awards, Second Division
N.R.A.B. (2d D.)

United States National Railroad Adjustment Board Awards, Trial Division
N.R.A.B. (3d D.)

United States Navy
USN

United States Navy Judge Advocate General Opinions
Op. JAGN

United States, Notes on United States Reports
Notes on

United States of America
U.S., US

United States Patent and Trademark Office, Official Gazette: Trademarks
O.G. TM

United States Patent Office, Official Gazette
Off. Gaz. Pat. Off., Off. Gaz.,
Off. Gaz. Pat. Office, O.G., O.G.
Pat. Off., Pat. Off. Gaz., P.O.G.,
Official Gazette USPO

United States Patent Quarterly
P.Q., U.S. Pat. Quar., U.S. Pat.
Quart., U.S.Pat.Q.

United States Patents Quarterly, Bureau of National Affairs
U.S.P.Q. (BNA)

United States Postal Service
USPS

United States Post Office Department Solicitor's Official Opinions
Op.Solic.P.O.Dep't.,
Op.Sol.P.O.D., Ops.A.A.G.,
P.O.D.

United States Public Health Service, Court Decisions
Pub. Health

United States Railroad Labor Board
U.S. R.R. Lab. Bd.

United States Railroad Labor Board Decisions
R.L.B.

United States Railroad Retirement Board Law Bulletin
R.R.B.L.B.

United States Register
U.S.Reg.

United States Reports
U.S.Rep., U.S. Reports

United States Reports, Lawyers' Edition
U.S. Rep. (L. Ed.), U.S. Sup. Ct.
(L.Ed.)

United States Revised Statutes
U.S. Rev. St., U.S.R.S.

United States Senate Committee Report
Sen. Rep., S.Rept., Sen.Rept.

United States Senate Concurrent Resolution
S. Con. Res.

United States Senate Resolution
S. Res.

United States Shipping Board Bureau Decisions
U.S.S.B.B.

United States Shipping Board Decisions
U.S.S.B.

United States Social Security Board Unemployment Compensation Interpretation Service, Benefit Series
Benefit Series, U.C.I.S.

United States State Department Bulletin
State Dept. Bull.

United States Statutes at Large
St., U.S. St. at L., United States
Stat., Stat. at L., Stat.
United States Supreme Court Bulletin, Commerce Clearing House
S. Ct. Bull. (CCH)
United States Supreme Court Digest Annotated
U.S. Dig. (L.ed.) Anno.
United States Supreme Court Reporter
U.S. Sup. Ct., U.S. Sup. Ct. Rep., U.S. Sup. Ct. R.
United States Supreme Court Reports
U.S., US, U.S.R., U.S.S.C. Rep.
United States Supreme Court Reports, Lawyers' Edition
U.S. Law. Ed., Law. Ed. Adv. Op., L.Ed. (Adv.Ops.)
United States Supreme Court Reports, Photo Reproduction Set by Baldwin
Bald. United States Sup.Ct.Rep.
United States Supreme Court Rule
Sup. Ct. R.
United States Supreme Court Slip Opinion Docket Numbers
USDk
United States Tariff Commission Publications
T.C. Pub.
United States Tariff Commission Reports
T.C.Rept.
United States Tariff Commission Reports, Second Series
T.C. Rept. 2d ser.
United States Tax Cases, Commerce Clearing House
U.S.Tax Cas. (CCH), U.S.T.C.

United States Tax Court
T.C., T. Ct.
United States Tax Court Cases
T.C.
United States Tax Court Reports
T. Ct. Rep.
United States Tax Court Memorandum
T. Ct. Mem.
United States Trademark Association Bulletin
Trademark Bull.
United States Travel Service
USTS
United States Treasury Department
U.S. Treas. Dept.
United States Treasury Regulations
Treas. Regs., U.S. Treas. Reg.
United States Treaties and Other International Acts Series
TIAS
United States Treaties and Other International Agreements
U.S.T., UST
United States Treaty Development
U.S.T.D.
United States Treaty Series
TS, T.S., U.S. Treaty Ser.
United States Veteran's Administration Administrator's Decisions
U.S.V.A.A.D.
United States Veterans Bureau Directors Decisions
U.S.V.B.D.D.
United States War Department, Decisions of Board of Contract Adjustment
War Dep. B.C.A., War Dept.B.C.A.

Universal
Univ.
Universal Human Rights
Univ. Hum. Rts., Univ. Human
Rights
Universal Postal Union
U.P.U.
Universit[y, ties]
U., U., Univ.
University Law College Journal, Rajputana University
U.L.C.J., Univ. L. Coll. J.
University Law Review
Univ. L. Rev., Univ. L.R., U.L.R.
University Microfilms International
UMI
University of Arkansas at Little Rock Law Journal
U. Ark. Little Rock L.J., UALR
L.J.
University of Baltimore Journal of Environmental Law
U. Balt. J. Envtl. L.
University of Baltimore Law Forum
U. Balt. L.F.
University of Baltimore Law Review
Ba. L.R., U. Balt. L. Rev., U.
Balt. L.R., U. Baltimore L. Rev.,
U.B.L.R.
University of Botswana, Lesotho and Swaziland Law Journal
U.B.L.S. L.J.
University of Bridgeport Law Review
U. Bridgeport L. Rev.
University of British Columbia Law Review
U. Brit. Col. L. Rev., U. Brit. Co-
lum. L. Rev., U.B.C. L. Rev.,
U.B.C. L. Rev.

University of British Columbia Legal News
U.B.C. L.N.
University of British Columbia Legal Notes
U.B.C. Legal N., U.B.C. Notes
University of California at Davis Law Review
U.C. Davis L. Rev., U.C.D. L.
Rev.
University of California at Los Angeles Law Review
C.L.A., UCLA L. Rev., Univ.
California Los Angeles L. Rev.,
U.C.L.A. Law R.
University of California, Los Angeles
UCLA
University of California Los Angeles-Alaska Law Review
U.C.L.A.-Alaska L. Rev.
University of Ceylon Law Review
U. Ceylon L.R., U.C.L.R.
University of Chicago Law Review
Ch. L., Ch. L.R., U. Chi. L. Rev.,
U. Chicago L. Rev., U. of Chi. L.
Rev., U.C.L.R., Univ. of Chicago
L. Rev.
University of Chicago Law School
UCHILS
University of Chicago Law School Record
U. Chi. L. Rec., U. Chi. L. Sch.
Rec., U. Chi. L.S. Rec.
University of Chicago Legal Forum
U. Chi. Legal F., U. Chi. Legal F.

University of Cincinnati Law Review
Cin. L. Rev., Cin. Law Rev., U. Cin. L. Rev., U. of Cin. L. Rev., U.C.L.R., Univ. of Cincinnati L. Rev., U.C.R.

University of Colorado Law Review
C.U.R., U. Colo. L. Rev., U.C.L.R., Univ. of Colorado L. Rev., U. Color. L. Rev.

University of Colorado School of Law
UCOSL

University of Dayton Intramural Law Review
Dayton

University of Dayton Law Review
U. Dayton L. Rev.

University of Detroit Journal of Urban Law
U. Det. J. Urb. L., U. Detroit J. Urban L., Urban L.J.

University of Detroit Law Journal
U. Det. L.J., U. Detroit L.J., U. of Detroit L.J., D. L.J.

University of Detroit Law Review
U. Det. L. Rev., U. Detroit L. Rev.

University of Detroit Mercy Law Review
U. Det. Mercy L. Rev.

University of Florida Journal of Law and Public Policy
U. Fla. J. L. & Pub. Pol'y

University of Florida Law Review
Fl. L.R., F.L.R., U. Fla. L. Rev., U. Florida L. Rev., U. of Fla. L. Rev., Univ. of Florida L. Rev.

University of Ghana Law Journal
U. Ghana L.J., U.G.L.J., Un. of Gh. L.J., Univ. of Ghana L.J.

University of Hawaii Law Review
U. Haw. L. Rev., U. Hawaii L. Rev.

University of Ife Law Reports, Nigeria
U.I.L.R.

University of Illinois Law Bulletin
U.Ill. L.B., U.Ill. L.Bull.

University of Illinois Law Forum
Law Forum, L.F., U. Ill. L.Forum, U.Ill. L.F., Univ. Ill. L. Forum, Univ. of Illinois L. Forum

University of Illinois Law Review
Ill LR, U. Ill. L. Rev.

University of Illinois Moot Court Bulletin
Moot Ct. Bull.

University of Iowa Law Review
U.Iowa L. Rev.

University of Kansas City Law Review
Kansas City L. Rev., K.C.R., U. Kans. City L. Rev., U. of Kans.City L. Rev., U. Kan. City L. Rev.

University of Kansas Law Review
Kan. L. Rev., U. Kan. L. Rev., U. Kan. L.R., U. Kansas L. Rev., U. of Kansas L. Rev., U.K.L.R.

University of Maine Law Review
Me. L., U. Maine L. Rev.

University of Malaya Law Review
U.M.L.R., U. of Malaya L. Rev.

University of Manila Law Gazette, Philippines
Univ. of Manila L. Gaz.

University of Maryland Law Forum
U. Mary. L. Forum, U.Md. L.F.

University of Miami Entertainment and Sports Law Review
U. Miami Ent. & Sports L. Rev.

University of Miami Inter-American Law Review
U. Miami Inter-Am. L. Rev.

University of Miami Law Center
UMLC

University of Miami Law Review
U. Miami L. Rev., U. of Miami L. Rev., U.M.L.R., Univ. of Miami L. Rev., Mi. L.

University of Michigan Journal of Law Reform
U. Mich. J. L. Ref., U. Mich. J. Law Reform, Univ. of Michigan J. of Law Reform

University of Missouri at Kansas City Law Review
K.C.R., U. Missouri at K.C.L. Rev., U. Mo.-Kansas City L. Rev., U. Mo. K.C. L. Rev., UMKC L. Rev., UMKCLR, Univ. of Missouri at Kansas City L.Rev.

University of Missouri Bulletin Law Series
U. Mo. Bull. L. Ser., Law Ser. Mo. Bull.

University of Missouri Law Bulletin
U. Mo. L. Bull., U. of M.L.B.

University of Nebraska College of Law
UNBCL

University of New Brunswick Law Journal
U. New Brunswick L.J., U.N.B. Law Journal, U.N.B.L.J., Univ. of New Brunswick L.J.

University of New Brunswick Law School Journal
U.N.B.L.S.J.

University of New South Wales Law Journal
U. New So. Wales L.J., U. News S. Wales L.J., Univ. N.S.W.L.J., U.N.S.W. L.J., U. New South Wales L.J.

University of Newark Law Review
Newark L. Rev., U. Newark L. Rev.

University of Osaka Prefecture Bulletin, Japan
Osaka Pref. Bull.

University of Pennsylvania Journal of International Business Law
U. Pa. J. Int'l Bus. L.

University of Pennsylvania Law Review
Pa. L., Pa. L. Rev., Pa LR, U. of P. L. Rev., U. of P. L.R., U. of Pa. L. Rev., U. Pa. L. Rev., Univ. of Pennsylvania L. Rev.

University of Pittsburgh Law Review
Pitts. L. Rev., P.L.R., U. of Pitt. L. Rev., U. Pitt. L. Rev., Pit. L., Univ. of Pittsburgh L. Rev.

University of Puget Sound Law Review
U. Puget Sound L. Rev.

University of Puget Sound School of Law
UPSSL

University of Queensland Law Journal
Univ. Q. L.J., U. Queens. L.J., U. Queensl. L.J., U.Q.L.J., Univ. of Queensland L.J., U. of Queensl. L.J.

University of Richmond Law Notes
U. Rich. L.N., Univ. of Richmond L. Not.

University of Richmond Law Review
Univ. of Richmond L. Rev., U. Rich. L. Rev., U. Richmond L. Rev.

University of San Fernando Valley Law Review
U. San Fernando V. L. Rev., U. San Fernando Valley L. Rev., U.S.F.V. L. Rev., Univ. of San Fernando Valley L. Rev.

University of San Francisco Law Review
SFLR, U. San. Fran. L. Rev., U. San Francisco L. Rev., U.S.F. L. Rev., U.S.F. L.R., Univ. of San Francisco L. Rev.

University of San Francisco Maritime Law Journal
United States F. Mar. L. J.

University of Santa Clara School of Law
SNCLAR

University of Santo Tomas Law Review
Santo Tomas L. Rev.

University of South Carolina Governmental Review
U.S.C. Govt'l. Rev.

University of Southern California School of Law Tax Institute
So. Calif. Tax Inst., United States Cal. Sch. L. Tax Inst.

University of Southern California Tax Institute
S.C.T.I., U. So. Cal. Tax Inst.

University of Tasmania Law Review
Tasmania L.R., U. Tas. L.R., U. Tasm. L. Rev., Univ. T. L.R., Univ. Tas. L.R., Univ. of Tasmania L. Rev.

University of Tennessee College of Law
UTLC

University of Texas School of Law
UTSL

University of the East Law Journal
U. East L.J., UE. Law J.

University of Toledo College of Law
UTOLCL

University of Toledo Intramural Law Review
U. Toledo Intra. L.R.

University of Toledo Law Review
To. L.R., Tol. L.R., Toledo L. Rev., U. Tol. L. Rev., U. Toledo L. Rev., Univ. of Toledo L. Rev.

University of Toronto Faculty of Law Review
U. Tor. Fac. L. Rev., U. Tor. Fac. L.R., U. Toronto Fac. L. Rev., U. Toronto Faculty L. Rev., U.T. Fac. L. Rev.

University of Toronto Law Journal
U. Toronto L.J., U.T.L.J., U. of Toronto L.J., Univ. of Toronto L.J.

University of Toronto School of Law Review
U. Tor. L. Rev., U. Toronto Sch. L. Rev.

University of Tulsa Law Journal, Tulsa, Oklahoma
Univ. of Tulsa L.J.

University of Washington Law Review
U. Wash. L. Rev.

University of West Los Angeles Law Review
U. West. L.A. L. Rev., U. West Los Angeles L. Rev.

University of West Los Angeles School of Law, Law Review
U.W.L.A. L. Rev., U.W.L.A. Rev.

University of Western Australia Annual Law Review
U. West. Aust. Ann. L. Rev., Univ. W.A. Ann. L. Rev.

University of Western Australia Law Review
U. of West. Aust. L. Rev., U. Western Aust. L. Rev., Univ. W.A. L. Rev., U.W. Austl. L. Rev., U.W.L.A. L. Rev., W.A.L.R., West. Aust. L. Rev., Univ. of West. Australia L. Rev.

University of Western Ontario Law Review
U. Western Ont. L. Rev., U.W.O. L. Rev., U.W.Ont. L. Rev.

University of Windsor Law Review
U. Windsor L. Rev.

University of Zambia Law Bulletin
U. Zambia L.B.

University Publishing Group
Univ. Pub. Group.

University Year for Action
U.Y.A.

Unofficial Reports
Unof.

Unreported New York Estate Tax Cases, Prentice-Hall
Unrep. N.Y. Est. T.C.

Unreported Travancore Decisions, India
Un. Trav. Dec.

Unreported Wills Cases, Prentice-Hall
Unrep.Wills Cas.

Update on Law-Related Education
Update

Upper Bench
Banc. Sup., U.B.

Upper Bench Precedents, Tempore Car. I, England
U.B.Pr., Up. Ben. Pr., Up. Ben. Pre.

Upper Burma Rulings
U.B.R.

Upper Canada
U.C., Up. Can.

Upper Canada Appeal Reports
U.C. App., U.C. App. (Can.), U.C. App. Rep.

Upper Canada Chamber Reports
U.C. Chamb. Rep., U.C. Cham., U.C. Cham. (Can.), U.C. Chamb., Chamb. Rep.

Upper Canada Chancery Chambers Reports
Cooper, Ch. Ch., Ch. Cham., Ch. R., Chy. Ch., Chy. Chrs., Chamb. R., Chan. Chamb., Ch.Chamb. (Can.)

Upper Canada Chancery Reports
U.C. Ch. (Can.), U.C. Ch. Rep., U.C. Chan., U.C. Ch.

Upper Canada Common Pleas
C.P.

Upper Canada Common Pleas Division Reports
U.C.C.P.D.

Upper Canada Common Pleas Reports
U.C.C. P., U.C.C. P. (Can.), Van. K. & H.

Upper Canada Court Records (Report of Ontario Bureau of Archives)
U.C.C.R.

Upper Canada Error and Appeal Reports
E. & A., U.C. Err. & App., U.C. Err. & App. (Can.), U.C.E. & A.

Upper Canada Jurist
U.C. Jur., U.C. Jur. (Can.)

Upper Canada King's Bench Reports
K.B.U.C.

Upper Canada King's Bench Reports, Old Series
U.C.K.B., U.C.K.B. (Can.), U.C.O.S.

Upper Canada Law Journal
U.C.L.J. (Can.), Up. Can. L.J., U.C.L.J.

Upper Canada Law Journal, New Series
U.C.L.J. N.S., U.C.L.J. N.S. (Can.)

Upper Canada Practice Reports
U.C. Pr., U.C. Pr. R., U.C.P.R., U.C.Pr.(Can.), U.C. Pract., P.R.

Upper Canada Queen's Bench Reports
U.C.Q.B.

Upper Canada Queen's Bench Reports, Old Series
O.S., U.C.Q.B. O.S., U.C.Q.B. O.S. (Can.)

Upper Canada Reports
U.C. Rep.

Upshur's Review of Story on the Constitution
Ups. Sto.

Upton on Maritime Warfare and Prize
Upt. Mar. W.

Upton on Trademarks
Upt. Tr. Mar.

Urban
Urb.

Urban Affairs Reporter, Commerce Clearing House
Urb. Aff. Rep., Urban Affairs Rep.

Urban Law and Policy
Urb. Law Pol., Urb. L. & Pol'y

Urban Law Annual
Urban L. Ann., Urban Law Ann.

Urban Law Review
Urb. L. Rev., Urban L. Rev.

Urban Lawyer
Urb. Law., Urban Law., Urban Lawyer

Urban Mass Transportation Administration
UMTA

Urling on Foreign Patents
Url. For. Pat.

Urling on the Office of a Trustee
Url. Trust.

Urling's Legal Guide for the Clergy
Url. Cl.

Uruguay
Uru.

US Bureau of Labor Statistics Bulletin
B.L.S. Bull.

Utah
U., Ut., Utah

Utah Administrative Rules
Utah Admin. R.

Utah Bar Bulletin
Utah B. Bull., Utah Bar. Bull

Utah Bar Journal
Ut. B.J., Utah B.J.

Utah Code Annotated
    U.C.A., Utah Code Ann.
Utah Constitution
    Utah Const.
**Utah Industrial Commission Bul-
letin**
    Utah I.C. Bull.
Utah Law Review
    ULR, U.L.R., Ut. L.R., Utah L.
    Rev.
Utah Laws
    Utah Laws
**Utah Public Utilities Commission
Report**
    Utah P.U.C.
Utah Reports
    U., Ut., Utah
Utah Reports, Second Series
    Utah 2d, U.2d

Utah State Bar Association
    Utah S.B.A.
Utah State Bulletin
    Utah Admin. Bull.
Utah Supreme Court Reports
    Utah
Utilities Law Reporter
    ULR, U.L.R.
**Utilities Law Reporter, Com-
merce Clearing House**
    Util. L. Rep. (CCH)
**Utilities Law Reports, Commerce
Clearing House**
    Util. L. Rep. (CCH)
Utilit[y, ies]
    Util.
Utility Section Newsletter
    Util. Sect. Newl.

V

Vacated; Same Case Vacated (used in Shepard's Citations)
V.

Vacating
Vac'g

Vagrancy
Vag.

Vaizey's Law of Settlements
Vaizey

Valen's Commentaries
Val. Com.

Valid; Decision or Finding Held Valid for Reasons Given (used in Shepard's Citations)
V.A.

Valparaiso
Val.

Valparaiso University Law Review
Valparaiso Univ. L. Rev., Val.U.L. Rev.,V.U.L.R.

Valuation Decisions
V.D.

Valuation Reports, United States Interstate Commerce Commission
Val. Rep., Val. Rep. I.C.C., V.R.

Van Diemen's Land Acts, Australia
Acts Van Diem.L., Van Diem.L.Acts

Van Fleet on Collateral Attack
Van Fleet, Coll. Attack

Van Heythuysen on Maritime Evidence
Van Hey. Mar. Ev.

Van Heythuysen's Equity Draftsman
V.H. Eq. Dr., Van Hey. Eq.

Van Heythuysen's Rudiments of English Law
Van Hey. Rud.

Van Koughnet's Reports (15-21 Upper Canada Common Pleas)
Van K.

Van Ness' Prize Cases, United States District Court, District of New York
V.N., Van N., Van Ness, Prize Cas.

Van Santvoord's Equity Practice
Van Sant. Eq. Pr.

Van Santvoord's Lives of the Chief Justices of the United States
Van Sant. Ch. J.

Van Santvoord's Pleadings
Van Sant. Pl.

Van Santvoord's Precedents
Van Sant. Prec.

Van Weytson on Average
Q. Van Weyt.

Vander Linden's Practice, Cape Colony
Van. L.

Vanderbilt
Vand.

Vanderbilt Journal of Transnational Law
Vand. J. Transnat'l. L., Vanderbilt J. Transnat'l L.

Vanderbilt Law Review
Vand. L. Rev., Vanderbilt L.R., V.L.R.

Vanderbilt Lawyer
Vand. Law.

Vanderbilt University School of Law
VANUSL

Vanderlinden's Laws of Holland
Vander L.

Vanderstraaten's Decisions in Appeal, Supreme Court, Ceylon
Vanderstraaten

Vanderstraaten's Reports, Ceylon
Vanderstr.

Various
var.

Various Years
V.Y.

Vatican City State
Vatican

Vattel's Law of Nations
Vatt., Vattel, Vattel, Law Nat.

Vaughan's English Common Pleas Reports
Vaug., Vaugh., Vaughan, Vaughan (Eng.)

Vaux' Recorder's Decisions, Philadelphia
Rec. Dec., Vaux, Vaux (Pa.), Vaux Rec. Dec.

Veazey's Reports (36-44 Vermont)
Veazey

Vehicle and Traffic
Veh. & Traf.

Vehicle Code
Veh. C.

Vehicles
Veh.

Venditioni Exponas (Lat.)
Vend. Ex.

Vendor and Purchaser
V. & P.

Venezuela
Venez.

Ventris' English Common Pleas Reports
Vent., Vent. (Eng.), Ventr.

Ventris' English King's Bench Reports
Vent., Vent. (Eng.)

Venue
Ven.

Verb
V.

Verbo
Vo.

Verified Statement
V.S.

Vermont
V., Vt.

Vermont Administrative Code
Vt. Admin. Code

Vermont Administrative Procedure Compilation
Vt. Admin. Comp.

Vermont Administrative Procedures Bulletin
Vt. Admin. Proc. Bull.

Vermont Attorney General Biennial Report
Biennial Rep.Vt.Att'y Gen.

Vermont Bar Association Committee on Continuing Legal Education
VTCLE

Vermont Bar Association, Reports
Vt. B. A.

Vermont Bar Journal and Law Digest
Vt. B.J. & L. Dig.

Vermont Constitution
Vt. Const.

Vermont Law Review
Vermont L. Rev., Vt. L. Rev.

Vermont Laws
Vt. Acts

Vermont Public Service Commission
Vt. P.S.C.

Vermont Railroad Commission
Vt. R.C.
Vermont Reports
V., Ver., Verm., V.R., Vt., Ver.
Rep., Vermont R., Vermont
Rep., Vermont Reports, Vermt.,
Vert., Vt. R., Vt. Rep.
Vermont Statutes
V.S.
Vermont Statutes Annotated
V.S.A., Vt. Stat. Ann.
Vernon and Scriven's Irish King's Bench Reports
Vern. & Sc., V. & S., Vern. & S.,
Vern. & S. (Ir.), Vern. & Scr.,
Vern. & Scriv.
Vernon's Annotated Missouri Rule
V.A.M.R.
Vernon's Annotated Missouri Statutes
Mo. Ann. Stat. (Vernon),
V.A.M.S.
Vernon's Annotated Texas Civil Statutes
Vernon's Ann. Civ. St.
Vernons' Annotated Texas Code of Criminal Procedure
Vernon's Ann. C.C.P.
Vernon's Annotated Texas Penal Code
Vernon's Ann. P.C.
Vernon's Annotated Texas Statutes
V.A.T.S.
Vernon's English Chancery Reports
Vern. Ch., Vern., Vern.(Eng.)
Vernon's Kansas Statutes Annotated
Kan. Ann., Kan. Subject
Ann.Vernon's

Vernon's Kansas Statutes Annotated, Code of Civil Procedure
Kan. Civ. Pro. Stat. Ann., Kan.
Civ. Pro. Stat. Ann. (Vernon)
Vernon's Kansas Statutes Annotated Criminal Code and Code of Criminal Procedure
Kan. Crim. Code & Code of
Crim. Proc. (Vernon)
Vernon's Kansas Statutes Annotated, Uniform Commercial Code
Kan. U.C.C. Ann. (Vernon)
Vernon's Texas Codes Annotated
V.T.C.A.
Verplanck on Contracts
Verpl. Cont.
Verplanck on Evidence
Verpl. Ev.
Versus (against) (Lat.)
V., Vs.
Vesey and Beames' English Chancery Reports
Ve. & B., Vea. & B., V. & B.,
Ves. & B. (Eng.), Ves. & Bea.,
Ves. & Beam., Ves. & B.
Vesey, Junior's English Chancery Reports
Ves. Jr. (Eng.), Ves. Jun., Ves.
Jr.
Vesey, Junior's English Chancery Reports, Supplement
Ves. Supp., Supp. Ves. Jun.,
Ves. Jr. Suppl, Ves. Jun. Supp.
(Eng.)
Vesey, Senior's English Chancery Reports
Ves. Sr. (Eng), Ves., Ves. Sen.,
Ves. Sr.
Vesey, Senior's English Chancery Reports (Belt's edition)
Belt Ves.Sen.

Vesey, Senior's English Chancery Reports, Supplement
Ves. Supp., Ves. Sr. Supp., Ves. Sr. Supp. (Eng.)

Vesey, Senior's English Chancery Reports, Supplement (Belt)
Belt.Sup., Belt. Sup. Ves., Belt's Supp. (Eng.), Belt Supp.

Veterans Administration/Department of Veterans Affairs
VA

Veterans Administration Procurement Regulations
VAPR

Veterans' Affairs, Veterans' Affairs Department
VA

Veterans' Affairs Decisions, Appealed Pension and Civil Service Retirement Cases
V.A.D.

Veterans and Veterans Laws
Vet.

Veterans' Bureau
V.B.

Veteres Intrationes
Vet. Entr. (or Int.)

Veterinarians
Veterinar.

Vicat's Vocabularium Juris Utriusque ex Variis Ante Editis
Vicat. Vicat Voc.Jur.

Vice-Admiralty
V.A.

Vice Chairman, Vice Chairperson, Vice Chairwoman
V Chair

Vice-Chancellor
V.C.

Vice-Chancellor's Courts
V.C.

Vice-Chancellor's Reports
V.C. Rep.

Vice President
VP

Victoria
V., Vict., Vic.

Victoria, Acts of Parliament
Vict. Acts, Acts Vict.

Victoria Law Reports
V.R. (Law)

Victoria Reports, Admiralty
V.C. Adm.

Victoria Reports, Equity
V.C. Eq.

Victoria University College Law Review
V.U.C. L.R.

Victoria University Law Review
Vict. U. L. Rev.

Victoria University of Wellington Law Review
Vict. U. Well. L. Rev., Vict. U. Wellington L. Rev., V.U.W.L. Rev., V.U.W.L.R., Vict. U.of Wellington L. Rev.

Victorian Admiralty
Vict. Admr.

Victorian Consolidated Statutes
Vict. C.S.

Victorian Equity
Vict. Eq.

Victorian Law
Vict. L.

Victorian Law Journal
Vict. L.J.

Victorian Law Reform Commissioner
V.L.R.C.

Victorian Law Reports
Vict. J. (Austr.), Vict. L.R., V.R.L., V.L.R.

Victorian Law Reports, Admiralty
V.L.R. (Adm.)

Victorian Law Reports, Equity
V.L.R. (E.), V.L.R. (Eq.)
Victorian Law Reports, Insolvency, Probate and Matrimonial
V.L.R. (I.P. & M.)
Victorian Law Reports, Law
V.L.R. (L.)
Victorian Law Reports, Mining
V.L.R. (M.)
Victorian Law Reports, Probate and Matrimonial
V.L.R. (P. & M.)
Victorian Law Times
Vic. L.T.,V.L.T., Vict. L.T.
Victorian Mining Law Reports
Vict. L.R. Min.
Victorian Planning Appeal Decisions
V.P.A.
Victorian Reports
Vict., V.R., Vict. Rep., Vict. Rep. (Austr.), Vict. R.
Victorian Reports (Admiralty)
Vict. Rep. (Adm.), V.R. Adm.
Victorian Reports (Equity)
V.R. (Eq.), Vict. Rep. (Eq.)
Victorian Reports (Law)
Vict. Rep. (Law)
Victorian Review
Vict. Rev.
Victorian State Trials
Vict. St. Tr.
Victorian Statute Law Revision Committee
V.S.L.R.C.
Victorian Statutes; the General Public Acts
Vict. Stat.
Victorian Statutory Rules, Regulations and By-Laws
Vict. Stat. R. Regs. & B.

Vide (see) (Lat.)
V.
Videlicet (that is to say) (Lat.)
Viz.
Vidian's Exact Pleader
Vid.
Vietnam Era Veterans' Readjustment and Assistance Act
VEVRAA
Vietnamese
V.
Vilas and Bryant's Edition of the Wisconsin Reports
Vil. & Br.
Vilas' Reports (1-5 New York Criminal Reports)
Vilas
Villanova
Vill.
Villanova Environmental Law Journal
Vill. Envtl. L.J.
Villanova Law Review
Vill. L. Rev., Villanova L. Rev., Vo. L.R., V.R.
Vincent on Criticism and Libel
Vinc. Cr. & Lib.
Vincent's Manual of Criminal Law
Vinc. Cr.L.
Viner's Abridgment of Law and Equity
Viner, Abr., Vin. Abr. (Eng.)
Viner's Abridgment of Law and Equity, Supplement
Vin. Abr., Vin. Supp.
Viner's Abridgment or Commentaries
Vin. Comm.
Vinnius' Commentary on the Institutes of Justinian
Vinn., Vinn. ad Inst.

Vinson on Slaughter's Products Liability: Pharmaceutical Drug Cases
PLPD
Vinton's American Canon Law
Vint. Can. Law
Virchow on Post Mortem Examinations
Virch. P.M.
Virgin Island Reports
V.I.
Virgin Islands
V.I., Virgin Is.
Virgin Islands Bar Journal
V.I. B.J.
Virgin Islands Code
V.I.C.
Virgin Islands Code Annotated
V.I. Code Ann.
Virgin Islands Rules and Regulations
V.I.R. & Regs.
Virginia
V., V.A., Va., Vir., Virg.
Virginia Act of the General Assembly
Va. Acts
Virginia Acts, Published By the Chancery Judges of Virginia (1785)
Chan. Rev.
Virginia Appeals
Va. App.
Virginia Bar Association Journal
Va. B. Ass'n J., Va. B.A.J.
Virginia Bar News
Va. Bar News
Virginia Bill of Rights
B.R.V.
Virginia Cases, by Brockenbrough and Holmes
Vir., Brock. Cas., Va. Cas.,Virg., Virg. Cas.

Virginia Circuit Court Opinions
Va. Cir.
Virginia Colonial Decisions, by Randolph and Barrandall
Va. Col. Dec.
Virginia Constitution
Va. Const.
Virginia Criminal Cases (3-4Virginia Reports)
Va. Cas.
Virginia Decisions
Va. Dec.
Virginia Environmental Law Journal
Va. Envtl. L.J.
Virginia Industrial Commission Opinions
Va. I.C. Ops.
Virginia Journal of International Law
Va. J.Int'l. L., Virg. J.Int'l. L.
Virginia Journal of Natural Resources Law
Va. J.Nat. Resources L., VJNRL
Virginia Law Digest
Va. L. Dig.
Virginia Law Journal
Va. L.J., Vir. L.J., Va. Law J., Virg. L.J.
Virginia Law Register
Va. L.Reg.
Virginia Law Register, New Series
Va. L. Reg. N.S.
Virginia Law Review
Va. L., Va. L. Rev., Va LR
Virginia Law Weekly Dicta Compilation
Va. L. Wk. Dicta Comp
Virginia Laws
L.V.
Virginia Reports
V., V.A., Virginia Rep., Va. Rep.

Virginia Reports, Annotated
Va. R. Ann., Va. Rep. Anno.
Virginia State Bar Association
Va. B.A., Va. Bar Assn.
Virginia State Bar Association Reports
Va. S.B.A.
Virginia State Corporation Commission
Va.S.C.C.
Virginia Supreme Court Reports
V.A.
Virginia Tax Review
Va. Tax Rev.
Virgin's Reports (52-60 Maine)
Vir., Virg., Virgin
Vishny's Guide to International Commerce Law
GICL
Visual Average Speed Computer and Recorder
V.A.S.C.A.R.
Vizard's Practice of the Court in Banc
Viz. Pr.
Vocational
Vocat.
Voce (word) (Lat.)
V.
Voets' (Jan) Commentarius and Pandectas
J.Voet, Com.ad Pand., Voet, Com.ad Pand.
Voice of America
V.O.A.
Void; Decision or Finding Held Invalid for Reasons Given (used in Shepard'sCitations)
V.

Void in Part; Decision or Finding Held Invalid In Part for Reasons Given (used in Shepard's Citations)
Vp.
Volk and Morgan's Medical Malpractice: Obstetrics and Neonatal Cases
MMON
Volume
V., Vol.
Voluntary
Vol.
Voluntary Employees' Beneficiary Association
VEBA
Volunteer
Vol.
Volunteer Firemen's Benefit
Vol. Fire Ben.
Volunteers in Service to America
VISTA
Volunteers in Technical Assistance
VITA
Von Holst's Constitutional History of the United States
Von H. Const. Hist.
Von Ihering's Struggle for Law
Von Ihr. Str. for L.
Voorhies' Criminal Jurisprudence of Louisiana
Voorh. Cr. Jur.
Voorhies' Louisiana Revised Statutes
Voorh. St.
Voorhies' New York Code
Voorh. Code
Voting Trust Certificate
VTC

Vroom's (G.W.D.) Reports (30-85 New Jersey Law)
Ve., Vr., Vroom, Vroom (N.J.),
Vroom (G.D.W.), Vroom (P.D.)

W

Waddilove on Marriage and Divorce
Wad. Mar. & Div.

Waddilove's Digest of Ecclesiastical Cases
Wad. Dig.

Wade on Acta Curiae Admiralatus Scotiae
Act.Cur.Ad.Sc.

Wade on American Mining Law
Wade Min., Wade, Am. Mining Law

Wade on Attachment and Garnishment
Wade, Attachm.

Wade on Retroactive Laws
Wade Retro. L.

Wade on the Law of Notice
Wade Not.

Wade's Cabinet Lawyer
Cab. Lawy.

Wage and Hour Cases, Bureau of National Affairs
W.H., W.H.Cas., Wage and Hour Cas. (BNA), WH Cases

Wage and Hour Division, United States Department of Labor
W. & H.

Wage and Hour Opinion Letter
WH Op. Letter

Wage and Hour Reference Manual, Bureau of National Affairs
W.H.R. Man.

Wage and Hour Reporter, Bureau of National Affairs
Wage & Hour Rep., W.H.R.

Wage-Price Law and Economics Review
Wage-Pr. L., Wage-Price L. & Econ. Rev.

Wage Stabilization Board
WSB

Wages and Hours Manual, Bureau of National Affairs
W.H.Man.

Wagner's Missouri Statutes
Wag. Stat., Wag. St., W.S.

Wait's Actions and Defences
Wait Act. & Def.

Wait's Annotated New York Code
Wait Co.

Wait's Law and Practice in New York Justices' Courts
Wait L. & P.

Wait's New York Digest
Wait Dig.

Wait's New York Practice
Wait Pr., Waits Prac.

Wait's New York Table of Cases
Wait Tab. Ca.

Wait's State Papers of the United States
Wait St. Pap.

Wake Forest Intramural Law Review
Wake Forest Intra. L.Rev.

Wake Forest Law Review
Wake For. L. Rev., Wake Forest L.Rev.

Walace's (J.W.) United States Circuit Court Reports
Wall.Jr., Walc. Jr. C.C., Wal. J.

Waler's Reports (14-16 New Mexico)
Walter.

Wales
W.

Walferstan and Bristowe's English Election Cases
W. & B.

Walford on Railways
Walf. Railw.

Walford's Parties to Actions
Walf. Part.

Walker and Elgood on Executors and Administrators
Walk. Exec.

Walker on Patents
Walk. Pat.

Walker on Wills
Walk. Wills

Walker's American Law
Walk. Am. Law

Walker's Banking Law
Walk. Bank. L.

Walker's Equity Pleader's Assistant
Walk. Eq. Pl.

Walker's Louisiana Digest
Walk. La. Dig.

Walker's Introduction to American Law
Walk. Int.

Walker's Michigan Chancery Reports
Walk., Walk. Ch., Walk. Ch.
Mich., Walk.Ch. Cas., Walker,
Wal. Ch., Walk. Chanc. Rep.,
Walk. (Mic.) Ch., Walk. Mich.,
Walk. Michig. Rep., Walker's
Ch. R.

Walker's Pennsylvania Reports
Walk., Walker, Walk. Pa.

Walker's Reports (96 and 109 Alabama)
Walk., Walker

Walker's Reports (1 Mississippi)
Walk., Walk. Miss., Walker

Walker's Reports (22-25, 38-51, 72-88 Texas; 1-10 Civil Appeals Texas)
Walk.,Walk. Tex., Walker

Walker's Theory of the Common Law
Walk. Com. L.

Wall on Litigation and Prevention of Insurer Bad Faith
LPIB

Wall Street Journal
Wall St. J.

Wallace
Wal., Wall.

Wallace, Junior, United States Reports
Wall. Jr.

Wallace, Principles of the Laws of Scotland
Wall. Pr., Wal. Prin.

Wallace, Senior, United States Reports
Wall. Sr.

Wallace's (J.W.) United States Circuit Court Reports
Wallace, Jr., Rept., Wall., Wall.
C.C.

Wallace's Nova Scotia Reports
Wall., N.S.R. Wall.

Wallace's Reports (68-90 United States)
Wall., Wall. Rep., Wall. S.C.

Wallace's Supreme Court Reports (68-90 United States)
Wall.

Wallace's The Reporters
Wall. Rep.

Wallace's United States Reports
Wal. U.S. Rep.

Wallford's Laws of the Customs
Walf. Cust.

Wallis' Irish Chancery Reports
Wall., Wall., Wallis., Wallis (Ir.)

Wallis' Irish Chancery Reports by Lyne
   Wallis by Lyne, Wall. Lyn., Wallis by L., Wal.by L., Lyne (Wall.), Wall. By L.

Wallis Philadelphia Reports
   Wall.

Walpole's Rubric of Common Law
   Walp. Rub.

Walsh's Irish Registry Cases
   Walsh.

Walter and Bates Ohio Digest
   W. & B. Dig.

Walter Code
   Walter C.

Walton on Husband and Wife
   Walt. H. & W.

Walter on Statute of Limitations
   Walt. Lim.

Wandell's New York Reports
   Wandell

Wandsworth Legal Resource Project
   W.L.R.P.

Waples on Proceedings in Rem
   Wap. Pr. R.

War Assets Administration
   W.A.A.

War Labor Board
   WLB

War Risk Insurance Decisions
   W.R.

War Trade Board Rulings
   W.T.B.R.

War Trade Regulations
   War Trade Reg.

Ward on Belligerent and Neutral Powers
   War. Bell.

Ward on Legacies
   Ward, Leg.

Warden and Smith's Reports (3 Ohio State)
   Warden & Smith, Ward. & Sm.

Warden's Reports (2-4 Ohio State Reports)
   Warden, Ward.

Warden's Weekly Law and Bank Bulletin, Ohio
   Warden's Law & Bk. Bull.

Ward's Justice of the Peace
   Ward Just.

Ward's Law of Nations
   Ward Nat.

Warehouse
   Wareh.

Ware's United States District Court Reports
   Ware's C.C. Rep., Ware's Rep., Ware.

Warrants
   War.

Warren
   Warr.

Warren, Gorham & Lamont Inc.
   WGLI

Warren's Adventures of an Attorney in Search of Practice
   War. Adv. Att.

Warren's Law Studies
   War. L. St.

Warren's Moral, Social and Professional Duties of Attorneys and Solicitors
   War. Prof. Dut.

Warren's Ohio Criminal Law
   War. Cr. L.

Warsaw Treaty Organization
   WTO

Warvelle on Abstracts of Title
   Warv. Abst.

Warvelle's Elements of Real Property
   Warv. El. R. P.

Warvelle's Vendors and Purchasers of Real Property
Warv. V. & P.
Warwick's Opinions, City Solicitor of Philadelphia
War. Op., Warwick's Op.
Waseda University, Institute of Comparative Law, Bulletin, Japan
Bull. Waseda Univ. Inst. of Comp.Law, Bull.Waseda U.Inst.Comp.L.
Washburn
Wash.
Washburn Law Journal
W. L. Jour., Washburn L.J., W.L.J., Wsb.
Washburn on Criminal Law
Wash. Cr. L.
Washburn on Easements and Servitudes
Wash. Ease., Washb. Easem.
Washburn on Real Property
Wash. R.P., Washb. Real Prop.
Washburn University School of Law
WUSL
Washburn's Reports (18-23 Vermont)
Washburn
Washburn's Vermont Digest
Wash. Dig.
Washburton and Hazard's Reports, Prince Edward Island
Wash. & Haz. P.E.I.
Washington
Wa., Wash.
Washington Administrative Code
Wash. Admin. Code
Washington and Lee Law Review
Washington and Lee L. Rev., W. & L., Wash. & Lee L. Rev., W.L.L.R.

Washington Annotated Codes and Statutes by Ballinger
Bal.Ann.Codes, Ballinger's Ann. Codes & St.
Washington Appellate Reports
W. Ap., Wa. A., Wash. App.
Washington Bar News
Wash. B. News
Washington Constitution
Wash. Const.
Washington County Reports
Wash. Co. R., Wash. Co. Repr., Wash. Co., Wash. Co. (Pa.)
Washington Decisions
Wash. Dec., W.D.
Washington Decisions, Second Series
W.D.(2d)
Washington Department of Public Works
Wash. D.P.W.
Washington Financial Reports, Bureau of National Affairs
Wash. Fin. Rep. (BNA)
Washington Jurist
Wash. Jur.
Washington Law Reporter, District of Columbia
Wash. L. Rep., Wash. Law Rep., Wash. L.R. (Dist Col), W.L.R.
Washington Law Review
Wa. L.R., Wash. L. Rev., Washington L. Rev., Wn.L.R., Ws.L., W.L.R.
Washington Laws
Wash. Laws
Washington Lawyer
Wash. Law.
Washington Legislative Service
Wash. Legis. Serv.
Washington Library Network (Bibliographic Utility Network)
WLN

Washington Monthly
Wash. Monthly

Washington Public Service Commission
Wash. P.S.C.

Washington Public Utility Commission Reports
Wash. P.U.R.

Washington Reports
Wa., Wash., Wn., W.

Washington Reports, Second Series
Wash.2d, Wn.2d

Washington Revised Code Annotated
Wash. Rev. Code Ann.

Washington State Bar Association
WSBA

Washington State Bar Association, Proceedings
Wash. S.B.A.

Washington State Bar News
Wash. St. B. News

Washington State Register
Wash. Admin. Reg.

Washington State Reports
Wash. St., Wsh., Wash.

Washington State Reports, Second Series
W.2d, Wa. 2d

Washington Supreme Court Reports
Wash

Washington Supreme Court Reports 2d Series
Wash 2d

Washington Territory Opinions
Wash. Ter., Wash. Terr., Wash. Ty., Wash.T.

Washington Territory Reports
W.Ty.R., W.T., Wash.Ter., Wash, Wash. Terr., Wash. Ty., Wash.T.

Washington University Journal of Urban and Contemporary Law
Wash. U. J.Urb. & Contemp. L.

Washington University Law Quarterly
Wash. U. L.Q., Washington Univ. L. Quart., W.L.Q.

Washington University Law Review
Wash. U. L. Rev.

Washington's Reports (16-23 Vermont)
Wash.

Washington's Reports (1-2 Virginia)
Wash., Wash.Va.

Washington's United States Circuit Court Reports
Wash. C.C., Wash. C.C.R., W.C.C.R.

Water Pollution Committee
W.P.

Waterman on Set-Off
Wat. Set-Off

Waterman on the Law of Trespass
Wat. Tres.

Waterman's Criminal Digest
Wat. Cr. Dig.

Waterman's Criminal Procedure
Wat. Cr. Proc.

Waterman's Justices' Manual
Wat. Just.

Waterman's United States Court of Claims
U.S. Crim. Dig.

Watermayer's Supreme Court Reports, Cape of Good Hope
W., Wat. C.G.H., Watermeyer., Wat.

Waterworks and Water Companies
Wat. wks.

Watkins on Conveyancing
Watk. Con., Watk. Conv., Wat. Con.

Watkins on Copyholds
Watk. Cop., Watk. Copyh., Wat. Cop.

Watkins on Descents
Watk. Des.

Watson on Arbitration
Wats. Arb.

Watson on Partnership
Wats. Part.

Watson's Clergyman's Law
Wats. Cler. Law.

Watson's Constitutional History of Canada
Wats. Const. Hist.

Watson's Medical Jurisprudence
Wats. Med. Jur.

Watson's Office and Duty of Sheriff
Wats. Sher.

Watson's Practical Compendium of Equity
Watson Eq., Wats. Comp. Eq., Watson.

Watson's United States Commissioners' Manual
Wats. Com. Man.

Watts and Sergeant's Reports, Pennsylvania
Watts & Ser., W.& S., Watts & S., Watts. & S. (Pa.), Watts & Serg., WS

Watt's Pennsylvania Reports
W., Wat., W., Watts., Watts (Pa.)

Watts' Reports (16-24 West Virginia)
Wat, Watts.

Wayne Law Review
Wayne L. Rev., Wayne L.R., Wn.L.R., Wn.L.

Ways and Means
W.M.

Weapons and Firearms
Weap.

Webb & Duval's Reports (1-3 Texas)
Webb. & D., Webb & Duval

Webb, A'Beckett & Williams' Equity Reports, Victoria, Australia
W.A'B. & W. Eq., V.R. Eq., Webb, A'B. & W. Eq.

Webb, A'Beckett and Williams' Insolvency, Ecclesiastical and Matrimonial Reports, Victoria, Australia
Webb, AB. & W.I.E. & M, W.A'B. & W.I.E. & M., V.R. (I.E. & M.), Webb, A'B. & W.I.P. & M.

Webb, A'Beckett and Williams' Mining Cases, Victoria, Australia
W.A'B. & W.Min., Webb, A'B. & W.Min.

Webb, A'Beckett and Williams Reports, Victoria, Australia
W.A'B. & W., Webb, A'B. & W.

Webb, A'Beckett and Williams' Victorian Reports, Australia
V.R.

Webb on the Judicature Act
Webb Jud. Act

Webb's Digest of Texas Criminal Cases
Webb Cr. Dig.

Webb's Kansas Pleading and Practice
Webb Pl. & Pr.

Webb's Railroad Laws of Maine
Webb. R.R.

Webb's Reports (6-20 Kansas)
Webb.

Webb's Reports (11-20 Texas Civil Appeals)
Webb.

Webb's Supreme Court Practice, English
Webb Supr. Ct. Pr.

Webster in Senate Documents
Webster In Sen. Doc.

Webster Patent Cases
Webster Pat. Cas. (Eng.)

Webster's Dictionary
Webst. Dict., Webster Dict.

Webster's International Dictionary
Internat. Dict., Webst. Int. Dict.

Webster's New International Dictionary
Webst. New Int. D.

Webster's New Patent Law
Web. Pat.

Webster's Patent Cases, England
Web. P.C., Web. Pat. Cas., Webster Pat. Cas., W.P. Cas., W.P.C., W.P.R., Webs., Webs. Pat. Cas.

Webster's Patent Reports, England
W.P.R.

Webster's Trial for Murder
Web. Tr.

Webster's Unabridged Dictionary
Webst. Dict. Unab.

Wedgwood and Homan's Manual for Notaries and Bankers
Wedg. & Hom.

Wedgwood on American Government and Laws
Wedg. Gov. & Laws

Wedgwood's Dictionary of English Etymology
Wedgw. Dict. Eng. Etymology

Week
Wk.

Weekblad voor Fiscaal Recht, Netherlands
Wbl.voor Fiscaal Recht

Weekly
Wkly

Weekly Benefit Amount
W.b.a.

Weekly Cincinnati Law Bulletin. Ohio
Week. Cin. L.B., Cin. Law Bull., Wkly. Cin. Law Bul.

Weekly Compilation of Presidential Documents
Weekly Comp. of Pres. Doc.

Weekly Jurist, Illinois
Week. Jur.

Weekly Law and Bank Bulletin
Week. Law & Bk. Bull., Law & Bk. Bull., L. & B. Bull

Weekly Law Bulletin and Ohio Law Journal
Week. Law. Bull.

Weekly Law Bulletin, Ohio
Weekly L. Bull., Bull. O, TS., Bull. (Ohio), Cin. Law Bull., Cinc. L. Bul., Cincinnati Law Bull., Law Bull., Ohio L. B., Ohio Law Bull., W. Law Bul., Weekly Law B., Wkly. L. Bul., W.L. Bull., W. Law Bul., W.L. Bull., Wkly. Law Bul., W.L. Bull. (Ohio), W.L.B.

Weekly Law Gazette, Ohio
Week. L. Gaz., Week. Law Gaz., Wkly. L. Gaz., W.L. Gaz., Gaz., Wkly. Law Gaz., W.L.G.

Weekly Law Magazine, England
Week. L. Mag.

Weekly Law Record
Week. L. Rec., Week. L. Record

Weekly Law Reports, England
Week. L.R., Week. L.R. (Eng.), Weekly L.R., W.L.R.

Weekly Law Review
Week. L. Rev.
Weekly Notes of Cases, Pennsylvania
Week. No., Week. No. Cas.,
Week. Notes Cas., Weekly N.C.,
Wk. N., Wkly. N.C., Wkly.
Notes Cas. (Pa.), W.N.Cas.
(Pa.), W.N.C., W.N.C. (Pa.),
W.N.Cas., Week. No., Week. No.
Cas.
Weekly Notes of English Law Reports
W.N., W.N. (Eng.), Weekly
Notes
Weekly Notes, Miscellaneous, England
W.N. Misc.
Weekly Notes, New South Wales
W.N.N.S.W.
Weekly Reporter, England
Week. R., Week. R. (Eng.),
Week. Rep., W.R., Week. Reptr.,
W.R., W.R., Week. Reptr., Wkly.
Rep.
Weekly Transcript Reports, New York
Week. Trans. Rep., Week.
Trans. Repts., W.T.R.
Weeks' Damnum Absque Injuria
Weeks D.A. Inj.
Weeks on Attorneys at Law
Weeks Att. at Law
Weeks on Depositions
Weeks Dep.
Weeks on Mines and Mineral Law
Weeks Min.
Weeks on The Mining Legislation of Congress
Weeks Min. Leg.
Weerakoon's Appeal Court Reports, Ceylon
Weer.

Wehmhoefer's Statistics in Litigation
SL
Weightman on Marriage and Legitimacy
Weight. M. & L.
Weightman's Medico-Legal Gazette
Weight. Med. Leg. Gaz.
Weights and Measures
Wts. & M.
Weinstock on Planning an Estate
PE
Weir's Criminal Rulings
Weir
Welfare
Welf., Welfare
Welfare and Institutions
Welf. & Inst.
Welfare and Institutions Code
Welf. & Inst. C.
Welfare Law
Welf. L.
Welfare Law Bulletin
Welfare L. Bull.
Welfare Law News
Welfare L. News
Welford on Equity Pleadings
Welf. Eq.
Wellbeloved on Highways
Well. High.
Wells on Instruction to Juries and Bills of Exception
Wells Inst. Juries
Wells on Replevin
Wells Rep., Wells, Repl.
Wells on the Jurisdiction of Courts
Wells Jur.
Wells on the Separate Property of Married Women
Wells Mar. Wom.

Wells' Questions of Law and Facts
    Wells L. & F.
**Wells' Res Adjudicata and Stare
    Decisis**
    Wells' Res. Ad.
**Wells' Successful Trial Tech-
    niques of Expert Practitioners**
    STT
**Wellwood's Abridgment of Sea
    Laws**
    Wellw. Abr.
**Welsby, Hurlstone and Gordon's
    English Exchequer Reports**
    Welsby H. & G., Welsb. H. & G.,
    Welsb., Hurl. & G., Welsby H. &
    G. (Eng.), W.H. & G.
Welsh's Irish Case at Siligo
    Welsh.
**Welsh's Irish Case of James
    Feighny**
    Welsh.
Welsh's Irish Registry Cases
    Wel., Welsh Reg. Cas., Welsh.
**Wendell's Blackstone's Commen-
    taries**
    Wend. Bl.
Wendell's Reports, New York
    W., Wen., Wend. R., Wend.
    Rep., Wendel, Wendell Rep.,
    Wendell's Rep., Wend., Wen-
    dell., Wend.(N.Y.), W.R.
Wendt's Maritime Legislation
    Wendt. Mar. Leg.
Wendt's Reports of Cases, Ceylon
    Wendt.
Wentworth's Office of Executors
    Went. Ex., Off. Ex., Off. Exec.
Wenzell's Reports (60 Minnesota)
    Wenz.
**Weskett's Complete Digest of the
    Theory, Laws and Practice of
    Insurance**
    Wesk. Ins., Weskett, lns.

West
    W.
West Africa
    W. A.
**West African Court of Appeal Re-
    ports**
    W. Afr. App.
**West African Court of Appeal, Se-
    lected Judgments**
    W.A.C.A.
**West African Economic Commu-
    nity**
    CEAO
**West African Law Reports, Gam-
    bia, Ghana and Sierra Leone**
    W.Af. L.R., W.A.L.R.
West Australia
    W.Austl.
West Bengal
    W. Beng.
West Coast Reporter
    W.Coast Rep., West Co. Rep.,
    West Coast Rep.
West Germany
    W. Ger.
West India
    W.I.
West Indian Law Journal
    W. Indian L.J., W.I.L.J.
West Indian Reports
    W.I.R.
West Indies
    W.I.
West on Patents
    West Pat.
West Publishing Company
    West
**West Publishing Company's
    Docket**
    Dkt., Docket
West Virginia
    West Va., W.Va.

West Virginia Acts
W. Va. Acts

West Virginia Acts of the Legislature
W. Va. Acts

West Virginia Attorney General Reports
O.A.G. West Virginia

West Virginia Bar
W.V. Bar, W.Va. Bar.

West Virginia Bar Association
West Va. B.A.

West Virginia Biennial Report and Official Opinions of the State Attorney General
Biennial Rep. & Op.W.Va.Atty's Gen.

West Virginia Code
W.Va. Code, WVC, Warth Code.

West Virginia Constitution
W.Va. Const.

West Virginia Criminal Justice Review
W.Va. Crim. Just. Rev.

West Virginia Law Quarterly
W.Va. L.Q., W.V.L.Q., W.V.L.Q.

West Virginia Law Review.
West Virginia L. Rev., W.Va. L. Rev., W.V.L., W.V.L.R.

West Virginia Public Service Commission Decisions
W.Va. P.S.C.

West Virginia Public Service Commission Reports
W.Va. P.S.C.R., W.Va. P.U.R.

West Virginia Reports
West Va., W.V., W.Va., W.Va. Law Reports, W.Va. Rep., W.V.R., W.V. Rep.

West Virginia State Bar Journal
W.Va. St. B.J.

West Virginia Supreme Court Reports
W.Va.

West on Extents
West Ext.

Westbury on European Arbitration
West

Western
W.

Western Australia
W. A., W.Aus., W.Austl., West. Aus.

Western Australia Acts
W.Austl. Acts

Western Australia Reprinted Acts
Repr. Acts W. Austl., W. Aust. Repr. Acts

Western Australia University Law Review
W.A.U. L.R., West A.U.L.R.

Western Australia Worker's Compensation Board Decisions
W.C.B.D. (W.A.)

Western Australian Annual Law Review
Annual L. Rev.

Western Australian Arbitration Reports
W.A.A.R., W.A. Arb. R.

Western Australian Industrial Gazette
W.A.I.G., W.Austl. Ind. Gaz.

Western Australian Justice of the Peace
W. Austl. J.P.

Western Australian Law Reform Commission
W.A.L.R.C.

Western Australian Law Reports
West Austr. L., W. Austl. L.R.

Western Australian Reports
W.A.R., West. Austl., W. Austl.,
W. Austl. R.
Western Australia State Reports
S.R. (W.A.)
Western District
W.D.
Western European Union
W.E.U.
**Western India States Agency Law
Reports**
W.I.S.A. Law Rep., W.I.S.A.
Law Reports, W.I.S.A.L.R.
Western Jurist
West. Jur., W.J.
**Western Labour Arbitration
Cases**
W.L.A.C.
Western Law Gazette
West. L. Gaz.
Western Law Journal, Ohio
W. L. Jour., W.L.J., West. Law
J., West. L.J., West. L.J. (Ohio),
West. Law Jour., Western Law
Jour.
Western Law Monthly, Ohio
West. Law M., West. Law
Month., West. L.M., West.
L.Mo., West. L.Month., Law
Mo., West. Law Mo., W.L.M.
Western Law Reporter, Canada
West. L.R., West L.R. (Can.),
W.L.R.
Western Law Review
West. L. Rev., West. Law. Rev.,
Western L. Rev.
Western Law Times, Canada
W.L.T., West. L.T.
Western Legal History
W. Legal Hist.
Western Legal Observer
West. Leg. Obs., West Legal Ob-
ser.

**Western New England Law Re-
view**
W. New Eng. L. Rev., West.
New Engl. L. Rev.
Western Nigeria Law Reports
W.N.L.R.
Western Nigeria Legal Notice
W.N.L.N.
Western Ontario Law Review
W. Ont. L. Rev., Western Ont.
L. Rev., West. Ont. L. Rev.
Western Pacific High Commission
W.P.H.C
Western Region
W.R.
**Western Region of Nigeria Law
Reports**
W.R.N.L.R.
Western Reporter, Canada
West. R., West. R., West. Rep.
Western Reserve Law Journal
Wes. Res. Law. Jo., Wes. Res.
Law Jrl.
Western Reserve Law Notes
Western Reserve L.N.
Western Reserve Law Review
W. Res. L. Rev., West. Res. L.
Rev., West. Res. Law Rev., West-
ern Res. L. Rev., W.R.I.
Western Samoa
W. Samoa
Western School Law Review
West. School L. Rev.
**Western State University Law Re-
view**
W. St. U. L. Rev., West. St. U.
L. Rev., West. State. U. L. Rev.
Western Virginia Law Review
West. Va. L. Rev.
Western Weekly, Canada
West. Wkly.
Western Weekly Digests, Canada
W.W.D.

Western Weekly, New Series, Canada
West Week N.S. (Can.)

Western Weekly Notes, Canada
West Week (Can.), West. Week. N., West Week N. (Can.)

Western Weekly Reports, Canada
West. Week. Rep., W.W.R.

Western Weekly Reports, New Series, Canada
W.W.R. (N.S.)

Western's Commentaries on the Laws of England
West. Com.

Western's London Tithe Cases
We., West. Ti. Cas., West, West. Tithe Cas.

Westin's Federal Tax Planning
FTP

Westin's Middle Income Tax Planning and Shelters
MIT

Westlake's Conflict of Laws
Westl. Confl.

Westlake's Private International Law
West. Pr. Int. Law, Westl. Priv. Int. Law, Westlake Int. Private Law

Westminster
W.

Westminster Hall Chronicle and Legal Examiner
Westm. Hall. Chron., W.H. Chron.

Westminster Review
West. Rev.

Westmoreland County Law Journal, Pennsylvania
Westmore Co. L.J. (Pa.), Westm., Westmoreland Co. L.J., Wes. C.L.J., Westm. L.J., West, Westmoreland

Weston's Reports (11-14 Vermont)
West, Weston

West's Annotated California Code
Cal. [subject] Code (West), Ann. Cal. Codes

West's Bankruptcy Reporter
B.R.

West's English Chancery Cases
West Ch., West Ch. (Eng.), West. Chy., W.R., We., West

West's English Chancery Reports tempore Hardwicke
West t. H., W. Rep., West. t. Hard., West t. Hardw., Cas.t.H., Cas.t.Hardw.

West's Federal Practice Digest
W.F.P.D.

West's Federal Practice Digest, Second Series
W.F.P.D.2d

West's Louisiana Civil Code Annotated
La. Civ. Code Ann. (West)

West's Louisiana Code of Civil Procedure Annotated
La. Code Civ. Pro. Ann.

West's Louisiana Code of Criminal Procedure Annotated
La. Code Crim. Pro. Ann.

West's Louisiana Revised Statues
LA.R.S.

West's Louisiana Revised Statutes Annotated
La. Rev. Stat. Ann. (West)

West's Minnesota Statutes Annotated
Minn. Stat. Ann. (West)

West's Opinions, City Solicitor of Philadelphia
West's Op.

West's Reports, English House of Lords
West H.L., We., West

West's Symboleography
West's Symb.
West's Wisconsin Statutes Annotated
Wis. Stat. Ann. (West)
Wethey's Reports, Upper Canada Queen's Bench
Weth., Weth. U.C., Wethey
Wharton and Stille's Medical Jurisprudence
Whar. & St. Med. Jur., Whart. & S. Med. Jur.
Wharton on Agency
Whar. Ag., Whart. Ag.
Wharton on Criminal Evidence
Whar. Cr. Ev., Whart. Cr. Ev., Wharton Crim. Evidence
Wharton on Evidence in Civil Issues
Whar. Ev., Whart. Ev.
Wharton on Innkeepers
Whar. Innk.
Wharton on Negligence
Whart. Neg.
Wharton on the Law of Domicile
Whar. Dom.
Wharton School, University of Pennsylvania
WHSUPA
Wharton's American Criminal Law
Whar. Am. Cr. L., Whar. Cr. Law., Whart. Am. Cr. Law., Whart. Cr. Law., Whart. Crim. Law., Wharton.
Wharton's Conflict of Laws
Whar. Con. Law., Whar. Confl. Law, Whart. Confl. Laws.
Wharton's Criminal Law and Procedure
Wharton, Crim. Proc.

Wharton's Criminal Pleading and Practice
Whart. Cr. Pl. & Prac., Whar. Cr. Pl., Whar. Cri. Pl.
Wharton's Law Dictionary (or Law Lexicon)
Whart. Law Lexicon, Whart. Law Dic., Whart. Law Dict., Whart. Lex., Whart. Lex., Wharton.
Wharton's Law of Homicide
Whar. Hom., Whart. Hom., Whart. Homicide
Wharton's Law of Negligence
Whar. Neg.
Wharton's Legal Maxims
Whar. Leg. Max.
Wharton's Pennsylvania Digest
Whar. Dig.
Wharton's Pennsylvanis Supreme Court Reports
Whart., Whar, Wharton., Whar., Wh., Whart. Pa.
Wharton's Precedents of Indictments and Pleas
Whar. Ind., Whar. Prec. Ind.
Wharton's Principles of Conveyancing
Whar. Conv.
Wharton's United States State Trials
Whart. St. Tr., U.S. St. Tr., Whart. State Tr., Whar. St. Tr.
Wharves
Whar.
Wheaton on Maritime Captures and Prizes
Wheat. Cap.
Wheaton's Elements of International Law
Wheat. Int. Law, Wheat. El. Int. Law.

Wheaton's History of the Law of Nations
Wheat. Hist. Law Nat., Wheat. Law of Nat.

Wheaton's International Law
Wh., Wheat. Int. Law.

Wheaton's Reports (14-25 United States)
W., Wh., Wheat., Wheaton.

Wheeler on Slavery
Wheel. Slav.

Wheeler's Abridgment of American Common Law
Wheeler Abr., Wheel. Abr., Wheeler, Am. Cr. Law

Wheeler's New York Criminal Cases
Wh. Crim. Cas., Wh. Cr. Cas., Wh., Wheel. Cr. C., Wheel., Wheel. Cr. Cas., Wheel. Cr. Ch., Wheeler C.C., Wheeler Cr. Cases, Wheeler Crim. Cas., Wheeler, Cr. Cas., Wheeler's Cr. Cases, Wheel. Cr. C.

Wheeler's Criminal Recorder (1 Wheeler's New York Criminal Cases)
Wheel. Cr. Rec.

Wheeling Bridge Case
Wheel. Br. Cas.

Wheelock's Reports (32-37 Texas)
Wheel., Wheel.(Tex.)

Whishaw's Law Dictionary
Whish L.D., Whishaw.

Whitaker on Liens
Whitak. Liens

Whitaker on Rights of Lien and Stoppage in Transitu
Whit. Lien

Whitaker on Stoppage in Transitu
Whit. St. Tr.

White and Tudor's Leading Cases in Equity, England
White & T. Lead Cas. in Eq. (Eng.), Wh. & Tud., White & Tud. L.C., L.C. Eq., White & T.L. Cas.,White & Tudor., White & T. Lead Cas. Eq., W. & T. Eq. Ca., W. & T. L. C., Wh. & T. L.C., Lead. Cas. Eq., Lead. Cas. In Eq.

White and Wilson's Texas Civil Appeal Cases
White & W. (Tex.), White & Civ. Cas. Ct. App., Willson Civ. Cas. Ct. App., White & W., White & W. Civ. Cas. Ct. App., Tex. A. Civ., Tex. A. Civ. Cas., Tex. App. Civ. Cas. (Willson), Tex. Civ. Cas.

White and Wilson's Texas Civil Cases
W. & W. C.C., W. & W. Cir. Cases, Court of Appeals, W. & W. Con. Cases, W. & W. Con. Rep., W. & W.

White on Supplement and Revivor
White Suppl.

White's Annotated Texas Penal Code
White's Ann. Pen. Code

White's Justiciary Court Reports, Scotland
White.

White's Land Law of California
White L.L.

White's New Collection of the Laws, etc. of Great Britain, France and Spain
White New Coll., White, Coll.

White's Reports (10-15 West Virginia)
White., White's Rep.

White's Reports (31-44 Texas Appeals)
White's Rep., White.

Whiteford on Charities
White. Char.

Whiteley on Weights, Measures and Weighing Machines
White. W. & M.

Whiteman's Digest of International Law
D.I.L. (White)

Whitemore on Adoption of Children
Whitm. Adopt.

Whitman's Massachusetts Libel Cases
Whitm. Lib. Cas.

Whitman's Patent Cases, United States
Whitman Pat. Cas. (U.S.), Whit. Pat. Cas., Whitm. Pat. Cas., Whitman's Patent Cases

Whitman's Patent Law Review
Whitm. Pat. Law Rev.

Whitman's Patent Laws of all Countries
Whitm. Pat. Law., Whit. Pat.

Whitmarsh on Bankrupt Law
Whitm. B.L.

Whitney's Land Laws, Tennessee
Whitney

Whittaker's Practice and Pleading, New York
Whitt.Pl.

Whittier Law Review
Whitt. L. Rev., Whittier L. Rev.

Whittlesey's Reports (32-4l Missouri)
Whittlesey

Whitworth's Equity Precedents
Whit. Eq. Pr.

Wight's Scottish Election Cases
Wight El. Cas., Wight., Wight.

Wightwick's English Exchequer Reports
Wight., Wightw., Wightw. (Eng.)

Wigmore on Evidence
Wigm. Ev., Wigmore, Evidence

Wigmore on Wills
Wig. Wills

Wigram on Discovery
Wig. Disc.

Wigram on Extrinsic Evidence
Wig. Ev.

Wigram on Loills
Wig.

Wilberforce on Construction and Operation of Statutes
Wilb. Stat.

Wilberforce on Statute Law
Wilberforce

Wilcox Condensed Ohio Reports (1-7 Ohio, Reprint)
Wilc.Cond., Ohio Cond. R., Wilc. Cond. Rep., Ohio Cond., Wilcox, Wilcox Cond.

Wilcox on Municipal Corporations
Wilc. Mun. Corp.

Wilcox's Lackawanna Reports, Pennsylvania
Wilcox

Wilde's Supplement to Barton's Conveyancing
Wilde Sup. (or Conv.)

Wildman on Search, Capture, and Prize
Wildm. Search

Wildman's International Law
Wildm. Int. L., Wildm. Int. Law

Wilgram and O'Hara on Wills
W. & O. Wills

Wilkins' Leges Anglo-Saxonicae Ecclesiasticae et Civiles
Wilk. Leg. Ang. Sax.

Wilkins on Drafting Wills and Trust Agreements
DWTA

Wilkinson on Limitations of Actions
Wilk. Lim.

Wilkinson on Replevin
Wilk. Repl.

Wilkinson on Shipping
Wilk. Ship.

Wilkinson, Owen, Paterson and Murray's New South Wales Reports
Wilk., Wilk. & Mur., Wilk. & Ow., Wilk. & Pat., Wilk.P. & M.

Wilkinson's Office of Sheriff
Wilk. Sh.

Wilkinson's Precedents in Conveyancing
Wilk. Prec.

Wilkinson's Public Funds
Wilk. Funds

Wilkinson's Texas Court of Appeals and Civil Appeals
Wilk.

Willamette Law Journal
W. L. Jour., Will. L.J., Willamette L.J., Willamette L.J., Wm. L.J., W.M.L.

Willamette Law Review
Willamette L. Rev.

Willamette University College of Law
WILUCL

Willan's Criminal Law of Canada
Will. Cr. L.

Willard on Real Estate and Conveyancing
Will. Real Est.

Willard's Equity Jurisprudence
Will. Eq. Jur.

Willcock on Medical Profession
Willc. Med. Pr.

Willcock on the Office of Constable
Willc. Const.

Willcock's Municipal Corporation
Willcock, Mun. Corp., Willc. Mun. Corp.

Willelmus Rex (King William)
W.R.

Willes' English Common Pleas Reports
Will., Willes (Eng.), Willes

William
Will.

William and Mary College Bulletin
Bull. Coll. Wm. & Mary

William and Mary Law Review
W. & M., W. & M. L. Rev., Wm. & Mary L. Rev., W.M.L.R., Will. & Mar., Wm. & M., Wm. & Mary, William & Mary L. Rev.

William and Mary Review of Virginia Law
Wm. & Mary Rev. Va. L., W.M.R.

William (King of England)
W., Wm., Will., Wil.

William Mitchell Law Review
William Mitchell L. Rev., Wm. Mitchell L. Rev.

William S. Hein & Co., Inc.
Hein

William the Conqueror's Laws
LL. Wm. Conq.

Williams' Abridgment of Cases, England
Will. Abr.

Williams and Bruce's Admiralty Practice
Will. & Br. Adm. Jur., Williams & B. Adm. Jur., Williams & Bruce Ad. Pr., Wms. & Bruce

Williams' Annual Register
    Wms. Ann. Reg., Will. Ann. Reg.
Williams' Bankruptcy Practice
    Williams B. Pr., Wms.
    Bank.,Will. Bankt.
Williams' Justice
    Will. Just.
Williams' Law Dictionary
    Will.L.D.
Williams' Massachusetts Citations
    Will. Mass. Cit.
Williams' Massachusetts Reports
(1 Massachusetts)
    Will.
Williams' Notes to Saunders' Reports, England
    Williams, Saund., Will. Saund.,
    Wms. Notes
Williams on Auctions
    Will. Auct.
Williams on Executors
    Wms. Exors., Will. Ex., Wms.
    Ex., Williams, Ex'rs., Wms.
    Ex'rs., Wms. Exs.
Williams on Executors, Randolph and Talcott Edition
    Williams, Ex'rs, R. & T. Ed.
Williams on Personal Property
    Wms. P.P., Williams, Pers. Prop.
Williams on Real Property
    Wms. R.P., Williams Pers. Prop.
Williams on Rights of Common
    Williams, Common, Will. Com.
Williams on Seisin of the Freehold
    Williams, Seis., Will. Seis.
Williams on the Settlement of Real Estates
    Will. Sett.
Williams on the Study of the Law
    Will. St. L.

Williams' (Peere) English Chancery and King's Bench Cases
    Peere Wms., PeereWilliams,
    Wms.P., Williams, Wms. Peere,
    Williams-Peere, Will.P., P.W.,
    P.Wms., P.Wms.(Eng.), Williams P.
Williams' Real Assets
    Will. Real Ass.
Williams' Reports (1 Massachusetts)
    Wms. Mass., Will. Mass., Williams
Williams' Reports (10-12 Utah)
    Williams
Williams' Reports (27-29 Vermont)
    Williams, Will.Vt., Wms. Vt.,
    Will.
Williams on Petitions in Chancery
    Will. Pet. Ch.
Willis-Bund's Cases from State Trials
    Will.-Bund St. Tr.
Willis on Equity Pleadings
    Willis Eq.
Willis on Interrogatories
    Willis Int.
Willis on Trustees
    Willis Trust., Willis, Trustees
Williston on Contracts
    Williston, Williston, Contracts
Williston on Sales
    Williston
Willmore, Willaston and Davison's English Queen's Bench Reports
    W.W. & D., Wilm. W. & D.,
    Willm. W. & D., Will. Woll. &
    D., Will., Woll. & Dav

**Willmore, Wollaston and Hodges'
English Queen's Bench Reports**
Willm. W. & H., Will. Woll. &
H., W.W. & H., W.W. & H.
(Eng.), Will. Woll. & Hodg.

**Wills, Estates and Trust Service,
Prentice-Hall**
Wills Est. & Tr.(P-H), Wills Est.
& Tr. Serv. (P-H), Wills, Est., Tr.

Wills on Circumstantial Evidence
Wills, Circ. Ev., Wills, Civ. Ev.

Willson's Civil Cases Court of Appeals, Texas
Willson Civ. Cas. Ct. App.

**Willson's Reports, (29-30 Texas
Appeals; 1-2 Texas Court of Appeals, Civil Cases)**
Willson

**Willson's Revised Penal Code,
Code of Criminal Procedure,
and Penal Laws of Texas**
Willson, Tex. Cr. Law

**Wilmington, Delaware, Board of
Public Utility Commission**
Wilmington, Del. P.U.C.

Wilmot on Mortgages
Wilm. Mort.

Wilmot's Digest of the Law of Burglary
Wilm. Burg.

**Wilmot's Notes and Opinions,
English King's Bench**
Wilmot's Notes, Wilm., Wilm.
Judg., Wilm. op., Wilmot's
Notes (Eng.)

**Wilmot's Notes of Opinions and
Judgments, England**
Not. Op.

Wilson
Wil., Wils.

**Wilson and Courtenay's Scotch
Appeal Cases**
W. & C., Wils. & Court.

**Wilson and Shaw's Scotch Appeal
Cases in the House of Lords**
W.& S., W. & S. App., Wils. &
S., Wils. & S. (Scot.), Wils. &
Sh., Wilson & Shaw

Wilson on Arbitrations
Wils. Arb.

Wilson on Fines and Recoveries
Wils. Fines

Wilson on Springing Uses
Wils. Uses

Wilson on the Judicature Acts
Wils. Jud. Acts

Wilson's English Chancery Reports
Wils. Ch., Wils., Wilson, Wils.
Ch., Wils. Ch. (Eng.)

**Wilson's English Common Pleas
Reports**
Wils., Wils. C.P., Wilson, Wils.
(Eng.)

Wilson's English Exchequer Reports
Wils. Exch., Wils. Exch. (Eng.)

**Wilson's English Privy Council
Reports**
Wils. P.C.

**Wilson's Entries and Pleading (3
Lord Raymond's King's Bench
and Common Pleas Reports)**
Wils. Ent.

Wilson's Exchequer in Equity Reports
Wilson

Wilson's Glossary of Indian Terms
Wils. Ind. Gloss.

Wilson's History of Modern English Law
Wils. Mod. Eng. Law

Wilson's Indiana Superior Court Reports
Ind. Super., Wilson Super. Ct. (Ind.), Wilson's R., Wils. Ind., Wils. Super. (Ind.), Wilson

Wilson's Parliamentary Law
Wils. Parl. L.

Wilson's Reports (48-59 Minn.)
Wils. Minn., Wilson

Wilson's Reports (1-3 Oregon)
Wils. Oreg., Wilson

Wilson's Reports (29-30 Texas Appeals; also 1-2 Texas Civil Appeals)
Wil., Tex. A. Civ. Cas. (Wilson)

Wilson's Revised and Annotated Statutes of Oklahoma
Wilson's Rev. & Ann. St.

Winch's Book of Entries
W.Ent., Winch. Ent.

Winch's English Common Pleas Reports
Winch, Winch (Eng.), Win.

Windsor Yearbook of Access to Justice
Windsor Y.B. Access Just.

Windt's Insurance Claims and Disputes
ICD

Winer's Unreported Opinions (New York Supreme Court, Erie County)
Win.

Winfield's Adjudged Words and Phrases, with Notes
Winfield, Words & Phrases

Wingate's Maxims
Win. Max., Wing., Wing. Max.

Winslow on the Plea of Insanity in Criminal Cases
Wins. Ins.

Winston's Law or Equity Reports, North Carolina
Win. Eq., Winst., Winst. Eq., Winst. Eq. (N.C.), Winst. L. (N.C.), Win.

Wisconsin
Wi., Wis.

Wisconsin Administrative Code
Wis. Admin. Code

Wisconsin Attorney General Reports
Ops. Atty. Gen. Wisc.

Wisconsin Bar Bulletin
Wis. B. Bull.

Wisconsin Board of Examiners in Chiropractic
Chir.

Wisconsin Board of Tax Appeals Decisions
WBTA

Wisconsin Board of Tax Appeals Decisions, Commerce Clearing House
WBTA-CCH Tax Reporter

Wisconsin Board of Tax Appeals Reports
Wis. B.T.A.

Wisconsin Conservation Commission
W.C.C.

Wisconsin Constitution
Wis. Const.

Wisconsin Industrial Commission, Workmen's Compensation Reports
Wis. I.C.

Wisconsin International Law Journal
Wis. Int'l L.J.

Wisconsin Labor Relations Board Decisions
Wis. L.R. Bd. Dec.

Wisconsin Law Review
Wi. L.R., Wis. L. Rev., Wisconsin L. Rev., W.L.R.

Wisconsin Laws
Wis. Laws

Wisconsin Lawyer
Wis. Law., Wisc. Law.

Wisconsin Legal News
Wis. Leg. N., Wis. L.N.

Wisconsin Legislative Service
Wis. Legis. Serv.

Wisconsin Public Service Commission Opinions and Decisions
Wis. P.S.C. Ops.

Wisconsin Public Service Commission Reports
Wis. P.S.C.

Wisconsin Railroad Commission Opinions and Decisions
Wis. R.C. Ops., Wis. R.C.R.

Wisconsin Reports
W., Wis., W.R., Wis. R., Wis. Rep., Wisc.

Wisconsin Reports, Second Series
Wis. 2d

Wisconsin State Bar Association
Wis. Bar Assn., Wis. S.B.A.

Wisconsin State Bar Association Bulletin
Wis. B.A. Bull., Wis. Bar Bull., Wis. S.B.A. Bull.

Wisconsin Statutes
Wis. Stat.

Wisconsin Statutes Annotated
W.S.A.

Wisconsin Student Bar Journal
Wisc. Stud. B.J.

Wisconsin Tax Appeals Commission Reports
Wis. Tax App. C.

Wisconsin Women's Law Journal
Wis. Women's L.J.

With Warrants
W.W.

Withdrawal
W/D

Withdrawn
W/D

Withholding
W.H.

Withholding Agent
W. A.

Without Warrants
X.W.

Withrow's American Corporation Cases
With. Corp. Cas., Withrow

Withrow's Reports (9-21 Iowa)
Withrow

Witkin's Summary of California Law
Witkin, Cal. Summary

Witness
Witn.

Witthaus and Becker's Medical Jurisprudence
Witthaus & Becker's Med. Jur.

Wittlesey's Reports (32-41 Missouri)
Whitt.

Witwatersrand Local Division Reports, South Africa
W.

Woerner's Treatise on the American Law of Administration
Woerner, Adm'n.

Wolcott's Reports (7 Delaware Chancery)
Wol.

Wolferstan and Bristow's Election Cases, England
Wolf. & B.

Wolferstan and Dew's Election Cases, England
W. & D., Wolf. & D.

**Wolffius' Institutiones Juris Natu-
rae et Gentium**
Wolff. Inst., Wolff. Inst. Nat.,
Wolffius, Wolffius, Inst.

**Wollaston's English Bail Court
Practice Cases**
Wol., W.P. Cas., W.P.C., Woll.
B.C., Woll.

**Wolstenholme and Cherry's Con-
veyancing Statutes**
W. & C. Conv.

Woman Offender Report
Woman Offend. Rep.

**Women Accepted for Volunteer
Emergency Service**
WAVES

Women and Law
Women & L.

Women Lawyers Journal
Women L. Jour., Women Law
J., Women Lawyer's J.

Women Organized Against Rape
WOAR

Women['s]
Women('s)

Women's Air Force
W.A.F.

Women's Law Forum
WLF

Women's Law Journal
Women L. Jour., Women's L.J.

Women's Law Reporter
Women's L. Rptr.

Womens' Laws
Laws Wom.

Women's Rights Law Reporter
Women Rights L. Rep., Women
Rts. L. Rep., Women's Rights L.
Rep., Women's Rights L. Rptr.,
Women's Rts. L. Rep., W.R.L.R.

**Wontner on Land Registry Prac-
tice**
Wont. Land Reg.

Wood and Long's Illinois Digest
W. & L. Dig.

Wood on Conveyancing
Wood Conv.

Wood on Fire Insurance
Wood Fire Ins., Woods, Ins.

Wood on Landlord and Tenant
Wood Land. & T., Wood. Landl.
& Ten.

Wood on Limitation of Actions
Wood, Lim.

Wood on Mandamus
Wood Man.

Wood on Master and Servant
Wood, Mast. & Serv.

Wood on Mercantile Agreements
Wood

Wood on Nuisances
Wood, Nuis.

Wood on Trademarks
Wood Tr. M.

**Woodbury and Minot's United
States Circuit Court Reports**
W. & M., Wood. & M., Woodb. &
M., Wood. & Minot, Woodb. &
Min. (C.C.), Woodbury & Mer.
C.C.R.

**Wooddeson's Elements of Juris-
prudence**
Wood. El.Jur.

**Wooddeson's Lectures on Laws of
England**
Wood. Lect., Wooddesson, Lect.,
Woodd. Lect.

Woodfall on Landlord and Tenant
Woodf., Woodf. Landl. & T.,
Woodf. Landl. & Ten., Woodf. L.
& T.

Woodfall's Celebrated Trials
Woodf. Cel. Tr.

Woodfall's Parliamentary Debates
Woodf. Parl. Deb.

Woodman and Tidy on Forensic Medicine
Woodm. & T. For. Med.

Woodman's Reports of Thacher's Criminal Cases, Massachusetts
Woodman Cr. Cas., Woodm. Cr. Cas.

Wood's Digest of California Laws
Wood's Dig.

Wood's English Tithe Cases in the Exchequer
Wood

Wood's Institutes of English Law
Wood Inst. Eng. L., Wood, Inst., Woods, Ins.

Wood's Institutes of the Civil Law of England
Wood Civ. L., Wood's Inst. Civ. L., Wood's Civ. Law

Wood's Institutes of the Common Law
Wood Com. L., Wood, Inst. Com. Law, Wood's Inst. Com. L.

Wood's Law of Railroads
Wood, Ry. Law

Wood's Manitoba Reports
Wood's R.

Wood's Mayne on Damages
Wood Mayne Dam.

Woods' Oriental Cases, Malaya
W.O.C.

Wood's Tithe Cases, England
Wood Ti. Cas., Wood Tit. Cas., Wood Decr.

Wood's Treatise on the Statutes of Frauds
Woods, St. Frauds

Woods' United States Circuit Court Reports
Woods, Woods C.C., Wood

Woodward's Pennsylvania Decisions
Woodw., Woodw. Dec., Woodw. Dec. Pa.

Woolf on Adulterations
Woolf. Adult.

Woolrych on Certificates
Woolr. Cert.

Woolrych on Criminal Law
Woolr. Cr.L.

Woolrych on Law of Waters
Woolr. L.W., Woolr. Waters

Woolrych on Law of Ways
Woolr. Ways

Woolrych on Party Walls
Woolr. P.W.

Woolrych on Rights of Common
Woolr. Com.

Woolrych on Sewers
Woolr. Sew.

Woolrych, on Window Lights
Woolr. Wind. L.

Woolsey's Introduction to International Law
Wool. Int., Wools. Int. L.

Woolsey's Political Science
Wools. Pol. Science, Woolsey, Polit. Science

Woolworth's Reports (1 Nebraska)
Woolw., Woolw. Rep.

Woolworth's United States Circuit Court Reports
Woolw., Wool., Wool. C.C., Woolw. Rep., Woolworth, Woolworth's Cir. Ct. R.

Worcester's Dictionary of the English Language
Worcester, Wor. Dict., Worcest. Dict.

Wordsworth's Election Cases, England
Words. Elect. Cas.

Wordsworth's Law of Elections
Words. Elect.
Wordsworth's Law of Joint-Stock Companies
Words. J.S.
Wordsworth's Law of Mining
Words. Min.
Wordsworth's Law of Patents
Words. Pat.
Wordsworth's Railway and Canal Companies
Words. Ry. & C.
Work Incentive Program
WIN, WIP
Worker's Compensation Board Decisions, Western Australia
W.C.B.D. (W.A.)
Worker's Compensation Cases, New Zealand
W.C.C. (N.Z.)
Workers' Compensation Commission Reports of Cases, New South Wales
W.C.R., W.C.R. N.S.W.
Worker's Compensation Reports, Queensland, Australia
W.C.R. (Qn.)
Workmen's Compensation
Work. Comp.
Workmen's Compensation Act
W.C.A.
Workmen's Compensation and Insurance Reports, England
W.C. & Ins. (Eng.), W.C. & Ins. Rep., W.C. & I.R., W.C. & I.Rep., W.C.Ins.Rep.
Workmen's Compensation Bureau
W.C.B.
Workmen's Compensation Cases
W.C.C.
Workmen's Compensation Division
Workmen's Comp. Div.

Workmen's Compensation Law Journal
W.C.L.J.
Workmen's Compensation Law Reporter, Commerce Clearing House
Workmen's Comp. L Rep. (CCH)
Workmen's Compensation Law Reports, Commerce Clearing House
Workmen's Comp. L Rep. (CCH)
Workmen's Compensation Law Review
W.C.L.R.. Workmen's Comp. L. Rev.
Workmen's Compensation Opinions, United States Department of Commerce
W.C. Ops.
Workmen's Compensation Reports
W.C. Rep.
Workmen's Compensation Supplement to Department Reports of Pennsylvania
Pa. W.C. Bd. (Dep.Rep.Sup.)
Works on Courts and Their Jurisdiction
Works, Courts
Works' Practice, Pleading, and Forms
Works, Pr.
World
World
World Arbitration Reporter
World Arb. Rep.
World Competition, Law and Economics Review
World Competition & Econ. Rev.
World Confederation of Labour
W.C.L.

World Federation of Trade Unions
    W.F.T.U.
World Federation of United Nations Associations
    W.F.U.N.A.
World Food Council
    WFC
World Health Organization
    WHO
World Intellectual Property Organization
    WIPO
World Law Review
    W.L.R., World L. Rev.
World Meterological Organization
    W.M.O.
World Peace Council
    WPC
World Peace Through Law Center
    WPTLC
World Peace Through Law Conference
    WPTLC
World Polity
    World Pol.
World Today
    World Today
World Trade Institute
    WTI
World Trade Law Journal
    World Trade L.J.
Worrall's Bibliotheca Legum
    Wor. Bib. Leg.
Worthington's General Precedent for Wills
    Worth. Prec. Wills
Worthington's Power of Juries
    Worth. Jur.
Wotton on Leges Wallicae
    Wott. Leg. Wal.
Wright
    Wr.

Wright on Criminal Conspiracies
    Wright Cr. Cons.
Wright on Friendly Societies
    Wright Fr. Soc.
Wright on Tenures
    Wright, Ten., W. Ten.
Wright's Advice on the Study of the Law
    Wright St. L.
Wright's Nisi Prius Reports, Ohio
    Wright N.P.
Wright's Ohio Reports
    W., Wright (Ohio C.), Wright R., Wright's Rep., Wright, Wright Ch., Wr. Ch., Wr. Ohio
Wright's Reports (37-50 Pennsylvania State Reports)
    Wright, Wr. Pa., Wr.
Wright's Tennessee Chancery Appeals Reports
    Tenn. Ch. Ap. Reps., Chy. App. Rep., Tenn. Chancery Appr., Tenn. Ch. App.
Writ of Certiorari Granted
    Cert. granted
Writ of Error Denied
    Writ of error den.
Writ of Mandamus Will Issue
    M.I.
Writer to the Signet
    W.S.
Wrongful Discharge
    Wrong. Disch.
Wyatt and Webb's Equity Reports, Victoria, Australia
    Wy. & W., Wyatt & W. Eq., Wy. & W., Wyat. & W. Eq., W. & W. (E.), W. & W. Eq.
Wyatt and Webb's Insolvency, Ecclesiastical, and Matrimonial Reports, Victoria, Australia
    Wyatt & W.I.E. & M.

Wyatt and Webb's Insolvency, Probate, and Matrimonial Reports, Victoria, Australia
Wyatt & W.I.P. & M.

Wyatt and Webb's Mining Cases, Victoria, Australia
Wyatt & W. Min.

Wyatt and Webb's Reports, Victoria, Australia
Wyatt & W., Wyatt & Webb, W. & W., W. & W. Viet, W. W.

Wyatt and Webb's Reports, Law, Victoria, Australia
W. & W. (L.)

Wyatt, Webb and A'Beckett's Equity Reports, Victoria, Australia
Wyatt, W. & A B. Eq., W. W. & A'B. Eq., W.W.& A'B. (E.)

Wyatt, Webb and A'Beckett's Insolvency, Ecclesiastical, and Matrimonial Reports, Victoria, Australia
Wyatt, W. & AB.I.E. & M., LW.W. & A'B. (I.E. & M.)

Wyatt, Webb, and A'Beckett's Insolvencey, Probate, and Matrimonial Reports, Victoria, Australia
Wyatt, W. & A'B.I.P. & M.

Wyatt, Webb and A'Beckett's Mining Cases, Victoria, Australia
Wyatt, W. & A'B.Min., W. W. & A'B (M.), W.W. & A'B. Min.

Wyatt, Webb and A'Beckett's Reports, Victoria, Australia
Wyatt, W & AB., W.W. & A'B., Wy.W. & A'Beck.

Wyatt's Dickens' English Chancery Reports
Wy. Dic.

Wyatt's Practical Register in Chancery
Wyatt Pr. R., Wyatt, Prac. Reg., Wy. Pr. R.

Wyman's Reports, India
Wyman

Wynne's Bovill's Patent Cases
Wynne Bov.

Wynne's Eunomus
Eun., Wynne Eun.

Wynne's Life of Sir Leoline Jenkins
Sir L. Jenk.

Wyoming
Wy., Wyo.

Wyoming Bar Association
Wyo. B.A.

Wyoming Constitution
Wyo. Const.

Wyoming Law Journal
W. L. Jour., W.L.J., Wy. L.J., Wyo. L.J.

Wyoming Lawyer
Wyo. Law.

Wyoming Public Service Commission Reports
Wyo. P.S.C.

Wyoming Reports
W., Wy., Wyo., Wyom.

Wyoming Session Laws
Wyo. Sess. Laws

Wyoming State Bar Association Proceedings
Wyo. S.B.A.

Wyoming Statutes
Wyo. Stat.

Wyoming Territory
Wyo. T.

Wythe's Virginia Chancery Reports
Va. Ch. Dec., Wythe, Wy., Wythe Ch. (Va.), Wythe (Va.)

Wythe's Virginia Chancery Reports, 2d edition
    Wythes C.C., Wythe's R.,
    Wythe's Rep.

Y

Yale Journal of International Law
Yale J. Int'l L.
Yale Journal of Law and Feminism
Yale J.L. & Feminism
Yale Journal of Law and Liberation
Yale J.L. & Lib.
Yale Journal of Law and the Humanities
Yale J.L. & Human.
Yale Journal of World Public Order
Yale J. World Pub. Ord.
Yale Journal on Regulation
Yale J. on Reg.
Yale Law and Policy Review
Yale L. & Pol'y Rev.
Yale Law Journal
Yale L.J., Y.L.J.
Yale on Legal Titles to Mining Claims and Water Rights
Yale Mines
Yale Review of Law and Social Action
Yale Rev. Law & Soc. Act., Yale Rev. Law & Soc. Act'n., Yale Rev. of L. and Soc. Action
Yale Studies in World Public Order
Yale St. Wld. Pub. Ord., Yale Stud. World P.O., Yale Stud. World Pub. Ord.
Yates-Lee on Bankruptcy
Yate-Lee
Yates' Select Cases, New York
Yates Sel. Cas. (N.Y.), Sel. Cas. N.Y., Yates Sel. Cas.

Year
Y.
Year Book (or Yearbook)
Yr.Bk. (Y.B.)
Year Book 5, Henry V
Quinti, Quinto
Year Book of Legal Studies Madras, India
Yb. of Leg. Stud.
Year Book of the European Convention on Human Rights
Y.B. Eur. Conv. On Human Rights, Y.B. Eur. Conv. on H.R., Yb. of the Eur. Conv. on Human Rights, Y.B. Europ. Conv. H.R.
Year Book, Ames Foundation
Y.B. Ames
Year Book, Canadian Bar Association
Can. Bar Year Book
Year Books, English King's Bench, etc.
Yearb.
Year Books, Ed. by Dieser
Y.B.
Year Books, Ed. by Maynard
Y.B.
Year Books of Edward I
Y.B.Ed.I.
Year Books, Selden Society
Y.B.(Sel.Soc.), Y.B.(S.S.)
Year Books, Rolls Series
Y.B. (Rolls Ser.), Y.B. (R.S.)
Year Books, Selected Cases
Y.B.S.C.
Yearbook, Commercial Arbitration
Y.B. Com. Arb., Y.B.C.A.

Yearbook of Air and Space Law
Y.B. Air & Space L., Y.B.A.S.L.

Yearbook of International Organizations
Y.B. Int'l. Org.

Yearbook of School Law
Y.B. Sch. L.

Yearbook of the Association of Attenders and Alumni of the Hague Academy of International Law
Y.B.A.A.A.

Yearbook of the International Law Commission
Y.B. Int'l. L. Comm'n., Y.B. Int. L. Comm.

Yearbook of the League of Nations
Y.B. League

Yearbook of the United Nations
U.N.Y.B., Y.B.U.N., Y.U.N.

Yearbook of World Affairs
Y.B. World Aff., Y.B. World Pol.

Yearbook on Human Rights
Y.B. Hum. Rts., Y.B. Human Rights

Yearbook on the International Court of Justice
Y.B.I.C.J.

Yeates' Pennsylvania Reports
Y., Yea., Yeates., Yeates (Pa.)

Yelverton's English King's Bench Reports
Yel., Yelv. (Eng.), Yelv.

Yerger's Reports (9-18 Tennessee)
Yerg., Yerg. (Tenn.), Yer.

Yool on Waste, Nuisance and Trespass
Yool Waste

York Antwerp Rules
Y.A.

York Legal Record, Pennsylvania
York Leg.Record, York Leg. Rec., York Leg. Rec. (Pa.), York Legal Record, Y.L.R., York

Young's Nautical Dictionary
Young. Naut. Dict., Younge & C. Exch.

Younge and Collyer's English Chancery Reports
Y. & C.C.C., Y. & C.Ch.Cas., Younge & Ch. Ch. Cas., Younge & C. Ch. Cas. (Eng.), Younge & C.Ch., Younge & Coll. Ch., You. & Coll. Ch., Y. & C. Ch., Y. & Coll., Y. & C.

Younge and Collyer's English Exchequer Reports
Younge & C. Exch. (Eng.), Younge & Coll. Ex., Younge & C. Exch., You. & Coll. Ex., Y. & C. Exch., Y. & C. Ex., See also New Chancery Cases

Younge and Jervis' English Exchequer Reports
Younge & J., Younge & Je., Younge & Jerv., Younge & J. (Eng.), Y. & J., You. & Jerv.

Younge's English Exchequer Reports
Younge., Younge Exch. (Eng.), You., Yo., Younge Exch.

Younge's Historical Sketch of the French Bar
Younge French Bar

Young's Maritime Law Cases, Nova Scotia
Young M.L.Cas.

Young's Nova Scotia Vice-Admiralty Decisions
Young Adm. Dec., Young Adm. Dec. (Nov.Sc.), Young V.A. Dec., Young Adm.

Young's Nova Scotia Vice-Admiralty Decisions, edited by Oxley
Oxley
Young's Reports (21-47 Minnesota)
Young
Youth Challenge Program
Y.C.P.
Youth Court
Youth Ct.

Yugoslav Law
Yugo.L., Yugoslav L.
Yugoslavia
Yugo.
Yukon Ordinances
Yuk. Ord.
Yukon Revised Ordinances
Yuk. Rev. Ord.
Yukon Territory
Yuk., Yukon Terr., Y.T., Y.T.

Z

Zabriskie on the Public Land Laws of the United States
Zab. Land Laws
Zabriskie's Reports (21-24 New Jersey)
Za., Zab. (N.J.)
Zambia Law Journal
Zambia L.J., Z.L.J., Zam. L.J.
Zambia Selected Judgments
S.J.Z.
Zane's Reports (4-9 Utah)
Zane.
Zanzibar Law Reports
Z.L.R.
Zanzibar Protectorate Law Reports
Z.L.R., Zanzib. Prot. L.R.

Zeidman's Legal Aspects of Selling and Buying
LASB
Zilla Court Decisions, Bengal, Madras, North West Provinces, India
Zilla C.D.
Zimbabwe
Zimb.
Zimbabwe Law Journal,
Zimbabwe L. J.
Zinn's Select Cases in the Law of Trusts
Zinn. Ca. Tr.
Zoning and Planning Law Reports
Zoning & Plan. L. Rep.
Zouche's Admiralty Jurisdiction
Zouch. Adm.

Addendum

Additional References and Cross References

A

ABA Journal
See: American Bar Association Journal

Accra and Gold Coast, Selected Judgments of the Full Court
See: Selected Judgments of the Full Court, Accra and Gold Coast

African States, Constitutions of
See: Constitutions of African States

A.K. Marshall's Kentucky Supreme Court Reports
See: Marshall's (A.K.) Reports

Alabama, Acts of
See: Acts of Alabama

Alabama, Code of
See: Code of Alabama

Albert Arbitration, (Reilly) Cairns' Decisions in the
See: Cairns' Decisions in the Albert Arbitration (Reilly)

Alberta, Revised Statutes of
See: Revised Statutes of Alberta

Alemanni, Laws of the
See: Laws of the Alemanni

Alexandra Case, by Dudley, Report of the
See: Report of the "Alexandra" Case by Dudley

Alfred, Laws of
See: Laws of Alfred

American Academy of Psychiatry and the Law, Bulletin of the
See: Bulletin of the American Academy of Psychiatry and the Law

American Bar Association Quarterly Newsletter
See: Quarterly Newsletter, American Bar Association

American Indian Tribes, Constitutions and Laws of the
See: Constitutions and Laws of the American Indian Tribes

American Patent Law Association, Bulletin of the
See: Bulletin of the American Patent Law Association

American Society of Composers, Authors and Publishers, Copyright Law Symposium
See: Copyright Law Symposium (American Society of Composers, Authors and Publishers)

American Society of International Law, Proceedings
See: Proceedings, American Society of International Law

American Stock Exchange, Rules of the
See: Rules of the American Stock Exchange

Ames Foundation, Yearbook
See: Yearbook, Ames Foundation

Amsterdam, Ordinance of
See: Ordinance of Amsterdam

Anderson, Ohio Revised Code Annotated
See: Ohio Revised Code Annotated, Anderson

Anglo-Soviet Law Association, Bulletin of the
See: Bulletin of the Anglo-Soviet Law Association

Annaly, Cases Tempore Hardwicke, King's Bench, England by
See: Cases Tempore Hardwicke, King's Bench, by Annaly

Antwerp, Ordinance of
See: Ordinance of Antwerp

Arabin, Sergeant, Decision of
See: Decision of Sergeant Arabin

Archbold's Practice, Chitty's Edition of
See: Chitty's Edition of Archbold's Practice

Arizona, Hoyt's Compiled Laws of
See: Hoyt's Compiled Laws of Arizona

Arizona, State Bar of
See: State Bar of Arizona

Arkansas, General Acts of
See: General Acts of Arkansas

Arkansas Statutes, English's Digest
See: English's Digest of the Arkansas Statutes

Arkansas, Statutes, Gantt's Digest of
See: Gantt's Digest of Arkansas Statutes

Arkansas Statutes, Sandels and Hill's Digest of
See: Sandels and Hill's Digest of Arkansas Statutes

Ashe's, Tables, Benlie at the End of
See: Benlie at the End of Ashe's Tables

Athelstan, Laws of
See: Laws of Athelstan

Australia, Acts of the Parliament of the Commonwealth of
See: Acts of the Parliament of the Commonwealth of Australia

Australia, Acts of the Parliament of
See: Acts of the Parliament of Australia

Australia, Business Law Cases for
See: Business Law Cases for Australia

Australia, Commonwealth Acts of
See: Commonwealth Acts of Australia

Australia, Commonwealth Arbitration Reports
See: Commonwealth Arbitration Reports, Australia

Australia, Ratcliffe and M'Grath's Income Tax Decisions of
See: Ratcliffe and M'Grath's Income Tax Decisions of Australia

Australia, Statutory Rules, Consolidation
See: Statutory Rules, Consolidation, Australia

Australian Broadcasting Tribunal, Policy Statements of the
See: Policy Statements of the Australian Broadcasting Tribunal

Australian Broadcasting Tribunal, Practice Notes of the
See: Practice Notes of the Australian Broadcasting Tribunal

Australian Capital Territory, Laws of
See: Laws of the Australian Capital Territory

Australian Capital Territory, Ordinances of
See: Ordinances of the Australian Capital Territory

Australian Capital Territory, Subsidiary Legislation of the
See: Subsidiary Legislation of the Australian Capital Territory

Australian Jurist, Notes of Cases
See: Notes of Cases, (Australian Jurist)

Australian Legal Monthly Digest
See: Australia, Legal Monthly Digest

Australian Parliament Acts
See: Australia, Commonwealth, Acts of Parliament

B

B. Monroe's Reports
See: Monroe's Kentucky Reports

Bacon, (Sir Francis), Aphorisms of
See: Aphorisms of Bacon (Sir Francis)

Bacon, Francis, Ritchie's Cases Decided by
See: Ritchie's Cases Decided by Francis Bacon

Baines, by Archbold, Acts on Criminal Justice
See: Archbold on Baines' Acts on Criminal Justice

Baldwin, Ohio Revised Code Annotated
See: Ohio Revised Code Annotated, Baldwin

Barton's Conveyancing, Bird's Supplement to
See: Bird's Supplement to Barton's Conveyancing

Bateson's Leicester Records
See: Leicester Records, by Bateson

Bavarians, Laws of the
See: Laws of the Bavarians

Bayly Moore's English Common Pleas Reports
See: Moore's (B.) English Common Pleas Reports

Beavan's English Railway and Canal Cases
See: English Railway and Canal Cases, by Beavan and others

Beawes' Lex Mercatoria Rediviva
See: Lex Mercatoria Rediviva, by Beawes

Bellingham's Trial, Report of
See: Report of Bellingham's Trial

Bendloe's or Benloe's Reports, England, Anonymous Reports
See: Anonymous Reports at End of Benloe or Bendloe, England

Bengal, Select Cases Sadr Diwani Adalat
See: Select Cases Sadr Diwani Adalat, Bengal

Benloe or Bendloe's Reports, England, Anonymous
See: Anonymous Reports at End of Benloe or Bendloe, England

Beor's Queensland Law Reports
See: Queensland Law Reports by Boer

Betrieb, Germany
See: Der Betrieb

Bigelow's Placita Anglo-Normannica Cases
See: Placita Anglo-Normannica Cases, Bigelow

Bihar and Orissa, India, Selected Decisions of the Board of Revenue
See: Selected Decisions of the Board of Revenue, Bihar and Orissa, India

Bilboa, Ordinance of
See: Ordinance of Bilboa

Bingham's New Cases
See: New Cases, (Bingham's New Cases)

Black Book of the Exchequer (Liber Niger Scaccarii)
See: Liber Niger Scaccarii, (Black Book of the Exchequer)

Blackstone, Ewell's Edition
See: Ewell's Editon of Blackstone

Blackstone on Real Property, by Leith's
See: Leith's Blackstone on Real Property

Blackstone's Commentaries Anthon's Abridgment
See: Anthon's Abridgment of Blackstone

Blackstone's Commentaries, Archbold's Edition
See: Archbold's Edition of Blackstone's Commentaries

Blackstone's Commentaries, Broom and Hadley's Edition
See: Broom and Hadley's Blackstone's Commentaries on the Law of England

Blackstone's Commentaries, by Chase
See: Blackstone's Commentaries by Chase

Blackstone's Commentaries, by Kinne
See: Blackstone's Commentaries by Kinne, edited by Devereux

Blackstone's Commentaries, Chase's Edition
See: Chase's Blackstone's Commentaries

Blackstone's Commentaries, Chitty's Edition
See: Chitty's Edition of Blackstone's Commentaries

Blackstone's Commentaries, Cooley's Edition
See: Cooley's Edition of Blackstone's Commentaries

Blackstone's Commentaries, Curry's Abridgment
See: Curry's Abridgment of Blackstone's Commentaries

Blackstone's Commentaries, Devereux's Kinne's Edition
See: Devereux's Kinne's Blackstone

Blackstone's Commentaries, Dickson's Analysis
See: Dickson's Analysis of Blackstone's Commentaries

Blackstone's Commentaries, Kerr's Edition
See: Kerr's Blackstone's Commentaries

Blackstone's Commentaries, Kerr's Student's Edition
See: Kerr's Student's Blackstone's Commentaries

Blackstone's Commentaries, Reed's Pennsylvania Edition
See: Reed's Pennsylvania Blackstone's Commentaries

Blackstone's Commentaries, Sharswood's Edition
See: Sharswood's Edition of Blackstone's Commentaries

Blackstone's Commentaries, Tucker's Edition
See: Tucker's Blackstone's Commentaries

Blackstone's Commentaries, Wendell's Edition
See: Wendell's Blackstone's Commentaries

Book of Ramsey (Liber Ramesien-sis)

See: Liber Ramesiensis, (Book of Ramsey)

Bosanquet and Pulley: Moore's (A.) Reports

See: Moore's (A). Reports, (1 Bosanquet and Pulley)

Bott on the Poor Laws, Pratt's Edition

See: Pratt's Edition of Bott on the Poor Laws

Bourke's Parliamentary Decisions, Lefevre's Edition

See: Lefevre's Parliamentary Decisions, by Bourke

Bracton, Coxe's Translation of Guterbach's

See: Coxe's Translation of Guterbach's Bracton

Bracton, James S., Digest of Maxims

See: Digest of Maxims by James S. Bracton

Breese's Reports, Appendix to Illinois

See: Appendix to Breese's Reports, Illinois

Brice on Ultra Vires, Green's Edition

See: Green's Edition of Brice on Ultra Vires

Bridgman's English Common Pleas Reports by Carter (same as Orlando Bridgman)

See: Carter's English Common Pleas Reports Tempore O. Bridgman (same as Orlando Bridgman)

Bridgman's (Orlando), English Common Pleas Reports

See: Orlando Bridgman's English Common Pleas Reports

Bridgman's (Orlando), English Common Pleas Reports, Bannister's Edition of

See: Bannister's Edition of O. Bridgman's English Common Pleas Reports

British Columbia, Consolidated Statutes of

See: Consolidated Statutes of British Columbia

British Columbia, Statutes of

See: Statutes of British Columbia

British Guiana, Official Gazette Reports

See: Official Gazette Reports, British Guiana

British Guiana, Reports, Dampier and Maxwell's

See: Dampier and Maxwell's British Guiana Reports

Brockenbrough and Holmes's Virginia Cases

See: Virginia Cases, by Brockenbrough and Holmes

Brockenbrough's Virginia Cases

See: Virginia Cases

Brooke's New Cases, Bellewe's Cases Tempore Henry VIII

See: Bellewe's Cases Tempore Henry VIII, Brooke's New Cases

Brook's New Cases, Translation of

See: Translation of Brook's New Cases

Brougham's Cases by Cooper

See: Cooper's Cases Tempore Brougham

Brougham's Select Cases by Cooper

See: Cooper's Select Cases Tempore Brougham

Brown's (David Paul), Speeches
See: David Paul Brown's
Speeches

Brown's English Chancery Reports, Belt's Edition
See: Belt's Edition of Brown's
Chancery Reports

Brown's Parliamentary Cases, England, Tomlins' Supplement
See: Tomlins' Supplement to
Brown's Parliamentary Cases,
England

Brown's Praxis Almae Curiae Cancellariae
See: Praxis Almae Curiae Cancellariae, Brown

Bruzard's Mauritius Reports
See: Mauritius Reports by
Bruzard

Buddhist Law, Leading Cases on
See: Leading Cases on Buddhist
Law

Burgundians, Laws of
See: Laws of Burgundians

Burma, Selected Judgments
See: Selected Judgments, Lower
Burma

Burn's Justice, Chitty's Edition
See: Chitty's Edition of Burn's
Justice

Burrill on Assignments, Bishop's Edition
See: Bishop's Edition of Burrill
on Assignments

C

C.P. Cooper's English Chancery Practice Cases (1837-38)
See: Cooper's English Chancery
Practice Cases

C. Robinson's Admiralty Reports
See: Robinson's Admiralty Reports

Cahiers de Droit
See: Les Cahiers de Droit

Caines' Reports, New York Term Reports
See: New York Term Reports,
(Caines' Reports)

California Advance Legislative Service, Deering's
See: Deering's California Advance Legislative Service

California Annotated Code, Deering's
See: Deering's Annotated California Code

California Code, Annotated, West's
See: West's Annotated California Code

California, Codes, Hittell's
See: Hittell's California Codes

California, Continuing Legal Education of the Bar, Extension, University of
See: Continuing Legal Education of the Bar, University of
California Extension

California, Decisions of the Industrial Accident Commission
See: Decisions of the Industrial
Accident Commission of California

California General Laws Annotated, Deering's
See: Deering's California General Laws Annotated

California General Laws, Hittell's
See: Hittell's California General Laws

California Law, Survey of
See: Survey of California Law

California Legal Filing Directory by Britton's Shepard
See: Britton's Shepard's California Legal Filing Directory

California, Opinions and Orders of the Railroad Commission
See: Opinions and Orders of the Railroad Commission of California

California, Public Utilities Commission, Decisions of the
See: Decisions of the California Public Utilities Commission

California, State Bar Journal of
See: State Bar Journal of California

California, Statutes and Amendments to the Code of
See: Statutes and Amendments to the Code of California

California, Statutes of
See: Statutes of California

Cambridge Philological Society Proceedings
See: Proceedings of Cambridge Philological Society

Camden's Britannia, Gibson's [Edition of]
See: Gibson's [Edition of] Camden's Britannia

Cameron and Norwood, (North Carolina), Conference Reports
See: Conference Reports by Cameron and Norwood, (North Carolina)

Canada, Appeal Cases
See: Appeal Cases in Canada

Canada, Conference of Commissioners on Uniformity of Legislation
See: Conference of Commissioners on Uniformity of Legislation in Canada

Canada, Consolidated Statutes of
See: Consolidated Statutes of Canada

Canada, Decisions of the Judicial Committee of the Privy Council re the British North American Act, 1867, and the Canadian Constitution
See: Decisions of the Judicial Committee of the Privy Council re the British North American Act, 1867, and the Canadian Constitution, Canada

Canada, Federal Court of
See: Federal Court of Canada

Canada Law Times, Occasional Notes
See: Occasional Notes, Canada Law Times

Canada, Proceedings of the Uniform Law Conference
See: Proceedings of the Uniform Law Conference of Canada

Canada, Railway Commission of
See: Railway Commission of Canada

Canada, Recent Laws
See: Recent Laws in Canada

Canada, Revised Statutes of
See: Revised Statutes of Canada

Canada, Statutes in the Reign of Victoria
See: Dominion of Canada Statutes in the Reign of Victoria

Canada, Statutes of
See: Statutes of Canada

Canada, Statutes of the Province of
See: Statutes of the Province of Canada

Canada, Statutory Orders and Regulations
See: Statutory Orders and Regulations, Canada

Canada, Supreme Court of
See: Supreme Court of Canada

Canada, Territories Law, Northwest Territories
See: Territories Law, Northwest Territories, Canada

Canada, Territories Law Reports
See: Territories Law Reports, Canada

Canada, Uniform Law Conference Proceedings
See: Proceedings of the Uniform Law Conference of Canada

Canadian Bar Association Yearbook
See: Yearbook, Canadian Bar Association

Canal Zone, Laws of the
See: Laws of the Canal Zone

Candy and Birdwood's Ceylon, Printed Judgments of Sind
See: Printed Judgments of Sind by Candy and Birdwood, Ceylon

Canterbury, Prerogative Court of
See: Prerogative Court of Canterbury

Cape of Good Hope, Cases in the Supreme Court
See: Cases in the Supreme Court, Cape of Good Hope

C.E. Greene, New Jersey Equity Reports
See: Greene's, C.E., New Jersey Equity Reports

Ceylon, Appeal Cases
See: Appeal Cases in Ceylon

Ceylon, Appeal Court Reports
See: Appeal Court Reports, Ceylon

Ceylon, Supreme Court
See: Supreme Court, Ceylon

Chadwyck, Healey and Landon's Somersetshire Pleas (Civil and Criminal)
See: Somersetshire Pleas (Civil and Criminal), edited by Chadwyck, Healey and Landon (Somerset Record Society Publications, 11, 36, 41, 44)

Chalmer's Bills and Notes, Benjamin Edition
See: Benjamin's Chalmer's Bills and Notes

Chandler's American Criminal Trials
See: American Criminal Trials, Chandler's

Channel Islands, Rolls of the Assizes in
See: Rolls of the Assizes in Channel Islands

Charles Hammond's Reports
See: Hammond's (Charles) Reports

Chesapeake Case, New Brunswick, Report of the
See: Report of the Chesapeake Case, New Brunswick

China, Republic of
See: Republic of China

Chitty's Archbold's Practice
See: Archbold's Practice by Chitty

Chr. Robinson's English Admiralty Reports
See: Robinson's English Admiralty Reports

Chr. Robinson's Reports, Ontario
See: Robinson's Reports (1-8 Ontario)

Chr. Robinson's Upper Canada Reports
See: Robinson's Upper Canada Report

Christopher Robinson's English Admiralty Reports
See: Robinson's English Admiralty Report

Church of Scotland, Acts of the General Assembly,
See: Acts of the General Assembly, Church of Scotland

C.L. Smith's Registration Cases
See: Smith's (C.L.) Registration Cases, England

Clarendon's (Lord) Orders
See: Orders, Lord Clarendon's

Clark's Jamaica, Supreme Court Judgments
See: Supreme Court Judgments by Clark, Jamaica

Coast Guard, United States Marine Safety Manual
See: Marine Safety Manual, Coast Guard

Coke on Littleton, Butler's Notes
See: Butler's Notes to Coke on Littleton

Coke on Littleton, Hargrave and Butler's Notes
See: Hargrave and Butler's Notes on Coke on Littleton

Coke on Littleton, Hargrave's Notes
See: Hargrave's Notes to Coke on Littleton

Coke upon Littleton, Hargrave and Butler's Edition
See: Hargrave and Butler's Edition of Coke upon Littleton

Coke upon Littleton, Hawkins' Abridgment
See: Hawkins' Abridgment of Coke Upon Littleton

Coke upon Littleton, Thomas' Edition
See: Thomas' Edition of Coke upon Littleton

Coke's Reports, Davis' Abridgment
See: Davis' Abridgment of Coke's Reports

Coke's Reports, Dunlap's Abridgment
See: Dunlap's Abridgment of Cokes' Reports

Coke's Reports, Parsons' Answer to the Fifth Part of
See: Parsons' Answer to the Fifth Part of Coke's Reports

Coke's (Sir Edward) Institutes of England (Commentary Upon Littleton)
See: Institutes of England, Sir Edward Coke (Commentary Upon Littleton)

Colorado Code of Civil Procedure, Dawson's
See: Dawson's Colorado Code of Civil Procedure

Colorado, Continuing Legal Education in
See: Continuing Legal Education in Colorado, Inc.

Colorado, Regulations, Code of
See: Code of Colorado Regulations

Colorado, Session Laws of
See: Session Laws of Colorado

Commercial Arbitration Yearbook
See: Yearbook, Commercial Arbitration

Common Bench Reports
See: Manning, Granger &
Scott's English Common Bench
Reports

Common Law and Equity Reports
See: Spottiswoode's English
Common Law and Equity Reports

**Common Pleas, England, Cases of
Practice in Common Pleas**
See: Cases of Practice in Common Pleas, England

Comparative Law Bureau Bulletin
See: Bulletin, Comparative Law
Bureau

Connecticut, General Statutes of
See: General Statutes of Connecticut

**Connecticut State Agencies,
Regulations of**
See: Regulations of Connecticut
State Agencies

Connecticut, Statutes of
See: Statutes of Connecticut

**Constant's Edition of Bott's Poor
Laws**
See: Bott's Poor Laws by Constant, England

**Cook and Alcock's Irish King's
Bench Reports**
See: Cooke and Alcock's Irish
King's Bench Reports

Cooke's Cases of Practice in Common Pleas by Bucknill
See: Bucknill's Cooke's Cases of
Practice Common Pleas, England

Copenhagen, Ordinance of
See: Ordinance of Copenhagen

**Copyright Society of the U.S.A.,
Bulletin of the**
See: Bulletin of the Copyright
Society of the U.S.A.

Cottenham's Cases by Cooper
See: Cooper's Cases Tempore
Cottenham

**Council of Europe, European
Treaty Series, Agreements and
Conventions of**
See: European Treaty Series,
Agreements and Conventions of
the Council of Europe

**Council of Europe, General
Agreement on Privileges and
Immunities**
See: General Agreement on
Privileges and Immunities of
the Council of Europe

**Court's Edition of Bott's Poor
Laws**
See: Bott's Poor Laws by Court,
England

Cowell's Institutions Juris Anglicani
See: Institutions Juris Anglicani
by Cowell

**Cowen, Hill and Edwards' Notes
to Phillips on Evidence**
See: Phillips' on Evidence,
Notes by Cowen, Hill and Edwards

**Cowen's, New York Reports,
Digest to**
See: Digest to Cowen's New
York Reports

Craigius' Jus Feudale
See: Craig (Sir T.), Jus Feudale

Criminal Law Commissioners, Reports of
See: Reports of Criminal Law
Commissioners

Crockford's English Maritime Law Reports
See: English Maritime Law Reports, by Crockford

Crompton's Star Chamber Cases, England
See: Star Chamber Cases by Crompton, England

Crumrine's Pittsburgh Reports
See: Pittsburgh Reports, Edited by Crumrine

C.W. Dudley's South Carolina Equity Reports
See: Dudley, South Carolina Equity Reports

D

D. Chipman's Vermont Reports
See: Chipman's Vermont Report

Dasent's Common Law Reports, England
See: Dasent's Common Law Reports, England

David Paul Brown's Speeches
See: Brown's (David Paul) Speeches

Davis' Irish King's Bench and Exchequer Reports
See: Davies' Irish King's Bench and Exchequer Reports

Day's Connecticut Reports
See: Connecticut Reports, by Day

Day's Edition of Comyn's Digest
See: Comyn's Digest, by Day

Delaware, Laws of
See: Laws of Delaware

Dieser Edition of Year Books
See: Year Books, Ed. by Dieser

District of Columbia, Appeal Cases
See: Appeal Cases, District of Columbia

District of Columbia, Bar Association of the
See: Bar Association of the District of Columbia

Domat's Civil Law, Strahan Edition
See: Strahan's Domat's Civil Law

Dow's Reports
See: Dow's House of Lords (Parliamentary Cases)

Dudley, Alexandra Case Report
See: Alexandra Case Report by Dudley

Dudley, Report of the "Alexandra" Case
See: Report of the "Alexandra" Case by Dudley

Durnford and East's Reports, Term Reports, English King's Bench
See: Term Reports, English King's Bench (Durnford and East's Reports)

Dwarris on Statutes, Potter's Edition
See: Potter's Edition of Dwarris on Statutes

E

E.B. Smith's Reports (21-47 Illinois Appeals)
See: Smith's (E.B.) Reports (21-47 Illinois Appeals)

E. Buchanan's Reports, Cape of Good Hope
See: Buchanan's (Eben J. or James) Reports, Cape of Good Hope

Earl of Coventry, Trial of the
See: Trial of the Earl of Coventry

Earnshaw's Gold Coast Judgments
See: Gold Coast Judgments, by Earnshaw

East Africa, Digest of Decisions of the Court of Appeal for
See: Court of Appeal for East Africa Digest of Decisions of the Court

East's Reports, Term Reports, English King's Bench, New Series
See: Term Reports, English King's Bench, New Series, (East's Reports)

Economic Stabilization Agency, Office of Price Stabilization, Rent Procedural Regulation
See: Rent Procedural Regulation, Office of Price Stabilization, Economic Stabilization Agency

Economic Stabilization Agency, Office of Rent Regulation
See: Rent Regulation, Office of Price Stabilization, Economic Stabilization Agency

E.D. Smith's New York Common Pleas Reports
See: Smith's (E.D.) New York Common Pleas Reports

Eden's English Chancery Reports Cases Tempore Northington
See: Cases Tempore Northington (Eden's English Chancery Reports)

Edward the Confessor, Laws of
See: Laws of Edward the Confessor

E.H. Smith's Reports
See: Smith's Reports (New York Court of Appeals)

Eldon's English Chancery Reports by Cooper
See: Cooper's English Chancery Reports Tempore Eldon

Eldon's Select Cases by Cooper
See: Cooper's Select Cases Tempore Eldon

England, Statutory Rules and Orders
See: Statutory Rules and Orders England

England, Statutory Rules and Orders and Statutory Instruments Revised
See: Statutory Rules and Orders and Statutory Instruments Revised, England

English Common Bench Reports
See: Manning, Granger and Scott's English Common Bench Reports

English Common Bench Reports, New Series
See: Manning, Granger and Scott's English Common Bench Reports

English Equity Cases Abridged
See: Equity Cases Abridged

English High Court of Chancery, General Orders of the
See: General Orders of the English High Court of Chancery

English King's Bench, Sessions Settlement Cases
See: Sessions Settlement Cases, English King's Bench

English King's Bench, Settlement and Removals Cases
See: Settlement and Removals Cases in English King's Bench

English Law Reports, Appeal Cases
See: Appeal Cases, English Law Reports

English Law Reports, Scotch and Divorce Appeals
See: Scotch and Divorce Appeals, English Law Reports

English Railway and Canal Cases, by Carrow, Oliver et al
See: Carrow and Oliver English Railway and Canal Cases

English Settlement and Removal Cases
See: Burrow's English Settlement Cases

E.P. Smith's Reports (15-27 New York Court of Appeals)
See: Smith's (E.P.) Reports

European Atomic Energy Commission, Treaty Setting Up the
See: Treaty Setting Up the European Atomic Energy Commission

European Commission of Human Rights, Collections of Decisions of the
See: Collections of Decisions of the European Commission of Human Rights

European Communities, Bulletin of the
See: Bulletin of the European Communities

European Communities Court of Justice, Protocol on the Statute of the
See: Protocol on the Statute of the European Communities Court of Justice

European Communities, Official Journal
See: Official Journal of the European Communities, O.J.

European Convention on Human Rights, Yearbook
See Yearbook of the European Convention on Human Rights

European Economic Community, Protocol on Privileges and Immunities of the
See: Protocol on Privileges and Immunities of the European Economic Community

Evans' Great War Prize Cases
See: Great War Prize Cases by Evans

Evans' Lord Mansfield's Decisions
See: Lord Mansfield's Decisions, by Evans

Evans' Mansfield's Decisions
See: Mansfield's Decisions, by Evans

Evans on Agency, Ewell's Edition
See: Ewell's Edition of Evans on Agency

F

Farresley's Modern Cases Tempore Holt
See: Modern Cases Tempore Holt, by Farresley (7 Modern Reports)

Federal Insecticide, Fungicide and Rodenticide Act, Notices of Judgment Under the
See: Notices of Judgment Under the Federal Insecticide, Fungicide and Rodenticide Act

Federal Trade Commission, Statutes and Court Decisions
See: Statutes and Court Decisions, Federal Trade Commission

Ferguson's (George, Lord Hermand) Consistorial Decisions, Scotland
See: Consistorial Decisions, Scotland, by George Ferguson, Lord Hermand

Finch's Chancery Cases, England
See: Cases Tempore Finch in Chancery, England

Finch's English Chancery Reports Tempore
See: English Chancery Reports Tempore Finch

Finch's Precedents in Chancery,
See: Precedents in Chancery, Edited by Finch

Fisher's English Digest, Chitty's Mew's Supplement to
See: Chitty's Mew's Supplement to Fisher's English Digest

Fisher's English Digest, Jacob's American Edition
See: Jacob's American Edition of Fisher's English Digest

Fitzgibbon's Irish Land Reports
See: Irish Land Reports, Fitzgibbon

Florence, Ordinance of
See: Ordinance of Florence

Florida, Annotations to Official Statutes
See: Annotations to Official Florida Statutes

Florida, Annual Report of the Attorney General
See: Annual Report of the Attorney General, State of Florida

Florida, Laws of
See: Laws of Florida

Florida, Railroad Commission for the State of
See: Railroad Commission for the State of Florida

Fordham Corporate Law Institute, Proceedings of the
See: Proceedings of the Fordham Corporate Law Institute

Forrester's English Chancery Cases Tempore Talbot
See: Cases Tempore Talbot, by Forrester, English Chancery

Foster's Crown Cases, Trial of the Rebels
See: Trial of the Rebels, (Foster's Crown Cases)

Foster's Legal Chronicle Reports
See: Legal Chronicle Reports, Edited by Foster

Fox's Decisions, Haskell's Reports for U.S. Courts in Maine
See: Haskell's Reports for U.S. Courts in Maine (Fox's Decisions)

France, Code Civil
See: Code Civil France

Francis Macnaghten's Bengal Reports
See: Macnaghten's (Francis) Bengal Reports

Fraser's Scotch Court of Session Cases, 5th Series
See: Scotch Court of Session Cases, 5th Series, by Fraser

Freeman's Buckner's Decisions (in Mississippi Chancery Reports 1830-43)
See: Buckner's Decisions (in Freeman's Mississippi Chancery Reports 1839-43)

Fries (John), Trial of
See: Trial of John Fries

G

G. Cooper's English Chancery Reports
See: Cooper's English Chancery Reports

G. Greene's Iowa Reports
See: Greene's Iowa Reports

Gaius and Ulpian, by Adby and Walker
See: Adby and Walker's Gaius & Ulpian

Gaius, Poste's Translation of
See: Poste's Translation of Gaius

Gaius, Tomkins and Lemon's Translation
See: Tomkins and Lemon's Translation of Gaius

Gales' Register of Debates in Congress
See: Register of Debates in Congress, Gales

Gardner's LeMarchant's Peerage Case
See: LeMarchant's Gardner Peerage Case

G.B. Shaw's Reports (10-11 Vermont)
See: Shaw's (G.B.) Reports

G.D.W. Vroom's Reports
See: Vroom's (G.D.W.) Reports

Geldert and Oxley's Nova Scotia Reports
See: Nova Scotia Reports, GEldert and Oxley

Geldert and Oxley's Nova Scotia Decisions by
See: Nova Scotia Decisions by Geldert and Oxley

Geldert and Russell's Nova Scotia Reports
See: Nova Scotia Reports, Geldert and Russell

General Agreement on Tariffs and Trade, Organization for Trade Cooperation of the
See: Organization for Trade Cooperation of the General Agreement on Tariffs and Trade

Genoa, Ordinance of
See: Ordinance of Genoa

George Washington University Law Center, Government Contracts Program
See: Government Contracts Program, George Washington University Law Center

Georgia, Annotated, Code of
See: Code of Georgia Annotated

Georgia Code by Clark, Cobb and Irwin
See: Clark, Cobb and Irwin's Georgia Code

Georgia, Code of
  See: Code of Georgia
Georgia Digest of Statute Laws by Cobb
  See: Cobb's Georgia Digest of Statute Laws
Georgia Laws, Cobb's New Digest
  See: Cobb's New Digest, Laws of Georgia
Georgia, Official Code Annotated of
  See: Official Code of Georgia Annotated
Georgia, Official Compilation of the Rules and Regulations of the State of
  See: Official Compilation of the Rules and Regulations of the State of Georgia
Georgia, Opinions of the Attorney General, State of
  See: Opinions of the Attorney General, State of Georgia
Ghana, Akan Laws and Customs Danquah
  See: Danquah, Akan Laws and Customs of Ghana
Ghana, Cases in Akan Law by Danquah
  See: Danquah, Cases in Akan Law of Ghana
Ghana, Divisional and Full Court Judgments
  See: Divisional and Full Court Judgments of Ghana
Ghana, Full Court Judgments
  See: Full Court Judgments, Ghana
Ghana, National Redemption Council Decree
  See: National Redemption Council Decree, Ghana

Gilbert's Reports, Cases in Equity, England
  See: Cases in Equity, Gilbert's Reports, England
Gildersleeve's New Mexico Reports
  See: New Mexico Reports (Gildersleeve)
Girard Will Case, Report of the
  See: Report of the Girard Will Case
Glanville by Beames
  See: Beames' Glanville
Goebel's Ohio Probate Reports
  See: Ohio Probate Reports by Goebel
Gold Coast Colony, and Colony of Nigeria, Renner's Reports, Notes of Cases
  See: Renner's Reports, Notes of Cases, Gold Coast Colony and Colony of Nigeria
Gold Coast Colony, Divisional Court Selected Judgments, Divisional Courts
  See: Divisional Court Selected Judgments, Divisional Courts of the Gold Coast Colony
Gold Coast Colony of Judgments
  See: Judgments, Gold Coast Colony
Gold Coast, Judgments of Divisional and Full Courts
  See: Judgments of Divisional and Full Courts, Gold Coast
Gold Coast Law, Cases in
  See: Cases in Gold Coast Law
Gold Coast, Redwar's Comments on Ordinances
  See: Redwar's Comments on Ordinances of the Gold Coast

Gold Coast, Renner's Reports
See: Renner's Gold Coast Reports
Gold Coast, Selected Judgments of the Divisional Courts
See: Selected Judgments of the Divisional Courts, Gold Coast
Goodeve and Woodman's Full Bench Rulings for Bengal
See: Full Bench Rulings for Bengal edited by Goodeve and Woodman
Gottshall's Ohio Miscellaneous Decisions
See: Ohio Miscellaneous Decisions, Gottshall
Great Roll of the Exchequer, Magnus Rotulus Pipae
See: Magnus Rotulus Pipae (the Great Roll of the Exchequer)
Green's Criminal Law Reports
See: Criminal Law Reports by Green

Griqualand, Reports of the High Court
See: Reports of the High Court of Griqualand
Grotius on War and Peace, Barbeyrac's Edition
See: Barbeyrac's Edition of Grotius on War and Peace
Grotius Society, Transactions of the
See: Transactions of the Grotius Society
Guam, Administrative Rules and Regulations of the Government of
See: Administrative Rules and Regulations of the Government of Guam
Guterbach's Bracton, Coxe's Translation
See: Coxe's Translation of Guterbach's Bracton

H

Hackworth's Digest of International Law by
See: Digest of International Law by Hackworth
Haggard's English Consistorial Reports
See: English Consistorial Reports by Haggard
Hamburg, Ordinance of
See: Ordinance of Hamburg
Hardwicke's Cases
See: Cases Tempore Hardwicke, England
Hardwicke's Cases by Lee and Hardwicke
See: Cases Tempore Hardwicke by Lee and Hardwicke, England

Hardwicke's Cases by Ridgeway
See: Cases Tempore Hardwicke, by Ridgeway, England
Hardwicke's Cases in King's Bench
See: Cases in King's Bench Tempore Hardwicke, England
Hardwicke's English King's Bench Reports by W. Kelynge
See: Cases Tempore Hardwicke (W. Kelynge, English King's Bench Reports)
Hardwicke's King's Bench Cases by Annaly
See: Cases Tempore Hardwicke, King's Bench, by Annaly, England

Hare's Vice-Chancellor's Reports, Appendix to Volume 10
See: Appendix to Volume 10 of Hare's Vice-Chancellor's Reports

Harper's South Carolina Constitutional Court Reports
See: South Carolina Constitutional Court Reports (by Treadway, by Mill, or by Harper)

Harper's South Carolina Constitutional Reports, Vol. 1
See: Constitutional Reports, South Carolina, Vol. 1, by Harper

Harper's South Carolina Reports, Riley's Edition
See: Riley's Edition of Harper's South Carolina Reports

Harris' Modern Entries, Evans' Edition
See: Evans' Edition of Harris' Modern Entries

Hawaii, Session Laws of
See: Session Laws of Hawaii

Hay & Marriott's Admiralty Decisions, England
See: Admiralty Decisions tempore Hay & Marriott

Hayford's Gold Coast Native Institutions
See: Gold Coast Native Institutions, by Hayford

H. Blackstone's English Common Pleas Reports (1788-96)
See: Blackstone's (H.) English Common Pleas Reports

Heiskell's Tennessee Reports
See: Malone (6, 8-10 Heiskell's Tennessee Reports

Henry Blackstone's English Common Pleas Reports
See: Blackstone's (H.) English Common Pleas Reports

Henry I, Laws of
See: Laws of Henry I

H. Finch's English Chancery Reports
See: Finch's (H.) English Chancery Reports

High Court of Justice of England and Wales
See: England and Wales, High Court of Justice

Hill and Denio's New York Reports, Lalor's Supplement to
See: Lalor's Supplement to Hill and Denio's New York Reports

Holdsworth's History of English Law
See: History of English Law, by W. Holdsworth

Holt's Cases (11 Modern Reports), England
See: Cases Tempore Holt (11 Modern Reports), England

Holt's King's Bench Reports, Farresley's Cases, England
See: Farresley's Cases in Holt's King's Bench Reports

Holt's King's Bench Reports (Holt's Reports), England
See: Cases Tempore Holt, King's Bench (Holt's Reports), England

Holt's Rule of the Road Cases
See: Holt's English Admiralty Cases

Home's, Decisions, Scottish Court of Session
See: Clerk Home's Decisions, Scottish Court of Session

Hopkinson Admiralty Decisions
See: Admiralty Decisions of Hopkinson in Gilpin's

Howell's Michigan Nisi Prius Reports or Cases
See: Brown's or Howell's Michigan Nisi Prius Reports or Cases
Howell's State Trials
See: Cobbett's (afterwards Howell's) State Trials
Howell's State Trials, Jardine's Index to
See: Jardine's Index to Howell's State Trials
Hughes Parson's Law
See: Parson's Law by Hughes
Human Reproduction and the Law, Reporter on
See: Reporter on Human Reproduction and the Law
Human Rights Yearbook
Yearbook on Human Rights

Hume on Crimes, Bell's Supplemented Notes to
See: Bell's Supplemented Notes to Hume on Crimes
Hume's Lectures, Notes from
See: Notes from Hume's Lectures
Hunter's (Robert) Edition of Encyclopedia Dictionary
See: Encyclopedia Dictionary, edited by Robert Hunter
Huxley's Second Book of Judgments, England
See: Second Book of Judgments, (Huxley), England
H.W. Green's New Jersey Equity Reports
See: Green's New Jersey Law and Equity Reports

I

Idaho, Session Laws of
See: Session Laws of Idaho
Illinois Annotated Statutes, Cothran's
See: Cothran's Annotated Statutes of Illinois
Illinois Annotated Statutes, Smith-Hurd's
See: Smith-Hurd's Illinois Annotated Statutes
Illinois Compiled Laws, Gross'
See: Gross' Illinois Compiled Laws
Illinois Courts Commission, Official Reports
See: Official Reports: Illinois Courts Commission
Illinois, Laws of
See: Laws of Illinois
Illinois Statutes, Cahill's
See: Cahill's Illinois Statutes

Illinois Statutes, Gale's
See: Gale's Statutes of Illinois
Illinois Revised Statutes, Hurd's
See: Hurd's Revised Illinois Statutes
Illinois Statutes, Hurd's
See: Hurd's Illinois Statutes
Illinois Statutes, Starr and Curtis' Annotated
See: Starr and Curtis' Annotated Illinois Statutes
India, Civil and Criminal Law Series
See: Civil and Criminal Law Series, India
India, Full Bench Decisions
See: Full Bench Decisions for India
India, Supreme Court Journal
See: Supreme Court Journal, India

Indian Appeals, Law Reports, Supplemental
See: Supplemental Indian Appeals, Law Reports

Indian Society of International Law, Proceedings of Conference
See: Proceedings of Conference, Indian Society of International Law

Indian Territory, Annotated Statutes
See: Annotated Statutes of Indian Territory

Indiana Administrative Rules and Regulations, Burns'
See: Burns' Indiana Administrative Rules and Regulations

Indiana Annotated Revised Statutes, Horner's
See: Horner's Annotated Revised Indiana Statutes

Indiana Annotated Statutes, Burns'
See: Burns' Annotated Statutes, Indiana

Indiana, Annual Report and Official Opinions of the Attorney General of
See: Annual Report and Official Opinions of the Attorney General of Indiana

Indiana Revised Statutes, Elliott's Supplement
See: Elliott's Supplement to the Indiana Revised Statutes

Indiana Revised Statutes, Gavin and Hord's
See: Gavin and Hord's Revised Indiana Statutes

Indiana Statutes Annotated Code Edition, Burns'
See: Burns' Indiana Statutes Annotated Code Edition

Indiana Statutes, Gavin and Hord's
See: Gavin and Hord's Indiana Statutes

Industrial Law Society, Bulletin of the
See: Bulletin of the Industrial Law Society

Industrial Property Law, Annual of
See: Annual of Industrial Property Law

Inter-American Bar Association, Conference Proceedings
See: Conference Proceedings, Inter-American Bar Association

Inter-American Commission on Human Rights, Annual Report of the
See: Annual Report of the Inter-American Commission on Human Rights

Internal Revenue Service, Announcements by the
See: Announcements by the Internal Revenue Service

International Arbitral Awards, Reports of
See: Reports of International Arbitral Awards

International Association of Law Libraries, Bulletin of
See: Bulletin of International Association of Law Libraries

International Bar Association, Bulletin of the
See: Bulletin of the International Bar Association

Isle of Man Constitution. Report of the Commission on the
See: Commission on the Isle of Man Constitution. Report

Israel, Selected Judgments of the Supreme Court of
See: Selected Judgments of the Supreme Court of Israel

J

Jamaica Supreme Court of Judicature Judgments
See: Judgments, Jamaica Supreme Court of Judicature

Jamaica Supreme Court Judgments, Clark's
See: Clark's Jamaica Supreme Court Judgments
See: Supreme Court Judgments by Clark, Jamaica

James' Nova Scotia Reports
See: Nova Scotia Reports (James)

Japan Commercial Arbitration Association, Quarterly of the
See: Quarterly of the Japan Commercial Arbitration Association

Jarman on Wills, Bigelow's Edition of
See: Bigelow's Edition of Jarman on Wills

J.B. Moore's English Common Pleas Reports
See: Moore's (J.B.) English Common Pleas Reports

J.B. Wallace's United States Circuit Court Reports
See: Wallace's (J.B.) United States Circuit Court Reports

Jessel's (Sir George) Decisions, Analysis and Digest
See: Analysis and Digest of the Decisions of Sir George Jessel

Jessel's (Sir George) Decisions, Analysis and Digest by A.P. Peter
See: Analysis and Digest of the Decisions of Sir George Jessel by A.P. Peter

J.J. Marshall's Kentucky Supreme Court Reports
See: Marshall's Reports

J.M. Moore's English Common Pleas Reports
See: Moore's (J.M.) English Common Pleas Reports

John Shaw's Justiciary Reports
See: Shaw's (John) Justiciary Reports

Johnson's Chase's United States Circuit Court Decisions
See: Chase's United States Circuit Court Decisions, edited by Johnson

Johnson's New Mexico Reports
See: New Mexico Reports (Johnson)

J.P. Smith, Law Journal
See: Smith's (J.P.) Law Journal

J.P. Smith's English King's Bench Reports
See: Smith's (J.P.) English King's Bench Reports

J.S. Green's Reports
See: Green's (J.S.) Reports

Judge Advocate General of Army, Bulletin of
See: Bulletin of Judge Advocate General of Army

Justinian, Code of
See: Code of Justinian
Justinian, Codex
See: Codex Justinian
Justinian, Digest of
See: Digest of Justinian
Justinian, Edicts of
See: Edicts of Justinian
Justinian Institutes
See: Institutes of Justinian
Justinian Institutes by Cooper
See: Cooper's Institutes of Justinian
Justinian Institutes by Holland
See: Holland's Institutes of Justinian
Justinian Institutes by Lyon
See: Lyon's Institutes of Justinian

Justinian Institutes by Ortolan
See: Ortolan's Institute de Justinian
Justinian Institutes, Sanders' Edition
See: Sanders' Edition of Justinian's Institutes
Justinian Pandects
See: Pandects of Justinian
Justinian Pandects by Pothier
See: Pothier's Pandectae Justinianeae, etc.
Justinianus, Codex
See: Codex Justinianus
J.W. Wallace's United States Circuit Court Reports
See: Wallace's (J.W.) United States Circuit Court Reports

K

Kansas Criminal Code and Code of Criminal Procedure
See: Criminal Code and Code of Criminal Procedure, Kansas
Kansas, Opinions of the Attorney General, State of
See: Opinions of the Attorney General, State of Kansas
Kansas Session Laws
See: Session Laws of Kansas
Kansas Statutes Annotated, Code of Civil Procedure, Vernon's
See: Vernon's Kansas Statutes Annotated, Code of Civil Procedure
Kansas Statutes Annotated Criminal Code and Code of Criminal Procedure, Vernon's
See: Vernon's Kansas Statutes Annotated Criminal Code and Code of Criminal Procedure

Kansas Statutes Annotated, Uniform Commercial Code, Vernon's
See: Vernon's Kansas Statutes Annotated, Uniform Commercial Code
Kansas Statutes Annotated, Vernon's
See: Vernon's Kansas Statutes Annotated
Keilway Reports by Dalison, England
See: Dalison's Reports in Keilway, England
Keilway's King's Bench Report, England by Dallison
See: Dallison's Reports in Keilway's King's Bench Report, England

Keilway's Reports by Benloe or Bendloe
See: Benloe or Bendloe in Keilway's Reports

Keith's Registrar's Book, Court of Chancery, Pennsylvania
See: Registrar's Book, Keith's Court of Chancery, Pennsylvania

Kelynge's (W.) English King's Bench Reports Tempore Hardwicke
See: Cases Tempore Hardwicke (W. Kelynge, English King's Bench Reports)

Kent's Commentaries by Kinne
See: Kent's Commentaries by Kinne, edited by Devereux

Kent's Commentaries by Kinne, edited by Devereux
See: Devereux's Kinne's Kent

Kent's Commentaries, Dickson's Analysis of
See: Dickson's Analysis of Kent's Commentaries

Kentucky, Continuing Legal Education, College of Law, University of
See: Continuing Legal Education, University of Kentucky College of Law

Kentucky Decisions, Sneed
See: Sneed's Kentucky Decisions

Kentucky Revised Statutes Annotated, Baldwin's
See: Baldwin's Kentucky Revised Statutes Annotated

Kentucky Statutes, Barbour and Carroll's
See: Barbour and Carroll's Kentucky Statutes

Kentucky Statutes, Bradford's
See: Bradford's Kentucky Statutes

Kentucky Statutes, Stanton's Revised
See: Stanton's Revised Kentucky Statutes

Kenyon's English Chancery Cases (Notes of King's Bench Cases)
See: Chancery Cases (Kenyon's Notes of King's Bench Cases), England

Kenyon's English King's Bench Reports
See: Kenyon's King's Bench Reports, England

King Canute, Laws of
See: Laws of King Canute

King's Bench Cases of Settlement, England
See: Cases of Settlement, King's Bench, England

King's English Chancery Cases
See: Cases Tempore King, Chancery, England

King's Select English Chancery Cases by Macnaghten
See: Cases Tempore King (Macnaghten's Select English Chancery Cases)

King-Farlow's Gold Coast Judgments and the Masai Case
See: Gold Coast Judgments and the Masai Case by King-Farlow

Kitchin's Reports of Cases Decided in the Supreme Court of South Africa, Griqualand West Local Division
See: Reports of Cases Decided in the Supreme Court of South Africa, Griqualand West Local Division, by Kitchin

Knight-Bruce, and Parker's Reports, Vice-Chancellor's Court
See: De Gex and Smale's Tempore Knight-Bruce and Parker Reports, Vice-Chancellor's Court

Kolze's Transvaal Reports
See: Transvaal Reports by Kolze
Konigsberg, Ordinance of
See: Ordinance of Konigsberg
Korea, Republic of
See: Republic of Korea

L

Lagos, Reports of Certain Judgments of the Supreme Court, Vice-Admiralty Court and Full Court of Appeal
See: Reports of Certain Judgments of the Supreme Court, Vice-Admiralty Court and Full Court of Appeal, Lagos
Lalor's Supplement to Hill and Denio
See: Hill and Denio's Supplement by Lalor
Law Reports, Privy Council, Indian Appeals
See: Law Reports, Indian Appeals
Lawting Court, Scotland, Acts of
See: Acts of Lawting Court, Scotland
Le Marchant, Gardner's Peerage Case, Reported by
See: Gardner's Peerage Case, Reported by Le Marchant
Leadam's Select Cases in the Court of Requests (Selden Society Publication, 12)
See: Select Cases in the Court of Requests, edited by Leadam, (Selden Society Publication, 12), England
League of Nations Yearbook
See: Yearbook of the League of Nations

Lee and Hardwicke's Cases
See: Cases Tempore Hardwicke by Lee and Hardwicke, England
Lee's Cases, England
See: Cases Tempore Lee, England
Lee's Cases Tempore Hardwicke, England
See: Cases Tempore Hardwicke, by Lee, England
Lefevre's Parliamentary Decisions by Bourke
See: Bourke's Lefevre's Parliamentary Decisions
Leges Alfredi
See: Laws of Alfred
Leges Allemanni
See: Laws of Allemanni
Leges Baiarum
See: Laws of Baiarum
Leges Canuti
See: Laws of King Canuti
Leges Edmundi
See: Laws of Edmund
Leges Ethelredi
See: Laws of Ethelred
Leghorn, Ordinance of
See: Ordinance of Leghorn
Littleton, Butler's Notes to Coke on
See: Butler's Notes to Coke on Littleton
Littleton, Coke on
See: Coke on Littleton

Littleton, Hargrave and Butler's Edition of Coke upon
See: Hargrave and Butler's Edition of Coke upon Littleton

Littleton, Hargrave and Butler's Notes on Coke
See: Hargrave and Butler's Notes on Coke on Littleton

Littleton, Hargrave's Notes to Coke on
See: Hargrave's Notes to Coke on Littleton

Littleton, Hawkins' Abridgment of Coke Upon
See: Hawkins' Abridgment of Coke Upon Littleton

Littleton, Tenures, Cary's Commentary on
See: Cary's Commentary on Littleton's Tenures

Littleton, Thomas' Edition of Coke upon
See: Thomas' Edition of Coke upon Littleton

Lomas's City Hall Reporter, New York City
See: City Hall Reporter (Lomas), New York City

Lombards, Laws of the
See: Laws of the Lombards

London, Calendar of Coroners Rolls of the City of
See: Calendar of Coroners Rolls of the City of London

London, Privilegia Londini (Customs of Privileges of London)
See: Privilegia Londini (Customs of Privileges of London)

Lord Kenyon's King's Bench Reports
See: Kenyon's English King's Bench Reports

Lord Mansfield's Decisions, by Evans
See: Mansfield's Decisions, by Evans

Lord Raymond's English King's Bench Reports
See: Raymond's (Sir T.) English King's Bench Reports

Lord Raymond's Entries
See: Raymond's Entries

Los Angeles, Bar Association Bulletin
See: Bar Association Bulletin, Los Angeles

Louisiana Acts of the Legislature
See: State of Louisiana: Acts of the Legislature

Louisiana, Benjamin's and Slidell's Digest
See: Benjamin's and Slidell's Louisiana Digest

Louisiana, Civil Code Annotated, West's
See: West's Louisiana Civil Code Annotated

Louisiana, Civil Code of
See: Civil Code of Louisiana

Louisiana, Code of Civil Procedure Annotated, West's
See: West's Louisiana Code of Civil Procedure Annotated

Louisiana, Code of Criminal Procedure Annotated, West's
See: West's Louisiana Code of Criminal Procedure Annotated

Louisiana, Court of Appeals, Parish of Orleans
See: Court of Appeals, Parish of Orleans, Louisiana

Louisiana, Opinions of the Attorney General of the State of
See: Opinions of the Attorney General of the State of Louisiana

Louisiana, Revised Statutes Annotated, West's
See: West's Louisiana Revised Statutes Annotated

Louisiana Revised Statutes, Voorhies'
See: Voorhies' Louisiana Revised Statutes

Louisiana Revised Statutes, West's
See: West's Louisiana Revised Statutes

Lower Canada, Consolidated Statutes of
See: Consolidated Statutes of Lower Canada

Lowndes and Maxwell's Bail Court Cases
See: Bail Court Cases, Lowndes and Maxwell

Lyndewood's Provinciale, Constitutiones Othoni
See: Constitutiones Othoni (found at the end of Lyndewood's Provinciale)

Lyne's Wallis' Irish Chancery Reports
See: Wallis' Irish Chancery Reports by Lyne

M

Macdonnel and Manson's Great Jurists of the World
See: Great Jurists of the World, by Sir John Macdonnel and Edward Manson

Macdonnel (Sir John) and Edward Manson's Great Jurists of the World
See: Great Jurists of the World, by Sir John Macdonnel and Edward Manson

Macclesfield's Cases (10 Modern Reports), England
See: Cases Tempore Macclesfield (10 Modern Reports), England

Mackeldey's Civil Law, Kaufmann's Edition
See: Kaufmann's Edition of Mackeldey's Civil Law

Macnaghten's Cases Tempore King (Select English Chancery Cases)
See: Cases Tempore King (Macnaghten's Select English Chancery Cases

Macnaghten's Select Cases in Chancery Tempore King, England
See: Select Cases in Chancery Tempore King, Ed., Macnaghten, England

Maine, Acts, Resolves and Constitutional Resolutions of the State of
See: Acts, Resolves and Constitutional Resolutions of the State of Maine

Maine, Laws of the State of
See: Laws of the State of Maine

Malaysia, Royal Commission on Non-Muslem Marriage and Divorce Laws in
See: Royal Commission on Non-Muslem Marriage and Divorce Laws in Malaysia

Malcolm, King of Scotland, Laws of
See: Laws of Malcolm, King of Scotland

Malcom's Laws
See: Laws of Malcolm

Manitoba, Consolidated Statutes of
See: Consolidated Statutes of Manitoba

Manitoba, Revised Statutes of
See: Revised Statutes of Manitoba

Manning, Granger and Scott's English Common Bench Reports
See: Common Bench Reports, Manning, Granger & Scott's, England

Mansfield's (Lord) Decisions, by Evans
See: Lord Mansfield's Decisions, by Evans

March's Translation of Brook's New Cases, England
See: Brook's New Cases, Translation by March, England

Marsden's Edition of Burrell's Admiralty Reports, England
See: Burrell's Reports, Admiralty, ed. by Marsden, England

Martin's Louisiana Term Reports
See: Louisiana Term Reports (3-12 Martin's Louisiana)

Martin's North Carolina Circuit Court Reports, United States Decisions
See: United States Decisions in Martin's North Carolina Circuit Court Reports

Martin's North Carolina Reports, Notes of Decisions
See: Notes of Decisions (Martin's North Carolina Reports)

Maryland Annotated Code
See: Annotated Code of Maryland

Maryland, Annual Report and Official Opinions of the Attorney General of
See: Annual Report and Official Opinions of the Attorney General of Maryland

Maryland Code of Regulations
See: Code of Maryland Regulations

Maryland Laws
See: Laws of Maryland

Massachusetts Acts and Resolves
See: Acts and Resolves of Massachusetts

Massachusetts Annotated Laws
See: Annotated Laws of Massachusetts

Massachusetts Code of Regulations
See: Code of Massachusetts Regulations

Massachusetts Digest by Bennett and Heard
See: Bennett and Heard's Massachusetts Digest

Massachusetts, Reports of the Attorney General, State of
See: Reports of the Attorney General, State of Massachusetts

Massachusetts, Statutes, Laws, of the Province of
  See: Statutes, Laws, of the Province of Massachusetts
Maynard's Year Books
  See: Year Books, Ed. by Maynard
McAdam's Marine Court Reporter
  See: (McAdam's) Marine Court Reporter
Methodist Church Cases, Report of
  See: Report of Methodist Church Cases
Mew's Supplement to Fisher's English Digest by Chitty
  See: Chitty's Mew's Supplement to Fisher's English Digest
Mews Reports, England
  See: Reports, Mews, England
Michigan Annotated Statutes, Howell's
  See: Howell's Annotated Michigan Statutes
Michigan, Biennial Report of the Attorney General of the State of
  See: Biennial Report of the Attorney General of the State of Michigan
Michigan Compiled Statutes by Dewey
  See: Dewey's Compiled Statutes of Michigan
Michigan Digest, Binmore's
  See: Binmore's Digest, Michigan
Michigan, Public and Local Acts of the Legislature of the State of
  See: Public and Local Acts of the Legislature of the State of Michigan

Michigan Reports, Binmore's Index-Digest
  See: Binmore's Index-Digest of Michigan Reports
Mill's South Carolina Constitutional Court Reports
  See: South Carolina Constitutional Court Reports (by Treadway, by Mill, or by Harper)
Mill's South Carolina Constitutional Reports, New Series
  See: Constitutional Reports, South Carolina New Series, printed by Mill
Minnesota Laws
  See: Laws of Minnesota
Minnesota, Opinions of the Attorney General, State of
  See: Opinions of the Attorney General, State of Minnesota
Minnesota Statutes Annotated, West's
  See: West's Minnesota Statutes Annotated
Minnesota Statutes, Bissell's
  See: Bissell's Minnesota Statutes
Mississippi Code, Hutchinson's
  See: Hutchinson's Mississippi Code
Mississippi General Laws
  See: General Laws of Mississippi
Missouri Digest, Barclay's
  See: Barclay's Missouri Digest
Missouri Laws
  See: Laws of Missouri
Missouri Rule, Vernon's Annotated
  See: Vernon's Annotated Missouri Rule
Missouri Statutes, Vernon's Annotated
  See: Vernon's Annotated Missouri Statutes

Missouri Statutes, Wagner's
> *See:* Wagner's Missouri Statutes

Mitford's Equity Pleading, Tyler's Edition
> *See:* Tyler's Edition of Mitford's Equity Pleading

Monroe's Acta Cancellariae
> *See:* Acta Cancellariae by Monroe

Monroe's Kentucky Reports (40-57) (Ben Monroe's Kentucky Supreme Court Reports)
> *See:* Ben Monroe's Kentucky Reports (40-57) (Ben Monroe's Kentucky Supreme Court Reports)

Montana Administrative Rules
> *See:* Administrative Rules of Montana

Montana Annotated, Revised Codes
> *See:* Revised Codes of Montana, Annotated

Montana, Continuing Legal Education, University of
> *See:* Continuing Legal Education, University of Montana

Montana Digest, Bishop's
> *See:* Bishop's Digest, Montana

Montana Laws
> *See:* Laws of Montana

Montana Public Service Commission Reports
> *See:* Public Service Commission Reports, Montana

Montana Public Service Commission Reports, New Series
> *See:* Public Service Commission Reports, New Series, Montana

Montana, Railroad and Public Service Commission of
> *See:* Railroad and Public Service Commission of Montana

Montana Revised Code
> *See:* Revised Code of Montana

Montana State Bar
> *See:* State Bar of Montana

Montesquieu's Spirit of the Laws
> *See:* Spirit of the Laws by Montesquieu

Moore's (Bayly) English Common Pleas Reports
> *See:* Bayly Moore's English Common Pleas Reports

Moore's Digest of International Law
> *See:* Digest of International Law by Moore

Morison's Dictionary, Tait's Index to
> *See:* Tait's Index to Morison's Dictionary

Morrison's Dictionary of Decisions in the Court of Session, Scotland
> *See:* Morrison's Dictionary of Decisions, Scotch Court of Sessions

Morrison's Dictionary of Decisions, Court of Session, Scotland, Brown's Supplement
> *See:* Brown's Supplement to Morrison's Dictionary of Decisions, Court of Session, Scotland

Morrison's Dictionary, Scotch Court of Session, Supplement
> *See:* Supplement to Morrison's Dictionary, Scotch Court of Session

Morton's Reports, Montriou's Supplement to
> *See:* Montriou's Supplement to Morton's Reports

Mundy
> *See:* Abstracts of Star Chamber Proceedings

Municipal Corporations, Reports of
See: Reports of Municipal Corporations

N

N. Chipman's Vermont Reports
See: Chipman's Vermont Reports
Napier's Irish Chancery Reports by Drury
See: Drury's Irish Chancery Reports Tempore Napier
Napier's Irish Selected Cases
See: Irish Selected Cases Tempore Napier
Natal Native Appeal Court Selected Decisions
See: Transvaal and Natal Native Appeal Court Selected Decisions
Natal, Reports of Cases in the Supreme Court of
See: Reports of Cases in the Supreme Court of Natal
National Association of Railway Commissions, Annual Proceedings of the
See: Annual Proceedings of the National Association of Railway Commissions
National Tax Association, Bulletin of the
See: Bulletin of the National Tax Association
Naval War College, International Law Studies
See: International Law Studies, Naval War College
Nebraska Annotated Statutes, Cobbey's
See: Cobbey's Nebraska Annotated Statutes

Nebraska, Reports of the Attorney General of the State of
See: Reports of the Attorney General of the State of Nebraska
Nebraska Revised Statutes
See: Revised Statutes of Nebraska
Nevada, Official Opinions of the Attorney General of
See: Official Opinions of the Attorney General of Nevada
Nevada Statutes
See: Statutes of Nevada
New Brunswick Consolidated Statutes
See: Consolidated Statutes of New Brunswick
New Brunswick Revised Statutes
See: Revised Statutes of New Brunswick
New Hampshire Laws
See: Laws of the State of New Hampshire
New Jersey Laws
See: Laws of New Jersey
New Jersey Prerogative Court
See: Prerogative Court, New Jersey
New Magistrates' Cases (Bittleston, Wise and Parnell)
See: Bittleston, Wise & Parnell's New Magistrates Cases
New Mexico Continuing Legal Education
See: Continuing Legal Education of New Mexico, Inc.

New Mexico Laws
See: Laws of New Mexico
New Mexico Laws, Prince's
See: Princes' New Mexico Laws
New South Wales Court of Review Decisions by Ratcliffe and M'Grath
See: Court of Review Decisions, Ratcliffe and M'Grath, New South Wales
New South Wales Public Acts
See: Public Acts of New South Wales
New South Wales Reserved and Equity Judgments
See: Reserved and Equity Judgments, New South Wales
New South Wales Statutes
See: Statutes of New South Wales
New South Wales Supreme Court Judgments for the District of Port Philip
See: Judgments of the Supreme Court of New South Wales for the District of Port Philip
New South Wales Workers' Compensation Commission Reports of Cases
See: Workers' Compensation Commission Reports of Cases, New South Wales
New York Attorney-General's Opinions
See: Attorney-General's Opinions, New York
New York City Bar Association Bulletin
See: Bulletin of the Association of the Bar of the City of New York

New York City Bar Association, Committee on Criminal Courts Law and Procedure, Bulletin
See: Bulletin, Committee on Criminal Court's Law and Procedure, Association of the Bar, City of New York
New York City, Bulletin, Committee on Criminal Courts' Law and Procedure, Association of the Bar
See: Bulletin, Committee on Criminal Courts' Law and Procedure, Association of the Bar, City of New York
New York City, Bulletin of the Association of the Bar of the City of New York
See: Bulletin of the Association of the Bar of the City of New York
New York Code, Bliss' Annotated
See: Bliss' Annotated New York Code
New York Code, Bliss'
See: Bliss's New York Code
New York Code, Wait's Annotated
See: Wait's Annotated New York Code
New York County Lawyers, Bar Bulletin
See: Bar Bulletin, New York County Lawyers'
New York, Judicial Council, Annual Reports of
See: Judicial Council, New York, Annual Reports
New York Laws
See: Laws of New York
New York Laws McKinney's Consolidated
See: McKinney's Consolidated Laws of New York

New York Laws McKinney's Unconsolidated
See: McKinney's Unconsolidated Laws of New York

New York Miscellaneous Reports
See: Miscellaneous Reports, New York

New York Miscellaneous Reports, Second Series
See: Miscellaneous Reports, Second Series, New York

New York, Official Compilation of Codes, Rules and Regulations of the State of
See: Official Compilation of Codes, Rules and Regulations of the State of New York

New York, Opinions of the Attorney General of
See: Opinions of the Attorney General of New York

New York Revised Laws
See: Revised Laws, New York

New York Statutes at Large, by Edmonds
See: Edmonds' New York Statutes at Large

New York Statutes, Edmonds' Edition
See: Edmonds' Edition of the New York Statutes

New York Transcript Appeals
See: Transcript Appeals, New York

New York University Conference on Charitable Foundations Proceedings
See: Conference on Charitable Foundations Proceedings, New york University

New Zealand Appeal Court Reports
See: Appeal Court Reports, New Zealand

New Zealand Appeal Reports
See: Appeal Reports, New Zealand

New Zealand Appeal Reports, Second Series
See: Appeal Reports, New Zealand Second Series

New Zealand Court of Appeals Reports
See: Court of Appeals Reports, New Zealand

New Zealand, Ordinances of the Legislative Council of
See: Ordinances of the Legislative Council of New Zealand

New Zealand, Reprint of the Statutes of
See: Reprint of the Statutes of New Zealand

New Zealand Rules, Regulations and By-Laws
See: Rules, Regulations and By-Laws Under New Zealand Statutes

New Zealand Statutes
See: Statutes of New Zealand

New Zealand Statutory Regulations
See: Statutory Regulations, New Zealand

New Zealand Worker's Compensation Cases
See: Worker's Compensation Cases, New Zealand

Newfoundland Revised Statutes
See: Revised Statutes of Newfoundland

Newfoundland Select Cases
See: Select Cases, Newfoundland

Nichale's English Railway and Canal Cases
See: English Railway and Canal Cases, by Nichale, etc.

Nigeria Federal Supreme Court Judgments
See: Judgments of the Federal Supreme Court, Nigeria

Nigeria Federal Supreme Court Selected Judgments
See: Selected Judgments, Federal Supreme Court, Nigeria

Nigeria Law Reports, Western Region
See: Western Region of Nigeria Law Reports

Nigeria, Renner's Reports, Notes of Cases
See: Renner's Reports, Notes of Cases, Gold Coast Colony and Colony of Nigeria

Nigeria Supreme Court Judgments
See: Judgments of the Supreme Court of Nigeria

NLADA (National Legal Aid and Defender Association), Briefcase
See: NLADA Briefcase

Normandy, Coutumes de
See: Coutumes de Normandy

North Carolina Digest, Battle's
See: Battle's Digest, North Carolina

North Carolina General Statutes
See: General Statutes of North Carolina

North Carolina Public Statutes, Battle's Revised
See: Battle's Revisal of the Public Statutes of North Carolina

North Carolina Revised Statutes by Battle
See: Bat.Stat.

North Carolina Session Laws
See: Session Laws of North Carolina

North Carolina Statutes, Battle's Revised
See: Battle's Revised Statutes of North Carolina

North Dakota Laws
See: Laws of North Dakota

North Dakota, Opinions of the Attorney General, State of
See: Opinions of the Attorney General, State of North Dakota

North West Territories Revised Ordinances
See: Revised Ordinances, North West Territories

Northern Ireland, Office of the Director of Law Reform
See: Office of the Director of Law Reform, Northern England

Northern Ireland Selected Decisions by Umpire for Respecting Claims to Benefit
See: Selected Decisions by Umpire for Northern Ireland, Respecting Claims to Benefit

Northern Ireland Statutory Rules and Orders
See: Statutory Rules and Orders of Northern Ireland

Northington's Cases (Eden's English Chancery Reports)
See: Cases Tempore Northington (Eden's English Chancery Reports)

Northington's English Chancery Reports, Eden's Edition
See: Eden's Edition of English Chancery Reports Tempore Northington

Northwest Provinces, Full Bench Rulings
See: Full Bench Rulings for Northwest Provinces

Northwest Provinces, Select Cases
See: Select Cases, Northwest Provinces

Northwestern Provinces, India, Circular Orders
See: Circular Orders, Northwestern Provinces, India

Notre Dame Annual Estate Planning Institute
See: Annual Notre Dame Estate Planning Institute

Nova Scotia Revised Statutes
See: Revised Statutes of Nova Scotia

Noye's (William) Grounds and Maxims of English Law
See: Grounds and Maxims of English Law by William Noye

Noye's (William) Maxims of the Laws of England
See: Maxims of the Laws of England by William Noye

O

Office of Price Stabilization, Economic Stabilization Agency, Rent Procedural Regulation
See: Rent Procedural Regulation, Office of Price Stabilization, Economic Stabilization Agency

Ohio Annotated Revised Statutes, Bates'
See: Bates' Annotated Revised Statutes, Ohio

Ohio Digest, Bates'
See: Bates' Digest, Ohio

Ohio Laws, Curwen's
See: Curwen's Laws of Ohio

Ohio Legislative Acts and Joint Resolutions
See: State of Ohio: Legislative Acts Passed and Joint Resolutions Adopted

Ohio, Opinions of the Attorney General of
See: Opinions of the Attorney General of Ohio

Ohio Revised Statutes, Curwen's
See: Curwen's Revised Statutes of Ohio

Ohio Revised Statutes, Swan and Sayler's Supplement
See: Swan and Sayler's Supplement to the Revised Statutes of Ohio

Ohio Statutes at Large, Chase's
See: Chase's Statutes at Large, Ohio

Ohio Statutes, Curwen's
See: Curwen's Statutes of Ohio

Ohio Statutes, Swan and Critchfield's Revised
See: Swan and Critchfield's Revised Ohio Statutes

Ohio Statutes, Swan and Sayler's Revised
See: Swan And Sayler's Revised Statutes of Ohio

Oklahoma, Opinions of the Attorney General of
See: Opinions of the Attorney General of Oklahoma

Oklahoma Statutes, Wilson's Revised and Annotated
See: Wilson's Revised and Annotated Statutes of Oklahoma

Old Book of Entries (Liber Intrationum)
See: Liber Intrationum, (Old Book of Entries)

Oldright's Nova Scotia Reports
See: Nova Scotia Reports, Oldright

Oleron, Jugemens d'
See: Jugemens d'Oleron

Oleron, Laws of
See: Laws of Oleron

Oleron, Les Jugemens d'
See: Les Jugemens d'Oleron

Ontario, Chancery Chambers' Reports
See: Chancery Chambers' Reports, Ontario

Ontario Court of Chancery, General Orders
See: General Orders, Ontario Court of Chancery

Ontario, Province of
See: Province of Ontario

Ontario Revised Statutes
See: Revised Statutes of Ontario

Orange Free State Native Appeal and Divorce Court Selection of Cases
See: Cape and Orange Free State Native Appeal and Divorce Court

Orange River Colony, Reports of the High Court
See: Reports of the High Court of the Orange River Colony

Oregon Annotated Codes and General Laws, Hill's
See: Hill's Annotated Oregon Codes and General Laws

Oregon Annotated Codes and Statutes by Bellinger and Cotton
See: Hill's Annotated Oregon Codes and General Laws

Oregon Annotated Codes and Statutes, Bellinger and Cotton's
See: Bellinger and Cotton's Annotated Codes and Statutes, Oregon

Oregon Miscellaneous Laws
See: Miscellaneous Oregon Laws

Oregon, Opinions of the Attorney General
See: Opinions of the Attorney General of Oregon

Oudh Select Cases
See: Select Cases, Oudh

P

Page's Ohio Revised Code Annotated
See: Ohio Revised Code Annotated, Page

Paley, on Agency by Dunlap's
See: Dunlap's Paley on Agency

Paris, Coutumes de
See: Coutumes de Paris

Parker's Reports, English Vice-Chancellor's Court by De Gex and Smale's
  See: De Gex and Smale's Tempore Knight-Bruce and Parker Reports, Vice-Chancellor's Court

Peake On Evidence, Randall's Edition
  See: Randall's Edition of Peake on Evidence

Peere Williams' English Chancery and King's Bench Cases
  See: Williams' (Peere) English Chancery and King's Bench Cases

Pennsylvania Laws, Dallas'
  See: Dallas' Laws of Pennsylvania

Pennsylvania Laws, Smith's
  See: Smith's Laws of Pennsylvania

Pennsylvania Laws of the General Assembly
  See: Laws of the General Assembly of the Commonwealth of Pennsylvania

Pennsylvania, Opinions of the Attorney General of
  See: Opinions of the Attorney General of Pennsylvania

Pennsylvania Statutes, Purdon's
  See: Purdon's Pennsylvania Statutes

Pennsylvania, Workmen's Compensation Supplement to Department Reports of
  See: Workmen's Compensation Supplement to Department Reports of Pennsylvania

Peter's Analysis and Digest of the Decisions of Sir George Jessel
  See: Analysis and Digest of the Decisions of Sir George Jessel by A.P. Peter

Peters' Edition of Haviland's Prince Edward Island Chancery Reports
  See: Haviland's Prince Edward Island Chancery Reports, by Peters

Peters' Reports Appendix, United States Reports
  See: Appendix to 11 Peters, U.S. Reports

Peters' Reports, Baldwin Appendix
  See: Baldwin, Appendix to 11 Peters

Petersdorff's Abridgment, Supplement to
  See: Supplement to Petersdorff's Abridgment

Petit Brooke
  See: Brooke's New Cases

P.F. Smith's Pennsylvania State Reports
  See: Smith's (P.F.) Pennsylvania State Reports

Phi Alpha Delta, Reporter
  See: Reporter, Phi Alpha Delta

Philippine Law, Gamboa's Introduction to
  See: Gamboa's Introduction to Philippine Law

Phillips' Famous Cases of Circumstantial Evidence
  See: Famous Cases of Circumstantial Evidence, by Phillips

Pike and Fischer's Administrative Law Reporter
  See: Administrative Law Reporter, Pike and Fischer

Pike and Fischer's Administrative Law Reporter Second
See: Administrative Law Reporter Second, Pike and Fischer

Pipe Roll Society Publications
See: Publications of the Pipe Roll Society

Pipe Roll Society Publications, New Series
See: Publications of the Pipe Roll Society, New Series

Plunkett's Cases in Chancery, England
See: Cases in Chancery Tempore Plunkett

Popham's Reports, Cases at the end of
See: Cases at the end of Popham's Reports

Portugal, Ordinance of
See: Ordinance of Portugal

Pothier on Obligations, Evans' Translation
See: Evans' Translation of Pothier on Obligations

Powell on Devises, Jarman's Edition
See: Jarman's Edition of Powell on Devises

Preston Edition of Sheppard's Touchstone
See: Sheppard's Touchstone, by Preston

Printed Decisions
See: Sneed's Kentucky Decisions

Printel Decisions, Sneed's Kentucky Decisions (2 Kentucky)
See: Sneed's Kentucky Decisions, (2 Kentucky) (also known as Printel Decisions)

Proceedings of Cambridge Philological Society
See: Cambridge Philological Society, Proceedings of

Proudfit's United States Land Decisions
See: United States Land Decisions by Proudfit

Prussia, Frederician Code of
See: Frederician Code of Prussia

Prussia, Ordinance of
See: Ordinance of Prussia

Puerto Rico Annotated Laws
See: Laws of Puerto Rico Annotated

Puerto Rico Laws
See: Laws of Puerto Rico

Puerto Rico Rules and Regulations
See: Commonwealth of Puerto Rico Rules and Regulations

Puffendorf's Law of Nature and Nations, Barbeyrac's Edition
See: Barbeyrac's Edition of Puffendorf's Law of Nature and Nations

Purdon's Digest of Pennsylvania Laws, Brightly's Edition
See: Brightly's Edition of Purdon's Digest of Pennsylvania Laws

Purdon's Pennsylvania Consolidated Statutes Annotated
See: Pennsylvania Consolidated Statutes Annotated, Purdon

Q

Q. Van Weytson on Average
See: Van Weytson on Average
Quebec Code Municipal
See: Code Municipal Quebec
Quebec Code of Civil Procedure
See: Code of Civil Procedure for
Quebec
Quebec, Province of
See: Province of Quebec
Quebec, Province of, Statutes
See: Statutes of Province of Quebec
Quebec (Reign of Victoria) Statutes
See: Statutes of Province of Quebec (Reign of Victoria)

Quebec Revised Statutes
See: Revised Statutes of Quebec
Quebec, Society of Criminology, Bulletin of
See: Bulletin of the Quebec Society of Criminology
Queensland Public Acts
See: Public Acts of Queensland
Queensland Workers' Compensation Reports
See: Workers' Compensation Reports, Queensland, Australia

R

R. Bell's Decisions, Court of Sessions, Scotland
See: Bell's Decisions, Court of Session
Ramsey Abbey Court Rolls
See: Court Rolls of Ramsey Abbey
Randolph and Barrandall's Virginia Colonial Decisions
See: Virginia Colonial Decisions, by Randolph and Barrandall
Randolph and Talcott's Edition of Williams on Executors
See: Williams on Executors, Randolph and Talcott Edition
Rastell's (John) Terms of the Common Laws and Statutes Expounded and Explained
See: Terms of the Common Laws and Statutes Expounded and Explained by John Rastell

Ratcliffe and M'Grath's Court of Review Decisions, New South Wales
See: Court of Review Decisions, Ratcliffe and M'Grath, New South Wales
Ratcliffe and M'Grath's Income Tax Decisions of Australia
See: Income Tax Decisions of Australia, Ratcliffe and M'Grath
Red Book of the Exchequer (Liber Ruber Scaccarii)
See: Liber Ruber Scaccarii, (Red Book of the Exchequer)
Reilly's Cairns' Decisions in the Albert Arbitration
See: Reilly's Cairns' Decisions in the Albert Arbitration
Reports of Patent Cases
See: Cutler's Reports of Patent Cases

Rhode Island General Laws
   See: General Laws of Rhode Is-
   land
Rhode Island Laws, Bartlett's In-
dex
   See: Bartlett's Index of the
   Laws of Rhode Island
Rhode Island Public Laws
   See: Public Laws of Rhode Is-
   land
Rhodes, Jus Navale Rhodiorum
   See: Jus Navale Rhodiorum
Rhodes Laws
   See: Rhodian Law
Rhodes, Laws of
   See: Laws of Rhodes
Rhodes, Schomberg's Treatise on
the Maritime Laws
   See: Schomberg's Treatise on
   the Maritime Laws of Rhodes
Ridgeway, Lapp and Schoales'
Irish Term Reports
   See: Irish Term Reports, by
   Ridgeway, Lapp and Schoales
Ridgeway's Cases Tempore Hard-
wicke, England
   See: Cases Tempore Hardwicke,
   by Ridgeway, England
Ridgeway's Irish State Trials
   See: Irish State Trials, Ridge-
   way's

Riggs' (J.M) Select Pleas, Starrs,
and Other Records from the
Rolls of the Exchequer of the
Jews (Selden Society Publica-
tion, 15),
   See: Select Pleas, Starrs, and
   Other Records from the Rolls of
   the Exchequer of the Jews, ed-
   ited by J.M. Riggs (Selden Soci-
   ety Publication, 15
Ripuarians, Laws of the
   See: Laws of the Ripuarians
R.M. Charlton's Georgia Reports
   See: Charlton's Georgia Reports
Robertson Report of Burr's Trial
   See: Burr's Trial, Reported by
   Robertson
Roccus' Maritime Law, Inger-
soll's Edition
   See: Ingersoll's Edition of Roc-
   cus' Maritime Law
Roper's City Hall Recorder, New
York City,
   See: City Hall Recorder
   (Roper's), New York City
Rotterdam, Ordinance of
   See: Ordinance of Rotterdam
Russell on Crimes, Greave's Edi-
tion
   See: Greave's Edition of Russell
   on Crimes

S

Sadr Diwani Adalat, Select
Cases, Bengal
   See: Select Cases Sadr Diwani
   Adalat, Bengal
Sadr Diwani Adalat, Select
Cases, Bombay
   See: Select Cases Sadr Diwani
   Adalat, Bombay

Sadr Diwani Adalat, Select De-
crees, Madras
   See: Select Decrees, Sadr Di-
   wani Adalat, Madras
San Francisco, Bar Association of
   See: Bar Association of San
   Francisco

Saskatchewan Revised Statutes
See: Revised Statutes of Saskatchewan

Saunders and Cole's Bail Court Reports
See: Bail Court Reports, Saunders and Cole

Saunders' Reports, England, Williams' Notes to
See: Williams' Notes to Saunders' Reports, England

Savannah Privateers, Trial of the
See: Trial of the Savannah Privateers

Savigny's Treaties on Obligations in Roman Law, Brown's Epitome and Analysis
See: Brown's Epitome and Analysis of Savigny's Treatise on Obligations in Roman Law

Sayles' Annotated Texas Civil Statutes, Supplement to
See: Supplement to Sayles' Annotated Texas Civil Statutes

Sayles's Select Cases in King's Bench under Edward I, England
See: Select Cases in King's Bench under Edward I, edited by Sayles, England

Scates' Purple's Statutes, Compilation
See: Purple Statutes, Scates' Compilation

Scotch Revised Reports
See: Scots Revised Reports

Scotch Session Cases, Tait's Index to
See: Tait's Index to Scotch Session Cases

Scotland, Act of the General Assembly, Court of
See: Court of Scotland, Act of the General Assembly

Scotland, Acts of the Parliament of (1124-1707) (1814-1875)
See: Acts of the Parliament of Scotland (1124-1707) (1814-1875)

Scotland, Decisions of the Commissioners Under the National Insurance (Industrial Injuries) Acts Relating to
See: Decisions of the Commissioners Under the National Insurance (Industrial Injuries) Acts Relating to Scotland

Scottish and Divorce Appeals
See: Scotch and Divorce Appeals

Scottish Land Court Report
See: Report by the Scottish Land Court

Scottish Land Court Reports, Appendices to
See: Appendices to Scottish Land Court Reports

Sea, Law of the
See: Law of the Sea

Sergeant and Lowber's English Common Law Reports
See: English Common Law Reports, (American Reprint edited by Sergeant and Lowber)

Seven Bishops, Trial of the
See: Trial of the Seven Bishops

Sheil's Cape Times Law Reports
See: Cape Times Law Reports, edited by Sheil

Shepard's California Legal Filing Directory by Britton
See: Britton's Shepard's California Legal Filing Directory

Shepard's Florida Legal Filing Directory by Hill
See: Hill's Shepard's Florida Legal Filing Directory

Shephard's Touchstone, Anthony's Edition
See: Anthony's Edition of Shephard's Touchstone

Shower's English King's Bench Reports, Butts' Edition
See: Butts' Edition of Shower's English King's Bench Reports

Sind, Ceylon, Printed Judgments, by Candy and Birdwood
See: Printed Judgments of Sind by Candy and Birdwood, Ceylon

Smith Law Journal
See: Law Journal, (Smith)

Smith's (C.L.) English Registration Cases
See: English Registration Cases

Smith's (C.L.) Registration Cases, England
See: C.L. Smith's Registration Cases, England

Smoult's Collections of Orders, Calcutta, India, Notes of Cases
See: Notes of Cases in Smoult's Collection of Orders, Calcutta, India

South Africa Official Reports
See: Official Reports, South Africa

South Africa Selected Decisions of the Native Appeal Court, Central Division
See: Selected Decisions of the Native Appeal Court, Central Division, South Africa

South Africa Selected Decisions of the Native Appeal Court, Transvaal and Natal
See: Selected Decisions of the Native Appeal Court, Transvaal and Natal, South Africa

South Africa Selection of Cases Decided in the Native Appeal and Divorce Court, Cape and Orange Free State
See: Selection of Cases Decided in the Native Appeal and Divorce Court, Cape and Orange Free State, South Africa

South Africa, Supreme Court Cases in the Eastern District's Local Division
See: Cases in the Eastern District's Local Division of the Supreme Court of South Africa

South Africa, Supreme Court Cases in the Griqualand West Local Division
See: Cases in the Griqualand West Local Division of the Supreme Court of South Africa

South Africa, Supreme Court, Griqualand West Local Division, Reports of Cases by Kitchin
See: Reports of Cases Decided in the Supreme Court of South Africa, Griqualand West Local Division, by Kitchin

South Africa Water Courts Decisions
See: Union of South Africa, Water Courts Decisions

South African Law Review, Butterworth's
See: Butterworth's South African Law Review

South African Republic, Official Reports
See: Official Reports, South African Republic
South Australia Acts
See: Acts of South Australia
South Australia Acts and Ordinances
See: Acts and Ordinances of South Australia
South Australia Public General Acts
See: Public General Acts of South Australia
South Carolina, Acts and Joint Resolutions
See: Acts and Joint Resolutions of South Carolina
South Carolina Annotated Code of Laws
See: Code of Laws of South Carolina Annotated
South Carolina, Annual Report of the Attorney General to the General Assembly for the State of
See: Annual Report of the Attorney General for the State of South Carolina to the General Assembly
South Carolina Public Statute Law, Brevard's Digest
See: Brevard's Digest of the Public Statute Law, South Carolina
South Carolina Code of Laws
See: Code of Laws of South Carolina
South Carolina Constitutional Reports, New Series, printed by Mills
See: Constitutional Reports, South Carolina New Series, printed by Mills

South Carolina Constitutional Reports, printed by Treadway
See: Constitutional Reports, South Carolina, printed by Treadway
South Carolina Constitutional Reports, Vol. 1, by Harper
See: Constitutional Reports, South Carolina, Vol. 1, by Harper
South Carolina Laws, Faust's Compiled
See: Faust's Compiled South Carolina Laws
South Carolina Public Laws, Grimke's
See: Grimke's Public Laws of South Carolina
South Dakota Administrative Rules
See: Administrative Rules of South Dakota
South Dakota, Biennial Report of the Attorney General of the State of
See: Biennial Report of the Attorney General of the State of South Dakota
South Dakota State Bar
See: State Bar of South Dakota
South-West Africa, Reports of the High Court of
See: Reports of the High Court of South-West Africa
Sparks's Diplomatic Correspondence of the United States
See: Diplomatic Correspondence of the United States, Edited by Sparks
Speers' South Carolina Reports
See: Spears' South Carolina Equity and Law Reports

Spottiswoode's Common Law and Equity Reports, England
> *See:* Common Law and Equity Reports, England

Spottiswoode's Common Law Reports, England
> *See:* Common Law Reports, published by Spottiswoode

St. Kitts
> *See:* St. Christopher Nevis

St. Louis Metropolitan Bar Association, Bankruptcy Reporter
> *See:* Bar Association of Metropolitan St. Louis Bankruptcy Reporter

St. Vincent Supreme Court Decisions
> *See:* Supreme Court Decisions, St. Vincent

Stair's Decisions, Scotch Court of Session, Dalrymple on
> *See:* Dalrymple on Stair's Decisions, Court of Session

Stair's Institutions, Brodie's Notes and Supplement to
> *See:* Brodie's Notes and Supplement to Stair's Institutions

Stair's Institutions, More's Notes on
> *See:* More's Notes on Stair's Institutions of Scotland

Stephen on the Principles of Pleading, Tyler's Edition
> *See:* Tyler's Edition of Stephen on the Principles of Pleading

Stephen's Digest of Evidence by Chase
> *See:* Chase on Stephens' Digest of Evidence

Stephen's on Evidence, Reynold's Edition
> *See:* Reynold's Edition of Stephen's on Evidence

Strange's Notes of Cases at Madras
> *See:* Notes of Cases at Madras, by Strange

Strange's Select Cases in Evidence
> *See:* Select Cases in Evidence, by Strange

Staundeforde's Les Plees del Coron
> *See:* Staundeforde's Pleas of the Crown

Staundford's Pleas of Crown
> *See:* Staundeforde's Pleas of the Crown

Style's English King's Bench Reports, Narrationes Modernae
> *See:* Narrationes Modernae (Style's English King's Bench Reports

Subversive Activities Control Board, Reports of the
> *See:* Reports of the Subversive Activities Control Board

Sugden's Irish Chancery Cases
> *See:* Cases Tempore Sugden, Irish Chancery

Sugden's Irish Chancery Reports by Drury
> *See:* Drury's Irish Chancery Reports Tempore Sugden

Swabey and Tristram's Reports, England, Tristram's Supplement
> *See:* Tristram's Supplement to 4 Swabey and Tristram Reports, England

Sweden, Ordinance of
> *See:* Ordinance of Sweden

Swift's Digest of Connecticut Laws, Revision of
> *See:* Revision of Swift's Digest of Connecticut Laws

T

T.B. Monroe's Reports (17-23 Kentucky)
See: Monroe's (T.B.) Reports (17-23 Kentucky)

Talbot's Cases, England
See: Cases Tempore Talbot, England

Talbot's Cases in Chancery, England
See: Cases in Chancery Tempore Talbot

Talbot's Chancery Cases, England
See: Chancery Cases Tempore Talbot

Talbot's English Chancery Cases by Forrester
See: Cases Tempore Talbot, by Forrester, English Chancery

Taney's Decisions, U.S. Circuit Court, Campbell's Reports
See: Campbell's Reports of Taney's Decisions, U.S. Circuit Court

Taschereau's Edition of Canada Criminal Acts
See: Canada Criminal Acts, Taschereau's Edition

Tasmania Acts
See: Acts of Tasmania

Tax Court of the United States, Rules of the
See: Rules of the Tax Court of the United States

Tennessee Annotated Code, Shannon's
See: Shannon's Tennessee Annotated Code

Tennessee Code, Thompson and Steger's
See: Thompson and Steger's Tennessee Code

Tennessee, Official Compilation Rules and Regulations of the State of
See: Official Compilation Rules and Regulations of the State of Tennessee

Tennessee, Opinions of the Attorney General
See: Opinions of the Attorney General of Tennessee

Tennessee Private Acts
See: Private Acts of the State of Tennessee

Tennessee Public Acts
See: Public Acts of the State of Tennessee

Tennessee Public Statutes, Shankland's
See: Shankland's Tennessee Public Statutes

Termes de la Ley, Les
See: Les Termes de la Ley

Texas Annotated Revised Civil Statutes, Batts'
See: Batts' Annotated Revised Civil Statutes, Texas

Texas Civil Appeals
See: Civil Appeals, Texas

Texas Civil Statutes, Vernon's Annotated
See: Vernon's Annotated Texas Civil Statutes

Texas Code of Criminal Procedure, Vernon's Annotated
See: Vernon's Annotated Texas Code of Criminal Procedure

Texas Codes Annotated, Vernon's
See: Vernon's Texas Codes Annotated

Texas General and Special Laws
  See: General and Special Laws
  of the State of Texas

**Texas, Opinions of the Attorney
General of**
  See: Opinions of the Attorney
  General of Texas

**Texas Penal Code, Vernon's Anno-
tated**
  See: Vernon's Annotated Texas
  Penal Code

**Texas, Professional Development
Program, State Bar of**
  See: Professional Development
  Program, State Bar of Texas

**Texas State Bar, Professional
Development Program**
  See: Professional Development
  Program, State Bar of Texas

**Texas Statutes, Vernon's Anno-
tated**
  See: Vernon's Annotated Texas
  Statutes

Themis, La
  See: La Themis

Theodorianus, Codex
  See: Codex Theodosius

Theodosianus, Codex
  See: Codex Theodosianus

Theodosius, Code of
  See: Code of Theodosius

Theodosius, Codex
  See: Codex Theodosianus

**Thompson and Cook's New York
Supreme Court Reports**
  See: New York Supreme Court
  Reports by Thompson and Cook

Tichborne Trial, Report of the
  See: Report of the Tichborne
  Trial

Tidd's Practice, Appendix to
  See: Appendix to Tidd's Practice

**Townshend's Notes to Ram's Sci-
ence of Legal Judgment**
  See: Ram's Science of Legal
  Judgment, Notes by Townshend

**Transvaal Colony, Witwaters-
rand High Court Reports**
  See: Reports of the Witwatersrand High Court, Transvaal Colony

**Transvaal, Official Reports of the
High Court**
  See: Official Reports of the High
  Court of the Transvaal

**Treadway's South Carolina Con-
stitutional Court Reports**
  See: South Carolina Constitutional Court Reports (by Treadway, by Mill, or by Harper)

**Treadway's South Carolina Con-
stitutional Reports**
  See: Constitutional Reports,
  South Carolina, printed by
  Treadway

**Tristram's Edition of Coote's Pro-
bate Court Practice**
  See: Coote's Probate Court Practice, Edited by Tristram

**Troubat and Haly's Practice,
Brightly's Edition**
  See: Brightly's Edition of
  Troubat and Haly's Practice

U

Uganda, High Court, Monthly Bulletin of Decisions
See: Monthly Bulletin of Decisions of the High Court of Uganda

Underhill on Torts, Moak's Edition
See: Moak's Edition of Underhill on Torts

Unification of Law Yearbook
See: L'Unification du droit Annuaive

Uniform Law Conference of Canada, Proceedings
See: Proceedings of the Uniform Law Conference of Canada

United Nations Disarmament Commission
See: Disarmament Commission, United Nations

United Nations Drug Supervisory Body
See: Drug Supervisory Body, United Nations

United Nations Economic and Social Committee
See: Economic and Social Committee, United Nations

United Nations Economic and Social Commission for Asia and the Pacific
See: Economic and Social Commission for Asia and the Pacific, United Nations

United Nations Economic Commission for Latin America
See: Economic Commission for Latin America, United Nations

United Nations Economic Commission for Africa
See: Economic Commission for Africa, United Nations

United Nations Economic Commission for Europe
See: Economic Commission for Europe, United Nations

United Nations Economic Commission for Western Asia
See: Economic Commission for Western Asia, United Nations

United Nations Economic Commission for Asia and the Far East
See: Economic Commission for Asia and the Far East, United Nations

United Nations General Assembly
See: General Assembly, United Nations

United Nations General Assembly Official Record
See: General Assembly Official Record, United Nations

United Nations General Assembly Resolution
See: General Assembly Resolution, United Nations

United Nations International Law Commission
See: International Law Commission, United Nations

United Nations International Trade Organization
See: International Trade Organization, United Nations

United Nations Yearbook
See: Yearbook of the United Nations

United States Air Force, Special Court-Martial
See: special Court-Martial, United States Air Force

United States, Annual Law Register of the
See: Annual Law Register of the United States

United States, Appeal Cases in the
See: Appeal Cases in the United States

United States, Appeal Cases of the different states of the
See: Appeal Cases of the different states of the United States

United States Army, Judge Advocate General, Procurement Division
See: Procurement Division, Judge Advocate General, United States Army

United States Army, Special Regulation
See: Special Regulation, United States Army

United States Army, Technical Manual
See: Technical Manual, United States Army

United States Bureau of Indian Affairs, Special Disbursing Agent
See: Special Disbursing Agent, United States Bureau of Indian Affairs

United States Coast Guard Marine Safety Manual
See: Marine Safety Manual, Coast Guard

United States Coast Guard, Special Court-Martial
See: Special Court-Martial, United States Coast Guard

United States Code, Annotated, Mason's
See: Mason's United States Code Annotated

United States, Constitution of the
See: Constitution of the United States

United States Court of Customs and Patent Appeals, Rules of the
See: Rules of the United States Court of Customs and Patent Appeals

United States Department of Agriculture, Service and Regulatory Announcement
See: Service and Regulatory Announcement, United States Department of Agriculture

United States Department of Commerce, Workmens' Compensation Opinions
See: Workmens' Compensation Opinions, United States Department of Commerce

United States Department of Labor, Wage and Hour Division
See: Wage and Hour Division, United States Department of Labor

United States District Court of Hawaii, Reports of the
See: Reports of the United States District Court of Hawaii

United States Food and Drug Administration, Notices of Judgment
>*See:* Notices of Judgment, United States Food and Drug Administration

United States Government Printing Office, Superintendent of Documents
>*See:* Superintendent of Documents, United States Government Printing Office

United States Internal Revenue Bureau, Excess Profits Tax Council Ruling or Memorandum
>*See:* Excess Profits Tax Council Ruling or Memorandum, United States Internal Revenue Bureau

United States Internal Revenue Bureau, Processing Tax Board of Review Decisions
>*See:* Processing Tax Board of Review Decisions, United States Internal Revenue Bureau

United States Internal Revenue Bureau, Processing Tax Division
>*See:* Processing Tax Division, United States Internal Revenue Bureau

United States Internal Revenue Bureau, Sales Tax Branch
>*See:* Sales Tax Branch, United States Internal Revenue Bureau

United States Internal Revenue Bureau, Sales Tax Rulings
>*See:* Sales Tax Rulings, United States Internal Revenue Bureau

United States Internal Revenue Service, Estate Tax Division
>*See:* Estate Tax Division, United States Internal Revenue Service

United States Internal Revenue Bureau, Solicitor's Memorandum
>*See:* Solicitor's Memorandum, United States Internal Revenue Bureau

United States Internal Revenue Bureau, Solicitor's Recommendation
>*See:* Solicitor's Recommendation, United States Internal Revenue Bureau

United States Internal Revenue Bureau, Tobacco Branch
>*See:* Tobacco Branch, United States Internal Revenue Bureau

United States Internal Revenue Bureau, Tobacco Tax Ruling
>*See:* Tobacco Tax Ruling, United States Internal Revenue Bureau

United States Internal Revenue Bureau, Tobacco Tax Ruling Term
>*See:* Tobacco Tax Ruling Term, United States Internal Revenue Bureau

United States Internal Revenue Service, Announcement by the
>*See:* Announcement by the Internal Revenue Service

United States Internal Revenue Service, Employment Taxes, Social Security Act Rulings
>*See:* Employment Taxes, Social Security Act Rulings, United States Internal Revenue Service

United States Internal Revenue Service, Special Tax Ruling
See: Special Tax Ruling, United States Internal Revenue Service

United States Interstate Commerce Commission, Valuation Reports
See: Valuation Reports, United States Interstate Commerce Commission

United States, Laws of the
See: Laws of the United States

United States Navy, Special Court-Martial
See: Special Court-Martial, United States Navy

United States Patent and Trademark Office, Official Gazette of the
See: Official Gazette of the United States Patent and Trademark Office: Trademarks

United States Patent Office, Official Gazette
See: Official Gazette, United States Patent Office

United States Trademark Association, Bulletin of
See: Bulletin of United States Trademark Association

United States Treasury, Decisions, Synopsis Series
See: Synopsis Series of the United States Treasury Decisions

United States, Treasury Department
See: Treasury Department, United States

United States Treasury, Synopsis Decisions
See: Synopsis Decisions, United States Treasury

United States Trials
See: Wharton's United States State Trials

University of California, Extension, Continuing Legal Education of the Bar
See: Continuing Legal Education of the Bar, University of California Extension

University of Denver College of Law, Program of Advanced Professional Development
See: Program of Advanced Professional Development, University of Denver College of Law

University of Kentucky College of Law, Continuing Legal Education
See: Continuing Legal Education, University of Kentucky College of Law

University of Montana Continuing Legal Education
See: Continuing Legal Education, University of Montana

Unreported Trust Cases, Prentice-Hall
See: Prentice-Hall Unreported Trust Cases

Upper Canada Appeal Reports
See: Appeal Reports, Upper Canada (1846-66)

Upper Canada Chancery Chambers Reports
See: Chancery Chambers Reports, Upper Canada

Upper Canada Consolidated Statutes
See: Consolidated Statutes of Upper Canada

Upper Canada, Special Lectures of the Law Society of
See: Special Lectures of the Law Society of Upper Canada

Utah Administrative Rules
See: Administrative Rules of the State of Utah

Utah Laws
See: Laws of Utah

Utah, State of, Bulletin
See: State of Utah Bulletin

V

Van Diemen's Land, Australia, Acts of
See: Acts of Van Diemen's Land, Australia

Van Heythuysen's Equity Draftsman, Hughes' Edition
See: Hughes' Edition of Van Heythuysen's Equity Draftsman

Van Santvoord's Equity Pleading, Moak's Edition
See: Moak's Edition of Van Santvoord's Equity Pleading

Vermont, Biennial Report of the Attorney General of the State of
See: Biennial Report of the Attorney General of the State of Vermont

Vermont Laws
See: Laws of Vermont

Vermont Statutes, Slade's Compilation
See: Slade's Compilation of the Statutes of Vermont

Vesey Senior's English Chancery Reports, Belt's Edition
See: Belt's Edition of Vesey Senior's English Chancery Reports

Vesey Senior's English Chancery Reports, Belt's Supplement
See: Belt's Supplement to Vesey Senior's English Chancery Reports

Vesey's Reports, England, Sumner's Edition
See: Sumner's Edition of Vesey's Reports, England

Victoria, Acts of the Parliament of
See: Acts of the Parliament of Victoria

Victoria, Reports of Cases - Supreme Court of
See: Reports of Cases - Supreme Court of Victoria

Virginia, Acts of the General Assembly of the Commonwealth of
See: Acts of the General Assembly of the Commonwealth of Virginia

Virginia, and West Virginia, Michie's Jurisprudence of
See: Michie's Jurisprudence of Virginia and West Virginia

Virginia, Bill of Rights of
See: Bill of Rights of Virginia

Virginia Code
See: Code of Virginia

Virginia Constitution
See: Constitution of Virginia

Virginia, Joint Committee on Continuing Legal Education of the State Bar and the Bar Association
See: Joint Committee on Continuing Legal Education of the

Virginia State Bar and the Virginia Bar Association
Virginia Laws
See: Laws of Virginia
Virginia Laws, Purvis' Collection
See: Purvis' Collection of the Laws of Virginia

Virginia Statutes, Hening's
See: Hening's Virginia Statutes
Visby, Laws of
See: Laws of Visby
Visigoths, Laws of the
See: Laws of the Visigoths

W

W.G. Shaw's Reports (30-35 Vermont)
See: Shaw's (W.G.) Reports
W. Jones' King's Bench and Common Pleas Reports
See: Jones, W. King's Bench Reports
W. Robinson's English Admiralty Reports
See: Robinson's Admiralty Reports
Wade's Acta Curiae Admiralatus Scotiae by
See: Acta Curiae Admiralatus Scotiae by Wade
Wade's (John) Cabinet Lawyer
See: Cabinet Lawyer by John Wade
Wales, Decisions of the Commissioners Under the National Insurance (Industrial Injuries) Acts Relating to
See: Decisions of the Commissioners Under the National Insurance (Industrial Injuries) Acts Relating to Wales
Ware's Daveis' District Court Reports (Volume 2)
See: Daveis' District Court Reports (2 of Ware)

Ware's Davies' District Court Reports (Volume 2)
See: Davies' District Court Reports (2 of Ware)
Warren Hastings, Trial of
See: Trial of Warren Hastings
Waseda, University Institute of Comparative Law, Bulletin
See: Bulletin, Waseda University Institute of Comparative Law
Washington Annotated General Statutes and Codes, Hill's
See: Hill's Annotated Washington General Statutes and Codes
Washington Annotated Codes and Statutes, Ballinger's
See: Ballinger's Annotated Codes and Statutes, Washington
Washington Annotated Revised Code
See: Revised Code of Washington, Annotated
Washington Laws
See: Laws of Washington
Washington Revised Code
See: Revised Code of Washington
Washington, State of, Office of the Attorney General, Opinions
See: Office of the Attorney General, State of Washington, Opinions

Webster, Professor, Trial for Murder
  See: Trial of Professor Webster for Murder

West Indian Court of Appeal Judgments
  See: Judgments of the West Indian Court of Appeal

West Virginia Acts of the Legislature
  See: Acts of the Legislature of West Virginia

West Virginia, and Virginia, Michie's Jurisprudence
  See: Michie's Jurisprudence of Virginia and West Virginia

West Virginia, Biennial Report and Official Opinions of the Attorney General
  See: Biennial Report and Official Opinions of the Attorney General of the State of West Virginia

Western Australia Reprinted Acts
  See: Reprinted Acts of Western Australia

Western Australia Statutes
  See: Statutes of Western Australia

Western Australia Worker's Compensation Board Decisions
  See: Worker's Compensation Board Decisions, Western Australia

Wharton's (George Frederick) Legal Maxims with Observations
  See: Legal Maxims with Observations by George Frederick Wharton

Wheaton's International Law, Dana's Edition
  See: Dana's Edition of Wheaton's International Law

White and Tudor's Leading Cases in Equity
  See: Leading Cases in Equity by White and Tudor

Whiteman's Digest of International Law
  See: Digest of International Law by Whiteman

William Blackstone's English King's Bench Reports
  See: Blackstone's (William) English King's Bench Reports

William Blackstone's English King's Bench Reports, Elsley's Edition
  See: Elsley's Edition of William Blackstone's English King's Bench Reports

William Kelynge's English Chancery Reports
  See: Kelynge's English Chancery Reports

William Robinson's English Admiralty Reports
  See: Robinson's English Admiralty Reports

William the Bastard, Laws of
  See: Laws of William the Bastard

William the Conqueror, Laws of
  See: Laws of William the Conqueror

Williams' (Peere) Reports, Cox's Edition
  See: Cox's ed. of Peere Williams' Reports

Wilson's (Sergeant) English King's Bench Reports
See: Sergeant Wilson's English King's Bench Reports

Windward Islands Court of Appeal Judgments
See: Judgments of the Windward Islands Court of Appeal

Wisconsin, Advanced Training Seminars, State Bar of
See: State Bar of Wisconsin Advanced Training Seminars

Wisconsin, Continuing Legal Education
See: Continuing Legal Education for Wisconsin

Wisconsin Laws
See: Laws of Wisconsin

Wisconsin, Opinions of the Attorney General of the State of
See: Opinions of the Attorney General of the State of Wisconsin

Wisconsin Statutes Annotated, West's
See: West's Wisconsin Statutes Annotated

Wisconsin Statutes, Sanborn and Berryman's Annotated
See: Sanborn and Berryman's Annotated Wisconsin Statutes

Wisconsin Statutes, Taylor's
See: Taylor's Wisconsin Statutes

Wisconsin Statutes, Taylor's Revised
See: Taylor's Revised Wisconsin Statutes

Witwatersrand High Court, Transvaal Colony, Reports
See: Reports of the Witwatersrand High Court, Transvaal Colony

Women, Laws of
See: Laws of Women

Wood's (Hutton) Decrees in Title Cases
See: Hutton Wood's Decrees in Tithe Cases

World Bank (International Bank for Reconstruction and Development)
See: International Bank for Reconstruction and Development (World Bank)

W.W. Harrington's Reports (31-39 Delawre)
See: Harrington's (W.W.) Reports

Wyoming, Opinions of the Attorney General of
See: Opinions of the Attorney General of Wyoming

Wyoming Session Laws
See: Session Laws of Wyoming

Y

Year Books, England, Selected Cases
See: Selected Cases, Year Books, England

Yelverton, Metcalf's Edition
See: Metcalf's Edition of Yelverton

Younge and Collyer's New Chancery Cases, England
See: New Chancery Cases, (Younge and Collyer)

Z

Zambia Selected Judgments
See: Selected Judgments of Zambia